D1064619

Patterns in the Dust

Contemporary American History Series
WILLIAM E. LEUCHTENBURG, GENERAL EDITOR

PATTERNS IN THE DUST

Chinese-American Relations
and
the Recognition Controversy,
1949–1950

NANCY BERNKOPF TUCKER

New York
Columbia University Press
1983

Library of Congress Cataloging in Publication Data

Tucker, Nancy Bernkopf
Patterns in the dust.

(Contemporary American history series)
Bibliography: p.
Includes index.
1. United States—Foreign relations   China.
2. China—Foreign relations—United States.   3. United
States—Foreign relations—1945–1953.   4. China—
Foreign relations—1949–1976.   I. Title.   II. Series.
E183.8.C5T836   1983   327.73051   82-14724
ISBN 0-231-05362-2
ISBN 0-231-05363-0 (pbk.)

The Andrew W. Mellon Foundation, through a special grant,
has assisted the Press in publishing this volume

Columbia University Press
New York *and* Guildford, Surrey

*Clothbound editions of Columbia University Press books are Smyth-sewn and
printed on permanent and durable acid-free paper*

Contents

Preface

A S witnesses to the disintegration of Nationalist forces in the path of onrushing Communist armies in later 1948, American officials had no choice but to reconsider the course of Sino-American relations. Since the end of World War II, Americans had been involved in Chinese affairs—giving aid to the government of Chiang Kai-shek as it fought an anticommunist civil war. But despite arms, ammunition, money, and supplies from the United States, the Kuomintang effort had faltered and by 1949 had reached its last days. The question arose, therefore, whether Washington would try to rescue the collapsing Nationalist regime or come to terms with China's communists.

President Harry S Truman and his Secretary of State, Dean Acheson, caught up in the calculations of cold war diplomacy and the management of domestic politics, refused to make rash judgments about events in the East. Attempting to explain the Administration's cautious approach to the Kuomintang debacle, Acheson likened it to a tree falling in the forest: the United States would have to wait until the dust settled before it could see ahead clearly.[1] Yet this was not a do-nothing policy as critics supposed;[2] the Truman-Acheson posture of passivity masked serious efforts to assess both the international repercussions of a new China policy and the tolerance of American interest groups and the public for a change of direction in Asia.

I trace here the patterns in the dust of China's fall—to see what officials thought they saw and what they might do. My analysis is of American reactions to the Chinese revolution, with an emphasis upon the issue of United States recognition of the People's Republic of China. The inquiry spans the eighteen months from January 1949, when the second Truman Administration took office and events in China heralded an imminent resolution of the civil conflict, to June 1950, when the Korean War brought reasoned analysis to an abrupt end. It covers a range of government actions, from assessment of the chances for accommodation with the Chinese Communists, through efforts to ascertain the views of Americans for whom America's relations with China—be it Communist or Nationalist—had special significance, to estimates of how much freedom public and Congressional opinion would grant policymakers. Ultimately, having investigated the impact of United States China policy upon Washington's allies and enemies, and having scrutinized the Kuomintang's potential for survival, Dean Acheson and the State Department devised a strategy.

My attempts to reconstruct the activities of China policymakers in 1949 and 1950 have profited greatly from the wealth of source materials now available to scholars. The U.S. State Department has recently completed declassifying most of its documents through the end of 1949 and has made a large collection of significant items accessible in the *Foreign Relations* series, which is now in print through the year 1951. Although no comparable resource exists on the China side, an enormous compilation of papers and oral history interviews given to Columbia University by China's Ambassador to the United States, V. K. Wellington Koo, provides fascinating insights into at least some of the workings of the Chinese Nationalist government in its months of decline. I have also been fortunate in securing permission to work in numerous private collections—corporate and personal—which have not hitherto been utilized by researchers in the field of American–East Asian relations.

At all stages my work has been rendered more interesting and agreeable by the assistance of a variety of scholars, archivists and persons whose own participation in the events of the period have kept memories surprisingly fresh after the passage of thirty years. Randall Gould, former editor of the *Shanghai Evening Post & Mercury*, John Cabot, American Consul General in Shanghai, and Philip Fugh, personal secretary to the late Ambassador John Leighton Stuart all generously shared with me their reminiscences and their papers. Others who patiently listened to my questions and sought to aid in my search included Philip C. Jessup, O. Edmund Clubb, Everett Case, John Melby, Henry Lieberman, Walter Sullivan, and General Albert C. Wedemeyer. Unusual in the business world, which more often refused my inquiries or lost my letters, Boise Cascade and the International Telephone and Telegraph Corporation kindly gave me access to their files and provided working space and even duplicating privileges. Francis T. Masterson, Executive Director of the Foreign Claims Settlement Commission, made time in his busy schedule to discuss the agency's operations and secure documentary materials for me from distant warehouses. Particularly appreciated, as other researchers can attest, were the efforts of special archivists to make the information over which they hold dominion easily accessible. Those at the Library of Congress Manuscript Division, the Diplomatic Branch of the National Archives and the Columbia University Manuscript Reading Room stand out in my memory. So, too, do the extras such as the invitation by Ann Robinson, Reference Librarian at New England College, to use the spare room in her house.

The financial support of the Harry S Truman Library Institute, the International Studies Association/Ford Foundation and the Colgate University Research Council also aided in the completion of this book. *The Pacific Historical Review* generously gave its permissions to reprint my article "An Unlikely Peace" in somewhat altered form as Chapter 6. Moreover, the skilled typing of Debbie Bell at Columbia's East Asian Institute and Rosalie Hiam and Pat Ryan at Colgate University speeded me through several revisions of the manuscript.

During the months of writing I benefited from opportunities to discuss my work with colleagues who gave of their time and their knowledge. In June 1978 I had the privilege of participating in the Mt. Kisco conference on American–East Asian relations and testing many of my hypotheses on fellow paper-writers and conference discussants. Although they did not always agree with my conclusions, I profited especially from the insights and encouragement of Michael Hunt, Waldo Heinrichs, Larry Weiss, Steven Goldstein, and Walter LaFeber. I am indebted also to Professors Heinrichs, George C. Herring, James W. Morley, and Andrew Nathan who painstakingly read the entire manuscript and urged changes in both style and substance. Similarly, a small group of Columbia University students, John D'Emilio, William McLaughlin, Duane Tananbaum, and Susan Stone Wong, read drafts of my work over a period of eight months and provided helpful suggestions as well as cheerful support.

The greatest debt is, of course, the hardest to acknowledge and no words can effectively describe the herculean efforts of Dorothy Borg, William E. Leuchtenburg, and Bruce Tucker in making this book a reality. Professor Leuchtenburg showed me that no task of research was too great to perform and no lines of prose too prized to be rewritten. Dorothy Borg, over the course of a long association, has helped me learn which questions to ask and tirelessly guided me toward the answers. Without the support and comfort she unfailingly offered, this task would have been far more difficult to accomplish. Bruce, my husband, gave unstintingly of his editorial advice, his strength, and his patience in times which were often trying. For their contributions I shall always be grateful.

A Note on Romanization

I have chosen to use the Wade-Giles system, which is in keeping with the source materials of the period 1945–1950. I have departed from this rule only where place and personal names have become more familiar in a different form as, for example, in Peking rather than Peip'ing or Peiching.

Nancy Bernkopf Tucker
January 1983

Patterns in the Dust

CHAPTER ONE
America's China Policy
On the Threshold

)━●━()━●━()━●━()━●━(

O N the same brisk January morning in 1949 that Dean Acheson took office as Harry Truman's third Secretary of State, Chiang Kai-shek, who had long symbolized Nationalist China, withdrew from his post as President of the Republic. The concurrence of these two events foretold how insistently China would intrude upon Acheson's years in the State Department and involve him ever more in Asian affairs and in the need to reformulate America's China policy. "Chiang was in the last stages of collapse," Acheson later recalled. "I arrived just in time to have him collapse on me."[1] In fact, by the time Acheson assumed his duties as Secretary the total rout of Nationalist authority on the mainland at the hands of the Communist Chinese, once a distant possibility, had become imminent. Renewed attempts to reach a negotiated settlement paralleled the flight of Kuomintang notables seeking sanctuary on the island of Taiwan early in 1949. Americans had to decide whether they, too, would accompany Chiang Kai-shek into exile or recognize the new authorities in Peking.

Neither Dean Acheson nor President Harry Truman wanted to make this difficult decision. There seemed to be only costs—and no benefits—for the Administration. Continuing to support the Nationalist Chinese would mean cutting the United States off from an overwhelming majority of Chinese people. It meant denying the revolutionary energies of an Asian society and rejecting a long sought peace. But to turn away from the so-called free Chinese to deal with an avowedly communist regime threatened to provoke partisan turmoil at home. Moreover, for men who had grown to political maturity since the Bolshevik revolution, such a choice required an unsettling ideological adjustment.

Then, too, Truman and Acheson did not relish the prospect of devoting time and attention to a reexamination of American interests in China. As 1949 began, they found themselves most often preoccupied with Soviet challenges in Europe or Republican opposition in Congress. China had been engulfed in civil war for years and, before that, had proven a weak and stubborn ally. What little either man knew about Chinese politics, and it was little indeed, suggested that the problems might be insoluble and thus energy might better be spent elsewhere. President Truman, who felt uncomfortable in the realm of foreign relations, readily agreed with the conviction of his Secretary of State that China remained a peripheral area of scarcely any enduring importance to the United States.

But in 1949, however much they wished it otherwise, Truman and Acheson found that China could not be ignored. The disintegration of Kuomintang rule would not proceed quietly, removed from the turbulence of postwar politics. Instead, as in Chinese opera, when the dissonance of gongs and cymbals compels an inattentive audience to focus on the stage, Mao Tse-tung's guns forced the President and Secretary to witness the death throes of a government and an era. The Nationalists could no longer maintain their military dominance or the façade of concern for people's rights and livelihoods. Revolutionary forces wrested power from Chiang Kai-shek and alarmed Washington by promising to solve China's age-old problems through a reorganization of the society according to communist dictates. President Truman and Secretary Acheson confronted in this development a possible threat to American security. How serious a danger depended on whether the victor proved to be a Chinese patriot or a puppet manipulated by Soviet power.

China's significance to the United States extended beyond cold war competition, encompassing America's relations with its allies as well. For instance, although far removed from Europe, China occupied a special place in the calculations of British statesmen. London looked to profitable investments in and trade with China to help stabilize a floundering economy. Acheson, for whom England's difficulties ranked barely below America's own, felt it imperative to weigh British interests in the balance of Sino-American relations.

The dissolution of a nominally Western-style government in China also had a potentially unsettling impact upon American friends in Asia. Long a battleground between expanding imperialist powers, the Pacific region after World War II lay exposed to a new round of exploitation. The United States possessed predominant influence but the Soviet Union, by virtue of geography, maintained a more salient presence. Truman and Acheson worried that failure of an allegedly democratic government in China would suggest to other Asian peoples either that the system itself didn't work or that the United States would not stand by its commitment to succor troubled allies. Particularly among the Japanese, whose status had rapidly changed from enemy to ally, Washington's reliability must not be open to question. Furthermore, in Tokyo as in London, economic imperatives complicated the issue. The China market lured Japanese businessmen in spite of the political risks such contacts involved.

Political risk, President Truman and Secretary Acheson knew, was not limited to developments abroad. In the United States the citizenry had grown disenchanted with a *pax Americana* that did not produce an abiding sense of security. World War II had not resolved global tensions and increasingly the public blamed Democratic politicians for the disordered state of international affairs. The Republican party consciously fueled the restiveness, in time turning to the so-called loss of China to prove that Truman, Acheson and others in the government had been soft on communism.

Given these pressures, the approaching Nationalist debacle plunged the Secretary and his staff into the unwelcome but ultimately unavoidable task of analyzing national objectives in the East. And during the eighteen months from January 1949 to the advent of the Korean War—months which would later, confusingly, take on the glow of that conflagration and of the "McCarthy massacres"—Acheson did actually devise a China strategy and set about implementing it. While critics accused the Department of doing nothing, and Administration rhetoric seemed to indicate that policy would await developments abroad, the Secretary proceeded to formulate and gather support for his plan. He moved cautiously, hampered by his own uncertainty and lack of knowledge—but still shielded by an absence of widespread public concern—as he secured allies and anticipated opposition along the way. From his perspective, there seemed ample time for prudence: America had not committed itself to the crusading zeal of later days, and for the moment the tenor of discussion remained open and diplomacy flexible enough to develop in a variety of directions.

Beginning early in 1949, the State Department, guided by Acheson, attempted to assess the degree of tolerance that domestic politics would allow for a new relationship with China.[2] Acheson entertained a lively distrust for amateurs who sought to interfere in the running of international relations. But although he believed that foreign affairs ought to be the preserve of an educated elite, he recognized that in a democracy the Secretary of State must at least appear sensitive to the expectations of the people and their representatives. The Department might look primarily outward, dealing with problems beyond the nation's borders, but it remained incumbent upon the Secretary to create an image of concern for domestic opinion. Having served as the State Department's liaison with Congress under Secretary Edward Stettinius from 1944 to 1945, Acheson possessed an uncommon awareness of the yearnings of legislators to play a significant role in foreign affairs. Acheson consequently conferred with members of Congress about China far more than his predecessors, even going so far as to modify Constitutional practice by promising formal consultation before implementing any decision regarding recognition of the Chinese Communists. Moreover, with pro-Kuomintang partisans determined to compel policymakers to save Chiang Kai-shek, it appeared wise to discover how many Americans actually shared their viewpoint. If countervailing pressures existed, they might well give Acheson more freedom to decide what the United States should do while reducing the political costs if he chose to shun the China Lobby. Ultimately the public would not determine policy: that would be the result of careful deliberation by experts; but the people would have to approve the direction taken. Department officers must convince them that the nation's welfare and safety would be protected. Acheson the patrician found such activity distasteful, but Acheson the clever bureaucrat resolutely undertook the task.[3]

The existence of an assortment of Americans with links to China made it somewhat easier for officials to gather opinion and exert influence beyond Department precincts. Businessmen, missionaries, and scholars received and accepted invitations to discuss proposed courses of action in Washington. Constant monitoring of stories by journalists reporting from China, as well as of those at home, provided insight into media positions and the events they covered. All this information increased the Secretary's ability to fashion a well-informed but independent approach to the Chinese situation.

The Administration welcomed the concern of businessmen whose enterprises committed them to activities in Asia. Harry Truman's relations with the corporate world had not always been smooth; his veto of the Taft-Hartley Act in 1947, for instance, alienated many who had been won over by his earlier struggle against John L. Lewis and the unions. At the same time, the economic imbalances of the 1940s had made necessary considerable collaboration between American government agencies and business. The Marshall Plan grew in part out of the need to keep export markets alive, and participation by private entrepreneurs in speeding European recovery secured enthusiastic encouragement. In 1949, the President again courted business interests, this time in behalf of his Point Four plan for assistance to underdeveloped areas of the world. Economic expansion in Asia received considerable emphasis in the early months of preparation for the new program.[4] It seemed essential, therefore, to work constructively with businessmen whose Chinese connections might spur other Asian investments and trade agreements.

The business community's interaction with the State Department on China policy reflected the unevenness of its investments and trade with that turbulent country. Corporations like General Electric, International Telephone and Telegraph, and First National Bank, which relied upon the government to help protect their Chinese holdings, apprised officials of their views and experiences. They expected support to counter the exactions of foreign authorities and rescue employees should civil war threaten them with bodily injury. In turn, company executives volunteered information on transactions in China and pledged cooperation if and when trade restrictions became necessary. None of the major corporations had massive assets at risk and, though their interests could not be considered negligible and they hoped to exert some influence on policies that would determine future profits, almost all assumed a compliant stance toward Department policy.

Missionaries sustained less intimate but still significant ties with American decision makers. Mission board representatives visited the State Department to lobby with officials and join in meetings analyzing events in China. Missionaries similarly interacted with foreign service officers in the field, and one member of the mission community, John Leighton Stuart, served as America's Ambassador to China from 1946 to 1949. American officials, nevertheless, often dismissed missionary views as naïve and self-interested. Stuart's appointment, according to press officer John Melby, "produced an atmosphere of unmitigated gloom" around the Embassy because of the effect his emotional Christianity was thought to have on his political judgment.[5] But missionaries with connections to thousands of parishes throughout the United States, where churchgoers gave nickels and dimes for enlightening the heathen, had unusual opportunities to mold popular views regarding China. Many Americans, including some in government, formed their earliest images of the Chinese from reports about the Christian "conquest" of Asia. Dean Acheson recalled years later, "Hardly a town in our land was without its society to collect funds and clothing for Chinese missions, to worry about those who labored in distant, dangerous, and exotic vineyards of the Lord, and to hear the missionaries' inspiring reports. Thus was nourished the love portion of the love-hate complex that was to infuse so much emotion into our later China policy."[6]

Scholars contributed more directly than either missionaries or businessmen to decision-making and to the process of communicating those decisions to the public. Senator Joseph McCarthy's virulent charges against Owen Lattimore of Johns Hopkins University, the alleged "architect of our Far Eastern policy," exaggerated his influence, but scholars did cooperate officially and unofficially with the government. Scholars, who had the leisure that State Department officials lacked to study Chinese affairs, could put information on contemporary events into perspective and help weigh trends. Forums such as the State Department's Round Table discussions of October 1949 provided opportunities to tap their expertise and, at the same time, bring them up to date on official attitudes.[7] Then they could and often did explain policies to wider audiences in magazine and journal articles. Individual scholars served in more regularized consulting capacities: Nathaniel Peffer, for one, secretly assisted with the preparation of the China White Paper.[8] And still more centrally, Dean Acheson prevailed upon his trusted friend Philip C. Jessup, an internationally known professor of law from Columbia University, not only to edit the White Paper but also to carry out a major reassessment of America's position in Asia. Important, in part, simply as a public relations gesture, the review did confirm Acheson's developing thoughts on the future of Sino-American relations.

Coverage of China in the press and on radio gave journalists a channel to policymakers not shared by other groups. The Department conducted formal surveys following particular issues and recorded the intensity and frequency of comment in the media. In addition, the staff and the Secretary read newspapers and magazines, passing notable stories and columns from desk to desk. Reporters writing in China supplemented the observations of foreign service dispatches, adding independent interpretations valued in Washington. For State Department officials, Dean Acheson included, the media also provided a ready means of access to the reading public, allowing difficult decisions to be analyzed and explained. Thus the press supplied the government with a way to inform the nation while keeping officials aware of which issues generated controversy and required elucidation or possibly rethinking.

Responsible in the end for formulating United States policy, Acheson invited—but did not necessarily use—the perspectives of others to supplement his own considerable talents and experience. A tall, imposing man with bushy brows and a carefully cultivated moustache, Acheson looked like a Secretary of State and came to his duties bearing an unusual history of involvement in diplomacy. During the tenures of James Byrnes and George Marshall, he had repeatedly served as Acting Secretary and had grown accustomed to dealing with foreign diplomats, as well as with Congress and American interest groups. He had also established a warm relationship with Harry Truman; their intimacy, when Acheson became Secretary, made him virtually the President's only advisor on international relations. The two men agreed on most policies and Truman especially appreciated, after his frustrating ordeal with the presumptuous Byrnes, Acheson's realization that, "while I leaned on him for constant advice, the policy had to be mine."[9] Within the Department, Acheson expected from and gave to his subordinates the same sort of cooperation and loyalty. When their recommendations diverged from his own analyses, he listened attentively although he was rarely persuaded. On China he had the good fortune to be supported by many of the people in the Department whose views he believed reliable.

Exploration of alternative approaches to China led State Department officials to examine not only the contemporary ramifications of Sino-American relations but also their wartime history. What they uncovered was a legacy of misunderstanding and contradiction which had significantly shaped contacts ever since.

Americans and Chinese, attributing erroneous motives and values to one another during the war, had produced little but animosity and discord. President Franklin Roosevelt, for instance, misjudging the basic nature of Chiang Kai-shek's regime, had hoped to promote an independent, democratic and pro-American China. Anxious about the power vacuum that would exist in Asia once Japan's forces had been disarmed and sent home, he wanted to build a Chinese state capable of controlling the East and keeping the Russians out. The American press, at least in the early years of the war, embellished Roosevelt's view of Chungking fighting on the front lines for freedom and democracy. The papers applauded Chinese resistance and touted Chiang as a fearless and indomitable leader.

The reality behind the United States partnership with Nationalist China bore little resemblance to Roosevelt's ideal. When America entered the war, Chiang and the Kuomintang envisaged it a savior rather than an ally.[10] The President, on the other hand, assumed that the Chinese would continue to tie down the Japanese armies while Americans fought to free Europe from fascist control. While Roosevelt chided Chiang for hoarding his arms and ammunition and urged him to keep the fight against Japan alive, the Generalissimo worried instead about the struggle with communist armies which would erupt as soon as the Japanese scourge lifted. American disenchantment with Chiang proceeded apace, accelerated by the Kuomintang's refusal to liberalize its regime.

Americans discovered that prospects for a strong and westernized China did not accord with Chiang's politics and policies. The Generalissimo spent most of his energies preserving his own authority. He kept inept generals in charge of his troops simply because they remained loyal supporters. He refused to equip soldiers in the field battling the Japanese lest he deplete his anticommunist stockpiles. When Roosevelt attempted to take the situation in hand by dispatching Joseph Stilwell to China in 1944, Chiang resisted the General's guidance and forced his recall to Washington.[11] Similar barriers frustrated those hoping to encourage nonmilitary reforms. Nationalist officials saw little value in American concepts of progress and, American observers lamented, obstinately ignored the desperate plight of China's starving millions. Chiang, even had he sympathized with China's peasantry, believed he could not attack his only reliable base of support in the privileged bastions of the landowning elite. To Roosevelt and then Truman, ineffectiveness and corruption seemed compounded by a stubborn callousness.

At war's end, in spite of these large areas of incompatibility, the United States remained Chiang's ally and sought to reconcile the Soviet Union and the Communist Chinese to his leadership. Initially this spurred concessions at the Yalta Conference of 1945. The United States urgently wanted Soviet participation in the last stages of the fight against Japan. Acquisition of Chinese territory could, it seemed, convince Stalin both to enter the war and to throw his support to the Kuomintang. In exchange for a treaty of friendship between Stalin and Chiang Kai-shek, the United States promised to persuade Nationalist officials to recognize the independence of Outer Mongolia and agree to joint control of the Chinese-Eastern railroad, the internationalization of Dairen, and the leasing of Port Arthur to Moscow. Six months later, in August 1945, as Japan capitulated and World War II ended, Chiang Kai-shek accepted Stalin's terms and secured a pledge that the Soviets would recognize his regime and not support communist elements in China.[12] Chiang felt certain—and the Americans hoped—that, having been abandoned by Moscow, Mao Tse-tung would now reach a compromise with the Kuomintang.[13]

Anxious to facilitate such an agreement, the Truman Administration struck upon the idea of a coalition government to be established through American mediation. Special emissary General George C. Marshall would, the President believed, resolve twenty years of civil conflict and bring about genuine cooperation. But neither the CCP nor the KMT desired an end to China's struggle which would require significant concessions, each anticipating a day when it could hurl overwhelming might at the other and emerge as the single ruling party in the nation. Temporary adjustments suited the Communists, who needed time to prepare for a final offensive against Chiang Kai-shek's far more numerous forces. However, the CCP rapidly lost faith in Marshall's impartiality as Truman, while asserting his nation's disinterestedness, consistently maintained its support for the Nationalist regime. The United States air-lifted Chiang's soldiers east and north from Szechuan during late 1945 and early 1946, allowing them to take control of key cities and position themselves in China's heartland. Not only did such activity alienate the Communists, but by strengthening the Kuomintang's hold on China, it inadvertently convinced Chiang that he had no need to compromise. CCP intransigence similarly drew encouragement from Soviet actions in Manchuria. The Russians violated their treaty pledges by providing the CCP with Japanese weapons and, more importantly, blocking Nationalist efforts to reimpose their authority before Mao's troops could occupy large stretches of the Northeast, which still lay behind Soviet lines. By January 1947, despite the ceasefire Marshall had worked so hard to secure, China drifted once again into warfare, and Truman recalled the mission to Washington.[14]

Failure of Marshall's efforts had a significant impact upon both President Truman and then Undersecretary of State Dean Acheson. Acheson, part of Marshall's rear echelon in Washington, had been privy to the frustrations the China mission experienced in such abundance. He had shared in the struggle to provide economic inducements for a coalition government which never really had a chance to end the civil war. When Marshall, a man both Acheson and Truman admired immensely, returned home in disgust, the hopelessness of compromise seemed to be affirmed. "Sincere efforts to achieve settlement," the General lamented, "have been frustrated time and again by extremist elements of both sides." It had not simply been communist irreconcilables at fault but the Kuomintang's "dominant group of reactionaries who have been opposed, in my opinion, to almost every effort I have made . . . [who], interested in the preservation of their own feudal control of China, evidently had no real intention of implementing" political reforms or making peace.[15]

The months of full-scale civil war that followed found the United States in an increasingly uncomfortable association with the Kuomintang. President Truman continued supplying weapons to Nationalist China in spite of serious reservations. American advice, however, went unheeded and American guns passed into communist hands with alarming rapidity. Chiang began the struggle with an enormous preponderance of force, and United States officers argued that astute management could prevent any short-term disaster. But Chiang demonstrated from the first, by insisting upon a reoccupation of Manchuria against American admonitions and despite severe logistic inadequacies, that he would orchestrate the fighting regardless of the cost.[16] The Kuomintang also made painfully clear that criticism of the government, even from an

avowed friend, General Albert C. Wedemeyer (whose remarks came at
the end of his fact-finding mission in August 1947), would elicit no
changes in KMT domestic or foreign policies.[17]

Chiang Kai-shek's inflexibility grew, in part, out of his conviction that
the United States could not afford to abandon him. The cold war had
divided the world into competing blocs and China, as part of the free
world alliance, played a crucial role in preventing communist expansion
eastward. Chiang believed firmly in the Nationalist regime's indis-
pensability to Washington even though the postwar Soviet-American
contest for world power had not been waged in Asia. Trouble had
erupted initially in Europe, where both Moscow and Washington saw
fundamental questions of national security at stake. Stalin insisted on
the creation of a buffer zone to protect his country's western border.
Washington, loath to watch free people pass under communist domination, convinced that avoidance of renewed depression demanded
open markets, and nervous about the political stability of Western Europe, challenged Soviet advances. An acrimonious confrontation developed, first over Poland, then Rumania, and soon, most particularly,
over Germany.

By January 1949 President Truman had committed Washington to a
host of anti-Soviet policies. For six months, since June 1948, American
aircraft had been supplying the besieged city of Berlin, successfully resisting a blockade that the Russians had imposed in order to prevent
establishment of a viable West German republic. The Marshall Plan,
inaugurated in 1948, had so effectively begun to rebuild the economies
of America's Western European allies that Moscow introduced its own
Council of Mutual Economic Assistance in January 1949 to mollify its
East European satellites. Overcoming a heritage of isolationism, the
United States verged on ratification of a mutual defense pact. This un-
precedented peacetime alliance, the North Atlantic Treaty Organization
(NATO), promised protection to twelve nations presumably in the path
of a rapacious Soviet Union.

As the United States became entangled in these cold war measures,
Chiang urgently insisted that China benefit from similar guarantees. The
perfect vehicle seemed to be the Truman Doctrine which the American
President had announced early in 1947. Once again, this was a policy
which had received its impetus from European developments, a response to a British declaration that, facing economic crisis, London could
not supply the $250,000,000 in assistance that Greece and Turkey re-
quired to maintain their freedom. Seeing an opportunity to force a
budget-cutting Congress into saving Europe from collapse, the President
and current Secretary of State George Marshall challenged all Americans

to fight for liberty. The United States must act, they asserted, not merely to save Greece or Turkey, but to stop communist advances everywhere.[18] To Chiang and his associates this suggested that despite its European origins the program would include provisions for China.

In reality, the President had not intended to expand the cold war beyond Europe, and after Acheson took office as Secretary of State, Administration policy continued to focus on rehabilitating the West. Neither Acheson nor Truman believed that American power could be productively applied everywhere, and neither thought that the United States had as serious a need to act in Asia as in Europe. Acheson tried to make clear that Washington had to respond to troubles abroad according to a set of ordered priorities:

> The United States, in my judgment, acts in regard to a foreign nation strictly in regard to American interests. . . . And if it is to American interest or those wider interests which affect it, to do one thing in one country and another thing in another country, then *that* is the consistency upon which I propose to advise the President, and I am not in the slightest bit worried because somebody can say: "Well, you said so and so about Greece, why isn't all of this true about China?" I will be polite. I will be patient, and I will try to explain why Greece is not China, but my heart will not be in that battle.[19]

Having once utilized global rhetoric, however, the White House and State Department found it almost impossible to channel the militancy the rhetoric engendered. Within the United States animosity toward the Soviet Union and fear of communist contagion grew. If America must meet such a palpable threat in Europe how safe, wondered a shocked nation, were we at home? The President's Executive Loyalty Program, promulgated just nine days after his speech on Turkey and Greece, suggested that the dangers of communism had assumed an unnerving immediacy. Abroad too, Chiang Kai-shek shrilly proclaimed that communist forces had made new inroads. The United States must, he declared, apply the Truman Doctrine to Asia. By January 1949 these concerns had begun to mesh as the disintegration of China came to be seen more and more as a domestic political issue.

Grasping at opportunities provided by developments in Asia, various individuals and interest groups proved exceedingly eager to set the Chinese civil war in a context of Soviet–American confrontation. Nationalist Chinese emissaries in Washington and New York couched pleas for aid in cold war verbiage.[20] Similarly, Chiang Kai-shek's American sympathizers, the so-called China Lobby, drew upon President Truman's own words to frustrate his intentions. Congressman Walter Judd

(R, MN), a former medical missionary in China and the most influential of Chiang's loyal exponents, declared to the House of Representatives as it considered aid appropriations: "We have to win in Asia, too, or we will ultimately lose in Europe. I cannot myself vote to put some $20,000,000,000 into holding the line on one front and then ignore another equally vital to our future."[21]

Republicans less concerned with Asia than Judd, but determined to recapture the Presidency after twenty years out of power, also linked the Administration's China policy to the cold war. The Grand Old Party, frustrated by Truman's totally unexpected victory over Thomas Dewey in November 1948, sought ways to discredit the President's authority. Utilizing charges that the Democrats harbored communists in the government and knowingly betrayed Chiang Kai-shek, the GOP hoped to overcome the attraction of Roosevelt's domestic legacy and scare the American public into voting Republican.[22]

The case of Alger Hiss came to symbolize the conflicts of the period. Hiss represented an educated elite which appeared to disdain a simpler America, his urbane New Dealism offending those who yearned for less government interference and expenditure. Hiss had been at Yalta, where, critics insisted, a sick and senile Roosevelt had made major concessions to Stalin. Indeed, the China Lobby literature maintained that Hiss "sat behind the worn and exhausted Roosevelt, then only a few weeks from his grave, whispering advice into his ear on the vital decisions which gave China, Poland and Eastern Europe to Stalin." In 1948 Whittaker Chambers explained that Alger Hiss had facilitated Stalin's "coup" at Yalta because he was a member of the Communist Party. Chambers, himself an apostate communist, claimed further that Hiss had been a spy who had passed confidential State Department files to him for transmission to Moscow. Chambers' prestigious position as an editor of *Time* magazine gave credence to his accusations, and classified documents which he had microfilmed and secreted in a hollowed-out pumpkin on his Maryland farm seemed to prove that an illicit connection with Hiss had existed. Since the statute of limitations upon the latter's purported treason had expired, Hiss faced charges of perjury for denying that he had seen and dealt with Chambers.[23] Thus, as Harry Truman's second term began, the Hiss case put to a test the President's characterization of the communists-in-government issue as a "red herring."[24] Further, it threatened to give credibility to a much broader indictment of the Democratic Party and its handling of world affairs.

China provided the perfect theater for Republican repudiation of Democratic leadership. Not only had the situation there declined precipitously, but members of the GOP and other Administration critics claimed that China policy had long been the preserve of the party in power. In truth, widespread lack of interest in China and the confusion of continual civil war had minimized Congressional influence and left the White House and State Department in almost complete control of Chinese affairs.[25] This situation persisted despite a brief flurry of concern occasioned by American Ambassador to China Patrick Hurley in 1945, when he demanded the recall of certain foreign service officers who he claimed had an overabundance of sympathy for the Chinese Communist forces. Although Washington withdrew the men in question, Hurley's embarrassing performance before a Congressional committee of inquiry following his resignation limited the repercussions of his charges.[26] Congress returned to its more usual attitude of indifference, allowing the executive branch to resume largely uncontested dominion over America's China policy. But the fact that Republicans in Congress had abdicated responsibility for developments in the East afforded Truman little solace; for, having dominated the field, the Administration alone appeared accountable.

As 1949 began, Truman became the object of increasingly bitter partisan attacks over China but he maintained a resolute determination not to be drawn further into the struggle there. He continued to send aid to Chiang, but with Nationalist fortunes so severely compromised by Nationalist actions, the President would not increase the nation's commitment. Rejecting a series of ever more desperate appeals, Truman and Acheson refused to send American ground troops to shore up Nationalist lines. Armed forces officials warned that the United States already lacked sufficient manpower to protect more important fronts in Europe because the military establishment had been so critically depleted by the postwar rush to demobilization.[27] Commitment to an effort as overwhelming as that in China appeared neither possible nor desirable. The American people would not approve such a campaign for an area that seemed of negligible economic, political, or cultural importance to them. Moreover, to avoid entanglement in the fighting by accident or manipulation, the President rebuffed suggestions that he significantly increase aid to the Kuomintang and direct Americans to supervise the distribution of it as in Greece. Having already spent great quantities of money on Chiang Kai-shek, the Administration, as well as most of Congress, opposed squandering additional funds. Repeatedly during 1947 and 1948 Congress further cut minimal appropriations for assistance to Nationalist China.[28]

Dean Acheson and Harry Truman welcomed rampant apathy toward China and mounting disenchantment with Chiang Kai-shek. Neither man wanted to be forced to adopt an active stance prematurely or perhaps, given the situation, at all. Compiling his list of urgent international problems in January 1949, the new Secretary of State did not include China, even though at that moment the CCP was engaging KMT armies in the most decisive battle of the civil war.[29] Over the closing months of 1948, the Department had reviewed its approach to China and dismissed any notion of implementing a more energetic policy. President Truman sustained this decision and refused to make a public declaration of support for the KMT as requested by Chiang Kai-shek or call a special session of the Eightieth Congress as urged by China-bloc Senator Styles Bridges (R, NH).[30] During February Acheson would explain to thirty members of Congress that what critics condemned as Administration passivity really was a positive choice to "wait until the dust settled." In truth, the State Department was not ignoring China; it was seeking the opinions of those concerned with China's future; it was simply doing so in a deliberate fashion shorn of the headline-making attributes of the Marshall Plan or Truman Doctrine.

The calm with which most policymakers approached events in China grew in large part from their perception of the country as an unimportant theater for the growing competition between Soviet and American interests. Stakes seemed critically high in Europe, in the Middle East, increasingly in Japan, but not in poor, overpopulated, underdeveloped China. George Kennan, while director of the State Department's Policy Planning Staff, argued that only four vital power centers required application of the containment doctrine. With the Soviet Union, the fifth nucleus, already lost to dark forces, the United States must protect itself, Great Britain, the Rhine valley, and Japan.[31] Dean Acheson, having watched the breakdown of Washington's wartime alliance with Moscow at first hand and having attended a series of fruitless postwar conferences, advocated firm resistance against Soviet expansion. He no longer believed negotiations could curb Soviet avarice. Instead, he thought, the United States must build strong armed forces and refuse to allow idealism about the United Nations to deter it from constant vigilance. But in China, Acheson continually emphasized, an overreaction by Americans to the revolution could trigger an ill-considered retaliation by the Soviet Union and total identification by the Chinese Communists with Moscow. He resolutely concluded that American policy must minimize both Russian and American involvement in China's future.[32]

Detention of America's Consul General Angus Ward and his staff in Mukden after November 1948 put Acheson's convictions to a severe test. The incident began when Chinese Communist officials became convinced that the Mukden consulate general ran an espionage network in the surrounding politically and militarily sensitive reaches of Manchuria.

Reversing initially friendly contact with American officials, Communist authorities suddenly cordoned off the American compound and proceeded to hold twenty-two people under house arrest until November 1949.

Throughout the months of Ward's ordeal, Acheson refused to be provoked into precipitous action. Early in 1949, the Secretary ascribed the Mukden incident and other such occurrences to the normal disorder accompanying revolution. He cautioned against repeating rumors that the staff in Manchuria suffered abusive treatment lest indignation occasion too brash an American response.

Even the events of November 1949, which so sharply challenged Washington, did not undermine the Secretary's determination to preserve State Department and White House composure. Perhaps needing some way to bring the episode to a close, the Chinese Communists seized upon an altercation at the consulate compound to charge Ward and three others with beating a former employee. Imprisonment of the four Westerners set the China Lobby and various patriotic associations in the United States aflame. Lobby organizers saw to it that sympathetic newspapers carried lurid stories about Ward's detention and berated the Administration. The *New York Daily News*, for instance, complained that "Stalin's Chinese stooges are making our Government look more foolish and impotent by the hour." The American Legion called stridently for military action. Harry Truman, distressed by the developments in China and the outcry at home, contemplated a rescue attempt or a blockade of coal shipments to Communist Chinese ports. Acheson, however, argued that violent tactics would risk far too much. Not only would Washington hand the CCP a powerful propaganda weapon but the blockade would probably be ineffective in light of China's economic self-sufficiency. An analysis by the Joint Chiefs of Staff of America's strengths and the possible costs involved supported Acheson's conclusions and a still angry Truman acceded to their combined advice. The Secretary turned instead to diplomacy, but his efforts to mobilize international assistance proved unnecessary when a CCP court quickly tried, convicted, and expelled the Americans.

The Ward incident illustrated the intricate balancing of forces that shaped American relations with China in 1949. Chinese Communist radicals, struggling with moderates desirous of relations with the United States, precipitated a crisis. American anticommunists responded with demands for military action calling the incident an example of unbridled Soviet treachery. The Russians probably did influence Chinese actions. John Paton Davies of the Policy Planning Staff pointed out that Moscow, preferring to keep Peking isolated, might have engineered the Mukden confrontation to embitter CCP relations with the United States. More-over, action could have been initiated independently by a Communist Party faction in Manchuria with close ties to Russian Communists. The Soviets also had more immediate motives for retaliating, given the pros-ecution in the United States of one Russian official as a spy and the arrest in October 1949 of three commercial representatives who had not registered as foreign agents. But ultimately Russian manipulation, if it existed, gave way to Chinese self-interest as Peking acted to defuse the dangerous situation. Chinese leaders, whether anxious to avoid sanc-tions, or shooting, or international obloquy, or simply fearful that Soviet support would dissipate, let the consular staff go. Americans, with a few notable exceptions, approached the entire incident cautiously. Press and radio comments, though in some cases quite belligerent, heated up only slowly during the year and returned to a more judicious posture as soon as the crisis ended. Most importantly, at the end of 1949, as at the beginning, the Administration and in particular the President, fol-lowing the stoic leadership of Dean Acheson, did not allow the en-counter to escalate and embroil the United States in a war.[33]

Despite Moscow's ideological affinity with the Communist Chinese and the Truman Doctrine's globalism, the cold war had not yet arrived in Asia.[34] On several occasions during the 1940s American officials had found their counterparts at the Kremlin willing to compromise Mao Tse-tung's interests to secure benefits for the Soviet Union. At Teheran in 1943 Stalin had called Chiang the best available leader in China, and he told W. Averell Harriman in 1944 that Mao and his followers could not be considered real communists.[35] During World War II, Moscow made three loans totaling $250,000,000 to Chungking, while providing Yenan with virtually no aid of any kind.[36] American observers reported few Russians in the Communist capital and no shipments of arms to help in the CCP's struggle. The Sino-Soviet Friendship Treaty signed in Au-gust 1945 came as a shock to the unprepared CCP, as did the various territorial and economic concessions that Stalin wrested from Nationalist negotiators in that and other agreements.[37] The Soviet Union, Truman concluded, preferred a divided and weak neighbor to a unified China under a dynamic Communist leadership.[38]

Moscow's willingness to limit its involvement in China by not stim-ulating the growth of the CCP and dealing instead with the Kuomintang safely allowed the United States to minimize its presence there as well. In fact, an increase in American aid to the Kuomintang risked provoking a degree of cooperation between the CCP and Moscow which both sides had so far resisted.[39] Truman and Acheson accepted the possibility that Mao Tse-tung could to some degree be independent of Soviet direction,

discriminating between adherence to an ideology and slavish acceptance
of foreign rule. Neither man believed, in January 1949, in a monolithic
worldwide communist conspiracy.[40] They found in Tito's dispute with
Stalin, which had led to Yugoslavia's expulsion from the Cominform in
June 1948, evidence that not all communists necessarily followed orders
from Moscow.[41] But even should China accept Soviet dominance, its
lack of raw materials and industrial resources would, as George Marshall
had told the Senate Foreign Relations Committee in February 1948, prevent it from becoming a first-rate military power in the foreseeable future.[42] Rather than posing a threat to the United States, China would
probably turn into a quagmire for the Russians—an eventuality that
Washington could enjoy from afar.

Acheson therefore sought a policy which would preserve American
flexibility. Without scuttling the Nationalists, he hoped to encourage
contacts with Communist leaders. His interest in the views and actions
of private groups involved in China took much of its impetus from such
expectations. Acheson's State Department urged businessmen, missionaries, educators, and others to continue their efforts among the
Chinese. He intended, over time, to make use of informal ties to improve
official relations. Although the Secretary lacked in Asian affairs the in-
tuitive understanding which served him so well in Europe, he did recognize that Washington had to overcome considerable resentment. For
whatever motives, the United States had effectively prolonged warfare
in war-weary China and had become identified with governmental ineptitude and corruption. Confronting this legacy and moving beyond
it would be a slow and difficult process. In the interim, Acheson would
try to convince the Communists in China that their future lay in jeopardy
only to the extent that they aligned themselves with the Soviets, and
Americans in the United States that their national interests would best
be served by maintaining contacts with China's Communists.

The Secretary discovered that, more than any other, this latter effort
plunged him into the maelstrom of domestic politics. Attacks upon the
Administration after the 1948 election increasingly tied China to charges
that Truman coddled communists. Not until after the Korean War
erupted would Truman and Acheson be intimidated by McCarthyite
witch-hunting in the capital, but there were those around the nation
who had tried in the months before to indict the Democrats for undermining Chiang Kai-shek. Acheson, contemptuous of these critics, had
the State Department listen instead to the missionaries, businessmen,
scholars, and newsmen who had not been identified with the China
Lobby for a sense of the public's temper. Usually inclined to disregard
the complaints of the uninitiated, he welcomed countervailing pressures

which would leave him free to follow his own conscience and sense of international imperatives.

On Inauguration Day 1949, as the sun shone upon crowds massing along Pennsylvania Avenue, the direction of American relations with China remained unsettled. Few watching the festivities spared a moment's thought to the tumultuous events occurring half a world away. Even the President and his incoming Secretary of State, if they worried about foreign problems, would have thought about Berlin or the North Atlantic Treaty, not Nanking or Shanghai. Yet their lack of interest could not survive unscathed through the disintegration of Nationalist rule. Many external factors would play a role in the eventual decision of whether to recognize China: the developing cold war between Russia and America; the extent of Mao's victory in China; the face that Chinese Communism turned toward the United States. Within America, too, various forces would exert pressures, sometimes compatible, sometimes conflicting with the inclinations of the Administration. Missionaries and businessmen with interests in China, the China Lobby, journalists, and media representatives who had been sending dispatches from the East, and the public which responded to those groups—all tried to influence American policy.

Increasingly harsh realities in China confronted Truman and Acheson. Both men found it necessary to take positions, but did so cautiously, sounding out the broadest range of opinion and struggling to keep their options open as long as possible. And in the actions they eventually took, they were guided in no small measure by the confluence of domestic and foreign views which, like it or not, they could hardly ignore.

CHAPTER TWO

International Influences
European and Asian Perspectives

)◄━◗◄━◗◄◗◄━◗◄◗◄━◗(

T HE crowded early days of 1949 immersed the Secretary of State in a round of activities designed to reaffirm the nation's alliances and make clear its continued resolve to counter America's adversaries. This meant, in essence, an immediate and almost all-encompassing focus on Europe, particularly a concentration on the German crisis and final ne-gotiation of a North Atlantic pact. Little time remained for other trouble spots—the traditional new secretary's speech on Latin America did not come until September—a situation made still more acute by Dean Ache-son's personal inclination to see events in Europe as dominant. But even as the Secretary and his staff devoted their attention to relations with the Soviet Union, Britain, and Western Europe, Asia thrust itself into their thinking.

Acheson realized that China could not be isolated from the interplay of global politics. London's economic woes placed a premium on British control of its prosperous colony at Hong Kong and other lucrative en-terprises inside China. Soviet challenges in the West also compelled Americans to be concerned about vulnerable areas in the East. Moreover the United States had acquired worldwide responsibilities as a result of World War II and ignored those obligations only at great peril. In Japan an American occupation force determined reform and rehabilitation pol-icies which impinged on and were unavoidably shaped by developments elsewhere. When policymakers disregarded protests against rebuilding Japan, for instance, they gave impetus to conclusion of a Sino-Soviet military alliance aimed directly against Japan and the United States. In effect they had accelerated a threat to Japan which reconstruction had been designed to retard. Clearly, policies could not be devised for China without taking international repercussions into account and, increas-ingly, American moves elsewhere in the world reverberated in China.[1]

I The British

Searching for a new balance of power and interests in the postwar world, the United States reluctantly found itself in conflict with Great Britain over the future of Asia. The British sought to salvage what remained of their once great empire and preserve vital sources of income for a faltering domestic economy. For the American government, anxiety over Britain's internal problems clashed with a growing conviction that colonialism no longer could stand in the way of national aspirations. The United States considered any effort to reimpose European control over Asian peoples to be nothing less than an invitation to communist subversion and revolution. Washington, therefore, sought to minimize Britain's part in Asian affairs—seeking London's acquiescence in or support of American politics, but denying Britain a substantive decision-making role.[2] With respect to China these conflicting expectations and desires ultimately produced opposing policies and strained the Anglo-American alliance.[3]

Questions about the future status of Western nations in Asia played a significant role in World War II politics and planning. As the Japanese marched southward, occupying much of East and Southeast Asia, they sought to secure the cooperation of local populations by arousing their anticolonial resentments. Japan promised that within a new Greater East Asian Co-Prosperity Sphere the entire area would achieve economic self-sufficiency and freedom from Western exploitation. Although promises of independence never materialized, because Japan needed the resources of its neighbors for its war effort, the Japanese succeeded in dislocating several old colonial regimes.[4] At the same time, United States policymakers began to argue against a postwar return to European dominance. Franklin Roosevelt told reporters in 1941 that "there never has been, there isn't now, and there never will be any race of people on earth fit to serve as masters of their fellow men." As soon as the war ended he hoped to see the principle of self-determination, embodied in the Atlantic Charter of 1941, realized universally.[5]

The attack on colonialism, mounted simultaneously if separately by the United States and Japan, seriously threatened Britain's position in the East. Although many British officials recognized the necessity of change in the imperial system, liquidation by Japanese attack or American order did not recommend itself to them. Winston Churchill, somewhat more belligerent than most of his government colleagues, reportedly declared that "Hongkong will be eliminated from the British Empire only over my dead body." Nevertheless, American efforts to curb British influence in Asia, coupled with the decline in London's power because of the war, forced British acknowledgement that predominance in China had passed to the United States. An official in Britain's Chungking Embassy observed during 1943 that China had become dependent on America and that:

> because we are not in a position to do otherwise, we have accepted this condition and have abdicated from the position of leadership which we have occupied in China for the past hundred years. China is by agreement regarded as in the American theatre of war, a decision the consequences of which seem to become more far-reaching every day; we are not in a position to keep pace with the United States in the furnishing of financial, economic and military assistance to the Chinese and their government; and in the diplomatic sphere, where ten years ago we naturally took the lead, we now wait anxiously to see what the American Government may do.[6]

Various Americans did not believe that Great Britain would so easily relinquish its position in China. Churchill seemed determined to reimpose his nation's authority and reclaim his countrymen's property. That property, in fact, substantially exceeded American investments and constituted an important input for the economy of the United Kingdom.[7] Given such strong motivation, these Americans believed, the British could be expected to utilize any means to protect themselves. In 1944 American Ambassador to China Patrick Hurley warned Franklin Roosevelt that he suspected the British of secretly dealing with the Chinese Communists.[8] Representative Mike Mansfield (D, Mt) reported from China that the British seemed to favor a weak postwar government that would be unable to resist reassertion of British privileges.[9] Hurley, General Albert C. Wedemeyer, and even John Paton Davies, a generally well-informed foreign service officer, agreed that, in Davies' words "the British oppose the unification of China by either Chiang or the Communists . . . and will be satisfied if they can have Chiang as a quasi-puppet in the area between the Yangtze valley and the Indochina border."[10] State Department personnel similarly believed that "there are reasons to take with a grain of salt a statement that the British are completely resigned to our having taken over the position they previously occupied in China." London could not, however, be allowed to interfere because of the "Chinese proclivity for playing off one power against another" and because the Americans did "not intend to relinquish . . . leadership."[11]

Early evidence that the United Kingdom would not docilely follow America's lead materialized during the war. President Roosevelt's insistence that China be treated and viewed as a powerful country (one of the "Big Four") Churchill considered to be the "great American illusion." That Washington "accorded China almost an equal fighting power with the British Empire, and rated the Chinese armies as a factor to be mentioned in the same breath as the armies of Russia," astounded him. The Prime Minister told Roosevelt that he thought American opinion overestimated China and although he himself "would of course always be helpful and polite to the Chinese" the President must not expect him to adopt a wholly unreal standard of values.[12] Anthony Eden similarly made it clear that he not expect China to be able to police a postwar Japan, and that he would be surprised if China itself avoided the turmoil of revolution.[13] America's efforts to exaggerate China's status seemed to many British observers a blatant attempt to increase American influence in China and insert a puppet vote in international decision-making councils.[14]

British activities in China during the civil war era departed even further from America's support of the Kuomintang regime. As the balance of power unequivocally shifted to the Communist forces, evidence of British disgust with the KMT and interest in the CCP mounted. According to British perceptions, the Nationalists had squandered their opportunity in China. By 1948 the Foreign Office no longer believed that KMT forces could be aided.[15] Sir Stafford Cripps, the British Chancellor of the Exchequer who early in World War II had imagined Chiang Kai-shek leading his country to a democratic and peaceful future, told Chinese Ambassador to Washington V. K. Wellington Koo in 1949 that he had heard too many reports of corruption and fascism in China. Indeed, Lady Cripps, a former KMT propagandist whose United Aid to China Fund had collected £703,000 for the Nationalists during the first year of its operation, had subsequently visited Yenan and been tremendously impressed by the CCP.[16] British Foreign Secretary Ernest Bevin told Koo that his government had become disillusioned with the Generalissimo and that he no longer sympathized with the KMT.[17]

Proof of this disenchantment had already come to the attention of American authorities in the form of an August 1949 British cabinet statement. The cabinet assumed that the CCP would soon dominate all of China and asserted that policy must be made in this context without holding out vain hopes for a KMT revival.[18] Outside the government the British press echoed official sentiment. The liberal *Manchester Guardian* judged the Kuomintang to be inept, brought down by its own actions. Even the conservative *Daily Telegraph* agreed that Chiang's "precarious foothold in Formosa" could not become the nucleus of a viable alternative to the Communist Chinese regime.[19]

Troubled relations between the Nationalists and the British merely enhanced disaffection. The Nationalist government, at the end of the war, had delayed reopening ports to British traffic, returning Yangtze valley property to British owners, and resuming payments on loans from London. Resisting the return of colonialism to China, Chiang Kai-shek tried to prevent British troops from accepting the surrender of Japanese forces in Hong Kong.[20] The British, suffering severe financial difficulties in the postwar period, responded minimally to Kuomintang appeals for assistance to fight its civil war.[21] Furthermore, the Kuomintang blockade of Chinese ports provoked British resistance. London maintained that the Nationalists could not effectively close the designated ports and that they simply wished to secure the rights of war without assuming the accompanying responsibilities dictated by international law. Great Britain declared that it would not support so transparent a sham and would convoy its merchant craft into Chinese Communist ports.[22] Finally, despite fighting which caught British property between Nationalist and Communist armies, the British sustained damage only at the hands of fleeing KMT soldiers and not as a result of CCP actions.[23]

Given all these problems in China, London came under increasing pressure to devise a new policy to protect British assets—most especially Hong Kong. American intelligence sources identified two primary areas of concern. Economically, China and Hong Kong occupied a position of some importance in Britain's financial and trading networks.[24] Hong Kong had developed into one of the world's great entrepots—significant not merely to the markets of China but to commercial intercourse throughout Asia. The colony's preservation as a Western outpost in a rapidly changing Asia involved critical political considerations as well. Evidence of British weakness could undermine the morale of Pacific Commonwealth nations and accentuate the vulnerability of moderate governments. Australia and New Zealand might well worry that Britain no longer would be able to guarantee them military and diplomatic support. In Malaya Chinese guerrilla forces could use a British setback against the Malay governing coalition. "It would," the United States Central Intelligence Agency feared, "create throughout the region the impression that the West is retreating before the new order in Asia, thereby causing a rush to support the Chinese Communists."[25]

The British government therefore undertook several parallel, if not always consistent, policies. It gave serious consideration to opening diplomatic relations with the Chinese Communists, thereby hoping to salvage its assets through compromise. Meanwhile, local officials did what they could to reduce the possibility of internal subversion in the crown colony. Additional military forces arrived from elsewhere in the Empire to provide a deterrent against outright attack. Although the government realized that it could not hope to defend Hong Kong against a concerted

Communist military campaign, it tried to make that assault appear un-necessarily costly. And finally, the British attempted to secure United States support both for the protection of Hong Kong and for its efforts to reach a *modus vivendi* with the CCP.[26]

Discussions between officials of the United States and Great Britain regarding developments in China became a regular feature of interna-tional affairs during 1949.[27] Washington wanted to maintain a united front among all Western powers so that economic embargo or nonre-cognition could be used if necessary to secure proper behavior from the incoming Communist regime. These measures could have no effect without British cooperation.[28] Moreover, should Britain recognize the CCP and the United States refuse to, the split between them could not help but delight the Soviet Union and worry vulnerable states world-wide. It also might jeopardize Congressional appropriations for British postwar recovery given the views of some pro–Chiang Kai-shek Rep-resentatives and Senators. William Knowland (R, Ca) suggested that Marshall Plan aid be discontinued if Britain opened relations with Pe-king.[29] Secretary of State Acheson thus devoted his energies to delaying any independent action by London. Foreign Secretary Bevin, on the other hand, hoped to convince the Americans that Britain's pragmatic view of Chinese affairs must rule, since no viable alternative to recog-nition would exist once the Communists succeeded in dominating the entire mainland.[30]

Ultimately, the impetus toward recognition of the Chinese Commun-ists proved more forceful than the desire to accommodate American policy. As late as September 1949 Ernest Bevin pledged that Britain would avoid appearing eager to establish diplomatic relations with the CCP. Instead London would endeavor to maintain close and continuous consultations with the United States, and so far as possible, adopt a parallel course of action.[31] But Anglo-American unity did not endure. Early in October, in response to Chou En-lai's invitation to foreign gov-ernments to establish mutually beneficial relations with Peking, London all but granted the CCP *de facto* recognition. Not only did the British thereby evidence a fair degree of eagerness to proceed with diplomatic intercourse, but they did so without giving Washington the slightest warning. President Truman felt that the British had not dealt fairly with him, and the State Department condemned the Foreign Office for con-fused administration of policy if not intentional deception.[32]

Nonetheless, American analysts realized that the British government had come under considerable pressure to move closer to the Chinese Communists. The U.S. State Department intelligence research staff ob-served in November 1949:

The persuasive case of the business interests and the old China hands for keeping open commercial channels in Communist areas has impressed the articulate China bloc in Parliament and important segments of the press. In fact, Britain is no longer debating the issue of recognition; the case has been made to the satisfaction of interested opinion in the country. It is the reluctance of other countries, particularly the United States, to come along that is responsible for British caution.

Indeed, the staff continued, recognition would occur almost unopposed in Britain.[33] As early as May 1949, the report noted, many members of Parliament had favored a British approach to the CCP regarding diplomatic relations.[34] The *Manchester Guardian*, the *London Times*, and the *Daily Telegraph* all had come to advocate recognition.[35] Business interests in China and England, organized through various Chambers of Commerce and the China Association of London, also appealed to the government to promote commercial ties with the CCP.[36] Paralleling these influential sectors of domestic opinion, the views of Britain's Asian Commonwealth partners and representatives in the East also favored recognition. At the November 1949 Singapore Conference of British military and diplomatic personnel in Southeast Asia, pro-recognition sentiment proved unanimous. India, Pakistan, and Ceylon, moreover, were expected to view British policy as a test of London's regard for Asian nationalism and willingness to work in an interracial Commonwealth community.[37]

In extending recognition on January 6, 1950, British officials did not imagine themselves to be acting contrary to long-term American policy. Although they realized that some discord had arisen over their precipitous response to Chou En-lai in October, they believed American distress reflected simply a disagreement over timing. London expected that the United States would follow suit in a matter of months—certainly after the November Congressional elections if not before.[38]

Events in Asia interfered with British expectations. Contrary to normal international practice, the Chinese did not exchange ambassadors with the British in January, but instead demanded resolution of various issues first. London's reluctance to support Peking's demand for admission to the United Nations generated considerable tension during the following weeks. Further complicating relations, the British repeatedly emphasized that their recognition of the Communist system in China did not mean approval. Designed to quiet U.S. Congressional complaint about Whitehall's action lest aid appropriations suffer, these declarations angered Chinese leaders. As a *London Times* commentator reflected: "We are, it seems, to make it clear that we are entering into the most reluctant relations with criminals with whom no honest dealings are possible. . . .

In fact we are to make recognition so humiliating, so insulting, and so absurd that no government, not even a Communist one, will accept it."[39] Yet by early June 1950 these frictions had eased somewhat, and until the Korean conflict erupted the two nations seemed to be advancing toward normalized relations.[40]

The difficulties that Britain encountered in China gave impetus to arguments opposing recognition in the United States. Pro-Nationalists like columnist Constantine Brown and radio commentator Walter Winchell contended that CCP behavior demonstrated the validity of their position. In fact, the British had gotten just what they deserved for pandering to Communists in Asia while demanding American money to protect them from communism in Europe. Advocates of recognition found the British dilemma disquieting. The *New York Herald Tribune*, which in November 1949 asserted that "despite bitterness aroused by the Ward case it seems wise to strive to maintain American influence in China, even at considerable risk," in May 1950 viewed the British experience as a warning to proceed slowly.[41]

In reality no real parallel existed between Great Britain's position in China and that of the United States. Some British and American officials saw London's extension of diplomatic recognition as a test of the response that a commitment by Washington would evoke in the United States and in China. But London had not provided the Kuomintang with millions of dollars in arms and ammunition and consequently had not earned the enmity that CCP leaders felt for Washington. The Party had cultivated relations with the British during the civil war years, seeing advantages for China and world communism in undermining Anglo-American unity. On the other hand, the United Kingdom's prestige, influence, and material resources had diminished significantly during World War II. The Chinese Communists, hoping to establish limited economic independence from the Soviet Union, could not expect an Anglo-Chinese tie to secure the advantages that would come from trade with the United States. Britain's friendship could be a useful asset, as when Mao Tse-tung warned Colonel David Barrett of the Dixie Mission that London would give him help if Washington did not. However, both the risks and the benefits of accommodation between Washington and Peking far outdistanced those that Sino-British normalization promised to yield.[42]

The United States in 1949 and 1950 faced a situation in Asia made more complex by Britain's wartime decline. The Empire which the British did not wish to relinquish had begun to disintegrate. Washington preferred to see it go and yet agonized over London's waning economic and political power. During the war, moreover, the United States had assumed a dominant place in Asia and this it refused to give up. Unwilling to face all contingencies alone, the American government wanted British support, but not an equal British voice in policymaking. When London indicated a staunch determination to preserve its assets in China, however, Washington had an opportunity to align itself with the British in an area clearly more important to them than to the United States. A decision to recognize the Communist Chinese promised not just the benefits of dealing with China but the chance to strengthen both Britain and the Anglo-American alliance.

II The Soviets

During the decade following World War II, the United States became increasingly obsessed with a phenomenon it referred to as "the international communist conspiracy." Americans envisioned a monolithic bloc headed by the Soviet Union seeking to destroy, through violent revolution or subversion, the "free world." This conviction in time came to dominate decision-making, significantly reducing the flexibility with which Washington approached international affairs. In Asia from 1948 to early 1950, however, the Soviet-American conflict had not yet ripened into cold war; fanaticism had not yet replaced reasoned analysis.[43] China, although clearly an arena of contention, seemed a questionable prize for the victor. The Chinese people, whether Communist or Nationalist, would need enormous amounts of aid to repair a war-ravaged society. A burden to its own leaders, China could not be a threat to the United States in the foreseeable future. Policy planners in Washington might hope that communism would turn out to be a passing infatuation, or that traditional tensions would destroy a Sino-Soviet alliance, but they also saw the advantages of encumbering an exhausted Soviet economy with Chinese demands.[44] Thus Washington contemplated the accession of a Communist government in Peking without feeling compelled to hurl brute force at it. And officials not yet repelled by a bamboo curtain entertained the possibility of opening diplomatic relations with a Chinese Communist regime.

Estimates of the degree to which Chinese Communism depended upon support from the Soviet Union differed. Some observers both inside and outside the government saw an intimate association, while others identified tensions that suggested an eventual Sino-Soviet split. Officials who agreed with the China Lobby and the Congressional China bloc visualized a Chinese Communist movement totally subservient to Moscow. To them Mao Tse-tung appeared to be a Soviet puppet willing to impose Moscow's requirements on an unsuspecting Chinese populace. Various scholars, businessmen, missionaries, and members of the government contended, on the other hand, that Mao and most of his colleagues were endowed with a strong sense of nationalism and would resist Russian domination. Ideological affiliation did not have to mean total submission of Peking to Moscow.[45]

Evidence establishing the closeness of the Chinese and Russian revolutions came less from concrete actions than from rhetoric.[46] Mao Tse-tung and other CCP leaders attested to their pro-Soviet orientation on many occasions. Liu Shao-ch'i, Deputy Chairman of the Politburo, in a widely publicized article reconciling nationalism and proletarian internationalism in November 1948 averred, "Neutrality is impossible. If you do not stand in the imperialist camp helping American imperialism and its stooges to enslave the world and your own nation, you must stand in the anti-imperalist camp." Mao Tse-tung some seven months later confirmed that "a third world does not exist," China would lean to the side of the Soviet Union against the exploitative West.[47] American Ambassador to China J. Leighton Stuart wrote the State Department that Mao could hardly have pledged a greater allegiance to the USSR.[48] Secretary of State Acheson, no doubt also reacting to Mao's hard-line position, declared in his letter of transmittal to President Truman which accompanied the China White Paper that:

> The Communist leaders have foresworn their Chinese heritage and have publicly announced their subservience to a foreign power, Russia, which during the last 50 years, under czars and Communists alike, has been most assiduous in its efforts to extend its control in the Far East.[49]

Despite the public declarations of fraternity, frictions complicated Sino-Soviet relations. The Chinese Communists had fought foreign domination too long to accept dictation from Moscow meekly. *Pravda* might contend that "the experience of the Communist Party of the Soviet Union is basically, fundamentally, and essentially *acceptable* to, and *compulsory* for, the Communist parties of all lands," but the Chinese had reasons to disagree.[50] In 1927 the CCP had suffered cruelly at the hands of Chiang Kai-shek because Stalin, far from the scene and locked in a power struggle, had insisted that the Communists continue a dangerous alliance with the Kuomintang.[51] Then, during the Sino-Japanese War, Moscow had provided Chiang with military assistance and signed a friendship treaty with him pledging that Russia would support only his authority in China.[52] At Yalta the Soviets had acquired control over Manchuria, which gave them the opportunity to strip China's major industrial base of factories and equipment. Although the Russians did give the CCP forces light arms taken from surrendering Japanese troops, no airplanes or tanks passed into Chinese Communist hands. Moreover, according to Lin Piao, commander in chief of the CCP's Manchurian campaign, the Russians provided no troops or advisors and took all their own weapons back to Soviet territory with them.[53] As the civil war increasingly promised a communist victory, even without Russian aid, Stalin counseled the CCP to stop at the Yangtze River and accept a divided nation.[54] At the same time his representatives pressed the Nationalist government to yield economic concessions in Sinkiang province before its power to do so disappeared.[55] Indeed, during the closing phases of the civil struggle, the Soviet ambassador, alone among the ministers of foreign governments in China, accompanied the fleeing Nationalists to Canton when Nanking fell to the People's Liberation Army.[56] Stalin hoped to serve Russian interests by balancing the KMT and CCP against each other. His efforts, predictably, inspired little Chinese Communist confidence in his knowledge of or concern with the security or prosperity of their movement.

United States foreign service officers and State Department personnel noted Sino-Soviet tensions with cautious pleasure. In May 1947 John Melby, on the Nanking Embassy staff, reflected that Chinese Communist declarations of loyalty to the USSR appeared reserved and that "there are even suggestions of wariness as to where Russian ideology ends and Russian nationalism begins. We have all seen," he continued, "too many examples of Russian, even official Russian, contempt for the Chinese as Chinese to assume that the Communists have not noticed it too."[57] John Paton Davies of the Policy Planning Staff, remarking upon "a strong odor of bad fish . . . emanating from Sino-Soviet relations" in January 1949, hypothesized a reluctance in Moscow to see the Chinese Communists achieve rapid victory. Far from happy to have a unified neighbor in the East, Stalin might be hoping that a Kuomintang government would survive in South China. Otherwise, Davies suggested, the Chinese Communists "will be able to throw their weight around in Southeast Asia more effectively than Moscow can. The spectre of a great autocephalous competitor may well have disturbed the Kremlin's dreams."[58] Observing the lack of Soviet enthusiasm even as Chinese successes drew accolades from Yugoslav, French, and Polish Communists, Ambassador Stuart also pointed to Moscow's possible discomfort over having a Chinese neighbor powerful enough to resist further Russian demands in Manchuria.[59]

In response to indications of conflict between the Soviet Union and the Chinese Communists, speculation regarding development of a

Chinese variety of Titoism abounded. The parallel seemed a natural one to observers who so recently had been confronted with a "rebel" communist government in Europe. As in the case of Marshal Josip Broz Tito, Mao Tse-tung had come to power without Stalin's assistance. The continuity of leadership in the Yugoslav Communist Party, emphasized by analysts in the American Embassy at Belgrade, held equally true for the CCP. So, too, did the fact of mass membership newly recruited, largely uneducated, and loyal to the Party for emotional and nationalistic reasons.[60] The potential for Titoism appeared to exist in China and promised to be in the best interests of the United States. In February 1949 the Truman Administration decided to relax export controls in favor of Yugoslavia because, as the Policy Planning Staff argued, Tito "is perhaps our most precious asset in the struggle to contain and weaken Russian expansion."[61] Similarly an independent communist regime in China could curb Soviet designs in the East. Care would have to be taken neither to be deceived by Mao nor to weaken his power by reacting too eagerly to signs of Chinese independence, but Shanghai Consul General John Cabot, a veteran of diplomatic service in Belgrade, concluded that the situation appeared even more favorable to the West in China than it had in Yugoslavia.[62]

Development of the appropriate United States China policy intrigued Washington planners and political commentators alike. The press and the government both devoted much time and attention to the question of Chinese Titoism. The European Division in the State Department argued that the United States could not encourage such a development, since it "will come only when the USSR's own ultimate selfishness and power lust have alienated the Chinese comrade."[63] John Cabot, on the other hand, believed that American policies could profoundly influence the timing of a Sino-Soviet split. "If Communist moderation and tentative pro-Western moves are met by rebuffs, further pressures, trade limitations, and vitriolic publicity . . . then Communists are likely to reason that [a] *modus vivendi* with [the] West is impossible," warned the Consul General. The United States must respond favorably enough to CCP approaches to support moderates in the Party, but not so enthusiastically as to convince them "that Westerners will accept anything to make profits." Meanwhile, he suggested that Americans leave China, thereby both eliminating an area of possible Sino-American friction and demonstrating that the Chinese would miss American contacts.[64]

Most official observers, in fact, emphasized that Washington should exploit every opportunity to encourage a Sino-Soviet split. Government councils incorporated this admonition in a variety of policy guidance papers produced by the Offices of Chinese and Far Eastern Affairs, the

Policy Planning Staff (PPS) and the National Security Council (NSC) during 1949 and 1950. John Davies maintained that the United States could accelerate the trend toward Titoism by recognizing a Chinese Communist government as soon as the Party established one.[65] Walter P. McConaughy, A. Sabin Chase, and Hendrik van Oss of the Shanghai Consulate concurred in this assessment, believing recognition and trade would permit the United States to take advantage of both Chinese good will toward Americans and rising anti-Soviet sentiment. The result would be either Titoism or, at least, a weakening of Sino-Soviet ties.[66] Moscow already viewed Chinese Communist yearnings for independence from tight Soviet controls with suspicion.[67] The Kremlin seemed eager to isolate China from contact with the United States and thereby force increased reliance upon its own power and authority.[68]

Large segments of the press also predicted Titoism in China and urged American action to speed its coming. From January through early May of 1949, the State Department noted almost constant discussion in the news media of strains between Mao and the Russians and the likelihood that Mao would not be a puppet of Moscow.[69] *Newsweek* and *Business Week*, for instance, considered trade and recognition possible devices to lure Mao away from Stalin, and the *Washington Post* suggested that a split would come as soon as the Chinese discovered how difficult the Russians could be to deal with.[70]

American observers, official and nonofficial, speculated that Mao's December journey to Moscow to negotiate a friendship treaty had initiated the learning process. At first, Mao's trip and the resulting treaty seemed to testify to Sino-Soviet intimacy. The *Philadelphia Inquirer* warned against basing United States policy on wishful thinking and calculated that, far from contemplating a split, Mao had gone to Moscow for marching orders.[71] So, too, the *Washington Star*, the *Baltimore Sun*, and others cautioned that Titoism in China now looked a remote possibility.[72] But as time passed it became apparent that the Communist negotiators faced some intractable problems. John Hightower of the Associated Press reported serious frictions over control of Manchuria.[73] The State Department noted rumors that Stalin's demand for five Chinese ports in addition to Port Arthur and Dairen had prompted a threat from Chou En-lai to resign rather than accede. State also received reports that the Soviets wanted to place large numbers of Russian "advisers" in China's secret police, army, and party—a move which again engendered Chinese resistance. Ultimately, the prolonged talks yielded definite guarantees of security, but only minimal levels of economic aid ($300 million in credits to be repaid with interest) and a continued Soviet presence in Manchuria.[74]

By the time Chinese and Soviet officials actually signed their agreements, the United States had devised a policy to cope with the situation. The National Security Council at the end of December 1949 concluded that Kremlin control over the Peking regime would increase in the immediate future and that China would "represent a political asset to the USSR in accomplishment of its global objectives." NSC 48/2, however, also held out the hope that sharp disagreements would develop between Peking and Moscow and enjoined the American government to be prepared to exploit them.[75] Meanwhile, the State Department acted to encourage discontent through propaganda. In January and February 1950 the Department planted news stories with C. L. Sulzberger of the *New York Times* highlighting Soviet imperialism and Mao's weakness in the face of Stalin's demands.[76] Secretary of State Acheson continued to emphasize publicly the disservice done to China's domestic welfare by Chinese Communist adherence to Moscow. Officials tried to promote Chinese dissatisfaction with the Soviets and encourage splits within the CCP between pro-Soviet and nationalistic factions. As economic conditions in China worsened, and Americans were sure they must, and evidences of Russian imperialism increased, the anti-Kremlin group could grow in influence.[77] A mysterious approach to American Economic Cooperation Administration officers by a supposed emissary of General Ch'en I regarding a coup d'état against Chinese Stalinist elements within the party complemented substantial intelligence that the CCP was, in fact, divided.[78] If the United States could help create a Chinese Tito out of Ch'en I or another prominent leader, communism in China might be more palatable. After all, in December 1949 the United States adopted a policy designed to "foster a heretical drifting-away process on the part of the satellite states" in Eastern Europe so as to weaken Soviet power. Nationalistic communists in Asia who could be lured away from Moscow would be valuable allies in further discouraging Soviet expansion.[79]

III The Japanese

Early in World War II bureaucrats and scholars in the State Department planned the reconstruction of a defeated Japan. To ensure that the Japanese would not rise up again, as the Germans had after the First World War, Japan would be forced to demilitarize and undertake extensive economic and political reforms.[80] General Douglas MacArthur, Supreme Commander of the Allied Powers in the Pacific (SCAP), set about achieving America's precontrived objectives in September 1945. First of all he abolished the Army and Navy Ministries and stopped all war-oriented industrial production. Then he energetically began the decentralization of industry and gave impetus to the growth of a labor movement. Finding the Japanese attempts at constitution-writing too tradition-bound, the General proposed a draft relying heavily on British and American models. Although he himself tended to rule autocratically, often refusing to cooperate with the United States State and Defense Departments and altering Japanese society by fiat, SCAP launched a wide-ranging series of democratic reforms designed to liberalize the entire life of the Japanese nation.[81]

Developments in other parts of the world, however, compelled the character of the occupation to change. By 1948 Moscow had clashed with Washington in Italy, Poland and Iran. Soviet presence along the northern rim of Asia boded ill there too. In China the Communists appeared to be destroying Chiang Kai-shek's Nationalist armies. Although some hope still lingered for a compromise, China would not serve as one of the great pro-American powers in the United Nations and international affairs, as Franklin Roosevelt had vainly hoped. The determination to pacify the Japanese slowed as these new realities became clear. Efforts to draw up a Japanese Peace Treaty in 1947–1948, having encountered Russian resistance, subsided as American planners chose to strengthen Japan's defenses against communism before risking a new initiative. No longer did it seem wise to leave Japan vulnerable when the Soviet Union and a Communist China would dominate East Asia and threaten international security.[82]

The vision of a Japan closely allied with the United States gained currency as the situation worldwide and in Asia darkened. In 1947 the State Department's newly created Policy Planning Staff (PPS) took up the matter of Japan's status in the face of Soviet pressures and deteriorating circumstances in China. George F. Kennan, PPS director, has noted in retrospect that "the nature of the occupation policies pursued up to that time by General MacArthur's headquarters seemed on cursory examination to be such that if they had been devised for the specific purpose of rendering Japanese society vulnerable to Communist political pressures and paving the way for a Communist takeover, they could scarcely have been other than what they were."[83] By the end of 1948, with Kennan's encouragement, the occupation had declared its radical reforms complete and turned its energies to reconstruction. To bring stability to Japan's economy, dissolution of the huge industrial and financial combines, the *zaibatsu*, ceased. The Japanese Communists, who had been granted political freedom, began to be purged from labor union leadership at SCAP command. And despite a prohibition, written into the Japanese constitution by Americans, against maintenance of "land, sea and air forces," SCAP encouraged the formation of a "National Police Reserve" of 75,000 men whose subsequent militarization progressed slowly but steadily.[84]

The reversal in United States policy, occasioned in part by growing Chinese Communist power and the uncertain future of the Nationalist Government, nonetheless angered and frightened the Chinese. To them Japan's ferocity had not diminished in memory merely because an end to the fighting had come. Japanese soldiers had killed some 11 to 15 million Chinese and destroyed approximately $60 billion worth of property. Individuals all over the country had vivid recollections of Japanese brutality. The Chinese people expected that Japan would be punished, that China would receive reparations to help regenerate its industrial sector, and that the Japanese would not again be a threat to their security.[85]

Opposition to America's decision to rehabilitate Japan became, in fact, one of the few issues around which Chinese groups of all political complexions could rally. Early warnings of the renewed imperialist threat began to fill the Chinese press in 1946. The United States seemed to be devoting resources to the revival of Japanese factories which could in turn fuel a new offensive capability. Moreover the funds being invested in Japan could better be put to use in rebuilding a China torn asunder by Japan's depredations. During the spring of 1948, university students took such concerns off the pages of newspapers and into the streets of several of China's largest cities. Even Nationalist officials voiced disapproval of plans to reduce reparations payments by the Japanese and to allow increases in Japan's levels of industrialization and standard of living.[86] The Chinese Communists, not circumscribed by dependence upon American support, railed far more loudly against Washington's efforts to re-create the terrifying strength of China's longtime nemesis. Propaganda teams accused the United States of fostering Japan's recovery as part of its nefarious scheme to monopolize the world's resources. Communist writer Kuo Mo-jo contended that "By now there is not the slightest shadow of a doubt that the American imperialists are building up Japan as an operational base in their projected counterrevolutionary war." The supposed American insistence that Chiang Kai-shek release the notorious war criminal Okamura Yasugi (Japanese Commander-in-Chief in China, 1944–45) suggested the imminence of renewed aggression upon a still-vulnerable China.[87]

Chinese Communist hatred for and dread of the Japanese did not, however, dictate isolation from Japan. The CCP eagerly sought a peace treaty with Tokyo. The Party wished to see American occupation brought to a rapid conclusion while Japan remained weak. The leaders also highly valued participation in the preparation and signing of the final accords, wanting a voice in the decision-making and the legitimacy to be gained by joining in such a significant international conclave. Furthermore, the Chinese Communists wanted to establish economic ties with Japan.

Unable to obtain from the Soviet Union machinery and other industrial commodities, Peking made it known that China would like to trade with the Japanese. Chang Tsung-ping, liaision for the Ministry of Industry and Commerce, told American Consul General O. Edmund Clubb that the CCP could supply coal and salt and wished to exchange these on a barter basis for textile and steel industry machine parts, newsprint, and medicines. An American representative of the Far Eastern Trading Company further informed Clubb that the CCP had expressed interest in using private United States companies to carry on this North China–Japan trade. He observed that his firm would be interested and that the Communists appeared avid to foster exchange with Japan.[88]

The Japanese mirrored Chinese enthusiasm for this trade link. Premier Yoshida Shigeru, although he had once told CBS newsman William Costello, "I hate communism so much I avoid even reading about it," sounded very different in 1949. Echoing the feeling of many Japanese, he declared: "I don't care whether China is red or green. China is a natural market, and it has become necessary for Japan to think about markets." Similarly, the conservative *Mainichi* daily newspaper attributed Japan's economic problems in large part to "the slump in trade with China." In December 1949 the Japan Management Association, made up of executives from the nation's banks, trading and manufacturing companies and government officials, publicized its study entitled "Measures to Boost Trade With China." The businessmen not only expressed optimism regarding trade volume but even entertained the possibility of concluding a trade pact with the CCP.[89]

The decision on whether to establish commercial relations between the Chinese Communists and the Japanese, however, remained in American hands. And to United States military and diplomatic authorities this issue appeared fraught with difficulties. The United States, they reasoned, could not condone a trade policy which might help the Communists tighten their hold upon 600 million innocent people. Moreover, these Americans worried about the possibility that Sino-Japanese trade might jeopardize Japan's freedom and democracy. On the one hand, commerce with the Chinese mainland might provide opportunities for slow infiltration of agents to aid the Japan Communist Party; on the other hand, Japan could become excessively dependent on Chinese goods and therefore be controlled politically by the CCP.[90] Chiang Kai-shek predicted that Japan would turn communist just as soon as the occupation forces departed.[91]

But commercial intercourse could not simply be dismissed on political grounds. Japan's and China's willingness to do business reflected the traditional economic interdependency of these two nations. Under SCAP supervision the Japanese economy made progress, but only slowly. In 1948 unfavorable trade balances, spiraling inflation, and low wages continued to hamper recovery.[92] Substantial dependence on American raw materials kept prices high and industry weak. In 1949, for instance, SCAP shipped coal from the United States to Japan at $24 per ton when China could supply the same material for $12 per ton. Some source nearer to the island nation had to be found for such commodities, and Japanese merchants looked to the plentiful and inexpensive markets of China. In fact, before the war China had taken more than 30 percent of Japan's exports and provided some 20 percent of its imports, including critical items such as coal, iron ore, and foodstuffs.[93] Once the occupation ended, American observers felt sure, Japan could be expected to reestablish that trading relationship.[94]

Apart from the natural affinity of Japan for China's resources, American officials had also to consider that, under the occupation system, support of Japan's economy had become a drain on the United States taxpayer. The Department of State's Office of Intelligence Research asserted in January 1949: "It has become increasingly clear that Japan is not likely to achieve a self-supporting economy without continued, if not increasing, US aid unless trade with northeast Asia, particularly China and Manchuria, can be restored."[95] Indeed, argued State Department officials in May, "Japan's economy cannot possibly be restored to a self-sustaining basis without a considerable volume of trade with China, the burden of Japan on the United States economy cannot be removed unless Japan's economy is restored to a self-sustaining basis . . . [moreover] U.S. interference with natural Japanese trade relations with China would produce profound Japanese hostility."[96]

American officials, lacking a fully satisfactory alernative, decided to gamble on the growth of trade between China and Japan. The National Security Council, having explored the possibilities, admitted that "Japan's natural dependence on China for food and industrial raw materials would provide the Communists with a potentially powerful leverage over Japan after the United States occupation and financial support had been withdrawn. This is a disadvantage," the Council concluded, "that must be incurred as a calculated risk unless the United States is willing to underwrite the Japanese economy indefinitely." SCAP must simply "encourage trade with China on a *quid-pro-quo* basis . . . avoid preponderant dependence on Chinese sources for Japan's critical food and raw material requirements," and make every effort to develop alternate markets elsewhere in Asia.[97]

In addition the United States might try to turn this necessary relationship to an even wider benefit. State Department analysts pointed out that "the USSR is the primary target of those U.S. economic policies designed to contain or turn back Soviet-communist imperialism, and not China or any of the Soviet satellites considered as individual countries. It would, therefore, be inappropriate to apply to the willing or unwilling partners of the USSR punitive or restrictive economic measures which are not being applied to the USSR itself."[98] At the same time, by aiding in the restoration of mutually beneficial trade relations between China and Japan, the United States "might bring about serious conflicts between Kremlin and Chinese Communist policy, and thereby tend to produce an independent Chinese Communist regime." In other words, the United States could not help but benefit from a situation in which the CCP needed Japanese imports to keep its economy functioning. Frictions with its Soviet mentors could develop, and conceivably the CCP might become more willing to establish normal trade and diplomatic contacts with the United States.[99]

Beyond these questions of trade, the implications for Japan's military and political security which American recognition of a Communist regime in China would bear worried American officials. William J. Sebald, director of the office of the United States Political Advisor for Japan, concluded on the basis of research and observation by his staff in Tokyo that political considerations in Japan presented no major obstacles to recognition. A strong undercurrent of pro-recognition sentiment existed among the Japanese people, and they took it as "a matter of course" that diplomatic relations would be opened between the United States and the mainland soon. This would surely be followed by Japanese recognition of the CCP. But as with the exchange of goods, diplomatic contacts with the Chinese Communists posed a security threat to Japan. A Chinese Communist mission in Tokyo would give the CCP direct access to the Japanese people. CCP participation in the Far Eastern Commission and negotiation of the peace treaty, the Americans asserted, would allow the Communists dangerous authority over Japan's future. Trade might be necessary to Japan's domestic stability, but American officials preferred not to see political relations develop. Japanese authorities, although helpless to enforce their opinions, disagreed. They believed that China could not be ignored and that their country could not afford to isolate itself from any part of Asia, even if that meant exposure to communism.[100]

American policymakers evaluating alternatives in Asia during 1949 and early 1950 found it impossible to divorce their decisions regarding China from those bearing upon Japan. Responsible for Japan's recovery and security and increasingly anxious to turn the erstwhile enemy into an ally, the United States worried about how recognition of a Communist Chinese regime would affect Japan. Economically, mainland China appeared indisputably important to the Japanese. Sino-Japanese interaction did involve a host of risks which the United States hesitated to take. A safer policy avoided possible Chinese contagion but slowed Japanese growth and prolonged the period during which the American public had to bear developmental costs. It also deprived Washington of a significant political advantage. A sheltered Japan could not reach out to the Chinese Communists and help win them away from Moscow. The CCP had already demonstrated its interest in trading with Japan. The Japanese themselves expected to carry on diplomatic relations with China and believed a reconciliation must come eventually. Thus State Department officials could see that, although an effort to isolate Japan from China might be successful temporarily, the costs would be high and in time the Japanese would probably initiate relations on their own. Japan's needs would be better served by a Sino-American link which would facilitate early contacts and trade.[101]

IV Recognition in a Global Context

The question of whether the United States should or should not recognize a Communist China touched broad areas of foreign policy decision-making. More than relations with the single, backward giant called China weighed in the balance. President Truman and Secretary of State Acheson could use the opportunity Mao Tse-tung presented to acknowledge the forces of Asian nationalism, to challenge the unity of the Soviet bloc, to reduce tensions with London, and to speed Japan's economic recovery. Government opinion in Britain, Japan, and India leaned toward recognition and trade and hoped that Washington could be persuaded to lead a common front in establishing these ties. Although some countries, especially in Southeast Asia, feared that recognition would enable China to plant subversive agents in embassies and legations, most saw more danger in attempting to deny reality. Even the French, whose struggle with Vietminh guerrillas seemed fated to attract Communist Chinese interference, favored diplomatic relations as the best way to try to limit that intervention.[102]

At home, many discussed the effects of American action on the decisions other nations would make. The dedicated communist fighters declared recognition unimaginable and threatened to force the Truman Administration to stop United States aid to any country that dared to deal with the enemy. Anglophobes found China policy a convenient new forum for condemning London and warned Truman not to follow Britain's example. Yet nonrecognition and embargo would be unpopular policies abroad, impossible to enforce with adequate international cooperation. The United States risked isolating itself by refusing to accept Communist domination of China. A moral crusade probably would not arouse sympathetic world opinion but rather irritate those who deemed recognition a practical device.

The United States clearly could not hope to please everyone, but special attention had to be given to the needs and desires of the British and the Japanese. Tokyo could not act without permission and would have to follow Washington's lead. American observers in Japan believed that opinion there favored trade and diplomatic contacts but identified salient threats to Japan's security in the contemplated links. London, on the other hand, acted independently. British recognition had been delayed by American pressure, but not for long. And early recognition by Washington would not only please London, but would also frustrate Soviet anticipation of an Anglo-American dispute.

Indeed, the burgeoning hostility between Washington and Moscow bore with some immediacy on the American decision. Recognition might disturb Russian plans to make of China a satellite. American business, missionary, and cultural contacts might ameliorate the impact of communization on China. Informed opinion divided regarding the Kremlin's preferences on the question of Sino-American relations. Some thought that the Soviets wanted to isolate China and thereby consolidate control over the huge nation. Others speculated that the Russians would like to see Chinese Communists obtain American economic aid, relieving Moscow of the responsibility and reducing Western preparedness against Communist subversion.

The advice that Acheson and Truman received from overseas in most cases urged recognition of the Communist Chinese. America's allies, especially Britain and Japan, counselled realism and warned against allowing an unthinking anticommunism to dictate policy. Sensitive to the ramifications for the Communist bloc as well as for the "free world" of any new relationship with China, the Secretary and the President sought throughout 1949 and into 1950 the views of foreign leaders and tried to reconcile America's domestic and foreign needs and obligations.

CHAPTER THREE

Chinese Communist Policy

Unexpected Avenue

)━━()━━()━━()━━(

CHINESE Communist attitudes helped determine America's reaction to the Chinese revolution. American policymakers, choosing between the Nationalists, the Communists, and neutrality, anxiously sought indications of how Mao Tse-tung and his party would behave. If the CCP put ideology first and sharpened doctrinal prejudices on the rough edges of past relations, hostility promised to breed hostility. Suggestions that room could be found for accommodation, however, occasioned interest in Washington about economic and political ties with the Communist Chinese. Throughout 1949 and 1950, the Truman Administration carefully followed developments on the mainland of China, trying to analyze changes in party policies and determine the chances of establishing a viable relationship between the two nations.

From the perspective of Chinese Communist leaders, foreign relations seemed inextricably intertwined with China's immense economic problems. When Communist armies marched to victory over the Nationalists during 1949, they brought to an end decades of warfare, but their struggle had just begun.[1] Chinese leaders faced enormous difficulties in rehabilitating and modernizing China's economy. They had to overcome generations of political inequality and earn for China an independent place among the world's powers. The leadership recognized that assistance would have to be sought abroad to accomplish all this. Although maintaining the Yenan spirit of self-reliance,[2] the Communists' shortage of adequate personnel and appropriate resources required them to supplement their own efforts with foreign aid.[3]

The Chinese turned first to the Soviet Union for guidance. Having studied communism under Soviet tutelage, China's communists expected Moscow to provide inspirational and practical help for domestic construction. In foreign policy, the CCP aligned China with the anti-imperialist bloc led by the Soviet Union. Communist leaders felt keenly the expectations of a hostile world that their revolution would collapse. As Mao Tse-tung observed, "The imperialists reckon that we will not be able to manage our economy; they are standing by and looking on, awaiting our failure."[4] Moscow appeared to be the only reliable commercial and political partner that the Chinese could find or would need.

Soviet assistance proved not to be an unmitigated blessing. Moscow entertained serious misgivings about the Chinese revolution and the emergence of a powerful communist neighbor on its long Asian frontier. Repeatedly Russian self-interest dominated over fraternal communist bonds and Stalin, in a variety of ways, intentionally and inadvertently acted to keep China disunited and weak. Although CCP loyalty remained strong, at times ideology alone closed the gap between Russians as communist cadres and Russians as manipulating foreigners.[5]

Virtually every member of the Chinese Communist Party had suffered the sting of foreign exploitation. Each had experienced debilitating anti-Chinese discrimination in his own country. The "Chinese and dogs not allowed" sign at the entrance to a Shanghai park had made a lastingly negative impact on many. They had lived through the violence of Japanese aggression and knew intimately the tales of nineteenth-century defeats by the French and the British. China had lost control of Taiwan, Korea, and Indo-China during their lifetimes. Scarring the landscape were factories and mines owned not by Chinese entrepreneurs, but by foreigners who drained China of wealth and shipped it abroad. These Chinese had not been born into a great and ancient civilization, but into the twilight years of an empire in decline and at the mercy of many enemies. Communism, as they encountered it in their youth, promised release from hopeless subjugation. Marxism-Leninism provided a western theory to explain why the West would crumble and socialist states would survive. When the CCP embarked upon civil war to win control of the country, it looked upon its enemies as pawns of foreign exploiters. Members of the Kuomintang had forfeited their birthright by clinging to the power of foreign capital and betraying China's sovereignty.[6]

With so powerful a legacy of foreign abuse, the CCP yearned for equality within the Communist bloc. Experience suggested that the best course might be expulsion of foreigners and isolation from all nations except those in the Soviet camp. Nestled in a communist coalition, China could benefit from Moscow's military strength and yet be free of the worst features of external control. But, if China elected exclusive dependence upon Russia, it would have to do without significant outside help in reconstruction and modernization of its economy. The Soviet Union, having sacrificed twenty million lives and important sectors of its domestic industry in World War II, could offer the Chinese only minimal assistance in the foreseeable future. Party leaders would have to make do with the materials and expertise the Chinese people themselves could provide. Indeed, the Russians would expect certain concessions in return for their help. Surprisingly reminiscent of earlier imperialistic depredations—joint stock companies for mining and aviation in Sinkiang, continued Soviet presence in Port Arthur and Dairen, and recognition of Mongolia's incorporation into the Soviet sphere of influence—they came as a shock to the Chinese. The CCP accepted such realities as the price for ideological alignment, but resentment brewed beneath the surface.[7]

Although adhering to the Soviet Union politically, China chose to keep its economic options open. CCP determination to make China a rich and powerful country made total self-reliance inadequate. And since Moscow could not give China sufficient machinery and the money to ensure rapid postwar recovery and growth, the temptation to seek trade and financing in Britain and the United States arose. Mao Tse-tung looked ahead to an era of development resembling Russia's New Economic Policy (adopted by Lenin in 1921) more closely than subsequent Stalinist models. China would benefit from utilizing the skills of its own bourgeoisie and the energies of its prosperous peasants. Similarly, if cooperation were carefully monitored, China could profit from the knowledge its foreign communities in Shanghai and other cities possessed. It might also, as approaches by Minister of Industry and Commerce Yao I-lin to American Consul General O. Edmund Clubb in Peking suggested, expand those economic contacts to include the supply of commodities and services which the Soviet Union could not provide.[8]

Such a policy did not win unanimous and unqualified support within the Chinese Communist Party. Deep-seated hostility against the imperialists stood as a barrier to relations. The capitalists, many Party leaders believed, would never treat them equally and simply wanted Chinese riches to prevent the impending collapse of Western civilization.[9] Laborers in the cities expecting instant wage increases demanded a redistribution of foreign wealth to meet their needs.[10] Many wished to shame and abuse the foreigners as well, and the newspapers carried public "apologies" by foreigners for a host of petty crimes.

Ideological imperatives also persuaded some Chinese Communist leaders that cooperation with the West, and most especially the United States, could not be countenanced. China would maintain a firm and unsullied commitment to the revolutionary forces of the world led by the Soviet Union. Moreover, in the face of Communist-bloc disruption in Europe, the CCP must reassure Stalin of Chinese loyalty. American talk of Mao's becoming another Tito appeared particularly dangerous and deserving of loudly articulated scorn.[11] But, although Mao shared this concern for protecting China's still-vulnerable revolution from Stalin's suspicious gaze, his adherence to ideological desiderata never became inflexible. Many of China's vital needs could not be met by Moscow and nationalism dictated that a conscientious ruler look elsewhere.[12] This did not mean abandoning the Sino-Soviet alliance, just modifying its application somewhat.

American behavior also presented a serious obstacle to diplomatic intercourse and trade in the late 1940s. The United States continued to interfere in the civil struggle by providing Kuomintang armies with aid. This had been true, except for a brief embargo, ever since the end of World War II, and statements by American Congressmen and military figures suggested that it would not end anytime soon. Although the United States protested Chiang Kai-shek's illegal blockade of Chinese ports, Nationalist persistence elicited no efforts by the Americans to convoy merchant craft into closed harbors. In fact, the Chinese Communists became convinced that the blockade had originated with American planners. Chinese intelligence sources, according to General Ch'en I, had traced it to Admiral Oscar C. Badger, Commander of U.S. Naval Forces in the Western Pacific. When the KMT coupled blockades with bombings of major cities, using American-made planes, Washington's complicity appeared undeniable.[13] In addition, evidence began to accumulate that the United States might try to prevent CCP "liberation" of Taiwan. For the Party leaders unification of China had a special, emotionally charged significance, and they had loudly proclaimed the commitment of their forces and their prestige to achievement of that goal. The United States, they knew, could effortlessly prevent vulnerable junk fleets from landing People's Liberation Army soldiers on Taiwan's coast; the United States seemed to be encouraging the Formosan independence movement and might try to reimpose Japanese control over the island. Indeed, Washington appeared determined to rearm Japan and foster the growth of Japanese power in Asia as a permanent threat to the Communist Chinese.[14]

American officials, at the same time, apparently nursed hopes that the CCP's victory would prove transitory. Dean Acheson, in his August 1949 letter of transmittal accompanying the China White Paper, talked freely of a future in which "the profound civilization and democratic individualism of China will reassert themselves and she will throw off the foreign yoke." To the Chinese Communists this sounded suspiciously like encouragement for saboteurs and the creation of a fifth column within the new China.[15] By early 1950 anticommunist guerrilla strength on the mainland, according to American estimates, had climbed to 1,667,000. The Communist New China News Agency maintained that the leaders of these covert forces and other special agents received training in spy schools operated by General Douglas MacArthur's staff.[16]

The Chinese Communists documented American involvement in such subversive schemes in Manchuria. The U.S. Navy through its External Survey Detachment had actually been collecting intelligence data in Manchuria ever since 1946. When Communist success became inevitable there during the closing months of 1948, the ESD chose to continue its operations from the Mukden consulate, providing Chinese agents with radio transmitters and secret codes. The espionage network did not last long. CCP authorities discovered it almost immediately after their takeover of the city. They arrested eight operatives, seized the radio equipment at the American consulate, and put Consul General Angus Ward and his staff under house arrest. Initially friendly approaches to Ward by the Communist mayor were forgotten, and the Americans remained incommunicado for most of the following year. Ward's belligerence and threatening statements by American newspapers and Congressmen, who did not know of the covert activities, served to worsen the tense situation. Ultimately the CCP put Ward and his compatriots on trial and then expelled them from China.[17]

Interest in dealing with the United States evinced by some members of the CCP persisted despite serious and repeated frictions between the two sides. During World War II, Mao Tse-tung had set aside hostility against the imperialist United States to seek aid in fighting Japan. The CCP had celebrated the Fourth of July 1944, praising American traditions of freedom and democracy, and soon thereafter welcomed a U.S. Army Observer Mission (dubbed the Dixie Mission) to Yenan.[18] At an August 1944 Central Committee meeting, Mao secured support for a policy of rapprochement with the United States. The Party would welcome military collaboration, capital investments and technical cooperation, diplomatic contacts, and the establishment of press and government information agencies in Yenan. Chou En-lai actually invited American Secretary of the Treasury Henry Morgenthau to visit Yenan, and the head of the army, Chu Te, proclaimed CCP willingness to put part of its forces under American command. Mao Tse-tung told American foreign service officer John Service that "Chinese and American interests are correlated and similar. They fit together, economically and politically. We can and must work together."[19]

To emphasize the need for cooperation between Washington and Yenan, Mao Tse-tung and Chou En-lai sought a meeting with President Roosevelt. The CCP had come to look upon America's President as a progressive leader and Mao hailed his reelection in 1944. Although Mao had never been outside China, the desire to bypass Ambassador Patrick Hurley and reach an understanding with the United States which would extend beyond wartime exigencies prompted an extraordinary offer. Mao and/or Chou En-lai would be willing to travel to Washington and talk with Roosevelt at the White House "as leaders of a primary Chinese party."

This startling Chinese proposal, designed to circumvent obstructive Americans and Nationalist authorities, failed to arouse enthusiasm in the United States. Meant to be secretly transmitted to Washington through Dixie Mission channels, it fell instead into Ambassador Hurley's hands. Hurley, who had initially come East as President Roosevelt's special agent, entertained a lively suspicion that the regular diplomatic and military personnel in China resented his unorthodox appointment and wanted to undermine his efforts at creating a coalition government. After discussing Chinese affairs with Stalin, he became convinced that the Soviets would not aid the CCP and that, therefore, the Chinese Communists had no choice but to accept Kuomintang peace terms. Any suggestion to the contrary by China specialists, the Ambassador considered insubordination. The Chinese Communists, meanwhile, harbored a growing distrust of Hurley. In 1944 during a brief visit to Yenan, he had presented Mao a liberal plan for military and political unification of China supplemented by American aid which at his behest both he and Mao signed. When Hurley then encountered Chiang Kai-shek's vehement opposition to the plan, he repudiated it. Obviously unreliable, Hurley became increasingly identified with Chiang and the Communists tried to avoid dealing with him, privately calling him *ta-feng* (big wind). Hurley's discovery of CCP attempts to skirt his authority occasioned a telegram to Roosevelt in which the import of the Mao-Chou démarche was obscured by his furious attack on foreign service officers in China. Coming as it did during preparations for Yalta, with trouble developing in Greece and Iran, and bearing Hurley's angry objection, the CCP proposal predictably was rejected by Roosevelt.[20]

Although the Communist Chinese leaders had been rebuffed, they still did not turn completely from thoughts of compromise with the United States. In March 1945 Mao told Service that the United States "is not only the most suitable country to assist [the] economic development of China; she is also the only country fully able to participate." The Chinese Communists cooperated with General George C. Marshall's mission in 1946 in renewed efforts to find a coalition solution to China's civil war. Chou En-lai assured Marshall that CCP policy remained flexible despite obvious ties with Moscow, explaining, "Of course we will lean to one side. But how far depends on you." In fact, on repeated occasions Chou made a point of dissociating the CCP from Soviet policies regarding China. He drew for Marshall an image of a democratized China cultivating free enterprise over an indeterminate but prolonged period. And he made clear that Mao continued to hope for an invitation to visit the United States.[21] Demonstrating their willingness to work with the Americans, CCP troops helped rescue downed airmen and Party leaders continued to fraternize with Dixie Mission representatives. The head of the observer group became so convinced of the Party's eagerness to reach out that he reported "If General Marshall's reactions toward the China problem are favorable and he appreciates the Communist point of view, the Communists will throw themselves in the lap of the United States."[22]

Chinese Communist politics would never have countenanced such total abandon, but apparently certain members of the Party did look forward to limited arrangements with the Americans. Despite troubled relations after the end of the Marshall Mission (January 1947), with ultimate CCP victory seeming increasingly inevitable, the Central Committee of the CCP in November 1948 declared that:

> The Chinese Communist Party, the People's Government of the Liberated Area and the Liberating Army are willing to cooperate with any nation, including the American Government, in establishing a peaceful and friendly relationship in China and to extend protection over the legal interests of all the foreign residents, including Americans in China; provided Chinese territorial integrity is maintained.[23]

Mao Tse-tung announced in April 1949—and reiterated in June—that the fundamental requirements for establishing diplomatic relations between China and all other nations consisted in "equality, mutual benefit, mutual respect for sovereignty and territorial integrity and, first of all, on no help being given to the Kuomintang reactionaries." Mao made no effort to exclude imperialist countries from this "invitation" to open official contacts with the new regime, but, as he told the Seventh Central Committee meeting in March 1949, he did not expect these governments to change their hostile attitudes and treat the Chinese properly.[24]

Chou En-lai and others in the upper echelon of the Party held out more hope. Chou personally headed a group trained to conduct relations with the Western powers. His protegés had modern, often overseas educations, competency in foreign languages, and experience in dealing with diplomatic affairs during World War II. Probably with the support of Yao I-lin and several influential generals, Chou argued that economic assistance from the United States, trade with Japan, and prevention of direct American entry into the civil war could be attained through cautious negotiation.[25] Chou's faction faced resistance from a hardline group which advocated a much closer alignment with the Soviet Union, but Mao, despite his own reservations, seemingly gave Chou at least moderate support.[26]

Policies designed to protect foreign interests in China issued from governing authorities throughout 1949. The CCP clearly wished to prevent serious incidents which might provoke American intervention. At the same time, correct and sometimes even friendly treatment of foreigners stood a chance of persuading American officials of the CCP's good intentions. Missionaries found that in many areas they could continue their activities. Businessmen received assurances that their productive enterprises would not be damaged and could contribute to the building of a strong, new China. In fact, various American entrepreneurs reported to their consulates in China that the CCP wanted to discuss increased trade and negotiate long-term contracts for a variety of commodities and services.

Having set the stage, the Communists initiated conversations with American diplomatic representatives in China. Huang Hua, one of Chou En-lai's experts on the Western barbarians, assumed the post of director of the Alien Affairs Office in Nanking in May 1949 and almost immediately contacted the American Ambassador J. Leighton Stuart. Stuart had been Huang Hua's teacher at Yenching University and so their talks could be conducted on an informal and friendly basis. Several meetings between Huang Hua and Stuart—and between Huang Hua and Stuart's trusted personal secretary, Philip Fugh—produced an invitation to the Ambassador to visit Peking, ostensibly for a trip to Yenching but actually to meet with Mao Tse-tung and Chou En-lai. Huang gave Stuart the impression that the Communist leaders hoped "very much" that he would come north.[27] Stuart received similar assurances that he would be welcomed by Mao and Chou through Ch'en Ming-shu, a leader of the Kuomintang Revolutionary Committee whose relations with top CCP figures Stuart believed to be quite good, and from other sources in Peking.[28] Even after Washington instructed Stuart not to go and Mao Tse-tung made his July 1, 1949 "lean to one side" speech, which appeared to preclude any Sino-American accommodation, Huang Hua again urged, in his own and Peking's behalf, that Stuart journey north to talk with Mao and Chou.[29]

Economic necessity underlay CCP approaches to American diplomats in China. China did not propose to break or weaken its political association with the Soviet Union but hoped to supplement that almost wholly political relationship with western economic ties. As Mao as-

serted in June 1949: "The Chinese people wish to have friendly cooperation with the people of all countries and to resume and expand international trade in order to promote economic prosperity." On May 31,
1949 American Assistant Military Attaché Colonel David Barrett received a message purportedly from Chou En-lai proposing just such an
arrangement. China, Chou observed, desperately needed aid to avoid
complete collapse, and the Soviets could not provide such assistance.
The liberal wing of the CCP, which Chou headed, believed that reconstruction must precede a turn toward communism and that America's
genuine interest in the welfare of the Chinese people could become a
basis for friendly relations between the two countries. When the United
States attempted to reply to Chou's démarche, even though he had not
requested a response and did not wish his name linked to the message,
Chinese Communist contacts rebuffed the effort. This encouraged speculation that the original communication had not come from Chou En-
lai.[30]

On the other hand, Chou's emphasis on China's material needs and
desire for trade with the United States found expression in statements
by several Communist officials. Minister of Industry and Commerce Yao
I-lin broached the subject of trade with American Consul General O.
Edmund Clubb in April 1949.[31] Even earlier Yeh Chien-ying, Mayor of
Peking, had suggested that China conclude trade treaties with the capitalist world to secure the necessities China lacked.[32] In June 1949, Ch'en
I, the Mayor of China's primary commercial center, Shanghai, told an
audience of cultural leaders that Communist China would welcome not
only normal trade with the United States and Great Britain, but also
loans and technical assistance.[33] Other local officials informed Ambassador Stuart, during his June visit to Shanghai, that they favored trade
and friendly relations with the United States.[34] Huang Hua, in talks
with Philip Fugh, declared that the CCP could not be isolationist in its
economic policies and would particularly require American help.[35]
Ch'iao Kuan-hua, the CCP's leading liaison official in Hong Kong, similarly emphasized the vital need of China for trade with the United
States.[36] Moreover, Americans received a report from the Peking leader
of the Democratic League, Chang Tung-sun, who operated often as a
source of information for the ambassador, that Mao Tse-tung, Liu Shao-
ch'i, and Chou En-lai all favored trade and foreign relations. However,
because of pressures from lower levels of the Party, where indoctrination
had produced a different attitude, they felt constrained to proceed
slowly.[37] Mao would have to convince them that: "In politics, severity
is necessary. In economics, give-and-take is permissible."[38]

Nonetheless, political imperatives tended to interfere with the realization of economic goals. If rapid rehabilitation and modernization required foreign support, then the CCP ought to have avoided creating problems in its dealings with foreign nationals and diplomatic representatives. Communist ideology and, more importantly, Chinese nationalism made such docile response impossible. The CCP demanded respect for China's independence and territorial integrity and would not condone perpetuation of any behavior that called these values into question.

As early as February 1947, the CCP announced that upon its accession to power it intended to abrogate all the "disgraceful" international agreements concluded by the Kuomintang after January 10, 1946. The CCP rejected these treaties, loans, and other accords because they had been entered into by the Nationalists after convocation of the Political Consultative Conference. The Communists maintained that the PCC, a multiparty conference organized to discuss establishment of a constitutional government in China, should have been consulted before the Nationalist government's acceptance of any new international obligations. Lacking approval of the PCC or its constituent parties, none of these agreements could be binding on a non-Kuomintang China.[39]

With promulgation of the Common Program in September 1949, the CCP broadened the criteria employed in judging treaties. No longer would agreements the Party chose to "recognize, annul, revise or reconclude" automatically be determined by their date of approval. Henceforth, all Nationalist accords would be analyzed on the basis of their contents to determine whether they inflicted the burdens of imperialism upon China or served the interests of the nation. Thus, agreements such as the 1942 United Nations Declaration continued to have validity in CCP eyes, whereas the Party condemned the 1943 Sino-American Treaty for the Relinquishment of Extraterritorial Rights in China as an unequal compact imposed on the Chinese people.[40]

The United States rejected the CCP's interpretation of treaty principles as a direct affront to international law. A state could not simply pick and choose which agreements it would honor if any equitable system of global relations were to survive.[41] Indeed, Washington pointed out, the United Nations considered a country's history of observing treaties as evidence of its willingness to discharge its obligations to the UN charter, and had refused Albania membership on the basis of its poor record in this regard.[42] The attitude of the Communist Chinese with respect to this matter angered American officials and produced a serious impediment to improvement of Sino-American relations.

The CCP similarly chose to make an issue of the status retained by representatives of foreign powers in China. Customarily, diplomatic personnel within a country undergoing revolution retained their privileges throughout the period of upheaval and for some months after inauguration of a new government. Only then, if the home government did not accord recognition to the new authorities, would they request that the foreign staff on their territory be withdrawn.[43] The Chinese Communists, possibly unaware of normal practice and very sensitive to real or imagined slights to China's sovereignty, chose instead to ignore the diplomatic status of foreign representatives. An American observer noted that "the Communists show the hesitancy and suspicion of a people who have long lived in inland isolation, feeling the anti-Communist world actively against them and the Communist world only passively for them."[44] They treated the diplomatic corps, including Soviet consuls, as ordinary individuals, on the grounds that none of the sponsoring governments had extended recognition to the CCP. They intended, it seemed, to use recognition of consular function as quid pro quo for obtaining de jure recognition of their national authority.[45] Moreover, the Communists insisted that all business conducted by foreigners with the Alien Affairs Bureau, the single agency that would deal with them, had to be transacted in Chinese. Although over time the ban on English lightened, reception and results remained more favorable for Chinese speakers.[46]

Communist Chinese determination to alter radically the superior attitudes and behavior of foreigners in China had some violent results as well.[47] In July 1949 Shanghai Vice Consul William Olive drove through a Chinese Communist parade in his jeep. The authorities arrested Olive and, ignoring his diplomatic status and the appeals from other American foreign service personnel, detained him for three days. During this time the police administered a brutal beating, kept Olive handcuffed for almost twenty-four hours, fed him nothing but bread and water, and finally forced him to sign a dictated apology. The CCP denied that Olive had been mistreated and accused him of beginning the fight in which he sustained his injuries. The Communist Chinese claimed that "the angry imperialist reaction to his case displays a century-old emotional pattern" which they intended to break. According to the CCP's *China Digest*:

> Imperialist foreigners enjoying special privileges under KMT protection have looked down upon the Chinese people as an inferior race, to be ordered about and kicked around. The behavior of Americans in postwar China—running over people without stopping their jeeps; beating and killing Chinese coolies and rickshaw boys; raping Chinese girls—climaxed the insolence of foreigners in the last century. Ordinary Americans coming to

China . . . begin to take their "superman" position for granted. When they are not so regarded, their reaction, at best, is to complain of being treated impolitely; and, at the worst, to curse and hit—as William Olive did in Shanghai.[48]

CCP efforts to deflate foreign—particularly American—arrogance nonetheless stayed within surprisingly moderate limits. Although in the throes of a massive revolution with bloodshed and terror on every side, China remained a relatively safe place for American officials, missionaries, and businessmen. Incidents such as the detention of and assault upon Vice-Consul Olive and the lock-in experienced by Randall Gould, editor of the *Shanghai Evening Post & Mercury*, happened infrequently, despite the lack of law and order in the country. The Chinese Communists repeatedly assured foreigners that the Party would protect their lives and their property. They specifically extended these guarantees to Americans even while the United States continued to intervene in and thereby to prolong the civil war. In addition to pledges, the Party actually provided assistance to Americans in trouble, warning only against efforts to retain unusual privileges.[49] Even then, the CCP provided special treatment for Ambassador J. Leighton Stuart, although he along with other American diplomats refused to acknowledge the authority of Communist officials. Huang Hua arranged a visit to Shanghai for the Ambassador and secured exemption for him from such traditional procedures as shop guarantees and baggage inspection upon his departure from China.[50] Americans, angered by and fearful of the well-publicized clashes between foreigners and the Chinese, nevertheless recognized that they fared surprisingly well under the circumstances.

Requisition of consulate property in Peking challenged the United States in yet another sensitive area of historic inequality. The particular property in question had been acquired by the United States under provisions of the 1901 Protocol forced upon China following foreign occupation of Peking in the wake of the Boxer Rebellion. In addition to imposing a staggering indemnity upon China, punishing the intelligentsia for collaboration in the Boxer uprising, and destroying the capital's fortifications, the Protocol expanded Peking's foreign legation quarter and garrisoned it. In subsequent years American officials had ceased quartering troops there and had converted the military barracks erected on this Protocol territory into offices of the Consulate General. A 1943 treaty concluded with the Nationalist government reaffirmed Washington's title to the land. For Chinese Communist leaders the intervening years apparently had not lessened the remembered humiliation of having foreign armies in Peking. They announced in January

1950 their decision to reclaim the garrison areas and to do so within a week of their proclamation.[51]

The United States reacted sternly to the prospect of imminent requisition. Standing on its treaty rights, Washington launched a heated protest and followed it with the threat that all official personnel would be withdrawn from China if Peking persisted in its planned action. The Americans offered to return a different tract with proper indemnification from Peking authorities but insisted that the specific plot mentioned by the CCP could not be ceded.

The Chinese Communists, while remaining adamant about reclaiming the former American, French, and Dutch barracks, did not anticipate serious repercussions from their position. The Peking Military Control Commission's requisitions order included the suggestion that "separate measures" could be formulated "to solve the problems in regard to the buildings arising from the taking over of the land." American Consul General O. Edmund Clubb further noted the possibility that Chinese Communist leaders wanted to use the barracks issue to convince foreigners to recognize their government. He observed that CCP officials had gone to the trouble of posting requisition notices at the British consulate general and then had ceremoniously removed them and exempted Britain when its initiation of diplomatic relations became official. Clubb speculated that the Communists may well have hoped to damage the prestige of the United States but certainly had not expected the complete withdrawal of all its representatives from China.[52]

Chinese Communist interest in establishing relations with the United States, in fact, did continue despite political conflicts between the two nations. A July 1949 New China News Agency broadcast sent in English to North America asserted that the Chinese people wanted to have relations with all countries willing to deal with them in a spirit of "equality and amity." The Common Program, adopted in September 1949, reiterated Mao Tse-tung's previously stated conditions of "equality, mutual benefit and mutual respect," along with the severance of ties with the Kuomintang, as the basis for opening diplomatic relations with China. The document cited even more liberal prerequisites for establishing commercial exchange, making no mention of the necessity to break all contacts with the Nationalist government first. Also in September, long-time veteran China newsman Tillman Durdin reported that, "while supporting friendship and general collaboration with Russia," Mao and Chou En-lai, "want, nevertheless to pursue a more independent line and particularly believe that Communist China should seek a working relationship with the United States and Britain in the interest of trade and other dealings of advantage to China." Both Mao and Chou invited foreign recognition of the new Communist regime upon its creation on October 1, 1949. Their messages, sent directly to Clubb for communication to Washington, carried Chou's admonition that "it is necessary that there be established normal diplomatic relations between the People's Republic of China and all countries of the world." Following the CCP bid for recognition, Chinese Communist newspapers reduced the volume of anti-American propaganda that they ordinarily printed. Teachers at Tsinghua University told students that, although "American diplomatic and commercial personnel must be treated as self-confessed spies, American businessmen as informers . . . American missionaries as hypocritical, violently anti-Communist, exploiters of [the] Chinese people," China must accept recognition so as to secure economic aid that only the United States could provide.[53]

Further explicating the views of CCP leaders, K'o Pai-nien addressed the issue of foreign policy in the pages of *Hsüeh-hsi*, the Party's most important journal. K'o's remarks, coming from a member of the Foreign Ministry staff and a Chou protegé soon appointed head of the American and Australasian Affairs Department, carried considerable weight. He indicated clearly that China would shun a middle-of-the-road course and maintain a close alignment with the Soviet Union in international affairs. This, however, did not preclude "peaceful cooperation" between China and the imperialist countries. Any nation willing to sever relations with the Kuomintang and approach the People's Republic of China with friendship and respect would be similarly treated. The law-abiding nationals of foreign countries, in any case, would find their property and interests protected by the new regime. Moreover, the Chinese "would like to do business with the people of imperialist countries" insofar as the governments in these states do not "bar us from trading with their people."[54]

Above all, then, for the Chinese Communists diplomatic relations must accord to the Chinese people a status commensurate with their new self-image. Ideological identification with the Soviet Union did not necessarily preclude contacts with the United States so long as such dealings promised to benefit China. Threats of withholding recognition could not win foreigners any special privileges. *De facto* recognition, seen as an imperialist contrivance designed to allow continued cooperation with the Kuomintang, would not be considered. But, observed the *China Digest*, the natural magnanimity of the Chinese would allow them to forgive the past crimes of an imperialist power if it approached the new nation in a spirit of true friendship and equality.[55]

At the end of 1949 and during the early months of 1950, Chinese Communist attention shifted from the recognition question to focus on consolidating the revolution. Communist bloc countries had already opened diplomatic relations with Peking, and several Western states had indicated their willingness to do so. Of more immediate importance to the Communist leadership was realization of a final military victory over Taiwan and gradual economic rehabilitation of the mainland. Mao Tse-tung foresaw three to five years of reconstruction before China could hope to launch a program of rapid development. To bring the resources of the entire population to bear, he assured the bourgeois class of entrepreneurs and skilled technicians that their energies would be used and they would not suffer discrimination.[56] Mao also journeyed to Moscow to negotiate an alliance with the Russians which would provide military security and some economic assistance for China. Provisions of the resulting treaty guaranteed protection against a renewed attack by Japan or any nation allied with Japan (i.e., the United States) and promised financial and technical aid.

Mao's trip to Moscow did not completely resolve China's problems. Within the CCP there continued to be those who felt chary about too close an alignment with the Soviets. A January 1950 approach to American officials in Shanghai, purportedly on behalf of General Ch'en I, seemed to confirm the strong impression many American observers had acquired that a moderate CCP faction feared Russian control. Ch'en supposedly desired to maintain contact with the United States after its diplomatic personnel departed from China. He anticipated the possibility, so the Americans were told, that Chinese Communist nationalists might eventually strike out against the Stalinists within the Party.[57]

Other evidence of anti-Russian prejudice among Party leaders and the Chinese people belied the image of nationwide euphoria with which Party propaganda organs greeted Sino-Soviet cooperation. Displays of Stalin's picture in the streets, the poor quality of Russian imports, and the arrogance of Russian technicians produced an undercurrent of dissatisfaction heightened sometimes by a general antipathy to foreigners, whether communist or not. Diplomatic and extraterritorial privileges enjoyed by the entire staffs of the Soviet trade missions in China after March 1950 may have aggravated these tensions. Ordinarily only one to three members of a trade group in any nation would have been granted such license. Anger also flared over the transfer of foodstuffs from Manchuria to the Soviet Union at a time when a serious shortage existed in China.[58] The scope of aid offered by Moscow did not entirely ameliorate these feelings. China's mammoth economic requirements would barely be touched by a Russian loan valued at US$300 million spread over a five-year period. In return for that meager sum the nation would not only have to pay interest but also grant concessions.[59] The

Chinese welcomed help from Russian experts in developing their resources but resented joint stock companies established to channel some of the profits directly to Moscow. Mao Tse-tung had vowed as early as 1936 that the Chinese Communist Party was "certainly not fighting for an emancipated China in order to turn the country over to Moscow!"[60]

The Sino-Soviet alliance, on the other hand, did afford the CCP a degree of protection for its Taiwan gamble. During December 1949 the remnants of the Kuomintang government, which had moved from Nanking to Canton and then to Chungking just ahead of advancing CCP armies, joined Chiang Kai-shek's entourage in Taiwan. Located a hundred miles from the Chinese coast, the island posed a difficult military objective for a force lacking naval and air power. Nevertheless, riding the crest of its unexpectedly rapid victory on the mainland, the People's Liberation Army vowed to overcome all physical barriers and drive the Kuomintang from its last bastion into the sea.[61] With a Soviet guarantee of military assistance in case the United States attacked China, the PLA had only to face the possibility that American intervention would render its Taiwan invasion force inadequate.

Signals from the United States appeared to conflict. Economic aid flowed from Washington agencies to Chiang Kai-shek, and the Nationalists continued to make arms purchases from American sources. Prominent Americans such as former President Herbert Hoover and Republican Senator Robert Taft (of Ohio) urged the government to use the Navy to prevent a CCP assault on Taiwan. Others suggested that the legal status of Taiwan remained at issue in the absence of a Japanese peace treaty and that in the interim the island should be declared a United Nations trusteeship under American administration. This would allow United States occupation forces to take over from the Kuomintang and prevent both an invasion and internal subversion.[62] President Truman seemed to reject these recommendations in his statement to the press early in January 1950. "The United States," he asserted,

> has no desire to obtain special rights or privileges or to establish military bases on Formosa at this time. Nor does it have any intention of utilizing its armed forces to interfere in the present situation. The United States will not pursue a course which will lead to involvement in the civil conflict in China. Similarly, the United States Government will not provide military aid or advice to Chinese forces on Formosa.

Not only had the President of the United States asserted that American troops would not be sent to preserve the Nationalist hold on Taiwan, but Truman had also acknowledged in his remarks that Taiwan belonged under Chinese control.[63] Soon thereafter Secretary of State Acheson added the observation that Taiwan could not be considered of vital concern to Washington and that it fell outside America's defensive perimeter in Asia.[64]

Corroborating these official declarations, and possibly of even more import to Chinese Communist analysts, a secret State Department guidance paper on Taiwan became public during January. The document indicated that the American government expected Taiwan's imminent fall and proposed to take no action to prevent it. Rather, authorities in Washington urged their foreign service representatives abroad to minimize Taiwan's significance whenever opportunities for such propaganda statements allowed. The leak, generated by General MacArthur's headquarters for domestic American political purposes, provided unintended support for President Truman's contention that the United States would not rescue the failing Nationalist regime.[65]

The Chinese Communists now confronted a serious dilemma. Fully committed to the "liberation" of Taiwan, they must have wanted to believe that the United States would not interpose military force to prevent realization of that goal. Statements by Truman and Acheson, dressed though they may have been in anti-Soviet rhetoric, seemed to indicate a willingness to let the Nationalists fend for themselves. But could the Americans be trusted? They had in the past demonstrated a perverse determination to stand by Chiang Kai-shek. During World War II and the subsequent year of Marshall's mediation, they had repeatedly rejected opportunities to work constructively with the Communist Party and remained tied to the uncooperative and corrupt Kuomintang. Even now, Truman and Acheson both had qualified their hands-off pledges with phrases like "at this time" and "in the present situation."

CCP leaders, therefore, sought to test American intentions. Between January and June 1950 they mounted a series of small-scale amphibious operations against selected island targets. Success in these ventures not only established the PLA's ability to carry out seaborne campaigns, but also bolstered their confidence that American forces would not intercede to help Kuomintang remnant units. This proved true even when victory in the Choushan Islands, off the Chekiang coast, meant the end of the Kuomintang blockade of Shanghai's shipping lines.[66] At the same time, with a similarly provocative intent the CCP waged a shrill anti-American propaganda campaign. Beginning with attacks on Truman's January 5 statement, the Chinese Communist press heaped charges of deceit and aggression upon American officials and their policies. No doubt MacArthur's decision to release Japanese war criminals before their prison sentences were completed aroused genuine fury, but angry responses to American talk of offering foodstuffs to hungry Chinese may have been more pointedly provocative in nature. CCP leaders probably resented Acheson's implication that they could not adequately feed their people, but charges that Americans "venomously hope that the Chinese people will die of famine" seem to be intentional exaggeration.[67] In any case, neither Chinese Communist rhetoric nor action produced any detectable change in American policy. Despite constant publicity about the upcoming Communist attack upon Taiwan, the United States made no threats of retaliation and no efforts to prevent the initial thrust.[68]

In addition to the CCP's belligerent tactics, probes on the diplomatic level continued as well. Although minor and muted, they suggested a willingness to deal with the United States. Consul General Clubb reported from Peking that his efforts to see a Foreign Ministry official before his departure from China had met with success. Although the Chinese Foreign Office had been apprised of his proposed topics of discussion through both the Alien Affairs Office and British intermediaries, they "could hardly be sure that there was not some concrete proposal in the offing." Apparently in hopes that the United States might further reduce or entirely sever its ties to Chiang Kai-shek, Clubb obtained his interview. Clubb, however, could not satisfy the Chinese Communist demand that American recognition of their regime and abandonment of Chiang precede the resolution of other problems. Still, the CCP, without compromising its position verbally, did make "semi-conciliatory" gestures. Peking, for example, permitted the Consulates General in the capital and in Shanghai to keep their radios in operation until they closed and, despite delays, allowed all official American personnel to leave China peaceably. Moreover, in May 1950 the Party released three American military pilots who had been accused of espionage and detained as prisoners of war. That same month, *Hsüeh-hsi* raised the issue of the place foreign enterprise could occupy in the new China. Reminding its readers of Lenin's positive views on the subject, the journal argued that to speed recovery and industrialization a carefully supervised foreign contribution would be beneficial.[69]

All the while, preparations for the Taiwan offensive proceeded steadily through the early months of 1950. The Chinese Communists did not allow fear of possible American moves to deter them, and from later developments it would seem that they had decided to believe American claims that the United States would remain uninvolved in Taiwan's future. A *Jen-min jih-pao* editorial immediately following the outbreak of war in Korea pointed out that as late as June 23, 1950 Acheson had reaffirmed Truman's hands-off Taiwan declaration made the previous January. Thus in June, as an outpouring of patriotic fervor in the press and on the radio accompanied a tripling in the number of soldiers massed in coastal provinces, the assault appeared imminent.[70]

Then suddenly with the eruption of fighting in Korea everything changed. President Truman, reacting to the Korean Communist threat, reflexively intervened in the nearby Chinese struggle. Determined to put a rapid end to Communist advances, lest the United States be plunged into general war, he dispatched the U.S. Seventh Fleet to the Taiwan Straits. The imminent PLA invasion of the island came to an abortive end. On June 28, Chou En-lai spoke confidently of liberating Taiwan regardless of any "obstructive action the United States imperialists may take," but he did not call for immediate mobilization. In the face of interference by sophisticated naval units with unrestricted access to Chinese commerce and industry near the coast, CCP leaders had little real choice except to postpone the invasion.[71] Their earlier preparations, abandoned as soon as the United States intervened, strongly suggests that when the CCP undertook them, its leadership did not expect any American action.

The United States response to the Korean War dispelled whatever interest Peking had had in an accommodation with Washington. Had America allowed the People's Liberation Army to "liberate" Taiwan, it would have demonstrated a willingness to respect China's sovereignty. But neutralization of the Straits illustrated, in Communist eyes, an ongoing determination to frustrate China's development as a strong and independent nation. Washington had accomplished precisely what Secretary of State Dean Acheson, in quieter times, had warned against. The United States had created an irredentist issue over Taiwan, focusing upon itself the anti-imperialist outrage that Acheson had hoped to see directed against Russia because of Soviet actions in Sinkiang and Mongolia.[72] For the CCP, economic need and the commercial utility of a Sino-American tie lost significance in comparison with Washington's unconscionable act.[73] Henceforth, the Chinese dedicated themselves to countering America's "armed aggression."

But before the resonance of gunfire obliterated reasoned conversation, the Chinese Communists had indicated a willingness to pursue limited economic cooperation and working, if not friendly, relations with the United States. Problems abounded—some such as the continued existence of a Nationalist government on Taiwan provoked serious tensions—yet the leadership in Peking had given Americans a variety of signals that, desiring economic advancement and a degree of independence from their Soviet alliance, it desired an accommodation. Washington officials, then, during 1949 and early 1950, did not find the CCP erecting insurmountable barriers to Sino-American relations. Although resolving differences would be difficult, progress had not appeared impossible.

CHAPTER FOUR

Kuomintang Decline

The Flickering Hope

)⬤()⬤()⬤()⬤(

IF the CCP and those who supported relations with the Party tried to exert influence upon American policymakers, so too did the groups opposing an accommodation between Washington and the Communist Chinese. A coalition of American and foreign interests, the advocates of continued United States identification with the Kuomintang, struggled purposefully through the late 1940s. However, their greatest enemy would prove to be not the Communist forces but the Nationalist regime they championed.

At the beginning of 1949 the National Government of China appeared to be crumbling. After decades of almost constant warfare, Kuomintang attempts to exterminate the Chinese Communists sputtered to a close in bitter defeat. In Manchuria, Chiang Kai-shek had futilely sacrificed some 400,000 of his best trained and equipped soldiers to a larger and logistically superior force. That same month, November 1948, overruling his advisors, Chiang had again engaged the Communists, this time in central China. The 65-day Huai-hai battle along a 200-mile front in which more than a million fighting men participated, saw ably commanded Communist legions encircle and destroy the government's troops. A Kuomintang relief column, overloaded with heavy arms and camp followers, was dispatched, but agile Communist units trapped this ponderous army behind rings of trenches. Then, after Generalissimo Chiang decided to bomb the column's valuable equipment rather than see it fall into enemy hands, the relief force, not surprisingly, surrendered.[1]

Diplomatic defeat paralleled military disaster. Madame Chiang Kaishek's mission to America in the autumn of 1948 for urgently needed aid was proving fruitless. Efforts by the Nationalists to cement an alliance in 1948 with Presidential candidate Thomas E. Dewey and Republican Party stalwarts for a time appeared more promising. With a sympathetic White House, it was thought, anti-Chiang bias in the State Department could be eliminated or at least circumvented. Truman's upset victory shattered these hopes. Thus the Nationalists were not surprised when the United States, along with France, Great Britain, and the Soviet Union, rebuffed their appeals to mediate the civil war in January 1949. Soon after, Mao Tse-tung denounced a Chiang Kai-shek New Year's Day peace plan as hypocritical, countering with eight terms of his own that were equally unacceptable to the Generalissimo. Whereas Chiang demanded preservation of the Kuomintang constitution, government, and army, Mao disposed of all these "bogus" institutions and insisted upon land reform, abrogation of "treasonable" treaties, and punishment of a list of war criminals which, of course, included Chiang Kai-shek.[2]

Driven by mounting desperation, the badly shaken Nationalists sought frantically in the months that followed to escape from the catastrophe of Communist takeover. As time passed and alternatives lost promise, hope focused on the single source of support that might stem the quickening tide. Although the United States had been an increasingly reluctant benefactor, Kuomintang leaders came to believe, with a certitude born of despair, that salvation lay with American aid and that they could convince or coerce the Truman Administration to cooperate. Pursuing this elusive goal, they fashioned ever more improbable stratagems to manuever their restive ally into a firm commitment.

As the country lurched from crisis to crisis, however, discord within the Chinese government hampered even this policy. While unity might not have preserved a noncommunist China, disunity simply ensured its demise. From the moment that illusions of possible victory dissolved at the close of 1948, the fiction of unified rule was abandoned.

Evidence of this decline appeared first in the voices within Chiang Kai-shek's governing coalition that called stridently for his resignation. As in 1927, when military misfortune made him politically vulnerable, failures of leadership in late 1948 encouraged his opponents. The New Year's peace proposal was, in fact, a final effort to preserve his formal governmental authority without acknowledging the enormity of Kuomintang losses. There were some in the Party, however, who feared complete collapse and were willing, even anxious, to try to bargain with the Chinese Communists. On January 21, 1949, heeding at last the often-tendered demands of these dissidents, Chiang Kai-shek turned his fragile government over to Vice President Li Tsung-jen, his long-time rival.[3]

American Ambassador John Leighton Stuart had reported during 1948 that a growing number in the Chinese government and military considered a negotiated peace with the Communists and formation of a coalition government desirable and achievable through mediation by the Soviet Union.[4] As the Generalissimo was implacably opposed, advocates of this view were among those calling for Chiang's retirement at the end of the year. Li Tsung-jen, upon assuming the presidency, immediately notified Soviet Ambassador N. V. Roschin that he would like to reopen discussions regarding Russian aid for a negotiated end to the civil war. At the same time, Li authorized the pro-Soviet General Chang Chih-chung to conclude a commercial agreement with the USSR in Sinkiang. Later, when a new cabinet was formed under Ho Ying-ch'in, Li's chosen President of the Executive Yuan, a man with nine years' experience as Chinese Ambassador to Moscow was named Foreign Minister. Encouraged by the momentary support of Sun Fo, who proclaimed himself to be pro-Soviet, and by at least part of the influential Political Study Clique, Li went so far as to offer the Russians Chinese neutrality in a forthcoming world war. In response Roschin demanded that Li also agree to form a genuinely cooperative relationship with Russia and eliminate American influence from China.[5]

At this juncture developments took a most peculiar turn, or so it seemed. Li appealed to John Leighton Stuart for support in his talks with Roschin. Stuart got, and communicated to Secretary of State Acheson, the impression that Li had tentatively agreed to a three-point accord incorporating the provision that China would cease to depend upon the United States. Yet here Li was, in the "incredible" position (as the Department of State put it), of asking Americans to help him throw them out. Subsequently, Li's diplomatic spokesman, Kan Chieh-hou, denied that talks with the Russians had ever gone so far. The Chinese had agreed to neutrality because they needed time and hoped to delay Mao Tse-tung's advance. Stuart's help, it had been hoped, would strengthen Li against Roschin's demands, which were indeed finally refused.[6] In any case, the National Government, whether under the direct command of Chiang Kai-shek or the shaky leadership of Li Tsung-jen, could not bring itself to jettison the United States. Some factions might entertain the illusion that Soviet promises were reliable, but a history of unmet guarantees made the government unwilling to abandon its one stable, if inadequate, source of aid.

Moreover, the Russian connection did not and could not serve to soften Chinese Communist peace terms, which clearly amounted to unconditional surrender by the Nationalists. Soviet influence upon CCP policies was at best tenuous, since Moscow had too often misjudged China's revolution and discouraged its leaders. Having cautioned them to discontinue military operations at the Yangtze River when success was within reach, the Russians were predictably ignored. The Nationalists' abiding belief in Soviet control over Communist activities in China testified to a prevailing misunderstanding of the Chinese Communist movement.[7]

Disagreement over negotiating directly with the CCP proved much more serious than that provoked by talks with the Soviet Union. Li Tsung-jen rapidly found himself confronted not only by adamant enemies, but also by uncompromising allies. Clinging to the idea of an "honorable peace," Sun Fo, who had been appointed President of the Executive Yuan by Chiang Kai-shek, moved it away from the capital and charged Li with exceeding his authority in accepting Mao's eight points as a basis for talks.[8] Although Li did have the support of members of the Political Study Clique, as well as that of his own Kwangsi faction and leftist elements such as the Kuomintang Revolutionary Committee, stubborn resistance on the part of traditionalists in the government and army made his task all the more difficult.[9] It was obvious that he could not command the Nationalist forces to stop fighting even if an agreement could be reached.

Li's impotence was all too apparent to the Communists. To them it seemed that Li was merely stalling for time while refurbishing his anticommunist alliances.[10] Perhaps, too, the knowledge that disunity would make Li's pledge hollow contributed to CCP intransigence. In any case, rejection of demands for complete surrender led, the very next day, to a Communist assault on the Yangtze front. When the front collapsed and the People's Liberation Army rolled south almost unopposed, the Chinese Nationalists were, as in the past, left clutching at elusive American help, bereft of any alternative.

Li Tsung-jen, confronted with the failure of his peace proposals, struggled with scarcely more success to maintain the authority of his presidency. As he had quickly discovered, the Generalissimo's retirement partook more of fantasy than reality. Chiang Kai-shek viewed his departure from office as an opportunity to lay the onus of failure on someone else's shoulders. Retirement was never meant to be resignation.[11] Thus, whether in retreat in Fenghua or Shanghai or on Taiwan, the Generalissimo continued to direct government operations, continued to guide military campaigns, and continued to lose the Chinese mainland to communism.

Chiang Kai-shek's ability to rule from a semi-secluded retirement hinged on two features of the Kuomintang political system: dictatorship and disunity. In 1924, the KMT's founder and the nation's revolutionary father-figure, Sun Yat-sen, allowed Soviet advisers to reorganize his following. Out of a weak political association, the advisers created a centralized party on the Bolshevik pattern. The new KMT embarked on military unification and then announced the beginning of a period of political tutelage. At that point inclination and events interfered. Instead of emerging six years later into an age of democratic institutions as Sun had planned, China continued under the domination of a single authoritarian party. Moreover, the party fell under the domination of a single authoritarian leader—Chiang Kai-shek.

Chiang came to power by a somewhat circuitous route. Initially a minor military figure with disreputable underworld connections, he was, as Sun's protégé and director of the Whampoa Military Academy, in a position to take advantage of, and occasionally help arrange for, misadventures among important contenders for party leadership. Although without government office through much of the 1930s, Chiang insinuated supporters into pivotal positions and increasingly exercised a dominant role in national affairs. By 1938, he had achieved the long-sought title of Kuomintang director-general (*tsung-tsai*), a recognition of his commanding, if not undisputed, status.[12]

Eleven years later, the weight of habit and the dearth of compelling alternatives within the system had given Chiang an unbreakable grip on Nationalist fortunes. The interim had shown him to be tenacious. Throughout the bleak Chungking days of World War II, Chiang had led China's resistance to Japanese brutality. Although the Communists, with some cause, denounced his corruption, inefficiency, and incompetence, and even suggested he might sign a separate peace with Japan, the Generalissimo had hung on.[13] In 1945, he emerged from the Szechuan highlands to reimpose, however tenuously, KMT rule over China.

Contrary to and yet coupled with this concentration of power, chronic disunity also existed in China. Though the Kuomintang had nominally united the nation in 1928, warlordism was never eliminated, regionalism flourished, and factions played havoc with internal party affairs. With an ancient, ofttimes scarlet history, factionalism in modern China splintered government leadership and rendered control of government policies a matter of personal relationship rather than official position. Destructive as they could be when major concerns were domestic and peaceful, the effects of factionalism on foreign policy for a government close to extinction were nothing less than disastrous.

Crowded into the framework of a single party, the Kuomintang, a multiplicity of alliances contended for influence.[14] The predominant groups were divided only roughly along the lines of China's most important governing units: the party, the army, and the government. The CC Clique, which was led by nephews of Chiang's revolutionary model, Ch'en Ch'i-mei, tended to dominate party affairs from its position in the KMT's Organization Department. It also exerted significant control over the administrative bureaucracy through educational and cultural institutions, its own secret service network (called the Central Statistical Bureau), and its ability to assign party members to government posts and supervise their performance. The Whampoa Clique was the strongest of the military groupings, deriving its preeminence from its tie with Chiang Kai-shek. Finally, the Political Study Clique (sometimes referred to as the Political Science Clique) concentrated its energies in the governmental and financial spheres. Less formally organized than the amorphous factions described above, the Political Study Group provided Chiang with a pool of experienced bureaucrats, industrialists, and bankers.[15]

These cliques and their complex subdivisions exerted power through their link to Chiang Kai-shek. As one observer put it:

> If we take the Kuomintang as a big Chinese family, then according to their respective positions, characteristics and styles, the Political Science Group may be compared to a middle-aged matron of great experience and worldly wisdom who, though only in the position of a concubine, still manages to make her weight felt within family circles by keeping the master of the house constantly under her control; the CC may be likened to the faithful wife of long standing who, though fundamentally well-beloved, nevertheless has to put up with the occasional whims and ill temper of the master; while the Fu Hsing Society [primarily Whampoa elements] is in the position of the unmarried daughter of the family who, though forced to adopt an attitude of coy reserve before the eyes of the world, still occupies a cozy corner in the heart of the old man.[16]

Chiang stood above all these alliances, utilizing the talents first of one and then another, keeping them constantly off-balance, never allowing any one to be strong enough to dominate the others completely or depose him. He dealt in much the same way with individuals, some of whom were attached to him directly and some of whom led independent followings and cooperated with him only sporadically. While Chiang exercised his control through a constellation of competing groups loyal to him, making his ouster difficult and his replacement impossible, others contested his authority through their own devoted factions. The foremost of these was the Kwangsi Clique, which in 1948, utilizing a temporary and unusually strong anti-Chiang alliance, put one of its own, Li Tsung-jen, into the vice presidency against the wishes—and the chosen candidate—of Chiang Kai-shek.[17]

The precise impact of factionalism in the broader context of policy formulation, however, remains unclear.[18] Lloyd Eastman in *The Abortive Revolution* concluded that the many internecine rivalries were rarely disputes based on policy differences. Rather, they were, as Liu Chieh-ch'ün claimed, "struggle[s] for the rice bowl."[19]

> There was not necessarily a conflict between the personal and impersonal goals of the faction members. But in Chinese society, where the *sheng-kuan fa-ts'ai* [to become an official and grow rich] mentality was deeply entrenched, the personal goals of the members usually—and especially after the faction had worked its way into power—began to overshadow their commitment to the impersonal goals. Chiang Kai-shek and his coterie provide, perhaps, the preeminent example of this strain between group principles and personal aggrandizement. Chiang himself seems to have been little concerned with personal enrichment and was probably firmly committed to broad national goals. Yet he also condoned flagrant corruption and notorious inefficiency on the part of his officials and military commanders as long as they remained loyal to him.[20]

Eastman and others have probably overstated Chinese indifference to abstract ideas; disagreements between cliques often arose from divergent political orientations and, at times, notably dissimilar plans of action.[21] Nevertheless, it is probably true that disputes, whether stemming from conviction or interest, were generally perceived to involve status and position. A viewpoint at variance with Chiang's, for example, was interpreted as a direct challenge to his authority and could not be dealt with as just an alternative solution for a complex problem.

The effects of these factional disputes within the Nationalist alliance were manifold. First, it proved impossible to have a strong, efficient, and determined government which could conduct a coordinated war or peace effort. Political decisions were tied up in an endless need to reconcile a variety of interests in each and every policy determination. When Sun Fo objected to a compromise peace which would fall short of Chiang Kai-shek's New Year's terms, he was able, at least initially, to divide the government because he possessed a personal following within the Kuomintang and had the support of the CC Clique. The Acting President of a nation at war had to journey from Nanking to Canton and cajole Sun to return to the capital and participate in national affairs.[22]

Even when a decision was reached and a policy or military manuever initiated, the government could never be certain that the policy or order would be carried out or in what form. The chief of staff for the Chinese armies found that his directives to field commanders were often countermanded by Chiang Kai-shek, who had the habit of flying to various battlefronts or telephoning instructions to mere captains and lieutenants.[23] Chiang, as Generalissimo, had appointed members of his trusted

Whampoa Clique to senior military positions, and their loyalty to him took precedence over their military ability and their integrity. Thus, even after his "retirement," he was able to overrule the directives of both civilian and military authorities. It was Chiang who rendered defense of the Yangtze River unmanageable, just as it was Chiang who forced General Pai Ch'ung-hsi to retreat into Kwangsi by ordering a withdrawal that left Pai's flank exposed.[24] Top army and navy officials told American observers that "if this situation continues, bloodshed may occur within the Nationalist army and navy because of divergent loyalties and directives." Almost constant disagreement over tactics and strategy was as disastrous to Nationalist forces as actual combat with People's Liberation Army units. Li grew so desperate that he proposed American command of his forces to eliminate the Generalissimo's interference.[25]

Li Tsung-jen's control of civil affairs was equally tenuous. He complained that members of his government would clear orders with the Generalissimo before implementing them.[26] Leader of a small clique based almost entirely in his backward and underpopulated province of Kwangsi, Li was forced to recruit members of other groups to fill pivotal posts in his administration.[27] He could not replace entrenched representatives of factions that looked to Chiang Kai-shek for guidance, as did the Whampoa cadets. Thus, when Chiang asserted his will, there was little that officials opposed to his actions could do. Chiang's July 1949 conference with President Elpidio Quirino at Baguio in the Philippines, at which he discussed the possibilities of a Pacific security pact, was reportedly not authorized by the government.[28] Similarly, the Generalissimo appointed General T'ang En-po Governor of Fukien to replace General Chu Shao-liang without the approval of Li or his administration. Chu, angered, left his post before T'ang was ready to take over, and in the interim Foochow fell to the Communists.[29] T'ang was also directed by the "Gimo" to arrest the Governor of a neighboring province, Chekiang, for having implemented Li's reform measures, such as releasing political prisoners, and for talking peace.[30]

Prominent among problems that Acting President Li was never able to solve was his dispute with the Generalissimo over control of China's finances. Chiang had directed the Bank of China to ship its assets to Taiwan in the autumn of 1948. The holdings at that time included gold bars, coins, U.S. and British banknotes, jewelry, and other items valued in all at $350 million (US). Although public outcry secured suspension of further shipments after removal of the gold was discovered in early 1949, Li could never recover the already displaced bank assets, nor could he control their disbursement. Short of funds to meet administrative expenses or even to pay front line troops, the Acting President, at best, was able to arrange only limited transfers from Taiwan. Chiang retained authority over expenditures, and Canton bankers believed that he personally cleared all payments over $60,000 (Canton).[31]

Conflict over financing continued throughout 1949, and late in the year the director of the Bank of China found himself under renewed pressure. The Generalissimo insisted that remaining assets be shipped to Taiwan while there was still time; Yen Hsi-shan, president of the Executive Yuan, wanted the stocks moved to Chungking to support the government when, as he expected, it shifted there; and Kan Chieh-hou served the Bank with a written order from Li Tsung-jen demanding funds for his imminent trip to the United States. In a quandary as to whom to obey, the governor of the Bank, Liu Kung-yun, consulted his predecessor, O.K. Yui, a continuing power behind the scenes, who counseled him to ignore all others and carry out the Generalissimo's orders.[32]

Interference in the course of government affairs became easier for Chiang during the summer of 1949. On July 26 the Standing Committee of the Central Executive Committee of the Kuomintang, the party's most important organ, established a Supreme Policy Council to serve, on an emergency basis, as a coordinating agency for government and party policies. Because he was Director-General of the KMT, Chiang Kai-shek was named chairman of this new organization and Li Tsung-jen vice-chairman, an arrangement that further circumscribed Li's already limited authority as President of the Republic.[33] Thereafter all government decisions had to be approved by the Council before implementation, giving the Generalissimo final control of foreign and domestic, civil and military affairs. Further, on August 1, 1949, also in his capacity as Director-General of the Kuomintang, Chiang set up his own "alternate government" in Taiwan. Although he claimed that this was a purely informal structure, it closely paralleled the administrative divisions of the Canton government. Moreover, this Director-General's office commanded the services of former Foreign Minister Wang Shih-chieh at a time when Li was unable to fill that post in his own cabinet. And Yui, the ex-Governor of the Bank of China who told Liu Kung-yun to obey the Generalissimo's orders, coincidentally was the financial adviser.[34]

Kuomintang dissidents who had joined together to force Chiang out of the presidency recognized as early as February 1949 that this would not effectively eliminate his influence. Efforts to convince the Generalissimo to leave China following his retirement proved fruitless. Li sent emissaries to the district of Fenghua to convince Chiang to go. Ho Ying-ch'in and Pai Ch'ung-hsi both appealed to American Ambassador Stuart for assistance, hoping that an invitation from the United States might lure the Generalissimo abroad.[35] The Americans did not comply, but these were, in any case, unprofitable maneuverings, for Chiang was determined to stay on the scene. If his strength was inadequate to save the mainland, he must at least be sure that no one else could. He devoted his abilities, which were considerable, to thwarting his opposition. Li Tsung-jen never had a chance.

Factional rifts, debilitating in China, similarly impaired the country's representation abroad. The proliferation of Chinese observers and intervenors in the United States, each making separate pleas for aid to various Chinese leaders, merely created confusion. Not only the major camps maintained such missions: Yen Hsi-shan sent a follower to protect the interests of the Shansi Military Clique; T. V. Soong and H. H. Kung ran personal networks from New York City; and beyond the frontier of KMT membership, minor parties like the Young China Party also had spokesmen on the scene.[36]

These factional politics placed severe strains on diplomatic relations, a fact that caused China's Ambassador to Washington, V. K. Wellington Koo, who claimed to be a nonpartisan, but was identified by others variously as an adherent of Chiang or Li, to complain bitterly.[37] Ignorant of the activities of other Nationalist Chinese, his efforts to organize publicity were hampered. Interviews with American leaders, which should have been arranged through the Embassy, occurred haphazardly. Koo was never able to surmount such obstacles; and because his ambassadorial rank made him technically responsible, he was often berated for ineffective or inefficient work.[38]

Chiang Kai-shek operated on a variety of levels in America. Within the Embassy itself he had a group of five officials, including the Minister-Counselor and the Military Attaché, reporting directly to him over the head of the Ambassador.[39] Moreover, at least one important U.S. Congressional leader was told that the Minister-Counselor, Ch'en Chih-mai, not Koo, was the real power in the Embassy.[40] Similarly, the Generalissimo designated H. H. Kung his special representative in the United States, an appointment which virtually established a second ambassadorship. However, Koo, whose diplomatic skills and command of English were considered irreplaceable, quashed this move by threatening to resign. In retrospect he realized,

that Dr. Kung's appointment, the proposal for which was made prior to the Generalissimo's retirement, was desired . . . to keep in direct and confidential touch with the Administration in Washington, entirely separate from the government channels in China. The Generalissimo's retirement from the presidency . . . was not a step taken completely by preference, and there was certainly a general sentiment among the Generalissimo's entourage to have him return to power one day. In order to do that, during the interim period, it was very important and essential that an independent line of communication and information be kept up.[41]

Perhaps most embarrasing and difficult for the Ambassador, however, was the sudden arrival in Washington of Madame Chiang Kai-shek on December 1, 1948.[42] Madame Chiang set up headquarters in Riverdale, New York, and neither informed the Embassy of her purposes nor used its services to conduct her business. Only rarely did she confer with Koo and then imparted as little information about her intentions as possible. Rather than tap his familiarity with the workings of American politics, she relied on her family—particularly H. H. Kung, Madame Kung, and their sons and associates. Koo found this personally galling and politically misguided. Madame Chiang, for instance, did not see the impropriety of appealing to Secretary of State George Marshall for aid when his retirement was imminent. She misinterpreted his friendship as encouragement and, worse yet, "it was as if it were expected that an American Secretary of State would have the same ability to carry through a personal decision in the United States as the Generalissimo had in China."[43]

If the Generalissimo's followers regarded Koo with suspicion, so too did Li Tsung-jen and his prime supporter in the United States, Kan Chieh-hou. The Shanghai newspaper *Shih Shih Hsin Pao* speculated that Kan's May 1949 trip to the United States had a special purpose, because Koo, an experienced diplomat, needed no help. Koo himself, however, noted that "no correspondence from Acting President Li Tsung-jen to the United States government or President Truman ever went through the Embassy."[44] Kan also made it clear to everyone that he considered the Ambassador to be working for Chiang's interests—interests that were now discredited and detrimental to China's welfare.

By confessing past errors of China's government and blaming its former leaders, Kan apparently hoped to convince Americans that Li, with creative new policies and a more liberal and honest staff, could be trusted to handle renewed aid.[45] His efforts, however, failed to have the desired effect on U.S. government officials. Kan's rhetoric and behavior merely deepened impressions of disunity and reinforced convictions in the White House and State Department that further aid to the Nationalists would be wasted.[46]

Factions competed in the United States with the same ardor with which they fought in China because the stakes were enormously high. Washington was not seen merely as the capital of a major world power but as the stage upon which China's vital struggle would be played out.

A military victory over the Chinese Communists was clearly impossible after the Huai-hai debacle in January 1949. At most, the remnants of the Kuomintang army might preserve a sanctuary south of the Yangtze River. To accomplish even this, however, American aid was believed to be essential. Though there were approaches to other Western powers, and even efforts to come to terms with the Soviet Union, none of these attempts was more than a subsidiary, stopgap measure. All important plans, and everyone's energies, were dedicated to eliciting support from the United States.[47]

Chiang Kai-shek felt certain that the United States would not finally abandon China. True, there might be painful defeats. The mainland might have to be sacrificed temporarily. But in the end, arms and money would be forthcoming.[48] Meanwhile the Communists would smash his Kuomintang adversaries, who, bereft of the funds and weapons he still controlled, would be unable to fight on.[49] For the future Chiang was convinced—and neither Koo in Washington nor American foreign service officers in China could disabuse him of the notion—that World War III would soon break out between the United States and the Soviet Union. During this confrontation, Chiang would reconquer China and thereby eliminate communism's eastern redoubt while the United States destroyed it in the West. Chiang was not alone in expecting a war, and similar views held by the Japanese, many Europeans, and several doomsayers in America reinforced Nationalist expectations. So, too, did the signing of the North Atlantic Treaty in April 1949, which the Chinese interpreted as a military alliance that would heighten world tensions and provoke a violent Soviet response. General Cheng Chieh-min, head of the KMT military secret service and Vice Minister of National Defense, told Wellington Koo in November 1949 that Chinese government policy was to conserve resources on Taiwan until World War III provided the KMT an opportunity to oust the Communists.[50]

Short of the hoped-for war, the Nationalists made other efforts to keep the United States involved and on their side. In September 1949 U.S. Consul General Walter P. McConaughy in Shanghai reported to the Secretary of State that the Chinese Air Force was dropping pamphlets over the city signed "Tiger Airforce Squadron." As McConaughy noted, this title bore a striking resemblance to Chennault's "Flying Tigers" and could only be interpreted as a flagrant attempt to involve the United States directly in China's struggle.[51] Similarly, the use of Japanese mercenaries to fight for the Nationalist armies and advise the government on economic matters, at a time when American troops occupied Japan and General Douglas MacArthur had responsibility for Japanese policies and actions, could not help but confirm suspicions that the United States was participating in the Kuomintang military effort.[52]

A still more imaginative plan called for indicting the USSR on the grounds it had disregarded its obligations under the 1945 Sino-Soviet Treaty of Friendship. The Russians had pledged themselves to give Chiang moral, military, and material aid and to abstain from aiding his enemies in return for substantive concessions by the Chinese government.[53] By accusing the Soviets of treaty violations in the United Nations, Chinese leaders hoped to arouse world sympathy for China. They also wanted to make clear that any government, coalition or communist, that emerged in China was a creation of the USSR and not an independent regime entitled to recognition.[54] But "in reality," the State Department's Policy Planning Staff believed, "the end purpose of the Chinese effort . . . is to involve us in an obligation of further support to the Chinese government."[55]

Foreign Minister Wang Shih-chieh broached the idea of bringing a case before the United Nations to then Secretary of State George C. Marshall in November 1948. Marshall warned that the disadvantages of raising the matter before the UN would almost certainly outweigh the advantages. Although the United States strongly believed that the USSR had surreptitiously aided CCP advances in Manchuria, three years of surveillance had yielded no concrete evidence. If the UN were to act at all, it would merely send an observer group whose chances of seeing more than the Americans had seen were slight, especially since it would inevitably be hampered by a Soviet member.

But, in spite of Marshall's negativism and Ambassador V. K. Wellington Koo's opposition, enthusiasm for such a policy increased among the leaders of the Kuomintang. It was hoped that, if the General Assembly would not vote sanctions against Russia—an admittedly unlikely prospect—it would at least censure Soviet behavior, thereby embarrassing the USSR and distracting international attention from repeated KMT military defeats. In February 1949, Sun Fo, President of the Executive Yuan, was reported to have called for a UN appeal as the only solution to China's problems. Though rarely agreeing on anything, Chiang Kai-shek and Li Tsung-jen were both eager to make this case and Yen Hsi-shan added his approval. Finally, to overcome the Foreign Ministry's hesitancy, the Legislative Yuan passed a resolution calling on the government to act.[56]

The Chinese, therefore, presented their strategy to Department of State officers with the expectation, however ill-founded, of eliciting a positive response.[57] Surprisingly, a sympathetic Deputy Undersecretary of State, Dean Rusk, encouraged them. Subsequently T. F. Tsiang, China's Permanent Representative to the UN, was informed that the United States would support a complaint based on treaty and UN Charter violations, though not a call for nonrecognition of a Chinese Communist regime.[58] In September, when he presented the National Government's case, Tsiang felt hopeful that a strong indictment would emerge. Beneath the surface of State Department good will, however, uneasiness began to spread during the autumn of 1949. Charles W. Yost (adviser to Ambassador-at-Large Philip C. Jessup), the Policy Planning Staff, and Minister-Counselor Lewis Clark all argued against American involvement in the issue. Nationalist Chinese unreliability made the potential for embarrassment too high, they said. Yost, moreover, thought that the damage such an entanglement would do to American relations with the Chinese Communists weighed strongly against it. By November, Tsiang had become aware that American support had slipped and would tolerate only a very weak resolution.[59] The subsequent measure, sponsored jointly by the United States, Australia, Mexico, Pakistan, and the Philippines, merely reiterated traditional formulas regarding China's independence and integrity without touching on Soviet actions or the matter of recognition.[60]

Meanwhile, events in China had significantly altered Nationalist assessment of their prospects at the UN. On October 1, 1949, a new Communist Chinese government had been created at Peking. The People's Republic promptly demanded membership in the General Assembly and China's permanent seat in the Security Council. Frightened by this challenge, the Nationalists desired simply to avoid controversy. Thus, on December 5 they allowed their complaint to be sent to the General Assembly's Interim Committee for further study. This retreat, however wise, seemed to State Department critics of the Kuomintang regime to be proof that their skepticism had been justified. Lewis Clark remarked to Jessup that "in this as in so many other heartbreaking experiences I have had with the Chinese in the past two years, the Chinese just seem unable to do anything positive themselves. They always want the United States to do it first and for them."[61]

Chiang Kai-shek's inauguration of a Pacific security pact similarly sought to manuever Washington into rendering the Nationalists more aid and support. Although the concept of an eastern association to parallel the fledgling North Atlantic Treaty Organization (NATO) had been discussed, no concrete plans existed in the spring of 1949. Chiang's enthusiasm for a military and political alliance, offering heightened stature in domestic affairs and enhanced legitimacy and forcefulness in dealing with the United States, struck responsive chords with Philippine

President Quirino and South Korea's Syngman Rhee, both of whom likewise occupied vulnerable political positions. Chiang and Quirino thereupon met in Manila in July to launch the Pact, and Rhee indicated that South Korea would adhere shortly. According to former Shanghai Mayor K. C. Wu and the Generalissimo's son, Chiang intended to utilize his allies to secure "indirect assistance" from the United States by asserting his more pressing need for whatever they might acquire.[62]

However, the United States, whose leadership a Quirino spokesman claimed indispensable to the project had already demonstrated its opposition. Secretary of State Acheson announced in May that America would not join a Pacific defense union, maintaining that internal disruption in Asia made such a plan premature. Nevertheless, State Department officials recognized that considerable interest existed in Asia for establishing cooperative relations. Secretly, therefore, they suggested that a noncommunist rather than an anticommunist, economic rather than military, association might be welcomed by Washington. Such a venture must also exclude Nationalist China, the Americans cautioned, lest the burden of an impossible crusade doom it to failure.[63]

Other Kuomintang efforts to win American cooperation could not so easily be avoided by the United States. One tactic, political as well as military, was the imposition of a seacoast blockade, coupled with selective bombing of American and Chinese Communist targets. Although damage inflicted upon the Communists did handicap industry in Shanghai, the major urban center in China, the Nationalists knew that they could not cause severe dislocation of Communist power.[64] Rather, they aimed at overwhelming a group which lacked personnel equipped to operate a huge city, thus embarrassing an enemy which could not adequately protect the people under its control, demoralizing the Westerners who remained in Communist territory, and ensuring that Western aid and trade would not establish a bridge between the CCP and the Nationalists' own wavering allies. As intensely as the Soviets, Chiang desired to keep the Chinese Communists isolated and dependent upon Russian aid.

Legally, the National Government could not proclaim a blockade. Belligerency status, a prerequisite, had never been granted to the Communist "bandits." To do so at that time, as Ambassador Stuart pointed out, would imply that Shanghai was in CCP hands by right of conquest, in which case it was doubtful that a Kuomintang declaration would have any effect there. Moreover, under a blockade, foreign shipping would automatically be entitled to the rights of neutrals in the conflict, thereby handicapping Nationalist naval patrols. Thus, on June 20, 1949 the Chinese government announced that, in its capacity as the only recognized ruling authority on the mainland, it had closed ports from Foochow to Manchuria to international traffic.[65] Western powers, however, could not honor what was so transparently a naval blockade unless it effectively stopped all trade, and this the Chinese navy was not equipped to do. Great Britain promptly made clear its determination to resist, threatening to convoy its merchant craft if necessary.[66]

The United States position proved less consistent. Although publicly declaring the blockade illegal, the Truman Administration made it clear to private shippers that entering closed ports was dangerous business and no escort service would be provided by the U.S. Navy. With Presidential direction and encouragement, the State Department maintained a hands-off policy, despite provocation (American commercial ships were shelled) and pleas from the Isbrandtsen Shipping Lines.[67]

The United States took a similar stand in the matter of raids conducted by the Chinese Air Force over heavily populated Chinese cities, particularly Shanghai. Although it was clear that the CAF was not restricting its strikes to military targets, and American foreign service officers reported "indiscriminate destruction" and "butchery of unknown numbers," the American government apparently limited itself to ineffectual protests.[68] For the United States the situation was especially difficult. Despite Chinese assurances that U.S. property would not be deliberately bombed, Department of State reports left no doubt that easily identifiable installations such as the Shanghai Power Company, which provided all of the electric power for the city of Shanghai, were being hit repeatedly.[69] Robert C. Strong, Chargé d'Affaires in Taipei observed, "In my opinion Chinese navy and CAF both have idea U.S. will not retaliate in any serious way almost regardless of what they do."[70] And Foreign Minister George Yeh's half-hearted attempts to justify attacks on the grounds that Shanghai Power's output was being used for military purposes merely reinforced Strong's view.[71]

At the same time, the United States was being blamed for these raids in Shanghai, for whose people the erratic destruction was "like someone pounding on [a] festering boil."[72] The Communists loudly decried imperialist murder: American-made planes dropping American-made bombs, purposelessly incinerating the congested wooden neighborhoods of the city.[73]

Yet, the Americans found it difficult to alter their position. The director of the State Department's Office of Chinese Affairs, Philip Sprouse, argued that:

> It should not be overlooked that the Chinese government, in effect, exists and maintains its representation in the UN solely because of American sup-

port and that it would probably collapse overnight if that support were withdrawn. It seems incredible, therefore, that we permit the Chinese government brazenly to do the damage to our position in China that it is doing. It is all the more incredible that we do not take stronger steps than we have already taken to make clear to that Government that, if it continues bombing attacks of this nature, we will stop all aid or at least all shipments of military supplies from this country. We cannot afford to let the Chinese Government take us further down the primrose path than it has already led us.[74]

What this analysis did not mention, what the Nationalists obviously were counting on, was the political threat the Truman Administration was thought to be facing should it abandon "the cause." In fact, power over China's future immobilized the United States government. The Chinese Nationalists, therefore, were gambling. If their supporters in the United States were adept, the stakes would continue to be too high for the Democrats. As time passed, the United States became more and more closely identified with the brutality of the bombings, more and more tied into the Kuomintang fight.

The use of pressure politics in the United States on behalf of the Nationalists was intense and purposeful, if poorly planned and coordinated. Approaching varied segments of American society to recruit friends and engender sympathy, the Chinese employed paid lobbyists as well as the energies of Nationalist officials and interested allies. The Chinese believed that, with their understanding of American political institutions and American ways of thinking, they could shape public opinion into a powerful pro-Kuomintang instrument as they had during World War II.

V. K. Wellington Koo vigorously pursued this objective. American educated, with an illustrious diplomatic career dating from 1912, the Ambassador was an astute, if idealistic, observer of the American scene.[75] He was convinced, perhaps to an exaggerated degree, of the efficacy of "enlightening the public" which "in a democracy like the United States," he believed, "was as important as informing the administration of the major issues and the significance of particular problems arising in one's country or between one's country and the United States."[76] Utilizing his post as senior representative and spokesman for his government, Koo lectured widely and wrote often on Chinese affairs and the need for foreign, that is, American aid. Impressed by the political influence American interest groups seemed to wield, he worked at winning the support of labor unions, veteran's organizations and women's clubs.[77] He met frequently with members of Congress, and repeatedly with State Department officials, even though he found many of them unsympathetic and unpleasant.[78] He was sensitive to the effect on prominent figures of ill-timed or poorly executed appeals and worked assiduously, although ultimately with little effect, to coordinate China's publicity work.

Most lobbying for the Nationalists, in fact, occurred outside the control of the Ambassador. Koo neither disbursed the funds nor had a say over the selection of agents to carry out propaganda efforts. In the case of William Goodwin, a paid lobbyist, his "letter of employment, of which the Embassy knew nothing, was drafted, revised, and approved by 'Riverdale,' even against the objection of the Director of the Chinese News Service, whose official business was to look after publicity, and who, in this case, was the hiring agent." "Riverdale" was, of course, Madame Chiang Kai-shek.[79]

The struggle for a "Free China" attracted a wide range of Americans. Anticommunist religious leaders, industrialists, and Congressmen publicized the crusade through such organizations as Alfred Kohlberg's American China Policy Association and Frederick McKee's Committee to Defend America by Aiding Anti-Communist China.[80] The Chinese Embassy kept in touch with many prominent participants in this so-called China lobby. Koo entertainted them, met with them at dinners arranged by Goodwin, Kohlberg, or McKee, and appeared at functions throughout the United States at the invitation of Henry Luce, *Time-Life* publisher, and others.[81] Members of Congress, whether cold warriors, anti-New Dealers, partisan Republicans, or sincere friends of China, became constant targets for Kuomintang appeals. Some, such as H. Alexander Smith, Republican Senator from New Jersey, traveled to China and corresponded regularly with government officials. These few supported their arguments for aid to Nationalist China with first-hand knowledge. But up-to-date "evidence" provided by the Nationalists also appeared in Congressional speeches of many who personally knew little about Chinese affairs.[82] On occasion, the Embassy even drafted such speeches.[83]

From their American sympathizers, the Nationalists solicited and received confidential information about the inner workings of government agencies. They ascertained who might be well-disposed to their cause, where bureaucratic squabbles might operate in their favor, and how best to rephrase an appeal which had already been modified or denied several times. Most helpful in providing such intelligence were Congressmen like Walter Judd, State Department representatives like John Foster Dulles, and the military. Koo found both Americaan military officers and the Defense Department willing, even anxious, to cooperate with him. Admiral Oscar C. Badger, special advisor on Far Eastern affairs at the Navy Department, virtually authored China's December 1949 aid request and then directed the timing and manner of its submission. The Assistant Secretary of Defense and his deputy provided Koo regular reports on top level policy discussions in the Department of Defense. They recounted secret debates in the National Security Council to him and disclosed the details of State Department and Pentagon planning.[84]

When emotional and political inducements failed to secure help, the Chinese Nationalists used less subtle means. Chiang Kai-shek maintained a secret fund in the United States under the control of Yü Kuo-hua, Deputy Executive Director of the International Monetary Fund. These monies were intended for special purposes, such as a payment to Colonel M. Preston Goodfellow to organize a foreign legion for China.[85] In September 1949, General Albert C. Wedemeyer was offered a large amount of money to serve as an adviser to the Chinese Government, the aim being, the State Department speculated, to ensure "U.S. involvement, together with U.S. military and economic aid."[86] And in March 1949, when the European desk in the Department of State opposed his efforts to secure U.S. tanks, Colonel David Li of the Chinese procurement mission in Washington asked Ambassador Koo "whether he should promise rewards to Am. officials." Koo noted in his diary:

> I warned him to be very careful lest it should cause scandals hurting the good name of the Ch. Gov't and damaging the prospects of further aid legislation by Congress. I told him I would rather not know the people he had in mind and the amounts they asked, and I particularly asked if he had the funds already remitted to him from China. He said none yet, but he had already reported to Col. Chiang Wei-kuo [Chiang Kai-shek's son] who had entrusted the purchasing mission to him.[87]

Whether money was actually paid to anyone is unclear, but there can be no doubt that a Chinese official considered such a tactic.

The importance that the Chinese placed upon these efforts at persuasion, whether overt or covert, sheds light on their conduct in other areas as well. If impressing American opinion, especially such opinion leaders as Congressional representatives, was the way to secure aid, then American sensibilities had to be catered to. Thus Hu Shih received an invitation to become Foreign Minister because of his standing in American eyes. Similarly, there was talk of establishing a liberal party to pose as a front for the Kuomintang government in hopes of impressing the United States. A liberal cabinet enlisting the services of virtually every Chinese who had a vigorous and honest reputation in Washington, would, it was hoped, seeve as a convincing example of Chinese unity and purpose.[88] Nationalists made requests for American guidance in reforming their political system to serve this end as well. They also promised that their vote in international tribunals would always support American policies even with regard to rebuilding Japan.[89] Perhaps the most striking example of such accommodation, however, was the Nationalist response to a United States publication popularly known as the China White Paper.

To explain and defend its China policy, the State Department published this study on August 5, 1949. Even before its release rumors of its contents sparked virulent criticism and acrimonious debate throughout the United States. Pro-Chiang elements accused the Truman Administration of stabbing their hero in the back. Not only had aid to Chiang been inadequate and the Yalta talks with Stalin a betrayal of China's interests, they said, but now "communist sympathizers" and "fools" in the State Department had written Chiang's obituary and condemned his still valiant armies. Even Democrats loyal to Truman, while pointing out the Paper's compelling arguments, were hard-pressed to justify publication of confidential reports.[90]

Ironically, the reaction of China's government lacked the bitterness so evident in America. Officials and their spokesmen in the news media denounced the document, decrying its effects on China's future. But the mood of the CC Clique newspaper, *Tien-feng jih-pao*, was one of dismay rather than resentment, as it cautioned:

> One must not put too much faith in one-sided words of diplomats. [The] Chinese government has undeniably inevitably made mistakes but not so serious as the White Paper would have us believe. Countries are not alike, thus Marshall and Wedemeyer proposals may have been fine for America but not for China. . . . Republicans and rest of American people still love China. We must so arrange our affairs that no White Paper can harm China's brilliant future.[91]

This calm on the part of the most anti-foreign elements in Chiang's Kuomintang coalition testified both to the Generalissimo's control and the pervasive agreement among all segments that American aid remained the ultimate and only barrier to total annihilation. Thus, a lengthy refutation of the White Paper must be postponed until United States Congressional opinion regarding China aid crystallized. Chiang revised the brief statement prepared by the Supreme Policy Council of the KMT and eliminated its querulous and anxious tone.[92] Venting fury at this American betrayal might bring momentary satisfaction, but the necessity of securing further support from these same Americans compelled restraint.

It is evident, therefore, that the leadership of Nationalist China looked to the United States for deliverance and that, as the painful months wore on, no other options were seriously entertained. Whether the Nationalists had a viable alternative is arguable, but if they did not, it only makes their behavior harder to understand.

Having demonstrated military ineffectiveness and political vulnerability, the Nationalists proceeded during 1949 and early 1950 to display their diplomatic ineptitude as well. In the face of disaster, Kuomintang leaders refused to work together, distrusting their colleagues and seeking to preserve what personal power they could. This disunity hampered innovative thinking, much as it convinced observers abroad that the Chinese government could not be energetic, honest, or efficient. Similarly, efforts to embarrass the United States into providing support, although somewhat successful in the Congressional realm, aggravated pivotal American officials and produced but meager results.

Nevertheless, dependence on American aid, absolute during World War II, had become addictive. In the subsequent years of civil strife, China's Nationalist leaders could not see around or beyond that precedent. They listened to the rhetoric of their supporters in the United States and seemed convinced by propaganda that they, in part, generated themselves. Even after Nationalist hopes of a Republican presidency were dashed in 1948, they—and particularly Chiang Kai-shek—persisted in the belief that the tide would turn and America would come to the rescue. When the entire Chinese mainland fell under the control of the Communists, reliance on ultimate United States assistance continued on the small island of Taiwan.

Nationalist attentiveness to and faith in the United States did not delight American officials. Those who would have preferred to give energetic support to the Kuomintang found it difficult to argue the efficacy of aid for such an obviously dependent regime. Each time China's Nationalist leaders offered a new concession designed to entice the Americans, the KMT's proponents suffered further embarrassment. Policymakers found one of the best arguments for establishing relations with the Chinese Communists to be the utter bankruptcy of the Kuomintang option.

CHAPTER FIVE
The China Lobby
A Dedicated Few

)◆◼◻◼◻◼◻◼◻◼◻◼(

THE amorphous collection of Americans who tried to help maneuver the United States into saving Chiang Kai-shek found themselves handicapped by their inept hero and confronted with popular indifference and powerful opponents. Dubbed the China Lobby by the New York Communist Party in 1949, the pro-Chiang coalition never actually formed a tightly organized lobbying group.[1] What center the Lobby had revolved around its representatives from Nationalist China who operated out of New York and Washington, D.C. Contacts between the Chinese and their American supporters tended to lack any formal unity. A few individuals worked as paid lobbyists, but the majority of Americans who aided the Nationalists did so informally. Prominent figures in industry, labor, publishing, the military, academia, and religion contributed their efforts. Most of the serious participants had served previously in other campaigns for China, or at least against communism.

China Lobbyists joined the crusade for such varied motives that adherents often had little affinity for one another. Max Ascoli, editor of *The Reporter* magazine, believed that in addition to the "honest men deeply concerned with the plight of the Chinese people and Chiang Kai-shek" the Lobby also included "fanatics possessed by the nightmare of a Communist conspiracy centering on some of America's highest leaders; and politicians who will stop at nothing in their hunt for power." Certain businessmen supported Chiang's fight because they had contracts with the Nationalist regime; others enlisted in the cause positive that their intimate identification with Kuomintang interests would exclude them from contacts with the CCP. Those missionaries who could not countenance compromise with atheistic communism also flocked to Chiang and labored to see him victorious on the mainland.

Whatever their reasons—selfless or self-seeking—members of the China Lobby dedicated their efforts to preserving the authority of

Chiang Kai-shek. They sought not merely to arouse sympathy for an innocent victim of foreign aggression, but to commit the United States to a long-term program of military and economic assistance. Above all, they exerted themselves to oppose recognition of and trade with the Chinese Communists. In pursuing these ends, proponents of Chiang's survival did not hestitate to condemn their opponents as fools and traitors. They toiled to make support for Chiang and loyalty to the American government synonymous; in time, they succeeded.[2]

In 1949 and early 1950, however, the China Lobby had not yet scaled the heights of power or publicity that McCarthyism and the Korean War would bring. Although fear had begun to twist American politics, the Lobby remained in its infancy. Its ability to attract prominent individuals from respectable professions testified to uneasiness in America rather than the strength of the China Lobby's own appeal. Lamentations about the betrayal of Chiang Kai-shek and the "loss" of China had yet to find much resonance within a public which had long since rejected Chiang and cared little about Asia. If in the 1950s and 1960s the China Lobby could destroy people and organizations and make intelligent discussion of China policy impossible, in the months between January 1949 and June 1950 it was still struggling for notice and a voice in national affairs.[3]

To win adherents and increase its influence the China Lobby attempted to seduce the American people with a special picture of the importance of Sino-American relations. The myth had originated with an adventuresome few who dared visit the distant reaches of Asia and others, who shared their obsession, perpetuated it. The myth spoke of great riches to be had in China and millions of souls to be saved for Christ. It described a barbarian people who labored diligently and exhibited a remarkable cleverness and aptitude for Western learning. Most importantly, it referred to the dark oppressions that imperialism visited upon the unfortunate heathen and extolled America's virtuous self-restraint. The American people, according to the myth, were, in fact, great friends of China. The United States, a nation above such base behavior, never indulged in territorial or economic exploitation of the Chinese. Moreover, the United States had helped protect China from dismemberment with its Open Door policy, for which the Chinese felt boundless gratitude.[4] Sino-American relations had always been good and, if preserved from the evil influences of alien ideologies, would continue to prosper.

The grains of truth behind the myth made it no less debilitating to American understanding of Sino-American intercourse. That China did have an enormous population did not mean that all those people had the desire for or resources with which to purchase Western goods. That the United States had not actually acquired spheres of influence in China did not erase the U.S. Navy's desire to force Imperial concession of Samsah Bay in Fukien province.[5] And that some Americans, captivated by Chinese culture and politics, did develop a special sensitivity toward the Chinese people did not change the far more prevalent indifference to and ignorance about China in the United States.

Those who "joined" the China Lobby believed in or at least utilized the myth of China. They spoke freely of a special relationship between the Chinese and Americans, and a few of them felt personally responsible for China. They emphasized the ties which had grown up over years of contact and cautioned that American security required a strong and free Chinese nation. Symbolizing China's endurance and future promise, Chiang Kai-shek became central to the argument fashioned by the China Lobbyists. Americans supported Chiang, the Kuomintang, and a free China, said the Lobby, so America's government must render the cause all possible assistance. Through newspapers, magazines, and radio, through the Congress and the Department of Defense, through means legal and on occasion illegal, they pressed this simple litany upon policymakers.

Certain publishers ranked among the leading proponents of the cause, giving the China Lobby a visibility disproportionate to its importance. Roy Howard (Scripps-Howard), William Randolph Hearst (Hearst Press), Robert R. McCormick (*Chicago Tribune*), William Loeb (*New Hampshire Morning Union*), and Henry Luce (*Time-Life*) flooded their newspapers and magazines with testimonials to Chiang Kai-shek and condemnation of the forces opposing him. Luce had a personal commitment, forged by his missionary heritage and a childhood spent in China. To the others China policy assumed importance rather because of its implications for the worldwide struggle against communism or as a vehicle for attacks on a Democratic President. Roy Howard may well have viewed China as a handy stick with which to beat upon Franklin Delano Roosevelt's New Deal legacy. Initially a Roosevelt supporter, he became alienated by the court packing plan of 1937. William Randolph Hearst similarly began as a friend but rapidly had become a dedicated foe of the New Deal. His attacks on China policy, however, stemmed as much from an uncompromising anticommunism as from a disgust with Truman's presidency. An ardent isolationist and nationalist, Colonel Robert McCormick joined the China crusade to fight against communism, Wall Street, and Great Britain. McCormick's position differed from the others: thanks to his Republican austerity, his promotion of Chiang Kai-shek did not extend to an advocacy of financial aid.[6]

Similarly, columnists found the China crusade attractive for varying reasons. Some wrote to suit the editorial policies of their publications, sharing a general political philosophy with their employers and assuming a comparable perspective on China. Others adapted themselves to an editorial slant merely to further their careers. Certain columnists used events in China as an excuse to drive home heartfelt opinions on communism or domestic political inequities. But for whatever reasons, these columnists wrote often about the situation in Asia and how the United States appeared to be abandoning the Nationalist struggle.

George Sokolsky no doubt epitomized the self-seeking information manipulator who found the China issue a congenial way to serve other interests. Although he had spent twelve years in China, during which he acquired an understanding of Communist and Kuomintang politics unmatched by anyone in the United States, there is evidence that Sokolsky did not care about the Chinese or their problems. At an early age, according to his biographer Warren I. Cohen, he had become "a man without principles, irresponsible, loyal to no one but himself as he fought to satisfy his appetite for power and status." The Nationalist crisis provided him a release for pent-up frustrations and resentments. His earlier, reasonable analyses presented no bar to inconsistent and unfounded attacks on American China policy. Since "his ultimate concern was to prevent another four years of Democratic Government," he blithely attacked the administration for giving aid to China one day and for not doing so the next. Along with others like him, Sokolsky used his anticommunism as a partisan tool.[7]

Henry Luce, though not above using China to bait New Dealers and further Republican politics, felt a sincere commitment to the Nationalists far beyond anything George Sokolsky entertained. A popular portrait of Luce has contended that "Chiang Kai-shek . . . was and would remain in a sense the most important man in Luce's life—his pride, joy, worry, and disaster." Luce devoted the resources of his publishing empire to preserve the dwindling prestige of the Kuomintang, believing he might effect a significant change in United States policy. Among "the various company elders and executives . . . there was partial agreement that he felt close to God—perhaps even a little chummy—and that the two were collaborating, in Luce's view, on the solution of world problems." Luce would champion the pro-American, Communist-fighting, Christian President of China whatever advertisers, politicians, correspondents, or critics might say. "He knew instinctively what has since become a public cliché: the power of the press to set the agenda of public discussion," and he put *Time-Life-Fortune* in the forefront of "Chiang's American army."[8]

Demands for military and economic aid to Chiang Kai-shek predominated in the Lobby's press commentary on China. In 1947, for instance, "A Report to the American People on China" written by William C. Bullitt at Henry Luce's behest called for $1,350 million to support the man who "bulks larger than any living American."[9] George Sokolsky, in July 1949, touted this hero as "Fighting Chiang" who from "his fortress in Formosa, will keep the Chinese Communists busy. He will scorch the earth, bomb cities, blockade ports, encourage piracy and stimulate civil war. *If we had a competent State Department, America would give him every aid!*"[10]

Chiang's loyal admirers disregarded the autocratic nature of his rule and the corruption practiced by his family, friends, and staff. Sokolsky pointed out on ABC radio in November 1948 that many American officials, after all, were corrupt too.[11] *Time*, in turn, dismissed the "holier-than-thou attitude that the U.S. could only associate itself with simon pure, double-distilled democrats conforming to the strictest tenets of the Anglo-Saxon moral code."[12] Henry Luce himself had dabbled with fascist totalitarianism—approving its dynamism and, of course, its anti-communism.[13] If in Chiang he could not have the former, at least he could support a dedicated proponent of the latter.

Moreover, the Kuomintang, however unethical, never abused American diplomats as did the Chinese Communists. China Lobbyists emphasized that the CCP ignored international practice, subjecting foreigners to demeaning imprisonment and even violence. The *Washington Daily News*, noting the loss to American prestige because "we keep turning the other cheek and get slapped every time we do it," declared that "no American official has any legitimate business in Red China."[14] "When," wailed the Scripps-Howard papers, "is the State Department going to put down its teacup, pull in its pinky, and start acting like the foreign office of a world power instead of the protocol division of a banana republic?"[15]

The pro-Nationalist media denounced talk of recognizing Communist China as the rankest treachery. "Recognition," warned Hearst's E. F. Tompkins, "would not only obliterate all hope of Western aid; it would demoralize Nationalist resistance and assure total Sovietization of China."[16] Chiang Kai-shek's forces, *Human Events* recalled, had struggled alongside ours in World War II, the United States having fought in Asia largely to rescue China from foreign domination.[17] But, Mark Sullivan lamented, incompetent, perfidious leadership at Yalta, not to mention those who sanctioned an eighteen-month arms embargo against the Nationalists beginning in 1946, had pushed China to the brink.[18] "The British would sell the Far East out to communism . . . to save the few chestnuts that Britain still has in China," but the United

States, William Loeb's *New Hampshire Morning Union* declared, must not tag along with British appeasement and pusillanimity.[19] Indeed, "American recognition of *a Communist Government in China*," Hearst's *New York Journal American* predicted darkly, "would . . . be tantamount to American acceptance of *a Communist World*."[20] Clearly, "any American official recommending recognition of that outfit should be impeached," concluded the Scripps-Howard *New York World Telegram*.[21]

Attacks no less forthright issued from a few businessmen. Whereas the majority of merchants and manufacturers in the United States who had an interest in China favored efforts to establish trade relations with the Chinese Communists, a small, vociferous group made their objections well-known.[22] Most of these individuals possessed economic ties with the Nationalist regime. Some believed that free enterprise faced a serious challenge from communist totalitarianism and that even its weaker manifestations must be protected at all costs. Many of them had never engaged in commerce with the Chinese, but found the Kuomintang struggle a worthy crusade. Frederick McKee, a Pittsburgh industrialist and philanthropist, belonged in this category. A foreign affairs activist, McKee joined the American Committee for Non-Participation in Japanese Aggression, the American Association for the United Nations, the Committee on National Affairs, Free World, Inc., and other such groups.[23] He helped to found and direct the China Emergency Committee and its successor, the Committee to Defend America by Aiding Anti-Communist China. In August 1949, in a statement before the House Committee on Foreign Affairs, McKee called China the "key to Asia" and warned that it could be saved only if China policymaking was taken out of the hands of defeatists in the State Department's Far Eastern Division.[24]

Alfred Kohlberg became so bitter and persistent a critic of United States China policy that he earned the epithet "the China Lobby man." Having made his not unappreciable fortune importing Chinese laces, silks, and embroidery, he cultivated a lifelong interest in Chinese affairs. During World War II Kohlberg became involved in the activities of the American Bureau for Medical Aid to China, United China Relief, and the Institute for Pacific Relations (IPR); but rather than focusing on China, he became enmired in a series of personal feuds. A "mild mannered unassuming little man who rarely raised his voice," Kohlberg charged that communists and their sympathizers had captured control of the IPR. When the IPR investigated and dismissed his accusations, he asserted that there had been a cover-up. His subsequent war against the IPR launched his prominent career as the guiding light of the American China Policy Association (ACPA) and the "man behind McCarthy."

The approaching victory of the Communists in China gave added impetus to his endeavors since he faced the loss of his embroidery business. The Communists, he knew, were not likely to allow the continued use of poor peasant piecework laborers to produce luxury goods for Westerners. Kohlberg therefore aimed a persistent propaganda barrage at the media and policymakers. He wrote prolifically for his own magazine, *Plain Talk*, and sympathetic publications such as *The China Monthly*. He also circulated pamphlets, press releases, and open letters to large audiences.[25]

The themes of betrayal and subversion keynoted Kohlberg's voluminous writings. He provided a unique explanation for the "infamous" concessions the United States had made at Yalta. Franklin Delano Roosevelt, Kohlberg contended, had offered control of Manchuria's railways and possession of Port Arthur and Dairen to Stalin entirely unbidden. He had done this out of anger and annoyance with Chiang Kai-shek, who had refused to turn his government as well as his armies over to General Stilwell's command.[26] Truman, Kohlberg believed, had continued Roosevelt's misguided policies. Between 1945 and 1948 he "has so completely lost the peace in Europe, in the Near East, in Korea, in China, and almost everywhere in the Far East, that I find our people turning almost in resignation to the thought of a third world war as a corrective for these errors." Kohlberg told the Senate Appropriations Committee that the United States must immediately launch a strong anticommunist world alliance and break diplomatic relations with "all nations and areas within the communist world."[27] The contagion must be stopped and, Kohlberg insisted, the critical battle would be fought in China.

Not quite as much in the limelight as Kohlberg or McKee, other businessmen also gave Chiang Kai-shek and the Kuomintang their support. William Reynolds of the Reynolds Metals Company carried the Nationalist government's entreaties for assistance to General Albert C. Wedemeyer. The Reynolds Company's interest in an aluminum plant in Taiwan no doubt contributed to his desire to keep the island under some sort of American "supervision."[28] Robert M. Harriss, a Texas and New York cotton broker, became a trustee of the Institute of Chinese Culture in Washington, D.C. and lobbied for the Kuomintang.[29] Executives of American President Lines, anxious for profitable new contacts with the Chinese Communists, hoped also to keep ties with the Kuomintang firm. Thus when "the boys in the Embassy" asked the shipping company for money to help carry out some intensified Congressional lobbying, APL reportedly contributed.[30]

Labor's opposition to economic or political dealings with the CCP had less to do with China than with a reflexive anticommunism. The American Federation of Labor (AFL) had a long history of such views. In the 1930s it took issue with the communist presence in the CIO unions, supported Martin Dies' House Un-American Activities Committee, and opposed United States recognition of the USSR.[31] In the 1940s, in its eagerness to prevent relations with communist foes of capitalism, the AFL became aligned with the China Lobby. Matthew Woll, conservative and fiercely anticommunist chairman of the AFL's foreign affairs affiliate, the Free Trade Union Committee (FTUC), in December 1948 urged that prompt and adequate aid be given to the legitimate government of China.[32] In July 1949, reiterating this call, Woll put the Committee on record against recognition of or trade with the CCP and led its membership in writing letters to Congress and distributing propaganda advocating aid to the Nationalists.[33] To an audience of some 1,800 business representatives at the National Foreign Trade Convention the following November, Woll declared that "purse-conscious" American businessmen "may for a short time cash in a bit, but they will be digging . . . all free men's graves by helping the Chinese Communists to consolidate their totalitarian dictatorship over four hundred million people."[34] Woll also joined the board of directors of the Committee to Defend America by Aiding Anti-Communist China as did David Dubinsky, president of the International Ladies Garment Workers Union and vice president of both the AFL and the FTUC. Jay Lovestone, one-time general secretary of the American Communist Party and anti-communist foreign affairs advisor to the AFL, served on the board of the Defend America Committee too. During 1949 the Committee on National Affairs, another organization led by Frederick McKee, distributed a letter by William Green, AFL President, which pledged union support for efforts to secure more aid to China.[35]

A small number of outspoken clergymen and several religious bodies, differing with most of their colleagues, strongly objected to American trade or diplomatic relations with the atheistic communists. The Christian leaders' concern over China sprang out of a century-old missionary effort there and, of course, the church's ideological war on communism.[36] Unwilling to compromise with the CCP in order to stay in China, they sought instead to help the Kuomintang regain its leadership of all the Chinese people. The conservative *Christian Herald*, calling for "all out aid to our ally Generalissimo Chiang Kai-shek," reminded its readers that Chiang not only appeared to be the only alternative to communism in China, but also "a devout Christian, a Methodist."[37]

Although most missionary bodies preferred to prolong their contact with the Chinese people whatever the circumstances, Catholic organizations generally took a public stand opposing relations with mainland

China. The Catholic Association for International Peace resolved, at its December 1949 convocation, that "any further move to recognize Red China would flout international morality, violate historical concepts of international law and the Charter of the United Nations, abandon our traditional open-door policy and our commitments to China, condemn the Chinese people to degrading subjugation, jeopardize the welfare and security of the United States and increase the threat to the peace of the world."[38] The Most Reverend Raymond A. Lane, Superior General of the Catholic Foreign Mission Society of America, embodied similar thoughts in his October 1949 appeal to Truman not to recognize a Communist-dominated China.[39] Moreover, China's first archbishop, Paul Yu-pin, espoused Chiang's cause unreservedly.[40]

The Jesuit magazine *America* throughout 1947, 1948, and 1949 called for more aid and American advisers for the Kuomintang.[41] Like the Luce publications, it too suggested that State Department thinking "follows somewhat too closely the pattern set by Moscow."[42] Moreover, it agreed with the China Lobby's secular press that "objections to aid for China on the grounds that China's present Government is 'corrupt' and inefficient, are now besides the point. We are in a crisis and cannot await even desirable reforms."[43] In October 1949, despite the declaration of a new government in Peking, *America* claimed to see "discontent within Red China." The magazine argued that "failure to obtain recognition from countries that could help China might crystallize resentment into effective opposition."[44] At the very least, American insistence "that Nationalist China's case be given a decent hearing [in the United Nations] before we join in the indecent rush to recognize in Asia the henchmen of our declared enemies" would let us "save our self-respect as the traditional champion of China's sovereignty and as the prime movers in setting up the United Nations."[45]

Other clergymen, such as the Reverend William R. Johnson, became active spokesmen for the China Lobby. Johnson joined the board of directors of the American China Policy Association and the Committee to Defend America by Aiding Anti-Communist China. He had been a missionary in China for thirty-five years and returned to the United States a firm supporter of the Kuomintang. In the December 1947 issue of *The China Monthly* he declared that there "remains a coterie of the Communist front stealthily working within the State Department which participates in the briefing of Ambassadors and Presidents in Chinese affairs. Thus they serve the purpose of our enemies rather than our own."[46] Johnson condemned this "top-ranking group of American saboteurs" for their "studied blindness . . . to Moscow's growing encroachments upon China," indicating that such behavior could be nothing less than treason.[47]

An even more prominent missionary voice rallied pro-Chiang Kai-shek sentiment from the halls of Congress. Before World War II, Walter Judd had served as a Congregationalist medical missionary first in Fukien and later in Shansi province. Upon his return to the United States, he undertook a nationwide speaking tour designed to arouse the American people to the danger of Japanese aggression. In fact, on the morning of December 7, 1941, he told a Minneapolis congregation that Japan would not hesitate to attack the United States—perhaps in the near future. Judd's ability to spellbind an audience from a pulpit or podium also served him well in the committee rooms of Congress. In 1939, having been called as a witness before the Senate Foreign Relations Committee, he impressed his listeners to such a degree that according to Senator Lewis B. Schwellenbach (D, Wash.) "it was the unanimous opinion of those present at that meeting that the testimony of Dr. Judd had been so outstanding, and had so clearly and exhaustively outlined the situation in the Far East, that there was no need to call any other witnesses upon the Chinese-Japanese problem." Judd freely used his personal experience in China to claim a peculiar understanding of the Oriental mind and the mysterious social and political institutions of the East. After Minnesota voters, by a two to one majority, sent their patriotic and prophetic minister to Washington in 1942, Judd rapidly convinced his colleagues in the House that he could interpret Chinese affairs to them.[48]

Judd's conservative missionary orientation attracted him early to the Christian Generalissimo Chiang Kai-shek. He never doubted that Chiang was laboring in China's best interests. The man and his party sincerely desired to establish democracy, he was certain. Furthermore, America's own security needs dictated support for Nationalist forces. Unless the State Department changed its policy and forcefully backed the Kuomintang, Representative Judd declared, "the communization of Asia and World War III are inevitable."[49]

The sincere concern with which missionary Judd viewed the civil war in China did not prevent politician Judd from recognizing the partisan use to which Chinese developments could be put. In April 1950, he boasted to his Minnesota constituency that he had supplied Joseph McCarthy with "much" of the material used in the Senator's initial speeches. "Communism charges," he asserted, "should be exploited by Republicans in this year's elections." Although he retreated from his voluble self-identification with McCarthyism soon after, he continued to denounce Administration China policy with a self-righteousness and a fire-and-brimstone certainty that made him influential beyond his House position.[50]

Several military figures assumed prominent places alongside Walter Judd in the effort to preserve the Nationalist regime on the mainland and later in Taiwan. Rejecting the contrary assessment of the Joint Chiefs of Staff, these men argued that important security considerations hung in the balance in Asia which demanded a thoroughgoing United States commitment. They envisioned communism and the Soviet Union as the primary threats in the post-World War II era and believed the loss of China to these "enemies" would jeopardize American development of Japan, the Philippines, and other interests in Asia. To some, particularly General Chennault, the thought that America might abandon Chiang Kai-shek called into serious question the entire World War struggle to rescue China from Japanese aggression. These military leaders also believed, based on their service in the Western Pacific area, that they understood how to preserve American influence in Asia better than did the politicians and bureaucrats in Washington. Among these military men were several of the highest ranking and/or best known military personalities of the period, including Douglas MacArthur, Claire L. Chennault, Charles M. Cooke, and Oscar C. Badger.[51]

General MacArthur had spent World War II immersed in the effort to defeat Japan and the postwar years preoccupied with Asian political problems. He had come to view "the lands touching the Pacific with their billions of inhabitants" as far more significant than Europe's "dying system," because the masses of Asia would "determine the course of history for the next ten thousand years."[52] Stationed in Japan during 1949 and 1950, he nonetheless made his opinions well known in the United States. Touching on the question of Kuomintang reform and reorganization, he told the chairman of the House Foreign Affairs Committee: "Desirable as such reform may be, its importance is but secondary to the issue of civil strife now engulfing the land, and the two issues are as impossible of synchronization as it would be to alter the structural design of a house while the same was being consumed by flame."[53] MacArthur's dedication to Chiang Kai-shek, an influential factor in United States Congressional deliberations about China, did not prevent him from entertaining some "heretical" notions about encouraging trade between American-occupied Japan and Chinese Communist forces on the mainland. However, at the same time, he continued his staunch support of the Nationalists. As late as June 1950, MacArthur stressed the strategic importance of Formosa to the United States even though President Truman and Secretary of State Acheson (using arguments earlier made by the General himself) had put the island beyond America's defensive perimenter in January.[54]

Chennault never demonstrated even the modicum of flexibility that MacArthur's responsibilities as head of SCAP encouraged him to display. Having become closely tied to Chiang's struggle against Japan, first as a volunteer flyer and then as a U.S. Army Air Corps General, Chennault championed the Kuomintang uncritically. He also reportedly took a more active role in the Chinese civil war. During 1949 American Consul in Shanghai H. R. Rutherford heard rumors alleging that Chennault's China Air Transport engaged in gun-running and commercial smuggling in collusion with top-ranking KMT officials. Rutherford contended that, "under the guise of militant anti-Communism, lie the real motives of self interest and self-enrichment."[55] Later in the struggle Chennault also stepped in to save two Chinese airlines from falling into Communist hands. He not only purchased their sixty-three planes and equipment, but when the CCP demanded that following recognition the British turn over assets of the airlines in Hong Kong, Chennault undertook a prolonged legal battle to block the Communist claims.[56]

Admiral Charles M. Cooke, like MacArthur and Chennault, developed his interest in the Nationalist Chinese while on active duty in the Pacific area. Cooke served as commander of the U.S. Seventh Fleet from December 1945 to February 1948. After retiring from the military he began to do some writing for the Hearst press, first on a free-lance basis and later as an International News Service (INS) correspondent in Formosa. In December 1949 he told the audience of *America's Town Meeting of the Air* that the Chinese communist regime was a "Russian puppet regime. Its recognition would greatly strengthen the onward march of Communism toward world conquest, and would spread dismay amongst freedom seeking people who depend upon the United States for strength and leadership." During 1950 he became head of a group of retired American officers organized into an American Technical and Military Advisory Group to the Chinese government. The primary purpose of this unit, apart from some financial transactions conducted for the KMT which were alleged to have been unorthodox, apparently was to use its former U.S. Armed Forces knowledge and connections to press the Truman Administration to increase aid to China.[57] In fact, Cooke warned Admiral Forrest P. Sherman, Chief of Naval Operations, repeatedly about a build-up of Soviet air strength on the Chinese mainland which when transferred to Formosa would make World War III "inevitable."[58]

Support for aiding a free China also came from the American Legion. An association of veterans, the Legion took an active part in political controversies of many types. At its annual convention in 1949, the membership passed a resolution opposing recognition of the Communists but, as the State Department immediately noted, not "by inference or thought" recommending assistance to the Nationalists. This proved true even though Secretary of Defense Louis Johnson and Assistant Secretary Paul Griffith, two of Chinese Ambassador Koo's staunchest sympathizers, had both served as American Legion presidents in the past and retained considerable influence in the organization. The *American Legion Magazine* also devoted attention to China, publishing in May of 1950 an article attacking any possibility that the United States might recognize the Chinese Communists.[59]

The Chinese-oriented academic community divided in its sympathies toward opposing forces in China. The majority of these specialists saw the future of the Chinese people as intimately wrapped up in revolution—a massive social, economic and political upheaval to which moderate reforms no longer provided an alternative. Chiang Kai-shek and the Kuomintang had clearly failed, in the view of these people, and the United States would best serve its own interests by severing all ties with their decaying dictatorship. A minority, however, rejected the judgment that Chiang must lose and China must fall to the Communists. Although never as voluble as other elements of the Nationalists' American coalition, these people also pressed the arguments for aid to the KMT and against recognition of the CCP.[60]

David Nelson Rowe, a China-born scholar, developed strong opinions about China's future. In April 1949 his article in *World Politics* entitled "Choice in China" urged the American government to do something for the Nationalists immediately and on a substantial scale. Rowe feared the creation of a Communist China permanently tied to the Soviet Union and increasingly a threat to the United States.[61] He had argued similarly in a brief paper sent to the State Department in January 1949 and would do so again in the pages of the *Virginia Quarterly Review* the following autumn. Rather than abandoning the Nationalists to the "Russian aggression which we had helped induce and legalize" at Yalta, Rowe demanded that the United States give the KMT aid, perhaps even set up a new Flying Tiger group for them in Formosa. But above all it must not recognize the Chinese Communists.[62]

The argument that Chiang could still be saved by American appropriations impelled other academicians to express their views publicly. At the State Department's Round Table Conference on China in October 1949, Kenneth Colegrove of Northwestern insisted that the Kuomintang could be salvaged. The United States, he later added, should not discard its anti-Japanese ally and try to hide this despicable act behind an elaborate whitewash known as the White Paper.[65] Similarly, Roscoe Pound, Dean Emeritus of the Harvard Law School, denounced United States China policy. Basing his view on eighteen months service as advisor to the KMT's Ministry of Justice, Pound charged that America's actions undermined China's efforts at realizing constitutional government for its people. He denied that the Kuomintang's energies had been sapped by factionalism and asserted that the party and its government would survive the onslaught of communism. The Dean brought his convictions and his considerable prestige to the board of directors of the ACPA.[64]

Prominent persons from other walks of life also added their energies to the pro-Nationalist crusade. Stanley Hornbeck, whose diplomatic career for almost thirty years had concentrated on Asia from posts in the East and as director of the Division of Far Eastern Affairs, expressed strong pro-Chiang sentiments. He warned the State Department in 1948 that "Communism in China is a child of Communism in Russia" and that if the United States did not aid China's leaders it would have "either misguidedly or willfully, left to Chiang Kai-shek *and chance* the defending of our western front." He ridiculed the possibility that the Chinese Communists might be friendly to America, permit equal commercial opportunities for Western merchants, or respect international law. Furthermore, he dismissed the arguments of Americans who were "undermining the position of . . . [China's Nationalist] government by vilifying it and parroting falsehoods with regard to it and criticizing it for possessing some of the same deficiencies that plenty of other governments with which we do business possess."[65]

Harold Stassen discovered the China crisis and Chiang Kai-shek's bandwagon in 1949. Having been defeated as the young people's candidate for President at the GOP convention in 1948, Stassen apparently needed a new issue to boost his political fortunes. Claiming to have studied China for twenty-five years—a fact which, the *New Republic* noted, his campaign in 1948 had never mentioned—Stassen proposed a MacArthur Plan for Asia. In addition to providing $1 billion a year for the economic development of vulnerable Asian states, Stassen urged a heightened propaganda campaign against communism. The United States should "bombard" Russia and its satellites with leaflets describing the glories of freedom in the West. He also maintained "that it would be unthinkable to recognize the Communist government in China and to withdraw recognition from the Nationalist government. Even though the last vestiges of military opposition disappears, in my feeling . . . a number of years should still go by before we recognize that new government."[66]

To exert pressure on behalf of the Nationalist government and army of China, Lobby activists employed a wide variety of tactics. The previously mentioned newspaper and magazine publicity made up but one aspect of their campaign. Letter writing, organizational work, strategically placed financial and political assistance, and personal interviews all contributed to their effort. Translating passion into action did not always proceed smoothly. Throughout 1949 and into early 1950 China Lobbyists found it difficult to cultivate interest in their propaganda efforts. Even with support from some important individuals, pro-Nationalist sentiment struggled against widespread opposition and apathy. At the forefront, moreover, the same figures appeared so often that it seemed easy to dismiss the entire Lobby as a tiny group of predictable crusaders.

The ACPA and the Committee to Defend America by Aiding Anti-Communist China labored to increase aid to the Kuomintang and prevent recognition of a CCP government. In the ranks and on the boards of directors of these groups, businessmen, writers, and the clergy could bring their reputations and energies to bear. The ACPA, in particular, charged by Alfred Kohlberg's enthusiasm, issued reams of propaganda. Some two thousand editors and publishers received Kohlberg's material regularly, although few of them actually used it. Virtually the entire U.S. Congress also found itself on the ACPA mailing list as did the State Department, where China-Lobby literature attracted little interest.[67] Public rallies, such as the one held by Frederick McKee's Committee to Defend America by Aiding Anti-Communist China in November 1949, brought the faithful together and sometimes won new converts. McKee invited Senator H. Alexander Smith to be guest of honor for the November Carnegie Hall protest against the imprisonment of Angus Ward in Mukden, but Smith could not attend.[68] Two other Congressional speakers, James G. Fulton (R, Pa.) and Earl T. Wagner (D, Ohio), gave credit for Ward's recent release to the Scripps-Howard press. A third, Senator Herbert R. O'Conor (D, Md.) lamented that America's China policy had "pulled the rug from under [Kuomintang] China's feet." Frederick McKee urged Truman to warn the British that American aid would cease if they opened diplomatic relations with the Chinese Communists. The attendees unanimously endorsed a resolution condemning Communist aggression in Asia and calling on the administration not to recognize Red China, but the small crowd, only 1,500 in a hall big enough for twice that number, reduced its potential impact.[69]

Organization officers and private individuals bombarded government officials and Congressmen with letters expressing their pro-Chiang viewpoints. They apprised the legislators of Kuomintang activities and American popular support for aid programs. The letter writers, such as

William Johnson, Alfred Kohlberg, William Goodwin, and Claire Chennault, put forth arguments based on moral and ideological grounds as well as practical politics and partisanship.[70] Letter-writing campaigns, mobilizing sympathizers throughout the nation, highlighted the activities of church groups. For example 77.2 percent of the total mail received by the President during 1948 on the issue of aid to China (in itself, however, a small sample) bore some religious identification, and of these 81 percent came from Roman Catholic sources.[71] Frequently, mailings included press clippings or studies written by pro-Nationalists. Senator H. Alexander Smith circulated throughout Washington his report on an autumn 1949 trip to Taiwan and Japan.[72] Chennault distributed his own notes on the China situation with suggestions for American action and copies of his *Way of a Fighter* during 1949. And the year before he had seen to it that a translation of Yen Hsi-shan's "Ways and Means to Cope With the Communists" reached members of Congress.[73] A grandiose reconstruction plan for Nationalist China similarly made the rounds during 1948. Formulated by Colonel W. Bruce Pirnie, at the request of the Chinese government, it provided a detailed description of how American aid funds could be used in China. Pirnie also made his China Lobby publicity debut in a *China Monthly* article which demanded that "those who for one moment hinder [the job of aiding China's war effort] . . . should be branded publicly as betrayers of United States security."[74]

The mass of information which passed from Chiang Kai-shek's supporters to Congressional, governmental, and community leaders generated secondary publicity as well. The most significant instance involved Alfred Kohlberg's cooperation with Joseph McCarthy. Kohlberg, seeing a perfect opportunity to enlarge his audience, took China-related materials compiled over years of anticommunist activity and provided them to McCarthy to fuel his attacks on the State Department.[75] Similarly William Goodwin claimed to have "laid the groundwork" for McCarthy's charges of Communist infiltration of the State Department.[76]

Personal visits supplemented correspondence. During 1949 Claire Chennault talked directly with virtually everyone of any importance in foreign policymaking in Washington, D.C. He saw 85 of the 96 Senators and spoke with all the relevant State Department officials short of Dean Acheson who, Chennault said, would not meet with him.[77] Ambassador Koo believed that the most effective influence could be brought to bear not by the Chinese themselves, but rather by properly inspired Americans.[78] Thus the Chinese encouraged Chennault and Walter Judd and others like them to publicize the Kuomintang struggle. Mrs. Hamilton Wright, a narcotics control activist, who asked Koo what she could do to help China in December 1949, followed his suggestion and called

Senators and Congressmen to express opposition to British recognition of Communist China.[79]

Direct contact, however, did not always have the desired effect. In November 1949 representatives of the Committee to Defend America by Aiding Anti-Communist China visited Ambassador-at-Large Philip Jessup. Jessup, unenthusiastic, described McKee's lengthy statement as "along the lines which are familiar through the publications of his organization and his other letters and statements to officials of the Department."[80] Judge Robert Patterson's telephone call to Dean Acheson in February had proven even less effective. Patterson, a close personal friend of the Secretary, had been prevailed upon to suggest to Acheson the dispatch of a Presidential investigatory commission to China. In response to the Secretary's reservations, Patterson conceded that he himself had not felt any particular ardor toward the proposal and "was merely complying with a request to him by some of the people there (presumably McKee and [Clark] Eichelberger) and that he had now discharged his commitment and would forget the matter."[81]

Frequent lunches and dinners brought China Lobby figures together with likely new recruits. Ambassador Koo hosted many such gatherings at which "the regulars" might plan strategy or sympathetic outsiders would be persuaded to listen to Kuomintang propaganda. Paid agent William J. Goodwin entertained members of Congress as an important feature of his public relations responsibilities. He believed that out of one hundred legislators he wined and dined in a year, some fifty were converted to the Nationalist cause.[82] Others also used such social occasions to present their views. The 14th Air Force Association, for instance, in promoting a new American Volunteer Group (Flying Tigers) for China invited nine Senators, fifteen Representatives, and a variety of businessmen to a January 1949 dinner in Washington.[83] Senator William F. Knowland (R, Ca.), to help Chennault promote his plan for saving the southern and western portions of China from communism, brought 28 Senators together with him over lunch in July.[84] Alexander Smith, homebound because of thrombophlebitis, had some small dinners to further Senator Knowland's amendment regarding additional military aid to anticommunist forces in China to be administered by an American commission on the Greek pattern. Smith believed his dinners "very productive" in convincing John Foster Dulles and Senator Arthur Vandenberg (R, Mich.) of the importance of the Knowland plan.[85]

Money played a significant role in China Lobby activities when mere contagious enthusiasm proved insufficient. The Nationalist Chinese hired individuals and a public relations firm to keep their cause in the news and before key policy figures. William J. Goodwin described his

duties as arranging "meetings between Chinese government representatives and businessmen, bankers, newspapermen, legislators and other
leading citizens with a view to increasing their interest in the need for
developing China as a future market for American business and also
with a view to getting help from the U.S. for the Chinese Nationalist
Government." Goodwin also "published letters—gave out interviews—
and made a few speeches."[86] Allied Syndicates, Inc., which became an
agent for the Bank of China during 1949 and 1950, performed activities
across the "entire gamut of the public relations field" all designed "to
prevent the recognition of the Chinese Communist government and the
consequent freezing, for that government's benefit, of the Bank of
China's assets" in the United States.[87] Alfred Kohlberg used funds
from his importing business to assist anticommunist writers to pay their
rent or buy food and clothes.[88] And Kohlberg made political donations
to China Lobby types as, for example, $1,000 to Senator Styles Bridges'
reelection campaign in 1948 and $500 to Joe McCarthy in 1950.[89]

Members and friends of the China Lobby also appeared at Congressional hearings on matters relating to China. In 1947 Senator Bridges
summoned Albert C. Wedemeyer, Walter Judd, William C. Bullitt and
Alfred Kohlberg before his Appropriations Committee to testify regarding aid to Chiang Kai-shek. General Wedemeyer, who had recently returned from his mission evaluating the situation in China, told the Committee that he favored military and economic assistance to the
Nationalists. The weight of his remarks and those of the other witnesses
helped convince the Senators to appropriate $20 million for China.[90] In
1949, a similar set of pro-Chiang supporters advocated aid to the Nationalists before the House Committee on Foreign Affairs. At those hearings Frederick C. McKee, in his capacity as chairman of the Committee
on National Affairs, warned that China "is the only place where there
are still 1,000,000 anticommunist troops under arms and where there
are sufficient natural barriers to block the Soviet advance."[91]

The Congressional China bloc provided frequent opportunities for
testimony, reports, and even special missions which would emphasize
the need for aid to Chiang's armies. William C. Bullitt, having visited
China in 1947 for Henry Luce, returned in 1948 for the Joint Committee
on Foreign Economic Cooperation. Styles Bridges arranged for another
visit later the same year by former Senator D. Worth Clark. Clark not
only had been an associate of Bridges in the Congress, but practiced
law with one-time New Dealer Thomas G. Corcoran, who also had ties
to China through T. V. Soong. Funding for Clark's mission came in part
from the Nationalist treasury—a good investment since his report declared that the only way "to rescue China from Communism" would

be "immediate and extensive direct military aid to the Nationalists."[92] Bridges also sponsored a Kohlberg trip to China in 1948 and helped distribute the resulting report.[93]

Trips to Asia served as an effective method to persuade novices or heighten the influence of veteran Chiang promoters. Having interviewed Kuomintang officials or American military personnel, a China Lobby spokesman could make appeals for aid or against recognition with more knowledge and certitude. If the traveler managed a confidential meeting with Chiang Kai-shek or Douglas MacArthur his prestige soared. Talks with MacArthur in particular ranked with visits to an oracle—the China Lobby bestowing on his words an almost sacred importance. Senator Tom Connally (D, Tex.) remarked in disgust, "Every time a Congressman or Senator goes out to that area, MacArthur grabs him and surrounds him with his staff and his people and they feed him and pet him and pamper him, and then he comes back over here wanting to tell everything MacArthur said. They want to let General MacArthur rule the whole Pacific, militarily, diplomatically, hermetically."[94]

During 1949 several important persons made the pilgrimage. Senator Smith travelled East specifically to dramatize the China crisis. After meeting with Kuomintang authorities and General MacArthur he wired Secretary of State Acheson that "it would be critically serious if [the] United States indicated any interest in or intent to recognize [the] Chinese Communist government."[95] Senator William Knowland met with MacArthur during 1949, as did Hearst columnist David Sentner. Impressed by Sentner's pro-Nationalist stories, Chennault had urged Hearst to dispatch his man to Asia and have him supply further copy with the special impact of first-hand experience.[96] Stewart Alsop also made the Pacific circuit armed with introductions from his brother Joseph to all the prominent personages in the China theater. He returned to write in the pages of the *Saturday Evening Post* that the United States courted disaster in Asia. "We have lost China," he maintained, "because we never took a really serious view of what was happening in China, and never developed a really serious policy to stop it."[97]

The idea that the United States, through stupidity and treason, had lost China tormented the China Lobbyists and shaped the terror they directed at their enemies.[98] The Alsops might have been unwilling to find traitors responsible for disaster in the East, but others in the formless pro-Kuomintang coalition blithely made accusations that in time would shatter careers and destroy lives. Not incompetence of Nationalist leadership, graft in the armed forces, or utter disillusionment among the people could explain communist successes to these stalwarts. They assumed an omnipotence of American arms and a bottomless bounty which the Truman Administration need only have redirected from Europe to Asia. That government decision makers insisted upon seeing China as of only secondary importance to national security and a hopeless quagmire besides meant that they had become communist pawns or prophets.

Between January 1949 and June 1950, however, China Lobby hysteria remained a fairly insignificant phenomenon. Letters, newspaper columns and radio speeches denounced the government's treatment of the Kuomintang but came from a predictable constituency and did not yet produce a visceral reaction in the State Department or the White House. Policymakers despite charges of subversion and espionage continued to evaluate events in China with sanity. In their search for a solution to America's China policy dilemma, few officials thought to turn to the China Lobbyists for advice. Still free of the fears that McCarthyism and the Korean War would engender, they regarded the strident pro-Chiang element as somewhat suspect and better ignored.

CHAPTER SIX

Missionaries

An Unlikely Peace

)━●━()━●━()━●━()━●━(

WITH the struggle in China intruding into partisan politics at home, Secretary of State Acheson had to be more than commonly concerned about the domestic repercussions of foreign policy formulation. He might first assess the views of allies, calculate the motives of Soviet adversaries, and examine conditions in China, but his Department also had to turn its attention to a varied group of American "China hands." In part this signified an instinct for self preservation. Unlike other members of the government, diplomats did not have a natural constituency to support them on controversial issues. This became all the more true when disputes involved questions of Asian politics about which few Americans possessed any information or interest. In 1945 the vulnerability of State Department China service officers had become apparent when Patrick Hurley charged them with being soft on communism. In 1949 Acheson and his staff sought to protect the Department. Beyond this, the Secretary put a high priority on maintaining his freedom of action despite the strident demands of the pro-Kuomintang coalition. If the same voices seemed to be raised over and over again in Chiang's behalf, perhaps the China veterans who had thus far been silent had a different perspective to offer.

The China hands also had the potential of serving Department interests in China. Many spent their lives in the East pursuing careers in the church, business, and journalism. Some had come to believe in a special place for Americans in China while others simply had committed their material and emotional resources so thoroughly that they could not imagine a life elsewhere. When politics threatened their position, they turned to parent organizations and officials in the United States to render them aid. Acheson and other policymakers, knowing the total dependence of these people upon decisions made in Washington, found them burdensome and vexatious at times. But their unique knowledge about their adopted homeland, however tainted with personal interests and lack of perspective, made them valuable in the confusing months of 1949 and 1950. Moreover, should the Truman Administration wish to maintain a presence in China, these Americans could act as unofficial channels of communication with the Chinese.

On October 1, 1949, when Mao Tse-tung officially established the government of the People's Republic of China, some four thousand missionaries resided on the mainland of China. The missionary community lacked internal unity; it consisted of a mixture of Catholics and Protestants, fundamentalists and modernists, pro-Nationalists and pro-Communists. But to outsiders, the community formed an easily identifiable and readily defined group: it was foreign, though it had sizable property holdings and other vested interests in China; it was Christian, attempting to proselytize Chinese in a state with a godless ideology; it symbolized, at least in part, the influence of governments hostile to the new regime.[1]

Missionaries had often been a disruptive element in Chinese foreign affairs during the nineteenth and twentieth centuries. Anti-Christian activities had provoked costly reprisals from foreign nations, some of which had used them as excuses to advance "barbarian" interests and erode Chinese sovereignty. As a result an antimissionary tradition developed and remained strong among many Chinese as late as the 1940s.[2] Thus, it would not have been surprising to many if the People's Republic of China had taken immediate action to rid itself of a dubious foreign presence. Yet, except in a small number of cases, neither the Red Army nor the Chinese Communist civilian authorities took such steps. The official attitude toward the missionaries between January 1948 and June 1950 drew notice for its restraint and tolerance.

The formulation of this apparently favorable policy occurred late in 1947, when the Chinese Communist forces shifted their military campaign from a localized to a nationwide offense. By year's end large areas north of the Yangtze, south of the Yellow River, and east of the Han River to the sea had fallen under Red Army control. Mao Tse-tung, confident of success, planned to establish a Central People's Government sometime in 1949.[3] Missionaries in the newly "liberated" provinces faced the prospect of living indefinitely under Communist rule. While in the early months many missionaries had fled south with the Kuomintang armies, others decided to stay. The Chinese Communist Party, faced with this active foreign community, could either work with or eliminate it.

In the eyes of many missionaries and Communists, Christianity and Communism were competing ideologies. The missionary represented an alternative to the state's authority. Catholicism's call for devotion to a higher spiritual power, represented by the Vatican, fundamentally challenged Communist totalitarianism. The social gospel of twentieth-century Protestantism, which prompted missionaries to perform secular good works, also seemed to deny the all-encompassing nature of the new government.[4] As members of a party fighting to establish its legitimacy, the Chinese Communists feared allowing another group to serve the people and improve their lives. Loyalties were not won easily or treated lightly.[5]

The American denominations became the most difficult segment of the mission community with which the Chinese Communist Party had to deal. They constituted the largest and probably the richest groups of missionaries in China. Following World War II, despite damage and disruption, the size and value of the American missionary enterprise in China remained large. The Foreign Missions Conference supervised some 2,246 missionaries. They made up 62 percent of the total number of Protestant missionaries in that country, and were allotted $8,445,404—23 percent of its entire world budget.[6] When the Communists assumed power in 1949, there were 236 Protestant mission schools and 248 hospitals scattered throughout China. The United Board for Christian Higher Education maintained thirteen Christian colleges, and another fifty theological institutes existed in various provinces. The YMCA supported work in forty urban centers. American Protestant property holdings in China were estimated to be worth more than $70,000,000. Catholic facilities and landownership were even more valuable, and the American share of this investment amounted to several million dollars and grew constantly.[7]

In view of their numbers, their wealth, and their religious mission, it is hardly surprising that until 1948 missionaries often met with brutal treatment from Chinese Communist forces. Between August 1945 and August 1948, the Communists reportedly killed nearly a hundred Catholic missionaries.[8] But this policy of violence began to change as the tide of war turned in favor of the Communists.[9] They were determined to create the broadest united front possible and prevent incidents which might put off victory. In March 1948, a New China News Agency spokesman announced that "Freedom of religion . . . is a fixed policy of the democratic government and the People's Liberation Army. All missionaries . . . will be protected, regardless of their nationality, as long as they abide by the laws and do not engage in subversive activities."[10]

Missionaries in virtually all parts of China reported that the takeover after 1949 by Red Army units proceeded in a peaceful and orderly fashion. The Party instructed soldiers to protect both the person and prop-

erty of foreign missionaries. Still more unexpectedly, some military commanders requested that missionaries help prevent local disorder.
Mission hospitals nursed wounded Communist soldiers, and at Linhsien, in Kwangtung province, medical missioners received a commend-
atory banner for their service to the Chinese people and the revolution.[11]

The first formal declaration on the status of religion in China came in
September 1949, when the CCP convened the national People's Consultative Conference, which approved the Common Program, a general
statement of the aims of the new coalition government. Article V provided for freedom of religion. Thereafter, the CCP usually resolved instances of alleged religious persecution in a way that protected religious
belief.[12] Despite the doctrinal incompatibility of communism and organized religions, the party had no intention of creating any Christian
martyrs in China.[13] It had "learned from the Russian experience that
efforts to completely stamp out religious groups provoke only . . . undue
resistance."[14] And as early as 1927, Mao Tse-tung had expressed his
belief that "It is the peasants who made the idols, and when the time
comes they will cast the idols aside with their own hands."[15]

In April 1950, a new decree asserted the principle of religious toleration. Issued by the government to all its agencies and printed in the
official newspaper, *Jen-min jih-pao*, it prohibited seizures of religious
buildings. When temporary use proved necessary, the decree required
prior consultation with missioners and restoration to them of the facilities at the earliest possible date.[16]

Also in the spring of 1950, the Party invited a group of Chinese Christians to meet with Chou En-lai in Peking. Intended to serve as a liaison
committee between the government and the churches, the Chinese
Christians were told that the Christian churches must henceforth "use
effective educational and propaganda methods to give all Christians a
clear understanding of the part played by American imperialism . . .
[in] using the church to cloak . . . nefarious imperialistic methods."[17]
In addition, the Christian organizations had to eliminate foreign personnel and stop using foreign funds. At least temporarily, no new missionaries would be allowed to enter China because the government
could not be sure of their political leanings. Foreign missionaries who
left on furloughs could not return. However, missionaries who did not
engage in political activity, particularly those who possessed technical
skills, could remain in China. Most missionary societies chose to see
this last provision as an invitation to stay. Perhaps China would welcome
expertise even if it carried a missionary label.[18]

Real conditions in the period from January 1948 to June 1950 often
differed sharply from the favorable circumstances prescribed by national

policy. Local officials were in many instances inexperienced and illiterate. As in earlier times, they confused Christianity with secret societies whose rituals and potentially dangerous clannishness the Chinese Communist Party continued to fear and prohibit.[19] Communist rhetoric, moreover, identified Christian missionaries with imperialism and that association fostered repression.

Missionaries in urban areas generally received better treatment than those in rural regions. Especially in the large coastal port cities of eastern China, where foreign news media and diplomatic representatives clustered, the likelihood of unfavorable publicity encouraged official leniency.[20] In addition, since plentiful housing and facilities for large public meetings existed in the cities, Communist workers there, unlike their counterparts in rural areas, did not need to requisition church buildings for their rallies.[21] In general, wherever large groups of foreigners located, there were fewer hardships. Small rural stations, particularly those inland, remained more likely to suffer at the hands of enthusiastic Communist cadres. Western China, therefore, commonly experienced stricter measures from the outset.[22]

In areas taken over early in the civil war, the Communists extended their control gradually. Missionaries in northern China, although they came under Communist authority in 1946 and 1947, did not have to endure the same restrictions as did those in other sections. Yenching University received permission to operate almost normally after "liberation," as did Peiping Union Medical College. Some missionaries obtained authorization to return to their mission fields after hasty pretakeover evacuations.[23] The majority of north China missionaries did not experience efforts to evict them from the People's Republic until November 1950.[24]

Predictably treatment meted out to the various denominations within the American missionary community did not prove uniform. While intramural debate occurred about the relative suffering of Protestant sects, virtually every mission report agreed that Roman Catholics endured the harshest regimen.[25] To many Chinese, the Catholic Church represented the most suspicious and exploitative foreign body in China. Roman Catholic compounds were much more secluded than the Protestant mission stations. The celibacy of priests seemed unnatural, and people thought nuns committed lechery and murder in the Catholic orphanges. Roman Catholics in the past had also taken special advantage of unequal treaties and extraterritoriality.[26] More recently, they had interfered with CCP military activities in southern Kiangsi at Kanchow, ensuring that under United States government pressure the Nationalists defended the city and Catholic holdings there. In addition the Catholics had become too closely aligned with Chiang Kai-shek. The Archbishop of China publicly supported the Nationalists, while the Vatican was inflexibly opposed to communism. Rigid controls maintained by Rome over all the Catholic orders in China, both foreign and indigenous, made papal antagonism appear even more threatening.[27]

Paramount, however, huge Catholic mission land holdings presented an immediate and concrete problem. In parts of Shensi, Hunan, and Kansu provinces their tremendous estates gave them control over powers of taxation and adjudication usually reserved to local government, and they reportedly operated militia units for self-protection.[28] The Party believed that it could not allow these large areas to remain under foreign control, nor afford to lose the income from the land.

Accordingly, the Communists strictly limited proselytizing activities of American Catholics. A missionary of the Brethren Church, Ernest Ikenberry, noted that since Catholic missioners rarely left their fields voluntarily, the CCP put agents in the Catholic mission compounds to discourage converts from coming in, thereby destroying the missionaries' effectiveness.[29] Catholics paid higher taxes than other missioners, had their property confiscated sooner, and were imprisoned first. As the Party implemented land reform in various sections of the country, Catholic missionaries suffered the violence that often accompanied redistribution. In Szechwan, where Protestants lived peacefully, Catholics were victimized because of their land holdings.[30]

Restrictions upon other missionaries at first proved minimal. Protestant missioners could usually move freely within their immediate communities, but few could journey inland or from one city to another.[31] Additional restrictions depended upon geographic location. As late as March 1950, a Presbyterian worker in Hunan wrote to her mission board that there had been no curtailment of religious activity in her hospital, but schools elsewhere in China had to eliminate religious courses, and in most places the Party barred Christian observances from school buildings.[32]

The change from toleration to restriction generally began with the arrival of civilian authorities who established local government and levied taxes. Athough demands on church property were not unusually harsh, such property no longer enjoyed exemption from the normal tax load and the new financial burden became intolerable for many mission societies. Buildings had to be leased to cut expenses, but nothing could be done to reduce employee salaries because under Communist law the workers could not be fired.[33]

Missionaries responded to communism in very different ways. Some Roman Catholics and Protestants believed that the Chinese variety differed from communism in Eastern Europe and would not be antireligious. The majority of Roman Catholic missionaries, even as they decided to remain in China, felt considerable hostility.[34] Similarly, the Protestant *Christian Herald,* one of the most influential of the religious papers in America, consistently described the Communists as satanic.[35] By contrast, others saw the Chinese Communists as socialists or even agrarian reformers. Exposed to the books and articles of American travelers in Communist areas, they often believed, along with other sectors of the American public, that the Chinese Communists were energetic young people, both intelligent and likeable. Unlike the Kuomintang, the CCP had remained free from corruption and carried out democratic reforms among the north China peasantry. If they genuinely avowed Marxism and, "there was some question as to whether the Chinese Communists were Communists . . . they . . . were a long way from Stalinism. . . . In a land of limited alternatives," many missionaries found they could relate to such "dynamic, spartan, popular, progressive, democratic, reformist and patriotic" people.[36]

Differences in opinion depended upon individual conceptions of the missionary's role. During the nineteenth and early twentieth centuries a sharp division between so-called fundamentalists and modernists developed in the religious world. The fundamentalists dedicated themselves to evangelism and dismissed educational and social services as wasteful and irrelevant. Modernists derived their impetus from the social gospel movement and hoped to win Chinese converts by ministering to both their secular and spiritual needs. Since social utility possessed virtue in China's own ethical systems, Christianity might best be received through socially useful services. In time, some of the missionaries who took this approach were devoting all their energies to what the fundamentalists considered nonreligious endeavors.[37]

Virtually all fundamentalists considered communism an unadulterated evil. A missionary could neither work with it nor under it. To modernists, however, there seemed to be similarities between Marxism and Christianity. Like Christianity, communism preached human equality and shunned profit and competition.[38] A member of the Presbyterian mission board noted that communism, like Christianity, was hypnotic, mysterious, and "truly a religion whether they care to call it that or not."[39] Many modernist missionaries believed that Christianity and communism actually vied for the souls of the Chinese people and that the latter appeared to be winning. The Western churches seemed totally unprepared to lead in rural reconstruction and to sustain a large-scale social welfare program, both of which the Chinese vitally needed. While some thought that Christianity had higher spiritual goals than helping the downtrodden, most felt that it should do more.[40]

As the Communist military advance continued, some missionaries believed the feasibility of independent action had ended, but that cooperative work with the CCP might be possible. A noted Congregationalist missionary pointed out in 1949 that "In some circles the mere thought of Communism is enough to make people hysterical or begin to think in iron-curtain terms. Such thinking may have its place in the political world, but if we resort to it in our Christian strategy, let us remember that we are thereby fencing ourselves in rather than being fenced out."[41] Those who followed this line of reasoning and decided to remain in China under the new regime found courage from many different sources. One was the desire to prove that Christianity had sufficient resiliency to meet the needs of the Chinese people. "I believe God would have me stay," declared a teacher at a mission school in Canton. "Communism has captured the imagination and loyalty of many thousands, giving them a creed and a cause for which to labor and fight with great zeal. . . . We have been too easy-going, smug and indifferent to the cries of a worn humanity hungering physically and spiritually. We have a message for such a time as this . . . . If Christianity means to us all we say it does, now is the time to prove it."[42]

For some, the appeals of Chinese Christians proved decisive. Such missionaries hoped to be able to maintain morale and provide the stability and confidence that the churches needed. Workers who feared that a foreign presence in the People's Republic would not be tolerated wanted to utilize whatever time they could find to help integrate the church more completely into Chinese life. Throughout the turbulent years of 1948 and 1949, favorable reports of good treatment in already communized parts of China convinced others that they could continue their own work indefinitely. Reinforcing these beliefs, the CCP issued positive statements about religious toleration and the protection of foreign missionaries. The fact that some of these missionaries had been part of previous evacuations and that many felt guilty about abandoning their converts made them much less willing to flee again.[43]

Other missionaries felt that none of these reasons appeared sufficiently compelling and decided to leave. Among them were the elderly and those in poor health. Missioners who had undergone internment in Japanese war camps often eagerly desired to go before People's Liberation Army soldiers arrived in their districts.[44] The U.S. State Department encouraged these decisions to leave. In January 1949 a consulate circular urged all nonessential inland personnel to withdraw to the safer port cities.[45] But while Washington worried about the personal safety of the missioners, many of them feared that they might jeopardize the welfare of Christian converts by remaining. They hesitated to cause these people embarrassment or political danger.[46]

Although each American-based mission society normally determined official policy in the United States, during this period the parent organizations did not want to deal with the difficult circumstances in China. Most denominations refrained from taking a public position on the future of mission work until late in 1948. When they did so, the majority decided to leave decisions to the missionaries themselves rather than order their stations to close down. Churches which had sizable financial investments in their mission fields and did not want to leave these unprotected, however, were less equivocal. Out of eleven large missionary boards which replied to a 1949 survey conducted by Frank T. Cartwright, chairman of the China Committee of the Foreign Missions Council, all but one said that its workers had been encouraged to stay in China.[47]

Whether to maintain missions in China had become a critical question, but the ultimate resolution of this issue depended on far-reaching non-religious developments in Sino-American relations. If the American government decided to continue its support of Chiang Kai-shek and refuse recognition to the Communists, then obstacles would probably increase to the point that missionaries would be forced to leave regardless of contributions which they were capable of making to the country. In the 1920s, when revolutionary upheaval provoked concern over the unequal treaty system, mission boards had tried to influence U.S. government policy.[48] Motivated in the 1940s by the desire to preserve their spiritual and financial interests in China, they once again launched a campaign to reach the decision-making centers of the United States government.

Both individual missionaries and organizations attempted to influence national leaders. Representatives of mission societies secured invitations to briefing sessions in Washington, D.C., and lobbied with members of Congress.[49] When the State Department created a special committee concerned with developments in China during 1949, letters from China missionaries urged the group to discontinue aid to Chiang Kai-shek, and if the CCP set up a national government, to recognize it.[50] The China Committee of the Foreign Missions Conference, an organization representing 26 denominations and 29,000,000 members in the United States, sent appeals to the chairmen of the House and Senate Committees on Foreign Relations.[51] Further emphasizing that these sentiments expressed the views of more than just a few individuals, the executive secretary of the China Committee forwarded to Senator Tom Connally a cablegram from 330 leaders of 180 Christian organizations in China protesting American aid to the Kuomintang.[52] Similarly, the Federal Council of the Churches of Christ in America, whose function it was to facilitate interdenominational cooperation, took up discussion of American policy toward China. At a meeting in Atlanta on December 6, 1949, its executive committee asserted:

> Such military assistance as the United States placed at the disposal of the Chinese Nationalists had proved unavailing. The reasons for this are many, but among the reasons is the fact that the civil war in China is not only a test of arms, it is also, in part, a social and political convulsion of revolutionary proportions. . . . It is a matter genuinely to be deplored that the United States, with its democratic tradition and its long established commitment to freedom for subject and dependent peoples, has become aligned in popular world opinion with the maintenance of the status quo rather than with the forces making for a new Asia.[53]

Missioners traveling in the United States as well as those at work in China asked church members to help press for recognition of the new Communist government. Particularly through circular letters from the field, China missionaries appealed to large numbers of parishioners at home. The Southern Presbyterian Missionary Board's correspondence department alone estimated that it distributed China letters to some 120,000 recipients during the 1940s, many of whom duplicated them for a still wider readership.[54] A survey made during the 1950s found that missionaries constituted the most common source of information and opinion on developments in China among the professionals and government officials interviewed.[55] Missionaries reported in their correspondence about the activities of the Kuomintang and Communist forces and about the treatment each side meted out to them. Going beyond recitations of the difficulties of daily living, they asserted that the Nationalists had ceased to offer an alternative for China and that the Western powers should come to terms with the CCP's leadership so that missionary endeavors could continue there.[56]

Demonstrating their personal commitment to future relations with China, missionaries continued to embark upon new assignments there throughout 1949. The Cleveland Conference of American Protestantism launched a vigorous drive to enlist added personnel for service in China. "Whatever happens," the Cleveland Declaration asserted, "we must do everything possible to help the churches maintain their witness and ministry." When the SS *General Gordon* obtained CCP permission to evacuate foreigners from Shanghai in September 1949 only sixty-six American missionaries departed, and twenty sailed on the ship's return voyage to take up new posts. As of December nearly two thousand

Protestant missioners from the United States, Canada, and Great Britain were still laboring in China alongside 192 Maryknoll missionaries and a smaller number of American Dominicans, Jesuits, and Vincentians.[57]

Not all mission workers agreed that recognition of a Communist government would serve church interests in China. Some remained staunchly anticommunist and others continued to rely upon the Christianity of Chiang Kai-shek to solve the nation's ills.[58] Many who had lost faith in the Nationalists nevertheless protested official church appeals to Washington to abandon the Kuomintang, fearing for the safety of clergymen still in KMT-controlled areas of China. For these reasons and more, leaders could not secure the support of a majority of the members of the Foreign Missions Conference, at its annual meeting in March 1950, in favor of a resolution advocating recognition of the People's Republic of China. The FMC's China Committee, however, prepared an informal statement which sixty-eight members signed. Submitted to the U.S. Congress and the State Department, this memorandum urged policymakers to "show that the American government is not opposing needed changes" and that the American people favor contacts with the Chinese. It insisted that:

> Everything which would aid in maintaining economic, cultural, political, and religious contacts with the people of China is necessary if we are to have a share in influencing the course of events there. . . . Recognition would help to keep open at least the political channel, but delay in recognition would make still more difficult the continuance of even our present contacts.[59]

Washington officials took note of and encouraged missionary interest in preserving church ties with the Chinese people. Involved in medical and educational enterprises as well as purely religious activities, the missioners provided Communist authorities with skills and services the revolutionary forces sorely lacked.[60] Should the United States want to open relations with a CCP government, missionaries would have created considerable goodwill for Americans and might have established useful contacts among Party leaders.[61] Indeed, the Communists too seemed to see the missioners as channels of communication. At a December 1949 meeting in Peking, a CCP spokesman coupled positive statements about social and relief assistance with suggestions that the missionaries and their home churches press Washington for recognition.[62] In the interim, missionaries supplied information to American foreign service officers and sensitized the American public to the difficulties that could be expected in the course of future Sino-American relations.[63]

From January 1948 to June 1950 the Chinese Communists and the American missionaries in China coexisted and to some extent cooperated. The CCP did not seek to oust the entire missionary community, nor did it launch a bloody purge to destroy all vestiges of Christianity. Reversing the antimissionary violence that prevailed until 1948, they instituted a policy of toleration. As Mao's confidence in military success grew, both missionaries and their property received protection. The Communists succeeded in utilizing missionary talent, as in the Linhsien hospital, and controlled evangelical activities without resorting to violence. Although American missionaries had initially been pessimistic about the continuance of their work under a Communist government, they seemed to regain hope from their experience with the People's Liberation Army and from the attitudes which the new regime adopted.[64]

American officials, consequently, found the missionary community to be a source of support for a policy of remaining in China and establishing relations with the Communist Chinese. Representatives of American Catholicism might oppose accommodation vigorously, but their numbers and organization did not approach the strength of the Protestant churches and mission orders. These, on the other hand, almost universally welcomed the opportunity to continue functioning in China, often placing emphasis on teaching the unlettered and curing the sick as much as on evangelizing the godless. When questioned by policymakers, they argued for an end to a fruitless and harmful association with Chiang Kai-shek. They spoke of realism in foreign affairs and urged Washington to accept communist rule, competing with it peaceably rather than prolonging the civil war. As missionaries, they might abhor life in a communistic society, but they recognized that isolating themselves from the people would more surely defeat Christianity in China.

CHAPTER SEVEN

Commerce in China
An End or a Beginning?

)━●━()━●━()━●━()━●━(

AMERICA'S refusal for thirty years to recognize the Communist government in China has often been explained as a victory of business interests over the purveyors of an anticapitalist ideology. Striving to protect free enterprise, business leaders joined a campaign not just to deny the Communist Chinese political and commercial intercourse with the United States, but also to strengthen the opposing Kuomintang forces of Chiang Kai-shek. At the financial core of the so-called China Lobby, American business supposedly contributed to pressures which imposed an anticommunist China policy upon the Truman Administration.

Actually, although communism's theoretical opposition to capitalism disturbed businessmen engaged in the China trade, it persuaded few to dispense with their Chinese connections. Rather, as merchants and manufacturers, they weighed the extent to which China's economic backwardness might introduce enough flexibility into Marxist doctrine to accommodate American commerce and industry. When developments in China indicated that expertise and merchandise from the United States would be welcomed, businessmen voiced support for recognition of the new authorities.

For policymakers in Washington the willingness of American commercial houses to exploit opportunities in China provided a twofold benefit. On the one hand, a decision to open relations with a communist government would not arouse the ire of this important segment of the American public. The Administration could count on business support rather than be forced to rebut its criticisms. On the other hand, the American economy constituted the single most important enticement for capturing Chinese Communist attention and cooperation. Officials and business leaders alike believed the CCP would be compelled to seek

American help in building a viable economic structure. Washington, therefore, could use the attractions of trade and aid to establish equitable relations with the communist regime.

Those who persevered in a desire to conduct business with the Chinese despite the growth of Communist control took consolation from reports of developments in areas already under CCP rule. CCP leaders repeatedly promised protection for foreign individuals and enterprises. Along with assurances that Chinese capitalists would be permitted to continue operating, the Communist Party invited American entrepreneurs to assist in modernizing China. Substantiating verbal guarantees, the Party provided tangible security by stationing guards at American-owned factories to prevent damage by fleeing Nationalist soldiers. Members of the U.S. Economic Cooperation Administration's mission in Tientsin reported to Washington: "We are very impressed by the conduct of the officers and men of the People's Liberation Army. All were extremely orderly and well-disciplined. They were evidently under very strict orders not to molest anybody, not to take anything, not to occupy any private properties if the owners objected."[1] Moreover, the New Democratic policies of Mao Tse-tung acknowledged that progress toward a communist economic system had to come slowly in such an underdeveloped country.

In contrast to these promising signs a multitude of practical difficulties confronted Americans. Even enthusiastic cooperation from the CCP could not overcome a poorly developed transportation network. The subsistence level at which most of the nation's people lived would keep markets depressed after peace arrived. Dissidents, moreover, threatened to prolong wartime instability through sabotage and resistence to innovation. War damage would require years of intensive rehabilitation by largely unskilled, if zealous Party members. Inflation, which made business relations under the Kuomintang so difficult, similarly would require careful controls administered by scarce technicians. And in fulfilling commercial contracts, barter would be necessary because the incoming authorities possessed little foreign exchange. Such problems in the past had kept investments in China modest. Although the majority of American businessmen lacked motivation to take substantial risks or forcefully contest government policy, they made their advocacy of trade and relations with the Chinese Communists known. Yet they imbued their support with moderation and caution. Exponents of continued trade with China outnumbered the pro-Kuomintang anticommunist opposition, but they never indulged in the histrionics of the China Lobby as they sought to make their views understood in Washington.

I A Legacy of Disappointments

American businessmen in China could contemplate Communist control
with a degree of equanimity because they had become so accustomed
to conflict and adversity. Whether as exploiters in the nineteenth century
or as victims of Kuomintang discrimination in the twentieth, they had
been forced to cope with ever-changing conditions rarely conducive to
successful money-making. They yearned for stability and watched anxiously for a Chinese leader who could, with some degree of assurance,
promise to modernize and industrialize the nation.

In the early days, business determination to secure overseas markets
had involved Americans in the forceful opening of China to the West.
The United States had shared in the privileges of the unequal treaty
system initiated in 1842. Americans had manipulated tariffs, repressed
wage scales, extracted indemnities, and peddled opium along with the
other foreigners who kept China always on the brink of real modernization—a semi-colony vulnerable to every device of Western exploitation. American businessmen, through this era, had lived in sheltered
urban enclaves, protected even more than the missionaries from Chinese
realities and unwilling to assess the damage that their good fortune
wreaked upon China's economy.[2] But isolation could not survive the
tumult of repeated twentieth-century revolutions, and businessmen responded by supporting the least constructive elements in China. Their
determination to preserve threatened privileges, such as extraterritoriality, accentuated the imperialistic nature of their presence in China.

Despite these obstacles, the United States and China had maintained
modestly lucrative trade relations for many decades. Indeed, during the
1930s, the United States ranked first among countries from which China
purchased goods. In the same decade it also moved from third to first
place as a market for Chinese exports. From 80 to 100 percent of China's
requirements of copper, leaf tobacco, and machinery came from the
United States as did 60 to 80 percent of the lubricating oils, ink, asphalt,
and typewriters. China supplied Americans with 80 to 100 percent of
their tea, seed oil, and fur imports, and 60 to 80 percent of the tung oil,
embroideries, sheep's wool, and human hair they utilized, making
China seventh among America's suppliers although it ranked only thirteenth as an export market.[3]

In comparison to American interest in trade, enthusiasm for investing
in China remained limited. Although by 1931 Americans had ventured
some $155.1 million in business investments and held $41.7 million in
government obligations, thereby ranking fourth among China's credi-
tors, the Japanese and British far outdistanced them. Rather than strug-

gling to maintain an Open Door, few Americans evinced any inclination to establish factories or own other sizable assets. By 1936, even though Americans had upped their share to an estimated $250 million, this still equaled just 20 percent of Great Britain's and 40 percent of Japan's interests (exclusive of Manchukuo).[4]

War further jeopardized trade and investment by Americans in China, not only because of the immediate disruption it brought, but also because it provoked thoughts of abandoning the China market entirely. From the very beginning of the conflict between China and Japan, in 1937, the Japanese interfered with industrial and commercial activities and violated the rights of American businessmen. The December 1941 internment of United States citizens and takeover of their enterprises climaxed an increasingly untenable string of events. Thereafter, discrimination and restriction turned into direct abuse of property as the occupation forces cannibalized machinery (taking parts and iron scrap for the war effort) and failed to make necessary repairs. When the extent of these damages became apparent with victory over Japan, companies such as China Car & Foundry, a General Electric Company subsidiary, found their investments not worth salvaging, particularly after weighing restoration costs against the vagaries of China's uncertain future.[5]

More often, American companies did choose to come back and even to expand. By the end of 1946, roughly 110 of 126 prewar members of the American Chamber of Commerce in Shanghai had resumed operations.[6] Chinese needs seemed massive and a prime economic rival, Japan, no longer contended for markets. British, French, and German concerns—likewise suffering war-wrought disabilities—could not compete with energetic American entrepreneurs. The American-owned Shanghai Power Company, for instance, undertook an extensive rehabilitation program and intiated a proposal for a United Power Company which could meet the growing requirements of metropolitan Shanghai.[7] Stanvac and Caltex similarly launched strenuous rebuilding programs, enlarging facilities and acquiring new properties. Shantelco, after sustaining extensive war damage, spent close to $9 million repairing its equipment and telephone network. By May 1949, it was operating at full capacity, exceeding pre-war standards. Shantelco, in just four years, had developed the most modern telephone system in the Far East. Pan American, General Electric, and other giants, through various subsidiaries, also had reentered and begun to enlarge their China markets.[8]

However, the reintroduction of a large-scale American commercial presence met resistance from Chinese officials. Desirous of continued United States military support, Kuomintang traditionalists nevertheless hoped to keep their allies out of China's economy. Chiang Kai-shek had demonstrated in his wartime book, *China's Destiny*, how fiercely he detested foreigners and how thoroughly he held them responsible for all China's ills.[9] Lest Confucianism once again be burdened with a rapacious imperialism, Kuomintang authorities imposed cumbersome regulations to restrain American-owned businesses and, where possible, eliminate them entirely. They kept exchange rates officially at 50 percent or less of black market rates to provide the government with revenue, inhibit inflation, and handicap foreign firms dependent upon these currency transactions. The purchasing power of American companies, correspondingly, fell in 1947 to just 20 percent of 1937 levels. In addition, Shanghai's foreign banks, including National City and Chase, lost their most important prewar source of income—exchange dealings and arbitrage.[10] Foreign branch operations were further discriminated against by prohibitions on remitting profits to the United States and by tax laws. American businesses were taxable at a flat rate of 30 percent of all net profits above $7 million (CN) (roughly $150[US]) while the scale for Chinese firms remained flexible, ranging from 4 to 30 percent, graduated on a ratio of profits to capital.[11]

Import provisions and monopolistic practices rendered competition still more difficult. The Kuomintang condoned two types of restrictive business combinations: state monopolies with official purchasing agencies abroad and semi-governmental corporations connected with the so-called favored families. While the Kungs, Soongs, Chiangs, Ch'ens, and state-run enterprises were exempted from licensing restrictions, the Nationalists in 1946 even barred American Christmas packages from entering, claiming that such luxury goods would unbalance China's trade. More critically, the long delays American businesses experienced in obtaining import permits led manufacturers in the United States to transfer their concessions to privileged outlets. T. L. Soong's Fu Chung Corporation took the Westinghouse International, Willys Motors, and Anaconda Copper dealerships from China-based American companies because of the preferential treatment Soong secured in quotas and licensing procedures. Such a properly related entrepreneur did not have to worry that his merchandise might lie on a Shanghai dock for months and then be denied entry entirely.[12]

Beset with trade and tax troubles, American businessmen in China struggled also to survive the demands of an increasingly restive labor force. The celebrated economies associated with utilizing cheap Chinese workers vanished under provisions of the newly created Bureau of Social Welfare, which raised wages and mandated provision of social services. Anticipating conditions under the Chinese Communists, Kuomintang government officials denied American companies the right to close down lest they throw large numbers of laborers out of work. One American company was compelled to pay salaries for at least seven months to employees doing absolutely nothing. Throughout 1947 labor and management relations worsened provoking between 2,000 and 2,400 disputes—twice the number in 1946.[13]

These problems embittered many American businessmen. Encouraged by the United States to continue and expand their activities as an adjunct to postwar aid-to-China programs, Americans encountered erratic restrictions and omnipresent corruption without effective recourse either to the Chinese or their own government.[14] The instant popularity among these businessmen of a letter to the editor of the *Shanghai Evening Post & Mercury* testifies to widely shared frustration:

> Before coming . . . I had the impression . . . that China was badly in need of reconstruction, and welcomed foreign efforts toward that end. . . . But . . . the Chinese neither want us—nor are grateful. . . . They discourage foreigners from doing business by discriminatory legislation, restrict freedom of movement by a phony visa system, refuse to return property stolen by the Japs which they have now taken over, and sell justice at so much per pound. . . . I therefore propose that there be initiated a "Let's Get to Hell Out of China" movement. . . . Let's stop all loans and aid immediately and . . . take with us the power and transportation systems, the water works, the buildings and paved streets, the telephone system, the hospitals and every other trace of our despised work here.[15]

And yet, large numbers of American businessmen withstood both the abuses of the Nationalist government and the insecurities of civil war, hoping still to realize the spectacular profits projected by the China mythmakers. Accustomed to China's perpetual disruption, American businessmen in Shanghai, Tientsin, and Canton managed to cope with surging inflation and martial law. Disgruntled though they might be by reality, they continued as generations before them had, to be beguiled by the magnetism of numbers. They looked eagerly ahead to a time of peace and order in which untold profits from a multitude of miraculously monied Chinese demanding knives and forks would fill their coffers.[16]

II Prospects Under Communism

As communism blanketed China, however, American industrialists and traders had to weigh their desire for profit not just against past disappointments and continuing instability, but against a threatening future.

For those whose business hinged on Nationalist connections there clearly would be no place in the new China, and they either liquidated, abandoned, or moved their holdings to Taiwan. Lacemaker Alfred Kohlberg and airline operators Claire Chennault and Whiting Willauer not only ended their economic ties with the mainland but actively joined the anticommunist struggle. Chennault and Willauer even managed, through a prolonged and complex legal battle, to deprive the CCP of control over China's small fleet of commercial airplanes. The majority of American firms, on the other hand, did not choose to flee from a Communist regime. Anderson, Meyer & Co., though fearful that a minority interest in the firm by KMT-associated Chinese would hurt prospects under a bitterly anti-Nationalist government, decided to risk staying on; and American President Lines hoped its valuable services would provide access to both Communist and Nationalist ports. Most American businessmen in China did not share these particular concerns, for they had not become too intimately identified with the Kuomintang. Yet they recognized that as foreign capitalists they, too, might be judged harshly by the CCP.[17]

American entrepreneurs, therefore, welcomed favorable reports about CCP behavior sifting south from areas taken over by the Communists earlier in the war.[18] Businessmen found tolerant treatment of missionaries significant, for they reasoned that commercial houses "represent less of a menace to Communism than the missions, and have more to offer." Optimism increased further as CCP policy pronouncements reached the foreign community through English-language broadcasts, press translations from the consulates, and word-of-mouth from Chinese colleagues and a small number of Chinese-speaking foreigners.[19] Thoroughly disillusioned with the Kuomintang, American businessmen in China, much as the Chinese people themselves, came to believe that things could hardly be worse under a Chinese Communist regime. In any case, ruthlessness and brutality did not seem to be imminent.

The CCP, in fact, quite consciously had moderated its early hostility to China's cities and their foreign business enclaves. In 1947 the Party ceased repressive takeover practices.[20] Although city dwellers made up only 20 percent of the population, this segment possessed the administrative, technological, and intellectual abilities vital to completing the revolution. Mao Tse-tung accordingly initiated a long-range effort to change urban China's image of the CCP and to insure peaceful transition to communism in the cities.[21] By 1949 the effort to focus some attention on urban conditions had become an injunction not to ignore the countryside, but, nevertheless, to recognize that "the center of gravity of the work of the Party and the army must be in the cities; we must do our utmost to learn how to administer and build the cities."[22]

At the same time, the Party developed a positive policy toward China's private business and industry. The main point of this new approach was to prevent disruption of urban productivity and avoid massive unemployment. At a North China Liberated Area Conference on Business and Industry attended by representatives of labor and private enterprise in May and June 1948, the latter heard that the new China would provide many opportunities for them. "The tasks and methods of social reform in the cities is completely different from land reform in the countryside," a *Hsin-hua* editorial maintained in the following month. Redistribution of such urban property as factories or warehouses, were it manageable, could serve only to alienate essential skilled personnel. Instead private entrepreneurs in communist regions received support through loans and tax incentives. CCP officials also placed large orders for goods to help private entrepreneurs over difficult periods. Radical labor demands, toward which the CCP at first had been exceptionally sympathetic, gradually were moderated. The Party even went so far as to guarantee the rights of factory owners who had fled before "liberation," hoping that they would return. Li Li-san, Ch'en I, and others reassured them that although the Party advocated communism, China was nowhere near ready to carry out a socialist revolution.[23] Emissaries traveled to Hong Kong carrying the message that China required help from Chinese capitalists merely to survive.[24] Twenty-five years hence, they said, when the New Democratic period of development ended and private ownership ceased, the government would be sure to give them appropriate compensation.

American businessmen found the encouragement given Chinese industrialists heartening, but declarations assuring their personal safety and enjoining People's Liberation Army soldiers from confiscating foreign-owned property seemed even more auspicious. Ambassador John Leighton Stuart wrote the State Department from Nanking that "the Chinese Communists have given so much publicity to these proclamations that it is apparent they regard them as important policy decisions."[25] Just before the takeover of Shanghai in May 1949, for example, pamphlets printed in English were distributed which urged all foreigners to stay in the city and continue operations.[26] In many instances CCP members freely acknowledged the country's desperate need for technical expertise that only foreigners could supply. Similarly, the Party told Americans that the new China would need to trade with the United States because no other country in the world could provide the goods vital to a modernizing economy. Authorities eagerly approached the

President of the American Chamber of Commerce in Tientsin and America's Consul General in Peking to discuss commercial exchange.[27]

Chinese Communist actions which eased the transition from KMT rule reinforced the effect of their policy statements. The Party rapidly restored transportation links between major cities and reopened supply lines from the countryside. In vital industries, protection leagues, secretly organized by the Party, emerged just before "liberation" to prevent sabotage of essential services. Firms such as Shanghai Power, accordingly, remained operational and undamaged.[28] The captain of the first American ship to visit Taku Bar after the CCP takeover reported friendly treatment and apparent enthusiasm for trade with the United States. In Shanghai the Military Control Commission reopened port facilities as rapidly as possible "in order to boost industrial production, strengthen the economy and insure the exchange of supplies."[29] Foreign business also found that the CCP managed currency and inflation effectively. Bank managers applauded the realistic provision of new codes which freed them from uncomfortable Nationalist strictures. In fact, Communist restrictions on travel and business practices rarely handicapped Americans more than similar Kuomintang prohibitions and seemed to old China hands to be administered more efficiently and honestly.[30] If the future appeared threatening, it nonetheless seemed that the spectre of socialism remained distant, and that meanwhile there was money to be made.

III Opinion in China

The favorable experiences of virtually all American businessmen during their first weeks under Communist control engendered widespread, if cautious, enthusiasm regarding future possibilities. Those who had passed into CCP hands willingly—and few found themselves trapped by unpredicted Kuomintang debacles—waited to see whether protection of foreign property could be translated into business contracts. Northwest Airlines entered into negotiations with the Chinese Communists to maintain and expand its flight schedule to Communist cities.[31] American President Lines dispatched ships to Shanghai as soon as the city's authorities reopened the harbor.[32] Shanghai Telephone, along with Shanghai Power, continued to service China's largest industrial city despite financial and supply problems. Similarly, National City and Chase Banks, Stanvac and Caltex Petroleum Companies, and a variety of smaller companies persevered in hopes of profit regardless of the political milieu.[33]

But the American business community in China realized that success in consolidating these economic ties with the new authorities depended heavily on United States government policies. Aid to the Kuomintang had to cease immediately. So long as the United States supported the corrupt and inept Nationalist government, American businessmen would be identified as enemies of the CCP. Flexibility in Chinese Communist attitudes suggested by their propaganda and behavior during early 1949 could develop into cooperation only if Americans stopped fueling the civil war. Moreover, to facilitate commercial exchange, the United States must establish diplomatic relations with the Communists whenever an official governing body emerged. If the United States refused to deal with the CCP, it would drive the Chinese into an unwanted dependency on Moscow. The Chinese Communists could not be expected to trade with a nation whose political loyalties challenged the very existence of their government. Progress in the political realm would have to come first.

Merchants and industrialists who had fallen under Communist rule with the advance of the People's Liberation Army generally advocated recognition. Having made the conscious choice to remain, despite repeated consular warnings that conditions under the CCP might be dangerous, these individuals urged American officials to improve relations with the incoming regime rapidly. In February 1949, the Foreign Merchants Association of Tientsin informed the British, French, and U.S. consulates that it had appealed to Tung Pi-wu and the North China People's Council for resumption of normal commercial activities.[34] Early that same month, C. V. Schelke, General Manager of Anderson, Meyer & Co., inveighed against the Kuomintang government and American aid to it before a sympathetic audience at the Shanghai American Chamber of Commerce. Echoing these sentiments the Board of the American Association of Shanghai, a largely business-oriented group, appealed to United States government authorities in May to stop arming and financing the KMT. More pointedly, in June 1949, the Shanghai Committee of the National Foreign Trade Council, through the President of its parent body in New York City, admonished the State Department to conform to prevailing conditions in China and recognize the CCP.[35]

Paul S. Hopkins, President of the American-owned Shanghai Power Company, became one of the most outspoken advocates of initiating discussions with the CCP and moving toward recognition. He was impressed by the sincerity and diligence of the new authorities, who "practiced austerity to the point of not using electric fans or elevators in the buildings which they occupy as offices or residences." Hopkins urged that the United States distinguish communism in Europe from the

Chinese variety which he deemed less closely allied with Moscow. He traced poor relations between the CCP and the United States not to ideological conflict, but to the aid Americans were supplying the KMT. Instead, he called upon the United States to end its misguided alliance with the Nationalists and act to break their blockade of China's coast. A prominent leader of the American business community, Hopkins spoke often at meetings between Shanghai's businessmen and Ambassador Stuart, members of the Embassy, and consulate staffs. Furthermore, his superiors in the United States passed Hopkins' observations on to State Department officials and recommended that they act on his suggestions.[36] Although Hopkins on occasion entertained doubts about the future of American concerns in China, he always returned to the belief that if the United States would deal fairly with the Chinese Communists some amicable arrangement could be reached.

Businessmen less emotionally committed to staying on the mainland than China-born Paul Hopkins found life under communism progressively more difficult. Whereas in late 1948 an observer noted "that the outstanding feature of this situation is that so few people of any category intend to leave and that they look to the future with an astonishing lack of alarm," time brought with it growing tension and anxiety.[37] Hemmed in by a coastal blockade and vulnerable to KMT bombs, Americans at the same time lived in an uncertain relationship to the legal authority of the ruling CCP. Heartened by recurring promises of protection, they nonetheless fell victim to waves of hopelessness in the face of sporadic discrimination and antiforeignism.

Especially distressing in the early days after the Communist turnover, strikes and other labor disturbances swept industrial and commercial concerns. Although these were not limited to foreign businesses, action taken against foreigners often proved more violent than that meted out to Chinese entrepreneurs. Workers saw in Communist propaganda a license to demand large wage increases in restitution for what they deemed historic imperialistic exploitation. The CCP, moreover, continued Kuomintang prohibitions against closing businesses, even unprofitable ones, so as to avoid unmanageable unemployment problems. Thus at a time when civil war had severely cut industrial productivity, employers had to raise already burdensome costs. When they resisted, their employees subjected them to sit-down strikes or far more brutal and intimidating lock-ins. Several instances of laborers incarcerating their employers without food for days occurred in the spring and summer of 1949. When the government finally began allowing foreigners to shut down and leave China, it insisted on compliance with a traditional custom of publishing this intention so that all debts could be settled before

the authorities granted exit visas. Laborers, therefore, had a virtual invitation to exact substantial severance bonuses, the refusal of which
brought on renewed violence and involuntary detention in China.[38]

Labor radicalism in the case of the *Shanghai Evening Post & Mercury*,
voice of the city's American business community, brought an abrupt
end not only to a pro-recognition editorial policy, but to publication of
the daily newspaper itself. Early in 1949, the editor, Randall Gould,
having become disgusted with Nationalist bungling and dishonesty,
joined his otherwise conservative paper with those who believed that
any change would bring improvement.[39] If conscience prevented de jure
recognition of the CCP, he argued that business affairs dictated dealing
with the authorities of an ever larger part of China on a de facto basis.[40]
Having welcomed the CCP to Shanghai, Gould nonetheless proved
blunt in treating conditions under its jurisdiction. His criticisms, during
June, of striking workers and Communist policies provoked printers at
the *Post* to stop publication and a series of lock-ins and bitter confron-
tations ensued. Gould responded to labor intimidation by closing the
paper down entirely.[41]

Incidents such as the *Shanghai Post* controversy temporarily shattered
the relative calm of America's commercial enclaves in China. Unlike
missionaries, who disregarded danger in pursuit of a holy reward, businessmen hesitated to invest their monetary ventures with an element
of personal risk. The exodus of businessmen from China preceded and
exceeded the departure of their religious compatriots. Impasses reached
with belligerent workers by Caltex, Stanvac, Anderson, Meyer & Co.,
and the U.S. Navy all suggested to the Shanghai American Chamber of
Commerce "that the time to liquidate and leave China is overdue." The
Chamber promptly alerted parent companies to "difficulties" it judged
"incomparably more hazardous and disturbing than those faced on December 8, 1941" and elicited from them a call for "repatriation of foreign
staffs insofar as possible."[42]

Conditions, however, improved during the following weeks despite
hostile Communist propaganda provoked by Washington's release of
the China White Paper. Consul General Walter P. McConaughy observed in mid-August that the Chamber of Commerce memorial had
exaggerated the peril in which Americans found themselves and that,
in fact, "there has been a definite easing in [the] authorities' manifested
attitude and treatment [of] local foreigners."[43] On August 19, 1949 the
Shanghai Military Control Commission promulgated regulations intended to moderate the labor radicalism disrupting the city. They permitted businesses to petition to close, allowed employers to fire incompetent or unsatisfactory workers, and set reasonable limitations on

severance pay. In some measure this shift could be traced to declining factory production levels which compelled the CCP to recognize that labor excesses would have to be curbed. Unrealistic bonus and severance pay demands, contrary to the assumptions of many American businessmen, had not been encouraged by Party officials.[44] Rather, as John Cabot judiciously observed:

> The Communists were caught by one of those inescapable contradictions which they consider characteristic of capitalism. Their dogma forced them to blame the employer and the foreigner for everything, even though for the moment both were desperately needed. Confiscation could and must wait. But the masses swallowed Communist propaganda and acted, to the Communists' great embarrassment.[45]

Hoping to reverse this trend, the CCP adopted a new policy. As early as April 1949, Liu Shao-ch'i had begun imposing discipline through unionization upon unruly workers in Tientsin. Utilizing employer trade associations and the fledgling unions, Liu mandated negotiation of labor contracts backed up by government or court arbitration. Decisions rendered by the People's Courts upon appeal by either side became binding. In August, the Party extended Tientsin's experiment to all territories under Communist control. Thereafter labor disputes, in theory, could not result in strikes which disrupted production. Of course, abuses did continue but, at the same time, instances of authorities compelling workers to settle disagreements multiplied.[46]

CCP efforts to restrain labor's activism reflected the leadership's interest in keeping certain foreign enterprises operating. This did not indicate a modification of ideology so much as a realization that in some areas practical needs could be more expeditiously met using Western resources. In the Common Program, the interim constitution adopted in September 1949, the Party accordingly called for restoration and development of commercial relations with all governments and peoples on the basis of equality and mutual benefit. The CCP would favor firms having Communist or pro-Communist connections when possible, but the primary emphasis would be on fulfilling the requirements of a modernizing economy. The U.S. Central Intelligence Agency observed in a January 1950 memorandum that "the cargoes carried by Isbrandtsen [Shipping Lines] are obviously of importance to the Communists, as indicated by the exorbitant freight rates which they are reported to be paying for this traffic. The Communists are even rumored to be giving Isbrandtsen additional financial protection for the unusual risks involved."[47] Not only did the CCP lack its own merchant marine and need the commodities American ships imported, but it desperately desired destruction of the Nationalist blockade. Kuomintang ships and mines had virtually sealed the port of Shanghai and the CCP lacked the resources to challenge this maneuver. Instead the Party tried to apply a modern variation of a traditional tactic: "using barbarians to control barbarians" [i i chih i]. It enticed American vessels to run the gauntlet. Commodity export restrictions made more liberal at Shanghai than at the relatively accessible harbor of Tientsin furthered this end as did the high prices cargoes could command upon arrival. Then too, trade with American companies decreased Chinese dependence on Soviet imports, which sometimes proved to be of inferior quality.

American financiers, industrialists, and traders did not, therefore, flee China without a second glance. By the time the evacuation ship SS General Gordon arrived in September, the number of businessmen who chose to leave proved far smaller than could have been expected after the July 31 Chamber of Commerce alarm.[48] To Paul S. Hopkins the essential nature of the service he provided outweighed personal inconvenience and insecurity.[49] IT&T believed sales opportunities justified retention of its American staff in China, at least for the immediate future.[50] When it became clear that the British government would support the efforts of its merchants and probably would extend recognition, that too became a reason to stay. American entrepreneurs in China did not wish to see the Chinese do business only with Russia, but they felt even more reluctant about giving up their markets to British rivals.[51] Moreover, the State Department encouraged Hopkins and others to remain with promises of aid and guarantees of prompt evacuation should that be necessary.[52]

Still more decisive pressures came from Communist authorities. They sought to have certain Americans stay so that important companies would continue to function smoothly. Some executives were detained as security for debts—which they considered ransom demands—or as protection against Nationalist bombing raids. The CCP also hoped to disrupt the Nationalist blockade by insisting on a level of continued operation which American managers could meet only by shipments of oil and raw materials from abroad.[53]

Of course, continued business contacts with the Communist Chinese did not require that American producers and traders reside in Communist China. Companies such as Shanghai Power and Universal Leaf Tobacco, having foreseen that conditions for foreigners might become hazardous, began grooming managerial teams of local personnel early in 1949.[54] These concerns hoped to protect their American employees and remove a source of friction from the scene, while conducting normal operations through Chinese hands. Similarly, American businesses based in Hong Kong, in September 1949, proposed barter transactions with the CCP utilizing $50 million in unspent U.S. Economic Cooperation Administration funds to finance trade credits. They visualized exchange supervised by a U.S. Commercial Company and conducted between reputable private Chinese enterprises and established American companies with offices in the British colony.[55]

Thus, although danger convinced many American businessmen to evacuate, it did not occasion a total liquidation of investments in China. Interest remained and commitment promised to revive if only Washington would provide security and protection through diplomatic channels. Newspapers and magazines reported Standard Oil's desire to trade, Chase Bank's willingness to carry on financial transactions, and a widespread businessmen's advocacy of diplomatic relations with the new authorities.[56] At the same time, merchants and manufacturers continued to hold in excess of $180 million in assets on the Chinese mainland.[57] In January 1950, the Shanghai Consulate General told the State Department that the great majority of American businessmen in China were still "thinking along the lines that recognition should and must come."[58] A Stanvac official, some two months later, renewed earlier pleas that the United States stop supplying military aid to the KMT and accept the fact that not even the opponents of communism on the mainland of China wished to see Chiang Kai-shek return.[59]

IV Reaction in the United States

Opinion among businessmen in the United States varied more than the views of those actually in China. Probably the greatest segment of the commercial world had no particular interest in the China market. Organizations such as the U.S. Chamber of Commerce and the National Association of Manufacturers took no stand on issues of American China policy.[60] A zealous minority of the business community adamantly opposed consideration of commercial or political exchange with the Communists. A larger group favored contacts with the CCP and publicized their views to a greater or lesser extent depending on conditions in China and their own degree of involvement there.

Pro-Nationalist forces in the United States decried all efforts to keep communication with the CCP open.[61] Those who had fled People's Liberation Army advances and others who had cultivated their anticommunism from safer offices in America joined forces to support several groups working for the KMT including the American China Policy Association and the Committee to Defend America by Aiding Anti-Communist China.[62] Around the nation small businessmen, most of whom had never traded with the Chinese, also wrote to Washington protesting any compromise with the CCP. The American Express Company, however, remained alone among the major firms with interests in China to discontinue all its operations there during 1949. And Republic Steel Corporation was one of the few companies to ignore CCP trade inquiries owing to the anticommunist views of its president.[63]

In contrast to these interests, virtually all of the major participants in Sino-American commercial intercourse wanted to arrange some sort of accommodation with the Communists. Despite contrary experiences in Eastern Europe, American businessmen hoped that the Communist Chinese would bypass ideological imperatives in order to secure the necessities that only the United States could make available.[64] Similarly, they anticipated improvement in this position if only the United States government would end its alliance with Chiang Kai-shek and resolve its differences with Mao.[65]

Such advocacy of trade and recognition failed to generate the heights of emotion exhibited by members of the opposition. Executives at General Electric and Bank of America had too many more important investments to watch over and expend political capital on. China interests, which did not weigh heavily in the overall holdings of such large corporations, and which had always been shaky, did not merit unusual protective measures. Directors of these companies also acutely felt their great distance from scenes of turmoil in China and hesitated to urge risky ventures on vulnerable employees. Even when such firms remained eager to do business with the Communist Chinese, they spoke with care and moderation about the future and shrank from pressing State Department officials into precipitous action. They believed recognition of the Chinese Communists to be sensible and, for their own affairs, advantageous, but in most cases they readily deferred to the judgments of American authorities.[66]

Not only did American companies indicate a willingness to serve United States government policy, the State Department viewed them as potential instruments for promoting a Sino-Soviet rift. National City Bank, U.S. Steel, and other concerns queried the Department regarding the propriety of proposed sales, contracts, and continued operations behind Communist lines.[67] The Department, in turn, gave its blessings to virtually all arrangements (except those involving strategic goods) hoping thereby to create a CCP dependency on American suppliers and American expertise. To provide control and information over destination and use of commodities such as petroleum, government authorities encouraged American firms to remain in China under Communist jurisdiction.[68] Paul Hopkins, president of Shanghai Power, believed that Communist leaders could be convinced of the importance of cooperation with the United States. Anxious to accomplish this, he volunteered to stay in China and see to it that SPC electricity kept flowing. But although Hopkins wished "in the interests of the Chinese people" to keep SPC functioning and recognized that his utility could be an important bargaining tool in talks with the Party, he objected to State Department plans to withhold fuel oil until the Communists made concessions. This would render the company "a political 'cat's paw'" under guidance which he deemed "incompetent." "If it really be [the] American intent to 'scorch earth' Shanghai," he recalled saying, "then I wanted to lead the stampede out of Shanghai and refused to sit in the hot ashes, with mobs of unemployed factory workers surging around a ruined city." Hopkins, and other businessmen as well, sought a profitable modus vivendi with the CCP and had no interest in economic warfare.[69]

Although advocates of trade and recognition did not indulge in the heated propaganda of the pro–Chiang Kai-shek elements, those most critically threatened by a lack of contact with the Communists did speak out. The China issue was particularly important on the West Coast where business interests habitually looked across the Pacific. Early in 1949 a United Press dispatch datelined San Francisco noted that from a yearly total of $2 billion in trade with the Orient nearly 25 percent would be lost if commerce with China ceased. But, UP disclosed, such losses would not be necessary because, according to its survey, West Coast importers and exporters were anxious to do business with the new Chinese Communist authorities. In November, a similar *San Francisco Chronicle* study discovered that while the "State Department mulls over recognition of [the] Chinese Communist government, local American and Chinatown export-import firms are trading in North China . . . [and moreover] are pressuring [the] State Department to recognize [the] Chinese Communist government right now."[70] So, too, union workers engaged in shipping, warehousing, and allied trades appealed to President Truman to initiate diplomatic and trade relations.[71] The Greater San Francisco Chamber of Commerce also urged the Truman administration to follow the realistic policy of extending recognition to the CCP since the "economic development of the entire Western portion of this country may well be at stake." The Chamber admitted that this might not be the choice Americans preferred, but deemed it "the only practical way to keep the door open, as well as to listen and observe what goes on behind the bamboo curtain."[72]

The argument that recognition was the only reasonable course to take won several influential adherents in business circles. The *Wall Street Journal* pointed out in December 1949 that much of the public hue and cry on the question of recognition rested upon a misunderstanding of what this act implied. Parallel to views expressed by Secretary of State Acheson and a variety of legal analysts, the newspaper insisted that the granting of diplomatic recognition did not act as a reward for good behavior or a stamp of approval, but merely as an acknowledgement that the nation in question "jolly well is there."[73] *Business Week*, having observed that Republicans in Congress wished to use China policy against Truman and Acheson, reminded its readers that "recognition is the strongest bargaining material we have left." To lure Mao Tse-tung away from Stalin, the United States would have to trade with and recognize the Chinese Communists.[74]

Realistically, businessmen believed, America's only hope in China would be patience and participation. William L. Bond, Pan American Airways Vice President for the Orient, faulted his government for not facing the fact that a Communist regime actually existed.[75] Even if the vast majority of Chinese were not themselves communists, the Vice President of National City Bank of New York predicted, the new government would survive because the only alternative to it was the selfishness and inefficiency of the most degenerate regime China had ever experienced. Accordingly, he contended that the best way to counter communism in China would be "to maintain and develop friendly relations," since "free contact with the democratic nations is evidently not a healthy condition" for communism "or the Russian Iron Curtains would not exist." In view of this, "to isolate China by blockade and/or non-recognition . . . is tantamount to forcing China into the hands of Russia and is obviously what Russia is praying for." Although more pessimistic about future opportunities by January 1950, National City officials intended to hold on for another month or two "to see what effect the British recognition of the Red government would have, in the hope that if the United States recognizes the present government some sort of quid pro quo would be agreed upon, making it possible for American business to continue in China."[76]

George G. Cobean, President of the Bulkley Dunton Paper Company S.A., one of the largest paper manufacturing companies in the United States and supplier of paper for Nationalist China's currency, considered dealing with the CCP a practical necessity. A participant on the popular radio broadcast *America's Town Meeting of the Air* in December 1949, Cobean argued that recognition had been accorded many revolutionary regimes in Latin America because it helped ensure the safety of property abroad. Nonrecognition would merely give the Chinese Communists immunity against liabilities they incurred in mistreating Americans and their interests.[77]

Those in favor of trade and diplomatic relations with the CCP also brought their views directly to Washington. They persuaded at least one member of Congress, Edwin C. Johnson, the Chairman of the Senate Committee on Interstate and Foreign Commerce, to present their views to the Secretary of State. Remarks at an August 1949 State Department Division of Commercial Policy meeting with nine executives from companies such as IT&T, C. V. Starr, and Chase National Bank indicated some enthusiasm for continued business relations with China if a modicum of security could be guaranteed.[78] To business representatives at the Department's Round Table Discussion during October such an improvement in conditions hinged almost entirely upon American willingness to recognize the Communist regime. William R. Herod, President of International General Electric, argued that the United States had "recognized everybody else," regardless of communist affiliations. Once the civil war ended and a government emerged, recognition and trade should follow. After all, to try to stop China's commerce with the free world and fail, as he contended such an effort certainly would, seemed quite ill-advised.[79]

The State Department also heard from a more voluble advocate of relations with the Communist Chinese during the autumn of 1949. Isbrandtsen Shipping Lines had persisted in servicing Communist cities even after Chiang Kai-shek declared those ports closed in June 1949. Encountering armed interference by Nationalist vessels, Isbrandtsen requested U.S. Naval protection. This the State Department refused, despite its previous denunciation of Chiang's blockade as illegal. President of the company Hans J. Isbrandtsen furiously protested to Secretary of State Acheson that although "it may be all right for a Department of our Government to attempt to carry water on both shoulders . . . impotency is certainly not what citizens have a right to expect of such expensive installations as government departments are today. . . . We can see no justification for our sleepless nights and your apparent complacency." To the press Isbrandtsen added that he might apply for permission to arm his ships and have the crews defend themselves.[80]

Closer to the center of policymaking, Roger D. Lapham also urged continued American business activity in China and rapid recognition of Chinese Communist control. Lapham, a former Mayor of San Francisco, a prominent industrialist, and Chief of the U.S. Economic Cooperation Administration's Mission to China from May 1948 to June 1949, considered his government's highest priority to be keeping Americans in China "willing and able to counteract . . . Moscow." This would require a diplomatic presence to protect American citizens, and that, Lapham pointed out, would compel the United States to deal formally with Chinese governmental authorities. "I cannot go along with those who think it is wrong in principle to even try to deal with the Chinese Communists on the assumption they are 100% followers of the Moscow Politburo and will remain followers indefinitely," Lapham said. His earlier advocacy of ECA aid to Communist-dominated areas had proven fruitless, but Lapham persisted in making policy recommendations to Washington officials. From mid-summer 1949 until the CCP seizure of Peking consulate property in January 1950, Lapham wrote and spoke in favor of recognition, appealing to public interest groups and, wherever possible, to his friends and former State Department colleagues.[81]

The consulate incident and Washington's decision to withdraw diplomatic representatives from China diminished the ranks of those advocating relations but did not silence them. Roger Lapham, although still favoring normalization and regretting that the United States had not managed to settle the Peking dispute, suspended his activities believing that the CCP had demonstrated its disinterest in the matter. The February 1950 issue of the *Farmer Reporter*, on the other hand, asserted a growing desire to trade with China among businessmen, workers and farmers, particularly in California. In May, the Far Eastern agent of Isbrandtsen Shipping Lines took an optimistic view of continuing commerce with the CCP and the 5th Annual Mississippi Valley World Trade Conference heard a call for trade combined with propaganda efforts designed to turn the Chinese people away from communism. As late as the summer of 1950, after the Korean War had erupted, according to an informal poll at the National Foreign Trade Convention, a variety of American firms continued to trade with mainland China.[82]

But by June 25, 1950 Washington had not opened diplomatic relations with Peking. This testified to the precedence, among American officials, of political over business-related interests. Faced with a complicated issue requiring careful manipulation, the State Department appeared to ignore the viewpoints of businessmen. In retrospect a veteran of the China market wryly observed:

> In twenty years as top financial officer of . . . [a large company] I have not observed that governments . . . use information in formulating foreign policy. . . . [Rather it is] used only to justify the policies and attitudes of the top people; the latter are convinced they know it all basically already; their way of fitting the news into the Procrustes bed of their established creeds is called "evaluation" which is just a euphemism or misnomer covering up their preconceived notions.

Similarly, Paul S. Hopkins complained that State Department officials never seemed to make use of his expertise or advice.[83]

In reality what the State Department heard most clearly from the business community was their willingness to abide by a politically dictated resolution of the China controversy. The opponents of trade and recognition, although strident and demanding, made up only a fraction of the commercial companies concerned. The advocates of normalization, numbering by far the larger segment of the financial, manufacturing, and trading interests involved in China, influenced by unstable conditions and the uncertainty of CCP intentions, moderated their arguments. They had experienced the unpredictable nature of the China market and, in most cases, had only relatively small-scale operations to protect. Recognition might well make their investments profitable, but few would suffer irreparably if all their China-based assets disappeared.

Nevertheless, trade with Communist China continued to be appealing and both large and small companies persisted in their efforts to deal with the CCP. Few expected any long-term accommodation with a system so avowedly anticapitalist and anti-American, but possibilities of lucrative relations for a period of time after the difficulties of transition subsided seemed good. The outcome would depend upon CCP actions and United States policy decisions. American authorities, businessmen agreed, must extend recognition if prospects were to remain bright.

And the CCP, in the throes of civil war, with the American government aiding their enemy, did talk with American businessmen about contacts and contracts for the future. This did not portend a modification of ideology or even a slackening of hostility toward a power allied with the despicable Kuomintang. Rather it signified a desire to benefit from American resources and skills if that could be arranged without unprincipled sacrifices. Thus labor radicalism might be curbed in the interests of production and progress, but workers would not be violently repressed lest the revolution itself be jeopardized. Moreover, American businessmen could be valuable pawns in Communist hands. There is little doubt that the CCP tried to use them as hostages to break the Nationalist blockade of Shanghai. The Party constrained them, by their presence at vital petroleum and utility installations, to provide protection against KMT bombing raids. And the pressure on American businessmen may have been in part a gamble designed to force United States recognition. The Chinese Communists believed that United States industry needed the China market to survive.[84] They may have thought, therefore, that they had an important lever with which to compel initiation of diplomatic relations on their own terms.

In Washington the commercial connection, therefore, appeared realistic and promising. If businessmen did not approach the issue of Chinese relations with the impassioned dedication of their missionary brethren, they nonetheless made clear their desire to buy and sell in China. Not merely potential supporters for future dealings with the CCP, businessmen indicated that they would willingly participate in America's efforts to entice Mao and his cohorts to cooperate with the United States and establish mutually beneficial diplomatic relations.

CHAPTER EIGHT

Journalists and the Media
Changing Times; Shifting Views

)━━()━━()━━()━━(

AMERICAN journalists in China inhabited a tumultuous world in which upheaval proved a constant companion. Whether early in the twentieth century when Sun Yat-sen and Yuan Shih-k'ai contended, or in the middle years when followers of communism triumphed over the once-revolutionary Kuomintang, China captivated the adventuresome. For correspondents in this ever-changing country, news became an endless succession of exciting disasters, peopled by a cast of villains and scoundrels who not only tortured China, but also repressed the journalists. Political and professional crises dominated the landscape, preventing the sweltering summers in Nanking and the frigid winters of Shanghai from growing tedious.

Editors in the United States, far removed from the enchanting Orient, did not develop similar enthusiasms. Peking and Canton datelines often succumbed to more compelling events in Europe or downtown Buffalo. Still, the American press did highlight resounding victories and momentous defeats, exploiting the anxieties of a nation perpetually at war. Its sporadic concern with China suited a readership whose own capricious interest in Asian affairs was easily satiated.

When the American publishing industry did acknowledge China's turmoil, the alarm echoed through the White House and State Department. Officialdom monitored the press and culled from it information and analysis to supplement the reporting of its own foreign service. Not only factual data but also the opinions of editors and columnists received careful deliberation and wide distribution. As the nation's papers began, during 1949, to take opposing stands on the question of diplomatic relations with the emerging Communist regime in China, they drew an attentive audience in Washington. Government observers noted those papers and magazines which came to favor or accept the necessity for recognition and those which vociferously opposed it. The media would, after all, interpret Washington's decision to the rest of the nation so its inclinations bore with substantial weight on the manner, timing and substance of Administration policy.

I Sojourning in a Land of Conflict

Chinese circumstances had for decades encouraged American newsmen to become involved, to an unusual degree, in trying to influence United States China policy. Between 1900 and 1925, journalists functioned as agents for both Chinese leaders and American interests. They publicized the compatibility of Chinese and American goals and tried to convince the United States to take an active part in China's affairs. In effect:

> they represented not only journals but, in a queer way, Western society, business interests, and even governments. They strutted about as unofficial plenipotentiaries, offering advice—solicited and unsolicited—carrying official messages, negotiating, lobbying, criticizing, applauding and even occasionally writing. Some had sanity, many had sympathy, but all had authoritativeness . . . because China . . . buffeted by political and institutional uncertainty and by Western pressure and domination . . . groped for anything and anyone who would bring her rest and refuge.[1]

Chinese leaders knew that foreign correspondents advocated Western penetration of their country, but they hoped to compensate for this by exploiting the newsmen's supposed contacts and mass audience. That experiment did not survive the pressures of the period. Reporters could not provide American support unencumbered by government and mercantile prerequisites, and the Kuomintang would not accept commercial and political strings. After 1925, the Nationalists grew impatient with their erstwhile allies and tried to deport those who, like George Sokolsky, Hallett Abend, and Rodney Gilbert, had become critical of the KMT revolution.[2]

Once the Kuomintang began to see newsmen as adversaries, it imposed broad-ranging controls. During the 1930s, censorship prevented one in three dispatches from leaving China. In the brief period from spring to early summer of 1933, censors cut some 20,000 words out of the stories of a single United States news agency. More damaging, they also adopted the practice of rewriting articles without informing correspondents who might not become aware of the changes until long after publication. Since such activities followed no set pattern, varying from day to day and region to region, both in subjects deleted and in enforcement, the correspondent functioned in an exceedingly fluid milieu. Those who repeatedly tried to send "objectionable" messages faced the ultimate censure of having their registration certificates rescinded by the Ministry of Foreign Affairs. This made it impossible to transmit material out of China (except by slow-going mail) because authorization to use telegraphic facilities depended on proper identification papers.[3]

The outbreak of war between China and Japan in 1937, however, not only produced an avalanche of news, but also once again aligned American journalists with the Kuomintang. While China succumbed rapidly to Japan's swift advance, Chiang Kai-shek emerged as the nation's symbol of unity and resistance. Leadership of the anti-Japanese cause had been forced upon him by dissidents in a dramatic kidnapping at Sian in December 1936, and in American press accounts of the struggle in Asia he assumed the stature of a courageous and indefatigable commander. The Generalissimo's Christianity and his Wellesley-educated wife appealed to an American public eager to find democratic allies in an increasingly fascist world. This, of course, became even more true after Pearl Harbor brought American soldiers to the Pacific.[4]

Reporters found the idyllic portrait of the Nationalist Chinese, which they had helped to create, remarkably resistant to criticism. A. T. Steele, *New York Herald Tribune* reporter, recalled that "with the world at war and things going badly on most fronts, editors at home were little interested in routine news from China—least of all stories about corruption, inefficiency and factional bickering. There were those, too, who felt it unsporting to flog an ally while he was down."[5]

Moreover, a state of war had encouraged the Kuomintang to sharpen censorship measures again, preventing disparaging stories from leaving China. Americans contended that the requirements of military secrecy alone did not dictate the zeal with which the KMT applied their rules. "Equal if not greater emphasis," observed the Office of Strategic Services in 1945, "is placed upon preventing the release of information or opinion that would weaken the power and prestige of the Government or the Party either at home or abroad."[6] In fact during 1945 the Nationalists, beginning with Darrell Berrigan of the *New York Post* and Harold Isaacs of *Newsweek*, refused entry visas to journalists whose writings had not been favorable to their regime.[7] To Nationalist officials the really significant struggle was not that being fought against Japan, where the power of American arms would be decisive, but rather the coming battle with Chinese Communism. The government, therefore, tried to deprive correspondents of the ability to hurt Kuomintang interests or provide the CCP with favorable publicity.

Efforts to prevent contact between American journalists and members of the Chinese Communist Party proved fruitless from the first. Edgar

Snow, author of one of the most influential studies of Mao Tse-tung and his communist forces ever written, journeyed to Pao-an, the CCP capital, in 1936. After spending three months in Shensi province conversing with Mao and many others, Snow related their story through articles in *New Republic, Pacific Affairs, Saturday Evening Post, Time-Life* publications, and then in his classic book *Red Star Over China*. Not only did Snow's work fascinate the American reading public but also, in translation, it informed the Chinese people of a movement about which they had previously been able to learn only the most negative details.[8]

Subsequently other American reporters visited the northwest and almost without exception wrote enthusiastic accounts of the energy and imagination they found among China's red "bandits." Repelled by the Confucian-fascist philosophy that the Nationalists espoused, these observers found they could identify with the egalitarian humanity and informal friendliness of Chinese Communist youths.[9] "Those weeks in Yenan were a time of laughter and gaiety," journalist Theodore White later recalled. "Those of us who have been so criticized for romanticizing the Chinese Communists can claim forgiveness . . . Chinese Communists were different then; we were not duped. . . . It was a time of good will—men open, warm, trusting . . . Yenan . . . embraced us as allies and friends."[10] Indeed, the Chinese Communists in need of American assistance were carried away by the sympathetic demeanor of American journalists, servicemen, and foreign service officers. The July 4, 1944 editorial in *Liberation Daily* declared:

> Democratic America has already found a companion, and the cause of Sun Yat-sen a successor, in the Chinese Communist Party and the other democratic forces. . . . The work which we Communists are carrying on today is the very same work which was carried on earlier in America by Washington, Jefferson and Lincoln; it will certainly obtain, and indeed has already obtained, the sympathy of democratic America.[11]

A sense of kinship so unexpected and so genuine led some Americans to believe that the CCP was not a real Communist party. Instead, they misleadingly characterized the Chinese Communists as "peasant agrarians" who were "no more Communistic than we Americans are."[12] Illusions of this nature proved short-lived and a more realistic picture of the Communists emerged during the postwar period, but the favorable impression made by the Chinese Communists on a variety of journalists continued to be influential.[13]

At the beginning of the civil war period, American journalists in China had had very different experiences with the KMT and the CCP. Newsmen felt disillusioned by what they had seen of Kuomintang mismanagement and corruption during the war with Japan. They had personally suffered under a strict system of censorship which often appeared unreasonable. Some, such as Teddy White and Hank Lieberman, had developed a thoroughgoing contempt for the Americanized members of the Kuomintang Chiang used to deflect United States demands for reform. On the other hand, reporters had visited Chinese Communist territory where they had observed effective reforms and popular enthusiasm. Moreover, they had been received with warmth, had been freely and eagerly provided with information, and had departed with their notes intact.[14] The vast majority of these correspondents had no particular sympathy for communism and hoped that some moderate remedy could be found for China's ills. But they perceived, if only dimly at first, that the Nationalist cause was doomed and that the revolution could not be stopped.[15] This point they made increasingly in their dispatches home where their warnings gave impetus to a growing uneasiness among American government officials.

Chinese Nationalist treatment of the press corps at the end of the Pacific war did not improve relations with American journalists. To be sure, the Kuomintang's less stringent censorship regulations after 1945 eliminated some resentment and areas of friction.[16] Furthermore, though military coverage continued to be burdensome because of the distance to war zones and primitive transportation and communications facilities, the Nationalists made limited efforts to keep Nanking-based newsmen informed through weekly press conferences. However, correspondents had to submit questions in advance as the Government Information Office instructed, and they found official releases, communiqués, and other public announcements generally unreliable. Extemporaneous probes at news sessions did not receive replies, further frustrating the reporters' efforts to use the government as a news source.[17]

In any case, minor efforts by officials to cooperate with correspondents did not disguise the depth of Kuomintang decay. Journalists observed and reported advancing demoralization and economic disintegration. Amos Landman, for example, recorded his experience in Shanghai,

> We saw the police terror, symbolized by students of our acquaintance who cringed whenever a police emergency van screeched past. . . . We heard numerous stories of the depredations of corrupt officials. . . . We saw how the middle class was robbed by the so-called . . . economic reform. . . . We watched the growing public hatred of the troops which were supposed to be defending the population from the Communists. . . . Two decades of war, of corruption, of galloping inflation had taken their toll.

By May 1949 virtually every American reporter in China had come to reject the Nationalists thoroughly.[18]

At the same time the CCP continued its liberal treatment of newsmen until the last months of the civil war. In 1946 the Party permitted John Roderick of Associated Press to stay in Yenan and broadcast his dispatches over North Shensi radio for pickup on the West Coast.[19] Jack Belden traveled in Communist as well as Nationalist areas of China after 1946, gathering information on the conditions of peasant life.[20] As late as October 1948, Henry Lieberman and four other correspondents in Changchun, Manchuria, having been put under house arrest by local authorities when the Communists moved into the city, were released and feted at the order of top Party leaders, General Yeh Chien-ying and Party deputy P'eng Chen.[21] In Hong Kong Party spokesman Ch'iao Kuan-hua assured reporters that the Communist authorities would continue to guarantee their safety and their ability to gather and report the news.[22]

Approaching victory called a halt to these freedoms. In January 1949, Seymour Topping, then a reporter for AP, attempted to join the CCP forces as they launched their push on Nanking and Shanghai. Since there were no other independent Western correspondents with the People's Liberation Army at that juncture, he hoped to make exclusive broadcasts over CCP radio as Roderick had done earlier. Unexpectedly the Chinese Communists, caught up in the final throes of the immense Huai-hai battle, refused to allow him to wander in or even traverse their war zone.[23] American journalists might or might not be spies, but they made perfect targets for Kuomintang snipers—a complication better avoided.[24]

Almost inevitably, cordial relations between the Chinese Communists and journalists from the United States deteriorated once the takeover of large cities put the Party astride China's communications centers. To the CCP's way of thinking the news media functioned exclusively to serve the interests of the people. This included dissemination of official policy statements and eulogies of war or labor heroes. During the early civil war years, serving the people had meant informing China's millions about the CCP, the Communist leaders, and the Party's goals. Press responsibility under a Communist regime did not allow for embarrassing accounts of the failings of Party leadership. Forced to cope with enormous new adjustments, the CCP found criticism by the foreign press intolerable. Doak Barnett discovered that authorities in Peking were inclined to consider American-style reporting "a plot . . . purposely to destroy the Chinese People's democratic revolution." American reporters however, refused to squander the opportunity to write about a great revolution by simply reiterating propaganda slogans.[25]

As early as 1948, Ambassador Stuart had found that CCP declarations of press freedom sounded hollow. In December, he wrote the State Department, that the Chinese would probably copy the Soviet model in dealing with newsmen. Promises of "full freedom to report full facts" merely meant facts as interpreted by Communist authorities. "Guidance of local military and political authorities" over "the activities of foreign correspondents . . . in so far as a state of war exists" worried the Ambassador in a country where war had become a "continuing condition. If and when the Nationalist Government is defeated, class war will certainly remain, not to speak of the cold war."[26]

These forebodings appeared justified when in February 1949, immediately on the heels of its march into Peking, the CCP launched a public attack on foreign reporters. Combining the texts of different stories written by AP and UP correspondents, the CCP found "evidence" that two newsmen had resorted to "sneers and slanders" to explain the gala welcome given People's Liberation Army troops in the city. The *People's Daily* highlighted popular protest against the insults; and the Committee of Journalists, a prepatory group for a new journalists' union, demanded expulsion of the men from Peking.[27] Although in succeeding weeks denunciations of the two "imperialists" softened, unrestricted newsgathering proved impossible.[28] Then, on February 27, 1949, official word came regarding the future status of foreign correspondents in Peking. Yeh Chien-ying, Director of the PLA and Peking's Military Control Commission, notified the seventeen resident reporters and the United States Information Service that: "Because of the present wartime state, all foreign news agencies and foreign correspondents are not allowed to carry on their activities in Peiping. All foreign nationals are not allowed to publish newspapers or magazines in the city."[29]

Foreign journalists found their operations restricted in Shanghai as well.[30] Imposition of the Nationalist blockade along China's coast put immense pressure on CCP officials trying to manage a huge and unmercifully demanding metropolis without the requisite skills. In June 1949 the British-owned *North China Daily News* printed a front page story which stated that the Kuomintang had mined the Yangtze approaches to Shanghai. The CCP, lacking means to sweep the river and frightened by such rumors, turned its wrath on the newspaper, which it accused of spreading false, imperialistic propaganda.[31]

The Party felt equally sensitive about criticism of its fledgling authority. Randall Gould, editor of the *Shanghai Evening Post & Mercury*, after welcoming the CCP to Shanghai in hopes of improved conditions,

sought in June to urge more rapid progress in setting out new regulations governing wage adjustments. Without guidelines, laborers virtually had run riot through the city, and Gould complained about lock-
ins which had occurred at Caltex Petroleum and the *Post* itself. When
workers in the printing plant—probably under CCP orders—refused to
publish the June 15 issue with the offending story on its front page,
Gould resolved not to kill the story, and the *Shanghai Evening Post &
Mercury* in effect ceased to exist.[32] The shaky municipal government
would not abide an unfettered, critical publishing house in Shanghai,
particularly with the city blockaded and subject to repeated aerial attacks. On July 4, 1949, without prior announcement, PLA authorities
imposed military consorship on all foreign correspondents.[33]

Anticipating harsh treatment from the Communists, American reporters found actual conditions surprising. The Communists, although
determined to curb the media, appeared unwilling to suppress the activities of foreign journalists entirely. Press regulations promulgated by
Shanghai authorities in July for the duration of the period of martial law
prohibited reporting on military affairs and related topics such as the
weather in certain strategic locations. At the same time, the Party did
not impose political censorship and allowed even derogatory dispatches
to leave China unaltered. The new regulations further relaxed travel
restrictions which had been imposed previously. The only really unpleasant result of the new regimen turned out to be delays—sometimes
as long as thirty hours—in sending stories. Communist authorities simply lacked sufficient manpower to carry out oversight procedures.[34] To
correspondents this meant inconvenience but not unemployment.

Similarly, prohibitions issued at the end of August handicapped, but
did not destroy, the ability of American newsmen to work in China.
The Party banned dissemination of news by all foreigners within the
country. The ruling affected not only American agencies such as AP and
UP; even the Soviet Union's Tass had to stop distributing its material.[35]
Clear warning had gone out that Communist China would not have an
open society. Nonetheless, reporters could and did continue sending
stories abroad.

Even in the face of prohibitions and censorship, a fairly general expectation survived among American correspondents that, once the CCP
government had been stabilized, newsmen would be able to function
freely again. With memories of wartime and early civil war experiences
supporting them, many stayed on to make the best of temporary inconvenience.[36] During the *Shanghai Evening Post & Mercury* dispute, a
group of American reporters approached Randall Gould to convince him
to allow them to constitute a new editorial board and start publishing

the paper once more.[37] Associated Press, late in 1949, assuming that circumstances would improve "in a matter of months," assigned Seymour Topping to open a new Peking bureau as soon as the CCP would admit him, presumably in early 1950.[38]

II Official Contacts in China and America

American correspondents, in fact, had little future in a Communist China. Whereas the CCP, facing enormous difficulties in modernizing a backward nation, would not tolerate inquisitiveness, let alone criticism, American newsmen persisted in asking questions, exposing errors, and attacking official decisions. Furthermore, American reporters had established close working relationships with United States government agencies in China. Reflecting Chinese Communist suspicions generated by this type of cooperation, a May 1949 article entitled "Beware of Journalistic American Imperialists" asserted that all United States correspondents were "spare parts of the road paving machine of American imperialists." Not simply newsgatherers, these American journalists, they believed, engaged regularly in intelligence and propagandistic activities as well.[39]

Reporters developed their contacts with American officials in China to gain information, not to provide Washington with data about the Communist revolution. Nevertheless, more than missionaries or businessmen, journalists did supply information to United States foreign service representatives and did discuss the implications of developments in China with them.[40] Journalists cultivated wide-ranging contacts in official circles, spoke regularly with influential Chinese and with members of the American community.[41] Their mobility—a condition not shared by the diplomatic corps—kept those hardy enough to take advantage of it at the center of events.[42] Correspondents visited the Embassy and consulates often, reporting on developments, passing along rumors which could not go into print, and sharing their informed judgments of controversial issues. In many instances, the opinions of these newsmen were valued highly and their assessments not only influenced the recommendations of foreign service officers in China, but were also telegraphed to the State Department for further consideration.[43] Although American reporters in China were not spies, they proved to be a significant asset to American officials.[44]

A similar relationshp existed between journalists and government agencies in the United States. State Department officers met frequently with members of the press. Acheson not only conducted routine formal press conferences, but also spoke privately with small groups of journalists every two to three weeks. These sessions, although designed by the Secretary to explain policies to reporters, also allowed him to become better acquainted with individuals and their views.[45] Other Department officials retained friendships made during service in China, as, for example, Livingston Merchant with Al Ravenholt of the *Chicago Daily News*, upon which basis they passed the correspondents' assessments on to colleagues and superiors.[46] Occasionally, too, journalists fresh from a trip to China would volunteer information and observations.[47] Thus, despite sometimes conflicting needs of story-conscious reporters and public-relations or security-minded officials, a fairly wide area of cooperation existed.[48]

The State Department looked upon the press as a source of information which could supplement the occasionally inefficient and always overburdened foreign service system of reportage. Seeking data and insights about developments in China, Department personnel read overseas news dispatches in many of the major papers. W. Walton Butterworth, Director of the Division of Far Eastern Affairs, considered A. T. Steele "the oustanding American journalist in China," a newsman who "knows of old China under Communist and Nationalist control." He therefore sent articles written by Steele to Assistant Secretary of State Dean Rusk, Undersecretary of State James Webb, and Secretary of State Dean Acheson.[49] The news office of the State Department conducted a more formal survey of dispatches from China by hooking directly into the news tickers of AP, UP, and Reuters. On occasion these commercial networks proved hours or even days faster than official cable traffic.[50]

American newspapers and magazines also provided Department analysts with a means of judging public opinion on a routine basis.[51] The Office of Public Opinion Studies regularly compiled reports of media opinion about developments in China and Administration China policy. These circulated among policymakers, some of whom found the synopses enlightening and helpful. Resources employed by the analysts included editorials from 71 newspapers, 36 syndicated columnists, 23 periodicals, 12 national foreign policy organizations, public opinion polls, radio commentators, and the *Congressional Record*. These sources, according to H. Schuyler Foster, director of the Public Opinion Studies Staff (POSS), provided the State Department with "as accurate a reflection of American nationwide opinion as possible."[52]

Even more interaction—direct and indirect—took place between journalists and Congressmen. In retrospect, Senator H. Alexander Smith (R, NJ), a pro–Chiang Kai-shek activist, saw newspapers and magazines as "basic, . . . the general groundwork upon which the Congressman builds his knowledge of current events."[53] Lacking independent sources, apart from occasional trips and personal correspondence, and rarely privy to State Department information, Congressmen had to rely upon journalists.[54] In addition to culling factual data from the newspapers, Congressmen and their assistants avidly read editorials and columns. James Reston, weighing the influence of newsmen on foreign policy, found that it was "exercised primarily through the Congress, which confuses press opinion with public opinion."[55] Cut off for much of the year from their constituents, members of Congress sought in the press a reflection of the views voters held on foreign affairs. In addition, perhaps for most legislators and their staffs, the major columnists provided ideas, insights, and policy analyses.[56]

Harry S Truman, on the other hand, consistently denied that newspapers or magazines exerted any appreciable influence on his thinking. At one time or another, he denounced almost every major paper in the nation as biased or factually unreliable. He often asserted that the press was controlled by special interests and his own experience in 1948 confirmed his conviction that, in any case, the media were against him. Editors, when not rebuked for unprincipled mismanagement of the news, earned Truman's scorn as armchair statesmen.[57] But much as he claimed to distrust editors, Truman saved his special obloquy for columnists. A pundit, the President asserted, was "never hampered by the facts. When he meets a fact he doesn't like, [he feels] he can . . . ignore it . . . or he can wring its little neck, distort its little body, and shape it into a grotesque something no whit resembling its original form."[58] Accordingly, Truman claimed that he dismissed "what the editorial writers and columnists say about me on the editorial page if I can get a fair break on the front page in the news columns."[59]

In truth, the President, although frequently and outspokenly critical of journalists and the media, recognized that they wielded a fair measure of influence in national affairs. Truman read some four to six local and New York newspapers daily and other regional papers on a regular basis.[60] When he traveled, he had his usual editions flown across the country to him. The President also received oral press summaries at his daily morning staff meeting and clippings from a variety of sources. Throughout his years in office, he enjoyed good relations with the White House press corps and made several reporters close friends.[61]

On foreign affairs the President used newspapers primarily to ascertain the attitudes of the public toward Administration policies. Truman had access to Policy Planning Staff, National Security Council, and foreign service assessments of conditions in China and so did not need to depend upon the press for information the way members of Congress did.[62] But as leader of the Democratic Party and a consummate politician, the President kept close watch on the China debate in the media. He might revile the Hearst and McCormick empires but Truman remained sensitive to their mass circulation and potential influence with the electorate. At the same time, though he recognized that they raised public awareness, he found their views of Administration policy to be invariably negative and often misleading. "It was my conviction," Truman later recalled, "that the major media of communication had failed in their responsibility to present facts as facts and opinion as opinion. It seemed to me that owners, publishers, and columnists of the press and radio were deliberately irresponsible."[63]

Whether for good or ill, then, the American government listened closely to what the journalistic community had to say about China during 1949 and 1950. The press supplied information and analysis which officials used in making policy. Newspapers and magazines, through their editorials, also seemed to provide insights into what the public—informed and uninformed—thought about Chinese affairs. If journalists did not exercise any direct control over policy decisions, by determining what the public and officials read they significantly influenced what Americans thought about and took action on.

III. Press Opinion and Government Assessments

During 1949 and early 1950, as civil war in China raged, the State Department's Public Opinion Studies Staff monitored American newspaper and magazine reactions to the crisis. Officials found emphasis on China erratic and media opinion generally divided. Apart from a "vocal minority" which remained consistently critical of Administration policy, surveys indicated that most commentators felt uncertain about Asia. This vagueness and lack of information about developments in China contrasted sharply with the definite opinions expressed regarding European affairs and the containment of communism in the West. The only policy that a hesitant majority would endorse throughout much of 1949 proved to be the cessation of American aid for the Kuomintang.[64]

Disillusionment with Chiang Kai-shek had begun for newsmen in the filthy alleyways of Chungking during the War and then had spread to the United States. Initially the Generalissimo had acquired an image as a staunch defender of democracy, his regime a patriotic front against fascism. In 1937 he and Madame Chiang appeared on the cover of *Time* magazine as man and wife of the year. But while Henry Luce continued to tout Chiang in the waning years of the conflict, other less partisan editorial writers found the overwhelming evidence of KMT corruption and mismanagement convincing. The *New York Herald Tribune*, America's leading Republican newspaper, reacting to Chiang's tarnished glory, warned in 1947 that "there is no hope in backing reactionaries in China in the belief that they can stop the Reds. In China, as elsewhere in the world, the United States must stand for democracy and not try to build frail dikes against communism with worn and useless feudal bricks."[65]

Having rejected their idyllic assessment of Chiang Kai-shek's regime, most commentators in the United States looked forward to the emergence of a new head of state who could salvage Nationalist fortunes. The *New Orleans Item* joined the chorus, noted by State Department observers, contending "that China could not be regenerated as long as Chiang remained in power."[66] When the Generalissimo actually withdrew from the presidency in January 1949, however, his departure disconcerted his American critics and dismayed his supporters. Both sides feared a sudden collapse of the Chinese government and a Communist takeover. The pro-Chiang Scripps-Howard newspaper chain, representing those who regularly called for aid to China, blamed Washington for the tragic situation brought about by Chiang's retirement. Jack Beall of ABC sharply criticized left-wing elements in the State Department for acquiescing in a Communist takeover of China.[67] But word from China made it clear that reality differed greatly from appearance. "Far from weakening his power in Chinese politics," Allen Raymond, Nanking correspondent of the *New York Herald Tribune*, reported, this move had "immeasurably increased it" by allowing him to "cast the onus for continuing warfare on communist enemies" and, Raymond could have added, on Vice-President Li Tsung-jen.[68] Within days, it had become clear that Chiang still controlled Kuomintang policies, and soon most American editors resumed their pleas for a fresh start in China. The politically liberal *St. Louis Post-Dispatch* lamented, "His military hopes are unfounded, his political judgment is disastrous. Chiang had better forget his personal fortune, and permit new leadership which China so sorely needs."[69]

Opposition to further American aid for the Kuomintang ballooned as Chiang's continuing ascendancy turned the defeats of 1948 into disaster in 1949. Jack Bell, commenting in the *Miami Herald*, opposed giving more money and equipment to "Chiang's tottering temple of corruption."[70] Little support greeted former ambassador William C. Bullitt's proposal that the United States send a fighting general with troops and enough cash to stem the CCP advance. The *St. Louis Post-Dispatch* reminded its readers that Bullitt's "emphatically extreme views on our Chinese relations are well enough known to be discounted by almost everybody."[71] Senator Pat McCarran's bill requesting renewed appropriations for China provoked heightened protest. The conservative voices of the *Denver Post* and the *Kansas City Star* joined the *Post-Dispatch* in arguing that "one and a half billion dollars is not going to do now what four billion dollars in the past eight years have miserably failed to do."[72] Elmer Davis of ABC radio considered Flying Tiger Claire Chennault's testimony to the Armed Services Committee a logical and forceful presentation of the case for saving South China. But State Department analysts noted that most of those commenting on Chennault's plans or on the request by fifty Senators for hearings on McCarran's bill did so unsympathetically. Even Robert McCormick's *Chicago Tribune*, a pro-Kuomintang Truman Administration critic, opposed wasting more money in China.[73]

That most editors and commentators objected to giving more aid to the Nationalists became clear in the stormy debates generated by Secretary of State Acheson's declaration that large-scale aid would benefit neither China nor the United States.[74] Although some long-term critics of America's China policy, such as columnist George Sokolsky, implied that State Department decisions originated in Moscow, the *New York Times*, which had consistently advocated aid to keep China out of Soviet hands, ruefully admitted that Acheson's viewpoint had to be accepted.[75] The *Louisville Courier-Journal* also found Acheson convincing, "We have burdens enough on our hands without frittering away our treasure in the East," it declared.[76] State Department analysts concluded, "Most commentators, while alarmed at the prospect of a Communist-dominated China, believe that Communist control cannot be prevented by U.S. aid at this time." During the succeeding months repeated plans for Kuomintang funding stirred up advocates and opponents, but the majority consistently decried further wastefulness in Chiang Kai-shek's behalf. Eric Sevareid's disparaging remarks reflected dominant opinion: "The Nationalist government has all but disintegrated. Its real headquarters, if it has any, is here in Washington where its lobbyists and American supporters are desperately busy trying to scare up another big American aid program for China."[77]

With a Nationalist debacle imminent, journalists increasingly considered future possibilities. Most observers saw the Administration's "watchful waiting" as appropriate for the moment, but a good number believed that the United States should retain some minimal contacts with the victorious Chinese Communists.[78] The moderate *Baltimore Sun* and the Republican *Boston Herald* agreed that China's "desperate need of trade with the West" might provide "a way in which we can exchange our trade for Chinese independence" of Russian political control.[79] Even

Stewart Alsop, who ordinarily exuberantly promoted Chiang's struggle, called for trade with the CCP. "It is a curious device," Alsop conceded, "to exchange oil, locomotives and diesel engines, sheet steel and trucks, against Chinese products plus freedom of movement in China, freedom of information in China, and a reasonably friendly attitude of the Chinese government. But it can be done." Moreover, Alsop reasoned, "to have what another nation wants is to be capable of influencing [the] policy of that nation."[80] Such contacts with the Communists did not necessarily mean abandonment of the Kuomintang. Hallett Abend and Ferdinand Mayer, writing in *Current History*, recommended that the United States "should not attempt to take in tow either of the two fragments into which the Chinese ship is splitting. Rather we should serve as a sheet anchor for each to keep from drifting ashore in the storm— the question of repair to be decided when the immediate tempest is over."[81]

Critics of United States government policy, however, demanded positive action from the State Department and increasingly attacked Acheson's betrayal of the Nationalist Chinese. In July Scripps-Howard columnist Clyde Farnsworth wrote from Taipei that a reorganization and regeneration of the Kuomintang war effort had made Chiang an even more worthy recipient of aid. During September, the *Baltimore News-Post*, a Hearst publication, ran David Sentner's series praising Chiang Kai-shek and calling for aid to his forces. But opposition to Administration policies by what the Department called the "vocal minority" more frequently was expressed in denunciatory columns and editorials as illustrated by the violent outcry following publication of the China White Paper. The *New York Sun* ranked the State Department's report among history's "record-making alibis." *Time*, more colorfully, accused America's diplomats of conducting a politically motivated autopsy while in Asia "the body was still stubbornly squirming with life." Jack Beall (ABC), Paul Harvey (NBC), Richard Harkness (NBC), Constantine Brown, the *New York Times*, Scripps-Howard, and Hearst publications all condemned the White Paper's effort to whitewash American sins of omission and commission. For a loyal minority Chiang Kai-shek and the Kuomintang remained objects of near veneration. An indictment such as the White Paper roused them to fury. Chiang remained the sole repository of their hopes for China's future.[82]

In contrast, most of those remarking upon publication of the White Paper welcomed the Administration's effort to explain the situation in China. Many, such as the *New York Herald Tribune*, *Baltimore Sun*, and radio commentators Charles Collingwood (CBS), Earl Godwin (NBC), and Elmer Davis (ABC), agreed with the Paper's conclusion that the impending Communist triumph followed from Nationalist Chinese, not American, failure. The *Washington Star* found the volume a "bleakly persuasive argument" and the *Washington Post* hoped that it would stop the "suicidal campaign" for increased United States involvement in the civil war.[83]

Speculation that Mao Tse-tung might become a more acceptable leader by turning into a Chinese Tito accelerated as greater numbers of editors and columnists rejected Chiang Kai-shek. Walter Briggs set forth the basic argument that Titoism would occur in China in his February 1949 *New Republic* article. Pointing to the similar patterns of communist development in China and Yugoslavia, Briggs concluded that the "Chinese are ardent nationalists. Historically they distrust Russia. Mao himself got his start in South China not because of, but in spite of, Moscow. His 'communization' has been far more moderate than Stalin's. In this respect Mao out-Tito's Tito." Moreover, he added, Stalin's lack of confidence in Mao, as indicated by his returning Mao's old enemy Li Lisan to Manchuria, no doubt irritated the Chinese leader immensely.[84] Other commentators who doubted that Mao would make China a Soviet satellite included the *Kansas City Times, Christian Science Monitor, Dayton News, Des Moines Register, Boston Herald, U.S. News and World Report, Portland Oregonian, Detroit Free Press, Magazine of Wall Street,* and Charles Van Devander of the *New York Post.*[85] AP foreign affairs analyst J. N. Roberts and Joseph Phillips in *Newsweek,* on the other hand, cautioned against visions of a Sino-Soviet split.[86] The *Saturday Evening Post* reflected the indecision many commentators felt. Although it published Edgar Snow's speculations that the Russians and Chinese would develop many points of friction, the editorial board declared that they were by no means as hopeful as Snow.[87]

Mao's July 1, 1949 declaration that China would lean to the side of the Soviet Union in international affairs dampened optimism concerning China's future behavior only momentarily. The *New York Times,* to be sure, indulged in gloomy forecasting. "Mao persists in putting himself on record in contradiction of his apologists in the United States. . . . There is nothing on record to suggest Mao doesn't mean exactly what he says and that he will . . . by any stretch of the imagination be friendly to the U.S."[88] Others, though, quickly recovered their equilibrium and reiterated earlier warnings of the *Nation* that "Chinese Communist leaders are not likely to welcome Russian interference in their affairs unless they are forced in that direction by an unfriendly West. . . . [Therefore] the extent to which China will pass into the Soviet orbit will be determined during coming weeks in Washington, not in Moscow."[89] Instead of reinforcing the Sino-Soviet alliance through ill-starred intervention, the *Washington Post* suggested, "policy makers should be thinking of ways and means of loosening and eventually breaking it."[90]

Recognition of a Communist Chinese government became the most frequently discussed device for weakening Mao Tse-tung's ties to the Kremlin. The *Minneapolis Star* thought that recognition combined with a cautious trade policy had a good chance of winning the Chinese from Russia.[91] The *New Republic*, demanding wisdom and boldness, urged the American government to outwit Russia by initiating relations with China since, "from the Soviet point of view, recognition of China by the West is less to be desired than dependence of China on Asia."[92] But the Public Opinion Studies Staff in their November 1949 report found that, although the largest number of observers expected eventual recognition, no dominant trend in opinion favoring or opposing that action had developed. The strongest sentiment uncovered by Department analysts indicated that commentators hoped the government would proceed "slowly and with caution."[93]

Significantly, despite a diplomatic confrontation engendering considerable outrage against the CCP during the autumn of 1949, press opinion remained mixed and commentators continued to believe diplomatic relations would in time be established between Peking and Washington. The isolation and subsequent imprisonment of Consul General Angus Ward in Mukden was an issue perfectly designed to arouse the patriotic fervor of American citizens. The ordinarily sober voice of the *New York Times* thundered, "We cannot afford, if we are to retain a shred of prestige anywhere in Asia, to let such men as Angus Ward . . . suffer any further as martyrs to our inability to decide what can and should be done. If the Chinese Communists are illiterate in the language of international diplomacy and decency, we will have to draw them a picture they can understand."[94] The *New York World Telegram* proposed that the picture be drawn by America's Pacific fleet. Reminding their readers of Teddy Roosevelt's stand against the Sultan of Morocco in 1904, the *World Telegram* and the seventeen other newspapers in the Scripps-Howard chain called upon President Truman to take a strong, unbending position.[95] Most other commentators abjured such a volatile response and agreed with the State Department's feeling that their colleagues appeared to be "trigger happy."[96]

The question of whether the United States should recognize Communist rule in China, therefore, continued to occasion discussion in the media. Many commentators reflected a practical view of diplomatic relations similar to the approach advocated by Secretary Acheson in a speech during September 1949. Barnett Nover argued for the *Denver Post* that reality required recognition. Otherwise, Nover and the *Post* insisted, the United States must pretend that "what has happened in China during the past year and what is happening there has not happened at all." The *Denver Post* and the *Baltimore Sun* both asserted that recognition was not a matter of friendship, sympathy, or endorsement. Nonrecognition, on the other hand, forced the United States to discard a useful link between the American and Chinese people.[97] Edward R. Murrow similarly contended that diplomatic recognition "sets up a system of communication whereby the views of this government can be made known privately to a foreign power, while our representatives can keep our government informed of trends and developments in countries to which they are accredited."[98]

Recognition might also be advisable, some observers contended, because it would signify America's willingness to make common cause with the peoples of Asia. Should the United States choose not "to keep a hand in the windows [sic] and a foot in the door, making it clear to as many Chinese as possible that their welfare is important to us and that we support their national ambitions," warned the *New Republic*, Americans would forfeit all the respect and affection of the Chinese people.[99] Worse yet, admonished the *Nation*, all of Asia, aware of the moderation with which the Chinese revolution had been conducted, would infer that the United States opposed the legitimate aspirations of popular revolutions everywhere.[100] Thus, Walter Lippmann concluded, "recognition of Red China is not a matter in which the President and Congress have free choice. . . . For how are we to cooperate in a policy to stabilize South Asia if, on the critical question of how to deal with Red China, we are determined not to cooperate with nations we wish to support?"[101]

In analyzing media views of the recognition issue, the State Department's opinion staff found not only a large number of moderate and widely read commentators who remained undecided but also smaller groups taking strong positions on either side of the question. The fewest number pressed for immediate recognition. Arguing that this would be the most "realistic and forthright" policy, the *Nation*, Jennings Perry of the *New York Compass*, and Max Lerner joined businessmen, university experts, and religious organizations in advocating early action. Among opponents of dealing with the CCP, the State Department identified the Scripps-Howard and Hearst chains. Although larger and more influential than the proponents of recognition, "this group," the POSS noted, "does not appear to be growing in size." Moreover, certain commentators who generally aligned themselves with the China policy critics had not indicated definite opposition to recognition. Ordinarily in the vanguard of pro-Chiang forces, both the Luce press and George Sokolsky had abstained from voicing their opinions. The McCormick press (*Chicago Tribune* and *Washington Times-Herald*) also abandoned its strictly pro-Nationalist stance, for while it rejected recognition as a policy serving British interests, it equally opposed nonrecognition.[102]

Although opposition and uncertainty continued into the new year, events during January 1950 encouraged many to resolve their indecision on China policy. On January 5, 1950 President Truman announced that the United States would not intervene in the Chinese civil war and would allow Taiwan to fall to the Communists. Secretary Acheson followed this declaration with a speech one week later which placed Taiwan outside the nation's defensive perimeter in Asia. The Administration's statements predictably engendered heated debate in the press— more so than China policy had occasioned in many years, noted the POSS. The *Philadelphia Inquirer*, long a critic of Administration China policy, asserted that Truman had given the Communists a "green light to seize Formosa." The *Omaha World Herald*, *Columbus Dispatch*, and the *Washington News* bitterly attacked the policy as "appeasement."[103] Department of State analysts, however, found that apart from "regular Administration opponents" the President's "decision has drawn an impressive array of support from editors, columnists, radio commentators and organizations." Among those applauding the President's stand POSS counted the *Washington Post*, *Atlanta Constitution*, *San Francisco Chronicle*, *Milwaukee Journal*, *New York Times*, *Christian Science Monitor*, *Dayton News*, and a host of others across the nation.[104]

By February 1950, despite Chinese Communist seizure of American consulate property in Peking, the State Department identified "a clear trend of thinking that recognition is inevitable, and will be the most realistic course for the U.S. to take." Those actively favoring recognition had, at the same time, increased in number and the vehement opposition remained, in comparison, a "small minority." Marquis Childs, for instance, had not expressed his views when the POSS compiled its November report, but by February he had emerged as an advocate of recognition.[105] Walter Lippmann, having found the Taiwan decision "clean and honorable," argued strongly for recognition in the near future.[106]

Responding to a crisis in China, President Truman and Secretary of State Acheson found that the policy they were formulating fit well within the bounds of majority press opinion. Editors and commentators had been shocked out of their admiration for Chiang Kai-shek by stories of ineptitude and corruption filed by correspondents in China. Throughout 1949 and early 1950, as the State Department gradually dissociated the United States from Chinese Nationalist war efforts, media agreement with the policy of disengagement grew. Despite provocative incidents, the great majority of observers rejected any thought of American military opposition to the Chinese Communists. As to the possibility of extending diplomatic recognition to those Communists, commentators expressed hesitancy and distaste, but over time came to accept the inevitability, even the necessity, of dealing with the CCP.

At the same time as majority opinion became more favorable toward a policy of recognition, a minority remained vehemently opposed to both disentanglement from the KMT and opening of relations with the CCP. Although State Department analysts consistently identified this group as small, they noted the influence that some members such as the Hearst and Scripps-Howard publishing houses exercised in the public domain. Thus even though the suggestions voiced by these dedicated proponents of the Kuomintang often were dismissed as unrealistic, the Administration kept a wary eye on them as it proceeded to devise a new China policy.

CHAPTER NINE

The Public, Congress, Scholars
Seeking the Limits

)◂▬▸()◂▬▸()◂▬▸()◂▬▸(

CONGRESSIONAL and public opinion, generally malleable, compliant, and permissive in response to Harry Truman's foreign policy initiatives, presented problems in regard to China. Although Congress as a whole displayed an almost complete indifference to Asia, certain voluble elements attempted to make China policy a test of America's wisdom and morality. The general public similarly ignored the distant demands of an unfamiliar place, but small numbers of dedicated China Lobbyists aroused dissension over Administration measures. The President and his Secretary of State, accustomed to leading, not following, the public and disdainful of the narrow vision it and its political representatives entertained in foreign affairs, chose to delay but not abandon realization of Administration objectives. Whereas informed opinion from businessmen or foreign observers contributed insights and information to the process of decision-making, these other constituencies functioned much more as barriers to dynamic policy planning. Truman and Acheson, therefore, expended time and energy during 1949 and early 1950 to ascertain the resistence Congress and the public would offer to new departures in China policy. Then they evolved strategies through which to educate and persuade the indifferent, the reluctant, and the ignorant of the proper course for American policy in China.

The views of America's electorate possessed an inherent importance which compelled officials to read and conduct polls to try to gauge the temper of the citizenry. But election campaigns rarely hinged on single issues, much less particular foreign policy developments, and surveys of public opinion revealed widespread ignorance and apathy about international relations.[1] In the midst of World War II an analyst found that interest in domestic affairs remained almost twice as great as concern with foreign affairs. During the Truman presidency, Americans gave their attention to strikes, inflation, housing shortages, and de-mobilization rather than to events occurring abroad. A 1947 Council on Foreign Relations study discovered that 3 out of every 10 American voters had no knowledge or awareness of United States foreign relations and that 65 out of every 100 admitted that they rarely discussed foreign affairs at all. In fact, although Americans had enthusiastically welcomed their country's membership in the United Nations, 31 percent could not describe the organization's functions in even the simplest terms in 1946. Pollsters found evidence of ignorance and apathy regarding Sino-American relations even more striking. For example, 60 percent of a group of adult Americans could not locate China on an outline map in 1942—this despite five years of war between China and Japan that had captured, sporadically, the front pages of the nation's press, in which the United States had been providing China with aid, and as a result of which, so the China Lobby would later claim, the United States had become involved in the Pacific War.[2]

A lack of information about modern Asia did not characterize the public alone. Ignorance of Kuomintang politics and of the development of Chinese Communism pervaded the Congress as well. The majority of Senators and Representatives shared with their constituents an almost complete indifference to China. If more conscious of foreign policy issues than the general citizenry, Congressmen nevertheless tended to subordinate their foreign-policy-making opportunities to involvement with concerns at home. Anxieties provoked by incidents which jeopardized the safety of Americans abroad subsided quickly under the press of domestic legislation. State Department officials desiring cooperation of Congressmen in the lengthy process of decision-making had to "be grimly determined to hunt them down and drag them there."[3]

The White House and the State Department might ignore an uninformed public but had to take notice of Congress, whatever its degree of enlightenment. Whereas China Lobbyists, however outspoken, could be overlooked among the millions of citizens who accepted Administration leadership, the Congressional China bloc, with its ability to form alliances with economy-minded and isolationist colleagues so as to obstruct Administration programs, demanded attention. The Administration begged, cajoled, and threatened legislators to secure support for its China policy, but always kept in mind the predominance of European over Asian interests. Bipartisanship made the Secretary of State's efforts easier in garnering votes for the Marshall Plan and the North Atlantic Treaty. As Acheson described the tactic, he would "say politics stops at the seaboard—and anyone who denies that postulate is a son-of-abitch and a crook and not a true patriot. Now if people will swallow that, then you're off to the races."[4] On China, however, the members of Congress gagged.

Confronted with a Congress and public generally ignorant about China and excitable because of cold war tensions, the Administration sought to prevent turmoil through propaganda. Having previously treated Chinese affairs with some of the same indifference that characterized attitudes among the citizenry and their legislative representatives, the White House and State Department belatedly undertook "educational" efforts in 1949. To give their informational activities wider currency and added weight, officials solicited help from interest groups and the academic world. The government invited businessmen, missionaries, and journalists to discuss policy alternatives with the appropriate agencies and disseminate Washington's views among their associates. Similarly, the State Department attempted to utilize the instructional abilities of China scholars to communicate with the nation. It asked sympathetic academics to participate in various Departmental meetings, hoping that, once cognizant of contemporary developments and the Administration's intentions, these individuals would become unofficial public spokesmen for the government.[5]

I The Public

Public awareness of developments in China, despite the crises of the 1940s, remained marginal. China's distance and strangeness kept concern at a minimum, and only grave individual disasters penetrated the general disinterest. Opinion polls taken throughout 1949 and early 1950 reflected this phenomenon. Although statistics on any specific question might suggest strong popular convictions, government analysts found the most dominant characteristic was the consistently large percentage of people with "no opinion." A telling example involved the State Department's major public relations effort—the China White Paper. The volume received considerable fanfare and press coverage upon its release in August, but a September 1949 Gallup poll revealed that 64 percent of those queried had never heard or read anything about the White Paper. Based on the results of this poll and another survey conducted by the National Opinion Research Center (NORC) in August 1949, the Office of Public Opinion Studies concluded that "the China area is one about which a great many people are either unable to express opinions or hesitant to make judgments. Uncertainty about what U.S. policy should be is pronounced."[6]

Popular ignorance and indecisiveness, in fact, characterized responses to most questions about China and American policy alternatives: 29 percent of a group questioned in November 1948 by NORC said that they took practically no interest in United States China policy, and by September 1949 that percentage had expanded to 38.[7] In a December 1948 Gallup poll, of the 79 percent of respondents who claimed to have read or heard about the Chinese civil war, 20 percent did not know the current status of the fighting and another 11 percent gave miscellaneous or vague answers. A mere 32 percent believed the CCP had been gaining ground and the Nationalists' situation had become desperate—this at a time when Kuomintang forces were sustaining their final, decisive defeat in the civil war.[8] In January 1949 on the question of whether the United States had aided Chiang Kai-shek's Nationalists sufficiently, 18 percent of the sample questioned had no opinion and an additional 15 percent had not heard of the civil war.[9] Similarly, after the publication and press coverage of the White Paper, 18 percent of those aware of the document's existence still had no opinion about the way their government had handled the situation in China, and in a second comparable group 25 percent could not decide whether the Truman administration had followed a sound policy.[10]

Regarding Chiang Kai-shek, American views also remained vague. In November 1948 a NORC survey revealed that 42 percent of the respondents did not know enough about Chiang Kai-shek's government to express an opinion about it.[11] In September 1949 Gallup pollsters found that 44 percent of their group either had no opinion about Chiang or had not heard of him. Thus, it is not surprising that findings in this same survey indicated that 31 percent of Gallup's respondents had no opinion about whether the United States should give aid to Chiang.[12] After the Nationalists had fled to Formosa and President Truman had publicly announced that the United States would not provide military assistance for defense of the island, 22 percent of those participating in a NORC inquiry had no opinion to express on the administration's decision. This proved true despite the very controversial nature of the President's position and the considerable coverage it received in the nation's media. Indeed, Dr. Gallup reported that only 49 percent of a February sampling showed any familiarity with the Formosa question. The staff of the Office of Public Affairs concluded that apparently "the agitation over Formosa among articulate observers did not equally affect the general public."[13]

On the issue of trade with the Chinese Communists, again a large number of people seemed to be confused or uninformed. A July 1949 Gallup poll revealed that 46 percent of those responding thought America should refuse to trade with the CCP, while 34 percent favored trade; 20 percent of the sample had no opinion on this issue. By November 1949 the opposition to trade had dropped to 33 percent, and those favoring continued trade had decreased to 29 percent. The group that had no opinion or claimed to be unfamiliar with events had grown to 38 percent.[14]

When pollsters focused on the central question of whether the United States should recognize the CCP, a sizable percentage failed to register an opinion. Although in each of six surveys a plurality opposed American recognition of the Chinese Communists, in only two did those opposed exceed 50 percent of the samples queried. Those who had no opinion, refused to answer, or did not know enough about the Chinese civil war to reply ranged from a low of 23 percent of the respondents in October 1949 to a high of 44 percent in early June 1950.[15] The apparent unwillingness of a large segment of the public to deal with the Chinese Communists did not, however, translate into convictions about what American policy should be. In separate polls conducted in August and September 1949, in response to the question "Is there anything the United States should do, in your opinion, to stop China from going Communist?" 36 percent of both groups approached replied no and 38 and 45 percent respectively did not know.[16]

State Department observers analyzing the above statistics remarked repeatedly upon the indecisiveness of public opinion and lack of information regarding China. Although surveys frequently revealed high proportions of people ignorant about foreign affairs issues, analysts believed that the consistency of sizable "no opinion" tallies in these polls showed "clearly . . . that there is not much public understanding of China policy." Moreover, the often large percentages of no opinion responses might actually be somewhat low, the Office of Public Affairs thought, because many individuals who "do not have positive suggestions of their own to make . . . will, nevertheless, take a position when they are presented with alternatives for action."[17] As for the majorities opposing trade and recognition, the Public Opinion Studies Staff noted in July 1949 that "these results apparently reflect the widespread distrust of dealings with any Communist regime—rather than considered opinions about our relations with China."[18] Bearing out this observation, the January 1950 NORC survey summarized the following reasons advanced for continuing America's diplomatic relations with Chiang Kaishek's regime:[19]

Oppose all Communism; should not recognize it:	30%
Recognition would strengthen Communists:	11
Recognition would help Russia:	7
Communists are aggressors, Chiang still there:	23
Chiang is anti-Communist, more friendly to us:	15
Miscellaneous reasons:	9
Don't know, vague, irrelevant reasons:	10
Total (some people gave more than one reason):	105%

Apathy and ignorance demonstrated in the polls reinforced the Administration's inclination to view public opinion as malleable rather than restrictive. Acheson and Truman both "thanked God" that the United States had been created a republic, not a democracy, so that elected representatives could "use their best judgment for the public interest"; for otherwise, by doing "what the people wanted, you'd go wrong every time."[20] George Elsey, among the President's chief advisers, worried less about errors generated by the public than its inability to provide any guidance at all. "You can't sit around and wait for public opinion to tell you what to do," Elsey observed. "In the first place there isn't any public opinion. The public doesn't know anything about it; they haven't even heard about it. The President must decide what he is going to do and do it, and attempt to educate the public to the reasons for his action."[21] George Kennan, head of the Policy Planning Staff and later a State Department consultant, considered professional diplomats an embattled elite surrounded by a world of foreign affairs ignoramuses.[22]

This disdain for the ability of the citizenry to determine policy, however, did not imply that the people could safely be left in the dark. The public, and indeed its representatives in Congress, needed to be led. Acheson recalled shortly after leaving the State Department that "almost 80 percent of your time, if you are on a policy job, is management of your domestic ability to have a policy."[23] Truman put it more graphically, quipping, "the President is . . . a glorified public relations man who spends his time flattering, kissing and kicking people to get them to do what they are supposed to do anyway."[24] Government's responsibility, then, in the view of its top officials of the time, was to originate programs, determine directions, and manipulate Congress and the public into volunteering their support.

Just two years earlier, in 1947, faced with economic crisis in Western Europe, the government had thrown its resources into creating national support for the Truman Doctrine. Aware of Congressional desires to trim the Federal budget and suspecting popular reluctance to become involved in long-term projects abroad, the administration used fear to produce unity. Greece and Turkey suddenly became the frontline in a struggle to preserve a free way of life from the evils of world communism. Administration officials met with Congress, lectured to the public, and encouraged newsmen to favor aid and to report Soviet imperialistic activities. The President also inaugurated a Federal Employee Loyalty Program to demonstrate to the nation that, as chief executive, he was determined to stop communism at home and abroad.[25] Opinion polls reveal that the public responded to these efforts. Gallup surveyors found that only 35 percent of their January 1947 sample approved of the way Truman handled the presidency; and, although his rating improved to 48 percent in February, his popularity did not reach 60 percent until after the Truman Doctrine propaganda campaign had begun. Poll data also show that the Administration succeeded in reversing an initial popular reluctance to have the government send military material and advisors to Greece or Turkey—turning 54 percent opposition into a 54 percent support over a period of eight months. Moreover, by September 1947, 68 percent of a sample group favored some form of American military intervention in the Greek situation—28 percent of these advocating a United Nations peacekeeping force with United States participation and 40 percent willing to have Washington, in cooperation with the UN, tell Russia "that any further move into Greece will be considered a declaration of war against the rest of the world."[26]

Forming a consensus on China policy did not elicit the same efforts as protecting Western Europe's security. Despite the global rhetoric of the Truman Doctrine speech, the President never intended to devote America's strength to fighting in Asia. The secondary nature of Chinese affairs in the scheme of American foreign relations made it easy for officials not to inform the public about developments in China. Thus in 1949, when the Nationalist debacle became imminent, the State Department and the White House confronted a confused audience unprepared for disaster and attuned to a cold war rhetoric of anticommunism. They needed guidance in understanding Chiang Kai-shek's fall and the Chinese Communist victory. Within limits, they approached the issue willing to listen to and accept the government's explanations.[27]

Policymakers, perceiving a hesitant but not inflexible public view of American China policy, cultivated support for disengagement from the Nationalists and eventual normalization of relations with the Communists. Poll data provided them with information on how best to neutralize opposition and accentuate areas of agreement. State Department analysts used published surveys and also contracted, on a confidential basis, for polls meeting their own specifications. Research then pinpointed zones of ignorance and illuminated the probable constraints which would be exercised by the very vocal pro–Chiang Kai-shek factions.[28]

In August 1949, the Department released its China White Paper whose letter of transmittal argued forcefully that the Kuomintang's imminent extinction had not been a product of American error. Washington had done all that it could, but Nationalist corruption and insensitivity to the needs of China's people had doomed American efforts.[29] Emphasizing the future, the State Department next launched a well-publicized review of the Asiatic situation and placed it under the direction of a prestigious nongovernmental committee. In a series of meetings with special interest groups during the summer and fall of 1949, the Department and the consultants hoped not only to ascertain possible reactions to recognition, but also to spread the word that such a policy might be in the nation's best interests.

American public opinion did not prevent United States recognition of the Chinese Communist regime. Official assessments of public views showed that the American people had few firmly held ideas about China policy. The State Department's Public Opinion Studies Staff found widespread ignorance and uncertainty, coupled with a clear preference for dealing with domestic problems and European concerns rather than with those of Asia. A majority of the American people, according to the polls, opposed opening diplomatic relations with the CCP, but surveys since January 1949 had indicated a similar lack of enthusiasm for aid to Chiang Kai-shek.[30] After President Truman, in January 1950, announced to the people that the United States would not send military aid to Taiwan to protect the Nationalists from a Communist takeover, a NORC poll showed 50 percent of the respondents approving of Truman's decision, only 28 percent disapproving, with 22 percent having no opinion.[31] The Administration therefore concluded that once the Nationalist regime had ceased to exist, opposition to recognition of the Communist Chinese government would most likely fade. Dean Acheson, moreover, trusted in his own abilities to persuade the nation once the time came. In view of popular confusion and indifference, had the government decided to push hard for early recognition, the public probably could have been convinced of the rightness of that policy. As it was, with Taiwan's fall imminent, the White House and the State Department decided to delay, seeing no particular reason not to await the most auspicious moment for action.

II Congress

Congress focused its attention on China policy at the behest of a small group of its members for whom developments in the East bore uncommon importance. This so-called China bloc worried about the future of Chiang Kai-shek and cooperated with the efforts of the China Lobby to perpetuate his Nationalist regime. Although Congress exercised little formal control over policy determinations regarding China, it possessed an unusual degree of influence in the late 1940s in the whole realm of foreign affairs. Since the most important postwar American policies required massive funding, Congress wielded ultimate authority over several critical issues. The China bloc, in turn, managed to ally itself with other dissenters from Administration programs and thereby exaggerate its own influence. An image of invincibility began to adhere to the group, even though in fact it secured only negligible appropriations for Chiang Kai-shek and barely kept an American commitment to the KMT leader alive.

Individuals outside Congress recognized the pivotal role that the legislative branch could play in developing America's China policy. As always, constituents appealed to their elected officials to support particular measures.[32] More significantly, the Chinese Nationalists viewed members of Congress as their most important resource in the United States. Chinese officials and hired lobbyists cultivated Senators and Representatives, hoping to swing their military aid votes, to induce them to speak out publicly on behalf of the Kuomintang struggle, and to acquire their assistance in exerting pressure on the Administration. The White House and the State Department, therefore, had to contend with a Congress primed from within and without to ask difficult questions about China.[33]

China policy became a Congressional battleground in the late 1940s only in part because of developments in China. A few members of Congress, such as Walter Judd (R, Minn.) and John Vorys (R, Ohio), had actually spent time there and felt a personal concern about the civil war and the Kuomintang cause. These men informed themselves about conditions in China and spoke often to their colleagues about the obligations the United States had toward its World War II ally.[34] Others joined the China bloc not because of any feeling for the Chinese people, but because they represented an anticommunist front. Styles Bridges (R, NH), for one, followed a variety of such causes, seeking to defend his own country against subversion or contagion.[35] Another group of Senators and Congressmen had their interest in China aroused by constituency pressures. Senator Pat McCarran (D, Nev.) labored to protect the silver producers of his state by urging appropriation of aid funds to China in silver and encouraging the Nationalist government's use of silver currency.[36]

By far the largest number in Congress participated in the China controversy for partisan reasons. Senator Tom Connally (D, Tex.), an Administration Democrat, supported every action President Truman took. The Robert Tafts and William Knowlands, on the other hand, opposed the White House and the State Department with a relish that their scant interest in China could not explain. They saw the Administration's ill-fated involvement in the Chinese civil war as a way to drive the "Democratic dynasty" out of power.[37] Convinced that Thomas Dewey would win the presidency in 1948, the Republicans had barely mentioned events in China during their campaign. Indeed, foreign policy matters assumed little importance in the race, and the Republicans avoided strong statements on issues like China so as not to commit their incoming leader to predetermined policies.[38] When Dewey lost, the Grand Old Party decided that the 1952 contest would have to be ruthless and that China offered a vulnerable area for attack.[39]

China could hardly have been an issue more perfectly designed for partisan controversy. Under the leadership of Arthur Vandenberg, internationalism and bipartisanship had characterized Congressional approaches to foreign affairs since World War II. A genius in compromise, coalition, and facesaving, the Republican Senator from Michigan worked astutely with President Truman to see that the United Nations, the Truman Doctrine, and the Marshall Plan gained Republican votes.[40] China policy, however, forgotten in the shuffle of pressing European and domestic crises, never earned sufficient status to merit party cooperation. The Administration made no effort to secure Republican support for its decisions, and the GOP barely challenged this Democratic preserve. Particularly when the war-hero General George C. Marshall went to China to settle its domestic turmoil, Republicans as well as Democrats felt content to let him do whatever he believed to be necessary. After Marshall's mission failed and the entire Roosevelt-Truman strategy appeared doomed, Republicans happily recalled that they had had nothing to do with the disaster.[41]

Criticism of the Administration's China policy, given impetus by Marshall's failure and Truman's victory, grew in volume and frequency through 1948, 1949, and 1950. Increasingly, certain members of Congress echoed the China Lobby theme that "the Chinese Communist conquest of Asia was not made possible in China." "It was engineered," Senator William Jenner (R, Ind.) declared, "right here in Washington, by the top policymakers of this Government."[42] In February 1949, 51 Republicans addressed a letter to President Truman inquiring about Administration plans to help noncommunist China. In March, 26 Republicans, joined by 24 Democrats (hoping to diminish growing partisanship) called for hearings on a proposal made by Senator McCarran to provide aid and

American advisors to the Kuomintang. Although some of the signatories did not favor McCarran's bill, they agreed that public airing of the China situation would serve the national interest. Senator Bridges, strongly supported by Knowland and McCarran, broadened the call in April by urging a full-scale investigation of United States China policy. From June to September 1949 the Senate debated confirmation of W. Walton Butterworth as the first Assistant Secretary of State for Far Eastern Affairs. Butterworth, having served as director of the Office of Far Eastern Affairs since September 1947, became the object of heated denunciations by the China bloc as "the symbol of failure and of a tragic era in our relations with China." Even Senator Vandenberg criticized the State Department for nominating a member of the old regime instead of bringing in a "fresh point of view."[43]

The discord developing between the executive and legislative branches of the government did not result entirely from disagreements concerning China. Dean Acheson, his aristocratic manner clashing with Congressional vanity, could not command the same loyalty or respect that Marshall had as Secretary of State.[44] Security questions, exacerbated by the Soviet Union's explosion of an atomic bomb years ahead of schedule and the discovery of communist spies in London and Washington, contributed to an atmosphere of suspicion and unease.[45] The House Foreign Affairs Committee, chronically ignored by the Senate and the Administration, chose the late 1940s to assert its importance in foreign policymaking by advocating actions and appropriations diametrically opposed to State Department and Senatorial decisions.[46] Despite creation of the post of Assistant Secretary of State for Congressional Relations in 1949, consultations between Congress and the Department did not proceed smoothly. State Department personnel, the Secretary foremost among them, tended to consider members of Congress ill-informed, motivated solely by the desire for election, and generally a bothersome group which distracted them from important work.[47] Accordingly, in January 1950, when the Administration announced it would not defend Formosa, Congress had not been included in the decision-making discussions. China Bloc Senators received their "forewarning" on the day of Truman's statement. Even if unintentional, such an oversight aggravated worsening relations by reminding Congress of its powerlessness in the realm of foreign affairs.[48]

Indeed, constitutionally Congress had no role in determining whether or not the United States would recognize the Chinese Communists. Since the White House could act independently, members of Congress who wished to voice an opinion on the subject had to operate as did members of other pressure groups. Senators and Representatives spoke with Administration officials, wrote letters, and made public statements expressing their viewpoints. They invited Ambassador Jessup's consultant group to parties and passed constituent mail on to State Department officers.[49] Although Walter Judd may have been the most verbose, lecturing across the country, others also spoke out frequently. Senator Pat McCarran, broadcasting regularly on Nevada radio, repeatedly discussed China policy.[50] Senator William Knowland complemented his Congressional responsibilities with ownership and editorial control of the *Oakland Tribune*, whose pages he used as a forum for discussing China. Knowland also appeared in open meetings on China policy and convinced Herbert Hoover to publicize his views about Formosa. Responding to the San Francisco Chamber of Commerce's advocacy of recognition for the Communist Chinese, Knowland made an outraged protest for which he secured national press coverage.[51]

Delegations of legislators met with State Department officials and occasionally with President Truman to be briefed on developments in China. China bloc members took these opportunities to chide government representatives on their misguided policies and present renewed demands for aid to Chiang Kai-shek.[52] Others, such as Senator Vandenberg, managed to use these sessions to modify Administration policy rather than attack it. In February 1949 Vandenberg objected to suspension of Economic Cooperation Administration aid to the Kuomintang, arguing convincingly that if the United States should "take *this* step at *this* fatefully inept moment, we shall never be able to shake off the charge that *we* are the ones who gave poor China the final push into disaster."[53]

Whereas other interested parties had to be content with this type of activity, Congress could exert more leverage by threatening to hold up or defeat legislation desired by the White House. Thus, China aid requests usually came up as amendments to European assistance programs which the President deemed essential for national and international stability—in 1947 in conjunction with Interim Aid, in 1948 with the European Recovery Program, and in 1949 as part of the Military Assistance Program. To assure itself of the votes needed to pass these measures, the Administration had to include provisions for Chiang's Kuomintang regime and could not follow its reasoned inclination to disassociate the United States from a losing cause. Further, to placate these Congressional critics Secretary of State Acheson promised Tom Connally that before taking affirmative action on recognition he would consult with the Senate Foreign Relations Committee.[54] Although the China bloc itself did not control a large number of votes, in alliance with economy-minded isolationists and legislators like John Taber (R, NY) and Kenneth S. Wherry (R, Neb.), it could present a formidable barrier

to approval of Administration plans.[55] Moreover, the China bloc occupied important positions in the Congressional bureaucracy from
which its members could exert a disproportionate degree of influence.
In the House, for instance, Representatives Judd and Vorys saw to it
that the Foreign Affairs Committee remained cognizant of developments
in China; and in the Senate H. Alexander Smith on the Foreign Relations
Committee and Styles Bridges and Pat McCarran on Appropriations
stridently supported requests for aid to China.[56]

Of those members of Congress who expressed an opinion on the subject, virtually all opposed recognition. As early as June 1949, twenty-
one Senators led by William Knowland addressed a letter to President
Truman urging him to state clearly that the Administration did not contemplate recognizing a Communist government in China. Recognition,
they declared, would be inconsistent with America's anti-Communist
stand in Europe. In May 1950 thirty-five Senators reiterated this plea.[57]
Representative Eugene O'Sullivan (D, Neb.) wrote President Truman
that, based on the volume of mail he had received, he believed the
people of Nebraska felt recognition would be a "vital blow to our real
Chinese friends and to religion," and Representative George Fallon of
Maryland said much the same about his constituents. Arguing most
vehemently against recognition in the Senate, Knowland, Bridges,
Smith, Jenner, and Homer Ferguson (R, Mich.) pointed to Moscow's
influence over the CCP and claimed that by opening relations with China
we would be granting world communism a stamp of approval. Senator
Knowland maintained, in October 1949, that in American history recognition had always meant approval of the Government recognized.
And Senator Bridges told colleagues that he did not think it would be
wise to allow China's subversive diplomats into the United States.[58]

Only a few Senators or Representatives dared voice a contrary view.
Worried about the attitude of the voting public, they feared the actions
of the China bloc—as Connally said to Knowland in January 1950: "You
are trying to get me to make a statement that you can quote."[59] Edwin
C. Johnson, Democratic Senator from Colorado and chairman of the
Interstate and Foreign Commerce Committee, nevertheless wrote Secretary Acheson in October 1949 that he favored recognition of the CCP.[60]
Utah's Elbert Thomas and Connally both declared recognition would
come as a practical matter.[61] Senator Warren Magnuson (D, Wash.),
speaking in January 1950, noted that all the information available to
Congress seemed to damn the Kuomintang thoroughly and that the CCP
did, after all, control China. The debate in the Senate, he asserted, had
been too one-sided.[62] Wayne Morse (Ind., Ore.) added the United States
might be isolating itself by refraining from an action that its allies seemed

anxious to take.[63] Arthur Vandenberg, although declaring his opposition to opening relations "at this immediate moment" conceded on January 9, 1950 that "realities may force an early abandonment of this position."[64]

Since forthright opposition to the China bloc occurred so infrequently, the bloc acquired an aura of great size and influence. In fact, this group and its sympathizers composed a minority in the Congress. Although the pro-Nationalists managed to keep aid to China flowing, the amounts of this assistance never approached the financing given Europe. Moreover, financial measures always issued from the Administration so as to placate the China sympathizers and facilitate passage of other measures, but time after time the economy-minded Congress cut them substantially. The China bloc failed in its efforts to have aid to China supervised on the Greek-Turkish pattern. Despite repeated calls for a thorough scrutiny of United States China policy, Congressional action did not materialize until after the Korean War erupted. The Senate Foreign Relations Committee actually pigeonholed a resolution submitted by Senator Knowland which would have created a joint bipartisan investigatory committee in the spring of 1949. Less than one-quarter of the Senate and perhaps one-eighth of the House persistently opposed the Administration's policies toward China, and far fewer than this did so because of developments in China. Furthermore, never once did the China bloc, any other member of Congress, offer a constructive, coherent, and rational program for China during the late 1940s.[65]

The advent of McCarthyism early in 1950 began the transformation of the China bloc from a relatively weak to a frighteningly powerful influence on American foreign policy.[66] Joseph McCarthy took charges that the Truman Administration had harbored communists and had thereby lost China and gave them lurid publicity. In April 1950 he captured headlines by accusing Owen Lattimore of being the Soviet Union's number one espionage agent in the United States. He revived the 1945 Amerasia case, renewing attacks on China-born foreign officer John Service. Ignorant of Chinese affairs and having no particular interest in the East, McCarthy used the issue to further his political career. The China Lobby and the China bloc, in turn, used the Senator, supplying him with information about his victims and the alleged Administration betrayals of Chiang Kai-shek.[67]

Long before the blight of McCarthyism took hold, however, the administration had received little help from the Congress. Members of the China bloc clamored for loyalty to discredited policies, and few other Congressmen voiced any opinion at all. Truman, Acheson and virtually all of the State Department staff dismissed the demands of the Nationalist partisans but found that minor concessions helped smooth relations with their Congressional critics. The Administration, therefore, remained tied, if loosely, to the Kuomintang long after enthusiasm for that connection had ceased to exist. Officials accepted this state of affairs, believing that with the fall of Taiwan to CCP troops, Congress, like the public, could be convinced that a new departure in China policy had become necessary.

III Scholars

World War II forced America's community of Asian scholars to abandon their antiquarian interests and deal with modern events. In the early 1940s wartime intelligence organizations, such as the Office of War Information and the Office of Strategic Services, solicited the help of historians and political scientists in trying to understand Asia. Instrumental in planning for the postwar occupation of Japan, university Asian experts also played prominent roles in attempting to assess the course of Chinese affairs. At the war's end, a group of specialists interested in pursuing their studies of modern China returned to the universities and set about changing traditional curriculums. Academics had habitually abjured the study of events occurring in twentieth-century China, dismissing anything that recent as journalism. Many resisted the postwar innovations, but by 1949 Columbia University had established its East Asian Institute and in 1956 a more conservative Harvard University had followed with its East Asian Research Center.[68]

Despite the undeveloped state of contemporary Chinese studies, the government looked to the academic world in 1949, as it had during the war years, for help in making China policy and in explaining it to the American people.[69] Having identified American interests with the fate of Nationalist forces in China for so long, the United States government suddenly had to explain why Chiang's demise would not jeopardize the nation's welfare and why the United States bore no responsibility for the disaster. Officials undertook two complementary strategies to reassure the populace. First they sought to explicate past policy by publishing the China White Paper. This heavily documented account of Sino-American relations in the modern era, however, addressed itself primarily to a scholarly audience. Its sheer size (1,054 pages) limited readership to some China Lobby types, a few reporters, and students of Chinese affairs. Philip C. Jessup, Ambassador-at-Large and a professor of international law at Columbia University, made the final editorial judgments regarding the volume, and China specialists such as

Nathaniel Peffer of Columbia University read over sections of the text.[70] Along with publication of the White Paper, Secretary of State Acheson announced that the government had decided to initiate a thorough study of America's future policies in Asia. To assure maximum objectivity, the review would be conducted not by State Department personnel, but by consultants. Ambassador Jessup headed the effort and selected the president of Colgate University, Everett Case, and the former president of the Rockefeller Foundation, Raymond B. Fosdick, to assist him.[71]

In conducting the 1949 reassessment, the consultants relied upon the views of a variety of scholars, as well as their own research and State Department documentation. Ambassador Jessup sent a letter soliciting opinions on American China policy to some fifty prominent people who "either had extensive personal experience in the Far East or have made the area or some part of it the field of their special activity."[72] Among those from whom Jessup requested memoranda, almost half held university posts.[73] In addition, a number of academics submitted their ideas to the consultants independently.[74] Since Case, Fosdick, and Jessup lacked any extensive prior exposure to China, the information so transmitted provided welcome background detail in what Everett Case came to call the "learning phase."[75]

The State Department also organized a Round Table Conference in October 1949 to discuss American China policy. With one of the consultants presiding, the twenty-five attendees received briefings by key diplomatic, military, and intelligence officers. Then the conferees, more than half of whom were academics, examined United States alternatives in the East.[76]

The issues of trade with and recognition of the Chinese Communists arose repeatedly during the sessions. As State Department observers noted, majority opinion favored both trade and recognition.[77] Kenneth Colgrove of Northwestern University alone among the scholars present argued that the Kuomintang had a future in China. Although the possibility that the CCP functioned as a tool of Moscow was suggested by one participant (and rejected by others), several of the university professors agreed that only by maintaining a presence in China could the United States hope to reduce Soviet influence. If it wanted to preserve its position in Asia, Washington must not appear to be "punishing the people of China for having a government that wasn't approved in advance by the United States," warned Owen Lattimore of Johns Hopkins. The scholars asserted that the response of the American public should Washington open relations with a Chinese Communist regime would not be a serious problem. Most believed that forthright leadership from the government would easily convince the people that trade and recognition best served America's interests. United States policy, Nathaniel Peffer of Columbia asserted, could not run contrary to "our better judgment" simply to please Henry Luce and the China lobbyists.[78]

China specialists, when not talking directly to policymakers, sought to reach officials, associates and the public through newspapers, magazine articles, and books. Owen Lattimore and John Fairbank outstripped their colleagues in such literary output. Lattimore, by 1949, had established himself as one of the nation's foremost experts on China. During World War II he had served as American adviser to Chiang Kai-shek, a position which gave him little chance to affect Chinese policy but an unusual opportunity to observe China's politics.[79] As director of the Johns Hopkins School of International Affairs in the late 1940s he had easy access to government officials and commented often on America's possible courses of action. Lattimore also lectured to public groups across the country, explaining conditions in China and attempting to make the American people understand that "China is a fact. The Chinese Communists are a fact . . . [and] American policy in Asia must start with the admission that these facts cannot be conjured out of existence, or be made amenable either to the tactics of blandishment or the tactics of the bludgeon."[80]

Less well-known, but increasingly respected by those in the China field, John Fairbank published ten articles and two books between late 1948 and mid-1950.[81] Like Lattimore, he had established links with the government through OSS-OWI service in World War II and spent 1945 and 1946 as the director of the United States Information Service. Fairbank, the quintessential instructor, tried to teach his countrymen about the realities of life in China, which differed so drastically from their own experience. Communism in China no doubt was "real Communism," he explained, but as long as it fed and clothed them it seemed to be "a relatively good thing for the Chinese masses."[82] "The greatest error Americans can make," he warned, "is to look at China but think only of Russian expansion." In fact "the Chinese Communist success helps Russia, but," he reasoned, it "cannot be equated with Russian conquest of China. We have to face up to the fact that the Communist movement is not only genuinely Communist, but also genuinely Chinese."[83] The United States must continue to maintain contacts with the Chinese people so that the latter would have an alternative to total dependence on the Soviets. "If the Chinese people are in reality falling victim to police terror and the Russian squeeze, we have to let them find it out for themselves." Meanwhile, Fairbank declared on *Town Meeting of the Air* in December 1949, "nonrecognition by us would play into Russian hands," creating an American-built Iron Curtain. Instead, he wrote in

January 1950, the United States ought to reject defeatist and isolationist policies and compete with Russia in China by granting recognition to the Chinese Communists.[84]

Scholars who believed that the American government should establish relations with the CCP outnumbered those who did not. The president of the Far Eastern Association reported to the members of the Senate Foreign Relations Committee and the House Foreign Affairs Committee that a pro-recognition speech by Cornell University's Knight Biggerstaff at the December 1949 meeting of the American Historical Association did not occasion a single dissenting remark.[85] The consultants found that, if some China specialists hesitated over the timing of recognition, almost all agreed it would be a necessary and intelligent policy.[86] L. Carrington Goodrich of Columbia University wrote Ambassador Philip C. Jessup that the United States should recognize the Chinese Communists and utilize American diplomats, businessmen, and missionaries to make known to the Chinese "our contrasting way of life."[87] On ABC radio in December 1949 Columbia professors C. Martin Wilbur and Henry DeVries spoke out in favor of recognition, emphasizing, as had Goodrich, the importance of keeping channels of communication open to the Chinese people.[88] Mary Wright in the *Foreign Policy Bulletin* urged contact with the CCP, counselling that "anti-foreign propaganda, which is nothing new in Chinese nationalist movements, should not stop us from making a realistic effort to come to terms." Her article, reprinted by the *St. Louis Post-Dispatch*, reached a varied public audience, and the State Department's Public Opinion Studies Staff (POSS) quoted from it in their weekly circular summarizing comment on China.[89]

State Department officials, in fact, took frequent note of academic opinion. The special opinion reports of POSS, as well as the Weekly Summaries of Comment on China, mentioned articles written by experts on Asia and often quoted from them. They also reported the sentiments of international affairs organizations and reproduced in detail the result of a Council on Foreign Relations poll concerning the issue of recognition.[90] Like articles and letters from journalists, those of academic observers of the Chinese scene also occasionally circulated around the Department. Although once the consultants arrived they tended to use most of this type of information for their own edification, they continued to disburse the most informative materials to professional colleagues.[91]

In 1949 and 1950, faced with the imminent collapse of Kuomintang China and the question of whether to extend recognition to the CCP regime, the Administration turned to the scholarly community for help in decision-making and public relations work. Officials often considered academics too inexperienced in practical affairs to be of much use to

government, but in the case of Chinese matters they found the insights
of an Owen Lattimore, who had resided in Chiang Kai-shek's Chungking residence during the war, or a Doak Barnett, who had traveled extensively among the Communists and Nationalists, to be extremely valuable. State Department officers also cooperated actively with the policy
reevaluation conducted by Jessup, Case, and Fosdick, aware not only
of its inherent importance, but also of the pressures it redirected away
from their own endeavors.

The government, in fact, considered the China scholars useful allies
in addressing the problems raised by public and Congressional objections to United States China policy. The China specialists took a very
practical approach to Chinese relations, asserting in strong, well-rea-
soned, and apolitical terms that Washington should maintain contact
with the Chinese people whether under Communist domination or not.
They pointed forcefully in a direction which, the State Department believed, public opinion did not bar and only a minority in Congress vehemently opposed.

The patterns which policymakers came upon in the dust scattered by
China's fall did not trace a consistent design easy to follow, and yet
gradually, officials could identify a direction most congenial to the preferences and imperatives of interest groups, foreign governments, the
Congress, and the public. Whether from informed or uninformed constituencies, opinion developed outside the halls of state automatically
suffered a discount in the minds of decision makers privy to special
sources of intelligence. China more than most problem areas, however,
left officials in need of extragovernmental support. Often ignorant about
Asian affairs, they found journalists and scholars helpful. Forced to
chose between a winning and losing side in a civil war where communism distorted the alternatives, they invited the observations of foreign governments, American businessmen, and even missionaries.
White House and State Department investigation established that the
Administration retained considerable flexibility in formulating and securing approval for its China policy. Should it decide to remain allied
to Chiang Kai-shek and abandon efforts to reach an accommodation with
the mainland regime, emphasizing the fearsome communist nature of
that Chinese government could heighten popular anxiety to the point
that Americans would welcome isolation from China. But if Washington
chose to recognize the Chinese Communists, it could capitalize on a
widespread willingness to accept relations with the CCP. It could, moreover, utilize the academic, business, religious, and journalistic communities to explain to a confused and generally indifferent citizenry and
Congress why dealing with the Communist Chinese would serve America's best interests.[92]

CHAPTER TEN

The State Department and the White House

A Decision Unrealized

)⬤▶()◀⬤▶()◀⬤▶()◀⬤▶(

WHETHER America would recognize the Communist regime in China hinged ultimately on the President of the United States and his foreign-affairs advisors. Editors and commentators, China Lobbyists, and even Congressmen could accomplish nothing unless they exerted influence on the Chief Executive. If businessmen wished to trade in China and missionaries to proselytize, they had to make the White House and the State Department aware of their concern. Thus, during 1949 and early 1950, each group pressed its opinions upon policymakers, hoping to prompt a decision which would advance its own interests.

Questions of China policy, however, competed for Truman and Acheson's attention with a host of domestic and foreign problems during this period. The President had to outmaneuver a Soviet blockade of Berlin, cope with an Arab-Israeli war in the Middle East, and worry about the growth of communist power in South America. In September 1949, he had to tell the American people that Moscow had exploded its own atomic bomb. Since America's scientific and military experts had put a Soviet breakthrough years in the future, it appeared that espionage had subverted the nation's security. And, indeed, cases of spying in the United States, as well as in Canada and Great Britain, contributed to a growing uneasiness. Economic imbalances in Europe and at home further alarmed the public. American monies still fueled Europe's war-shattered economies and kept Japan's from collapsing. A recession during the first half of 1949 in the United States and threats of depression concentrated thinking still more upon the West and away from developments in China. Limited resources had to be used where they would serve America's most important goals.[1]

American officials also assigned China a low priority in the hectic

months between January 1949 and June 1950 because of personal inclination. The State Department and the White House shared an Atlantic
orientation. Neither Harry Truman nor Dean Acheson possessed any
particular knowledge or understanding of China, and both considered
the increasing amount of time that this Asian nation demanded of them
an imposition. During the eighteen months from January 1949 to June
1950, when the issues of trade and recognition came to the fore, each
sought to serve the best interests of the United States. Yet they approached Chinese affairs without the vigor or imagination that earlier
had produced a European Marshall Plan.[2]

The President took an erratic part in making and administering China
policy. His career had always been tuned almost exclusively to internal
politics, and as chief executive he gave the State Department considerable freedom to guide the nation's foreign relations.[3] In George C.
Marshall and Dean Acheson he had secretaries of state whose judgment
and intelligence he respected and relied upon.[4] Particularly with regard
to China, Truman kept only marginally informed and rarely intervened.[5]
On the occasions when he did intercede his motives included the desire
to preserve America's prestige, to protect the nation against communist
encroachments, and to defend Administration programs against partisan opponents. In the spring of 1947 Truman sided with his military
advisors in ending the arms embargo designed to make Chiang Kai-shek
more amenable to compromise with the CCP.[6] In 1949 he became infuriated by the detention of Consul General Ward in Mukden and, had
the State Department not restrained him, the President might have followed through on his threat to blockade China's coast.[7] Truman probably also vetoed Ambassador Stuart's proposed trip to Peking in the
spring of 1949 to talk with Mao Tse-tung and Chou En-lai. The President
had already committed his Administration to a gradual disassociation
from the Kuomintang but objected to any action which would imply
eagerness to deal with the CCP. As President, he feared jeopardizing
vital European legislation by antagonizing pro-Chiang members of Congress. Stuart remained accredited to the Nationalist regime and could
not properly discuss relations with officials in Peking. Truman, in fact,
wanted the Ambassador to stop in Canton to reestablish contact with
KMT authorities before he returned to the United States. Here again
State Department officials interceded lest such a trip further alienate the
CCP and give the KMT false hopes.[8]

The President nurtured and took pride in the anticommunist image
that he gave his Administration. He delighted in describing his spring
1945 meeting with V. M. Molotov and the harsh warning about Russian
behavior that he had given the Soviet Foreign Minister. His determi-

nation to enhance America's world power during his presidency led him to oppose any efforts by the Soviets to expand their own influence abroad. "The USSR," he affirmed, "has engaged the United States in a struggle for power, or 'cold war,' in which our national security is at stake and from which we cannot withdraw short of eventual suicide." Truman's attitude grew not only out of his personality and patriotism, but also out of his desire to impress the American public. A worthy successor to Franklin Roosevelt must provide dynamic leadership and Truman found the rhetoric of cold war anticommunism a congenial way to reach the people. In his efforts to sell the Truman Doctrine, for instance, the President exaggerated the menace and proposed a campaign to rescue the world from rapacious Soviet communism.[9]

In fact, Harry Truman maintained a more flexible approach to the China problem. Guided by State Department analyses provided through Dean Acheson, the President refused to cut the United States off from possible accommodation with the Chinese Communists.[10] Despite his rhetoric, he did not see the communist world as monolithic and entertained doubts as to the degree of control Moscow had over the CCP. During 1949 he remarked to Senator Arthur Vandenberg "that the Russians will turn out to be the 'foreign devils' in China and that the situation will establish a Chinese government that we can recognize and support."[11] In June, therefore, he approved a guarded but not uninterested reply to Chou En-lai's démarche.[12] Remarking upon a message from his old friend former Congressman Maury Maverick, in which Maverick had recommended that the American government should find a way to negotiate with and recognize the Chinese regime, Truman called it "the most sensible letter I've seen on the China situation."[13] Truman also expressed interest in retaining an American presence in areas passing over to the Chinese Communists.[14] He did not relish the prospect of recognizing a CCP government but accepted the possibility that this might become necessary.[15] In an October 19, 1949 press conference Truman refused to discuss the circumstances under which the United States would consider recognizing the CCP. He made his reluctance clear, adding, "I hope we will not have to recognize it." However, he did not rule recognition out. After meeting with the China consultant group in November 1949, the President told his Secretary of State that he had gotten fresh insights and a better understanding of the China imbroglio. In fact, he found merit in the suggestion that Washington attempt to exploit Sino-Soviet frictions by having economic and political relations with China as it did with Yugoslavia.[16]

Truman's willingness, however grudging, to contemplate future relations with the Communist Chinese proceeded also from his disillusionment with the Kuomintang. He had tried to cooperate with and support Chiang Kai-shek's regime, only to watch it disintegrate because of ineptitude and corruption. He had sent one of the men he most admired to attempt a reconciliation in China but was forced to watch George Marshall grow ever more frustrated and finally fail. "The Generalissimo's attitudes and actions," Truman reflected, "were those of an old-fashioned warlord, and, as with the warlords, there was no love for him among the people. There is no doubt in my mind that if Chiang Kai-shek had been only a little more conciliatory an understanding could have been reached."[17] Early in 1949 the President seriously entertained the possibility of ending military aid to the Nationalists, and only the objections of Congressional representatives deterred him. Even then he instructed the National Security Council not to expedite shipments.[18] Soon thereafter he endorsed the White Paper project to clarify developments in China for the American people, absolve his administration of responsibility for the disaster, and loosen Washington's ties with the Nationalist government.[19] When Congress appropriated $75 million to be used in the general area of China, the President thwarted pro-Chiang partisans by using the funds elsewhere in Asia.[20] By December 1949 he had thrown his weight behind the State Department in NSC deliberations and rejected the idea of providing last-minute military succor to the remnants of Chiang's army on Taiwan.

Although Harry Truman reserved the final decision-making power to himself as President, the State Department enjoyed primary responsibility for fashioning an American China policy. The national military establishment contributed observations and exerted influence through the NSC, but ultimately it could not overrule recommendations from diplomatic officials. In its deliberations the Department of State suffered less from the interference of the military, although on occasion this proved troublesome, than from the dearth of expertise on China within its own ranks. China specialists had always been scarce, but the resources had been further depleted by Patrick Hurley's purge in 1945. The China staff both in Washington and in the field had a heavily European background and orientation. W. Walton Butterworth, who served as Director of the Office of Far Eastern Affairs and later became Assistant Secretary for the Far East, had been stationed in Spain before his brief and unwelcome sojourn in China. Although an excellent administrator and a highly competent foreign service officer, he had only a marginal familiarity with China. Philip C. Jessup, put in charge of evolving a new China policy in the summer of 1949, had been associated with the Institute of Pacific Relations, but had never devoted any particular attention to Asian matters. His special field of interest, international law, more accurately meant law in the Western world. Similarly, men such as John Cabot, Consul General in Shanghai, and John Melby, press officer in Nanking and later a compiler of the White Paper, plunged into a volatile situation in a country whose language they did not speak and of whose history they had no knowledge. The China Division within the State Department actually operated under the Assistant Secretary for European Affairs until a reorganization in 1949.[21]

The tendency to view China from a European perspective sharpened the obvious parallel between America's earlier decision to recognize the Soviet Union and the pending question regarding China. For sixteen years the United States had refused to acknowledge the existence of a communist government in Russia. In the interim American companies had done business with the Soviets and commercial interests in the United States had become dissatisfied with the restraints imposed on trade expansion by the lack of diplomatic relations. Finally, in 1933 Franklin Roosevelt reversed the government's policy, having obtained from Moscow's representative several guarantees.[22] To some Truman Administration officials Russia's subsequent noncompliance with these promises testified not merely to Soviet duplicity but to the probable dishonesty of the Communist Chinese as well. Moreover, they argued that the United States had obtained few real benefits from recognition. Others countered that the prolonged period of nonrecognition had achieved nothing except to make the United States look foolish. The Soviet Union had survived quite well without Washington's coopera-tion. The American Ambassador in Moscow asserted that prompt rec-ognition might have allowed Americans to influence the course of events in Russia or, at the very least, permitted them to prepare the people and government of the United States for the threat to democratic insti-tutions developing under Russian Communism. In any case, the Am-bassador noted, the use of long-delayed recognition as a bargaining device had not rendered the Soviets more willing to abide by pledges made in 1933 than they would have been in 1917. Recognition, he main-tained, should be treated as a technical matter and extended to Com-munist China so that the United States could function there as it did in Russia's Balkan satellites and in Latin America.[23]

State Department officials tried to assess the effect that opening dip-lomatic contacts with the CCP might have on America's international relations. Washington had hoped to create a unified front among the Western powers which would delay recognition of the CCP until certain minimum standards of behavior had been adhered to. As time passed the desire of various governments, especially Great Britain's, to press ahead with relations for economic and other reasons splintered the coalition.[24] The United States, Department analysts believed, increasingly appeared obstinate in refusing to adopt a policy which its allies favored and clinging to one which had proved fruitless in dealing with the USSR. Not only did Washington seem unreasonable and impractical to European observers,[25] but in Asia the United States began to be seen as an opponent of nationalism. Although various Asian governments viewed the Communist Chinese with apprehension, they nonetheless felt pride in the success of an Asian neighbor. In an era of anticolonial struggles, the image of a resurgent China chasing the foreigners out won sympathy throughout the region.[26] American efforts to protect these countries against communism by containing it threatened to isolate the United States.[27]

Nonrecognition of the Chinese Communists by the United States, moreover, jeopardized Japan's postwar recovery. Americans feared the influence of communism on the Japanese, who in the midst of an economic, political, and psychological crisis appeared vulnerable to subversion and intimidation. But at the same time, Japan's traditional links with the mainland Chinese, if allowed to revive, promised a more rapid recovery and one that would substantially lighten the financial burdens being placed on the American people. To facilitate this contact, however, Washington must not delay too long lest British merchants close the Americans and Japanese out of China's markets.[28]

American officials also considered the impact of recognition on the Communist bloc. The United States risked strengthening the Soviet camp by recognizing and trading with a Russian satellite state. If American business supplied China's enormous demands, that would permit Moscow to direct its resources elsewhere. On the other hand, if the United States did not sell goods to China, the drain on Russia's economy might slow its growth and a weakened Soviet state would be less dangerous in Europe. Cyrus L. Sulzberger, writing in the *New York Times* after a series of briefings by John Paton Davies of the Policy Planning Staff, noted Washington's belief that "instead of gaining an area replete with the sinews of power, the USSR is tending to acquire a major interest in a morass of misery where famine is a calendrical occurrence." According to Sulzberger the government felt that, once having established "a truly cozy relationship with Mr. Mao," the Russians would find they could not "provide the necessary cadre and assistance for the Chinese," and so would "wear themselves out . . . just as General Chiang did."[29]

But the possibility that Mao Tse-tung might develop into another Tito caught the imagination of the State Department staff and made diplomatic relations with China appealing. If the Chinese were to follow an independent path, their disaffection would effectively embarrass the

Soviet bloc and decrease the worldwide threat of communism. To bring Sino-Soviet tensions to the fore more quickly, the United States must reduce Peking's dependency upon the Soviet Union. American commodities and technical expertise proferred along with diplomatic contacts would be vital. Moreover, Americans could best exploit rifts in the communist alliance if they resided in China and observed developments there directly. In March 1949 the National Security Council, with President Truman's approval, adopted a State Department recommendation that the United States follow a liberal trade policy designed to lure China away from Moscow's embrace.[30]

Speculation on the willingness of the Chinese Communists to maintain some freedom from Soviet domination and reach an accommodation with the United States shaped much of the recognition debate. CCP behavior which appeared alternately conciliatory and provocative produced a great deal of uncertainty. Lewis Clark, American Minister Counsellor in Canton, found the Communist Chinese thoroughly unscrupulous and believed that they followed orders from the Kremlin.[31] O. Edmund Clubb, Consul General in Peking, credited the CCP with much more nationalistic fervor and contended that the Party's determination to serve China's interests would produce a degree of independence from Moscow that the United States could exploit.[32] Ambassador J. Leighton Stuart vacillated between images of the Chinese Communists as puppets and as patriots.[33]

State Department analysts realized that differing assessments of the CCP stemmed, in part, from disunity within the Party. An influential faction had aligned China closely with the Soviet Union, but there also existed a moderate group which sought better relations with the United States. American observers—official and unofficial—hoped that the United States could strengthen the moderates by satisfying China's economic needs. Since the Soviet Union could not provide China with an equal quantity, quality, or variety of goods, the pro-Moscow hard-liners ought to suffer by comparison. The State Department, therefore, kept American service representatives in areas passing under communist control so that CCP moderates could make contact with them.

Repeated anti-American incidents, however, led to discouragement. The CCP refused to acknowledge the status of American diplomatic personnel in China, because the United States had not recognized their regime and U.S. representatives remained accredited to the Nationalists. Whether perceived as arrogance or inexperience or extreme sensitivity about Chinese sovereignty, this attitude produced anger and frustration among American officers. Subsequent occasions of violence, the holding of consulate staffs incommunicado, and the denial of exit visas all gave impetus to the conviction that, despite CCP guarantees protecting foreigners in China, Americans were in danger.

Concern grew also among private American citizens in China. Businessmen, missionaries, and journalists had refused evacuation and lingered in areas falling to the Chinese Communist armies. They had hoped to establish ties with the incoming authorities, who would require expertise and goods for building a new nation. CCP propaganda promised that their lives and property would be safe and that their skills would be needed in the months ahead. But labor violence, travel bans, and press restrictions escalated apprehension into fear.

Nevertheless, many Americans, inside and outside the government, argued that recognition of a CCP regime would improve conditions. Observers noted that for a massive revolution, capping decades of warfare, the situation in China involved surprisingly little violence against foreigners. Widespread retribution for past acts of exploitation, real or imagined, did not erupt. Daily life in China had not become filled with terror.[34] Instances of discrimination and intimidation happened to all foreigners; Americans suffered more simply because their government continued to supply the Kuomintang. If this pointless intervention in the Chinese civil war stopped, as the American community in China urged, then the primary cause of anti-American feeling would disappear. Missionaries appealed to the State Department and the President to give them the opportunity to work in China by recognizing the CCP regime. Businessmen told American officials that they anticipated expanding trade relations if only Washington would provide the security of diplomatic relations. The Director of the Office of Far Eastern Affairs observed that some of the disagreeable conflicts based on CCP refusal to acknowledge the status of American diplomats were no doubt occasioned by Washington's own attitude. So concerned were officials not to grant de facto recognition prematurely, they instructed representatives in China not to use formal titles in addressing CCP authorities and not to attend official functions.[35]

Far removed from the danger zone themselves, officials at the State Department hesitated over the proper response to disturbances in China. They repeatedly issued warnings to Americans not yet under Communist control and provided evacuation facilities to those who wished to leave CCP territory.[36] They reduced staffing at some consulates and decided to close others. The State Department also worried about the potential trouble inherent in espionage operations and tried to curb these.[37] But although anxious to protect American citizens, throughout 1949 and into 1950 officials encouraged businessmen to remain in China and spoke of the contribution that missionaries made in keeping channels of communication open between the Chinese and American people. They welcomed American willingness to maintain enterprises in China and sought to keep American diplomatic outposts there as well.[38]

Given foreign and domestic pressures, the State Department preferred to move slowly regarding relations with China. If the United States waited for the dust to settle, events might render decision unnecessary. Neither Truman nor Acheson wanted to facilitate consolidation of communist control over the Chinese people. At the same time, they objected to continuing support of a Kuomintang regime which despoiled the nation for private gain and in the end would probably lose to the Communists anyway. They chose to disengage from the KMT and move toward relations with the Communists, postponing any forthright action until a national government had been declared and substantial resistance to the CCP ceased.

For American policymakers ties with Chiang Kai-shek proved exceedingly difficult to sever. However willing for practical reasons some State Department officers might be to contemplate recognition of the Chinese Communists, such a compromise with their anticommunist principles provoked considerable anxiety. American awareness that China desperately needed fresh leadership had led to momentary acceptance of a myth which characterized the Chinese Communists as agrarian rebels and reformers. When that illusion was dispelled, Americans had to choose between supporting Chinese Communism or perpetuating Chiang Kai-shek's rule. Efforts to aid Li Tsung-jen in his challenge to Chiang's leadership or to promote a coup d'état by General Sun Li-jen demonstrated the degree of disgust felt in Washington with Chiang's misrule. The Generalissimo's authority, however, remained so pervasive and Li and Sun's power so weak that alternatives did not exist. American analysts also feared that a new government on Taiwan would not win diplomatic recognition internationally and would be perceived as an American puppet regime. The United States therefore continued to aid Chiang rather than be blamed for removing the single figure resisting the CCP advance.[39]

Political turmoil in the United States discouraged the Democratic Administration from adopting a more adventuresome policy. With the national welfare dependent upon Republican votes in Congress for European aid and defense plans, President Truman sought to minimize conflict over China. The Republican Party, on the other hand, frustrated in the 1948 presidential election, had launched an intensive search for issues that would embarrass the Democrats. Looking back at the campaign which had culminated in Harry Truman's victory, Republican leaders identified bipartisanship as a major part of the problem. Since World War II, the GOP had repeatedly subordinated its political interests to support Administration foreign policies in the name of national security. Even those concerned about developments in China had subdued their criticism anticipating a Dewey victory and not wanting to foreordain their candidate's policy. Once Dewey lost, however, the Republicans abandoned discretion and attacks on China policy mounted.

In fact, the China issue fit perfectly with Republican charges that the Democrats had spent sixteen years in the White House coddling communism. Although Harry Truman had himself given impetus to the growth of a red scare in the United States through the publicity attending the Truman Doctrine, the Democratic Administration became a victim of developing anticommunist hysteria. Republicans argued that in China the United States threatened to abandon not merely a trustworthy World War II ally, but also an important front in the global struggle against communism. How could the President expect Congress to appropriate billions to stop Russia in Europe when it allowed the Soviets a free hand in Asia? Worse yet, some Republicans suggested, subversives in the State Department had actually encouraged the Communist takeover in China. During World War II they had attempted to supply the CCP with weapons, and during the Marshall Mission they had tried to force Chiang Kai-shek into a coalition government. Clearly, these Republicans asserted, Washington, not Nanking, had lost the Chinese civil war.[40]

During the autumn of 1949 attempts to devise an American policy to reverse this trend and save the Kuomintang came from the military establishment. General MacArthur, exhorted the President to help Chiang Kai-shek stop communism by providing funds and military guidance.[41] Defense Secretary Louis Johnson, nursing presidential ambitions, urged the Joint Chiefs of Staff to declare Taiwan strategically vital to the United States. He contended that their refusal to recommend even a fact-finding mission to the island resulted from subjection to unwarranted political pressures and did not represent a strictly military assessment of the situation.[42] Past positions of the Joint Chiefs on China did suggest a lack of conviction behind their hands-off policy. Repeatedly since 1945, the JCS had advocated an active military involvement by the United States in China. In 1945 they had suggested a virtual protectorate, with special economic and military privileges being accorded to the United States in exchange for assistance.[43] During 1947 and 1948 they pressed scaled-down plans upon the President, claiming that even small amounts of help would strengthen Nationalist morale while it discouraged the CCP. The Joint Chiefs rejected any thought that the CCP might develop an independent nationalist stance, calling the

Party "Moscow inspired" and dismissing its members as "tools of Soviet policy." Therefore, the JCS warned in December 1948 that, should the mainland fall completely under Chinese Communist control, denial of Taiwan to Kremlin-directed exploitation would be critical in protecting important sea routes in the Western Pacific.[44]

The disparity between America's military strength and its global objectives, which became increasingly apparent during 1949, diminished JCS enthusiasm for opposing the Soviet Union in China. Not only had the Soviet Union exploded its own nuclear device, thus increasing the United States' long-term vulnerability, but also the military services had to deal with a $14.4 billion budget ceiling for the fiscal year 1950 and a projected $13 billion ceiling for 1951. The JCS insisted upon a $21–23 billion appropriation and declared $16.9 billion the barest minimum necessary for protecting the country. Worried about an inability to hold Western Europe and the Middle East in the event of war with Russia, the Joint Chiefs could not allot limited resources to a marginal adventure in Asia.[45] In 1947 they had ranked the Far East last in regional strategic importance to the United States and China thirteenth (third from last) on a list of countries significant to national security.[46] By 1949 they reluctantly affirmed that an American military occupation of or intervention in Taiwan would not be in the national interest.[47]

In fact, the Administration had increasingly seen the fall of Taiwan as the solution to its recognition problem. Once the last Nationalist stronghold dissolved, Republicans and China lobbyists would have no alternative to propose to diplomatic relations with Peking. Accepting Communist authority would not then carry with it the stigma of abandoning an ally. Recognition would again become the practical mechanism by which a government received acknowledgment so that ordinary dealings between states could continue. The Truman Administration prepared quietly for the end of Kuomintang resistance and resumption of relations with a viable regime in China.

Both Truman and Acheson perceived keenly that the forthcoming Kuomintang collapse must not appear to be an occurrence that the United States could have prevented. This dictated that every government action be invested with extreme caution. Repeatedly, despite the desire to sever ties with Chiang Kai-shek, the Administration agreed to renew assistance programs. On February 3, 1949, for instance, the National Security Council recommended that with the recent CCP victories in China and the initiation of peace talks by the Nationalist government, American aid should stop. Upon consultation with Congressional leaders, Truman and Acheson chose instead to delay arms shipments surreptitiously. It would not do, warned Senator Vandenberg, for the

United States to seem to be pushing the Chinese over the brink.[48] In July 1949 the State Department reconsidered its decision not to request aid for the Nationalists as part of the Mutual Defense Assistance Act so as not to "exacerbate the controversy" over China. Instead, officials secured money to be used at the President's discretion in the China area, thereby making no commitment that the funds would be spent in Chiang's behalf but avoiding the criticism of a negative approach to the issue.[49] Similarly, the Administration hesitated to tell the American people about the corruption and ineptitude of Chiang's regime. Dean Acheson yearned to make a public statement about the real situation in China in response to a February 1949 letter from 51 Republicans demanding reexamination of American policy.[50] The State Department as early as November 1948 had considered releasing a detailed indictment of Kuomintang mismanagement. In April 1949, it finally began the task of compiling the White Paper which it published during August. Even then Secretary Acheson chose to emphasize the point that the debate in China had been beyond American control. Neither critics at home nor allies abroad could be allowed to think that the United States had not followed through on its obligations.[51]

In spite of the necessity for dissimulation, Dean Acheson strove to adhere to a policy of disengagement from the Kuomintang. If abrupt action could not be taken, the State Department would implement a gradual separation. In addition to finding ways to slow arms shipments after February 1949, Acheson also took a strong stand in March against Senator McCarran's $1.5 million proposal for military assistance to the Kuomintang. The Secretary told British Foreign Secretary Ernest Bevin in April that he expected China Aid Act funds to cease as of the beginning of June and that thereafter the United States would take a more realistic stand regarding China. In fact, Acheson rebutted several subsequent Nationalist aid requests.[52]

United States military and intelligence estimates regarding the future of the Kuomintang reinforced the turn toward realism. The rapid disintegration of almost all KMT armies convinced observers that the Nationalists simply would not fight. Not only did prospects seem bleak on the mainland, but as early as August 1949 the Secretary of State informed the NSC that the Kuomintang would not even be able to hold on to Taiwan despite economic and political support from Washington.[53] A Central Intelligence Agency assessment of October 1949, concurred in by the State, Army, Navy, and Air Force Departments, and reaffirmed in March and April 1950, maintained that only United States military occupation and control could prevent Taiwan's subjugation before the end of 1950.[54] Faint hopes that Taiwan could be defended, not because of Chiang's soldiers but because the CCP had no amphibious capability, faded with the 1950 island campaign. On Hainan, the second largest of the offshore islands, Kuomintang troops dissolved before the CCP forces. Morale in Taiwan plummeted. The American consulate staff in Taipei predicted that the end would come sometime during the summer.[55]

Secretary Acheson brought these dire warnings to the attention of his foreign service officers and the Congress. In December of 1949 he dispatched a circular telegram which predicted the elimination of Kuomintang power in Taiwan and asked that American diplomatic personnel deemphasize the importance of this development.[56] At an executive session of the Senate Foreign Relations Committee during January 1950, he again asserted that the fall of Nationalist China could not be prevented. In March, after the Kuomintang had staged costly bombing raids over Shanghai, Acheson told the Senators that he believed the CCP would be "criminally crazy if they did not put an end to it just as soon as possible."[57] Indeed, Acheson himself had been so angered by the KMT action and the government's belligerent response to American protests that he considered an abrupt halt to all further aid. But with the final resolution of the problem so close at hand the Department chose not to make any move which might bring the Truman Administration further domestic political retribution.[58]

The Administration had been under almost constant attack from a voluble coalition of Republicans and China Lobbyists since the final collapse of Nationalist resistance on the mainland in December 1949. Strident demands that the United States take decisive action to protect Taiwan issued from Senators Knowland and Taft and former President Herbert Hoover.[59] Secretary of Defense Johnson and General MacArthur pressed the Joint Chiefs of Staff to reverse their earlier position and call for a survey of Kuomintang military needs. In response to their urgings, coupled with the availability of new funds under the Military Assistance Act and the supposed improvement of conditions on Formosa, the JCS proposed a program of "modest" and "closely-supervised" military aid.[60]

The State Department, which had ruled out the use of American forces to protect Taiwan as early as October 1948, argued against direct intervention to salvage the Kuomintang cause.[61] At best the JCS proposal would postpone Taiwan's fall by a year while incurring considerable damage to American prestige and exciting anticolonial hatreds not only in China, but also among peoples elsewhere in Asia. The political price, Acheson contended, could not be justified. The State Department, in fact, had already recommended that Military Assistance Act funds be used in China for informational programs and for military purposes only in Southeast Asia. After Acheson's forceful presentation JCS Chairman Omar Bradley conceded that the political liabilities of aid to the Nationalists might outweigh the military benefits.

President Truman, concurring with the position taken by his Secretary of State, decided to allow Nationalist China to fall. During the autumn of 1949, whatever misgivings he had had about disengagement from the Kuomintang had dissipated. Evidence of KMT moral and political bankruptcy in the pages of the White Paper, in reports from the State Department, and in the words of the China consultant group became overwhelming. Truman approved the National Security Council's paper providing for political and economic support for the Nationalists but making no provision for military assistance. Even this economic aid, financed under existing legislation, would expire in the middle of February 1950.[62] Communist conquest, Truman believed, would follow soon after.[63]

Having decided not to prevent the imminent fall of Taiwan, the President made a public declaration of his government's disengagement policy. On January 5, 1950 he announced that the American government did not intend to acquire special concessions in Taiwan nor would it intercede to prevent a takeover. Nine million dollars in unexpended military aid funds would still be available to the Kuomintang but no further military assistance would be forthcoming.[64] Seven days later the Secretary of State, in a speech at the National Press Club, put Taiwan outside America's defensive perimeter in Asia. The United States did not want to incur the anti-imperialist resentment of the Chinese people which should rightfully be directed at Soviet activities in Manchuria and Mongolia, said the Secretary. And, observed Tom Connally, the Administration's Senate spokesman, the American people did not want to be plunged into another war—particularly not to save Taiwan.[65]

Predictably, Nationalist sympathizers did not accept this policy as definitive. In Congress the China bloc secured an extension until June of the deadline for expenditure of remaining economic assistance funds by holding Korean aid legislation hostage.[66] Secretary of Defense Louis Johnson persisted in obstructing what he believed a misguided abandonment of an American ally. For months he had been warring with the State Department, denying it access to Defense Department information and personnel. He had objected to publication of the White Paper and refused to provide documents for the volume. He even created obstacles to the dispatch of an American ship to evacuate foreigners from Shanghai on the grounds that the CCP might capture the vessel. During the early months of 1950 he advocated military aid and intervention on Chiang Kai-shek's behalf and continued to keep Kuomintang officials apprised of policy developments within the American military establishment.[67] The Joint Chiefs also reiterated proposals for military aid to Taiwan and, although they still unanimously opposed direct intervention under existing circumstances, they secretly devised plans envisioning denial of Taiwan to the Soviets in case of war. From abroad, too, retired Admiral Charles M. Cooke and General MacArthur called for a reversal of the President's stand.[68]

Even within the State Department Secretary Acheson encountered dissent. The Secretary had been convinced that a Taiwan free of Chiang Kai-shek's control could exist only under the CCP. His interest in a Taiwan autonomy movement, evinced early in 1949, had dissipated when his special emissary Livingston Merchant and ECA observers attested to Chiang's iron grip on the island.[69] Two October 1949 meetings of the State Department's top advisors on China policy reached a consensus that the United States should not initiate either diplomatic or military maneuvers to stop the inexorable demise of the Nationalist regime.[70] Nevertheless, during the early months of 1950 some of these same officials reintroduced schemes to rid Taiwan of both Chiang and communism. George Kennan, consultant and former head of the Policy Planning Staff, advocated a Teddy Roosevelt style venture using American soldiers to throw the Generalissimo out and create an independent Chinese government.[71] Dean Rusk revived earlier ideas of making Taiwan a United Nations trusteeship territory. The United States, he suggested, should interpose its navy in the Taiwan Straits until the UN could consolidate its control on the island.[72] John Foster Dulles, newly arrived in the Department as special consultant on the Japanese peace treaty, agreed with Rusk's vision of a neutralized Taiwan.[73] The Secretary of State, however, rejected these stratagems just as he had rebuffed previous devices to rescue the Kuomintang. The end of Chiang Kai-shek's scourge finally appeared in sight and Dean Acheson had no intention of tampering with this long anticipated development. On June 23, 1950 he told the press that the United States would stand by its nonintervention policy.[74]

The Secretary's disgust with the Kuomintang played a significant role in his desire to disassociate the United States from the Nationalists. He had confronted the crisis in China with virtually no prior experience in Asian affairs and no interest in the area. Having served in Washington during the ill-fated Marshall Mission, he did begin his term as Secretary with the determination that he would fare better than had General and Secretary of State George Marshall. Indeed, whereas the Chinese Nationalists assumed that Marshall continued to direct China policy in the

Department during 1949, Acheson's exposure to the disillusionment of a man he so highly respected had much more influence than did the man himself.[75] Acheson also met with repeated instances of Kuomintang duplicity and incompetence during the early days of his administration. He became convinced of the party's financial deceit, its inability to rule, even its incapacity to unite in pursuit of a common goal. Increasingly, Acheson told the American people that the Nationalists deserved the fate that had befallen them. The United States, after all, could not be expected to supply the determination the KMT armies lacked or the loyalty its people had decided to give to the opposing Communist forces.[76]

America's responsibility, Acheson believed, no longer rested in supporting a discredited regime, but rather in finding ways to reconcile United States interests with those of the incoming government of China. According to Assistant Secretary Butterworth, the State Department on several occasions signalled the CCP that Washington "looked forward to formal, regularized relations with them; not intimate but proper."[77] Early in 1949 the Secretary accepted Department recommendations that American consulates remain open in Communist territory and that the Embassy stay in Nanking even after the KMT authorities withdrew from the city.[78] Acheson directed Ambassador Stuart to approach CCP leaders to try to clear away misunderstandings and improve relations.[79] With the Secretary's approval the Department made it clear to American businessmen that commercial exchange with the CCP did not contradict government policy, that on the contrary both businessmen and missionaries with important interests in China should remain there.[80] The Secretary also attempted to play down incidents of friction between Americans in China and the CCP. Even when the CCP went so far as to seize American consulate property in Peking, the Secretary refused to consider this a reason to stop progress toward normalization. The United States did pull its remaining representatives out of China, but to avoid further frictions rather than to sever contacts. Before his departure Consul General O. Edmund Clubb received instructions to approach the Communist government and try again to resolve Sino-American differences.[81] Washington continued to accept the idea that the CCP would soon obtain Nationalist China's seat in the UN and reassured the Secretary General that no veto would be cast: "The whole Peking regime," Acheson told Trygve Lie, "was an improvisation that scarcely knew what it was doing, or what repercussions its acts had internationally." It would begin to understand its position better, the Secretary hoped, when Soviet pressures on China made it realize the advantages of dealing with the United States.[82]

In deciding to move toward normalization and not create a Chinese irredentist struggle over Taiwan, the Secretary of State chose a course of action which gained support from much of the diplomatic establishment. State Department studies of recognition policy and precedents regarding treaty abrogation illustrated that the United States could preserve its interests and yet compromise with the CCP.[83] The consultants, Ambassador-at-Large Philip Jessup, Everett Case, and Raymond Fosdick, who had been brought into the Department specifically to deal with Chinese affairs, favored disengagement from the KMT and recognition of the CCP. Ambassador Jessup proposed that during his Far Eastern trip, early in 1950, he should undertake exploratory conversations with Mao Tse-tung.[84] Members of the Economic Cooperation Administration's China Mission, having returned to private vocations, continued to tout the benefits of recognition.[85] State Department officials, including Assistant Secretary Butterworth and his Deputy Livingston Merchant, Director of the Office of Chinese Affairs Sprouse, and co-author of the White Paper John Melby, advocated recognition with varying degrees of enthusiasm. A consensus reached in Department meetings during October described the appropriate attitude as not "eager" but "realistic." So, too, foreign service officers O. Edmund Clubb in Peking and John Cabot in Shanghai took note of the problems involved in opening relations but, adding that relations and trade might serve as bargaining tools, concluded that recognition would be a far wiser policy than nonrecognition. Robert Strong, Chargé in Taipei, urged the Department not to overlook the "mainland and its potentialities" and Walter McConaughy, Cabot's successor, argued that the CCP did not want to drive all Americans out. Washington, he contended, should strengthen the position of American businessmen and missionaries so as to maintain an American presence in China.[86]

State Department annoyance with constant pressures from Republican partisans and China Lobby interests also generated enthusiasm for disengagement. The repetitiveness of pro-Nationalist articles, letters, and visits led State Department officers to disregard much of this material. Sometimes it elicited an embarrassed sympathy for those who tried to paint the Nationalist cause in victorious colors—a reaction Chinese Ambassador Wellington Koo found discomforting. At other times the criticism and entreaties engendered annoyance.[87] Rumors and hearsay evidence indicated that Kuomintang notables, especially the Soongs, had invested large sums of United States aid in American real estate. Dean Rusk initiated a Department investigation in hopes that evidence regarding Nationalist financial abuses could be used to help defend the Department's China policy. Although this study produced

nothing concrete enough to use, officials continued to view KMT practices with suspicion. Assistant Secretary Butterworth noted the striking
similarity between KMT arms requests made on December 23, 1949 and
JCS proposals presented to the NSC that same day.[88] Even advocates
of continued aid for the Nationalists objected to the attitudes of Chiang
and his supporters. John Foster Dulles, for instance, chided a Kuomintang spokesman about the Party's demonstrated lack of conviction and
willingness to fight. It was wrong, he declared, to attempt to bargain
temporary resistance on Taiwan for a promise of eventual American aid.
Moreover, rumors that Chiang Kai-shek and other leaders had already
made escape plans would not help the Nationalist cause in the United
States.[89]

In Congress, too, the Administration's new departure obtained support. Demands by Senators Knowland and Smith that the United States
intervene in Taiwan, even occupy the island, failed to stir any enthusiasm among their colleagues. Instead, tired of strident Republican demands for Acheson's resignation, and weary of listening to diatribes on
China, Senate Democrats caucused and voiced virtually unanimous approval of Truman's hands-off-Formosa policy.[90]

Opinions opposing aid to the KMT and favoring a new beginning
with mainland China also came to the government from important elements in the missionary and business communities, influential sectors
of the press, and most prominently from members of the academic
world. A Round Table Conference held at the Department during October 1949 yielded a majority in favor of recognition; and the Council
on Foreign Relations, in a select poll of informed citizens nationwide,
produced a pro-recognition vote as well. Although public opinion surveys did not favor recognition, they did indicate a generalized disgust
for Chiang Kai-shek and a desire to see aid to his forces cease. More
significant, from the Department's perspective, analyses of nationwide
discussions of China policy by newspaper editors and commentators
and a variety of public figures indicated a trend toward accepting recognition as inevitable. Establishing diplomatic relations with the Communist Chinese might not be an especially desirable policy, but a growing sector of what the State Department identified as the "articulate"
population considered it a practical and realistic one.[91]

Dean Acheson then, upon whose recommendations the President relied, found no significant domestic resistance and considerable—if soft-
spoken—support for his China policy. Anxious to sever ties with the
Nationalists, he found widespread agreement that the Kuomintang
could not be saved and that the United States should, in any case, not
try. Hoping to normalize relations with the Chinese Communists, he

discovered indecision and uncertainty, but also increasing recognition that such a development must come. An outspoken opposition certainly existed, and it became passionate at times, but Acheson perceived it as small in numbers and part of the same group that consistently objected to Truman Administration policies. As to public opinion, Acheson paid it little heed and felt certain that when the time came he could persuade the people to acquiesce in actions the government deemed in their best interests.[92]

British attitudes also, no doubt, exerted a considerable degree of influence on Acheson. The British appealed to Acheson's sense of the practical and reasonable in foreign affairs. Acheson, in any case a notable Anglophile, found London's reaction to the Communist takeover in China far more sensible than the often emotional response of his countrymen. The Secretary appreciated as well the extent of British involvement in China and respected London's need to protect its investments and its position in Hong Kong. Beginning only shortly after he became Secretary of State, Acheson initiated regular and secret meetings with British Ambassador to the United States, Sir Oliver Franks, for consultation on "any international problems we saw arising." Acheson, therefore, remained in close touch with the development of British policy regarding China and the arguments which interests in London advanced for recognition of the CCP.[93]

Acheson himself conceived of recognition policy as a utilitarian device and not as a means by which to show moral censure. Supported by the Policy Planning Staff, the Division of Far Eastern Affairs, and the Office of Chinese Affairs, Acheson asserted that recognition should not be viewed as a political weapon. In September 1949, just days before the expected establishment of a Communist regime in Peking, the Secretary set forth his views at a meeting of the Pan American Society in New York. Although his remarks bore appropriately upon recurrent events in the western hemisphere, the implications for China did not escape notice. Emphasizing that extending recognition in essence meant acknowledging facts, Acheson insisted that

> we maintain diplomatic relations with other countries primarily because we are all on the same planet and must do business with each other. We do not establish an Embassy in a foreign country to show approval of its Government. We do so to have a channel through which to conduct essential government relations and to protect legitimate United States interests.[94]

Recognition, viewed as an instrument facilitating international discourse, carried with it no need for hasty action by American officials. Conscious of Republican opposition to opening diplomatic relations with the CCP and the President's resultant hesitancy, the Secretary of State willingly delayed substantive approaches to Peking. The State Department saw Congress and the public as manageable should trouble arise but discerned no need to provoke confrontation. Once the refugee regime on Taiwan fell to Chinese Communist assaults, Republicans and China lobbyists would cease to have an issue. There would be plenty of time to extend recognition when no threat of political ruin for Democratic election prospects remained.

Moreover, conditions in China continued to be unstable and the State Department did not yet have a clear picture of the degree to which the Communists would compromise on outstanding issues. Officials had concluded in September "that the withholding of recognition would [not] be a matter of such serious consequence as to affect appreciably the stability of the new Communist government or afford an effective lever for achieving other than limited objectives." Nevertheless, the United States would try to "obtain the maximum advantages possible."[95] In October, therefore, Washington had announced three criteria which it expected the CCP to fulfill in order to qualify for recognition. The regime should 1) have effective control of the territory it claimed to govern, 2) acknowledge its international obligations, and 3) rule with the consent of the Chinese people. Officials hoped that the Communists would desire American recognition enough to meet these requirements even though Party leaders had already declared their intention to abrogate all existing Sino-American treaties because of their unequal provisions.[96] By March 1950 the State Department found that the CCP not only had secured widespread cooperation and thoroughgoing control, it also continued adamantly to denounce its international obligations. The Department, aware that commercial and political agreements would have to be altered in any case, reduced its recognition criteria. In a speech to the Commonwealth Club of San Francisco, Acheson contended that improvements in relations between the United States and China depended solely on the treatment that the CCP accorded to American representatives and private citizens in China. The following month this point received further emphasis in the Department's publication of a speech delivered by the U.S. Ambassador to India. Denying that the delay in recognition had anything to do with the Peking government's communist ideology, he redefined the United States interpretation of the CCP's international obligations in terms potentially more acceptable to the Party. Washington wanted the Chinese "to treat American nationals in a manner prescribed by international customs established after a hundred years of experience in international intercourse." Thus, as Taiwan's fall neared, the State Department moved to eliminate other obstacles to recognition. With the source of CCP hostility toward the American government—aid to the Nationalists—about to disappear, prospects for better treatment of Americans under Chinese Communist rule looked promising.[97]

The State Department's hope that normalizing relations with China would encourage frictions between the CCP and the Soviet Union similarly allowed time for a gradual development toward recognition. A Sino-Soviet split would not occur in the immediate future, but, Acheson believed, it must come and Americans should be ready for it. The Department, therefore, devoted its resources to comparing Chinese Communism and Titoism, even posting John Cabot from Belgrade to Shanghai so as to have an expert observer on the scene. It planted stories in the press during Mao Tse-tung's negotiations with Stalin in February 1950 emphasizing Soviet imperialism. Repeatedly, speeches by American officials called the Communist Chinese puppets, hoping to shame them into a show of anti-Russian nationalism.[98]

At the same time, Acheson worked to avoid any escalation in Sino-American tensions. He favored retaining American business and missionary enterprises in China because they provided informal channels of communication to the Chinese Communists. They also demonstrated on a small scale the benefits that relations with the United States could yield. The Secretary resisted the temptation to view CCP violations of internationally accepted behavior as an excuse to end all contacts with them. When China Lobbyists and Republican critics of Administration policy demanded American aid for the Nationalists on Taiwan, Acheson adamantly opposed this intervention in the civil war. As the Secretary cautioned members of the Senate Foreign Relations Committee, "in and of itself . . . the island of Formosa is not a great question in American foreign policy, but it may become a very great question if it obscures or changes or interferes with what we are trying to do in regard to China." In other words, Acheson refused to allow "historic Chinese xenophobia" to be deflected from Russia to the United States because of some foolish adventure in Taiwan. More importantly, he did not propose that the United States go down to defeat with Chiang Kai-shek on a small island off the coast of China when an opportunity still existed to come to terms with Communist authorities in Peking.[99]

China would not be the ally that Americans of earlier periods had sought, but, Acheson thought, it might be possible to prevent the Chinese nation's becoming an unequivocal enemy of the United States. To this end, Washington would have to disentangle itself from Chiang Kai-shek's embrace and, Acheson told the Senators, "do everything [it] can to separate [the CCP] from Moscow." For, the Secretary observed, "whoever runs China, even if the devil himself runs China, if he is an independent devil that is infinitely better than if he is a stooge of Moscow."[100]

Recognition of China's Communist government, then, promised to accomplish a variety of objectives. It would allow Washington to improve its image in Asia and alleviate tensions which had developed with Great Britain over China policy. Opening diplomatic relations with the CCP might give impetus to Chinese Titoism or at least strengthen moderate elements within the Chinese Communist Party. Recognition, with the regular intercourse it implied, raised expectations of expanding trade and an ongoing role for American businessmen in the China market. Missionaries, too, foresaw the possibility of continued activities once normal relations had relieved tensions between Americans and the Chinese. Above all, recognition meant that the United States would not lose contact with the Chinese people and become isolated form one-quarter of humanity.

Realization of this goal, however, would not be easy, and the Truman Administration proceeded cautiously. Neither the President nor his Secretary of State wanted to make the issue of recognition a political battleground. China's overall insignificance to the United States did not warrant jeopardizing European aid or the Administration's domestic programs. So long as an opposition existed which could point to Chiang Kai-shek's regime as an alternative to Peking, Truman and Acheson would wait. When Taiwan had fallen and the dust had finally settled, there would be plenty of time to approach the Chinse Communists and convince the American people to face reality.

Epilogue

)━●━()━●━()━●━()━●━(

THE guns which exploded into action along Korea's 38th parallel on June 25, 1950 shattered more than just the morning calm. Any real prospect of normalization in relations between the United States and Communist China abruptly ended. Shocked by what appeared to be a naked display of Soviet puppetry, American officials marshaled their resources and responded with force.[1] Although intelligence had reported substantial Soviet military assistance flowing to North Korea, Truman, Acheson, and others in the Administration had refused to believe that fighting might break out at any moment. When it did, they found themselves instantly on the defensive at home as well as in Asia. The flexibility in American policy that Dean Acheson had managed to retain, in spite of pressures from the China Lobby and some members of his own staff, vanished. Asia, it had become brutally obvious, would no longer be exempted from the main arena of conflict between Washington and Moscow. Lacking any evidence of Chinese involvement, the White House and State Department nevertheless assumed that, by virtue of the Sino-Soviet Friendship Treaty signed in February 1950, Peking had connived in the North Korean assault. Suspecting the worst about the CCP's position, the Truman Administration abandoned thoughts of recognition.[2]

The din of battle also drowned voices of moderation among the Communist Chinese. Early in June 1950 party leaders anticipated an imminent end to their civil war. One final push against Taiwan and the Kuomintang would collapse, bringing a long awaited peace. Fighting in Korea, however, triggered an American decision to intercede once again in the Chinese conflict by placing its Seventh Fleet in the Taiwan Straits. Not particularly concerned about developments in Korea, at least at first, Peking was infuriated by United States intervention in the closing phase of China's civil war. Not only did the American action frustrate a long and bitterly sought conclusion of the revolutionary struggle by preserving Chiang Kai-shek's regime, but to the CCP it proved beyond doubt the deceitfulness of the world's foremost imperialistic power. Earlier American pledges to refrain from precisely such a measure appeared to have been lies. Diplomatic intercourse with Americans no longer seemed palatable to even the most conciliatory Communist leaders.

Only among the Nationalist Chinese and their supporters did the Korean War engender delight. If the fighting would just last long enough, they reasoned, the Kuomintang might succeed in thoroughly reentangling American wealth and power in Nationalist affairs. Harry Truman and Dean Acheson had, during 1949 and the early months of 1950, made clear their desire to be rid of obligations to the regime on Taiwan. But the war gave pro–Chiang Kai-shek elements in the United States a new opportunity to play on public fears of Communist onslaught. The political costs of appearing soft on communism compelled the President and his Secretary of State to shield the Kuomintang for the duration of the Korean conflict. It also, Chiang knew, prohibited recognition of a Communist government in China at least until Communists stopped killing South Korean and American boys on the Korean peninsula.

Confronted with aggression in Korea, Washington reacted almost reflexively in dispatching the U.S. Seventh Fleet to the Taiwan Straits. American intelligence agencies had predicted that a Communist attack upon Taiwan would occur during 1950, perhaps as early as July. Once war erupted on the Korean peninsula, the prospect of fighting along the Chinese coast became intolerable. American officials wanted the Korean conflict localized, Communist expansion halted, and American strength clearly demonstrated.[3] To achieve these ends the State Department and the JCS urged at the first conference following news of the invasion that President Truman freeze the Chinese situation. The Seventh Fleet, they suggested, should not only prevent CCP attacks upon Taiwan but must also keep Chiang Kai-shek from raiding the mainland. On June 26 Truman instructed his Secretary of Defense to implement this policy by alerting General Douglas MacArthur.[4]

The rapidity with which the United States took action on the Straits question followed from prior planning and discussion by the Joint Chiefs. In December 1949 the military had been overruled in National Security Council deliberations when President Truman had decided, in effect, to allow the Nationalists to succumb to a CCP assault. But, having agreed as early as 1948 that Taiwan did not present so acute a national security problem as to warrant direct American intervention, the JCS went on to explore the ramifications of that position. They concluded, with apparent agreement from the Department of State, that in the event of war the United States would deny Moscow use of Taiwan as a base for offensive operations. If the Chinese Communists acting alone did not pose a severe threat to American interests because of their military weakness, CCP moves in conjunction with or as a cover for Soviet advances posed a grave challenge.[5] Unwilling to reveal the substance of emergency war plans, the President and Secretary of State nonetheless hinted at this determination by qualifying their January 5, 1950 announcement of the government's decision not to intervene on Chiang's behalf. Truman inserted the phrase "at this time," and Acheson explained that an attack upon the United States in Asia could radically alter perspectives and policies.[6]

Truman's June decision to intervene in the Chinese civil war reflected sensitivity to domestic politics as well as concern about a Soviet presence in Taiwan. On January 12, 1950 Secretary of State Acheson had appeared before the National Press Club in Washington and discussed future policy considerations in Asia. Basing his remarks upon earlier recommendations made by General Albert C. Wedemeyer, MacArthur, and the Joint Chiefs, Acheson outlined American commitments. He emphasized that limits existed to the nation's resources and put Korea and Taiwan outside America's defensive perimeter. In essence, those states must henceforth protect themselves (with United Nations assistance); the United States could not watch over them.[7] Pro-Nationalist sympathizers immediately castigated Acheson and, venting their displeasure, joined forces with economy-minded legislators to defeat an Administration-sponsored Korean aid bill. Representative Donald L. Jackson (R, Ca) reflected Republican outrage, contrasting the need to strengthen Formosa ("if we are going to have any kind of policy at any time in the Pacific") with foolish efforts to protect South Korea, which he described as "a Bataan without a Corregidor, a Dunkerque without a flotilla, a dead-end street without an escape."[8]

Truman and Acheson found that only by placating the China bloc could Korea's economy be saved from imminent collapse. Extension of an earlier China Aid Act appropriation from February 15 to June 30, 1950 made $104 million in residual funds available to Chiang. More importantly, this Administration-sponsored action implied an intimate connection between two vulnerable Asian entities and suggested a continuing American obligation to them. When war broke out in Korea, protection of Taiwan appeared compulsory and Truman acted. Even so, Republican critics looked back at the National Press Club speech and called it an invitation to the Soviet Union to hurl its puppet troops southward.[9] Senator Robert A. Taft demanded Acheson's resignation in July, and Kenneth S. Wherry, Senate Republican floor leader, echoed that call in August. According to Wherry, "The blood of our boys in Korea is on [Acheson's] shoulders, and no one else [sic]."[10]

Not all Americans lashed out at Truman and Acheson when North Korea attacked the South, though. Rather, the President, as he had hoped, engendered widespread enthusiasm with his prompt aid to the beleaguered South Koreans. Public opinion polls indicated national agreement that the time to stop communism in Asia had arrived and that Truman had met the challenge courageously. The percentage of those approving the President's performance, according to pollster George Gallup, jumped nine points from June to July 1950: 81 percent of those questioned specifically about Korea favored the commitment of American troops. Senator Styles Bridges, though a long-time opponent of the Administration, told newsmen he thought Truman's decision a "damned good action." Many others, including Senators William F. Knowland and H. Alexander Smith and former Republican presidential candidate Thomas Dewey, joined Bridges in praising the rapid White House response. In the House of Representatives, Truman's June 27 report on the crisis recieved a standing ovation from all but one of the 319 members present.[11]

The war instantly coalesced support around a President who had been under attack for both his foreign and domestic policies. Although excitement would wane as the fighting dragged on, the country's initial reaction combined relief and euphoria. The pent-up anxieties of a frustrating cold war finally could be released, the issue joined and, it was thought, a quick victory over communism secured. Truman and Acheson welcomed popular support but soon discovered that support cultivated for an anticommunist crusade narrowed their choices on other foreign issues. If the American people must resist communist expansion and fear communist subversion, they could not be expected to condone policies flexible enough to initiate relations with a communist giant like the People's Republic of China.

For the Nationalist Chinese the struggle in Korea had come as if by magic at the last possible moment before disaster engulfed them. Chiang Kai-shek had anticipated a war for years, envisioning a worldwide Soviet-American holocaust. No matter who tried to disabuse him of the idea, he clung tightly to this conviction. Chiang felt certain that when conflict flared the United States would be forced, as it had been in World War II, to rescue the Generalissimo from his enemies. In the spring of 1950 with an invasion force assembling along the Chinese coast and an army on Taiwan already virtually defeated by its own low morale and inept commanders, the Nationalist regime neared extinction. But as had happened in the past, providence intervened—war suddenly broke out and Harry Truman put the Seventh Fleet in the Straits. If not quite the clash Chiang had expected, it sufficed nonetheless to preserve his otherwise doomed government.

The Kuomintang and its supporters jubilantly set about exploiting their good fortune. As Senator H. Alexander Smith (R, NJ) noted in his diary: "It was all very wonderful and an answer to a prayer. . . .The saving of Formosa was clearly God guided." Chiang Kai-shek's agents, sensing the change of atmosphere in Washington, alerted the Generalissimo to renewed prospects for aid.[12] But the Generalissimo did not need to be told that a miracle had happened. Acting immediately, he offered Nationalist troops to the United Nations defense coalition, hoping to link Taiwan's future even more closely with that of South Korea.[13] During July Chiang hosted a MacArthur visit to his island fortress which concluded with release of a joint communique celebrating their common view of developments in Northeast Asia. To heighten the significance of the trip, MacArthur shrouded it in secrecy, keeping the details of talks even from the State Department.[14] Henry Luce's *Time* magazine publicized the mutual admiration of Chiang and the American commander, noting in one of several articles MacArthur's observation that, "If we had dreamed that the Communists would take China, we would have swallowed Chiang K'ai-shek, horns, cloven hooves and all . . . if that was the way we felt about him. Personally I have great respect for Chiang."[15] MacArthur then went on in an August letter to the Veterans of Foreign Wars to argue yet again the strategic necessity of perserving that "unsinkable aircraft carrier and submarine tender," Taiwan.[16]

Truman and Acheson resisted the Nationalists' embrace but found themselves overwhelmed by events. Although willing to dispatch U.S. naval units to the Taiwan Straits, the President strongly objected to appropriating new funds for the Kuomintang. According to notes made by Philip C. Jessup at the June 26 Blair House conference, Truman asserted "that we were not going to give the Chinese 'a nickel' for any purpose whatever . . . that all the money we have given them is now invested in United States real estate."[17] The Administration rejected Chiang's offer of troops to fight in Korea, recalling their less-than-striking performance on the Chinese mainland. As Dean Rusk observed to Chinese Ambassador Koo, "if there had been some question a few months ago whether the forces on Formosa were in fact able to defend the island against an all-out Communist attack, then it would perhaps be unwise to spare troops at this time."[18] When MacArthur proposed his trip to Taiwan, the State Department attempted to dissuade him, and Truman tried to neutralize the impact of the visit by soliciting a pledge from the General that henceforth he would follow Administration policy. Shortly thereafter the VFW letter appeared without prior clearance by Truman, Acheson, Secretary of Defense Johnson, or the JCS, and the President ordered it officially withdrawn.[19] In September Acheson chastised the American minister in Taipei, Karl Rankin, for misrepresenting the Administration's attitude toward the Kuomintang. Instead of boosting Nationalist hopes Rankin should remind the regime that Taiwan's legal position continued to be tenuous. Dean Rusk similarly told Rankin, "We do not wish to make any commitment to Chinese authorities as to how long this relationship will extend into the future."[20]

Neutralization of the Straits had been intended as a temporary expedient, and neither Acheson nor Truman wanted to see their emergency measure become permanent policy.[21] Evolution in that direction, however, accelerated, encouraged whenever possible by the KMT, the China Lobby, and an assortment of others concerned about the spread of communism. Although Truman still intended to extract the U.S. Navy from the Taiwan stalemate when war in Korea subsided, Washington became more and more involved in the preservation of Chiang's regime.

Within the State Department, Acheson confronted repeated urgings from a growing number of his subordinates to do something positive about Taiwan's future. Dean Rusk, Assistant Secretary for Far Eastern Affairs, had long been more sympathetic to the Nationalist plight than the Secretary. Although rejecting George Kennan's cowboy-style tactics favoring use of American troops to oust Chiang, Rusk too promoted the idea of a new government on Taiwan shorn of the Generalissimo and content to limit its rule to the island. In conjunction with Ambassador-at-Large John Foster Dulles, Rusk had, in May, advocated introduction of a United Nations trusteeship arrangement. Acheson rebuffed such proposals, but after the war broke out Dulles and Rusk renewed their efforts to prevent communist control of the island through a "two Chinas" policy; that is, one China on the mainland and another separate entity offshore. Philip C. Jessup, Ambassador-at-Large and Acheson's close friend, added his support to their plan of having the United Nations hold a plebiscite which, they expected, would free Taiwan of domination by Kuomintang mainlanders. Jessup felt no more partial to the disintegrating regime of a tyrannical Chiang Kai-shek than he had on the eve of conflict in Korea, but the exigencies of war against communism persuaded him that Washington should try to save Taiwan.[22]

Members of the military establishment also exerted strong pressures for a commitment to Taiwan. During the early weeks of crisis in Korea, the President and Secretary had to restrain MacArthur, Secretary of Defense Louis Johnson, and the Joint Chiefs of Staff, all of whom advocated coastal bombing to prevent a Chinese Communist assault across the Taiwan Straits.[23] General Omar Bradley, chairman of the Joint Chiefs of Staff, worried about the island's position should Korea fall and on July 27 the Chiefs agreed that, regardless of developments to the north, Taiwan ought to be defended.[24] By August Truman, in response to Peking's repeated threats against the island and pressures at home, felt compelled to approve a $14 million military assistance package to strengthen Nationalist defense forces.[25]

American government planning to meet the Korean Communist military challenge spurred elaboration of Washington's support for Chiang Kai-shek. Whereas before the Korean War military leaders could not justify using limited assets in an area of marginal significance, the conflict altered both the estimates of Asia's importance and the resources available. Investment in weaponry and manpower escalated with the war and illustrated in practice that the economy could tolerate a larger defense sector.

Debate over defense budgets had captured much attention in the years following World War II. Although anxieties over Soviet behavior had led to restoration of the draft in 1948, budgets for the military establishment remained low. Secretary of State Marshall, among others, argued that American rearmament might well trigger an arms race with Moscow.[26] Policymakers, such as the chairman of Truman's Council of Economic Advisors, Edwin G. Nourse, feared that spending on weapons would necessitate debilitating cutbacks in domestic programs, an eventuality that would compromise national security even more fundamentally than a lack of conventional forces.[27] Defense Secretary Johnson had himself become committed to budget trimming to advance his political fortunes in an era of economizing, thereby depriving the armed forces of a prime spokesman for increased spending. As late as the spring of 1950, President Truman approved a proposed $13.5 million ceiling for fiscal year 1951. At a May 4 press conference, moreover, he contended that the military budget would actually decline in fiscal year 1952 because world conditions had stabilized.[28] But tight budgets could not be sustained once the outbreak of war necessitated rapid and sizable rearmament.

The Korean conflict, having broken down political and financial barriers to massive arms expenditures, gave impetus as well to a more thoroughgoing shift in the nature of America's defense structure. In January 1950, the President had responded to alarm generated by the fall of China and explosion of a Soviet atomic device by authorizing a review of the nation's military capabilities. Together with his decision to sanction development of the hydrogen bomb, Truman sought to assess the United States' non-nuclear forces. The resulting study, presented to Truman in April 1950, recommended huge defense increases, arguing that as much as 20 percent of the gross national product could safely be appropriated to the military without jeopardizing the economy. This effort not only was possible, the responsible State/Defense committee contended, but vital in light of Moscow's determination to control the world.[29] Harry Truman, however, did not accept the committee report, referring it to the National Security Council for further analysis and barring any public mention of its contents. Wedded to traditional economic theory, the President did not trust the report's budgetary manipulations. He also rejected its grim view of an immediate Soviet threat, preferring to emphasize recent American successes in Europe and the Middle East.[30]

When the North Koreans launched their attack on the South, NSC 68 (as the State/Defense study came to be called) suddenly became more palatable to Truman and other Administration skeptics. The emergency quickly overcame fiscal conservatism and forged a clearer commitment to defense-related propositions such as the strategic significance of Taiwan. Fears that the Soviet Union might accompany confrontation in Korea with aggression in various other trouble spots throughout the world convinced policymakers to launch a series of preventive buildups. Truman, who had rejected the NSC 68 presumption of urgency in April as he had rebuffed Nationalist Chinese demands for aid since January, found the pressures set in motion by the Korean War irresistible. Although the President and his Secretary of State attempted to preserve their freedom of action, the war hardened American policy appreciably.[31]

Similar efforts to withstand mounting anticommunist fervor on the part of some businessmen, academics, and missionaries did not fare much better. Americans, stunned by the ferocious North Korean attack, tended to dismiss the possibility that they had witnessed the start of a civil war and to attribute the fighting to scheming Soviet agents. Communism, it seemed, had proven its monolithic nature and those who had believed the Chinese would retain independence from Moscow's direction found their arguments considerably weakened. Furthermore, the government, which with Acheson's assent had encouraged Sino-American commercial relations, interceded suddenly with far tighter restrictions. Goods which might be used to fuel the North Korean advance could no longer be sold to China.[32]

A few voices, nevertheless, insisted that contacts with Peking be maintained and even widened. During the summer of 1950, according to an informal survey at the National Foreign Trade Convention, a variety of

American firms continued to trade with the mainland. Peter Hopkins, president of the Shanghai Power Company, still asserted the proposition he had long defended, that only through commerce could the United States hope to woo the Chinese Communists away from Moscow. The State Department, acting out of fear of the American public, he believed, was making a serious mistake in forswearing diplomatic relations with China. Similarly Ernest T. Weir, chairman of the board of directors of the National Steel Corporation and the Weirton Steel Company (which together ranked as the sixth largest steel producer in the country) urged recognition in a pamphlet he distributed during February 1951. Weir claimed to kave carried on a survey among European leaders and to be speaking for them as well as for big business interests in the United States. His position merited particular notice in view of his generally conservative politics.[33]

Delegates to the Second Annual Student Conference on United States Affairs also emphasized the importance of American relations with Peking. The students, representing fifty-two colleges and universities and meeting under the auspices of West Point Military Academy and the Carnegie Corporation of New York, though condemning communist expansion, agreed that the United States should be conciliatory toward Communist China, negotiate an end to the Korean conflict, not oppose China's entry into the United Nations, and accept whatever that institution recommended regarding Taiwan's future status. These resolutions, approved by the conferees, were subsequently sent to the State Department.[34]

An occasional religious leader also spoke out for continuing contacts with mainland China. The Reverend John A. MacKay, president of Princeton Theological Seminary, chose to ignore worsening conditions for American missionaries in China and advocated the opening of diplomatic relations with Peking. MacKay asserted that the war had not made the case favoring recognition any less valid. If the conflict necessitated delay, the President should be sensitive to changing conditions and at the earliest moment reverse course.[35]

Such views, however, found little resonance in America during the summer and autumn of 1950. War in Korea had released the floodgates of a red scare surpassing that of the 1920s. The alacrity with which the nation rose to fight communism demonstrated how thoroughly cold war anxieties had penetrated the popular mind. Charges that members of Truman's Administration had been soft on communism dated back to the 1945 Amerasia case. Revelations about the activities of Judith Coplon and Klaus Fuchs and allegations against Alger Hiss served to spread insecurity just as Americans grappled with the fact that Soviet scientists had developed an atomic bomb far sooner than had been anticipated. In February 1950, Joseph McCarthy, a Republican Senator from Wisconsin desperately in need of a campaign issue, decided to capitalize upon the pervasive sense of uncertainty and unease. McCarthy brutally attacked the government for harboring communists and launched a witchhunt that in time would destroy lives and jeopardize democratic institutions. Not until after disillusionment with the Korean War had set in, though, did McCarthy's rampage carry all reason before it. Prior to that it had seemed that the Tydings subcommittee of the Senate Foreign Relations Committee would curb McCarthy and the instant unity engendered by the war itself would silence him. But reverses on the battlefield provided the Senator with new opportunities, and the reign of terror he subsequently imposed in Washington forced Truman and Acheson to take fewer and fewer innovative actions.[36]

Options also had been diminished for American policy because of the international impact of the Korean War. A variety of nations, including France, Japan, Belgium, Turkey, and Australia, welcomed Truman's decisive stand against communist aggression in Korea. The British not only applauded the President's resolve, they put naval units in Northeast Asian waters at his disposal.[37] As gratifying as such support seemed, particularly when the United Nations Security Council promptly voted its endorsement of the resistance effort, drawbacks existed. To Truman and Acheson, American credibility became an ever more important element of the Korean imbroglio. Compromise to avoid prolongation of the bloodshed grew less and less acceptable. Washington must be seen to live up to its commitments even though explicit guarantees concerning Korea had never been tendered. American policymakers could not rid themselves of the apprehension that a failure to endure in Korea would weaken alliances throught the free world.[38]

Vigorous prosecution of the war had to be paralleled by anticommunist policies on the diplomatic front. Acheson believed efforts to conciliate the Chinese Communists or negotiate with the Soviets would undermine United Nations cooperation and determination. Although he had hoped to extend diplomatic recognition to Peking, circumstances no longer permitted advances toward a communist power. But America's diplomatic hard line, prompted in part by this desire to prevent any weakening of the coalition's resolve, did not evoke a similar response among some important European and Asian powers. Both Britain and India launched peace initiatives during July and August, which an annoyed Acheson rebuffed.[39] London and Paris, meanwhile, objected to the Taiwan Straits intervention and sought to settle the island's anomalous position through United Nations action.[40] The British re-

peatedly urged Truman Administration officials to expedite Communist
Chinese entry into the world organization, describing it as a positive
step toward peace.[41] Truman and Acheson, however, while feigning
interest in negotiated solutions, felt increasingly that bargains could not
be struck with Chinese or Soviet aggressors.

Developments in Japan also contributed to a stiffening of Truman's
and Acheson's attitudes. Recognition of the Communist regime in China
had seemed a wise policy in part because of Japan's economic crisis and
the positive contribution trade with the mainland promised to make in
remedying that situation. Once the war effort in Korea turned Japan
into America's staging area, the Japanese began reaping huge, unan-
ticipated profits. Procurement contracts pumped millions into Japanese
industry, and production, previously stalled at low levels, surged
ahead.[42] War, at the same time, brought an intensified concern about
Japan's security. The risk of communist subversion, which had been an
unavoidable concomitant of trade with China, no longer seemed necessary or tolerable. Finally the Korean conflict demonstrated that, as
George Kennan and others had argued, Japan must be firmly tied to the
United States to help protect American interests in the Pacific basin.
Tokyo, therefore, had to be assured that Washington would not stint
in efforts to stop communist expansion.[43]

The war similarly reduced the interest in and ability of China's leaders
to maintain flexible policies. Treatment of Americans in China, for instance, worsened appreciably after June 27, rendering a continued presence there untenable. The Communist Party's earlier desire to utilize
missionaries for their technical skills and perhaps as a channel of communication to Washington abruptly ended with the United States response to events in Korea. In the spring of 1950 American missionary
personnel throughout China suddenly faced charges of spying and sabotage. Possession of a radio transmitter, a gun, or letters from people
in political disfavor became evidence sufficient for denunciation and
expulsion. Some missionaries (probably fewer than fifty) found themselves under house arrest or convicted of espionage and sentenced to
prison.[44] The great majority (close to 2,000) applied for and ultimately
obtained exit permits.[45] Once slow and seemingly reluctant to throw
the missionaries out, the CCP now ejected them without hesitation.
Finally, on December 29, 1950, thirteen days after the government of
the United States froze Chinese assets in America, the administrative
council of the People's Republic of China ordered all Christian organizations to sever connections with American mission boards.[46]

From Peking's perspective American intervention in the Taiwan
Straits had ended any possibility of normalization in Sino-American re-

lations. Chinese Communist leaders bitterly denounced Washington's duplicity and imperialism. President Truman's January declaration that the United States would not rescue Chiang Kai-shek had been exposed as a lie, Mao intoned. The CCP, on the verge of total victory, had to draw back in outraged frustration. Chou En-lai pointed futilely to the wartime Cairo and Potsdam Declarations in which the United States had affirmed China's historic title to Taiwan. The Communist Chinese, he warned, would not rest until they had thwarted this latest American aggression and recovered Taiwan.[47]

Despite their rhetoric, CCP leaders knew that the intercession of American forces had rendered their imminent attack on Taiwan impossible. Although Chou kept the threat of eventual CCP invasion alive, he did not call for immediate action. General Ch'en I, commander of the Taiwan assault army, exhorted his soldiers to continue their training but to give attention to national economic reconstruction as well. Over the next few weeks the concentration of troops opposite Taiwan diminished, leaving in place just enough men to offer initial resistance if a KMT attack occurred.[48]

Rather than continue plans for "liberating" Taiwan, the Chinese Communists shifted their attention to Korea and the unexpectedly negative developments there. After the initial North Korean sweep covering half of South Korea in three weeks, a steady U.S. armed forces buildup convinced CCP leaders that the war would be prolonged. Peking, nevertheless, did not yet contemplate Chinese participation in the struggle. The Korean conflict had no immediate impact on Chinese interests and although Chinese leaders gave rhetorical support to Pyongyang, they abstained from further action until August.

During the summer of 1950, however, the CCP began to worry about Washington's objectives. Should MacArthur's forces cross the 38th parallel and attempt to reunify Korea, Peking believed Chinese security would be seriously jeopardized. China chose initially to express its dismay by giving support to Soviet diplomat Jacob Malik's appeal for a negotiated settlement. When Chou En-lai failed in his efforts to arrange a compromise through the United Nations, the CCP adopted a stronger approach. Late in September the Chief of Staff of the People's Liberation Army told India's Ambassador to China that Peking could not "sit back with folded hands and let the Americans come to the border." Chou En-lai issued similar warnings publicly and, privately, cautioned the Ambassador that, if MacArthur pushed north of the 38th parallel, China would intervene. Although these alarms reached American officials, Washington ignored them and sent its soldiers plunging onward toward the Yalu River. One week later Chinese "volunteers" began secretly to infiltrate the northernmost reaches of Korea and soon after engaged United States forces. By late November, in the midst of MacArthur's "end the war" offensive, CCP troops smashed through United Nations lines.[49]

The bloodshed in Korea ended all prospects of Sino-American normalization in the foreseeable future. Relations, which had been strained since America's intervention in the Taiwan Straits, totally snapped. The United States' neutralization of Taiwan had embittered Chinese Communist leaders, confirming their suspicions of United States rapacity. Washington, intending U.S. naval activities in the Straits to be temporary, tried to signal Peking that an eventual improvement in relations might still be possible. But reassuring words about America's absence of territorial ambitions or lack of desire for special privileges on Taiwan impressed no one in the Chinese capital.[50] And then with the entry of Communist Chinese armies into the Korean conflict in October 1950, the Truman Administration, stunned by the ferocious offensive and enmired in subsequent months of costly fighting, found its alternatives obliterated by the carnage.

Notes

ABBREVIATIONS

BCC	Shanghai Power Company Papers, Boise Cascade Company Archives
BFO	British Foreign Office Records
CA Records	Records of the Office of Chinese Affairs, 1945–1950
CPR	U.S. Consulate General translation service, Chinese Press Review (Hong Kong, Nanking, Shanghai)
CPS	Chinese Press Survey, Millard Publishing Co. (Shanghai)
CR	*Congressional Record*
FBIS	Foreign Broadcast Information Service
FCSC	Foreign Claims Settlement Commission (China Claims Program and War Claims Files)
FRUS	U.S. Department of State, *Foreign Relations of the United States*
Hoover	Hoover Institution on War, Revolution and Peace, Stanford
HST	Harry S Truman Library, Independence, Mo.
LC	Library of Congress
OSS/State Department Reports	OSS/State Department Intelligence and Research Reports
PPS Records	Records of the Policy Planning Staff, 1947–1953
RG 59, NA	General Records of the Department of State, Record Group 59, National Archives Building, Washington, D.C.
RG 84	China Post Files, Record Group 84
RG 319	Army Intelligence Document Files, Record Group 319
SW	*Selected Works of Mao Tse-tung*

Weekly Summary   Weekly Summary of Comment on China, Office of
                        Public Opinion Studies, 1943–1965

White Paper   Lyman P. Van Slyke (intro), *China White Paper, August
                        1949*

WNRC   Washington National Records Center, Suitland, Md.

PREFACE

1. Dean Acheson, *Present at the Creation*, p. 306; Tang Tsou, *America's Failure
in China, 1941–1950*, p. 499.

2. China-bloc Senator William Knowland declared a year later: "The Far Eastern Division of the State Department has had no intention, in my opinion of
helping the non-Communist government of the Republic of China survive. Since
it refused to collapse when they predicted it would some four years ago, they
have been more interested in saving face than they have been in saving freedom." *CR* (January 5, 1950) 96(1):81.

1. AMERICA'S CHINA POLICY

1. Acheson, *Present at the Creation*, pp. 257, 305; Dean Acheson, *Power and
Diplomacy*, p. 72. This chapter has drawn on several studies of Dean Acheson's
career: Robert H. Ferrell and David S. McLellan, "Dean Acheson: Architect of
a Manageable World Order," in Frank J. Merli and Theodore A. Wilson, eds.,
Makers of American Diplomacy, pp. 219–48; Lloyd C. Gardner, *Architects of Illusion*,
pp. 202–344; Norman A. Graebner, "Dean G. Acheson," in Graebner, ed., *An
Uncertain Tradition*, pp. 267–88; Philip Hamburger, "Profile: Mr. Secretary;"
David S. McLellan, *Dean Acheson: The State Department Years*; Oscar W. Perlmutter, "Acheson and American Foreign Policy: A Case Study in the Conduct
of Foreign Affairs in a Mass Democracy" (Ph.D. dissertation); Gaddis Smith,
Dean Acheson.

2. Analysts do not agree on the issue of how much influence the public or
interest groups actually have on foreign policy making. Some, such as G. William
Domhoff in his article, "Who Made American Foreign Policy 1945–1963?" in
David Horowitz, ed., *Corporations and the Cold War*, pp. 25–69, have contended
that large corporations virtually dictate American foreign policy. Others consider
economic interest groups as merely the most important extragovernmental ac-
tors on a stage from which relatively little effective pressure is actually brought
to bear, e.g. Bernard C. Cohen, *The Influence of Non-Governmental Groups on Foreign Policy Making*, p. 11, and Lester W. Milbrath, "Interest Groups and Foreign
Policy," in James N. Rosenau, ed., *Domestic Sources of Foreign Policy*, pp. 213–
30. A detailed study, *American Business and Public Policy* (New York: Atherton
Press, 1963) by Ithiel de Sola Pool, Raymond Bauer, and Anthony Dexter, agrees
that pressure groups do not have the degree of influence traditionally attributed
to them which, the authors are quick to point out, does not mean that they have
no effect. I believe that interest groups do help define the parameters within
which policymakers may act, and sometimes exert positive, constructive influ-

ence on the decision-making process. Historian Ernest May argues the point well, "That public officials study the mail, read newspapers and consult polls is itself evidence that they do care about public opinion. Looking back through American history, one can almost count on one's fingers the number of occasions when American statesmen made major decisions that they thought contrary to the public will." "An American Tradition in Foreign Policy: The Role of Public Opinion," p. 117.

3. Dean Acheson, *A Citizen Looks at Congress*, pp. 86–87; Warren I. Cohen, "Acheson, His Advisors, and China, 1949–1950," in Dorothy Borg and Waldo Heinrichs, eds., *Uncertain Years: Chinese-American Relations, 1947–1950*, pp. 50–51; Graebner, "Acheson" p. 276; Perlmutter, "Acheson and Foreign Policy," pp. 149–51; Princeton Seminars, July 8–9, 1953, Dean Acheson Papers, HST. The Princeton Seminars were meetings of those who had become involved in the making of foreign policy during the Truman Administration. They were held during 1953 and 1954 at the Institute for Advanced Studies, Princeton, N.J. Participants discussed various issues of note including China policy.

4. Harry S Truman, *Memoirs*, 2:230–39; Stephen E. Ambrose, *Rise to Globalism*, p. 175.

5. John F. Melby, *The Mandate of Heaven*, pp. 138, 181.

6. Acheson, *Creation*, p. 8.

7. The Round Table discussion included 25 participants (among them State Department representatives, military officers, scholars, businessmen, and philanthropists) who reviewed the most pressing problems of Sino–American relations. The sometimes contentious·debates can be followed in United States Department of State, *Transcript of Round Table Discussion on American Policy Toward China, October 6, 7, and 8, 1949*.

8. The China White Paper, published in August 1949, consisted of 1054 pages of narrative history and documents which attempted to explain and justify American policy toward China. Originally it appeared under the title *United States Relations With China With Special Reference to the Period 1944–1949* but quickly became known as the White Paper.

9. Truman, *Memoirs*, 2:430; Ernest R. May, *The Truman Administration and China*, pp. 29–30.

10. Novelist Han Suyin, married at the time to a Kuomintang officer stationed in Chungking, described the reaction she observed to news of Pearl Harbor: "The military council was jubilant. Chiang was so happy he sang an old opera aria and played 'Ave Maria' all day. The Kuomintang government officials went around congratulating each other, as if a great victory had been won. From their standpoint, it was a great victory. . . . At last, at last America was at war with Japan. Now China's strategic importance would grow even more. American money and equipment would flow in; half a billion dollars, one billion dollars. . . . Now America would have to support Chiang, and that meant U.S. dollars into the pockets of the officials, into the pockets of the army commanders, and guns . . . for the coming war against Yenan." Quoted in Michael Schaller, *The United States and China in the Twentieth Century*, p. 70.

11. Barbara Tuchman, *Stilwell and the American Experience in China*.

12. Lyman P. Van Slyke (intro), *China White Paper*, pp. 113–17.

13. Actually Chiang felt confident that he could convince Stalin to restrain the CCP because the Soviet leader would want to protect the concessions secured at Yalta. Akira Iriye, *The Cold War in Asia*, p. 122.

14. Steven I. Levine, "A New Look at American Mediation in the Chinese Civil War," pp. 349–75; *White Paper*, pp. 127–229, 686–89 (this and subsequent references are to the Van Slyke edition).

15. Personal Statement by the Special Representative of the President (Marshall), January 7, 1949, in *White Paper*, pp. 686–89. Re impact on Acheson see *Creation*, p. 210, and on Truman, *Memoirs*, 2:90.

16. *White Paper*, pp. 131–32, 146, 336–37, 358–59.

17. Albert C. Wedemeyer, *Wedemeyer Reports!* pp. 381–404, 461–79; *White Paper*, pp. 257–59, 815–16. Wedemeyer, felt compelled to point out that "considerable time and effort are spent in blaming outside influences and seeking outside assistance" when instead the KMT must "effect immediately drastic, far-reaching political and economic reforms. Promises will no longer suffice. Performance is absolutely necessary."

18. Walter LaFeber, *America, Russia and the Cold War 1945–1975*, pp. 50–59; Ernest R. May, *"Lessons" of the Past*, pp. 42–50.

19. Graebner, "Acheson," p. 281; Ambrose, *Globalism*, p. 153. Note the contrary emphasis on globalism in Thomas G. Paterson, "If Europe, Why Not China?" pp. 19–38, and the recent debate over the extent of containment in Eduard M. Mark, "What Kind of Containment?" pp. 96–109; John L. Gaddis, "Was the Truman Doctrine a Real Turning Point?" pp. 386–402, and "Containment: A Reassessment," pp. 873–87; Eduard M. Mark, "The Question of Containment," pp. 430–41.

20. Walter E. Millis, ed., *The Forrestal Diaries*, p. 285; Tang Tsou, *America's Failure in China*, p. 452.

21. House Committee on Foreign Affairs, *Hearings on Emergency Foreign Aid*, 80th Cong., 1st sess., 1947, p. 239.

22. Robert A. Divine, *Foreign Policy and U.S. Presidential Elections*, pp. 225–26, 242; Athan G. Theoharis, *The Yalta Myths*, pp. 63, 68–69. See also chapter 9.

23. Eric F. Goldman, *The Crucial Decade and After*, pp. 101–6; Allen Weinstein, *Perjury, passim;* W. A. Swanberg, *Luce*, pp. 3, 196–97, 216–32, 284–89; Ross Koen *The China Lobby in American Politics*, pp. 57, 80–83, 99; Acheson, *Creation*, pp. 250–52, 359–61. According to the *New York Times*, Hiss had been nothing more than a technician at Yalta. March 17, 1955, p. 79.

24. Transcripts of Presidential Press Conferences, August 5, 1948, Harry S Truman Papers, HST.

25. James Fetzer, "Congress and China, 1941–1950" (Ph.D. dissertation), pp. 35–37; Koen, *China Lobby*, p. 87; H. Bradford Westerfield, *Foreign Policy and Party Politics*, pp. 245–49.

26. Koen, *China Lobby*, pp. 66–73; Tsou, *America's Failure*, pp. 343–44; Joseph W. Esherick, ed., *Lost Chance in China*, pp. 354–58, 387.

27. Truman, *Memoirs*, 2:91.

28. Fetzer, "Congress and China," pp. 155, 161; Tsou, *America's Failure*, p. 475; Princeton Seminars, July 15–16, 1953, Acheson Papers, HST; see also chapter 9.

29. Princeton Seminars, July 22–23, 1953, Acheson Papers, HST; Smith, *Dean Acheson*, p. 108.

30. Tsou, *America's Failure*, pp. 486–93.

31. George F. Kennan, *Memoirs*, p. 359.

32. As the Secretary would later observe: "We must not undertake to deflect from the Russians to ourselves the righteous anger, and the wrath, and the

hatred of the Chinese people which must develop. It would be folly to deflect it to ourselves. We must take the position we have always taken—that anyone who violates the integrity of China is the enemy of China and is acting contrary to our interests." Dean Acheson, "Crisis in Asia," p. 115; Acheson, *Power*, pp. 41–42; Graebner, "Acheson," pp. 273–74; McLellan, *Dean Acheson*, pp. 134, 144–45, 163, 172; Smith, *Dean Acheson*, pp. 417–24; David S. McLellan and David C. Acheson, eds., *Among Friends*, pp. 121–22.

33. *New York Daily News*, November 18, 1949, p. 47; FRUS (1949)8:963–1051; "Allegations of Espionage in Mukden Denied," *Department of State Bulletin* (July 11, 1949) 21:36; "No Response from Chinese on Release of Angus Ward and Staff; Consul General Clubb Sends Letter to Chinese Authorities," *ibid.*, November 21, 1949, pp. 759–60; Meeting with the President, November 14, 1949, CA Records, Box 14: 1948–49, folder: Ward Case, Mukden, 1949, 1950, RG59, NA; Memorandum on Consul General Angus Ward, November 18, 1949, Central Intelligence Agency, Washington, D.C.; "Angus Ward Released by Communists: Secretary Acheson Sends Personal Letter to Thirty Nations," *Department of State Bulletin* (November 28, 1949) 21:779–80; "Living with the Chinese Communists," pp. 5–7; "Angus Ward Summarizes Mukden Experiences," *Department of State Bulletin* (December 26, 1949) 21:955–56; "American Spy Ring in Mukden," pp. 17–18; "Facts About Ward Case," pp. 6–8; "American Espionage Ring in Manchuria," pp. 9, 24; "Idle Reflections on the Question of Recognizing the Chinese Communists," John F. Melby to W. Walton Butterworth, CA Records, Box 16, folder: Recognition 1949, RG 59, NA; John P. Davies, "Mr. Ward, the Russians and Recognition," November 17, 1949, PPS Records, Box 33: Chronological File, folder: Chronological 1949, RG 59, NA; Bernard Gwertzman, "The Hostage Crisis—Three Decades Ago," pp. 41–44, 101–6.

34. Akira Iriye, "Was There a Cold War in Asia?" pp. 7, 9–14; Iriye, *Cold War*, pp. 164, 171.

35. Herbert Feis, *Churchill-Roosevelt-Stalin*, pp. 407–8.

36. Tsou, *America's Failure*, pp. 104, 183.

37. Esherick, *Lost Chance in China*, pp. 344–45; Herbert Feis, *The China Tangle*, p. 358; James Reardon-Anderson, *Yenan and the Great Powers*, p. 103.

38. Donovan, *Conflict and Crisis*, p. 150; Richard J. Walton, *Henry Wallace, Harry Truman, and the Cold War*, p. 66; see also chapter 2 below for an extended discussion of the Soviet role in China.

39. Iriye, *The Cold War*, p. 141; Iriye, "Was there a Cold War," pp. 9–10. See also chapters 2 and 3.

40. David E. Lilienthal, *Journals*, 2:525; A. H. Vandenberg Jr. and Joe A. Morris, eds., *The Private Papers of Senator Vandenberg*, pp. 559–60; Acheson, *Power*, p. 129.

41. See chapter 2.

42. Tsou, *America's Failure*, p. 394.

2. INTERNATIONAL INFLUENCES

1. Dorothy Borg puts it succinctly: "The American people and the American Government tended, far more than has been recognized, to look upon developments in Eastern Asia not as separate from but as an integral part of global

developments. The corollary to this theory is that, contrary to a widely held assumption, the motives underlying our policy in Eastern Asia may more often than not have been the same as those which formed the basis of our policies toward the rest of the world." Dorothy Borg, *American Policy and the Chinese Revolution 1925–1928*, p. xiv.

2. The United States virtually shut Britain out of the Japanese occupation, thereby creating what British Foreign Secretary Ernest Bevin called the "Monroe sphere" of the Pacific. Churchill, on the other hand, was willing to trade a role in Japan for sanctity of the Empire. Britain did play a more active role in Southeast Asia during the postwar period. Christopher Thorne, *Allies of a Kind*, pp. 678–79; Herbert Feis, *Contest Over Japan*, p. 90; Gabriel Kolko, *The Politics of War*, p. 465.

3. Brian Porter in the preface to *Britain and the Rise of Communist China* maintains: "Greater differences arose between the British and Americans over Far Eastern problems than over any others—apart, perhaps, from the short-lived Suez affair—in which they have been involved since the war."

4. John K. Fairbank et al. *East Asia: The Modern Transformation*, pp. 765–73.

5. Thorne, *Allies of a Kind*, pp. 102–3. Emphasis on the dangers of nationalist conflicts with colonialism in Asia continued. For example see: NSC 48/1, "The Position of the United States with Respect to Asia," December 23, 1949, Department of Defense, *United States-Vietnam Relations 1945–1947*, VB2: Justification of the War—Internal Commitments, Truman Administration 1945–1952, Book 1, 1945–1949, pp. 247–48. By this time, however, the United States had become concerned not just with satisfying "the fundamental demands of the nationalist movement[s]" but also with "minimizing the strain on the colonial powers who are our Western allies." NSC 48/2, NSC 48/1 revised conclusions, December 30, 1949, *U.S.–Vietnam Relations*, VB2, Bk. 1, p. 271.

6. Thorne, *Allies of a Kind*, pp. 13 (quote), 16, 209–11; 893.00/4-1445 Hurley, Ambassador in China (temporarily in Iran), FRUS (1945)7:330–31. Note: the decimal file system indicates not merely the file number (here 893.00), but also the date on which the item was sent (here 4-1445, which is April 14, 1945). Re concurrence with Churchill's view by other Britons: Thorne, pp. 558, 705, 709; and D. C. Watt, "Britain and the Cold War in the Far East, 1945–1958," p. 92. Re extent of British decline during World War II: Thorne, pp. 675–76, and Kolko, *Politics of War*, pp. 488–96.

7. According to the British Foreign Office the value of British commercial property in China in 1941 equaled £300 million to which "must be added invisible earnings." Although they had not deducted war damage from this total the value was still "very considerable." Indeed, American analysts noted that the British had invested large amounts of money in rehabilitating their properties after the war. Moreover, these analysts found that, because of the war-related liquidation of Britain's foreign holdings elsewhere, investments in China "bulk even more heavily in the smaller total remaining." "The Situation in China," April 5, 1949, Annex I, British Embassy to the Department of State, FRUS (1949)9:839; "Current British Policy Toward Communist China," OIR 5111, November 15, 1949, pp. 2–3, 13–15, Reel 4, Part 3: China & India, OSS/State Department Reports. Somewhat lower investment figures appear in Mayhew, *House of Commons Debates* (May 3, 1948) 450, cols. 890–91. A comparison of British and American investments in China in 1931 by Christopher Thorne puts Britain's China holdings at 5.9 percent of that country's overseas investments whereas United States

investments there comprised only 1.3 percent of total American foreign holdings. Thorne, *Allies of a Kind*, p. 17.

8. Feis, *China Tangle*, pp. 410–11; Michael Schaller, *The U.S. Crusade in China*, p. 199. In the mid-1940s British interest in the CCP paralleled the agrarian-myth convictions of many American observers. O. M. Green, *Yorkshire Post*, December 19, 1949, wrote that "Communism is but the modern name for China's oldest problem—the grievances of peasant against landlord." The *Times* expressed similar opinions, January 25, 1945, November 6, 1945 and January 6, 1946, as cited by Porter, *Britain and Communist China*, pp. 5–6. John Keswick, of Jardine Matheson and various wartime diplomatic posts, described CCP philosophy as agrarian revolt based on the San Min Chu I of Sun Yat-sen. Most important, Sterndale Bennett, head of the Far Eastern Department of the Foreign Office, also accepted this interpretation. Thorne, *Allies of a Kind*, p. 559. D. C. Watt, however, contends that the Far Eastern Office staff "rarely succumbed to the myth." When individuals did it was due to their "inexperience." Watt, "Britain and the Cold War," p. 93.

9. 893.00/1-1645, Representative Michael J. Mansfield of Montana to President Roosevelt, January 3, 1945, FRUS (1945)7:2–26.

10. 893.00/1-1044 "American Chinese Relations During the Next Six Months," Memorandum by John Paton Davies, Second Secretary of the Embassy, Nanking, FRUS (1944)6:697; 893.00/1-1044 "The Chinese Communists and the Great Powers," Memorandum by Davies, FRUS (1944)6:667–69; Memorandum by Davies to Chief of the Division of Chinese Affairs, Vincent, November 14, 1944, PSA China White Book, Lot 565, FRUS (1944)6:692–93; 893.00/1-1044 "The Generalissimo's Dilemma," Memorandum by Davies, FRUS (1944)6:724–27; 761.93/1-2645 "China and the Kremlin," Memorandum by Davies, FRUS (1945)7:155–57; 893.00/12-2444 Appointed Ambassador in China, Hurley, FRUS (1944) 6:748–49; Feis, *China Tangle*, p. 212n4; 121.893/8-647, #47 Albert C. Wedemeyer to Secretary of State and 893.00/8-1347, Memorandum by First Secretary of the Embassy in China, Ludden, to Wedemeyer, FRUS (1947)7:712, 717; and Albert C. Wedemeyer, *Wedemeyer Reports!* pp. 188, 281.

11. #1790 George C. Marshall, China, to President Truman, November 21, 1946, Marshall Mission Files, Lot 54-D270, FRUS (1946)10:557. This telegram carried the message that the British Ambassador in China had told Ambassador Stuart that Britain recognized the United States had taken over its position in China. To this Colonel Marshall S. Carter, General George C. Marshall's Washington liaison, replied at Secretary Acheson's request with the "grain of salt" quote in the text. #86246 Carter to Marshall, November 23, 1946, Marshall Mission Files, Lot 54-D270, FRUS (1946)10:561.

The British insisted that they wanted a strong, unified China. 741.93/11-1846, #1898 Stuart, Nanking, FRUS (1946)10:549. But a small group of experienced China hands in the Far Eastern Division of the Foreign Office, including John Pratt and G. F. Hudson, "thought policy predicated (as was that of the United States) on the emergence of a strong central government, however desirable that might seem, to be based on so great an improbability as to verge on the absurd." Watt, "Britain and the Cold War," p. 93.

12. Winston Churchill, *The Hinge of Fate*, pp. 133–34, and see Churchill's *Triumph and Tragedy*, p. 701, which reprints his contemporary comment: Churchill to Foreign Secretary, August 23, 1944: "That China is one of the world's four Great Powers is an absolute farce." See also Schaller, *U.S. Crusade*, p. 222.

13. Feis, *Churchill-Roosevelt-Stalin*, p. 124. The United States insisted on a variety of measures: (1) that China be a signatory, with the United States, the United Kingdom and the Soviet Union, of the Moscow Declaration, October 30, 1943; (2) that China be a signatory of the Cairo Declaration, December 1, 1943; (3) that China participate in the Dumbarton Oaks talks, 1944; (4) that China be a sponsor of the United Nations Conference on International Organization, San Francisco, 1945; be included among the formulators of the UN Charter; and be given a permanent seat on the Security Council. *White Paper*, p. 37.

14. Porter, *Britain and Communist China*, p. 14. Roosevelt believed that in any Anglo-American dispute China would wholeheartedly support the United States. He welcomed Chinese suspicion of British motives and Churchill's provocative condescension toward the Chinese. The Kuomintang leadership reinforced FDR's image. During her 1942–43 visit to the United States, Madame Chiang told Harry Hopkins that "China would line up with us [the United States] at the peace table." Tsou, *America's Failure*, pp. 38–41.

15. 893.50 Recovery/12-948, #5174 Douglas, Ambassador in the United Kingdom, FRUS (1948)8:683–84.

16. Thorne, *Allies of a Kind*, pp. 68, 193–94; V. K. Wellington Koo Oral History Collection, 1(section 8):460–64, East Asian Institute, Columbia University (hereafter Koo Oral History), and same conversation recorded in V. K. Wellington Koo Papers, Conversations #79, Sir Stafford Cripps, British Chancellor of the Exchequer, September 15, 1949, Box 130: Memoranda of Conversations, Butler Library Manuscript Division, Columbia University (hereafter Koo Papers). United Aid to China began its operations in 1942.

17. Koo Oral History, J(sec 1):8–9, and Koo Papers, Conversation #78, Ernest Bevin, British Foreign Secretary, September 16, 1949, Box 130: Memoranda of Conversations.

18. 893.00/8-1749, Dispatch #1357 Douglas, London, with enclosure "Memorandum Prepared in British Foreign Office: China," FRUS (1949)9:56–61.

19. 893.00/5-1649, Dispatch #838 Erle R. Dickover, Counselor of Embassy, London, RG59, NA. *Guardian* story dated April 25, 1949; 893.01/10-1849, #1655 Ringwalt, London, RG 59, NA; Robert Boardman, *Britain and the People's Republic of China*, pp. 112–13.

20. Porter, *Britain and Communist China*, pp. 13–14; 740.00119PW/8-1645 Hurley to Secretary of State, and 740.00119PW/8-1645, #1371 Hurley, and 740.00119PW/8-1845, #6 British Prime Minister Attlee to President Truman, FRUS (1945)7:500–4; Thorne, *Allies of a Kind*, p. 558.

21. Ernest Bevin, *House of Commons Debates* (December 9, 1948) 459:col. 566; George D. Hopper, Hong Kong, to J. Leighton Stuart, Nanking, "Report on Conditions in Hong Kong: Summary of Political Conditions for the Month of January 1949," February 12, 1949, folder: 350 Hong Kong Government—Political, Consul General Hong Kong, RG 84, WNRC; Andrew Roth, "China and the 'Foreign Devils,'" p. 296; 761.93/1-2645, "China and the Kremlin," FRUS (1945)7:155. Indeed in May 1949 London protested the use of requisitioned British ships for KMT troop transport and in the autumn of 1949 disputed the use of Hong Kong waters for Chinese military preparations. Evan Luard, *Britain and China*, pp. 76–77.

22. 893.00/6-2749 Memorandum by the Director of the Office of Far Eastern Affairs, Butterworth, FRUS (1949)9:1110–12. Re convoying see: 841.85/10-1849 Memorandum by the Secretary of State to the President, FRUS (1949) 9:1150–

52; Andrew Roth, "How the Communists Rule," p. 488; and Memorandum by R. H. Hillenkoetter, Director of Central Intelligence to the President, January 12, 1950, Harry S Truman Papers, President's Secretary's Files, Intelligence, folder: Central Intelligence Memorandum 1950–1952, HST. According to figures presented in Parliament, British ships were interfered with by the Nationalists on 16 occasions between September 1, 1949 and January 6, 1950. Moreover, Ernest Bevin told the House of Commons in May 1950 that British interests suffered more from the blockade than from CCP taxes and other restrictive measures. Boardman, *Britain and the People's Republic*, pp. 13, 29.

23. Boardman, *Britain and the People's Republic*, p. 12. The Nationalists not only resented the British for their colonialist attitudes, their resistance against the blockade, and the meager postwar aid appropriations London made for Chiang's forces, they also were aware of British reservations regarding China's international position. Although Anthony Eden assured T. V. Soong in July 1943 that Britain wanted a strong, unified China, Soong told Secretary of State Cordell Hull in August that the Chinese knew London did not wish to accord China "Big Four" status. Feis, *China Tangle*, p. 96n2.

24. Although British trade with China amounted to only about 1% of total United Kingdom trade in 1948, in a period when the nation was experiencing a balance of payments problem and straining to boost export volume, the China trade was especially difficult to lose. This was the opinion of American analysts who also noted that the volume of trade between China and the Commonwealth nations multiplied China's commercial importance to the British four times. In addition they pointed to the value of potential trade.

OIR 5111, November 15, 1949, pp. 11–12, Reel 4, Pt 3, OSS/State Department Reports. The British government also emphasized the China market myth: "Finally, in the long term, the potentialities of China under a strong and efficient Government as a source of raw material and food-stuffs and as an export market should not be forgotten. It would be a misfortune should at some future time these potentialities be realized if the western world were then cut off from what might become available." 893.00/8-1749, Dispatch #1357, FRUS (1949)9:59.

25. "Factors Affecting the Status of Hong Kong (to September 1950)," ORE 78-49, October 4, 1949, Central Intelligence Agency, RG 319, WNRC; #392 Political Report for November 1949, by K. L. Rankin, Consul General, December 20, 1949, folder: 350 Hong Kong Government—Political, Consul General Hong Kong, RG 84, WNRC. The Malayan uprising began in June 1948 as a consequence, British intelligence thought, of Soviet direction following the Calcutta Conference of the World Federation of Democratic Youth. Watt, "Britain and the Cold War," p. 89.

26. Memorandum by R. H. Hillenkoetter, Director of Central Intelligence, January 9, 1950, Truman Papers, PSF, Intelligence, folder: Central Intelligence Memorandum 1950–1952, HST; ORE 78-49, pp. 6–8, RG 319, WNRC; Lewis W. Douglas, American Ambassador to London, to Ernest Bevin, July 22, 1949, attachment to 893.00/8-1749, Dispatch #1357 Dickover, London, RG 59, NA.

27. Boardman, *Britain and the People's Republic*, pp. 33–39; 893.00/6-248 Memorandum of Conversation by the Assistant Chief of the Division of Chinese Affairs, Sprouse, FRUS (1949) 8:77–79; Douglas to Bevin, July 22, 1949 and Bevin to Douglas, July 22, 1949, attachments to 893.00/8-1749, Dispatch #1357, Dickover, London, RG 59, NA; John M. Hightower, "U.S., Britain Likely To Link Policies on China and Far East," p. 1B; Hightower, "Acheson To Discuss New

U.S. Policy in Far East with Bevin This Week," p. 1B; 893.00/11-449 Memorandum Merchant (FE) to Sprouse (CA), RG 59, NA. In addition, according to Arthur Ringwalt, Chief of the Division of Chinese Affairs, 1946–48, and Secretary of the American Embassy in London, 1949–57, it had been State Department practice, for many years, to station a relatively senior China service veteran in London to keep in touch with the Foreign Office. Arthur Ringwalt Oral History Interview, June 5, 1974, HST.

28. Office Memo Butterworth to Rusk, July 29, 1949, folder: Evacuation 1949, Box 14: 1948–1949, CA Records, RG 59, NA; "Far Eastern Problems Requiring an Urgent Solution," Memorandum transmitted by Douglas to Bevin, July 22, 1949, attachment to 893.00/8-1749, #1357 Dickover, London, RG 59, NA; Position Paper for Bevin Conversations, copies in Boxes 14 and 16, CA Records, RG 59, NA; 693.419/7-2649 #2956 Douglas, RG 59, NA; 693.419/9-1249 Aide-Memoire, British Embassy to Department of State, FRUS (1949)9:877; 693.419/12-3149, #4667 Department of State to American Embassy, London, RG 59, NA. The British initially favored a common front as well. 893.01/1-2749 Excerpts from telegram from British Foreign Minister to British Embassy, Washington, handed to Sprouse (CA) by Graves, Counselor of British Embassy, April 9, 1949, RG 59, NA; 841.503193/4-549 "The Situation in China," FRUS (1949)9:839–40.

29. Barnett Nover, "Far East Plan Drags," p. 14; 893.01/11-749 Memorandum of Conversation, and 893.01/11-949 Memo Brown to Battle, in which John Kee, Chairman of the House Foreign Affairs Committee predicts a threat to Korean Aid and ECA legislation, RG 59, NA.

30. The British remained pragmatic despite frictions with the Chinese Communists. CCP propaganda attacked Great Britain for imperialistic intentions and CCP guns attacked British ships in the Yangtze River for alleged imperialistic behavior. For details of the *Amethyst* Incident, in which a British ship intruded into a battle zone and became trapped under CCP fire, see: "Withdraw Foreign Armed Forces, Say Chinese People," April 30, 1949, and "British Vessels Invade Yangtze," April 27, 1949, *New China News Agency Weekly Bulletin* (May 3, 1949) no. 100, p. 4; "The Way to Establish Diplomatic Relations with New China," *China Digest* (May 17, 1949) 6:5; Dispatch #1, George Hopper, Hong Kong to Lewis Clark, Canton, May 10, 1949, folder: 350 Hong Kong Government—Political, Consul General Hong Kong, RG 84, WNRC; Porter, *Britain and Communist China*, pp. 26–27. Mao Tse-tung, "On the Outrages by British Warships—Statement by the Spokesman of the General Headquarters of the Chinese People's Liberation Army," April 30, 1949, in *SW*, 4:401–3.

31. "Summary of US-UK-French Conversations Relating to China, Formosa, Hong Kong, and Macao," September 9–17, 1949, folder: 1949, Box 16, CA Records, RG 59, NA.

32. "Proclamation of the Central Government of the People's Republic of China," and "An Official Communication from Chou En-lai," *NCNA Weekly Bulletin*, October 4, 1949, pp. 3–4; 893.01/10-1749 Meeting with the President, RG 59, NA; 893.01/10-1849 Office Memo Sprouse (CA) to Butterworth (FE), RG 59, NA. The British reply suggested that pending study of the situation "informal relations should be established between His Majesty's Consular Officers and appropriate authorities in territory under control of the Central People's Government for the great convenience of both Governments and promotion of trade between the two countries." OIR 5111, November 15, 1949, p. 1, Reel 4, Pt 3,

OSS/State Department Reports. President Truman noted that the Soviet Union considered the British response equivalent to recognition.

33. This paragraph relies heavily on the OSS/State Department Report "Current British Policy Toward Communist China," OIR 5111, November 15, 1949, Reel 4, Pt. 3. Quote taken from p. 4. The Chinese Nationalists also believed that recognition was a very popular policy in the United Kingdom. Koo Oral History, J(sec. 1):42–49. The British public expressed reservations in a November 28, 1949 Gallup Poll. The question and responses were as follows: Do you think that Britain should recognize the Government set up in China by the Chinese Communist Party, that is, should we send an ambassador and have dealings with this Communist Government?

	Yes	No	Don't Know
Conservative voters	23	59	18
Labour voters	34	37	29
Liberal voters	37	37	26
Total	29	45	26

Source: Porter, *Britain and Communist China*, p. 162

34. Even Conservative Party leadership tended to support government policy with only a minority favoring comprehensive anticommunist programs. Boardman, *Britain and People's Republic*, pp. 11, 25; and Porter, *Britain and Communist China*, pp. 14–17.

35. See *Manchester Guardian*, April 25, 1949, *London Times*, October 5, 1949 and *Daily Telegraph*, September 16, 1949, cited by OIR 5111. The U.S. State Department was apprised of British press opinion by the U.S. Embassy in London. See for examples: 893.01/10-649, Dispatch #1586 Arthur Ringwalt, First Secretary of the Embassy, London, and 893.01/10-1849, Dispatch #1655 Ringwalt, London, and 893.01/10-2849, Dispatch #1725 Ringwalt, London, and 893.01/11-2349, #A-2175 Douglas, London, and 893.01/12-149, #A-2268 Douglas, London, and 893.01/12-2349, #A-2442 Holmes, London, RG 59, NA.

36. The China Association was established in 1889 and functioned like a chamber of commerce. In 1949 it had 197 member firms and 230 individual members. Its president in 1948 was Lord Inverchapel and in 1950 became Sir Horace Seymour, both of whom were former ambassadors to China. Porter, *Britain and Communist China*, p. 153. Re pro-recognition and pro-trade sentiment in the British business community: "Report on Conditions in Hong Kong—Summary of Political Conditions for the Month of January 1949," February 12, 1949, Hopper, Hong Kong to Stuart, Nanking, RG 84, WNRC; 893.00/3-1749 Memorandum from Sprouse (CA) to Butterworth (FE), RG 59, NA; 841.503193/4-549 "The Situation in China," FRUS (1949)9:839; 693.0031/7-1649, #523 Smyth, Tientsin, FRUS (1949) 9:969; Boardman, *Britain and the People's Republic*, p. 31. CCP treatment of the British business community, according to newsman Andrew Roth, surpassed that given Soviet businessmen. Roth, "China and the 'Foreign Devil,'" p. 296.

37. British efforts to inform the Commonwealth and hear members' views: 893.01/10-2149, #4353 Douglas, London, RG 59, NA; Porter, *Britain and Communist China*, pp. 37–38; Lord Strang, *Home and Abroad*, pp. 239–50. Although

Asian Commonwealth opinion is usually seen as prorecognition there was some speculation in the Southeast Asia Division of the U.S. State Department that Malaya and Thailand might prefer trade without recognition. 893.01/9-1549 Office Memo Reed (SEA) to Butterworth (FE) FRUS (1949)9:85-86.

38. 75819 (F16699/1023/10) Foreign Office Minute by Scarlett, November 4, 1949, BFO; 75819 (F16527/1023/10) Minute by Franklin, November 4, 1949, BFO; Boardman, *Britain and the People's Republic*, pp. 39-40. France also reportedly believed that a French compromise with Mao Tse-tung would be acceptable to the United States, 893.00/11-449 Memo Jack D. Neal (SY) to O'Sullivan (PSA) and Sprouse (CA), RG 59, NA. American reporters maintained on many occasions that some understanding on a joint Anglo-American China policy had been reached. See for examples: Benjamin Welles, *New York Times*, London Dispatch, May 18, 1949, Weekly Summary, May 12-18, 1949; Constantine Brown, May 26, 1949, Weekly Summary, May 26-June 1, 1949; Hearst press, July 6, 1949, Weekly Summary, July 7-13, 1949.

39. Purcell in *London Times*, January 26, 1950, cited by Boardman, *Britain and the People's Republic*, p. 47. Churchill told the House of Commons: "One has to recognize lots of things and people in this world of sin and woe that one does not like." *House of Commons Debates* (November 7, 1949) 469:2225. The Chinese Communists agreed with Purcell's assessment. "Diplomacy and Friendship," *People's China* (January 16, 1950) 1:3; "Communist Press Supports Chou En-lai," Articles and Speeches, January 17, 1950, section: Far East, China, January 19, 1950, p. PPP-3, FBIS; "Struggle to the End for the Realization of Premier Chou En-lai's Statement," *Jen-min jih-pao*, January 17, 1950; "No Illusion About Imperialism," *China Digest* (January 26, 1950) 7:14; "British Failure to Break with Kuomintang Remnants Bars Way to Diplomatic Relations with China," Hsinhua *Daily Bulletin*, #38, May 26, 1950; "The Real Intentions of the British Government," *Jen-min jih-pao*, May 28, 1950. Re importance of British abstention on UN vote, January 13, 1950, see J. P. Jain, *China in World Politics*, pp. 36-37.

40. Boardman, *Britain and the People's Republic*, pp. 51-53. Re British troubles after recognition: O. M. Green, "Shanghai Faces Ruin," pp. 16-17; and Boardman, *Britain and the People's Republic*, pp. 43, 45-46. Public reaction to these problems: Porter, *Britain and Communist China*, pp. 39-40. The degree of British suffering may well be exaggerated in the literature. Hong Kong, for example, continued to exist and trade also proceeded.

41. Walter Winchell, ABC, March 12, 1950 and Constantine Brown, March 11, 1950, Weekly Summary, March 9-15, 1950; Constantine Brown, April 15, 1950, Weekly Summary, April 13-19, 1950; *New York Herald Tribune*, November 24, 1949, Weekly Summary, November 24-30, 1949, and May 23, 1950, Weekly Summary May 18-24, 1950. Others who saw British efforts to carry on business with the CCP as a failure included: Jay G. Hayden, North American Newspaper Alliance, April 17, 1950 and Polyzoides of the *Los Angeles Times*, April 15, 1950, Weekly Summary, April 13-19, 1950.

42. Schaller, *U.S. Crusade*, p. 199; 893.01/11-849, #2389 Bacon, Nanking, FRUS (1949)9:181.

43. The controversial question of when the Cold War came to Asia is discussed by Akira Iriye, "Was There a Cold War in Asia?" pp. 3-24.

44. 893.00/6-2749, #1620 Kohler, Chargé d'Affaires, Moscow, RG 59, NA; 893.00/7-1649, #2796 Cabot, Shanghai, FRUS (1949)8:439; 893.00/7-2749, #829 Clark, Canton, RG 59, NA.

45. At least some analysts in the State Department's Office of Intelligence Research believed that Mao would fill a position in China akin to East European satellite leaders. "The Status of Mao Tse-tung as Theoretician and Leader," OIR 5101, December 22, 1949, pp. 4–10, Reel 4, Pt. 3, OSS/State Department Reports. See also "Prospects for Soviet Control of a Communist China," ORE 29-49, April 15, 1949, CIA, RG 319, WNRC.

46. Little material assistance passed from the Soviet Union to the Chinese Communists. In October 1949 Liu Shao-ch'i acknowledged USSR aid in training personnel and rehabilitating industry and railroads in Manchuria. During July 1949 Moscow concluded a trade agreement with the CCP authorities in Manchuria. The Soviets promised machinery, motor vehicles, paper, and medicine in exchange for foodstuffs. This was, however, a period of food shortages in China and the agreement was not universally applauded in China. Moreover, much of the damage to industry and transportation in Manchuria had been done by the Russians. 661.9331/8-249, #A-155 Hopper, Hong Kong, RG 59, NA; 661.9331/8-449, #3017 McConaughy, Shanghai, RG 59, NA; 661.9331/8-1149, #1337 Clubb, Peking, RG 59, NA; "USSR—A Friend in Need," *China Digest* (August 24, 1949) 6:7; 761.00/10-1749 Weekly Selection from State Department to Certain Diplomatic and Consular Officers, RG 59, NA. Contradictory reports came from Tientsin: 693.0031/3-2949, #181 Smyth, Tientsin, and 693.0031/4-2649, #1379 Cabot, Shanghai, RG 59, NA. Re anger about food going to USSR: Secretary of State to Certain Diplomatic and Consular Officers, December 20, 1949, file 350 Miscellaneous—Political, Consul General Hong Kong, RG 84, WNRC; and 661.9331/11-2549, #972A Wellborn, Tientsin, RG 59, NA.

47. Liu Shao-ch'i, "Lun Kuo-chi chu-i yü min-tsu chi-i," [On internationalism and nationalism] (Hong Kong: Hsin-min chu-i ch'u-pan she, 1949), and English translation in the *Collected Works of Liu Shao-ch'i, 1945–1947*, pp. 123–51. Although Liu gave the speech on November 1, 1948, *Pravda* did not publish it until June 1949. American Ambassador Stuart speculated that the delay indicated that the Soviets were only slowly becoming prone to recognize the CCP as a genuine member of the Communist bloc. 893.00B/6-1049, #1258 Stuart, Nanking, FRUS (1949)8:379. Mao Tse-tung, "On People's Democratic Dictatorship," *China Digest* (July 13, 1949) 6:3–8 and reprinted in Mao, *SW*, 4:411–24. The Division of European Affairs of the U.S. State Department considered this speech an indication of how firmly Mao's movement adhered to the Soviet bloc. 893.00/8-149 "Observations on the Development of Communism in the USSR and in Eastern Europe with Regard to Their Applicability to the Chinese Communist Movement," Memorandum Thompson (EUR) to Butterworth (FE), RG 59, NA. The *New York Times* similarly saw this as confirmation of Mao's hostility to the United States. *New York Times*, July 3, 1949, Weekly Summary, June 30–July 6, 1949.

48. 893.00/7-649, #1443 Stuart, Nanking, FRUS (1949) 8:405–7. Stuart had expressed similar views on other occasions. In March 1949, although noting reservations made by the Chinese as to their independence, Stuart called a New China News Agency editorial evidence that the "Chinese Communists are wittingly or unwittingly tools of Soviet expansion." 893.00/3-2249, #628 Stuart, Nanking, RG 59, NA.

49. Secretary of State Dean Acheson to President Harry S Truman, July 30, 1949, Letter of Transmittal, in *White Paper*, p. xvi.

50. "Prospects for Soviet Control of a Communist China," ORE 29-49, RG 319, WNRC.

51. In 1927 Stalin's power struggle with Leon Trotsky drew China policy into the debate over Stalin's leadership. See Conrad Brandt, *Stalin's Failure in China*.

52. Text of the Treaty of Friendship and Alliance Between the Republic of China and the U.S.S.R., August 14, 1945, *White Paper*, pp. 585–87, and see pp. 116–26. Re CCP shock when news of the treaty became public see Warren I. Cohen, *America's Response to China*, p. 182. Re Russian aid to Chiang: John P. Davies noted that between 1937 and 1944 the CCP received no material assistance from the USSR; all of it went to the KMT. Some of this aid was used in maintaining the blockade around the CCP territories in northwestern China. 893.00/1-1044 "The Chinese Communists and the Great Powers," FRUS (1944)6:668. The Soviets subsequently asserted that between 1942 and 1945 the CCP leadership made efforts to arouse anti-Soviet nationalism and distrust for the USSR among Party members. Chinese Communists who had been educated in Russia suffered repression. The Soviets also alleged that a faction, headed by P'eng Chen and Lin Feng, had "maliciously distorted the role of the Soviet army [in Manchuria] and spread slander about the U.S.S.R." P'eng and Lin both held high Party positions—P'eng served as director of the Central Committee's Organization Department 1943–44 and of the Northeast China Bureau in Harbin, 1945–46. Excerpts from "Proletarian Internationalism is the Banner of the Workers of All Countries," *Kommunist*, May 1964, quoted in *China Quarterly* (July/September 1964) 19:191; James P. Harrison, *The Long March to Power*, pp. 293, 321, 337, 381, 383; O. B. Borisov and B. T. Koloskov, *Soviet-Chinese Relations*, pp. 118–20.

53. Re Yalta Conference and China see *White Paper*, pp. 113–16. Re developments in Manchuria see *ibid.*, pp. 589–98; and John Gittings, *The World and China*, p. 149. For a first-hand American look at the Manchurian situation see Paul Paddock, *China Diary*.

54. Stalin advised the CCP to compromise with Chiang on several occasions. Mao Tse-tung, "Speech at the Tenth Plenum of the Eighth Central Committee," September 24, 1962, and "Talks at the Cheng-tu Conference," March 10, 1958 in Stuart Schram, ed., *Chairman Mao Talks to the People*, pp. 102–3, 191. Kuo Mo-jo, Lin Piao and K'ang Sheng all made similar statements about Stalin's attitude. Schram, *Mao Tse-tung*, p. 245; Kuo Mo-jo, " 'Pai-wan-hsiung-shih kuo ta-chiang' tu Mao chu-hsi hsin fa-piao-te shih-tz'u," ["'An Army of One Million Crosses the Great River' upon reading one of the newly published poems of Chairman Mao,"], p. 10; Lin Piao, "Chung-kuo jen-min ke-ming chan-cheng-te sheng-li shih Mao Tse-tung ssu-hsiang-te sheng-li," and Tang Tsou's comments in *America's Failure in China*, p. 326; Joint Publications Research Service 49826, February 12, 1970, p. 27, Washington, D.C. (hereafter JPRS); Gittings, *The World and China*, p. 150; John Leighton Stuart Diary, January 4, 1949, Washington, D.C. Corroboration for this also comes from Yugoslav sources: Vladimir Dedijer, *Tito Speaks*, p. 331, and Milovan Djilas, *Conversations with Stalin*, p. 182; *White Paper*, pp. 72, 94–95.

55. Concessions desired by the USSR included mining, trade and civil aviation monopolies. 893.00/2-1549, #389 Stuart, Nanking, RG 59, NA; 661.9331/3-149, #48 Paxton, Tihwa, RG 59, NA; 661.9331/3-149, #494 Stuart, Nanking, RG 59, NA; 661.9331/3-249, Dispatch #58 American Embassy Nanking, RG 59, NA; 661.9331/3-1649, #904 Cabot, Shanghai, RG 59, NA; 661.9331/3-1649, #895 Cabot, Shanghai, RG 59, NA; 661.9331/3-3049, Dispatch #71 American Embassy Nanking, RG 59, NA; 893.00/4-2649, Dispatch #6 Cabot, Shanghai, RG 59, NA; Shui Chien-tan, "A Study of the Sino-Soviet Local Commercial Pact," *Ta Kung*

Pao, Shanghai, February 5, 1949, *CPS*, vol. 2, no. 5, February 11, 1949. American observers were provided plentiful evidence of CCP bitterness over USSR activity in Sinkiang, Manchuria, and Outer Mongolia. See for example: 893.00/6-2049, #2354 Cabot, Shanghai, and 893.00/7-2049, #2860 Shanghai, and 893.00/12-349, #2194 Clubb, Peking, RG 59, NA.

56. A CCP political agent for the Shanghai-Nanking area told Li Tsung-jen on February 1, 1949 that Mao Tse-tung and colleagues were puzzled by the move of the Soviet Ambassador to Canton and, the agent hinted, feared Russia was trying to prevent peace. 893.00/2-349, #302 Stuart, Nanking, FRUS (1949)8:104; and 893.01/4-1549, #214 Clark, Canton, RG 59, NA.

57. John F. Melby, *The Mandate of Heaven*, p. 205.

58. 893.00/1-2549 John Paton Davies to George Kennan, RG 59, NA; Herbert Feis interview with John Paton Davies, February 12, 1954, Herbert Feis Papers, Box 15, folder: John P. Davies, LC.

59. 893.00/1-2749, #237 Stuart, Nanking, FRUS (1949)8:88–89; 893.00/1-2749, #A-46 Kohler, Moscow, RG 59, NA.

60. "Origins of Titoism and Prerequisites for its Recurrence," Dispatch #162 Cavandish W. Cannon, American Embassy Belgrade, Yugoslavia, April 25, 1949, folder: 350 Miscellaneous, Consul General Hong Kong, RG 84, WNRC. Report which emphasizes the differences between China and Yugoslavia and regards Titoism unlikely but not impossible see: 893.00/9-2849 Office Memo Freeman (CA) to Butterworth (FE) with enclosure "Long Term Prospects of Chinese Communism," OIR 5020 (PV), RG 59, NA. See also Chalmers Johnson, *Peasant Nationalism and Communist Power*, pp. 156–75 and *passim*. The Division of Chinese Affairs forwarded a copy of Belgrade's "Origins of Titoism and Prerequisites for its Recurrence" to Hong Kong to assist the American Consul General there in analyzing the CCP and its future.

61. "Economic Relations Between the United States and Yugoslavia," PPS #49, February 10, 1949, cited by Lorraine M. Lees, "The American Decision To Assist Tito," pp. 414–15.

62. #2796 Cabot, Shanghai, July 16, 1949, cited by Thompson in 893.00/8-149 Thompson to Butterworth, p. 5, RG 59, NA. *U.S. News & World Report*, May 6, 1949 also thought Russian influence in China less potent than in Eastern Europe. Weekly Summary April 28–May 4, 1949; and #363 Peking to Department of State, March 8, 1949, file 510.1 China—Communist, RG 84, WNRC.

63. 893.00/8-149 Thompson to Butterworth, RG 59, NA. On the other hand, Foy D. Kohler, interim Chargé d'Affaires of the U. S. Embassy in Moscow, advocated United States encouragement of Titoism in the Far East. He was not, however, optimistic about the result. 761.00/4-649, Dispatch #202 and 893.00/4-1949, #971 Kohler, Moscow, RG 59, NA, latter telegram also in FRUS (1949)8:249–51.

64. 893.00B/5-3149, #1917 Cabot, Shanghai, and 893.00B/7-1649, #2796 Cabot, Shanghai, FRUS (1949)8:357, 436–40 (quote p. 438).

65. Created by Secretary of State George C. Marshall in 1947, the Policy Planning Staff's mandate called for the formulation of long-range foreign policy designs by a group unencumbered with routine State Department responsibilities. The National Security Council also originated in 1947 but as part of the National Security Act which provided, in addition, for a unified Department of Defense, a Central Intelligence Agency, and a Joint Chiefs of Staff. The NSC's primary function was to advise the President. 893.00/8-3149 Jessup to Fosdick with at-

tached memo by Davies, RG 59, NA; PPS 39/2, "United States Policy Toward China," February 25, 1949, PPS Records, Box 2: PPS Studies #34-63, RG 59, NA, which subsequently became NSC 34/2 when approved by the Council and the President, March 3, 1949; NSC 41, FRUS (1949)9:829–34; NSC 48/2, *U.S.-Vietnam Relations*, VB 2, Bk. I, pp. 247–48; #1994, Nanking, September 3, 1949, CA Records, Box 16, folder: 1949, RG 59, NA.

66. 793.02/1-550, #99 McConaughy, Shanghai, FRUS (1950)6:268; Airgram INTEL, Acheson to Certain Diplomatic and Consular Officers, December 20, 1949, folder: 350 Miscellaneous—Political, Consul General Hong Kong, RG 84, WNRC.

67. Consul General Clubb speculated that Mao's violently anti-American rhetoric of spring 1949 was occasioned by his need to disprove Titoist rumors. 893.00/6-2249, #1058 Clubb, Peking, FRUS (1949)8:pp. 394–95; and 893.00/7-2049, #1195 Clubb, Peking, RG 59, NA. Mao Tse-tung himself noted that "Stalin suspected that ours was a victory of the Tito type, and in 1949 and 1950 the pressure on us was very strong indeed." *SW*, 5:304 (quote April 25, 1956). Mao had, of course, given Stalin some reasons for his suspicions. In an October 1938 report to the Sixth Plenum of the Central Committee of the CCP Mao denied the universality of Marxist abstract ideology. He called for a Sinification of Marxism and declared that the Chinese "must put an end to writing eight-legged essays on foreign models." Stuart Schram, *The Political Thought of Mao Tse-tung*, p. 112. The State Department also had reports that the USSR was worried about the spread of Titoism: 761.00/10-1749 and 761.00/12-149 Weekly Selection from State Department to Certain Diplomatic and Consular Officers, RG 59, NA.

68. 893.01/12-249, #1828 Vincent, Bern, Switzerland, RG 59, NA; Marquis Childs, February 3, 1950, Weekly Summary February 2–8, 1950 and Walter Lippmann, February 14, 1950, Weekly Summary February 9–15, 1950. The Soviet boycott of the United Nations in early 1950 prevented the problem of Chinese membership from being worked out and, therefore, contributed to China's international isolation. For similar speculation re the Ward Incident see: "Mr. Ward, the Russians, and Recognition," November 17, 1949, PPS Records, Box 33: Chronological File, folder: 1949, RG 59, NA.

69. See introductions to Weekly Summaries for: December 30, 1948–January 5, 1949; January 13–19, 1949; January 27–February 2, 1949; February 3–9, 1949; February 17–23, 1949; February 24–March 2, 1949; March 31–April 6, 1949; April 21–27, 1949; and April 28–May 4, 1949. For journalists' views on Titoism see ch. 8.

70. *Newsweek*, May 9, 1949, Weekly Summary May 5–11, 1949, and *Business Week*, February 25, 1950, Weekly Summary March 9–15, 1950, and *Washington Post*, December 20, 1949, Weekly Summary December 15–21, 1949.

71. *Philadelphia Inquirer*, December 19, 1949, Weekly Summary December 15–21, 1949.

72. *Washington Star* and *Baltimore Sun*, December 19, 1949, Weekly Summary December 15–21, 1949 and similar views noted in introduction to Weekly Summary December 22–28, 1949.

73. John Hightower, December 18, 1949, Weekly Summary December 15–21, 1949. Consideration of Titoism continued: *Watertown Times*, January 21, 1950 and Drew Pearson, ABC, January 22, 1950, and Gabriel Heatter, MBS, January 20, 1950 went so far as to say there might be a Sino-Soviet shooting war in time. Weekly Summary January 19–25, 1950.

74. Re Soviet demands: 661.93/1-2550, #335 Secretary of State to Embassy in

France, FRUS (1949)8:294–96; 661.93/2-1150, #584 Secretary of State to Embassy in France, FRUS (1949)8:308–11; Memorandum R. H. Hillenkoetter, Director of Central Intelligence, January 4, 1950, Truman Papers, PSF, Intelligence, folder: Central Intelligence Memorandum 1950–52, HST. Mao Tse-tung commented some years later that the effort to commit Stalin to aid China was like taking "meat out of the tiger's mouth." John Gittings, "New Light on Mao," p.761. Allegedly Khrushchev in 1956 admitted that "Stalin faced Mao Tse-tung . . . with a series of economic demands smacking of colonialism. He insisted that he, Stalin, must have the final word on the development of Communism within China as he had in other countries of the Soviet bloc. Mao was extremely embittered by Stalin's insistence on jointly controlled companies and mining and industrial concessions. . . . Had it not been for the hardness of U. S. policy towards Communist China the Peking government might well have decided to break openly with Moscow as Marshall Tito did in 1948." John Gittings, "The Origins of China's Foreign Policy," in David Horowitz, ed., *Containment and Revolution*, pp. 212–13. However much Soviet activity in Manchuria angered Mao and other CCP leaders, observed Consul General O. Edmund Clubb in Peking, a Titoist break from the Soviet bloc could mean loss of the area because of heavy Russian influence there. 893.00/6-1149, #996, RG 59, NA; and 893.00B/12-2349, #2341 Clubb, Peking, FRUS (1949)8:645.

75. NSC 48/1, "The Position of the United States with Respect to Asia," December 23, 1949, *U.S.-Vietnam Relations*, VB2, Bk. I, 1945–49, pp. 243–44. NSC 48/2, discussed by Iriye in "Was There a Cold War in Asia?" pp. 19–20.

76. 661.93/1-2550, #335 and 661.93/2-1150, #584, FRUS (1949)8:294–96, 308–11. The State Department had engaged in similar activities at an earlier date. During 1949 Consul Robert C. Strong at Tsingtao placed a Department pamphlet entitled "The Soviet-Yugoslav Dispute" in hands likely to bring it to the attention of Communist leaders. He requested six additional copies for comparable disposal. Strong to W. Bradley Connors, Acting Director USIS, Shanghai, March or April 1949, File 300, Tsingtao, RG 84, WNRC.

77. Re Acheson's references to Soviet imperialism see "United States Policy Toward Asia," *Department of State Bulletin* (March 27, 1950) 22:467–72; "Soviet Penetration in North Areas of China," *ibid.*, February 6, 1950, pp. 218–19; "Soviets Exploit Sinkiang Oil and Mineral Resources," *ibid.*, April 10, 1950, p. 568. According to the State Department's opinion analysts Secretary Acheson's January 12, 1950 National Press Club speech, in which he discussed Soviet imperialism in Asia, increased "hopes for Chinese Titoism." Many observers have also stressed the value of propaganda in deepening any differences between Russia and the Chinese Communists. Department of State, American Opinion Reports, February 13, 1950, Office of Public Opinion Studies 1943–65, Box 33, folder: China 1949–1952, RG 59, NA. 793.00/2-450, #571 Chase, Shanghai, FRUS (1950)6:304n3; 793.00/1-2650, #430 McConaughy, Shanghai, *ibid.*, pp. 296–300; "New Light on Chinese Communism from a Disillusioned Party Member," OIR 4910(PV), March 22, 1949, Reel 4, Pt. 3, OSS/State Department Reports; 893.00/11-249 Stuart, Nanking to Butterworth (FE), RG 59, NA. Contemporary perceptions of who belonged to which faction were not always consistent. In a secret report (#10) from the American Consulate at Dairen, October 15, 1948, Liu Shao-ch'i was cited as disliking the USSR and favoring an independent CCP. Elsewhere Liu appeared as leader of pro-Soviet group. 893.00/3-1549, Dispatch #37 Cabot, Shanghai to Stuart, Nanking, RG 59, NA.

78. Rumors about Ch'en I's anti-Soviet attitudes, his ambition and his pop-

ularity encouraged American interest in Ch'en as a possible Titoist. Nothing ever came of contacts between Ch'en's alleged emissary Chou Ming-hsun and Americans of the Economic Cooperation Administration's China Mission. 761.00/1-350, #6 Secretary of State to Peking Consul General, FRUS (1950)6:269–70; #346 McConaughy, Shanghai, January 21, 1950, Truman Papers and FRUS (1950)6:289ff; 793.00/1-2150, #127 Secretary of State to Shanghai Consul General, FRUS (1950)6:294; 793.00/1-2650, #430, FRUS (1950)6:296–300; 793.00/2-1250, Memorandum by John P. Davies, PPS, FRUS (1950)6:305–6.

79. NSC 58/2, "United States Policy Toward the Soviet Satellites in Eastern Europe," December 8, 1949, and "Yugoslavia, A Current Problem," November 1949, Truman Papers, both cited by Lees, "Decision To Assist Tito," pp. 420–21.

80. Occupation planning began in April 1942 and "flourished under a policy of benign neglect . . . within the State Department where everyone was involved and wanted to be involved in the German settlement." The Joint Chiefs of Staff ignored Japan too. Conference of Scholars on the Administration of Occupied Areas, 1943–1955, April 10–11, 1970, pp. 4–5, transcript available from Harry S Truman Library. Re occupation reforms see: Hugh Borton, "The Allied Occupation of Japan," pp. 307–428 and Kawai Kazuo, Japan's American Interlude.

81. Re MacArthur's independence: George F. Kennan, Memoirs 1925–1950, p. 370.

82. Michael Yoshitsu, "Peace and Security for Japan," (Ph.D. diss.), pp. 30–35.

83. Kennan, Memoirs, p. 376, and see also pp. 373–93; and Conference 1943–1955, pp. 4, 53, 108.

84. Re reversal of the occupation: Hugh Borton, Japan's Modern Century, pp. 478–79. According to Japan scholar Robert E. Ward, American business groups applied strong pressure for an end to deconcentration efforts. Conference, 1943–1955, p. 26. Re the efforts of American labor leaders to rid Japanese unions of communism: Howard Schonberger, "American Labor's Cold War in Occupied Japan," pp. 249–72. Re militarization: Herbert Passin, The Legacy of the Occupation—Japan, p. 24; Fairbank, et al. East Asia, p. 820; 794.00/7-750 Summary Report by Dulles, FRUS (1950)6:1232. According to Tatsumi Eiichi, Prime Minister Yoshida's confidential military affairs advisor, had Japan's economy been stable in 1946 and 1947 and had there been a need for armed forces, the Prime Minister would have favored them. Yoshitsu, "Peace," pp. 108–9.

85. Johnson, Peasant Nationalism pp. 31–70, and Suzanne Pepper, Civil War in China, pp. 72–78.

86. Dorothy Borg, "America Loses Chinese Good Will," p. 43; Thurston Griggs, Americans in China, pp. 42–43; 893.00/5-2748, #187 Cabot, Shanghai, FRUS (1948)7:260–62; 893.00/6-348, #1242 Cabot, Shanghai, ibid., pp. 271–72; 893.00/6-748, #1278 Pilcher, Shanghai, ibid., p. 279; 893.00/6-948, #237 Clubb, Peking, ibid., pp. 280–81; 740.0011PW (Peace)/6-248, #255 Stuart, Nanking, FRUS (1948)6:800.

87. Kuo Mo-jo, "Closer Ties Between China and USSR," pp. 6, 23; 893.00B/7-649, #1447 Stuart, Nanking, FRUS (1949)8:409; 893.00B/3-3049, #70 Stuart, Nanking, transmitting Memorandum by Director of the Nanking Branch of the USIS, Josiah W. Bennett, on "The Nature of Chinese Communist Anti-American Propaganda," ibid., pp. 211–16; Allen S. Whiting, China Crosses the Yalu, pp. 35–36.

88. "Considerations Relevant to the Formulation of Conditions for U. S. Recognition of a Communist Government of China," OIR 5009 (PV), July 1949, p. 12n2, Reel 4, Part 3, OSS/State Department Reports, and Press Review, *Wen Hui Pao*, January 11, 1950, #176 Shanghai, January 12, 1950, Philip C. Jessup Papers, Subject Files 1924–1959, Box 137: Attacks on Jessup, folder: Attacks by Communist Press & Radio 1950, LC. And in the same folder see also #101 Clubb, Peking, January 13, 1950, and #205 Shanghai, January 13, 1950. "U. S. Intrigues to Conclude A Separate Peace with Japan," Hsinhua *Daily Bulletin*, #32, May 18, 1950; "Oppose U. S. Plot to Turn Japan Into Base for Aggression," *Jen-min jih-pao*, May 15, 1950. Chang Tsung-ping acted on behalf of Yao I-lin, the Minister of Industry and Commerce, 693.0031/4-3049, #736 Clubb, Peking, and 693.9431/4-3049, #732 Clubb, Peking, FRUS (1949)9:974–77. Efforts to send a Chinese trade mission to Japan proved abortive. 693.9431/7-649, #235 Houston, Tokyo, and 693.9431/7-949, #1148 Clubb, Peking, RG 59, NA. Consul General O. Edmund Clubb reported rumors that the CCP was so anxious to trade with Japan that the Party was considering smuggling. 893.01/4-1949, #661 Clubb, Peking, RG 59, NA.

89. William Costello, "Could Japan Go Communist?" p. 554; 693.9431/12-1949 Office Memo Allison (NA) to Butterworth (FE), RG 59, NA; and 893.01/12-549, Dispatch #849 William J. Sebald, Office of the United States Political Advisor for Japan, Tokyo, RG 59, NA.

90. Aid to the Japanese Communist Party by the CCP worried American foreign service officers, particularly since JCP leader Nozaka had spent twelve years in Yenan and was an intimate friend of Mao Tse-tung. Stewart Alsop to Marty, January 14, 1950, Joseph and Stewart Alsop Papers, Box 27: Special Correspondence, folder: SEP January–June 1950, LC. Evidence of CCP interest in the welfare of the JCP was rife. See for example: "The Path of Liberation of the Japanese People," *Jen-min jih-pao*, January 17, 1950; "Oppose MacArthur's Oppression of the Vanguard of Japanese Patriots—the Communist Party of Japan," *Jen-min jih-pao*, June 9, 1950; "MacArthur's 'Purge' in Japan is Utterly Illegal, Declare Chinese Communists," Hsinhua *Daily Bulletin*, #50, June 14, 1950.

91. 611.94A/1-1550 Memorandum of Conversation by Ambassador-at-Large Philip C. Jessup, FRUS (1950)6:281.

92. Borton, *Japan's Modern Century*, p. 478.

93. Beech Keyes, "M'Arthur Aides Favor Trade With Red China," *St. Louis Post-Dispatch*, September 1, 1949, p. 1B; and "The Effect of a Communist Dominated China on Other Areas of the Far East," OIR 4867, January 24, 1949, pp. 5–6, Reel 4, Pt. 3, OSS/State Department Reports.

94. NSC 41, "United States Policy Regarding Trade with China," February 29, 1949, Harry S Truman Papers, PSF, Box 205: National Security Council Meetings, no. 35, March 3, 1949, HST, also appears in FRUS (1949)9:829–34.

95. OIR 4867, pp. 5, 11. According to a Gallup Poll increased American aid to Japan was not a popular idea among the citizenry. Poll takers asked: "Do you think the United States should do more to help Japan get back on her feet?" The responses were: yes 37 percent, no 57 percent, no opinion 12 percent. Survey #439-K, April 19, 1949 (questions asked March 19–24), *The Gallup Poll: Public Opinion 1935–71*, 2: (1949–58):807. Between 1947 and 1952 the United States gave Japan $2 billion just to prevent starvation. Fairbank, et al., *East Asia*, p. 822.

96. 893.00/5-1049, "Considerations Supporting State Department's Policy Conclusions Regarding Trade with China," RG 59, NA. Not all opinion agreed

that important economic advantages would accrue to Japan through United States recognition of Communist China. See 893.01/12-549, Dispatch #849, RG 59, NA.

97. NSC 41, Truman Papers, p. 9, HST, and FRUS (1949)9:831; 893.00/5-1049, "Considerations," RG 59, NA. Trade contacts between Communist China and Japan during 1949 approached $9,500,000 in such commodities as copper wire, sheet steel, cotton seeds and peanuts. 893.01/12-549, Dispatch #849, RG 59, NA.

98. 893.00/5-1049, "Considerations," RG 59, NA.

99. NSC 41, Truman Papers, pp. 6–7, HST and FRUS (1949)9:830; 693.9431/5-1149, #306 Smyth, Tientsin, RG 59, NA. The suggestion that trade be used as a lever to secure release of Angus Ward, American Consul General being detained in Mukden, and Messrs. Smith and Bender, downed American flyers, was rejected by the State Department. Such action, noted Willard Thorp, the Assistant Secretary of State for Economic Affairs, ran contrary to NSC 41 and might prove embarrassing if ineffective, as he predicted it would be. 693.9431/11-1649 Memorandum Thorp to Butterworth (FE), FRUS (1949)9:998–99.

100. 893.01/12-549, Dispatch #849, RG 59, NA; Michael Yoshitsu, "Tokyo Tilts Toward Peking: 1951–1952," unpublished manuscript. The Far Eastern Commission which met in Washington supposedly had responsibility for formulating policies to govern Japan. Its members were Australia, Canada, China, France, India, the Netherlands, New Zealand, the Philippines, the Soviet Union, the United Kingdom, the United States, and after 1949, Burma and Pakistan. Actually the FEC had virtually no power.

101. In fact Yoshida had tried to secure an understanding rather than a treaty with the Kuomintang so as to keep future options open but was stymied by bureaucratic errors. In 1952 Japan recognized the Republic of China as *the* government of China. Yoshitsu, "Tilting"; Borton, *Japan's Modern Century*, p. 510.

102. France on recognition: Memorandum of Conversation, Ambassador Bonnet with Secretary Acheson, March 13, 1949, Dean Acheson Papers, Box 65: Memoranda of Conversations 1950, HST; 893.01/5-2049, #2084 Bruce, Paris, RG 59, NA; 75814 (F13118/1023/10) Sir Maberly E. Dening, British Assistant Undersecretary of State for Foreign Affairs to H. Ashley Clarke, Paris, August 31, 1949, BFO. Canada: F6968/1023/10, #626 Stevenson, Nanking, May 12, 1949, BFO. India: F6904/1023/10, #599 Stevenson, Nanking, May 10, 1949, BFO; 893.01/11-249, #2354 Bacon, Nanking, RG 59, NA; 893.01/11-749 Meeting with Pannikar, FRUS (1949)9:177–79. Philippines: 893.01/9-2849, #4087 McConaughy, Shanghai, RG 59, NA; 893.01/12-2049, #2880 Cowen, Manila, FRUS (1949)9:234. Indonesia: 893.01/11-2349, #2652 Cowen, Manila, RG 59, NA. Burma: 893.01/10-3149, Dispatch #424 Embassy, Rangoon, RG 59, NA; 893.01/12-2049, #A-505 Day, Rangoon, RG 59, NA. Vietnam: 893.01/10-549, #111 Gibson, Hanoi, RG 59, NA. Southeast Asia in general: 75819 (F16589/1023/10) Sir Malcolm MacDonald, Singapore, #919, November 4, 1949, and #405, November 5, 1949, BFO.

3. CHINESE COMMUNIST POLICY

1. Mao Tse-tung remarked, "To win countrywide victory is only the first step in a long march of ten thousand *li.*" *SW*, 4:374.

2. *Tzu-li keng-sheng*, self-reliance, implies a preference for advancement with-

out external aid but does not preclude accepting assistance from abroad or studying foreign models. The CCP merely meant to retain the initiative and have alternate plans ready if aid did not materialize. James Reardon-Anderson, *Yenan and the Great Powers*, p. 11. Mao Tse-tung made this point often: *SW*, 3:191, 257; 4:371, 408.

3. Liu Tu-wen, the public relations and political officer for the People's Liberation Army in Tientsin, told American officials in a private interview on the day after takeover that the CCP lacked adequate personnel to manage large cities and would therefore welcome advice from the foreign population of Tientsin. Foreigners, he added, should be patient and judge the CCP on its actions and not on propaganda. #74 Tientsin, January 16, 1949, Box 2315: Tsingtao, file 350: Correspondence, China Post Files, RG 84, WNRC; 893.01/6-2949, #197 Callanan, Hankow, RG 59, NA.

4. *SW*, 4:422.

5. See chapter 2 for an extended discussion of Sino-Soviet frictions.

6. Stuart Schram, *Mao Tse-tung*, pp. 47, 73; Michael Hunt, "Mao Tse-tung and the Issue of Accommodation with the United States," in Borg and Heinrichs, eds., *Uncertain Years*, pp. 189–93.

7. The CCP emphatically rejected the idea that the USSR would demand special rights in Manchuria since "the days of Russian imperialism are over." Joseph W. Esherick, ed., *Lost Chance in China: The World War II Dispatches of John S. Service*, pp. 344–45, and report by Service, "Chinese Communist Expectations in Regard to Soviet Participation in Far Eastern War," March 14, 1945, p. 349. Re Mao's expectation that Outer Mongolia would be part of a Communist Chinese nation see Edgar Snow, *Red Star Over China*, p. 96, and Guenther Stein, *The Challenge of Red China*, p. 443.

8. Mao and others frequently asserted that China could not eliminate capitalism and introduce socialism since the country had not yet developed adequately. *SW*, 2:353; 4:168, 421. A June 1950 CIA analysis emphasized the moderation of Mao's report to the CCP Central Committee, June 6, 1950. Foreign Broadcast Information Division of the CIA, Harry S Truman Papers, President's Secretary's Files, Intelligence File, Box 251: Central Intelligence Reports, folder: June 1950, HST, for text of Mao's speech see *SW*, 5:29–30. See also *Jen-min jih-pao*, editorial, March 17, 1949; 893.00/5-1749, #848 Clubb, Peking, RG 59, NA and for the speech Clubb refers to, Li Li-san, "Policy Towards Private Capital," p. 9. At this time Li served as vice chairman of the Chinese Federation of Labor.

9. Mao Tse-Tung observed that, "The economic power of U.S. imperialism . . . is confronted with unstable and daily shrinking domestic and foreign markets. The further shrinking of these markets will cause economic crises to break out. . . . Irreconcilable domestic and international contradictions, like a volcano, menace U.S. imperialism every day [and have] driven the U.S. imperialists to draw up a plan for enslaving the world, to run amuck like wild beasts in Europe, Asia and other parts of the world." Mao *SW*, 4:172; John Gittings, "New Light on Mao," pp. 755, 757, 759; 893.00/12-548, #227 Paddock, Dairen, RG 59, NA; 611.9311/8-849, #1317 Clubb, Peking, RG 59, NA; 611.9331/8-2749, #917 Jones, Nanking, RG 59, NA; Hunt, "Mao Tse-tung," p. 227; John Leighton Stuart Diary, July 30, 1949, Washington, D.C.

10. The unruly behavior of the urban workers caused the CCP considerable trouble. Mao warned that "a sharp distinction should be made between the correct policy of developing production, promoting economic prosperity, giving

consideration to both public and private interests and benefiting both labor and capital, and the one-sided and narrow-minded policy of 'relief,' which purports to uphold the workers' welfare but in fact damages industry and commerce and impairs the cause of the people's revolution." *SW*, 4:203. See also ch. 4.

11. The Cominform's condemnation of Tito required some response from the CCP and in July 1948 the Central Committee endorsed its decision. Liu Shao-ch'i in his speech "On Internationalism and Nationalism" vigorously set forth a two-camp picture of the world and also attacked Tito. But Mao and Liu's statement came months late, in November 1948. Little other public comment was made on the Cominform action, Liu made no mention of Yugoslavia's domestic policies, Mao did not attack Tito explicitly, and the Central Committee chose November for its very liberal statement regarding recognition. Liu Shao-ch'i, "Lun Kuo-chi chu-i yü min-tsu chu-i" [On Internationalism and Nationalism] and in *Jen-min jih-pao*, November 7, 1948; Mao Tse-tung, "Ch'üan shih-chieh ke-ming li-liang t'uan-chieh ch'i-lai fan-tui ti-kuo-chu-i-te ch'in-lüeh," *Jen-min jih-pao*, November 4, 1948; Hunt, "Mao Tse-tung," p. 210; 893.00B/8-3048, #375 Stuart, Nanking, FRUS (1948)7:442.

12. The argument that Mao for ideological reasons would not have contemplated an "understanding" with the United States is cogently made by: Steven Goldstein, "Chinese Communist Policy Toward the United States; Opportunities and Constraints, 1944–1950," in Borg and Heinrichs, eds., *Uncertain Years*, pp. 235–78; Steven I. Levine, "If My Grandmother Had Wheels She'd Be a Trolley," pp. 31–32; Okabe Tatsumi, "The Cold War and China," pp. 224–51. The opposing case, which I find more persuasive, holds that Mao coupled his ideological principles with a streak of nationalistic practicality. The argument which emphasizes Mao's concern with rebuilding China and his willingness to seek American aid to do so is made by: Hunt, "Mao Tse-tung," pp. 185–233; Lawrence Weiss, "Storm Around the Cradle" (Ph.D. diss.); James Hsiung, *Ideology and Practice* (New York: Praeger, 1972); and James Reardon-Anderson, "The Case for the 'Lost Chance in China,'" pp. 33–34.

13. 893.801/8-749 Shanghai, FRUS (1949)9:1126; Mao, *SW*, 4:449; "US Imperialists Behind KMT Bombing of Civilian Population," Hsinhua *Daily News Release* #283, February 10, 1950, pp. 50–51 (hereafter DNR); "More 'Malice Raids' on Nanking & Shanghai," DNR #294, February 23, 1950, pp. 113–14; "American Imperialism Behind KMT Bombings," DNR #302, March 3, 1950, pp. 11–12; "More Evidence on American Interference in China," DNR #324, March 25, 1950. Endorsement of the blockade by Republican Senators and reports that the State Department discouraged Northwest Airlines from servicing Shanghai gave impetus to such suspicions. Andrew Roth, "How the Communists Rule," p. 489.

14. 793.02/1-550, #99 McConaughy, Shanghai, FRUS (1950)6:264–67; Joint Weeka #9, from State, Army, Navy, Air (SANA), Nanking, March 18, 1949, p. 4, file 350.2 Joint Weeka Reports, Consul General Hong Kong, China Post Files, RG 84, WNRC; "U.S. Activities in Taiwan Denounced," Peking in Mandarin, May 29, 1949, section: Far East, China-Communist Controlled, May 31, 1949, p. CCC-1, FBIS.

15. *White Paper*, p. xvi; Mao, *SW*, 4:428, 451. The CCP accused the U.S. Vice-Consul in Tihwa, Douglas S. Mackiernan, of encouraging bandit resistance in the province of Sinkiang. "Former U.S. Vice-Consul in Tihwa Engaged in Espionage Activities," DNR #272, January 30, 1949, pp. 1–2.

16. "Guerrilla Activities on the Chinese Mainland," Truman Papers, George

M. Elsey Files, Subject Files, Foreign Relations C-H, Box 59, folder: Foreign Affairs - China Lobby, HST; "'Imperialists' Train Special Agents," Peking, in Cantonese to China and Overseas, March 21, 1950, section: China, March 22, 1950, p. BBB-1, FBIS; "American Imperialists Train Spies for Sabotage on Chinese Mainland," New China News Agency *Daily Bulletin*, #2 (April 4, 1950), pp. 2–3.

17. There is clear confirmation that ESD operated in Manchuria and continued to do so from elsewhere in China after the Mukden center closed in 893.00/9-1349, #1095 Strong, Canton, RG 59, NA; John M. Cabot Diary, June 23, 1949, Cabot Family, Washington, D.C. For Communist charges see: "Amercan-Directed Spy Ring Uncovered in Manchuria," NCNA *Weekly Bulletin* (June 21, 1949) #107, p. 4 and *China Digest* (June 28, 1949) 6:17–18; "American Espionage in Manchuria; 8 Spies Confess," NCNA *Weekly Bulletin*, (December 6, 1949) #131, p. 5; "Facts About the Ward Case," and "American Espionage Ring in Manchuria," pp. 6–9, 24. Re the Ward Incident from America's perspective: Meeting With the President, November 14, 1949, Box 14: 1948–49, folder: Ward Case, Mukden 1949, 1950, CA Records, RG 59, NA; "Living with the Chinese Communists," pp. 5–7; *Department of State Bulletin* (July 11, 1949) 21:36; (September 26, 1949) 482; (November 21, 1949) 759–60; (November 28, 1949) 799–800; (December 12, 1949) 907; and (December 26, 1949) 955–56; Herbert W. Briggs, "American Consular Rights in Communist China," pp. 243–46.

18. Cohen, *America's Response*, p. 174. In July 1944 the United States sent a mission to Yenan to learn more about the CCP and possible use of its guerrilla units against Japan. This U.S. Army Observer Group (known as the Dixie Mission because it served in rebel territory) combined military and political advisors under the command of Colonel David Barrett and later Colonel Ivan Yeaton. John Service filed a series of reports between July and November 1944 which related CCP interest in cooperating with Washington. Schaller, *U.S. Crusade*, pp. 181–90, 228–29; Esherick, *Lost Chance in China, passim*; and David Barrett, *Dixie Mission*.

19. The August 1944 meeting produced a document entitled "On Diplomatic Work" which set forth the types of collaboration foreseen. It remained secret until published by the Russians in *Problemy Dal'nego Vostoka* [Problems of the Far East], (March 24, 1972) 1:184–87, cited by Esherick, *Lost Chance*, pp. 291–92, and translated in JPRS 57230, October 12, 1972. Mao's observation recorded by John S. Service, August 27, 1944, is in Esherick, p. 307. Morgenthau had put the Treasury Department in a position of supervising aid to China from 1938 to 1941. Thereafter, disgust with Kuomintang corruption and preoccupation with Germany had taken him away from Chinese affairs. Chou hoped to reinterest him on the CCP side. Letter Chou to Morgenthau, November 13, 1944. On Morgenthau's concern with China see Schaller, *U.S. Crusade*, pp. 24–28, 36–38, 72–75, 95–98, 154. Re American command of CCP forces, Schaller, p. 168.

20. Barbara Tuchman, "If Mao Had Come to Washington in 1945," in *Notes from China*, pp. 77–112. The proposal was transmitted January 9, 1945, through the U.S. Military Observers Mission in Yenan to General Albert C. Wedemeyer in Chungking. With Wedemeyer visiting Burma, the message automatically went to Hurley. So, too, did a second message of January 11 which quoted Chou En-lai as saying that "General Hurley must not get this information as I don't trust his discretion." Esherick, *Lost Chance*, pp. 331–32; Hunt, "Mao Tse-tung," pp. 194–95; *White Paper*, pp. 74–78; Schaller, *U.S. Crusade*, pp. 204–9.

21. John Service, "The Views of Mao Tse-tung: America and China," March

13, 1945, Esherick, *Lost Chance*, p. 373; "China and U.S. Foreign Policy," p. 68; #137, Marshall to President and Secretary of State, February 1, 1946, FRUS (1946)9:151–52.

22. Colonel Ivan Yeaton, December 20, 1945, quoted in Reardon-Anderson, *Yenan and the Great Powers*, pp. 293–94. This was true despite the fact that Yeaton, a Chiang Kai-shek–approved anticommunist, "suspected a lie behind everything the Chinese Communists told him." Schaller, *U.S. Crusade*, p. 228.

23. Central Committee Statement, November 21, 1948, John D. Sumner Papers, Box 3, folder: Shanghai, file (1), HST. For a detailed catalogue of the difficulties in Sino-American relations after WWII see Goldstein, "Chinese Communist Policy," in Borg and Heinrichs, eds., *Uncertain Years*, pp. 235–78. Contrary to the interpretation given here, Goldstein maintains that no relations between the United States and China were possible because of Chinese Communist ideological commitments.

24. Mao, *SW*, 4:371, 402, 408. The *China Digest* headlined Mao's April statement in its May 17, 1949 edition as "The Way To Establish Diplomatic Relations with China," p. 5.

25. Tillman Durdin, *New York Times*, September 17, 1949, p. 5. Chou En-lai's team included Chang Han-fu and his wife, Kung P'u-sheng; Ch'iao Kuan-hua and his wife, Kung P'eng; Huang Hua, and K'o Pai-nien. For information on their careers see Donald W. Klein and Anne B. Clark, *Biographic Dictionary of Chinese Communism*, 1:27–30, 179–82, 393–95, 442–44. Re Chou's background see *ibid.*, pp. 204–19 and Hsu Kai-yu, *China's Gray Eminence*, which unfortunately skims over the late 1940s and early 1950s period in four pages. The influential generals probably included: Yeh Chien-ying, Nieh Jung-chen and Ch'en I. Klein and Clark, *Biographic Dictionary*, 1:104–13; 2:696–702, 1004–09; 893.00/12-1548, #549 Clubb, Peking, FRUS (1948)7:648–49.

26. Re factions in the CCP see Durdin, *New York Times*, September 17, 1949, p. 5 and September 18, 1949, p. 26; 893.00/5-1849, #1050 Stuart, Nanking, RG 59, NA; Dispatch #266 Jenkins, Hong Kong, September 22, 1949, p. 4, Box 912, file 350.21: Communists Non-Chinese, RG 84, WNRC; 893.00/12-3149, #5461 McConaughy, Shanghai, RG 59, NA; 793.00/2-450, #571 ConGen, Shanghai, FRUS (1950)6:304*n*3; Donald S. Zagoria, "Mao's Role in the Sino-Soviet Conflict," pp. 141–46; *Kommunist* on anti-Soviet faction, *China Quarterly*, (July/September 1964) 19:191. Although an August 1948 United States intelligence assessment denied the existence of a split within the CCP, indications in these sources and Mao Tse-tung's own words confirm that there were conflicts. Mao noted that, "apart from uninhabited deserts, wherever there are groups of people, they are invariably composed of the Left, the Middle, and the Right. This will still be the case after thousands of years." "Make a Class Analysis of Factionalism," p. 3; "Biographic Data on Members of the Politburo and the Central Executive Committee of the Chinese Communist Party," OIR 4729, August 20, 1948, p. 1, Reel 4, Pt. 3 China & India, OSS/State Department Reports.

27. Stuart Diary, entries for May 6, 13, 17 and 31, June 6, 17, and 28 record contacts with Huang Hua. Stuart Diary entries for June 23, 26 and 28 note other sources of comment on the proposed trip. In a July 14, 1949 cable to the Secretary of State Stuart wrote, "according to my friends in Peiping, Mao openly stated that I would be welcome in Peiping," and further "Mao-Chou counted on entertaining me and talking to me during this ostensibly private visit to Peiping." U.S. Senate, Committee on Foreign Relations, *The United States and Communist*

China in 1949 and 1950, p. 10n28. See also documentation in FRUS (1949)8:741–802.

28. Chou Yu-k'ang, an old friend of Stuart's and relative of Stephen Tsai, treasurer of Yenching University, informed Stuart that he had been told in Peking that Huang Hua had been sent to Nanking precisely because of his relationship with Stuart. Stuart Diary, June 26, 1949. The Democratic League and Kuomintang Revolutionary Committee were independent political associations outlawed under Nationalist rule and willing to cooperate with the CCP. Both were composed of intellectuals and liberal politicians who possessed some standing in China and some of whom had friendships with Chinese Communist leaders. Their reliability as reporters on CCP activities and attitudes was considered quite good. Ambassador Stuart and other foreign service personnel saw a few of them often. Although one or two warnings exist in the cable traffic as to the possibility that the CCP might use these individuals as channels to feed misinformation to the United States, comment to the contrary abounds. It should be noted, however, that to some degree these "non-Party democrats" were suspect in Mao's eyes. Their willingness to act as intermediaries with the Americans suggested that they believed in the existence of a third road between socialism and capitalism for China. Mao made clear in his July 1, 1949 speech that no such road existed. These also would have been the people who as believers in "democratic individualism" had been marked as subversives in Dean Acheson's *White Paper* transmittal letter of August. 893.00/8-349, #1694 Jones, Nanking, RG 59, NA; 893.00/7-349, #2600 Cabot, Shanghai, FRUS (1949)8:1195; 102.22/8-1949, #3344 McConaughy, Shanghai, *ibid.*, p. 1277; Mao, *SW*, 4:374. Carsun Chang, *The Third Force in China*, p. 279. A cable declassified for me (in sanitized form) indicates that Mao's suspicions were justified. Certain, unnamed, reputable liberals intended to carry on anti-Soviet covert activities. 893.00/5-1449, #378 Clark, Canton, RG 59, NA.

29. Stuart Diary, July 21, 1949. Ch'en I, Mayor of Shanghai, after Mao's July 1, 1949 speech, also purportedly hoped that Stuart would clear up misunderstandings between the CCP and Washington when he returned there. This was according to Ch'en Ming-shu who reported a conversation with Ch'en I in a letter to Philip Fugh. Stuart Diary, July 30, 1949.

30. Mao, *SW*, 4:408. American Consul General O. Edmund Clubb, Ambassador Stuart, Lewis Clark and State Department personnel all treated the Chou démarche as genuine. Some, like Clark, attributed devious motives to it but did not suggest that the intermediaries had perpetrated a hoax. The message passed from Chou En-lai's secretary and other Chinese Communists who claimed to be acting in Chou's behalf to Michael Keon, a United Press reporter. Keon had been in some trouble with the CCP after the takeover of Peking for what the Party termed his slanderous attacks on the Chinese people. I believe that his slightly unsavory standing would not have disqualified Keon for his secret mission, but would actually have provided an extra degree of protection so far as Chou En-lai was concerned. The documentation of the Chou démarche appears in FRUS (1949)8, as follows: 893.00/6-149, #917 Clubb, Peking, pp. 357–60; 893.00/6-249, #928, Clubb, pp. 363–64; 893.00B/6-649, #534 Clark, Canton, p. 370; 893.00/6-749, #1229 Stuart, Nanking, pp. 372–73; 893.00/6-2249, #1058 Clubb, pp. 394–95; 893.00/6-2449, #1073 Clubb, pp. 397–98; 893.00/8-1849, #1369 Clubb, p. 497. See also Robert Blum, "The Peiping Cable," pp. 8–10, 53.

31. 693.0031/4-3049, #736 Clubb, Peking, FRUS (1949)9:976–77.

32. 893.00/2-549, #184 Clubb, Peking, FRUS (1949)9:1058.

33. 893.00/6-659, #2010, Cabot, Shanghai, FRUS (1949)8:370; 761.00/6-1049 Weekly Report by Office of Intelligence Research, RG 59, NA.

34. 893.00B/6-1949, #1325 Stuart, Nanking, FRUS (1949)8:763.

35. 893.00B/6-949, #1250 Stuart, Nanking, FRUS (1949)8:377.

36. 893.00B/6-749, #311 Hopper, Hong Kong, FRUS (1949)8:373; Klein and Clark, *Biographic Dictionary*, pp. 179–81.

37. 893.00/5-2849, #1129 Stuart, Nanking, RG 59, NA and in FRUS (1949)8:350; 893.00/7-349, #2600 Cabot, Shanghai, RG 59, NA. See also discussion of labor problems in ch. 4.

38. Memorandum by General Ch'en Ming-shu, Chairman of Kuomintang Revolutionary Committee, Shanghai branch, RG 59, NA and in FRUS (1949)8:774.

39. International obligations, declared the CCP, "are nothing but unequal treaties, brutally and forcibly imposed upon [the Chinese people] by imperialist gunboats and aggressive wars, or signed by the traitorous KMT government in order to obtain imperialist aid in launching its criminal civil war against the Chinese people." "New China Enters World Diplomatic Stage," *China Digest* (October 19, 1949) 7:2; NCNA, *The Truman Doctrine in China* (China, 1949), Appendix B. The Central Committee of the CCP issued the statement regarding abrogation of treaties February 1, 1947. On the PCC see *White Paper*, pp. 135–44. The CCP supposedly lacked certified treaty texts and feared secret protocols. 893.00B/12-1349, #5200 McConaughy, Shanghai, FRUS (1949)8:628.

40. The Chinese People's Political Consultative Conference proclaimed the CCP's Common Program on September 29, 1949. This document set forth, in general terms, the aims of the new government in domestic and foreign affairs. Article 3 pledged that the new authorities would "abolish all prerogatives of imperialist countries in China," and Article 55 discussed the regime's intention to "examine the treaties and agreements" concluded by the Kuomintang. *Common Program and Other Documents of the First Plenary Session of the Chinese People's Political Consultative Conference* (Peking, 1950). Hungdah Chiu, "Suspension and Termination of Treaties in Communist China's Theory and Practice," *Osteuropa-Recht*, September 1969, pp. 173–79, Vertical File, East Asian Collection, Hoover Institution on War, Revolution and Peace, Stanford, Ca. The CCP wanted to replace the KMT at the UN; see Shih-chieh chih-shih Ch'u-pan she (comp), *Chung hua Jen-min Kung-ho Kuo tui-wai kuan-hsi wen-chien chi* [Collected Documents on the Foreign Relations of the People's Republic of China], vol 1, 1949–1950, pp. 85–86, and English translation and discussion, "Premier Chou En-lai's Telegram to UNO," and "A Test for United Nations," *China Digest* (November 30, 1949) 7:3; "Struggle to the End for the Realization of Foreign Minister Chou En-lai's Statement," *Jen-min jih-pao*, January 17, 1950. For text of 1943 Sino-American treaty see *White Paper*, pp. 514–17.

41. According to accepted Western usage as put forth by Professor Hersh Lauterpacht, noted British authority, "[c]hanges in the government or in the constitution of a state have . . . no effect upon the continued validity of its international obligations." Chiu, "Suspension and Termination of Treaties," p. 173; Briggs, "American Consular Rights," pp. 253–57.

42. 761.00/2-349, #60 Acheson to Clubb, Peking, RG 59, NA and in FRUS (1949)9:11.

43. Though states commonly recognize the continuance of diplomatic au-

thority, international law does not dictate that they do so. Dorothy Rae Dodge, "Recognition of the Central People's Government of the People's Republic of China" (Ph.D. diss.), p. 198; 893.01/5-1349, #1019 Stuart, Nanking, RG 59, NA.

44. Roth, "Peiping's New Look," p. 274; 893.01/5-1349, #1019 Stuart, Nanking, RG 59, NA. Mao himself confessed to a haphazard study of world affairs and the United States in *SW*, 1:303; 3:13, 18; Hunt, "Mao Tse-tung," pp. 228–29. The April 1949 invasion of Ambassador Stuart's bedroom by PLA soldiers illustrated the ignorance of the rank-and-file regarding proper procedures. High-level officials subsequently made embarrassed apologies to Stuart. See FRUS (1949)8:723–25, 730, 737–38, 742, 748–49, 798–99.

45. #158 Clubb, Peking to AmEmb Nanking, February 7, 1949, Box 2315: Tsingtao, file: 350 Correspondence, RG 84, WNRC; Joint Weeka #3, February 4, 1949, RG 84, WNRC; 124.936/5-749, #955 Stuart, Nanking, FRUS (1949)8:739; 701.0093/8-1549, #1788 Jones, Nanking, *ibid.*, pp. 814–15. Diplomatic officers in Nanking were, after all, accredited to the Kuomintang government. Moreover, American officials generally followed the same procedure; they did not use titles in addressing communications to CCP authorities lest they give impression the United States was granting the CCP de facto recognition. 124.93/5-949, #337 Clark, Canton, FRUS (1949)8:740; 124.936/5-749, #583 Secretary of State to Stuart, *ibid.* 743; 125.7146/5-1849, #896, Clubb, Peking, *ibid.*, pp. 1084–85; 125.0093/5-2749, #330 Acting Secretary to Clubb, *ibid.*, pp. 1085–86. Re recognition of consuls as quid pro quo 125.6336/2-2349, #76 Clark, Canton, *ibid.*, p. 939.

46. Seymour Topping, *Journey Between Two Chinas*, p. 82; Dispatch #266 Jenkins, Hong Kong, September 22, 1949, Box 912, file 350.21 Communists Non-Chinese, RG 84, WNRC.

47. Even pro-American Chinese agreed with this CCP effort although they deplored the occasional violence. On June 15, 1949 a newspaper associated with Ch'en Ming-shu, the *China Daily Tribune*, ran an editorial entitled "Please Stop Acting Like Overlords." 893.9111RR/6-1749, #2316 Cabot, Shanghai, FRUS (1949)8:1171–72.

48. "Is New China Anti-Foreign?" *China Digest* (July 27, 1949), 6:11; Briggs, "American Consular Rights," p. 246. For documentation on Olive Incident see FRUS (1949)8:1199–1222. Although William Olive clearly received harsh treatment, he did behave belligerently and his beating occurred while he was resisting the police. Other unpleasant incidents included Angus Ward's imprisonment allegedly for beating a former consulate employee, occupation of the consulate general in Shanghai by ex-Navy employees demanding severance pay and bonuses, the detention of U.S. servicemen charged with espionage in the Tsingtao area, and the refusal of exit visas to an American military attaché in Nanking and a consular official in Shanghai. Briggs, "American Consular Rights," pp. 246–48; "U.S. Protests Siege of Consulate General at Shanghai," *Department of State Bulletin* (September 19, 1949) 21:440–41; 893.00/12-849 Memo Butterworth (FE) to Secretary of State, RG 59, NA; "Statement on the Release of Two U.S. Airmen," DNR #368, May 9, 1950, p. 56; "Chinese Communists Refuse Exit Visa for American Military Attaché," *Department of State Bulletin* (November 7, 1949) 21:709–10. Documentation on these incidents available FRUS (1949)8:933–1051 (Ward-Mukden), 1214-82 (Shanghai Consulate General), 838-57 (Military Attaché Nanking).

49. Pledge by Commander Nieh Jung-chen of the Peking-Tientsin Garrison

Headquarters reported in 893.00/1-1849, #81 Smyth, Tientsin, RG 59, NA; pledge by Lin Piao, PLA commander in the Peking-Tientsin area reported in 893.00/2-1349, #175 Clubb, Peking, RG 59, NA; pledge by Chang Han-fu, chief of the foreign affairs department of the Shanghai military control commission reported in 893.00/5-3149, #1907 Cabot, Shanghai, RG 59, NA. Warnings against special privileges accompanied pledges. 893.00/8-2349, #3391 McConaughy, Shanghai, RG 59, NA. See also Roth, "China and the 'Foreign Devils,' " p. 296. Re Randall Gould see ch. 4.

50. 124.931/7-2349, #1590 Stuart, Nanking, and 123 Stuart, #1603 Stuart, Nanking, July 24, 1949, FRUS (1949)8:796-97, 799-800; John Leighton Stuart, *Fifty Years in China*, pp. 250-55. Every person leaving China had to have a business of recognized standing take responsibility for any debts discovered after his departure. This was required under both KMT and CCP administrations. V.K. Wellington Koo Oral History Collection, 1 (sec. 6):307, East Asian Institute, Columbia University; 123 Stuart, #1526, July 14, 1949, FRUS (1949)8:785. Re mistaken assumption by State Department that this procedure was unique with CCP, see 123 Stuart, #833, Secretary of State to Stuart, July 15, 1949, and #890, Secretary of State to Stuart, July 27, 1949, FRUS (1949)8:788, 803-4.

51. Re the Boxer Rebellion and the resulting international settlement see Chester Tan, *The Boxer Catastrophe*. Re sensitivity of CCP to imperialist nature of the barracks land see: DNR #263, January 21, 1950, p. 91, DNR #266, January 24, 1950, p. 107, and DNR #268, January 26, 1950, p. 117; "The Peking Military Control Commission Upholds National Sovereignty by Taking Over Alien Barracks," *Jen-min jih-pao*, January 19, 1950.

52. 125.7141/1-1050 Memorandum by the Acting Secretary of State James E. Webb to the President, Dean Acheson Papers, HST and FRUS (1950)6:270-72; 125.7141/1-1050, #65 Clubb, Peking, *ibid.*, pp. 274-75; 125.7141/1-950, #56, Clubb, Peking, *Ibid.*, p. 275; 602.0093/1-2050, #157 Clubb, Peking, *ibid.*, pp. 286-89; 602.0093/1-2050, #108 Secretary to ConGen Peking, *ibid.*, p. 306; "Communists Take U.S. Property in China," *Department of State Bulletin*, January 23, 1950, pp. 119-23; "Peking MCC Requisitions Foreign Barracks in City," and "Sophistries, Slanders and Threats of U.S. State Department," DNR #261, January 19, 1950, pp. 77-79. The latter article reiterated CCP willingness to work out problems having to do with the requisition order.

53. "Demands of People Now Being Realized," Peking NCNA, English morse code to North America, July 6, 1949, section: Far East, China, p. BBB-2, FBIS. Common Program, Articles 56 & 57. Durdin, *New York Times*, September 17, 1949 p. 5. Allen Whiting makes the distinction between conditions for recognition and trade in *China Crosses the Yalu*, p. 24. 893.01/10-1149, #1724 Clubb, Peking, FRUS (1949)9:121-22; 893.01/10-149, #1666 Clubb, Peking, FRUS (1949)8:544-45; 793.00/10-249, #1665 Clubb, Peking, FRUS (1949)9:93; 893.01/10-2749, #1836 Clubb, Peking, *ibid.*, pp. 148-49. Chou's message was addressed to Clubb without using his official title. The same invitation was distributed to other Western and to East European nations. It is perhaps worthy of note that Huang Hua had told Philip Fugh in May 1949, according to the latter's report, "that it would be up to the USA, when time came, to make [the] first move in establishing relations with People's Democratic Government." Lo Lung-chi, leader of the Democratic League also said the CCP did not intend to sue for recognition. *The United States and Communist China in 1949 and 1950*, p. 7; 893.00/7-1949, #848 Clubb, Peking, RG 59, NA.

54. K'o Pai-nien, "The Foreign Policy of New Democracy," pp. 13–15, reprinted in English as "New China's Foreign Policy," *China Digest* (November 2, 1949) 7:7–9.

55. "New China Enters World Diplomatic Stage," *China Digest* (October 19, 1949) 7:3.

56. "National Budget for 1950," *China Digest* (December 14, 1949) 7:28; Mao Tse-tung, "The Struggle for a Basic Turn for the Better in the Financial and Economic Situation of the State," June 6, 1950, report to the Third Plenary Session of the Seventh Central Committee, DNR #404, June 14, 1950, p. 79. See also ch. 4.

57. 793.00/1-350, #6 Secretary of State to ConGen Peking, FRUS (1950)6:269–70; 793.00/1-2150, #346 McConaughy, Shanghai, HST and FRUS (1950)6:289–93; 793.00/1-2150, #127 Secretary to ConGen Shanghai, *ibid.*, p. 294; 793.00/1-2650, #430 McConaughy, Shanghai, *ibid.*, pp. 296–300; 793.001/1-2750, #447 McConaughy, Shanghai, *ibid.*, pp. 300–2; 793.00/2-2550 Memo by John P. Davies, PPS, *ibid.*, pp. 305–6.

58. 893.00/3-849, #363 Clubb, Peking, RG 59, NA; 893.00/11-1549, #4782 McConaughy, Shanghai, RG 59, NA; Strobe Talbot, trans., *Khrushchev Remembers*, p. 243; Pepper, *Civil War in China*, pp. 212–16; "Soviet Designs in Communist China," November 23, 1949, Truman Papers, George M. Elsey Files, Box 59, Subject File (Foreign Relations, C-M), folder: Foreign Affairs—China, HST; 761.93/12-1649, #5250 McConaughy, Shanghai, FRUS (1949)8:632–36; Whiting, *China Crosses the Yalu*, p. 180*n*38; *Kommunist* on anti-Soviet faction, *China Quarterly* (July/September, 1964) 19:191. Re excusing Russian "imperialism" see Chao Yi-ya, "Kuo-chi chu-i hsueh-hsi t'i-kan" [Study Principles of Internationalism], pp. 7–9; Paul Paddock, *China Diary*, p. 135. Allen Whiting suggests that criticism of Soviet behavior may have been the impetus for creation of the Sino-Soviet Friendship Association in China. Whiting, p. 179*n*33.

59. The Far Eastern Division of the Department of State estimated that railroad rehabilitation in China proper alone would require approximately US$300 million in imported material and equipment. An even larger quantity of capital goods would be needed from abroad if an attempt were made to restore Manchuria's industrial sector. (An unspecified American government study cited by Allen Whiting estimated the replacement value of Japanese industrial equipment removed by the Russians from Manchuria at $2 billion. Whiting, *China Crosses the Yalu*, p. 29.) State further noted that when victorious, the CCP would have neither significant foreign exchange reserves nor any prospect of sizable foreign credits. 693.0031/7-1349 Office Memo Butterworth (FE) through Rusk (G) to Secretary, RG 59, NA. "Probable Developments in China," ORE 45-49, June 16, 1949, p. 19, Central Intelligence Agency, RG 319, NA. According to an informant "whose information we believe reflects at least some access to inside Communist circles," Mao went to Moscow seeking financial aid in the amount of US$5 billion. In addition to this he wanted machinery and equipment for domestic reconstruction and for the invasion of Taiwan. 793.00/1-2150, #346 McConaughy, Shanghai, HST, and in FRUS (1950)6:291. The not entirely convincing argument has been made that $300 million was welcomed by the CCP as all that such a backward country could use in its first five years of constructive activity. Chang Nai-chi, "Two Ways and One Way: The Greatness of the Sino-Soviet Treaty of Friendship," Peking in Mandarin, March 9, 1950, section: Articles and Speeches, March 13, 1950, p. PPP-3, FBIS. State Department analysts noted Mao's failure

to mention Soviet aid in his June 6, 1950 speech to the Central Committee as evidence of Chinese dissatisfaction. OIR IM-305, June 14, 1950, Truman Papers, PSF, HST.

60. Schram, *The Political Thought of Mao Tse-tung*, p. 419. Re displeasure about join stock companies see Ti Ch'ao-pai, "The Meaning and Method of Sino-Soviet Economic Cooperation," *Jen-min jih-pao*, April 21, 1950. An October 1954 communiqué resulting from the visit of Soviet Party Secretary Nikita Khrushchev and Premier Nikolai Bulganin to Peking announced that all Sino-Soviet joint stock companies would be dissolved as of December 21, 1954. That this was some 25 years earlier than specified in the 1950 accords indicates considerable Chinese dissatisfaction with the arrangements which could be vented once Stalin had died. Whiting, *China Crosses the Yalu*, p. 180n39.

61. " 'C-in-C Says' Army Certain to Free Taiwan, Preparing Intensively," DNR #300, March 1, 1950, pp. 1-2. Chu Te speaking at a meeting of the Taiwan Democratic Self-Governing League asserted "the liberation of Taiwan has become the most pressing task of the people of the entire country and we must fulfil [*sic*] it with all our power."

62. Herbert Hoover to Senator William Knowland, December 31, 1949, released to the press by Knowland January 2, 1950. *New York Times*, January 3, 1950, p. 1. Text appears in *CR*, 96, 81st Cong., 2d sess., 1950, p. 83; "Reds Scorn American Aid to Taiwan," Peking, English morse code to North America, January 3, 1950, section: China, January 4, 1950, p. BBB 1-2, FBIS. "Chiang Kai-shek Considers Handing Over Taiwan to MacArthur," NCNA *Daily Bulletin* #30, May 16, 1950, p. 3; "U.S. Imperialists Never Learn," p. 3. 794A.00/5-3150 Memorandum by the Deputy Special Assistant for Intelligence (Howe) to W. Park Armstrong, Special Assistant to the Secretary of State for Intelligence and Research, FRUS (1950)6:318-19.

63. *Public Papers of the Presidents: Harry S. Truman* (Washington, D.C.: Government Printing Office, 1964), p. 11.

64. Dean Acheson, "Crisis in Asia," p. 115.

65. Tsou, *America's Failure*, pp. 529-31.

66. For coverage of the Hainan campaign see NCNA *Daily Bulletin* #9 (April 17, 1950), #13-16 (April 21-26, 1950), #19 (May 1, 1950), #21 (May 3, 1950), #24 (May 8, 1950), #27 (May 11, 1950), and #29 (May 15, 1950). Re takeover of Tungshan Island see #32 (May 18, 1950). Re takeover of the Choushan (Chusan) Islands see #32-35 (May 18-23, 1950). Re takeover of islands in the Wanshan group see #43 (June 5, 1950). *Jen-min jih-pao* hailed the Hainan and Choushan triumphs as harbingers of victory over Taiwan in its April 21, 1950 and May 21, 1950 issues.

67. For examples see: "No Smoke-Screen Round Taiwan," p. 4; "American Committee for a Democratic Far Eastern Policy Exposes Truman's Statement on Taiwan," *Jen-min jih-pao*, January 14, 1950; Hu Chiao-mu's comments on Acheson's January 12, 1950 National Press Club Speech, "Crisis in Asia," and Chou En-lai's response to Acheson's March 15, 1950 Commonwealth Club speech both appear in *Chung Hua Jen-min Kung-ho Kuo tui-wai kuan-hsi wen-chien chi*, 1:92-94, 109-11; "American Lies and the Truth About Asia," *Jen-min jih-pao*, March 18, 1950; "A Mosquito and the Fortress of Peace," *People's China* (April 1, 1950) 1:3-4; Statement of the Chinese People's Relief Association, NCNA *Daily Bulletin* #24 (May 8, 1950), pp. 1-2.

68. General Su Yü, "Liberation of Taiwan in Sight," *People's China* (February

16, 1950) 1:8–9, and his remarks summarized in DNR #282, February 9, 1950, p. 42; "C-in-C," DNR #300, pp. 1–2 and message to the people of Taiwan from the Taiwan Democratic Self-Governing League, *ibid.*, pp. 2–3; "Liu Shao-ch'i's May Day Address," pp. 5–10 and the English-language text in DNR #361, May 1, 1950, pp. 1–9.

69. 123 Clubb, O. Edmund, April 11, 1950, FRUS(1950) 6:329; 793.00/6-250 Memorandum by Charlton Ogburn, Bureau of Far Eastern Affairs, *ibid.*, pp. 352–53; O. Edmund Clubb Oral History Interview, p. 72, HST; "Wen-t'i chieh-ta [Questions and Answers]," p. 18. Few countries in those days allowed a diplomatic post to send its own radio messages. Paddock, *China Diary*, p. 44; 119.2/12-1449, #2490 Secretary of State to McConaughy, FRUS (1949)8:1301–2.

70. Editorial, *Jen-min jih-pao*, June 29, 1950.

71. Whiting, *China Crosses the Yalu*, pp. 20–22, 62–64. For Truman's June 27 statement see *Public Papers, Truman* p. 492. For Chou's remarks on June 28 see *Chung Hua Jen-min Kung-ho Kuo tui-wai kuan-hsi wen-chien chi*, 1:130–31, and for English text see *People's China* (July 16, 1950) 2:4.

72. "The Formosan Problem," March 3, 1949, Acheson statement to NSC, FRUS (1949)9:295; Dean Acheson, "Crisis in Asia", p. 115; Dean Acheson testimony in Executive Session, March 29, 1950, U.S. Cong., Senate, Committee on Foreign Relations, *Reviews of the World Situation, 1949–1950* pp. 273–75.

73. On May Day 1950 Liu Shao-ch'i had spoken of China's redirecting resources to peaceful economic reconstruction after the Taiwan campaign. DNR #361, p. 3.

4. KUOMINTANG DECLINE

1. Lucien Bianco, *Origins of the Chinese Revolution*, pp. 177–78.

2. See *White Paper*, pp. 920–21; "Statement on the Present Situation by Mao Tse-tung, Chairman of the Communist Party of China, January 14, 1949," *SW*, 4:315–19; 893.00/1-849, #61, Stuart, Nanking, FRUS (1949)8:22–23; 893.00/1-1049, Memorandum of Conversation by Director of the Office of Far Eastern Affairs (Butterworth) to the Acting Secretary of State, *ibid.*, pp. 27–29; 893.00/1-849, #43, Acting Secretary of State to Stuart, Nanking, *ibid.*, pp. 41–42.

3. Bianco, *Origins*, pp. 177–78; and James P. Harrison, *The Long March to Power*, pp. 423–25. On Kuomintang members who desired Chiang's resignation, see FRUS (1948)7:625–27; and "Pai Chung-hsi Extends His Influence into the Nanking-Shanghai Area," *Hai Chao* (Tide Weekly), Shanghai, February 11, 1949, CPS, vol. 2, no. 6, February 21, 1949.

Over the next 18 months events moved rapidly. In retrospect it is easy to see the glaring mistakes. Yet evidence of developments beneath the surface is harder to unearth, and much remains concealed in still inaccessible Kuomintang and Chinese Communist archives.

4. 893.00/1-2349, #150, Stuart, Nanking, FRUS (1948)7:56–57; 893.00/2-548, #232, Stuart, Nanking, *ibid.*, p. 77.

5. Discussion of factions in the Kuomintang follows. V. K. Wellington Koo Oral History Collection, 1 (sec. 4):205, East Asian Institute, Columbia University (hereafter Koo Oral History); Shui Chieh-tan, "A Study of the Sino-Soviet Local Commercial Pact;" "Says Pro-USSR Policy is Bound to be Changed if Peace Talks

Break Down," *Ta Kung Pao*, Shanghai, April 20, 1949, CPR, #875, April 20, 1949; Joint Weeka #10, from State, Army, Navy, Air (SANA) Nanking, March 25, 1949, p. 2 file 350.2 Joint Weeka Reports, Consul General Hong Kong, China Post Files, RG 84, WNRC.

6. 893.00/1-2349, #197, Stuart, Nanking, and 893.00/1-2349, #94, Acheson to Stuart, RG 59, NA; Statement by Kan Chieh-hou, August 24, 1949, folder: 75.6 U. S. White Paper on China 1949, V. K. Wellington Koo Papers, Butler Library Manuscript Division, Columbia University (hereafter Koo Papers). The British Assistant Under Secretary of State for Foreign Affairs (FE) believed the Chinese were trying to frighten the United States into intervention. 893.00/2-249, #388, Holmes, UK, FRUS (1949)8:99–100.

7. Chang Chih-chung told Philip Fugh on January 4, 1949 that the Soviets had advised the CCP to stop at the Yangtze River. John Leighton Stuart Diary, January 4, 1949; Gittings, *The World and China*, p. 150. See also my ch. 2.

8. Lu Ying-hua, "The Delicate Relations Among Li Tsung-jen, Sun Fo, and Chang Chih-chung," "Peace Talks in Progress," *Ta Kung Pao*, Shanghai, April 11, 1949, CPR, #868, April 9–11, 1949. For Sun Fo's peace terms see Joint Weeka #12, April 8, 1949, p. 3, file 350.2, Consul General Hong Kong, RG 84, WNRC. Sun Fo was Sun Yat-sen's son by his first marriage. He served in a variety of government positions including the presidency of the Legislative Yuan and from November 1948 to March 1949 the presidency of the Executive Yuan (China's cabinet). Although he had opposed Chiang from time to time, in 1948 he was Chiang's candidate for the vice presidency against Li. See Howard L. Boorman and Richard C. Howard, eds., *Biographical Dictionary of Republican China* 3:162–65.

9. Editorials and news reports favorable to the concept of peace talks appeared frequently in the *Ta Kung Pao*, organ of the Political Study Clique. Comment hostile to a compromise peace was as prominent in the leading CC Clique newspaper *Shun Pao*. See for example, "Some Thoughts on the Peace Talks," *Ta Kung Pao*, Shanghai April 13, 1949, CPR, #870, April 13, 1949, and "Surrender or Otherwise," *Shun Pao*, Shanghai, April 19, 1949, CPR, #874, April 19, 1949. On the affiliation of the *Ta Kung Pao* with the Political Study Clique see, Han Ssu, *K'an! Cheng-hsüeh hsi* [*Look! The Political Study Clique*], p. 14; and Pepper, *Civil War in China*, pp. 436–40. On the *Shun Pao* see Walter Sullivan, "Chiang Aides Seen in New Maneuver," p. 8.

10. Mao, *SW*, 4:341–45, 351–59, 383–85; "Feverish Kuomintang War Activity Behind the 'Peace Front,' " North Shensi Radio, February 9, 1949, *New China News Agency Weekly Bulletin*, no. 89, February 15, 1949, (hereafter NCNA).

11. In Chiang's parting speech, he used the Chinese *yin-t'ui* meaning withdrawal, instead of the stronger *tz'u-chih* which would have meant resignation. See Koo Oral History, I (sec.1):6. Philip Fugh, former secretary to John Leighton Stuart, American Ambassador to China 1946–49, in a personal interview, July 21, 1977, described the Generalissimo's action as asking Li to be his representative in charge of the presidency. Li Tsung-jen personally contended throughout 1949 and even after Chiang resumed the presidency on March 1, 1950, that Chiang was acting illegally. "The function of 'acting' is for the official position of the president and not for you as an individual. Furthermore, after your retirement you became a private citizen without any further concern with the function of the presidency. Without an election by the National Assembly you have no legal ground to become again the President of China." Open Letter Li

Tsung-jen, NYC, to Chiang Kai-shek, Formosa, February 28, 1950, Box 221: Li Tsung-jen 1949–51, Koo Papers; and see Li Tsung-jen Oral History Collection, 4 (pt. 7, ch. 52):52–53, Chinese Oral History Collection, Butler Library Manuscript Division, Columbia University (hereafter Li Oral History).

12. The title *tsung-tsai* was, for all practical purposes the same as *tsung-li*, but the latter had been reserved in perpetuity to honor Sun Yat-sen. See William Tung, *The Political Institutions of Modern China*, p. 173; and Ch'ien Tuan-sheng, *The Government and Politics of China*, p. 120. On Chiang's early career see Brian Crozier, *The Man Who Lost China*, pp. 3–212, and P. Y. Pichon Loh, *The Early Chiang Kai-shek*.

13. The Hundred Regiments Offensive, launched August 20, 1940 by 400,000 troops of the Communist Eighth Route Army against Japanese forces in five northern provinces, was designed to keep the Sino-Japanese war alive and to prevent pessimistic or pro-Japanese elements in the KMT from engineering a peace settlement. Chalmers Johnson, *Peasant Nationalism*, p. 57; and Mao, "Expose the Plot for a Far Eastern Munich," *SW*, 3:27–28.

14. There were also minor political parties in Nationalist China, such as the Democratic League and the Young China Party, but they had little power and were generally insignificant. For a brief description of these organizations, see *The China Handbook 1950* (New York: Rockport Press, Inc., 1950), pp. 254–59.

15. Discussions of the cliques within the Kuomintang suffer from a lack of concrete data and a desire to fit a fluid situation into manageable static units. Contemporary observers with an obvious need to understand the inner workings of the party, Chinese Communist intelligence agents, forewarned their readers that factional alignments among the Nationalists were too changeable and complex to be reliably reported. See the foreword to "Biographies of Kuomintang Leaders," mimeographed by the Committee on International and Regional Studies, Harvard University, February 1948, originally a confidential CCP publication entitled "A List of the Various Cliques Among Members of Central Committees Elected by the Sixth Congress of the Kuomintang," August 31, 1945. Nevertheless, for a brief treatment of the subject, see Tien Hung-mao, *Government and Politics in Kuomintang China*, pp. 45–72; Ho Lien Oral History Collection, ch. 12, Chinese Oral History Project, Columbia (hereafter Ho Lien Oral History).

16. Huang Pin, "Faction Strife in the Kuomintang," *New Hope Weekly*, Shanghai, no. 6, March 21, 1949, Dispatch #53, John M. Cabot, Consul General Shanghai, 893.00/4-149, RG 59, NA. The *New Hope Weekly* was controlled by the army which goes far in explaining the favorable way in which the Fu Hsing Society is described.

17. For a detailed discussion of the background of the Kwangsi Clique see Diana Lary, *Region and Nation*. Owen Lattimore notes that Chiang never ruled as an absolute dictator because he constantly needed to reconcile conflicting factions. Owen Lattimore, Comments at East Asian Institute Research Luncheon, March 30, 1979, Columbia University.

18. Efforts to explain factionalism relying on generalizations about Chinese social traits and political behavior have stirred some controversy in recent years. See Lloyd Eastman, *The Abortive Revolution*, pp. 283–313; Andrew J. Nathan, *Peking Politics*, pp. 27–58; Richard H. Solomon, *Mao's Revolution and the Chinese Political Culture*.

19. Liu Chien-ch'ün, *Fu-hsing Chung-kuo ko-ming chih lu* [The Way to Regenerate the Chinese Revolution] (n.p., 1934), p. 39, quoted in Eastman, *Abortive*

Revolution, p. 305. Liu Chien-ch'ün was secretary to General Ho Ying-ch'in, a loyal follower of Chiang Kai-shek, and a leader of the fascistic Blue Shirts organization. He also trenchantly criticized the Kuomintang, hoping to convince the leadership to adopt reform measures for the good of the party. See Liu Chien-ch'ün, pp. 32–37.

20. Eastman, *Abortive Revolution*, p. 304.

21. "There has been much criticism of the Chinese government, both as to organization and as to personality. Such criticism, in China as elsewhere, is only partially justified. My own judgment is that while the moral level of officials should be raised, their intellectual level is even more in need of lifting and broadening. . . . Often I sat in cabinet meetings listening to discussions, indulging in the pastime of trying to fix the era to which the mentality of those present belonged. It was easy to detect German, Japanese, French, British or American educational backgrounds. But most common was the mentality of the old literatus, the one who mistook phrases for facts and decisions. If you told such a mind that it was out of date, the accusation would be resented." Tsiang Ting-fu Oral History Collection, p. 236, Chinese Oral History Project, Columbia; and see Ho Lien Oral History, pp. 164–65.

22. On March 7, 1949 Sun Fo finally did resign and was replaced by Ho Ying-ch'in, but by then Li had been to Canton (Feb.22) and Sun had returned the Executive Yuan to Nanking (Feb. 28). Koo Oral History, I (sec. 1):7–9; *New York Times*, February 19, 1949, p. 4; February 21, p. 1; February 22, p. 12; February 25, p. 7; Li Oral History, 4 (pt. 7, ch. 48):10–11.

23. Li Tsung-jen maintained that upon his return to Ch'i-k'ou in Fenghua, Chiang had seven radio broadcasting stations erected from which he could direct military operations. Moreover, the Chief of the General Staff, Ku Chu-t'ung took orders only from Chiang. Li Oral History, 4 (pt. 7, ch. 49):6. In a March 4, 1970 interview, Chang Fa-kuei told V. K. Wellington Koo that there were occasions during the civil war when the Minister of National Defense was not informed of the whereabouts of troops taking orders directly from the Gimo. Koo Oral History, J (sec. 4):282. See also Wu Kuo-cheng (K. C. Wu) Oral History Collection, ch. 2, p. 70, Chinese Oral History Project, Columbia (hereafter Wu Oral History).

24. It was understood, Ambassador Koo notes, that the Gimo's order to General Liu An-chi, one of his favorite pupils from Whampoa Military Academy, to withdraw south from the Kukong sector had, in large part, precipitated Pai's withdrawal from Hunan to Kwangsi. Koo continues, "it was quite evident to the Generalissimo, to General Liu, as well as to the outside world, that this order to withdraw would cause General Pai's line of defense against the Communists to crumble. It may be that the Generalissimo felt this last attempt would be useless anyway, that it would be mere sacrifice to no purpose, and therefore he wanted to save his troops as much a possible." Koo Oral History, J (sec. 1):39–40; 893.00/9-1749, #709 Karl L. Rankin, RG 59, NA. Chiang biographer Brian Crozier blames this military debacle on the "provincial egotism" of the Governor of Kwantung Yu Han-mou, who was trying to save his 50,000 regulars and keep Pai out of his province. Crozier, *Man Who Lost China*, pp. 341–42. However, Yu was known to be a loyal follower of Chiang.

25. According to Li and Pai in a September 12, 1949 interview with an American official, Chiang Kai-shek's interference was exemplified by withdrawal of

air support over the battleground at Hengyang and removal of ammunition from Canton to Taiwan. Proof of the latter, they asserted, was the explosion of the transport ship *Kaohsiung* en route. Office Memo Butterworth (FE) to Humelsine (S/S), September 14, 1949, folder: Military Developments in China, CA Records, RG 59, NA. General Barr reported to the U.S. Department of the Army that, "In an interview on 25th Jan with General Tang En-po [*sic*], Defense Commander of the Nanking-Shanghai area, he stated that he was not going to obey the orders of Li Tsung-jen to discontinue work on defense installations in the Shanghai area, nor was he going to lift martial law as directed. He said he would also refuse to obey the instructions of any Communist influenced government. . . . He is strong Generalissimo man obviously not in sympathy with the policy being pursued by the present Peace Party in Nanking but he cannot hope to hold Shanghai under the circumstances." CYF771 GAGA, January 26, 1949, JUS-MAGCHINA, Shanghai, Barr to Dept. of Army for Maddocks, folder: Military Developments, CA Records, RG 59, NA. Quote in text from Message COM-NAVWESPAC, April 19, 1949, folder: Political Trends in China, CA, RG 59, NA. Also see Yin Shih, *Li-Chiang Kuan-hsi yu Chung-kuo* [The Li-Chiang Relationship and China], pp. 103–28, and Liang Sheng-chün, *Chiang-Li Tou-cheng Nei-mu* [The Inside Story of the Struggle Between Chiang and Li], pp. 29–169; and 893.001/8-2349, #1012, Clark, Canton, FRUS (1949)8:501–2.

26. U.S. Minister-Counselor Lewis Clark told Li Wei-kuo in a September 12, 1949 conversation, that before his departure from Canton, he had met with a depressed Li Tsung-jen. No important decision was possible without first consulting the Gimo and securing his approval. Koo Oral History, I (sec. 8):478–79 and Notes of Conversation, 1949, #77, September 15, 1949, Koo Papers. A reporter from the *New Hope Weekly*, Shanghai, April 4, 1949, reported that the Lo Hsia airfield in East Chekiang was handling at least three flights per day as opposed to its normal one per month, and that all were high civilian and military missions. Shao Sheng, "Sidelights on Chikow," CPS, vol. 3, no. 5, April 7, 1949. Similarly, Associated Press in Nanking reported that the Gimo was in daily telephone contact with key economic, military, and political people "who remain personally loyal to him even while supposedly under the direction of Acting President Li." *New York Times*, February 20, 1949, p. 19.

27. The leadership of the Kwangsi Clique was essentially oligarchic. Li Tsung-jen and Pai Ch'ung-hsi remained at the forefront throughout its history. Li Chi-shen was something of a mentor in the early years but later moved away into other affiliations such as the Kuomintang Revolutionary Committee. In the 1920s Huang Shao-hsiung shared power, maintaining the sanctity of Kwangsi while Li and Pai "crusaded" in the north. Although disagreements led him to sever intimate associations with the clique (he was replaced by Huang Hsü-ch'u), he often cooperated with Li in subsequent years. Below this level of leadership, however, there were few men of any particular talent. Shih Fen-wu, "Li Tsung-jen and His Following," *Sinwen Tienti* (Newsland) Shanghai, May 10, 1949, CPS, vol. 4, no. 3, May 21, 1949; *The Far Eastern Bulletin*, Hong Kong, CPS, vol. 4, no. 2, May 11, 1949; Huai Hsiang (pseud), *Lun Li Tsung-jen yu Chung-Mei Fan-tung P'ai* [A Discussion of Li Tsung-jen and the Sino-American Reactionary Clique], *passim*; Laȝy, *Region and Nation*, pp. 34–42, 157–58.

28. Liang,*Chiang-Li*, pp. 156–63; John Leighton Stuart Diary, July 16, 1949; "Prospects for Renewed Peace Negotiations Between the Chinese Communists

NOTES FOR PAGES 66–68

and the Kwangsi Clique," OIR 5017(PV), July 25, 1949, p. 5, Reel 4, Pt. 3, OSS/State Department Reports; 893.001 Chiang Kai-shek/7-1149, #715 Clark, Canton, FRUS (1949)8:423.

29. Koo Oral History, I (sec. 8):497 and J (sec. 3):181. Wu Kuo-chen maintained in his oral history interview that "I think future historians will be interested to know . . . how much influence Chiang still wielded after his official stepping-down from the Presidency. I can tell you that. Retirement or not, he was still the Government of China. . . . Take my own case. Chiang told me he wanted me to remain as Mayor of Shanghai. If Li had wanted to remove me, he simply could not have done it." Wu Oral History, p. 106.

30. Li Tsung-jen Oral History, 4 (pt. 7, ch. 49):8–9; and Joint Weeka #8, March 11, 1949, p. 3, Joint Weeka #9, March 18, 1949, p. 13, file 350.2, Consul General Hong Kong, China Post Files, RG 84, WNRC.

31. Estimates of the amount of gold transferred varied considerably, reaching a high of $300 million in the remarks of the Chairman of the Senate Foreign Relations Committee, Tom Connally, on September 8, 1949. Press Conference, September 8, 1949, Speech File, 1949, Papers of Senator Tom Connally, LC; Koo Oral History, J (sec. 4):281; Tillman Durdin, "Nationalist Funds Dwindle in China," p. 12; and Li Oral History, 4 (pt. 7, ch. 51):8.

32. Liu Kun-yun described the situation as *yi-kuo san-kung*; that is, three kings ruling one country. Koo Oral History, I (sec. 4):117–18. Re Li's shortage of funds: Pai reportedly approached Hankow's U. S. Consul General with a desperate appeal for financial aid. Joint Weeka #6, February 25, 1949, file 350.2, Consul General Hong Kong, China Post Files, RG 84, WNRC.

33. *China Handbook 1950*, p. 239; Li Oral History, 4 (pt. 7, ch. 51):5; 893.001 Chiang Kai-shek/4-2949, #301 and 893.001 Chiang Kai-shek/5-149, #303 and 893.00/6-1449, #585 and 893.00/6-1949, #613, Clark, Canton, FRUS (1949)8:286–88, 383, 390.

34. China Briefs from Chungking in Cantonese, July 20, 1949, section: Far East, China, July 21, 1949, p. BBB-5, FBIS; "Tsungtsai Office Opened at Taoshan," from Chungking in Cantonese, August 3, 1949, FBIS, August 4, 1949, pp. BBB-2-3; "Prospects for Cooperation Between Chiang Kai-shek and Other Non-Communist Leaders in China," OIR 5050(PV), September 19, 1949, p. 2, Reel 4, pt. 3, OSS/State Department Reports.

35. Joint Weeka #7, March 4, 1949, p. 2; Joint Weeka #8, March 11, 1949, p. 2, file 350.2, Consul General Hong Kong, China Post Files RG 84, WNRC; Memorandum of Conversation with General Ch'en Ming-shu, 893.00/3-1149, Dispatch #36, Cabot, Shanghai to Stuart, Nanking, RG 59, NA; 893.001 Chiang Kai-shek/2-2149, #440, Stuart, Nanking, FRUS (1949)8:142; John Leighton Stuart Diary, February 20 and 21, 1949; Topping, *Journey Between Two Chinas*, p. 58.

36. Koo Oral History, I (sec. 4):120, and J, (sec. 1):34–35. H. H. Kung, a banker and businessman, held posts in the Nationalist government as Minister of Industry and Commerce and Minister of Finance. He was also the husband of Soong Ai-ling, Mme. Chiang Kai-shek's eldest sister. T. V. Soong, a younger brother of Madame Chiang, also held the post of Finance Minister as well as other important government positions. Thus both men were "related" to the Generalissimo and though they did not always agree with him or serve his interests, they remained prominent figures in Chinese Nationalist politics. See Boorman, *Biographical Dictionary*, 2:263–68; 3:137–40, 149–53.

37. "I was not taking sides between the Generalissimo and General Li, except

that so long as the Generalissimo proposed to do something which would be in the interest of China, I would be on his side, as I had always been. . . . My position would also hold true if General Li was doing something for the good of China." Koo Oral History, J (sec.2):165, and I (sec. 3):80. See also Chu Pao-chin, "V. K. Wellington Koo: The Diplomacy of Nationalism," in Richard D. Burns and Edward M. Bennett, eds., *Diplomats in Crisis*, p. 131. Koo also noted that, whereas Li's representative in the U. S., Kan Chieh-hou, and Yen Hsi-shan's representative, P'an Ch'ao-ying, were telling Congressional leaders that Koo spoke only for Chiang, the Gimo's followers, noting how much aid he had rendered Kan, believed Koo had joined Li's camp. Koo Oral History, I (sec. 8):490–91.

38. Koo Oral History, vols. I and J, *passim*; letter Koo to George Yeh, July 20, 1949, folder: L21.a. George Kung-chao Yeh 1949–54, Koo Papers. Control of propaganda activities was uncoordinated not only in the U. S.; in China it was shaped by the Department of Information of the Foreign Ministry, the News Bureau of the Executive Council, the Defense Department, the Chinese News Bureau, and the Publicity Bureau of the President's Office. Koo Oral History, I (sec. 4):173.

39. This coterie, revealed by Senator Wayne Morse's disclosure of a series of secret cables from the Chinese Embassy in Washington to an unspecified, but obvious, destination in China, consisted of Chen Chih-mai, the Minister-Counselor; Brigadier General Peter T. K. Pee (Pi Tsung-kan), Military Attaché; Lt. General P. T. Mow (Mao Pang-tsu), Chinese Air Force Procurement Mission; W. K. Lee (Li Wei-kuo), Delegate to the Far East Commission; and K. H. Yu (Yü Kuo-hua), Deputy Director of the World Bank. Copies of the cables were published in the *CR*, vol. 98, pt. 3, 82nd Cong., 2d session, April 10, 1952, pp. 3970–72, and vol. 98, pt. 5, June 6, 1952, pp. 6740–67. The subjects covered in these regular reports included information culled from the U. S. press and some received from friendly Congressional leaders. That the group was not delighted with Ambassador Koo was clear: January 17, 1950 "We think that Koo is not the ideal person." Again April 4, 1950 "Our diplomatic . . . officers are not at their posts and those who stay in America are not suitable persons to discharge their responsibilities." Folder: China Lobby, 1949, 1952, Styles Bridges Papers, New England College Library, Henniker, N. H.; Paul P. Kennedy, "Senate Gets 'Files' On Secret Activity in U. S. to Aid Chiang," *New York Times*, April 11, 1952; Senator Wayne Morse, "China Lobby;" Drew Pearson, "Cables Show Chiang's War Effort;" and "Morse Seeks 'Lie' Probe of Chiang Envoys," p. 3.

40. Confidential memo from JAW to Senator Taft, March 1, 1948, Alphabetical File, folder: China 1948–49, Legislative Papers, Robert A. Taft Papers, LC.

41. Koo Oral History, H (sec. 2):61–65; see also I (sec. 4):151–52.

42. Koo did not learn of Madame Chiang's imminent arrival from authorities in Taiwan until the same day that the U. S. State Department Press Officer announced the visit. In the same telephone call, November 26, 1948, from Vice Minister of Foreign Affairs George Yeh, Koo was reportedly told her visit was taking place despite the strong protests of Foreign Minister Wang Shih-chieh and efforts by the Gimo to dissuade her. She was instructed by Chiang to stay in Washington a maximum of two weeks and make all arrangements through the Embassy rather than the Kungs. Koo Oral History, H (sec. 3):81.

43. Koo Oral History, H (sec. 3):110; J (sec. 2):96.

44. *Ibid.*, I, (sec. 3):81; Hu Nung-chih, "Will Kan Chieh-hou Become Foreign

Minister?" *Shih Shih Hsin Pao* (connected with H.H. Kung's son David) Shanghai, May 15, 1949, CPR, #894, May 18, 1949. Li's view of Koo emerges clearly in the following: "My appointment of Dr. Kan as my personal representative to the United States in May, 1949, was due to Dr. Wellington Koo's neglect of his duties in Washington. Ambassador Koo took instructions only from Mr. Chiang. . . . Had I removed him from his position, he certainly would have rejected my order." Li Oral History, 4 (pt. 7, ch. 53):5, and similar comments ch. 48, p. 23, and ch. 50, p. 12.

45. Kan described the tactic as *ch'ang shuang huang*; that is, one person singing in two voices or playing a double role to one end. He told Koo on June 22, 1949 that though forced to condemn Chiang Kai-shek's performance as China's leader, he wasn't at all opposed to the Generalissimo. Koo Oral History, I (sec. 4):185–87; (sec. 8):491.

46. Koo Oral History, H (sec. 2):65; J (sec. 3):241–42. "Our American friends both in the Administration and on Capitol Hill . . . feel confused. The State Department regards the situation here as a 'miniature China' reflecting the disunity in our country." Koo to George Yeh, January 6, 1950, folder: Yeh 1949–54, Koo Papers.

47. Interview, Philip Fugh with the author, July 21, 1977. Koo advised T. L. Soong, Chinese Representative on the Board of Governors of the International Bank for Reconstruction and Development (and also a brother of Mme. Chiang), "as a general guide so often followed in our foreign policy, [the Nationalists should] . . . lean on the side of the American view where the British insist upon an opposite stand. We have to depend more upon U. S. for financial and economic aid which U. K. is unable to give us at present." V. K. Wellington Koo Diary, February 4, 1949, Koo Papers.

48. Interview with Philip Fugh, July 21, 1977.

49. Chiang "is reluctant . . . to provide [Li Tsung-jen and regional military leaders] . . . with sufficient material to permit them to offer an independent resistance to the Communists that is effective enough to threaten his own position of preeminence. . . . These objectives seem to have conditioned Chiang's strategic concepts—his refusal to defend the Yangtze line, his unwillingness to aid in the defense of the inland regions of the south, southwest, and northwest China, and his preference for defending the coastal regions of Kwangtung and Fukien and Formosa—as well as his persistent interference in Li Tsung-jen's efforts to revitalize the resistance against Communism in China." OIR 5050(PV), Reel 4, Pt. 3, OSS/State Department Reports; and see Li Oral History, 4 (pt. 7, ch. 49):18; (ch. 52):12; 893.00/7-2349, #1805, Clark, Canton, FRUS (1949)8:453.

50. Re imminence of WW III see: OIR 5050(PV), pp. iv, 6, Reel 4, pt. 3, OSS/State Department Reports; 893.001 Chiang Kai-shek/12-148, #489, Stuart, Nanking, FRUS (1948)7:625–27; 611.94A/1-550, Memorandum of Conversation by Ambassador at Large (Jessup) on talk with Chiang Kai-shek, January 16, 1950, FRUS (1950)6:280–83; Cantel #1281 to Secretary of State, November 25, 1949, file 350, Consul General Hong Kong, China Post Files, RG 84, WNRC; 893.00/5-949, #1565, Confidential Decimal File, RG 59, NA; Andrew Roth, "Chiang Under Fire," p. 35; Interview with Philip Fugh, July 21, 1977; Koo Oral History, I (sec. 3):65–66; (sec. 8):479; J (sec. 2):90–94, 131, 139. Li also based his policies on the imminence of WW III according to Koo; see Koo Diary, February 24, 1949, Koo Papers. Re role of Atlantic Pact in coming of WW III: the KMT-connected newspaper *Sinwen Tienti* maintained that the war would be brought on by Soviet

attempts, which the Atlantic Pact made unavoidable, to consolidate its position in Eastern Europe, and that it would occur within the year. Kung Sun-wang, "Peace Talks in China Before the World's Gathering Storm," *Sinwen Tienti*, Shanghai, no. 67, April 21, 1949, CPR, #877, April 21, 1949, pp. 12–15; *Inside the Chinese Communists* (connected with KMT secret service) Shanghai, no. 2, April 1, 1949, CPR, #862, April 1, 1949, pp. 11–12; "Safeguarding World Peace," *Ta Kung Pao*, Shanghai, April 5, 1949, CPR, #864, April 5, 1949, pp. 3–4.

51. 893.00/9-649, #3659, McConaughy, Shanghai, RG 59, NA; "Chinese 'Tiger Air Force' Not Related to American 'Flying Tiger,' " *Department of State Bulletin* (October 3, 1949) 21:515.

52. T. V. Soong is credited with the decision to use Japanese technical personnel for economic development projects. Chen Yi, "T. V. Soong's New Mission," *Niu Shih* (*Newsweek*) (connected with KMT), Shanghai, no. 20, May 19, 1949, pp. 11–13, CPR, #898, May 24, 1949. The CCP contended that General MacArthur recommended Horiuchi Kanjō and others to Soong, see "Henchmen of the Invading Americans," Peking in Japanese, July 24, 1949, FBIS section: Far East Articles and Speeches, July 26, 1949, pp. 1–17. The CCP also claimed to have captured major Japanese war criminals fighting with Yen Hsi-shan's army. See "Japanese Generals Captured at Taiyuan," Shengyang in Japanese, May 3, 1949, FBIS, section: China-Communist Controlled, p. CCC-3. Further, the Chinese Communists noted a July 18, 1949 Yen Hsi-shan speech calling for "international volunteers" including Japanese and using U. S. aid. Yen was the former Governor of Shansi and was serving as President of the Executive Yuan in July. "Kuomintang Trying to Recruit 100,000 Japanese Mercenaries," NCNA *Bulletin*, no. 114, August 19, 1949, p. 3. An undated, unsigned memorandum claiming to represent the views of the people of Shansi province and calling for Japanese volunteers because of Japan's proximity to China appears in the Claire L. Chennault Papers, Freedom Cause-Correspondence, "Raising of 100,000 International or Japanese Volunteers to Prevent the Spread of Communism in China by Using American Military Aids," Reel 12, LC. Also see Donald Gillin, *Warlord*, pp. 286–88.

53. Immanuel C. Y. Hsu, *The Rise of Modern China*, p. 707; and Tsou, *America's Failure*, p. 284.

54. Koo Oral History, J (sec. 1):11–12, 28.

55. Memo Dean Rusk to Philip C. Jessup, September 8, 1949, Country and Area Files, folder: China 1949, PPS Records, RG 59, NA.

56. Koo Oral History, H (sec. 1):38, 40–42, and J (sec. 1):11–12.

57. That this occurred only shortly after publication of the White Paper on China (discussed hereafter) gave Ambassador Koo added reason to anticipate a poor reaction.

58. Koo Oral History, J (sec. 1):16–29; Conversation with Assistant Secretary of State Dean Rusk, #80, September 21, 1949, Box 130: Notes of Conversation 1949, Koo Papers.

59. 761.93/9-749 Memorandum Fosdick to Jessup, Rusk, Hickerson, Butterworth, Bancroft, Freeman, and 761.93/10-349 Memorandum Clark to Jessup, and 761.93/11-1149 Memorandum Noyes to Jessup, and 761.93/11-1149 Memorandum Yost to Jessup, RG 59, NA; Koo Oral History, J (sec. 1):61; Memorandum Rusk to Jessup, September 8, 1949, PPS Records, RG 59, NA.

60. Tsou, *America's Failure*, pp. 521–22.

61. 761.93/11-749 Memorandum Clark to Jessup, RG 59, NA. Stuart expressed

similar views, see *White Paper* Annex 144, The Ambassador in China to Secretary Marshall, September 20, 1947, pp. 830–31; and also Koo Oral History, J (sec. 1):74–75.

62. "Chiang and Quirino in Philippine Talk," *New York Times*, July 10, 1949, pp. 1, 20, and "Anti-Red Bloc Plan of Chiang, Quirino," *ibid.*, July 11, 1949, p. 8; Ku Jen, "The Influence of American Aid and the Pacific Pact on the Peace Talks," *Ho Ping Jih Pao* (KMT Army related), Shanghai, April 13, 1949, CPR, #872, April 15, 1949, p. 9; "Developments in the Pacific Pact Plan," *Shih Shih Hsin Pao* (connected with David Kung), Shanghai, May 18, 1949, CPR, #895, May 19, 1949, p. 1.

63. 890.20/7-1549 Memorandum by Policy Information Officer of the Office of Far Eastern Affairs (Fisher) to Butterworth, FRUS (1949)7: 1160–64; 890.20/7-2949, #633, Acheson to Embassy in Korea, FRUS (1949) 7:1177–78; 890.20/8-1249, #A-75, MacDonald, Taipei, FRUS (1949)7:185. See also *ibid.*, pt. 2, *passim*.

64. By late October of 1949, Shanghai industry was operating at only 30 to 40 percent of normal capacity in spite of shipments made by blockade runners. Dispatch #88, November 8, 1949, file 510 Trade Relations, Consul General Hong Kong, China Post Files, RG 84, WNRC.

65. 893.801/6-2449, #1373, Stuart, Nanking, RG 59, NA; and "Blockade of Reds in China Ordered," *New York Times*, June 21, 1949, p. 1.

66. Great Britain maintained that the Chinese Nationalist decree closing ports occupied by insurgents without the maintenance of an effective blockade was simply an attempt to secure the rights of war without assuming the accompanying responsibilities dictated by international law. 893.00/6-2749 Memorandum by the Director of the Office of Far Eastern Affairs (Butterworth) FRUS (1949)9:1110–12. Re British convoying of merchant craft, see 841.85/10-1849 Memorandum by the Secretary of State to the President of the United States, *ibid.*, pp. 1150–52; Roth, "How the Communists Rule," p. 488; and Memorandum by R. H. Hillenkoetter, Director of Central Intelligence, to the President of the United States, January 12, 1950, President's Secretary's Files, Intelligence, folder: Central Intelligence Memorandum 1950–52, Papers of Harry S Truman, HST.

67. 393.115/9-1449, #939, Secretary of State to Consul General Rankin at Hong Kong, September 16, 1949, FRUS (1949)9:1133–34; Memorandum of Conversation with the President by Acting Secretary of State James E. Webb, October 1, 3, 1949, Memoranda of Conversations with the President 1949–52, Records of the Executive Secretariat, Lot Files, RG 59, NA; Dean Acheson, "Attacks on United States Shipping by the Chinese," p. 908.

68. 893.00/10-1549, #4351, McConaughy, Shanghai, RG 59, NA.

69. 793.00/2-650, #131, Acheson, Secretary of State to Embassy in China, FRUS (1950)6:306–7. The February 6, 1950 attack on the Riverside plant of the Shanghai Power Company caused severe damage estimated at $4,150,000 (US). It put approximately 40 percent of the company's generating capacity out of commission for an estimated twelve-month period during which SPC expected to lose an additional $970,000 (US). "Synopsis of Telephone Conversation between Mr. Gehrels in Shanghai and Messrs. Robertson and Kopelman in New York," January 24, 1950, Box 271-26, and Troy L. Perkins, Officer in Charge, Political Affairs, Office of Chinese Affairs, State Department, to W. S. Robertson, American and Foreign Power, New York, March 18, 1950, communicating confidential information from Gehrels in Shanghai, BCC. On the day before the

attack, KMT leaflets warned Shanghai residents to keep away from all utilities. Cablegram from Gehrels in Shanghai to Ebasinet, New York, February 6, 1950, Box 226-34. Yet, in May 1949, John M. Cabot, American Consul General in Shanghai, had secured a Nationalist promise, which he verbally communicated to Paul S. Hopkins of SPC, that the company would not be attacked. Paul S. Hopkins, "Memorandum Regarding Shanghai Power Company's Position in Shanghai, China," March 21, 1950, Box 268-14, BCC. Similar problem faced by Stanvac: 893.00/12-3049, #5456, McConaughy, Shanghai, RG 59, NA; "Pootung Terminal Damage Protested by State Department," *Stanvac Meridian* (March, 1950), p. 1, Mobil Oil Corporation Archives, New York.

70. 793.00/2-150, #194, Strong, Chargé in China, FRUS (1950)6:307n4.

71. 793.00/2-1050, #248, Strong, Chargé in China, FRUS (1950)6:307–8. The State Department had received indications that the Nationalists were firing upon highly visible United States property as early as May 1949. A cable from Consul General John M. Cabot in Shanghai reported: "Consulate offices have been repeatedly hit during afternoon by rifle and machine gun fire. All but two possible cases are clearly Nationalist side. Majority of cases appear accidental if utterly irresponsible but [in] several instances it can only be deliberate despite American flags on pole and both entrances. . . . If Department wishes it can quote me to press as saying, Nationalists have wantonly fired on American flag, that is the simple fact." Folder: B75.1 U. S. Diplomats in China, Koo Papers.

72. 793.00/2-150, #514, McConaughy, Consul General Shanghai, FRUS (1950) 6:302–3.

73. Paul S. Hopkins, Shanghai to K. R. MacKinnon, July 8, 1949, Box A: 271-27; and *Ta Kung Pao* editorial, Shanghai, February 13, 1950, Box 268-14, BCC.

74. 293.114/2-1650, Memorandum by the Director of the Office of Chinese Affairs, Philip Sprouse, to Deputy Assistant Secretary of State for Far Eastern Affairs, Livingston Merchant, FRUS (1950)6:312.

75. At the age of twelve, Koo began his western-oriented education at the Anglo-Chinese Junior College in Shanghai (*Chung-hsi shu-yüan*). Later he attended the talent fostering school (*Yü-ts'ai*) and St. John's University in China and the Cook Academy and Columbia University in the United States. At Columbia he earned his B.A. and both an M.A. and Ph.D. in political science. His diplomatic career followed soon after with an appointment as English secretary to the then Foreign Minister W. W. Yen (August 1912). In 1915, when only 27 years old, he became Minister to the United States. Subsequently, he represented China at the Versailles Conferences of 1919, in the League of Nations, as Minister to Great Britain and France, and at a host of international conferences. Boorman, *Biographical Dictionary* 2:255–59, and Chu Pao-chin, "V. K. Wellington Koo," in Burns and Bennett, eds., *Diplomats in Crisis*, pp. 125–29.

76. Koo Oral History, H (sec. 2):70.

77. On Koo's efforts to influence the AFL-CIO, the Federation of National Women's Clubs, and the Veterans of Foreign Wars through prominent persons such as Perle Mesta, American Minister to Luxembourg, Mrs. Hamilton Wright, crusader for narcotics control, and Fanny Holtzmann, New York lawyer, see Koo Oral History, I (secs. 4 and 8).

78. Koo was especially distressed by the attitude of W. Walton Butterworth, Assistant Secretary of State for Far Eastern Affairs, who seemed to take "glee" in making him uncomfortable. "I felt Butterworth looked upon me as if I were the Soviet Ambassador, judging from the caution and reserve he assumed, so

unusual for an American diplomat in his attitude and action toward an accredited Chinese representative. I have not experienced quite the same situation in my 35 years of dealing with Americans." Koo Oral History, H (sec. 4):148–49 (taken from Koo Diary, January 13, 1949), and (sec. 1):36, J (sec. 2):132. On the attitudes of Acheson and Webb, see Koo Diary, February 15, 1949 and March 3, 1949 respectively.

79. Koo Oral History, I (sec. 8):466–68; (sec. 4):144–46.

80. See chapter 5.

81. Koo Diary and Oral History, *passim*. Other Chinese Officials who dealt with politicians and the press included H. C. Kiang of the Chinese Delegation to the UN, who wrote to Joseph Alsop, November 25, 1949: "I think I do not have to say how much we shall appreciate it if you and your brother will write about our [UN] case for the better information of the people in this country." General Correspondence, folder: China lobby, Joseph and Stewart Alsop Papers, LC.

82. Senator Smith's papers are filled with correspondence he exchanged with various Kuomintang notables. He also circulated a report on his autumn 1949 trip to the Far East among his Congressional colleagues, and sent copies to State Department personnel, the White House, newspaper publishers, and reporters, among others. See especially Box 98, H. Alexander Smith Papers, H. Seeley Mudd Manuscript Library, Princeton University. Representative Walter Judd of Minnesota was generally credited with being *the* China expert in Congress, a distinction he accepted proudly. See Floyd R. Goodno, "Walter H. Judd: Spokesman for China in the United States House of Representatives," (Ph.D. diss.). Others normally associated with the China bloc in Congress were less directly motivated by China's plight. Nevada Senator Pat McCarran, for example, could not, in Wellington Koo's view, help but represent the interests of his silver-producing state, which would benefit if China's silver needs were met. Koo Oral History, I (sec. 3):84–85; (sec. 4):132–35; (sec. 6):263.

83. Koo Oral History, J (sec. 5):395.

84. Re Admiral Badger's role: Koo Oral History, I (sec. 5):159–73; Koo Diary, December 9, 20, 22, 27, and 30, 1949; and Notes of Conversation, #86 Admiral Oscar C. Badger, December 20, 1949, Box 130, Koo Papers. Re Defense Department and the assistance Koo obtained from Louis Johnson, Secretary of Defense, Paul Griffith, Under Secretary and later Assistant Secretary of Defense and Colonel Victor O'Kelliher, liaison between the Department and the Chinese Embassy see: Koo Oral History, I (sec. 4):172; (sec. 5):244–45, 249–50; vol. J (sec. 2): 94, 112–13; (sec. 3):160, 184–86, 223–24, 234–35; and Koo Diary, June 8, 1949, Koo Papers. W. Walton Butterworth, for one, noted the similarity between the KMT appeal and the JCS recommendation for aid submitted on the same day. 894A.00/12-2849 Memorandum by Assistant Secretary of State for Far Eastern Affairs, FRUS (1949)9:461–62.

85. Koo Oral History, J (sec. 5):396; Koo Diary, January 4, 1950, Koo Papers; 893.20/7-2549, #815, Clark, Canton, FRUS (1949)8:455. During WW II, M. Preston Goodfellow, a deputy director of the OSS, served in Axis occupied Europe and Asia as a guerrilla movement organizer. In 1946 he was attached to the commanding General's headquarters in Korea as a political adviser. Although he returned to newspaper publishing later that year, his interest in anticommunist activism remained strong. According to Koo, he continued assisting the Rhee government in training undercover operatives for work in North Korea.

New York Times Biographical Edition (September 1973) 4(9):1476; Koo Diary, January 4 and 12, 1950, Koo Papers.

86. Analysis of Pawley Memorandum by W. W. Stuart and Philip D. Sprouse, folder: Civilian Advisors to China, CA Records, RG 59, NA. In a personal interview, November 30, 1977, General Wedemeyer confirmed to me that the Chinese government had solicited his services, but that he never actually filled the position.

87. Koo Diary, March 2, 1949, Koo Papers.

88. The individuals most often mentioned, in addition to Hu Shih, were James Y. C. Yen, famous for his rural reform and educational projects, and K. C. Wu, the widely admired Mayor of Shanghai. Koo Oral History, J (sec. 2):101. Re reform plans: 894A.00/7-1849, #292, Edgar, Taipei, FRUS (1949)8:442–43; 893.00/8-1349, Dispatch #38 Clark, Canton, RG 59, NA, in which General Ho Ying-ch'in suggests that "U. S. advice and supervision" would convince "the Old Man" to stop interfering in government affairs.

89. 124.93/6-1349, #576 Clark, Canton, FRUS (1949)8:699. See also "Chiang Kai-shek Considers Handing Over Taiwan to MacArthur," NCNA *Daily Bulletin* (May 16, 1950)30:3.

90. See Lyman P. Van Slyke's Introduction to the Stanford University Press edition of the *White Paper* for a concise discussion of the background of and reception given to State Department publication 3573, *United States Relations with China, With Special Reference to the Period 1944–1949*.

91. 026CHINA/8-1049, #906 Clark, Canton, and 026CHINA/8-1549, #387 MacDonald, Taipei, RG 59, NA.

92. 026CHINA/8-1849, #981 Clark, Canton, and 026CHINA/8-2549, #A-84 Edgar, Taipei, RG 59, NA; "Draft of Reply to White Paper Finished," August 14, 1949, Chungking in Mandarin, FBIS, section: China, August 1, 1949, p. BBB-1.

5. THE CHINA LOBBY

1. On January 29, 1949, the New York State Communist Party told its members that "a strong Chinese lobby is at work in Washington . . . trying to influence our Government authorities to continue support of the anti-democratic and unpopular Kuomintang elements." This probably was the source of the term China Lobby. Ross Koen, *The China Lobby in American Politics*, p. 27. Kohlberg believed it had originated with the New York Communists. Joseph Keeley, *The China Lobby Man*, p. 114.

2. Cabell Philips defined the China lobby not as a "tight and tangible conspiracy of possible sinister intent," but rather as a "loose conglomeration of persons and organizations which for various reasons are interested in China." The members are people "who passionately believe American policy to be wrong; who think that American withdrawal from China has caused a needless and dangerous break in the dike against communism." Cabell Philips, "Is There a China Lobby?" p. 7D; Max Ascoli, "Starting the Job," p. 2; Koen, *China Lobby*, p. 29.

3. Victims of the Lobby's activities included John Service, John Paton Davies, Owen Lattimore, E. H. Norman (who committed suicide), John Carter Vincent,

and the Institute of Pacific Relations. Richard Kagan, Introduction, to Koen, *China Lobby*, p. xiii; Koen, *passim*; E. J. Kahn Jr., *The China Hands*; Owen Lattimore, *Ordeal By Slander*; O. Edmund Clubb, *The Witness and I*; Gary May, *China Scapegoat* (Washington, D.C.: New Republic Books, 1979).

4. For the Chinese view of American behavior see: Michael Hunt, *Frontier Defense*.

5. This occurred during the same period that the Open Door notes pledged America's respect for China's territorial and administrative integrity. See A. Whitney Griswold, *The Far Eastern Policy of the United States*, p. 83.

6. Publisher Roy Howard headed the Scripps-Howard chain of 29 newspapers. In 1933 he could scoff at opposition to recognition of the Soviet Union: "I think the menace of Bolshevism in the United States is about as great as the menace of sunstroke in Greenland or chilblains in the Sahara." But by the late 1940s he was alerting Americans to Communism's ever-present danger. William E. Leuchtenburg, *Franklin Delano Roosevelt and the New Deal*, pp. 205–6; *New York Times*, November 21, 1964, pp. 1, 29.

William Randolph Hearst's anticommunism and enthusiasm for Germany's fascistic experiments set him against American recognition of the USSR in 1933. In 1934 he launched a virulent anticommunist campaign in his newspapers and began branding anyone who opposed him as "communistic." In the late 1940s, although incapacitated by a stroke, he continued daily supervision of the editorial and general content of his eighteen newspapers and nine magazines, encouraging an anti-Chinese Communist, pro-Nationalist bias in their pages. John Tebbel, *The Life and Good Times of William Randolph Hearst*, pp. 327–43; Ferdinand Lundberg, *Imperial Hearst*, pp. 343–47, 355–63; Edmund D. Coblentz, ed., *William Randolph Hearst: A Portrait in His Own Words*, pp. x, 170–71; *New York Times*, August 15, 1951, p. 20; *ibid.*, April 1, 1955, p. 17; Morton Gordon, "The American Press and Recent China Policy, 1941–49," (M.A. thesis), p. 138.

7. Warren I. Cohen, *The Chinese Connection*, pp. 260, 266, 282, 287–89. Other pro-Nationalist columnists included Joseph and Stewart Alsop, Clyde Farnsworth and Edgar Ansel Mowrer. A student of the period has described Mowrer as "one of the most caustic anti-Truman-Acheson columnists, who turned out column after column, and espoused the clarion call of the Asia-Firsters and the new isolationist sentiment to the nation." Floyd R. Goodno, "Walter Judd: Spokesman For China in the United States House of Representatives" (Ph.D. diss.), p. 346n145.

8. W. A. Swanberg, *Luce and His Empire*, p. 2 and *passim*; Theodore H. White, *In Search of History*, pp. 206–7; see also pp. 126–30.

9. Swanberg, *Luce*, p. 265; William C. Bullitt, "A Report to the American People on China," pp. 35–36, 139–51. Before this trip Bullitt had never expressed a negative opinion on China policy. Koen, *China Lobby*, p. 89. His association with Luce, however, dated back to 1941 and he shared many of the publisher's views on America's strength and future and the threat of communism. Lloyd C. Gardner, "William C. Bullitt: Thomas Jefferson in Moscow," in his *Architects of Illusion*, pp. 22–25.

10. George Sokolsky, "Chiang Speaks His Mind," editorial, *New York Daily Mirror*, July 11, 1949, George Sokolsky Papers, folder 18: Scrapbooks, Butler Library Manuscript Division, Columbia University.

11. Radio broadcast, November 21, 1948, Sokolsky Papers, Box 10: Broadcasts.

12. Swanberg, *Luce*, p. 266.

13. *Ibid.*, p. 71.

14. "Get Out Of Red China," *Washington Daily News*, editorial, November 24, 1949, p. 8.

15. *El Paso Herald-Post* editorial quoted in *New York World Telegram* and in *Washington Daily News*, November 22, 1949.

16. E. F. Thompkins column in *Baltimore American*, June 19, 1949, Weekly Summary, June 16–22, 1949.

17. Henry P. Fletcher, "China and Bipartisanism," *Human Events* (December 14, 1949) 6:1 p. 1, Robert A. Taft Papers, Subject File 1950 E–F, Box 986, folder: Foreign Policy, LC. Ross Koen lists this newsletter as among the foremost periodicals creating a favorable climate of opinion for the Chinese Nationalists in the United States. Koen, *China Lobby*, p. 50. See also *Chicago Tribune*, editorial April 22, 1949, p. 8. The *Tribune* liberally used American China Policy Association material and other anti-Administration sources. Frederick T. C. Yu, "The Treatment of China in Four Chicago Daily Newspapers," (Ph.D. diss.), p. 186.

18. Mark Sullivan, "China's Plight and U.S. Guilt," Styles Bridges Papers, File 81, folder 80: Speech Material China, New England College Library, Henniker, New Hampshire.

19. "A Nail in the Coffin of Free China," *New Hampshire Morning Union*, editorial, July 2, 1949, Bridges Papers, *ibid.* Bridges entered this column into the *Congressional Record*.

20. *New York Journal American*, editorial, November 29, 1949, p. 18. Italics in the original.

21. *New York World Telegram*, editorial, November 15, 1949, p. 22.

22. See ch. 7.

23. Koen, *China Lobby*, p. 53.

24. U.S. Congress, House Committee on Foreign Affairs, *Hearings: Military Assistance Act of 1949*, 81st Congress, 1st sess., August 8, 1949, pp. 287–90. According to an FBI study McKee contributed $3,242.52 to the China Emergency Committee in 1949. Federal Bureau of Investigation, "Persons and Organizations Known to be Engaged in or to Have Been Engaged in Propaganda and Lobbying Activities on Behalf of the Chinese Nationalist Government with the Financial Support of that Government," August 31, 1951 (hereafter FBI Report), Harry S Truman Papers, President's Secretary's Files, HST.

25. Keeley, *China Lobby Man*, pp. 4, 11, 21–25, 55–70, 75–103, 196–206. See also Alfred Friendly, "Man Behind the Man Who Is Accusing Lattimore," pp. 1, 3; Edward A. Harris, "The Men Behind McCarthy," pp. 10–11; Malcolm Hobbs, "Chiang's Washington Front," pp. 619–20; Koen, *China Lobby* pp. 48–52; FBI report, August 31, 1951, pp. 10–11.

26. Koen, *China Lobby*, p. 58; Alfred Kohlberg, "Stupidity and/or Treason," p. 151.

27. Alfred Kohlberg statement, June 10, 1948, U.S. Congress, Senate Committee on Appropriations, *Hearings: H.R. 6801—ECA*, 80th Congress, 2d sess., pp. 533–36. Copy in Bridges Papers, File 27, folder 166.

28. Analysis of Pawley Memorandum by W. W. Stuart and Philip Sprouse, Records of the Office of Chinese Affairs, folder: Civilian Advisors to China, RG 59, NA. Wellington Koo, China's Ambassador to the United States, noted that Leonard Hsu, a Reynolds Metals representative, was pushing for an Export-Import Bank loan to expand Taiwan's aluminum industry in regard to which Reynolds had signed a contract with the Chinese National Resources Council

in 1948. The Reynolds Company had contracted to operate, on a partnership basis, aluminum plants acquired by the Chinese government from Japan at the end of World War II. William Reynolds, Koo also noted, knew Truman well and was a member of the U.S. National Resources Board. V. K. Wellington Koo Diary, February 9, 1949, V. K. Wellington Koo Papers, Butler Library Manuscript Division, Columbia University; *New York Times*, August 8, 1946, p. 33; *ibid.*, March 22, 1948, p. 2.

29. Harris, "Men Behind McCarthy," p. 11; Hobbs, "Chiang's Washington Front," p. 620. Harriss faced charges for illegal lobbying activities.

30. 893.00/6-649 Office Memorandum, Fulton Freeman to Philip Sprouse, RG 59, NA.

31. Leuchtenburg, *FDR*, p. 205; Philip Taft, *The A.F. of L. from the Death of Gompers to the Merger*, pp. 430–32. The AFL's anti-socialist policy began with Samuel Gompers. In 1918, Gompers warned the U.S. Peace Commission "he who temporizes with Bolshevism . . . [is] commiting an unspeakable crime against civilization itself." In 1933, when FDR took steps to recognize the USSR, William Green, AFL president, submitted a brief in opposition. Philip Taft, *Defending Freedom*, pp. 2–5.

32. AFL Weekly News Service, December 31, 1948, Weekly Summary, January 13–19, 1949. At its annual convention in 1944, the AFL established the Free Trade Union Committee to raise $1 million to "assure prompt and practical assistance to the workers of the liberated countries in Europe and Asia . . . to organize free democratic unions." This was consciously conceived of as an anticommunist alliance. The AFL contributed $24,965 to it in 1948, $32,400 in 1949 and $19,135 in 1950. Taft, *AFL*, pp. 342–43; *New York Times*, June 2, 1956, p. 19.

33. *New York Times*, July 5, 1949, Weekly Summary, June 30–July 6, 1949. The 1949 and 1953 AFL conventions attributed CCP victory to financial and military aid from the Soviet Union. The AFL, therefore, demanded "that recognition be denied to any government *forcibly imposed on any people with the aid of a foreign power*." Taft, *AFL*, pp. 404–5, italics in the original; "Soviet Plans Further Aggression from its China Base," *Labor's Monthly Survey* (April–May 1950) 2:5 sent by Senator Knowland to President Truman, May 15, 1950, Truman Papers, Official File 150 (1947)-150 Misc. (1948), Box 633, folder: 1950–1953, HST.

34. Philip Horton, "The China Lobby—Part II," p. 11; Matthew Woll, "The Key to Stable Prosperity," *Report of the Thirty-Sixth National Foreign Trade Convention, October 31, November 1 and 2, 1949*, p. 118. The CIO at its convention that same month took no position on the question of recognition of Communist China. It had, however, recently emerged from a massive purge of its left wing and at its 1948 convention adopted a foreign policy stand of which one enthusiastic supporter exclaimed, "There is no pussy footing in this resolution. There are no weasel words. . . . We say to the Soviets, 'If you want peace, cooperate with the United States of America.'" James R. Prickett, "Some Aspects of the Communist Controversy in the CIO," p. 312; Paul Jacobs, *Old Before Its Time*, excerpted in Jerold S. Auerbach, ed., *American Labor*, p. 406. Re elimination of communists from the CIO, see Bert Cochran, *Labor and Communism*, pp. 98, 145–47, 297–320, 379n6; R. Alton Lee, *Truman and Taft Hartley*, p. 76; William E. Leuchtenburg, *A Troubled Feast*, p. 15; Leuchtenburg, *FDR*, p. 282.

35. "The China Lobby: A Case Study," p. 950. Jay Lovestone, secretary of the Free Trade Union Committee, had been a founder of the American Communist Party. By the 1940s he had changed his views radically and had become

a prophet of the dangers of communist totalitarianism. As such he also headed the AFL's "labor CIA." Cochran, *Labor and Communism*, p. 318; Taft, *AFL*, pp. 343–44; Koen, *China Lobby*, p. 53; Horton, "The China Lobby–Part II," p. 11. Other labor leaders engaged in the pro-Chiang fight were: members of the ACPA board of directors A. Philip Randolph, president, and Ashley L. Totten, secretary-treasurer, Brotherhood of Sleeping Car Porters (AFL), Frank R. Crosswaith (ILGWU), and labor lawyer Louis Waldman. Victor Riesel, a labor columnist, was a director of the Committee to Defend America by Aiding Anti-Communist China. "The China Lobby: A Case Study," p. 951.

36. Historians have erroneously tended to treat missionaries as a unified group which gave "Chiang and his wife and the Kuomintang their full, uncritical, and passionate support." Harold Isaacs, *Images of Asia*, p. 162. Examples of this tendency include: Barbara Tuchman in *Stilwell and the American Experience in China*, p. 188; Lewis H. Purifoy in *Harry Truman's China Policy*, pp. 15, 68; and Nathaniel Peffer, *The Far East*, p. 221. Re the friendship between some missionaries and the KMT, see James C. Thomson, *While China Faced West*.

37. *Christian Herald* (March 1949) 72:18, and (March 1950) 73:16. The *Christian Herald* was the most successful mass magazine in independent Protestant circles. Marty, et al. *Religious Press in America*. Although generally an advocate of massive intervention in China, the *Christian Herald* was less inflexible than some other pro-Chiang voices. In March 1949, for example, it said: "This revolution in China would have come even if Karl Marx had never been born." *Christian Herald*, (March 1949) 72:11. See Raymond Whitehead, "Christian Response to People's China: Documentation of a Moral Failure," (Th.D. diss.), pp. 13–15.

38. "The CAIP on China," *America* (December 17, 1949) 82:330.

39. Raymond A. Lane, Superior General of the Catholic Foreign Missionary Society, Maryknoll, NY, to President Truman, October 12, 1949, Harry S Truman Papers, Official File 544, Box 1383, HST; "U.S. Obligations in China and the Far East," draft statement of the Catholic Association for International Peace, Sub-committee on Asia, November 1949, Philip C. Jessup Papers, Box 54, folder: Case, Everett C., LC.

40. 893.404/3-2549 Memorandum W. Walton Butterworth to Secretary of State and Memorandum Butterworth to Acting Secretary of State, October 5, 1949, RG 59, NA. The Archbishop traveled widely, seeking support for the Nationalist government. In this regard he visited President Truman in November 1947 and January 1949. Through U.S. Representative John W. McCormick he requested an appointment with Secretary of State Acheson in March 1949 and met with Acting Secretary James Webb in October 1949. Recognizing his political influence, the CCP added the Archbishop's name to their list of war criminals in January 1949.

41. Among the articles published by *America* were "China Cannot Wait Longer" (November 8, 1947) 78:144; "China Faces a Hard Year" (January 17, 1948) 78:422; "Help China Now" (March 20, 1948) 78:674; "The Chinese Nationalists and the U.S." (December 3, 1949) 82:265. *America*, a Jesuit journal of opinion, was established in 1909 and generally had been moderate in its tone and positions. In the 1930s, however, it took a conservative turn. Marty, et al., *The Religious Press*.

42. "Time Runs Short in China," *America* (January 31, 1948) 78:482.

43. "China's New Day," *America* (April 10, 1948) 79:3.

44. "Fall of Canton," *America* (October 29, 1949) 82:85.

45. "The Recognition Bandwagon," *America* (November 5, 1949) 82:119.

46. Koen, *China Lobby*, p. 59; William R. Johnson, "The United States Sells China Down the Amur," pp. 412ff, also condensed in the *CR* (March 25, 1948) 94(appendix):1909–10.

47. Koen, *China Lobby*, p. 60; William R. Johnson, *China, Key to the Orient*, pp. 7, 28, William R. Johnson Papers, Box 29, folder 33, Yale Divinity Library Archives, Yale Divinity School, New Haven, Connecticut; "The China Lobby: A Case Study," p. 951. Other religious leaders who were active in the China crusade included John Cronin and James W. Fifield. The Reverend Cronin, secretary of the Catholic Welfare Conference in Washington, D.C., helped Alfred Kohlberg launch his magazine *Plain Talk*. The Reverend Fifield served as one of the directors of the ACPA and was active in the organization. Fifield also headed the Spiritual Mobilization Movement which various people, including Senator H. Alexander Smith, considered at least a partial solution for China's leadership problems. In May 1948, allegedly at the suggestion of American Ambassador J. Leighton Stuart, an informal bipartisan Congressional committee invited Ch'en Li-fu, Vice President of the Legislative Yuan and leader of a staunchly conservative KMT clique, to attend the Moral Rearmament World Assembly for Ideological Preparedness in California. General Ho Ying-ch'in, one-time Minister of War, had attended an MRA Assembly at Niagara Falls in 1947 and similarly claimed a spiritual awakening as a result of its ideological message. Ch'en remarked upon his experience: "I have become convinced . . . that the most effective answer to communism is the moral force of a superior ideology. . . . It is not enough to try to meet the red menace with economics, politics, or military strength alone." John Roots, "Strategy Number 6: Giving the Patriots of China and India an Ideology to Inspire the Millions, Multiply Men of Moral Fibre in Their Governments, and Win the Battle for the Mind of Asia," draft of a chapter of a book Roots was preparing under *Reader's Digest* auspices, pp. 6–9. Smith Papers, Box 98, folder: Correspondence re Far East 1949 #1. On this subject see correspondence between Smith and John Roots, and between Smith and Kenaston Twitchell in *ibid.*; William M. Leary Jr., "Smith of New Jersey" (Ph.D. diss.), pp. 134–35.

48. This section discussing Walter Judd draws heavily on Floyd R. Goodno's previously cited dissertation "Walter Judd: Spokesman for China in the House of Representatives," pp. 8–23, 62–66. Schwellenbach quote, p. 23n54 taken from the *CR* (76th Congress, 1st sess., 1939) 84 (pt. 10):10753. Judd became one of the Congress's most sought-after speakers, delivering well over one hundred addresses each year. The *New York Times* in 1952 noted that he rated as an Asian expert not only with Republicans (consulting periodically with President Eisenhower and his staff), but also with many Washington Democrats. Goodno, "Judd," pp. 68, 360 and *New York Times*, July 29, 1952, p. 1. The *Times* itself credited Judd with "outstanding integrity." His denunciation of the August 1949 State Department report on China, therefore, was not made "lightly" and "must necessarily add to the already considerable mistrust with which the *White Paper* has been received." Goodno, "Judd," p. 281 and *New York Times*, editorial, August 22, 1949, p. 20.

49. Goodno, "Judd," pp. 205, 228, 238, and quote from p. 294.

50. *Ibid.*, pp. 316–20, 418, 420. At the Republican National Convention in 1960, Theodore White observed that using his "old fashioned Minnesota Populist

knack of heating the political blood . . . Judd made the rafters roar and the benches shake." Theodore White, *Making of the President, 1960*, p. 206.

51. Re Badger see ch. 4.

52. Walter Millis, ed., *The Forrestal Diaries*, pp. 17–18.

53. U.S., Congress, House Committee on Foreign Affairs, *Hearings: United States Foreign Policy for a Post-war Recovery Program*, 80th Congress, 2d sess., 1948, p. 2044. MacArthur was stationed in Asia from 1935 to 1951. During that time he did not return to the United States.

54. Tsou, *America's Failure*, p. 559; Keyes Beech, "M'Arthur Aides Favor Trade with Red China," p. 1B; 693.9431/5-2749, #331 State Department to American Consulate, Peking, RG 59, NA; Dispatch #727, Office of the U.S. Political Advisor for Japan, Tokyo, October 20, 1949, Consul General Hong Kong, file 510: Trade Relations, Box 912, China Post Files, RG 84, WNRC; Memorandum on Formosa by General of the Army Douglas MacArthur, Tokyo, June 14, 1950, FRUS (1950)7:161–65. President Truman's speech was delivered January 5, 1950 and Acheson's at the National Press Club on January 12, 1950.

55. 693.0031/4-1949, #205 American Consul General, Shanghai, to Michael Lee, Registrar China Trade Act, RG 59, NA. General Chennault joined with the other pro-Nationalists who dismissed KMT ethical weaknesses as irrelevant to the serious situation at hand: "Corruption comes and goes in all postwar eras, in all countries and . . . is no alibi for lack of affirmative action on the part of the U.S." Claire L. Chennault, "Eleventh Hour in China," p. 273.

56. Claire L. Chennault to Robert A. Taft, January 14, 1950, Taft Papers, Legislative Papers, Box 573: Ch-Ci, folder: China—W. Bruce Pirnie, LC. Also see Claire L. Chennault Papers, Pt. IV, CATI which covers the details of the case, its legalistic implications, and Chennault's victory. Reel 12, LC. For detailed explication of Chennault's views see *Way of a Fighter*.

57. Cooke had to be reminded by the Chief of Naval Operations that retired officers should not accept emoluments from foreign governments. John L. Gaddis, "The Rise and Fall of the 'Defensive Perimeter' Concept: United States Strategy in the Far East, 1947–1951," in Borg and Heinrichs, eds., *Uncertain Years*, p. 88n78. *America's Town Meeting of the Air*, December 6, 1949, New York City, Bridges Papers, File 81, folder 78: Speech Material China; Koen, *China Lobby*, pp. 44–46; Analysis of Pawley Memorandum, CA Records, RG 59, NA. Cooke had expressed interest in a strong American commission to guide United States policy and action in China as early as November 1948. Transcript of Teletype Interview by Frank M. Bartholomew, UP vice president for the Pacific area with Admiral Charles M. Cooke, USN retired, November 22, 1948, Smith Papers, Box 98, folder: Correspondence re Far East #1.

58. Gaddis, "Defensive Perimeter," p. 88.

59. Memorandum Crosby (PL) to Yost, September 1949, Box 1, Lot File 53D211, Jessup Papers, State; Koo Oral History, J(sec. 3):186; Weekly Summary, April 27–May 3, 1950, article by Judith and Arthur Hart Burling. Arthur H. Burling of Covington and Burling, the law firm of which Dean Acheson had been a partner, also served on the board of directors of the Committee to Defend America by Aiding Anti-Communist China. "The China Lobby: A Case Study," p. 950.

60. Ross Koen lists the pro-China Lobby academics as follows: David N. Rowe, William McGovern, Karl Wittfogel, Kenneth Colegrove, and George E.

Taylor. McGovern testified before the House Committee on Foreign Affairs in 1948 that "to suppress the Commies, the immediate need is military supplies and techniques." Taylor, although listed by Koen, expressed sentiments in his article "An Effective Approach in Asia" not generally voiced by true believers: "The Chinese Communist regime will have to be recognized, but there is no need to hurry about it. We should obviously trade with a Communist China to the extent that such trade is necessary for the economic recovery of Japan." George E. Taylor, "An Effective Approach in Asia," p. 41; Koen, *China Lobby*, pp. 93, 116, 248n6.

61. 893.00/4-2649 Office Memorandum W. Walton Butterworth to Dean Rusk, RG 59, NA. "Choice in China" sent to James E. Webb, Undersecretary of State, prior to publication by the Managing Editor of *World Politics*. 893.00/3-1349 William T. R. Fox to Webb, RG 59, NA.

62. "China Policy Today: Long-run Certainties and Short-run Choice," January 3, 1949, Dean Acheson Papers, Box 27: State Department, folder: China, HST; David N. Rowe, "Where Can We Stand in Asia?" pp. 539–43; *Boston Herald*, December 19, 1949, Weekly Summary, December 22–28, 1949.

63. U.S., Department of State, *Transcript of Round Table Discussion On American Policy Toward China*, pp. 101–2. Kenneth Colegrove, Professor of Political Science, Northwestern University, Evanston, Illinois, to Philip C. Jessup, October 17, 1949, Philip C. Jessup Papers, Box 61: Pace-Parody, 1953-48, LC. Colegrove was more properly a Japan specialist.

64. "Damning Indictment," *New Hampshire Morning Union*, editorial, July 7, 1949, Bridges Papers, File 81, folder 80; Koen, *China Lobby*, p. 53; NANA, January 18, 1949, Weekly Summary, January 13–19, 1949.

65. Stanley Hornbeck to W. Walton Butterworth, February 19, 1948, Stanley Hornbeck Papers, Box 42, Hoover; "The Asiatic Muddle: Its World Wide Repercussions," speech by Stanley Hornbeck to the 28th Annual Business and Professional Men's Group, University of Cincinnati, 1949, Hornbeck Papers, Box 51, folder: American Attitudes Toward China, Hoover; H. Alexander Smith Diary, December 6, 1948, Smith Papers; Richard D. Burns, "Stanley K. Hornbeck, The Diplomacy of the Open Door," in Burns and Bennett, eds., *Diplomats in Crisis*, pp. 91–117; Stanley Hornbeck, "Recognition of Governments," pp. 181–92. Hornbeck's influence on Department officers in 1949–1950 would have been diminished by memories of what John Paton Davies described as his "overbearing and sometimes vindictive" nature probably produced by "a suppressed realization that his recognition as a great scholar-statesman was thwarted by his own inadequacies." Gregory Prince, "The American Foreign Service in China, 1935–1941," (Ph.D. diss.), pp. 195–96.

66. "An Old China Hand," *New Republic* (May 2, 1949) 120:8; U.S. Department of State, *Round Table*, p. 129; John H. Fenton, "Asia Aid Program Urged by Stassen," p. 1; George Eckel, "Talk With Soviet Urged by Stassen," p. 24, "Iron Curtain Gap Cited by Stassen," *New York Times*, February 22, 1950, p. 8. According to Ross Koen, Stassen was one "of the most extreme pro-Chiang critics of American China policy." Koen, *China Lobby*, p. 139.

67. Harris, "Men Behind McCarthy," p. 10; 893.00/8-1749 Memo Sprouse (CA) to Yost (S/A), and 893.00/8-2449 Memo Sprouse to Jessup, and 893.00/4-2649 Memo Butterworth to Rusk, RG 59, NA.

68. Smith Papers, Frederick C. McKee to H. Alexander Smith, November 19,

1949 and Smith reply, November 23, 1949, Box 98, folder: correspondence re Far East 1949 #2.

69. Victor Lasky, "Rally Warns U.S. to Bar Recognition of Red China," *New York World Telegram*, November 29, 1949, Bridges Papers, File 81, folder 49: Speech Material China and Formosa 1950; Senator Herbert R. O'Conor's Carnegie Hall Address, p. 3, Hornbeck Papers, Box 69: Clippings 1948–1949.

70. Kohlberg's letters appear everywhere. See for examples: Kohlberg to Robert A. Taft, June 12, 1948, June 14, 1949 and January 5, 1950, Taft Papers, Legislative Papers, Box 573, Ch-Ci folders: China 1948–1949 and 1950 China-Formosa, LC. Kohlberg to Styles Bridges, Bridges Papers, File 29: 1950–51, folder: China Lobby. For McKee letters see: McKee to John Steelman, August 11, 1949, with enclosures analyzing *White Paper*, Truman Papers, Official File 150 (1947)- 150 Misc (1948), Box 633, folder: China White Paper, HST. McKee to Philip C. Jessup, June 1949, March 16, 1950 and March 23, 1950, Jessup Papers, General Correspondence, Box 48, folder: Chronological File, June 1949 (CFM-Paris), LC. McKee to Dean Rusk, Deputy Undersecretary of State, 893.00/6-2349, RG 59, NA. Senator William Knowland to Henry E. North, President of the San Francisco Chamber of Commerce, Smith Papers, Box 98, folder: Correspondence re Far East #2. In this letter Knowland asked North to have the Chamber rescind its stand favoring trade with and recognition of the Chinese Communists. William R. Johnson to Senator Tom Connally, April 14, 1949, with Kohlberg material attached. Thomas Connally Papers, Box 277, folder: S.1063 Senator McCarran, LC.

71. John Hedley, "The Truman Administration and the 'Loss' of China" (Ph.D. diss.), pp. 168–202; 893.01/11-749 Memorandum McFall (H) to Secretary of State, November 29, 1949, RG 59, NA; in RG 59, Box 7028, folder: 893.01/11- 149 to 893.01/12-3149 there appear a large number of requests from members of Congress for information to answer constituent inquiries and opinions on the question of recognition.

72. Those who received this report included Senators Guy Gillette (D, Ia), Edward Martin (R, Pa), Styles Bridges (R, NH); Philip Jessup and his fellow consultants Raymond Fosdick and Everett Case; George Kennan; Jack McFall; Dean Acheson; Louis Johnson, Secretary of Defense; Matthew Woll; James Reston of the *New York Times*; former President Herbert Hoover. Smith Papers, Box 98, folder: China Trip 1949.

73. Chennault Papers, Reel 12, Freedom Cause—correspondence, LC. Among those receiving Chennault's notes were Hubert Humphrey, Robert A. Taft, Henry R. Luce, and Sidney Souers, the Executive Secretary of the National Security Council. Among those receiving *Way of a Fighter* was Roy W. Howard. Chennault's plan for solving China's declining position was to establish a sanitary zone from Ninghsia in the northwest to Kwangsi in the southeast along which line a strong defense with American aid could be made. 893.00/6-649 Memorandum of Conversation—Chennault with W. Walton Butterworth and Philip Sprouse, RG 59, NA.

74. W. Bruce Pirnie, "Who Hamstrings U.S. Military Aid to China?" *The China Monthly* (October 1948) 9:288–91, cited by Koen, *China Lobby*, p. 77; Taft Papers, Legislative Papers, Box 573: Ch-Ci, folder: China—W. Bruce Pirnie, LC; Pirnie to Senator Tom Connally, March 25, 1948, with enclosure "A China Recovery Program," Connally Papers, Box 179: Legislation 80th Congress—Foreign Re-

lations, LC. Pirnie was Senior Economic Advisor to the Kwangtung and Kwangsi Provincial Governments and President of Pirnie, Lee & Co., Fed., Inc., USA, the negotiating agents for reconstruction of Kwangtung, Kwangsi, Hunan and Hupeh provinces.

75. "The China Lobby: A Case Study," p. 953; Friendly "Man Behind the Man," pp. 1, 3. See Appendix B in Koen, *China Lobby*, pp. 221–29, or State Department *Employee Loyalty Investigation*, part 2, pp. 1641–46 for evidence of Senator Joseph McCarthy's dependence on Kohlberg's material. This evidence is embodied in "Comparison of McCarthy and Kohlberg Charges Against Institute of Pacific Relations and Associated Personnel," submitted by Owen Lattimore as Exhibit 71 to the Tydings subcommittee.

76. "The China Lobby: A Case Study," p. 955.

77. Koo Oral History, J(sec. 2):90; Hobbs, "Chiang's Washington Front," p. 620; Geraldine Fitch, *China Lob-Lolly*, pp. 10–11, copy in Bridges Papers.

78. Koo Oral History, J(sec. 5):394.

79. *Ibid.*, J(sec. 1):79–80. Mrs. Wright called Senator Fulbright and Mrs. Vandenberg immediately.

80. 893.00/11-2949 Memorandum Philip C. Jessup, New York, to W. Walton Butterworth, RG 59, NA.

81. 893.00/2-149 Memorandum, RG 59, NA. Eichelberger became involved in a variety of international organizations and served with Frederick McKee in the American Association for the United Nations. Eichelberger had also been a State Department consultant during WW II and advised the U.S. delegation to the San Francisco conference in 1945. *Who's Who in America, 1948–49* (Chicago: A. N. Marquis Co., 1948), 25:724.

82. Charles Wertenbaker, "The China Lobby—Part I," p. 18; *Washington Post*, September 18, 1949, p. 1. For examples of such dinners see Koo Oral History, I(sec. 2):32–33, 39 and (sec. 7):333.

83. William C. Arthur, Executive Vice President, to Chennault, February 2, 1949, Chennault Papers, Reel 10, Pt. III, U.S. 14th Air Force, folder: 14 Air Force Association, Inc, LC.

84. Chennault Papers, Reel 12, Freedom Cause—Correspondence, LC.

85. H. Alexander Smith to H. Kenaston Twitchell, Switzerland, August 15, 1949, Smith Papers, Box 98, folder: Correspondence re Far East 1949 #1.

86. "The China Lobby: A Case Study," p. 955; FBI report, August 31, 1951, p. 3. Goodwin wrote to Senator Robert A. Taft on several occasions in 1949. Among the most interesting letters is the one of March 12, 1949 in which he tells "Bob" that he will, from time to time, send memoranda on subjects of interest to Taft and which may have an important effect on his 1950 election campaign. That campaign, Goodwin notes, was the most important thing on the horizon and nothing must be overlooked which could aid Taft. Taft Papers, Box 696, folder: Foreign Policy 1949, LC. Other paid lobbyists included: Maurice Williams, Joseph Paull Marshall, Dale Miller and Norman Paige. FBI report, August 31, 1951, p. 6 and Koo Oral History, J(sec. 2):166.

87. "The China Lobby: A Case Study," pp. 943–44; Wertenbaker, "China Lobby," p. 21. President David B. Charney of Allied Syndicates noted that conversations with media representatives and civic organization executives was one of its key methods of operation.

88. Keeley, *China Lobby Man*, p. 208.

89. *Ibid.*, p. 6; "Who Is Alfred Kohlberg?" *St. Louis Post-Dispatch*, editorial, September 22, 1949, p. 2E; Edward A. Harris, "Aid-China 'Angel' A Donor to Bridges Campaign Fund," pp. 1, 6; "The China Lobby: A Case Study," p. 952. The election was in 1948. The donation was made October 3, 1947. Bridges denied that Kohlberg's contribution had anything to do with his efforts during 1947–1948 to obtain a $125 million appropriation for China. Rather, he and Kohlberg were intimate friends and the contribution was made on that basis. McCarthy returned Kohlberg's 1950 contribution to avoid renewed attacks upon Kohlberg and his beneficiaries by Drew Pearson. Keeley, *China Lobby Man*, p. 7.

90. U.S., Congress, Senate Committee on Appropriations, *Hearings: Third Supplemental Appropriations Bill for 1948*, 80th Congress, 1st sess., pp. 119–87. Senator Vandenberg had this reduced to $18 million in the full Senate. *CR*, (December 19, 1947) 93:11679–11680. Wedemeyer, not strictly a China Lobbyist, became increasingly pro-Chiang in public statements. Koen, *China Lobby*, p. 115.

91. U.S. Congress, House Committee on Foreign Affairs, *Hearings: The Military Assistance Act of 1949*, 81st Congress, 1st sess., (July 28–August 8, 1949) 5:287.

92. Wertenbaker, "China Lobby," p. 19; "Report of D. Worth Clark, Consultant to the Appropriations Committee, U.S. Senate, on Financial, Economic and Military Conditions in China and Recommendations Concerning Future Aid," Clark Clifford Papers, Subject File, Box 3: China, Coal Case, folder 2: China, HST; Confidential Memorandum on the China Lobby, June 12, 1951, Truman Papers, President's Secretary's Files, Subject File, Box 161: China Lobby, HST. Accompanying Clark on the trip was Edward B. Lockett, a former *Time* correspondent, who wrote the mission's report. Wertenbaker, "China Lobby," pp. 10, 19.

93. Alfred Kohlberg to Styles Bridges, May 12, 1948, Smith Papers, Box 96, cited by James Fetzer, "Congress and China, 1941–1950," (Ph.D. diss.), 1969, p. 118*n*65; Kohlberg made this letter public as an ACPA release, May 23, 1948. Koen, *China Lobby*, p. 94.

94. Press Conference, January 13, 1950, Connally Papers, Speech File 1950, Box 570, LC. Both William Randolph Hearst and Robert McCormick treated MacArthur as a hero in their newspapers. Hearst helped boom MacArthur for the Presidency. Stassen suggested a massive economic plan for Asia based on the Marshall Plan in Europe, the Asian version to be called the MacArthur Plan. *New York Times*, April 1, 1955, p. 17 and August 15, 1951, p. 20; John H. Fenton, "Asia Aid Program," p. 1; Eric Goldman, *The Crucial Decade—and After*, p. 154.

95. Leary, *The Dragon's Wings*, p. 141; H. Alexander Smith to Dean Acheson, October 2, 1949, Smith Papers; H. Alexander Smith Oral History, p. 159, Columbia University.

96. Claire L. Chennault to William Randolph Hearst, San Simeon, Ca., June 24, 1949, Chennault Papers, Reel 12, Freedom Cause—Mr. Sentner, LC.

97. Joseph and Stewart Alsop Papers, Box 4: General Correspondence, folder: March 1949, and Box 57: Travel File, folder: Far East 1949, LC; Stewart Alsop, "We Are Losing Asia Fast," p. 29.

98. The "Who lost China?" literature is sizable. Perhaps the principal spokesman for the charge that incompetence, greed, and treason brought disaster in Asia is Anthony Kubek in his *How the Far East Was Lost*.

6. MISSIONARIES

1. The shattering events of World War II and the upheaval caused by revolution in 1949 have overshadowed historical writing about China during the 1940s. This is particularly true of the annals of missionary endeavor. The literature describing individual experience is plentiful. Among the many personal accounts are Robert W. Greene, *Calvary in China*; Harold H. Martinson, *Red Dragon over China*; Dorothy S. McCammon, *We Tried to Stay*; Sara Perkins, *Red China Prisoner*; Myra Scovel, *The Chinese Ginger Jars*; and Sister Mary Victoria, *Nun in Red China*. Serious appraisal of missionary activities and influences, as well as Chinese Communist policy, on the other hand, is almost nonexistent. Moreover, historians, looking at the many years of Sino-American contact, have almost always been more interested in the impact American missionaries have had on China than in the impact these American China missionaries have had on the United States. Liu Kwang-ching, both in his *Americans and Chinese* and in the Harvard seminar papers he selected and edited for *American Missionaries in China*, focuses on missionary contributions made to China. This is true also of James C. Thomson Jr.'s *While China Faced West*. Jessie Lutz's *China and the Christian Colleges*, concentrates on how the Christian educational enterprise served and survived in China, and Richard C. Bush Jr.'s *Religion in Communist China* looks at missionaries only briefly and in the context of general religious developments in modern China. *Missionary Enterprise in China and America*, edited by John K. Fairbank, deals largely with the nineteenth and early twentieth centuries and does not cover missionary interaction with the Chinese Communists. "Protestant Missions in Communist China," a Ph.D. dissertation by Creighton Lacy, does change the focus somewhat, discussing at length problems encountered during the Chinese Communist takeover and missionary responses to them. In fact, Lacy's study, conducted through questionnaires addressed to former China missionaries, is among the best sources of information on missionary experiences. But, like the earlier works, it is about happenings in China and does not examine the missionary attempt to influence American government policy. Very few studies deal with the latter subject, the most notable being Dorothy Borg's comprehensive *American Policy and the Chinese Revolution* and Paul Varg's *Missionaries, Chinese and Diplomats*. However, these works do not analyze the critical period from January 1948 to June 1950, during which the Chinese Communist Party fought its way to victory and established a new regime.

2. Bush, *Religion in Communist China*, pp. 66–67.

3. Tsou, *America's Failure*, pp. 463, 477.

4. Paul A. Carter, *The Decline and Revival of the Social Gospel*, pp. 3–16.

5. Creighton Lacy, "Protestant Missions in Communist China" (Ph.D. diss.), p. 645.

6. See the correspondence from the secretaries of the member organizations of the Foreign Missions Conference to Rowland M. Cross, secretary of the China Committee of the Foreign Missions Conference, October 7–27, 1949, Papers of the National Council of the Churches of Christ in the U.S.A., Division of Overseas Ministries, China Program files, New York City (hereafter China Program files).

7. There are no exact figures on American Catholic holdings in China because the records were destroyed by the Japanese and the Communists. It is known

that the value was several million dollars and that after a late start in the China field in 1918, American Catholic participation rapidly increased. Interview with Reverend William J. Coleman, archivist, Maryknoll mission, November 20, 1974; "Report on Protestant Missions," *Monthly Report: A Monthly Newsletter* (Shanghai, China, December 31, 1949) 7:21–23; "Statement by Eugene E. Barnett regarding the YMCA in China," Young Men's Christian Association Archives, National Headquarters, New York City.

8. Between V-J day and March 29, 1949, there were 83 Catholic missionaries killed by the Communists and another 13 reported missing and presumed dead. Most of the 96 died before April 1948, at which time the Communists declared that missionaries were not to be molested. *New York Times*, March 29, 1949, p. 9.

9. Frank T. Cartwright, "Protestant Missions in Communist China," p. 302; Lutz, *China and the Christian Colleges*, p. 445.

10. "Swiss Missionaries Convicted as Spies," March 17, 1948, section: Far East, China, p. BBB-2, FBIS. The NCNA and various CCP leaders reiterated such declarations thereafter, see "Protection to Churches," *China Digest* (December 14, 1948) 5:15, and Liang Yin, "The Liberation Army and the Church," *ibid.* (January 11, 1949) 5:15–16.

11. Homer Bradshaw to United Presbyterian Church in the U.S.A., June 21, 1950, United Presbyterian Church in the U.S.A., Central files, Interchurch Center, New York City (hereafter Presbyterian files); Bush, *Religion in Communist China*, p. 51; John and Frances Hamlin and Richard Bryant to China board secretaries and friends of China, in *China Bulletin*, November 10, 1948, p. 1; Lacy, "Protestant Missions," pp. 291, 335, 339, 390, 415; Spencer Coxe, "Quakers and Communists in China," pp. 152–55; "Missionary Hails China Rebels," *North China Daily News*, January 3, 1949, p. 5.

12. John K. Fairbank, et al., *East Asia*, p. 862; Ralph Mortenson, "China Bible House Still Going Strong," pp. 3–4.

13. Kenneth Scott Latourette, *Christianity in a Revolutionary Age*, 5:397.

14. Bush, *Religion in Communist China*, p. 29.

15. Mao Tse-tung, "Report of an Investigation into the Peasant Movement in Hunan," *SW*, 1:23–59.

16. Bush, *Religion in Communist China*, p. 104.

17. Arthur S. Olsen, "Visiting Team in Peking," p. 3.

18. According to a *China Bulletin* report of June 19, 1950, Chou En-lai said missionary teachers could return to China at a later unspecified date. Bush, *Religion in Communist China*, pp. 41–42; Olsen, "Visiting Team in Peking," pp. 2–5.

19. Mary Backus Rankin discusses the Ku-t'ien incident of 1895, in which the local inhabitants of Ku-t'ien (Fukien province) interpreted the conflict between Christians and the local secret society as intersect rivalry. The residents of the town hoped that members of the two societies would annihilate each other. "The Ku-t'ien Incident," p. 51.

20. Theodore Ainsworth Greene, "What of Our China Mission?" *Forward Through the Ages*, American Board of Commissioners for Foreign Missions Annual Report, 1949 (Boston, 1950), p. 66; *New York Times*, October 12, 1949, p. 16; China Letter, Lucile and Francis P. Jones, September 15, 1949, Box 19, William R. Johnson Papers, Yale Divinity Library Archives, Yale Divinity School, New Haven, Conn. (hereafter YDL).

21. Lacy, "Protestant Missions," pp. 517–19; "Report on Protestant Missions," *Monthly Report*, p. 20.

22. Edward J. Bannan to United Presbyterian Church in the U.S.A., October 10, 1949, Presbyterian files; Lacy, "Protestant Missions," pp. 335, 361, 447, 477.

23. Lacy, "Protestant Missions," p. 317; Lutz, *Christian Colleges*, pp. 446, 450; 893.00/4-2549, #5 Cabot, Shanghai, RG 59, NA; T. H. P. Sailer, Honorary Secretary, Missionary Education Movement, to Dean Acheson, September 2, 1949, RG 59 NA; Dr. Bliss Wiant, Yenching University to Frank T. Cartwright and Mr. Evans, June 6, 1949, Johnson Papers, Box 19, folder 318; "Missionaries Said Unmolested in Red-Occupied Towns," *North China Daily News*, February 10, 1949, p. 4; P. W. Parker, chairman, China Medical Board, New York, to Kenneth S. Latourette, November 21, 1949, Kenneth Scott Latourette Papers, Box 49, YDL.

24. Lacy, "Protestant Missions," p. 308.

25. *Ibid.*, pp. 313, 359; Martinson, *Red Dragon Over China*, p. 298; "Religious Intolerance in Communist China," OIR 4657, April 9, 1948, pp. 6–10, Reel 4, pt. 3, OSS/State Department Reports.

26. Lacy, "Protestant Missions," p. 517; George Nye Steiger, *China and the Occident*, pp. 93–98; Varg, *Missionaries, Chinese and Diplomats*, p. 45; Edmund Wehrle, *Britain, China and the Antimissionary Riots*, pp. 127–30; Wu Chao-kwang, *The International Aspect of the Missionary Movement in China*, p. 191.

27. Frederick B. Hoyt, "The Summer of '30," pp. 231–36; Lacy, "Protestant Missions," pp. 313, 359, 392, 395, 465–66, 618; OIR 4657, April 9, 1948, p. 10, Reel 4, pt 3, OSS/State Department Reports.

28. "China," *The Harvest*, Report of the Executive Secretary of the Divison of Foreign Missions, Board of Missions and Church Extension of the Methodist Church (Cincinnati, 1948), p. 141; "Report on Protestant Missions," *Monthly Report*, p. 17.

29. Transcript of an interview with Ernest Ikenberry, January 1972, Claremont College China Missionaries Oral History Project, Columbia University, Special Collections, Butler Library Manuscript Division, New York City.

30. McCammon, *We Tried to Stay*, p. 140.

31. *New York Times*, October 12, 1949, p. 16; "Report on Protestant Missions," *Monthly Report*, p. 23.

32. Mary Muriel Boone to United Presbyterian Church in the U.S.A., March 20, 1950, Presbyterian files: *Reports and Journals of the Annual Meeting of the Board of Missions, The Evangelical United Brethren Church, 1949* (Dayton, Ohio, 1950), p. 55.

33. Lutz, *Christian Colleges*, p. 454; W. E. Hines to International Committee of the YMCA, February 16, 1950, YMCA Archives.

34. John F. Donovan, *The Pagoda and the Cross*, pp. 178–81. On the other hand, according to American Bishop James E. Walsh, Papal Nuncio Anthony Riberi in Nanking in October 1949 recommended immediate recognition by the Vatican of the new Peking government so as to protect the church in China. 893.01/10-1049, #4232 McConaughy, Shanghai, FRUS (1949)9:116. See also Memorandum of Conversation, Father Thomas A. O'Melia with Raymond B. Fosdick, October 3, 1949, Box 2, Lot File 53D211, Philip C. Jessup Papers, Department of State, Washington, D.C.

35. Raymond L. Whitehead, "Christian Response to People's China" (Ph.D. diss.), pp. 7, 65.

36. Fox Butterfield, "A Missionary View of the Chinese Communists (1936–39)," *passim*; Kenneth E. Shewmaker, *Americans and Chinese Communists*, pp. 265–266.

37. Butterfield, "Missionary View," pp. 178–79; Jessie Lutz, ed., *Christian Missions in China*, pp. 11–16.

38. Butterfield, "Missionary View," p. 155; "Challenge of Communism to the YMCA in Asia," talk given to the staff meeting of the World Alliance of the YMCA, Geneva, Switzerland, August 12, 1952, YMCA Archives.

39. Interview with Nathaniel Bercovitz at Occidental College, Los Angeles, July 6, 1953, Presbyterian files.

40. Calvin H. Reber Jr., "South China Mission," *Reports and Journals, The Evangelical United Brethren Church, 1949*, p. 64.

41. Whitehead, "Christian Response," p. 11.

42. Alice H. Schaefer to United Presbyterian Church of the U.S.A., May 13, 1949, Presbyterian files.

43. Bush, *Religion in Communist China*, p. 49; Lacy, "Protestant Missions," pp. 315–17, 362, 398, 427–30, 468–69; John Oss, *Mission Advance in China*, p. 139; *Reports and Journals, The Evangelical United Brethren Church, 1949*, p. 57; 893.00/2-1049, #73 Strong, Tsingtao, RG 59, NA; Professor Roberts, St. John's University, Shanghai to Dean Kerr, Philips Exeter Academy, November 17, 1948, RG 59, NA; Rowland M. Cross, "The Christian Response to Revolutionary Change in China," p. 2, Rowland M. Cross Papers, Box 1, Hoover.

44. Women's Division of Christian Service, Methodist Church, *Tenth Annual Report*, pp. 123–24.

45. E. E. Walline to Wallace C. Merwin, in *China Bulletin* (January 15, 1948), p. 1; Lutheran Global Missions, *Report*, 1948 (New York, 1949), p. 36; John M. Cabot, "To All Organizations Registered at the American Consulate in Shanghai," November 3, 1948, YMCA Archives.

46. Lacy, "Protestant Missions," p. 431; McCammon, *We Tried to Stay*, pp. 135–37.

47. Out of eleven large missionary boards which replied to a 1949 survey conducted by Frank T. Cartwright, chairman of the China Committee, all but one said that its workers had been encouraged to stay in China. Cartwright, "Protestant Missions in Communist China," p. 304; "National News: American Methodist Mission in China," *China News Letter* (July–August 1949), p. 10; *Reports and Journals*, 1949, p. 57; "Principles Governing the Relations Between the National Committee and the Secretaries of the Associations Affected by Fighting," in Minutes of the National Cabinet Meeting, November 9, 1948, YMCA Archives. The United Board for Christian Colleges and the Princeton-Yenching Foundation agreed to keep western educational institutions functioning in China. Sidney D. Gamble, President, Princeton-Yenching Foundation, to H. Alexander Smith, Senator, June 8, 1949, H. Alexander Smith Papers, Box 98, folder: Correspondence re Far East #1, Seeley Mudd Manuscript Library, Princeton University, Princeton, N.J.

48. Borg, *Chinese Revolution*, pp. 68–94. Political scientists have studied the the relationships of nongovernmental groups to foreign-policy making, and some have concluded that large religious, civic, and fraternal associations lack any direct influence. Religious pressures, argues Bernard C. Cohen in *The Influence of Non-Governmental Groups on Foreign Policy Making*, pp. 6–16, are only effective in purely sectarian matters. Other observers have disagreed. In *The End*

of Extraterritoriality in China, Wesley R. Fishel (pp. 137, 275*n*) discusses the origins of the Porter Resolution of 1927, which called on the President to negotiate a "wholly equal and reciprocal" treaty with China to replace the long-standing unequal treaties. Although the resolution was named after Representative Stephen G. Porter, Fishel says that "there is every reason to believe that its phrasing was strongly influenced by missionary interests." Its wording, he notes, closely parallels a letter sent by Dr. A. L. Warnshuis, secretary of the International Missionary Council, to the chief of the State Department's Division of Far Eastern Affairs, Nelson T. Johnson, on December 27, 1926. Furthermore, in response to an inquiry by Fishel, Warnshuis said that he had been in frequent contact with both Porter and the State Department.

49. "Conversations at State Department, Washington, D.C. with Ambassador Stuart and Shanghai Consul General Cabot," notes by Eugene Barnett, August 23, 1949, YMCA Archives. Re September 1949 meeting, see Bruce S. Greenwalt, "Missionary Intelligence From China" (Ph.D. diss.), p. 312. Re lobbying with Congress, see for example: Lewis Hoskins, American Friends Services Committee, to Senator Robert Taft, January 13, 1950, Robert Taft Papers, Subject File 1950 E–F, Box 986, folder: Foreign Policy, LC.

50. Frank T. Cartwright to Special Policy Committee and Dr. Philip C. Jessup, September 23, 1949, China Program files; Jessup to Cartwright, October 4, 1949, Philip C. Jessup Papers, Box 48, folder: Chronological File, October 1949, LC; Jessup to Wynn C. Fairfield, Foreign Missions Conference, New York, November 16, 1949, LC. Letters also were addressed directly to the Secretary of State: 893.00/7-2949 Reverend Ward McCabe, St. Andrews Church, Wellesley, Ma. to Acheson, RG 59, NA, and 893.01/11-2949 Frank W. Price, Missionary of the Presbyterian Church and Secretary of the Church of Christ in China to Acheson, RG 59, NA.

51. Frank T. Cartwright and Rowland M. Cross to John Kee and Tom Connally, May 3, 1949, China Program files. By the end of June Cartwright had received only three letters protesting this action. Cartwright to William R. Johnson, June 27, 1949, Johnson Papers, Box 19, folder 318, YDL.

52. Rowland M. Cross to Tom Connally, November 18, 1949, China Program files.

53. As of August 1948 the Federal Council of the Churches of Christ in America had 28,127,107 members in 26 denominations. Its constituency overlapped that of the older Foreign Missions Conference and differed slightly from the latter. In 1950 both organizations joined the new National Council of the Churches of Christ in the U.S.A. George F. Ketcham, ed., *Yearbook of American Churches, 1949*; Federal Council of the Churches of Christ in America, "The Churches and American Policy in the Far East," p. 306.

54. Greenwalt, "Missionary Intelligence," p. 5.

55. Harold Isaacs, *Images of Asia*, pp. 50–51.

56. Betty and John Fairfield, Congregationalists, Foochow, to Friends, August 23, 1949, Greenwalt, "Missionary Intelligence," pp. 308–9; "MacKay Asks U.S. to Recognize Chinese Regime," p. 1.

57. Greenwalt, "Missionary Intelligence," p. 290; Cross, "The Christian Response," pp. 9, 11, Cross Papers, Box 1, Hoover; C. F. and E. S. Johannaber, China Letter #5, December 1949, Johnson Papers, Box 19, YDL. Ralph A. Ward, Resident Bishop of the Methodist Church, Shanghai wrote to supporters in America, May 13, 1949, that though some missionaries had gone home, the

Methodist presence in China remained strong. Johnson Papers, Box 19, folder 317, YDL. "Report on Protestant Missions," *Monthly Report*, December 31, 1949, p. 24; Interview with Reverend Coleman, November 20, 1974.

58. Opposition to recognition similarly found expression in letters to government officials. 893.00/10-1749 Most Reverend Raymond A. Lane, Superior General, Catholic Foreign Mission Society of America to President Truman, RG 59, NA; 893.01/11-3049 Reverend R. A. McGowen, Executive Secretary, Catholic Association for International Peace to Secretary Acheson, RG 59, NA. According to Alfred O. Hero Jr., Director of the World Peace Foundation and author of numerous works on the role of public opinion in foreign-policy making, however, in the 1940s the Catholic hierarchy was much less articulate on world issues than the Protestant leaders. *American Religious Groups View Foreign Policy*, p. vi.

59. Memorandum to the Secretary of State Dean Acheson, chairman of the House Committee on Foreign Affairs, chairman of the Senate Committee on Foreign Relations, Representative Walter Judd, Director of Chinese Affairs at the Department of State Philip Sprouse, April 26, 1950, China Program files; Rowland M. Cross, Secretary, China Committee, to Friends, March 31, 1950, Cross Papers, Box 1, Hoover, and copy in China Program files.

60. Evidence that officials considered missionary ventures in China to be good for American interests and tried to encourage them can be found in the following: 893.00/3-849 Memorandum of Conversation by Leo J. Callanan, Consul General, Hankow, RG 59, NA; 893.48/3-1859 Philip Sprouse, Chief, Division of Chinese Affairs, to Magnus I. Gregersen, President, American Bureau for Medical Aid to China, May 10, 1949, RG 59, NA, and Dean Acheson to Paul V. McNutt, Chairman, United Service to China, April 13, 1949, which was referred to in the previous item and reportedly stated that the Secretary hoped private organizations would continue undiminished their activities in China; Elmer A. Fridell, Secretary for China, Japan, and the Philippines, American Baptist Foreign Missions Society, to Kenneth S. Latourette, New Haven, and Dr. Alton L. Miller, Boston, August 17, 1949, Latourette Papers, Box 35, folder: ABFM Foreign Department, Correspondence Part III 1948-53, YDL; P. W. Parker, Chairman, China Medical Board, New York, to Kenneth S. Latourette, New Haven, November 21, 1949, Latourette Papers, Box 49, folder: China Medical Board, YDL.

61. This reliance on socially progressive work to gain CCP acceptance highlighted missionary approaches to remaining in China. See the decision to stay made by boards, October 1949, and the policy adopted by the Northern Presbyterian Mission Board, November 1949, cited by Greenwalt, "Missionary Intelligence," pp. 315–16.

62. 893.01/12-349, #2183 Clubb, Peking, RG 5, NA.

63. Contrary views have been expressed about the degree to which missionaries and foreign service officers interacted. John Melby, who served in the Nanking Embassy and traveled elsewhere in China, has maintained that missionaries were too parochial to have been good sources. In his diary he recorded that the inland missionary was one of two kinds: "One group seldom strays from its compounds and has not the faintest notion of what is going on in the vicinity. The other, the politically minded group, is invariably allied with the right wing of the Kuomintang and accepts its dicta without question." *Mandate of Heaven*, p. 219. In a personal interview March 26, 1977 Melby added that not even John Leighton Stuart, American Ambassador to China and a missionary himself, paid much attention to them. A variety of other sources contradict this

assessment: see 893.00/12-149 Memorandum from R. Anderson to Fulton Freeman and Troy L. Perkins, RG 59, NA; 893.00/1-2649, #17 Memorandum by Howard E. Sollenberger, RG 59, NA; Gregory Prince, "The American Foreign Service in China," (Ph.D. diss.), writes that missionaries did not often provide information but when they did "foreign service officers did not hesitate to use it." p. 76n 37.

64. Renssler W. Lee III, "General Aspects of Chinese Communist Religious Policy," pp. 161–73.

7. COMMERCE IN CHINA

1. Tientsin Regional Office, ECA Report, January 10–31, 1949, p. 5, Allen R. Griffin Papers, Box 2, folder: General Situation Report Tientsin, Hoover.

2. Debate over the extent to which Western imperialism impeded China's economic development has occupied China scholars for decades. The classic condemnation of Western impact appears in Harold Isaacs, *The Tragedy of the Chinese Revolution* chs. 1 and 2. Andrew J. Nathan in "Imperialism's Effects on China," pp. 3–8, argued that this "interpretation of imperialism's effects on China was simplistic and misdirected." Robert F. Dernberger has gone so far as to maintain that Western enterprise introduced scientific, managerial, and organizational skills, equipment, and new tastes and demands, all of which were beneficial to China's economic development. See, "The Role of the Foreigner in China's Economic Development, 1840–1949."

3. Ethel B. Dietrich, *Far Eastern Trade of the United States*, pp. 10, 37–39. The portion of total United States trade accounted for by trade with China never exceeded 1.9% of total United States exports or 3.4% of total imports in the prewar period. The United States, on the other hand, supplied approximately 16–26% of China's total imports and took 11–26% of China's total exports, acting as China's most important single trading partner. 893.01/11-2849 Memorandum of Consequences of Non-recognition for U.S.-China Trade, RG 59, NA; Memorandum on United States Interests in China, Folder: China 1949, Box 173: China-1, Foreign Affairs File, President's Secretary's Files, Harry S Truman Papers, HST.

4. In 1930 British investments totalled $1,189.2 million and Japanese were $1,136.9 million. Dietrich, *Far Eastern Trade*, pp. 43–44; C. F. Remer, *Foreign Investments in China*, pp. 76, 276–81; David Horowitz, ed., *Corporations and the Cold War*, p. 17.

5. Dorothy Borg, *The United States and the Far Eastern Crisis of 1933–1938*, pp. 505–8. American businessmen were interned for the duration of the war under what China Electric Company employees conservatively described as "very unpleasant conditions." "The Story of the China Electric Company," *The International Review of the International Telephone and Telegraph Corporation* (February 1946)2:21, International Telephone and Telegraph Corporation Archives, New York City. Re China Car & Foundry see General Electric Company, War Claim under Public Law 87-846, Exhibits Schedules C and F, China General Electric, FCSC.

6. Dorothy Borg, "The China Market," p. 150. The major American businesses in postwar China included Stanvac—Standard Vacuum Petroleum Co., a joint

venture of Standard Oil of New Jersey and Socony; Caltex—California Texas Oil Co., a joint venture of Standard Oil of California and the Texas Co.; Shanghai Power Company—subsidiary of the American and Foreign Power Co.; Shantelco—Shanghai Telephone and Telegraph, a subsidiary of IT&T; Anderson, Meyer & Co.—a subsidiary of International General Electric Co.; National City Bank of New York; Chase National Bank; American President Lines; Robert Dollar Co.; and Northwest Airways.

7. Henry W. Bradbury, "Shanghai Power Company," article prepared for Ebasco International Inc. in 1973, pp. 4–5, Box 382–29, BBC. The United proposal was first made by Paul S. Hopkins, President of SPC, to deal with the serious power shortage created by wartime bombing and cannibalizing of generating plants in Shanghai. SPC itself could produce no more than 60,000 kilowatts compared to a prewar output of 170,000 kw and the local Chinese and French-owned companies had no capacity at all. The idea of pooling resources caught the imagination of Economic Cooperation Administration China Mission chief Charles Stillman but was greeted less enthusiastically by the management of Ebasco International and the leadership of the Kuomintang. Plans were delayed and finally abandoned because of the CCP advance into Shanghai. Comments on the History of the United Power Company Proposal by John Kopelman of Ebasco International at a January 18, 1951 meeting, Box 271-35; "Summary of Various Reports Covering United Power Company Project, Shanghai, China, May 1948," Box 266-31; J. P. Anderson, "United Power Company Preliminary Estimates, September 21, 1948," Box 266-36, BCC.

8. Esso Standard Eastern Inc. Claim CN-0288, Vol I, Exhibit A: Description of Claim, p. 2, FCSC. Caltex (Asia) Ltd., Claim CN-0249, Vol I, Introduction, p. 6, FCSC. IT&T Corp. and International Standard Electric Corp. Claim CN-0285, Proposed Decision, p. 4, and Supporting Document, p. 3, FCSC. Oil company activity in postwar China was part of a world-wide expansiveness. According to Mira Wilkins: "At home, [the major oil companies] had antitrust difficulties. Abroad, they faced expropriation . . . political instablity, labor difficulties, dollar shortages, restraints on trade and payments, investment control laws, legislation excluding their participation, foreign government intervention in their business, and so forth. They had a backlog of harrowing memories of experiences in the 1930s, including the expropriations in Bolivia and Mexico, and of property losses in Europe and Asia during the war years. Yet, such obvious deterrents to foreign investments notwithstanding, the major oil companies expanded abroad in every single facet of their business. Energy requirements were rising; profits were to be made; despite the obstacles, the U.S. oil enterprises hoped to take advantage of the opportunities." Wilkins, *The Maturing of Multinational Enterprise*, pp. 314–15.

9. Chiang Kai-shek, *China's Destiny*. This book originally came out in 1943.

10. In August 1947, for example, new KMT regulations established "official" and "open" market exchange rates. While the "official" rate for importers of cotton, wheat, coal, etc. stayed at $12,000(CN) to $1(US), the "open" market was determined daily by an Exchange Equalization Board. By April 1, 1948 this rate had climbed to $500,000(CN): $1(US). Of course, even these figures bear no resemblance to black market rates. Esso Standard Eastern Claim, Exhibit A, pp. 7–8, FCSC; "Review of the Present Economic Condition of China," pp. 505–7; and Florence C. Smith, "Business in China Today," p. 12, clipping from folder sent by Smith, Executive Secretary of the American Chamber of Commerce,

Shanghai, to Arthur Ringwalt, Chief of the Division of Chinese Affairs, State Department, July 8, 1947, in the files of the Far East-American Council of Commerce and Industry, New York City (hereafter FEACCI).

11. Walter Gordon, "A New Chinese Wall," p. 54.

12. Borg, "The China Market," pp. 152–53; Gordon, "New Chinese Wall," pp. 49–53; Smith, "Business in China," pp. 3–7, 17, FEACCI; Harley Stevens, "Business and Politics in China," p. 298. Guenther Stein, a former correspondent for the *Christian Science Monitor* and former editor of the *China Air Mail*, conducted a series of interviews with a cross-section of traders, manufacturers, bankers, etc. with experience in East Asia. His results, which were presented in a paper to the Tenth Conference of the Institute of Pacific Relations, Stratford-Upon-Avon, England, September 1947, as "American Business with East Asia," recited instances of such KMT abuses and observed: "Even the most hardened 'Old China Hands,' who have long been used to what they consider the traditional hazards of their business . . . administrative inefficiency and corruption, seem to agree that no time they can remember has been beset with quite so many and quite so formidable difficulties as the present." p. 2.

13. Pepper, *Civil War in China*, p. 108; "Review of the Present," p. 507; Telegram #123, H. A. Bieling, Shanghai to New York, May 1, 1949, Caltex Claim, Exhibits, 1(14), sec. 4, FCSC.

14. Gordon, "New Chinese Wall," p. 51.

15. "L.G.T.H.O.O.C.," Letter to the Editor, *Shanghai Evening Post & Mercury*, October 30, 1946, republished in response to letters and personal requests, November 2, 1946, Smith clipping folder, FEACCI. Cases of property occupied by the KMT after V-J Day and not subsequently returned to American ownership were numerous. Among them: General Electric Company, War Claim under Public Law 87-846, Exhibits Schedule D: GECO as successor-in-interest to International General Electric, FCSC.

16. "In short, if businesses were planned entirely on paper, it would appear sheer folly to hope for survival in the Orient today. In actual practice, however, these seemingly insuperable obstacles are overcome in one way or another." Robert U. Frondorf, "Ault & Wiborg (Far East)," p. 57. "There is not much profit by present standards but we want to stay in it as some day [it] may be important." W. Stoy Elliot, to Seattle Office, #288, October 22, 1948, Box 15, folder: Lumber Operations, Robert Dollar Papers, Bancroft Manuscript Library, University of California, Berkeley.

17. Re Anderson, Meyer & Company's concern over some of its shareholders: 893.5043/7-1449, Memorandum of Telephone Conversation, Mr. Everlett, Vice President of IGE with S. C. Brown, Commercial Policy Division, State Department, RG 59, NA. The President of American President Lines was quoted in the *New York Herald Tribune*, June, 1949, as seeing good prospects for business relations with the Communists. Thereafter, APL struggled to convince Ambassador Koo that President Killion had been misquoted, but at the same time would not agree to a public retraction of those remarks. V. K. Wellington Koo Oral History Collection, I (sec. 4): 154; (sec. 5):210-13, East Asian Institute, Columbia University.

18. Favorable reports such as: Maxwell Stewart, "America's China Policy," p. 175; 611.9331/2-1549, #A-125 Cabot, Shanghai, RG 59, NA; Julian Schuman, "Shanghai Business Asks Quick Peace with Reds," pp. 1, 3; J. R. Kaim, "Trade Prospects in China," pp. 122–24. Kaim observed: "In North China the Com-

munists showed they were in no hurry to destroy anything that might prove useful for their own purposes." Of course, there were also negative reports: Caltex Claim, p. 8, and Joint Weeka #7, from State, Army, Navy, Air (SANA) Nanking, March 4, 1949, p. 6, file 350.2 Joint Weeka Reports, Consul General Hong Kong, China Post Files, RG 84, WNRC.

19. Randall Gould, "China Outlook: A Business View," p. 91. Translations of the Chinese press by the American Consulate in Shanghai were done according to seven categories: (1) references to the United States, (2) references to other major countries, (3) economic matters, (4) political matters, (5) military matters, (6) special items, e.g. China's international or cultural problems, and (7) labor. W. Bradley Connors, United States Information Service chief in China in 1949, estimated that the consulate translations covered at least 90% of the themes used in the Chinese press at the time. Translations were made by thoroughly tested and experienced personnel and were checked by other qualified translators. Ruth B. Chrone, "An Inquiry Into a Possible Relationship Between Propaganda and the Fall of Shanghai, 1949" (Ph.D. diss.). Chrone was an information specialist with the foreign service in Shanghai from January 1949 to April or May, 1949. Information about the Chinese Communists was widespread. For example: "Although listening to Communist radio forbidden, references to Communist broadcasts made openly by Chinese who . . . give greater credence to latter than to government communiques." 893.00/12-3048, #514 Smyth, Tientsin, RG 59, NA; Letter Louise Willauer to her family, no. 1, November 7, 1948, Folder: Family Letters, Items: CAT-China (1), Whiting Willauer Papers, Seeley Mudd Manuscript Library, Princeton University; Interview with Arthur Rosen, former vice-consul for commercial affairs in Shanghai, February 4, 1976.

20. On enemy occupation of the cities and Mao's injunction to encircle the cities from the countryside, see Mao Tse-tung, *Lun hsin chieh-tuan* [On the New Stage] (n.p.: Chieh-fang she, 1939), a report to the Sixth Plenum of the Sixth Central Committee in October, 1938, ch. 3. Extract appears in Schram, *The Political Thought of Mao Tse-tung*, pp. 288–90. The new policy appeared formally in the following proclamation: "Tung-pei-chü kuan-yü pao-hu hsin shou-fu ch'eng-shih chih-shih" [Directive of the Northeast Bureau on Safeguarding the Newly Taken-Over Cities] issued June 10, 1948 and included in the compilation, Liu Shao-ch'i, et al., "Hsin min-chu chu-i ch'eng-shih cheng-ts'e [The New Democratic City Policy], pp. 37–43. By mid-1948 the CCP controlled 586 cities including large centers such as Harbin in Manchuria and Loyang in Honan. Pepper, *Civil War*, p. 332.

21. *Ibid.*, p. 331; Mao Tse-tung, "Mu-ch'ien Hsing-shih ho Wo-men ti Jen-wu" [The Present Situation and Our Tasks] December 25, 1947, in collection with the same title, also appears in Mao, *SW*, 4:157–76. In this report to the Central Committee Mao presented his four slogans which were to guide urban policy: (1) develop production, (2) make the economy prosper, (3) consider both public and private, (4) benefit both labor and capital. The significance of this document is discussed by William Bruggar, *Democracy and Organisation in the Chinese Industrial Enterprise*, p. 67, and by Robert Loh, *Businessmen in China*, pp. 2–3; *New York Times* March 25, 1948, p. 25; Tillman Durdin, "China Reds Warn Against Brutality," p. 12.

22. Mao, "Report to the Second Plenary Session of the Seventh Central Committee of the CCP, March 5, 1949," *SW*, 4:363.

23. See Hsin-hua she editorial quoted in Pepper, *Civil War in China*, p. 351; Jen Pi-shih, "Kung-shang-yeh cheng-ts'e," p. 34; Li Li-san, "Kuan-yü fa-chan sheng-ch'an lao tzu liang li cheng-ts'e te chi-tien shou-ming," in Liu Shao- ch'i, et al., and noted in Pepper, p. 372, and see also pp. 349–51, 368; and Loh, *Early Chiang*, pp. 1–15. The Chinese Communists also tried to forestall the exodus of prominent Chinese by mailing policy statements promising protection for property and freedom of trade and business directly to them. For example: Mimeographed circular, December 20, 1948, Headquarters of the East China People's Military Zone of the People's Liberation Army, 893.00/12-2148, #277 Strong, Tsingtao, RG 59, NA. Re loans and orders: "State Orders Help Privately Owned Workshops in Tientsin," New China News Agency *Daily Bulletin*, #43, June 5, 1950; "With Government Help, Private Factories All Over China Overcome Difficulties," *ibid.*, #47, June 11, 1950. Re growth of private sector see "Development of Private Industries in Peking," *Hsinhua Daily News Release*, #278, February 5, 1950, p. 24; "Private Industry in Peking & Tientsin Forges Ahead," DNR #296, February 25, 1950, p. 123. In a fine, 1981 dissertation, Larry Weiss argues that before the Korean War, the CCP followed moderate policies designed to expedite rebuilding of the nation. See Weiss, "Storm Around the Cradle: The Korean War and the Early Years of the People's Republic of China, 1949–1953."

24. 893.00/6-1549, #1018 Clubb, Peking, RG 59, NA, and Loh, *Early Chiang*, pp. 10–12. Both Clubb and Loh indicate that the CCP was successful in enticing capital and capitalists to come back. This was not true, however, in the case of Ch'en Kuang-fu (K. P. Chen), a prominent Shanghai banker. Although he hoped to return to Shanghai after fleeing to Hong Kong in April 1949, he did not do so, despite invitations from Mao in 1949, 1950, and 1951. Ch'en Kuang-fu Oral History, ch. 12, pp. 132–33, Chinese Oral History Project, Butler Library Manuscript Division, Columbia University, New York City.

25. See 893.00B/12-2948, #520 Stuart, Nanking, FRUS (1948)7:700–3. Stuart believed that all proclamations promising fair treatment to law-abiding foreigners were patterned on a September 25, 1948 decree to the residents of Tsinan. ("Regulations for Entering the City Proclaimed by the Tsinan Municipal Control Committee," *Kuan-yü ch'eng-shih cheng-ts'e te chi-ko wen-hsien* [Some Documents on City Policy] [n.p.: Hua pei hsin hua shu-tien, 1949], pp. 8–9.) Such declarations were printed in the communist press, broadcast over North Shensi radio and even sent out through the mails, as for example, the provisional law promulgated by Lin Piao, Commander of the Peking-Tientsin front and delivered to firms in Tientsin in December 1948. ("The Eight Point Provisional Law of the Peking-Tientsin Front Line Command and of the People," issued December 22, 1948, *ibid.*, pp. 45–46); Walter Sullivan, "Chinese Reds Urge U.S. Firms to Stay," pp. 1, 12; "Protect Foreign Industry Slogan in Peiping," *North China Daily News*, January 25, 1949, p. 2, Reel no. 291 (hereafter NCDN); Joint Weeka #2, January 28, 1949; #74, January 16, 1949, Tientsin, recounting reassurances given by Liu Tu-wei, Public Relations and Political Officer of the PLA in Tientsin, Box 2315 Tsingtao, File 350 Correspondence, RG 84, WNRC; and also Tineca 333, January 18, 1949, James T. Ivy, ECA, Tientsin to ECA, Shanghai, Box 1, Roger D. Lapham Papers, Hoover.

26. Recollection of Darwin L. McMillan, Caltex marketing executive in China, provided to the author by J. M. Voss, Chairman of the Board, Caltex Petroleum Corporation, New York City; see also William M. Leary, Jr. *The Dragon's Wings*,

p. 217 re Pan Amercan's experience. Bryner and Company, agent for Northwest Airways and American President Lines in China, found the CCP eager to establish trade and shipping services to Taku Bar, and to initiate air routes to communist cities not hitherto serviced. See Joint Weeka #13, April 15, 1949, RG 84, WNRC, and *New York Times*, March 15, 1949, Weekly Summary, March 10–16, 1949.

27. 611.9331/6-149, #1919 Cabot, Shanghai, RG 59, NA. 893.00/6-1149, #996 Clubb, Peking, RG 59, NA; Joint Weeka #12, April 8, 1949, p. 12, RG 84, WNRC; #573 Acheson to Shanghai, Nanking, Hong Kong and Canton, April 1, 1949, File 510.1, Folder: North China Trade—Petroleum, RG 84, WNRC; 893.6363/5-2649, #1835 Cabot, Shanghai, RG 59, NA. Re the CCP's overall interest in establishing trade relations with the United States, see 693.0031/3-2549, #167 Smyth, Tientsin, RG 59, NA; 693.0031/5-1149, #307, Smyth, Tientsin, RG 59, NA; 693.0031/4-3049, #736 Clubb, FRUS (1949)9:976–77; 761.00/6-1049, Weekly Report by Office Of Intelligence Research for certain diplomatic and consular officers, RG 59, NA; Acheson to Certain American Diplomatic and Consular Officers, August 29, 1949, file 510 Trade Relations, Consul General Hong Kong, RG 84, WNRC; 693.0031/10-2149, #867 Smyth, Tientsin, RG 59, NA; 393.1115/9-1949, #3932 McConaughy, Shanghai, FRUS (1949)9:1342-43.

28. Pepper, *Civil War in China*, pp. 390–93. See also IT&T Corporation, *Annual Report for the Year 1949* (New York), p. 16, IT&T archives: and "Problem for Chinese Communists," p. 128. The orderliness of the Communist takeover was a surprise to businessmen; see: "China: Economic Conditions, Situation in Recent Months," p. 15; "Businessmen in China," p. 1459. The Monthly Report of the SPC for June 1949 noted: "The rapid return to normality after the changeover coupled with the new local government's declared intention to give every assistance possible in developing local industries created a feeling of optimism among industrialists. Consequently, some factories which had been shut down for some time made plans to resume operations while others planned to extend existing plants." Shanghai Power Company Monthly Report, June 1949, Box 271-29, BCC.

29. "S. S. Fillmore Arrives from Taku Bar," p. 1; Walter Sullivan, "Shanghai Freezes All Bank Accounts," p. 12.

30. In June 1949, referring to the PLA's Provisional Regulations Governing Foreign Trade in East China and in September after promulgation of the Provisional Measures Governing the Collection of Business Taxes in Shanghai by the People's City Government, the American Consulate General informed the State Department that the measures were quite reasonable. 693.0031/6-2349, Dispatch #309 AmConGen, Shanghai, RG 59, NA. Other comment comparing CCP favorably to KMT: 893.83/6-949, Memorandum of Telephone Conversation, K. R. MacKinnon, President, Ebasco International, with Philip Sprouse, Division of Chinese Affairs, State Department, RG 59, NA. "Dollar in Red China," p. 67; columns by Walter Sullivan in the *New York Times*, June 4, 1949, dispatch from Shanghai, Weekly Summary June 2–8, 1949, pp. 11–12 and June 13, 1949, Weekly Summary June 9–15, 1949, p. 11. In the latter dispatch Sullivan observed that American businessmen find themselves supporting the CCP "regime whose moderate businesslike policies have been in marked contrast to their predecessors." Similar statements as late as October 1950, John Kopelman, Vice President of Ebasco International to K. R. MacKinnon, October 19, 1950, Box 271-76, BCC.

Businessmen also noted the contrast between the behavior of CCP troops and that of the KMT soldiers. "Retiring Government Troops Seize Foreign Property for Billets," p. 1.

31. "NWA Plans to Continue in China," p. 2; 893.00/10-1049, #4238 Mc-Conaughy, Shanghai, RG 59, NA. State Department objections to NWA plans were based on an unwillingness to have the CCP establish an "internal mechanism of high value to consolidation [of] their political control of area." The Department was prepared to support NWA and Pan Am in restoration of international service to Shanghai. 811.79693/8-1249, #1631 Secretary to Mc-Conaughy, FRUS (1949)9:1299–1300.

32. *New York Times*, June 12, 1949, sec 5, p. 9. At Tangku, the port of Tientsin, an American ship was the first to call after the CCP took over the harbor, and during the first half of 1949 (the CCP moved in on January 16, 1949) American ships accounted for 38.51% of the total tonnage which served the port. 693.0031/11-1549, Dispatch 442, American Consulate General, Shanghai, RG 59, NA.

33. Shantelco maintained nearly normal service during the changeover to CCP rule. The company subsequently received public and governmental commendations for its conduct during this period. IT&T Corporation, *Annual Report* 1949, p. 16. Even after the company was forced to turn management over to its Chinese staff, operations continued. Manager's Monthly Letter, June 1950, George Kiang, Vice President and General Manager, Shanghai to C. B. Allsopp, c/o International Standard Electric, Tokyo, Japan, IT&T Archives. Re optimism of business based on China's needs: John Cabot, Shanghai Consul General to Leverett Saltonstall, U.S. Congress, January 20, 1949, John Cabot Papers, folder: China Correspondence 1948–1949, Manchester, Mass.

34. Robert S. Allen, "U.S. Oil Firms Shipping to Reds in China," p. 1B. Re optimism about staying in 1949, see for example: "2,500 U.S. Businessmen Sticking It Out in Shanghai," p. 3, comments by Alfred Holter, President of American Securities Corporation, and "Unlimited Commercial Potential of Far East," p. 1, comments by P. O. Matthews, manager of the Orient Lines. Ault & Wiborg, which specializes in printing inks and equipment, began exporting to China in 1896 and established its Shanghai branch in 1916. In subsequent years it endured civil war and Japanese takeover only to conclude in 1948 that "the company can look back on over thirty years of successful business in the Orient, and, barring a cataclysm far greater than the recent war, it plans for the future years with confidence." A & W (FE) remained in China and eventually lost its Shanghai assets in the December 1950, nationalization of American property. Frondorf, "A & W," pp. 52–59; Ault & Wiborg Co (FE) Ltd., Claim no. CN-0492, Memorandum Walter E. Monagan, Director, General Claims Division, to Andrew T. McGuire, General Counsel, May 12, 1970, FCSC; 693.0031/3-249 Clark, Tientsin, forwarding letter sent February 22, 1949, RG 59 NA.

35. Appeals to the State Department to stop aid to the KMT were made by the Board of the American Association of Shanghai (893.00/5-1249, #1624 Cabot, Shanghai, RG 59, NA) and by American businessmen in Tientsin via Hyman Hodes and Robert Smyth (#426 December 10, 1948, to which Robert A. Lovett called Clark Clifford's attention. Folder 2: China, Box 3: China, Coal Case, Subject File, Clark M. Clifford Papers, HST). These views were communicated by Secretary of State Acheson to President Truman at a May 13, 1949 cabinet meeting. Folder: Cabinet Meetings January 3-December 30, 1949, Set I, Box I, Matthew J. Connelly Files, Harry S Truman Papers, HST. 893.801/6-3049 Merrill C.

Gay, Assistant Chief, Division of Commercial Policy, State Department, to Eugene P. Thomas, President, NFTC, NYC, enclosing June 25 message from the the China Committee of the NFTC in Shanghai, RG 59, NA.

36. Paul S. Hopkins to K. R. MacKinnon, July 8, 1949, Box A: 271-27; and Hopkins to MacKinnon, September 22, 1949, Box A: 271-27; and quote taken from Hopkins to Robertson, September 21, 1949, Box A: 271-27, BCC; 893.6463/ 8-649, #3076 McConaughy, Shanghai, for Robertson from Hopkins; 893.6463/8-1949, W. S. Robertson, American and Foreign Power, NYC to W. Walton Butterworth, Assistant Secretary of State, RG 59, NA. Perhaps Hopkins' least hopeful period followed the February 6, 1950 bombing of SPC. Memorandum of Conversation, Situation of American Businessmen in Shanghai Who Might Be Denied Exit Permits by Communist Authorities, March 24, 1950, Memoranda of Conversations—1950, Papers of Dean Acheson, HST.

37. Dorothy Borg, Shanghai to friends in the United States, November 8, 1948, Box 124, Philip C. Jessup Papers, LC; "Communism's March Through China," pp. 125–29; Maxwell Stewart, "America's China Policy," pp. 174–75; Seymour Topping, "American Businessmen in China Expressing Desire to Trade with Communists." Pessimism came to Tientsin as early as April 1949, but it did not cause businessmen to leave. #134, Tientsin, April 7, 1949, file 510.2, folder: North China-Tientsin-conditions, RG 84, WNRC. Among the concerns affected by strikes and lock-ins were the Yee Tsoong Tobacco Company, Anderson, Meyer & Co., and Stanvac. 393.1115/5-349, #A-278 Cabot, Shanghai, FRUS (1949)9:1254; 893.6363/6-2349, #2442, and 6-2349, #2448, and 6-2449, #2460, Cabot, Shanghai, RG 59, NA.

38. Lynn and Amos Landman, *Profile of Red China*, p. 69; Caltex Claim, vol 1, exhibit 16, sec IF, American Chamber of Commerce Circular T/14, 3 Sets of Measures for Disposal of Labor-Capital Affairs Resolved by the All-China Federation of Labor, July 1949, translation of *Liberation Daily News* article, November 27, 1949, reprinting text, FCSC. Even before this, John M. Cabot informed the State Department that authorities had shown an increasing disposition to intervene in difficult cases. #2642, July 7, 1949, FRUS (1949)9:1261–65.

39. "Lost in a Dust Cloud," editorial, *Shanghai Evening Post & Mercury*, April 20, 1949, Box 4, Randall Gould Papers, Hoover; Interview with Randall Gould, August 1976. American Ambassador Stuart in December, 1948, however, considered the *Post* to be much more optimistic about the CCP than "either Embassy or responsible American business and evangelical interests." 893.00/12-1848, #2572 Stuart, Nanking, RG 59, NA.

40. International law provided that de facto recognition could be extended without withdrawing recognition from the de jure government. L. F. Oppenheim, *International Law*, 7th ed. (1920) 1:145–56, par., 75g. The CCP made it quite clear, however, that it would accept nothing less than de jure recognition and a complete severing of relations with the KMT. Common Program, Article 56, cited by O. Edmund Clubb, "Chinese Communist Strategy in Foreign Relations," p. 163; *New York Times*, May 1, 1949, p. 4.

41. See: Interview with Randall Gould, August 1976; Randall Gould, "If You Fight You May Get Hit," preliminary draft report to C. V. Starr, Box 4, Gould Papers, Hoover; FRUS (1949)8:1226, 1244-47, 1252, 1274-75. For further details on the *Post* situation see ch 8.

42. Paraphrase of July 31, 1949 memorial to the Department of State from the American Chamber of Commerce, Shanghai, Files of the National Foreign Trade

Council, New York City (hereafter NFTC); also quoted 393.1115/7-3149, #2976
McConaughy, Shanghai, FRUS (1949)9:1278–81. Present at the meeting called
by the State Department on August 4 to discuss the memorial were representatives of Caltex, Stanvac, National City Bank, Chase National Bank, Bank of
America, IT&T, Anderson, Meyer & Co., and American & Foreign Power Co.
393.1115/7-3149, Memorandum RG 59, NA. Meeting reported to Shanghai as
393.1115/7-3149, #1555 Acheson to McConaughy, FRUS (1949)9:1286–87. Re
evacuation by major companies: "Caltex in China, May 1949-January 1952,"
point 5, Recollections of Darwin L. McMillan, provided to the author by J. M.
Voss; 383.1115/8-149, #2982 and 012.3/8-949, #1558, RG 59, NA—both Caltex;
"Overseas Employees Are Leaving China," p. 4, Mobil Oil Corporation Archives, New York City; Henrietta M. Larson, et al., *History of Standard Oil Company (New Jersey)*, p. 778; 393.115/7-2749, #1484 Department to Shanghai, RG
59, NA. Some of the business community's pessimism was due to the effectiveness of the Nationalist blockade which slowed business activity in Shanghai
considerably. By mid-July approximately 70% of the imports bound for that port
were being held up in Hong Kong. "China: Economic Conditions," p. 15. Re
various problems with workers see FRUS (1949)8:1179, 1184–86.

43. 393.1115/8-1649, #3264 McConaughy, Shanghai, FRUS (1949)9:1298–99;
#2642, July 7, 1949, Cabot, Shanghai, *ibid.*, pp. 1261–65.

44. Pepper, *Civil War in China*, pp. 403–4. Re presumed discriminatory treatment: The National City Bank of New York was the only foreign bank in Shanghai to be assessed a particular liquidation tax. The Bank believed that this was
because of its dollar holdings which the CCP needed. "It was and is a transparent
pretext for acquiring foreign currency; and the basis and the amount are alike
fictitious. The City Bank has properly looked upon this tax as a mere arbitrary
exaction; a condition precedent to the final certificate of dissolution; an unreasonable but definite requirement before permission might be given to Mr. Harn-
den to leave. In short, it is blackmail or ransom and has no other financial or
legal significance." First National City Bank Claim, Shearman & Sterling &
Wright to Arnold, p. 6, FCSC.

45. Speech by John M. Cabot, Asilomar, California, December 10, 1949, p. 8,
Cabot Papers. Cabot told the State Department in July 1949: "I do not believe
on basis of information now available to Consulate General that [this] . . . is
part of a deliberate plan of Communists. So far, it appears to me part of normal
pattern of revolution." #2642, July 7, 1949, FRUS (1949)9:1261–65. A Caltex
interview with Shanghai authorities made it clear, so Consul McConaughy reported, that "government by labor" was an unwelcome development, but that
the CCP was reluctant to move against this politically critical group. They said
they would do so but only slowly. 393.1115/9-1449, #3839 McConaughy, FRUS
(1949)9:1337–38; Pepper, *Civil War in China*, p. 400.

46. Kenneth Lieberthal, "Mao Versus Liu?" pp. 509–17; Pepper, *Civil War in
China*, pp. 403–4; Landman, *Profile*, p. 69; 893.00/8-949, #3288 McConaughy,
Shanghai, RG 59, NA; 893.5043/9-149, #3580 McConaughy, RG 59, NA; Roth,
"How the Communists Rule," p. 491; 893.6363/12-849, #1025 Wellborn, Tientsin, RG 59, NA. In December 1949, Paul S. Hopkins and William F. Flanley,
Vice President and General Manager of the Shanghai Telephone Company, reported that the CCP had been pressuring labor to "produce more" and "cut out
troublemaking." There had, in fact been, a "notable improvement in relations
with the communist authorities during the past two or three months, which

were illustrated by two rate revisions in close succession at the end of November, improved access to the Director of the Bureau of Public Utilities, and a more realistic attitude by the authorities toward foreign-owned public utilities." Memorandum to William S. Robertson, American & Foreign Power Company, New York, December 18, 1949, Box: 271-27, BCC. Some abuses, however, continued. See 393.1115/9-949, #1076 Strong, Charge in China, FRUS (1949)9:1332.

47. Quote from Memorandum re Nationalist attacks on U.S. shipping, R. H. Hillenkoetter, Director, Central Intelligence Agency to the President, January 12, 1950, folder: Central Intelligence Memorandum, 1950–1952, Intelligence Files, President's Secretary's Files, Truman Papers, HST. The Common Program of the Chinese People's Political Consultative Conference, which was passed at the first plenary session on September 29, 1949, appears in *Chung-hua jen-min kung-ho-kuo fa-ling hui-pien* [Collection of laws and decrees of the People's Republic of China] 1949–1950, 1:19, and see also Jerome Alan Cohen, "Chinese Law and Sino-American Trade," pp. 128–29. Re use of Communist or pro-Communist concerns: 611.9331/8-249, #580 Smyth, Tientsin, RG 59, NA. Re variable trade restrictions: 611.9331/9-1449, Memorandum of Conversation, Mr. Rosenhirsch, International Commodities Corporation, NY, with C. T. White and S. C. Brown, Commercial Policy Division, State Department, RG 59, NA. Re quality of Soviet goods: 693.0031/10-2149, #867 Smyth, Tientsin, RG 59, NA. Re continuing encouragement to domestic capitalists: Loh, *Early Chiang*, pp. 6–10. A Peking radio broadcast of June 4, 1950, which described the two-week economic conference then under way in the capital, hinted that steps would be taken to control the encroachment of state trading organizations on private enterprise. This and Mao's June 6 speech calling for tax reductions and the preservation of private enterprise lifted the pessimism of foreign businessmen just a little. *New York Times*, June 5, 1950, p. 5, and Walter Sullivan, "News That Comes from Inside China," p. 5. The pessimism had been contributed to by measures such as the April 15, 1950 order abolishing the use of English and Western accounting practices in all businesses in China. *New York Times*, April 16, 1950, p. 4.

48. Only a very few large companies suspended operations completely at this time. The American Express Company did so as of September 30, 1949. American Express International Banking Corporation, Claim no. CN-0340, Proposed Decision, June 30, 1970, Finalized August 20, 1970, p. 1. FCSC. An American official of the Yee Tsoong Tobacco Co. maintained that pressures on American businessmen were designed not to drive them out but to rectify Shanghai's dire economic problems by forcing companies to contribute funds. 893.00/8-449, #3046 McConaughy, Shanghai, RG 59, NA. The S.S. *General Gordon* left Shanghai on September 25, 1949 with 363 Americans out of 1,220 passengers. A *New York Times* reporter in Shanghai observed that the evacuation ship had been arranged at a time when relations between the business community and the CCP were at the lowest ebb to date. "Since then the situation has eased and about 1,000 Americans here and many more in Nanking and elsewhere along the Yangtze Valley have elected to remain." *New York Times*, September 26, 1949, p. 13.

49. Hopkins was probably the most consistently optimistic and most thoroughly dedicated to China of all the American businessmen there. In part, his son Peter Hopkins suggests, this may have been because he was the only executive born in China and felt a very personal responsibility toward the country. His attitude was reflected in an April 25, 1949 telephone conversation with K.

R. MacKinnon, as MacKinnon later related: "It is a very tangled situation with exchange yesterday at 400,000:1, but Paul is in excellent spirits, and gave me a loud laugh at the idea of his abandoning Shanghai at this time. He said he will not let the people of Shanghai down." K. R. MacKinnon to John Kopelman, April 26, 1949, Box 268-14, BCC; Interview with Peter Hopkins, July 11, 1977.

50. Re IT&T see 811.503193/8-2449, Memorandum of Conversation by John F. Shaw, Division of Commercial Policy, Department of State, FRUS (1949)9:1312–16.

51. "International Outlook," *Business Week*, March 19, 1949, p. 119; Andrew Roth, "Shanghai Awaits the Communists," p. 72; 893.01/10-2649 Edwin C. Johnson, Senator, Colorado, Chairman Committee on Interstate Commerce to Secretary of State, RG 59, NA.

52. On encouragement to stay in China by State Department see below note 69. Also in the spring of 1949, before the fall of Shanghai, SPC executives consulted American authorities in China as to future plans. "The conclusion of those discussions were that the discontinuance of power service prior to the fall of Shanghai would accelerate the surrender, cause economic and political chaos with probable heavy loss of life; that the continuance of the service served no war purpose; that its continuance being essential to the survival of Shanghai might serve as a welcome bridge for an approach to the Communists by the American interests in China." "Memorandum Regarding Shanghai Power Company's Position in Shanghai," Box 268-14, BCC. John M. Cabot, Consul General in Shanghai, believed that the Department had pretty much encouraged key Americans to stay (#2642, July 7, 1949, FRUS [1949]9:1264 and John M. Cabot Diary, July 11, 1949, Cabot Family, Washington D.C.) and despite the Department's firm denial that this was so (893.00/7-749, #1373 Secretary of State to Cabot, FRUS (1949)9:1265–66), Cabot explained: "While Consul General gave no specific guarantees . . . and no positive encouragement, impression created . . . that key personnel should remain." 893.00/7-1149, #2693, Cabot, Shanghai, FRUS (1949)9:1266.

53. As of October 5, 1949, eighteen American businessmen remained in Shanghai "more or less against their will" according to Consul Walter P. McConaughy. The overt reason for this was labor problems, but McConaughy speculated that the real reasons included a desire to ensure competent management of American firms, continued supplies of vital commodities (e.g., petroleum, oils and lubricants), ongoing negotiations for air service and the presence of skilled personnel. Actually not all 18 wanted to leave China. 393.1115/10-449, #4201 McConaughy, and 393.1115/10-749, #4208 McConaughy, FRUS (1949)9:1350–53; W. R. Herod to Secretary of State, March 13, 1950, Box: 268-14, BCC. Detention by the CCP became a really frightening problem only after all U.S. diplomatic personnel were withdrawn in mid-March 1950. Receiving no support from the State Department, a small group of American business executives planned to escape by sea if they could not obtain exit visas within 30 days. Such an extreme step did not prove necessary. Memorandum of Conversation, March 24, 1950, HST; Warren Tozer, "Last Bridge to China," pp. 74–75. Re breaking blockade see #2646 Bacon, Nanking, December 23, 1949, FRUS (1949)9:1361–62. Shanghai's Director of Public Utilities told Y. K. Whang, Adminstrative Manager of SPC, that military authorities had decided not to permit American businessmen to return home until after Taiwan had been taken lest they report on the seriousness of Shanghai's situation and the effects of KMT

bombing. A. S. Gehrels, Shanghai to W. S. Robertson, NY, February 19, 1950, Box: 266-34, BCC.

54. 393.1115/7-2749, #1484 State Department to Shanghai, transmitting message for Seitz, Washington Representative Stanvac to W. P. Coltman, Shanghai manager Stanvac, RG 59, NA; 393.1115/9-1449, #3839 McConaughy, Shanghai, FRUS (1949)9:1337–38. Tozer, "Last Bridge to China," p. 72; 393.1115/7-3149 Memorandum of Conversation, Meeting with Business Executives at the State Department, August 4, 1949, RG 59, NA; 893.6363/9-649, #476 Hawthorne, Tsingtao, FRUS (1949)8:1143. The American staff of the Universal Leaf Tobacco Company left Chinese employees in charge as of September, 1949. They withdrew only as far as Hong Kong, however, hoping to be able to return—a hope not abandoned until August, 1950. Universal Leaf Tobacco Co. of China, Fed. Inc., USA, Claim no CN-0357, Form 780, Paragraph 13, FCSC.

55. Tillman Durdin, "New Plan Offered on China ECA Fund," p. 16. During optimistic periods Hong Kong-based American businessmen felt it "quite certain that American firms will be able to do business, big business, as long as they supply the things that the Communists want according to terms dictated to them. The terms are not likely to be too bad financially, but it seems to be a growing pattern that the trade will have to come through Japan or Hong Kong or someplace other than directly from the U.S." Bob Potter, Eastman Kodak Co. Wholesale Office, Hong Kong to Mr. Porter, President of the Peoples Banking Co., Oberlin, Ohio, November 1, 1949, forwarded to Senator Robert Taft, Subject file 1949: En-F, Robert Taft Papers, LC.

56. For example see: Robert S. Allen, "U.S. Oil Firms Shipping to Reds in China," p. 1B; *New York Times*, November 28, 1949, p. 28 which mentions Standard Oil, National City Bank, Chase Bank, Anderson, Meyer & Co., and Eastman Kodak.

57. In December 1950 the United States government blocked Chinese Communist assets in America, equal to some $76.5 million, under the Foreign Assets Control Regulations issued as a result of President Truman's declaration of a state of national emergency owing primarily to the Korean War. The People's Republic of China, in response, moved against American assets under their jurisdiction. Re December 28, 1950 "freezing order" which was promulgated by the State Administrative Council as Tsun Tsai 412 see Caltex Claim, Exhibit no. 16, sec 1B, p. 2, FCSC, for text. Between 1966 and 1972, under the provisions of Title V of the International Claims Settlement Act of 1949 as amended by Public Law 89-780 in 1966, the U.S. Foreign Claims Settlement Commission determined the amount and validity of claims by American nationals against the Chinese. All claims accepted for this program were based on the period following October 1, 1949. The FCSC entertained a total of 576 claims, rendering favorable decisions in 384 cases, totaling $196,861,834. The nine highest corporate claims were certified as follows:

1. Shanghai Power Company	$53,832,885
2. Esso Standard	27,026,602
3. Caltex Limited	15,443,700
4. IT&T Corporation	7,765,315
5. General Electric Company	4,546,200
6. International Standard Electric Corp.	3,228,853

7. Western District Power Co. Shanghai	1,758,685
8. First National City Bank	1,562,145
9. Shanghai Wharf and Warehouse Company	1,042,862

Charles H. Bayar, "China's Frozen Assets in the US," pp. 31–44; Nancy Ross, "Disputed China Claims Involve Bonds, Plot," p. 1E; "China Claims Program," FCSC. On March 1, 1979, U.S. Treasury Secretary Michael Blumenthal announced in Peking that China had agreed to pay Americans 41 cents on the dollar to settle outstanding claims. *New York Times,* March 2, 1979, p. 1.

58. 793.02/1-650, #98 Consulate General Shanghai, FRUS (1950)6:263n9.

59. Ernest B. Price, Stanvac, Hong Kong, to Philip C. Jessup, March 5, 1950, Box 61: Prentice-Prasser 1953–48, Jessup Papers, LC.

60. However, an ex-president of the National Association of Manufacturers at a December 1949 panel discussion at the Congress of American Industry in New York saw no objection to doing business with the Chinese Communists if payment for delivered goods could be assured. *New York Times,* December 9, 1949, p. 27.

61. China Air Transport, for instance, refused CCP overtures to resume service. Whiting Willauer, partner to Claire Chennault in CAT, wrote his wife, Louise, that, "the only exception would be if the USA would virtually order us to go back in to keep from creating a vacuum for the Russians to fill. There would have to be quite some inducements even then." Letter, June 28, 1949, Folder: China 18A (1948–1950), Items: CAT-China (1), Willauer Papers. Willauer's anticommunism and critical opinion of American China policy were widely known.

62. See ch. 7.

63. 611.9331/9-1449, Memorandum of Conversation, Mr. Stefan, Republic Steel Corp., with C. T. White and S. C. Brown, Commercial Policy Division, State Department, RG 59, NA. American Express International Banking Corporation, Claim CN-0340, Final Decision August 20, 1970, FCSC. Re small-business protests, see for example: Frank E. Midkiff, Secretary, Community Affairs Division, Chamber of Commerce of Honolulu to President Truman, November 25, 1949, Folder: July–December 1949, Official File 150 (1947)-150 Misc (1948), Truman Papers, HST; Charles M. Skinner, C. M. Skinner Co., Minneapolis, Minn. to President Truman, December 2, 1949, *ibid.*; A. S. Gross, Master, The National Grange, Washington, D.C. to President Truman, January 5, 1950, *ibid.*

64. On poor treatment of American business in Eastern Europe, see 893.00/12-648, #A-294 Stuart, Nanking, RG 59, NA. Both OIR 4848 "Chinese Communist Commercial Policy," January 17, 1949, pp. 32–33, Reel 4, Pt. 3 China and India, OSS/State Department Reports, and 611.9331/3-1549, #415 Clubb, Peking, RG 59, NA, hold out expectations of better conditions in China because of the country's huge requirements. Ambassador Stuart put it succinctly: "Best hope protecting American interests lies in growth Communist recognition own needs for American goods and technical assistance. As these needs become more acute, Communist manner and policy toward Americans may be expected to improve." 893.01/5-2749, #1123 Stuart, Nanking, FRUS (1949)9:30.

65. Interview with Randall Gould, August 1976; John Leighton Stuart Diary,

Washington, D.C.; Interview with John M. Cabot, former Consul General in Shanghai, November 29, 1977 and John M. Cabot Diary, *passim*.

66. "Facts that Dim Forecast of Big Trade with China," p. 17; "The Dollar in Red China," pp. 64–67.

67. 611.9331/6-1049, L. P. Gainsborough, President, Login Corp. (export-import firm with extensive Far Eastern interests), San Francisco to James E. Webb, Undersecretary of State (wishes to trade but wants to conform to policy); 611.9331/6-2949, M. Miller, Cole Laboratories, Inc., Long Island City, New York to State Department, RG 59, NA; 611.9331/6-2749, Memorandum of Conversation, Mr. Sibbett, Van Nouhuys & Co., San Francisco with S. C. Brown, Commercial Policy Division, State Department, RG 59, NA (has contracted with several large firms interested in selling and installing complete plants in China); 611.9331/12-249, Memorandum of Telephone Conversation, Mr. Meininger, Ford Motor Co., with S. C. Brown, Commercial Policy Division, State Department, RG 59, NA; Shearman & Sterling & Wright to Elting Arnold, Acting Director, Foreign Assets Control, U.S. Treasury, January 3, 1956, First National City Bank, Claim no. CN-0440, Supporting Documentation, FCSC; Inquiry by Armco Steel Co. 611.9331/12-249, Memorandum of Conversation by Stephen C. Brown, Office of Chinese Affairs, State Department, FRUS (1949)9:971–73; Inquiry by U.S. Steel Export Co., 693.0031/7-649, Memorandum of Telephone Conversation, RG 59, NA. Harold M. Bixby, Pan American Vice President, for example, after recommending against continued operations in China, indicated his willingness to proceed if the government wanted Pan Am's assistance. He then traveled to Washington to discuss a CCP offer with State Department officials and subsequently instructed his subordinates not to conclude a deal because of Department objections. Leary, *Dragon's Wings*, pp. 217–19. Similarly, Northwest Airlines withdrew from negotiations with the CCP, which were aiming toward establishment of a domestic airline, at the State Department's request. Memorandum by State Department, Executive Secretary's Files: NSC 41/ 1, FRUS (1949)9:892. Petroleum companies agreed to restrict Chinese imports to civilian requirements but refused to go further unless the government restricted all exports to Communist China. The Secretary of State agreed to continued sales hoping to keep the CCP coming back for more. 693.119/4-2549, #841 Secretary to Cabot, Shanghai, FRUS (1949)9:937.

68. Paul S. Hopkins, Shanghai to K. R. MacKinnon, Ebasco International, New York, April 28, 1949, Box: 268-15, BCC; Tozer, "Last Bridge to China," p. 68.

69. Even before the war ended, interest in peacetime economic development of China was evidenced by the United States. John Loftus, special assistant to the Director of the Office of International Trade Policy in the State Department, wrote: "In China there are great possibilities. . . . Concession rights are being sought." "Petroleum in International Relations," *Department of State Bulletin* (August 5, 1945) vol. 13, cited in Michael Tanzer, *The Political Economy of International Oil and the Underdeveloped Countries*, pp. 52–53. Postwar expansion by Caltex in China was "spurred on by the military forces of the United States which . . . maintained large forces in the China theatre, and which relied upon . . . [Caltex] and another American oil company [Stanvac] for its principal supplies of petroleum produce." Caltex Claim, 1:6–7, FCSC. During 1946 the U.S. Army-Navy Petroleum Board helped American companies by providing transportation and

storage facilities to them. OIR 4217, "Estimate of the Petroleum Situation in China," May 7, 1947, p. 19, Reel 4, Pt. 3, OSS/State Department Reports. When in 1948 and 1949 it became necessary for the State Department to issue evacuation orders to Americans in China, it took care "not to suggest that key American personnel in commercial, industrial, religious and philanthropic enterprises should leave or that American citizens having substantial interests in China should abandon those interests." Executive Secretariat Files: NSC 34, Memo by Acting Secretary of State Robert A. Lovett to Executive Secretary of the NSC (Souers), January 12, 1949, FRUS (1949)9:1215; 611.9331/4-749 Memorandum of Conversation, RG 59, NA.

American businessmen in China, therefore, turned to the government expecting assistance as conditions in China worsened: "as individuals enmeshed in an increasingly difficult situation due to the actions of our government we feel we have the right to seek clarification of the government's attitude, especially as the majority of American businessmen were encouraged to remain at their posts by the Department and assured of its full support." Statement of the American Chamber of Commerce in Shanghai, August or September, 1949, Box A: 271-27, BCC.

70. 611.9331/2-1549, #A-125 Cabot, Shanghai, RG 59, NA. The UP dispatch mentioned in this telegram ran under the title "U.S. Merchants Get Ready for Trade with Red Regime," and was written February 9, 1949. It was carried by four Shanghai and one Nanking Chinese language newspaper. It also appeared as "Coast Will Trade with Reds in China," *New York Times*, February 10, 1949, p. 43. See also *San Francisco Chronicle*, June 15, 1949, Weekly Summary, June 16–22, 1949, p. 6; Erich Nielson, *San Francisco Chronicle*, November 6, 1949, Weekly Summary, November 10–16, 1949, pp. 7–8. Among the firms concerned were Connell Brothers, Getz Brothers and Frazar and Hansen; 893.01/12-2949, B. T. Rocca, President, Pacific Vegetable Oil Corporation, San Francisco to Secretary of State, RG 59, NA.

71. Resolutions favoring trade and diplomatic relations were sent to the White House by the San Francisco branch of the National Union Marine Cooks & Stewards, March 4, 1950 (adopted unanimously January 12, 1950) and by the Warehouse, Processing and Distribution Workers Union, Los Angeles Local, in April 1950. Other maritime unions agreed with this position—MCS, MEBA, MFCW, ILWU. See Folders July–December 1949 and Misc. 1950, Box 634, Official File 150 (1947)-150 Misc. (1948), Truman Papers, HST. The NUMCS leadership reportedly was Communist-dominated. See James R. Prickett, "Some Aspects of the Communist Controversy in the CIO," p. 300n2. The crew of the SS *Canada Mail*, American Mail Lines, also urged recognition in an April 15, 1949 resolution sent to Dean Acheson. They noted that jobs for seamen would be lost without the China trade. 893.01/4-1749 Letter Charles L. Wolf, Recording Secretary, SS *Canada Mail*, to Secretary Acheson, RG 59, NA.

72. Minutes of the Board of Directors Meeting, October 6, 1949, 17:158–59, Greater San Francisco Chamber of Commerce Collection, California Historical Society Archives, San Francisco, California.

73. The *Journal* editorial also pointed out that Communists do not learn good manners by being unrecognized. They would continue to do just as they pleased regardless of their international status. "To Recognize or Not," editorial *Wall Street Journal*, December 1, 1949, p. 8. "Clearly," the paper proclaimed at an earlier date "the Chinese Communists are the rulers of China. . . . To pretend

anything else is to refute reality." "Chinese Puzzle," editorial, *Wall Street Journal*, October 4, 1949, p. 6.

74. "International Outlook," *Business Week*, February 4, 1950, p. 96. See also "Asia Plan: Forget Formosa, Beef Up South," *Business Week*, January 14, 1950, pp. 101–2, and "International Outlook," *Business Week*, January 21, 1950, p. 115 and February 25, 1950, p. 127.

75. William Langhorne Bond to J. T. Towers, October 20, 1949, cited in Leary, *Dragon's Wings*, p. 219.

76. Memorandum of China Situation—Mid-October 1949, James A. MacKay, Vice President, National City Bank of New York, October 18, 1949, Box A: 271-27, BCC. MacKay's January comments were made at a metting of twenty representatives of American firms still maintaining interests in China. Minutes of the meetings are unavailable, but notes made by one participant indicate that MacKay and John Kopelman of SPC said that their firms would stay. Al Schumacher of Chase Bank, on the other hand, emphatically declared "that there was no future for any American banking business in China . . . and he was strongly recommending to his Board to close up shop in China, taking whatever loss is necessary . . . in order to get out." The notes further describe the other representatives at the meeting as divided. Kopelman, Vice President, to MacKinnon, January 9, 1950, Box A: 271-26, BCC. After CCP seizure of U.S. consulate property in Peking conditions deteriorated. SPC though still operational in June 1950 had largely been taken over by CCP authorities. Kopelman, Vice President, McQuiston, Minturn & Kelly, New York, June 8, 1950, Box A: 271-26, BCC.

77. Draft and Official Statements of George C. Cobean, Partner in Bulkley Dunton & Co., president Bulkley Dunton Paper Co., S.A., *America's Town Meeting of the Air*, December 6, 1949, File 81, Folder 78: Speech Material China, Styles Bridges Papers, New England College Library, Henniker, New Hampshire.

78. 893.01/10-2649 Johnson to Secretary, RG 59, NA; 811.503193/8-2449 Memorandum by Shaw, FRUS (1949)9:1312–16. Participating in this discussion along with representatives of IT&T, C. V. Starr, Chase National Bank, Caltex, National City Bank of New York, Stanvac, Bank of America, Anderson, Meyer & Co., American & Foreign Power, NFTC and the American Chamber of Commerce were members of the Department's Division of Chinese Affairs and Ambassador Stuart and Consul General Cabot, both of whom were newly returned from China. Cabot told the businessmen that although immediate prospects were bad largely because of the blockade, "The attitude of responsible party members . . . is believed to be one of wanting to use for their own purposes the business know-how of the foreign community . . . [and that therefore they] would extend to certain private foreign interests a definite role for a period of years in China's foreign economic development."

79. U.S. Department of State, *Round Table*, pp. 168, 331–39, 421–39. A business representative at the conference remarked to China consultant Raymond Fosdick that abandonment of American consulates in China amounted to a policy of "scuttle and run." 893.01/10-1849 Fosdick to Jessup, RG 59, NA.

80. Re request for naval protection #939 Acheson to Hong Kong, September 16, 1949, transmitting September 14 telegram from Isbrandtsen Co., NYC. The request was refused in reply September 14, 1949, Hong Kong Files, 350 Misc-Political, RG 84, WNRC. See also *New York Times*, October 2, 1949, p. 13; 893.801/

9-2149, Hans J. Isbrandtsen to Dean Acheson, RG 59, NA. On October 5, 1949, the Shanghai American Chamber of Commerce protested to the State Department the lack of protection being provided United States shipping to and from Shanghai. *New York Times*, October 6, 1949, p. 10.

81. Quotes taken from Memorandum of Explanation of Lapham's September 8, 1949 Commonwealth Club of Northern California Speech "The Chinese Situation As I Saw It," December 28, 1949, Box 3, Personal Files, John D. Sumner Papers, HST. For text of Commonwealth Club Speech see #13589, Greater San Francisco Chamber of Commerce Collection, California Historical Society Archives. The previously mentioned resolution adopted by the San Francisco Chamber favoring recognition was based on Lapham's speech. Re suggestion that ECA aid be continued to Communist territories see #449, November 26, 1948 Lapham, Shanghai to ECA Administrator, Washington, D.C., PSF, Subject Files—Foreign Affairs, Box 173 (China–1), Folder: 1948, Truman Papers, HST. President Truman, on January 14, 1949 ordered all ECA assistance halted as soon as an area fell under CCP control. FRUS (1949)9:610, 614–15. Re Lapham not advocating recognition after the January seizure of property in Peking: Substance of a Talk on China and the Far East made by Roger D. Lapham before the Northwest Group of the IPR. March 6, 1950, Box 3 Personal Files, Sumner Papers, HST.

82. Lapham Talk before the Northwest Group of the IPR, March 6, 1950, Box 3 Personal Files, Sumner Papers, HST; *Farmer Reporter*, February 1950, Weekly Summary, February 9–15, 1950; *Export Trading Shipper*, May 8, 1950, Weekly Summary, May 18–24, 1950; *New York Times*, May 15, 1950, Weekly Summary, May 11–17, 1950; *Report of the 37th National Foreign Trade Convention*, pp. 207–11.

83. Letter John Ahlers, former Vice President and Treasurer, C. V. Starr & Company, Inc., New York, to the author, January 28, 1977; Interview with Peter Hopkins, July 11, 1977.

84. 893.00/12-548, #227 Paddocks, Dairen, RG 59, NA. The USSR had been predicting United States economic collapse since the end of the war. 611.9331/8-849, #1317 Clubb, Peking, RG 59, NA.

8. JOURNALISTS

1. Mordechai Rozanski, "The Role of American Journalists in Chinese-American Relations, 1900–1925," (Ph.D. diss.), pp. 1–2, 191–92 (quote), 359–78. Rozanski ably describes the intricate and the sometimes unsavory activities of American journalists in early twentieth century China.

2. Re journalists as the forerunners of imperialism see Yang Shou-jen, "Hsin Hu-nan," in Chang Nan and Wang Jen-chih, eds., *Hsin-hai ko-ming ch'ien-shih-nien chien shih-lun hsuan-chi* ["New Hunan," Selections of topical articles from the decade preceding the 1911 revolution] (Peking, 1960–63), cited by Rozanski. Re the activities of one of America's most controversial China adventurers, see Warren Cohen's delightful account of George Sokolsky in *The Chinese Connection*, pp. 72–87, 91–291.

3. Eastman, *Abortive Revolution*, p. 27, and J. J. Timperley, "Makers of Public Opinion About the Far East," pp. 223–25. The regulations governing issuance

of registration certificates to foreign newspaper reporters were promulgated by the Foreign Affairs Ministry on March 3, 1933.

4. On the Sian incident and the united front, see Schram, *Mao Tse-tung*, pp. 192–200, and Lyman P. Van Slyke, *Enemies and Friends, passim*. Examples of laudatory Chiang Kai-shek literature of the 1930s and early 1940s abound. Among the most telling are the writings of Edgar Snow who would later reject "weak China's strong man." In 1938, even after his exposure to Mao Tse-tung and Yenan, Snow considered Chiang's "leadership secure, dynamic, and progressive, his personal courage great, and the benevolent influence of his wife very strong." But as China's continued weakness in the postwar period encouraged the United States to look to Japan as an ally, Snow denounced Chiang and became "Mao's Mr. America." For Snow's pro-Chiang essays see "Weak China's Strong Man," pp. 402–8; "China's Fighting Generalissimo," pp. 612–25. See also Jerry Israel, "Mao's Mr. America," pp. 116–17.

5. A. T. Steele, *The American People and China*, p. 23.

6. "Scope and Operation of Censorship in China," R&A 2336S, January 19, 1945, p. 1, Reel 2, Pt. 3, OSS/State Department Reports.

7. Koen, *The China Lobby*, p. 118.

8. Before visiting CCP territory, Snow had acquired a modest fluency in Chinese and become acquainted with such prominent people as Mme. Sun Yat-sen. In 1932 he reported the Japanese attack on Shanghai and in 1935, while teaching at Yenching University, familiarized himself with the Chinese student movement against Japanese aggression. *Red Star Over China* communicated his great sympathy with China's problems and enthusiasm for possible solutions through an inspiring characterization of the Chinese Communists he met. At the same time, Snow pointed to their Soviet ties and never attempted to disguise their dedication to communism. In its first edition the book sold 15,000 copies. John K. Fairbank, Introduction, to *Red Star Over China*; Shewmaker, *Americans and Chinese Communists*, pp. 54–58; Israel, "Mao's Mr. America," pp. 107–22.

9. Shewmaker, *Americans and Chinese Communists*, pp. 265–329; Steele, *American People and China*, pp. 23–27; Schram, *Mao Tse-tung*, pp. 226–27. Examples of the literature sympathetic to the CCP include: Theodore White and Annalee Jacoby, *Thunder Out of China*; Agnes Smedley, *Battle Hymn of China*; Guenther Stein, *The Challenge of Red China*. Examples of literature critical of the KMT include: Pearl Buck, "A Warning About China," pp. 53–56; E. O. Hauser, "China Needs a Friendly Nudge," pp. 28–29. Re KMT Confucian-fascist leanings, see Chiang Kai-shek, *China's Destiny*, and Eastman, *Abortive Revolution, passim*.

10. Theodore White, *In Search of History*, pp. 182–83.

11. Schram, *Mao Tse-tung*, p. 226; Robert G. Sutter, *China-Watch*, pp. 12–13.

12. Tang Tsou cites these comments by the *New York Times* and Harrison Forman in his extended examination of the American image of Chinese Communism. Tsou, *America's Failure*, pp. 176–236. The *New York Times* quote comes originally from "The Chinese Crisis," November 1, 1944, p. 22, and the declaration by Forman was taken from his *Report From Red China*, p. 177. Tang Tsou's discussion, considered "perceptive" by some, also has been criticized by Shewmaker and Schram for its "sharp and partly gratuitous personal attacks on some of the journalists and diplomats who shaped the American image of China in the 1930s and 1940s." Schram, *Mao Tse-tung*, p. 226n (quote) and Shewmaker, *Americans and Chinese Communists*, pp. 297–98. Harrison Forman was not a novice on the China scene. Beginning in 1930 he spent much of his time in China and

contributed to publications such as *Collier's, Life, Harper's,* and the *New York Herald Tribune.* See Overseas Press Club of America: *Who's Who in Foreign Correspondence, 1950–51* (New York, 1952). Similar misconceptions about the CCP were shared by the midwestern Republican isolationist press. In an editorial on November 4, 1945 the *Chicago Sunday Tribune* called them "the Chinese equivalent of Iowa farmers," pt 1, p. 20. See Morton Gordon, "The American Press and Recent China Policy, 1941–1949," (Masters thesis), pp. 1–46, 67–83, 91–102.

13. The *New York Times* acknowledged its error September 17, 1946 in "Topics of the Times," p. 6.

14. Interview with Randall Gould, August 1976; White, *In Search,* p. 73; Interview with Henry R. Lieberman, *New York Times,* January 15, 1979. Chiang himself disliked and distrusted English-speaking, Western-educated Chinese, especially T. V. Soong. Comments by Owen Lattimore at luncheon meeting, March 30, 1979, Columbia University, East Asian Institute.

15. Re search for a third road: Tom Englehardt, "Long Day's Journey," pp. 101–04.

16. Although Henry Lieberman wrote that there was no censorship, other evidence indicates quite the contrary. The *Shanghai Evening Post & Mercury* apologized to its readers for a patchy appearance brought on by unpredictable and unreasonable official cutting exercises. Henry R. Lieberman, "The Correspondent Versus the News in China," p. 11. "It Isn't the Heat—It's the Censorship," *Shanghai Evening Post & Mercury,* May 21, 1949, p. 1; Box 4, Randall Gould Papers, Hoover; Interview with Randall Gould August 1976; Landman and Landman, *Profile,* p. 15; *New York Times,* April 26, 1949, p. 3.

17. Lieberman, "The Correspondent," pp. 11, 69–72; Steele, *American People and China,* p. 45.

18. Englehardt, "Long Day's Journey," pp. 98–99; Landman and Landman, *Profile,* pp. 4–7. Re question of objectivity Bernard C. Cohen maintains that "policy advocacy takes place in the news columns of the press [as well as on the editorial page]. . . . Despite some apparent belief that this practice has been engaged in only by the McCormicks and the Hearsts, it is a more general phenomenon, pursued regularly by the more independent reporters and analysts, and, at times when the issues at stake seem very great, by a majority of the foreign affairs correspondents. . . . This is by no means a minority viewpoint; foreign affairs correspondents generally perceive and accept this role for the press, even when they do not define their own efforts in these terms." Cohen, *The Press* and *Foreign Policy,* pp. 37–39.

19. Topping, *Journey,* p. 28.

20. Jack Belden recounted his experiences in *China Shakes the World.* Before his Chinese civil war assignment, Belden had been a correspondent in wartime Burma, North Africa and China.

21. Interview with Henry R. Lieberman, January 15, 1979.

22. 893.00/1-449, #A-1096 Cabot, Shanghai, RG 59, NA.

23. Topping, *Journey,* pp. 28–43.

24. On American journalists thought to be spies: Roth, "Peiping's New Look," p. 274; "Chinese Communists and the Foreign Press," p. 788. Topping assured his CCP contact that he was not afraid of danger but was told: "You don't care, but we do care about you passing through there." Topping, *Journey,* p. 42; Roth, "China and the 'Foreign Devils,'" p. 296.

25. Fan Cheng-ching of the Shanghai Cultural Control Committee made the CCP viewpoint clear in a speech June 23, 1949. Dismissing the possibility of impartial reporting he said, "We allow freedom of the press to those who serve the interests of the people and won't allow freedom of the press to those who don't serve this interest." Thomas L. Kennedy, "The Treatment of Americans in Red China Prior to the Korean War: A Study of Selected Cases," (masters thesis), p. 151. See also *Chieh-fang jih-pao* [Liberation Daily], editorial, July 12, 1949, cited by Landman and Landman, *Profile*, p. 92; A. Doak Barnett, *China on the Eve of Communist Takeover*, p. 352.

26. 893.00/12-3148, #A-321, Stuart, Nanking, RG 59, NA.

27. The two reporters were Spencer Moosa of AP and Michael Keon of UP. Although accused of American imperialistic activity, neither man was an American. Keon was Australian, Moosa British. 893.00/2-1149, #368 Stuart, Nanking, RG 59, NA; "Press Freedom in Red China Looks Unlikely," *North China Daily News*, February 12, 1949, p. 3, Reel #291 (hereafter NCDN); Roth, "Peiping's New Look," p. 275; Barnett, *On the Eve*, pp. 342, 352.

28. A. Doak Barnett, *Chicago Daily News*, February 17, 1949, Weekly Summary February 17–23, 1949.

29. "Peiping Foreign Newspapermen Silenced," North Shensi radio, New China News Agency in English morse code to North America, February 27, 1949, section: Far East, Communist-controlled China, February 28, 1949, p. CCC-1, FBIS; #315, Clubb, Peking, February 27, 1949, Box 2315: Tsingtao, File 350: Correspondence, China Post Files, RG 84, WNRC; Fred Hampson, "China Reds Gag Reporters," p. 1; Jean Lyon, "When the Communists Entered Peking," pp. 80–81; Joint Weeka #7, from State, Army, Navy, Air (SANA) Nanking, March 4, 1949, p. 5, file 350.2: Joint Weeka Reports, Consul General Hong Kong, RG 84, WNRC; Barnett, *On the Eve*, p. 338. Not all of the seventeen were Americans or employed by American publications: A. Doak Barnett (*Chicago Daily News*), Walter Bosshardt (*New Zurich Times*), James Burke (*Time, Life, Liberty*), Chang Lin (Agence France Presse), Hetta Empson (*London Observer*), Alfred Harding (*Hartford Times*), William Hogan (Catholic News Service), Michael Keon (UP), W. Lewisohn (*London Times*), Jean Lyon (*New York Times*, North American Newspaper Alliance), Spencer Moosa (AP), E. Nystrom (*Stockholm Daily*), Frank Robertson (*Daily Mail, Christian Science Monitor, New York Star*), Andrew Roth (*Nation, Star Weekly*—Canada), Mrs. F. Roth (*Rotterdam General Daily*), A. T. Steele (*New York Herald Tribune*) and John Vincent (Kemsley newspapers).

30. Pledges such as those made in an off-the-record interview of a Chinese Communist spokesman in Hong Kong by a Reuters correspondent, November 29, 1948. 893.00/1-349, #A-1096 Cabot, Shanghai, RG 59, NA. Re Shanghai: Fred Hampson, "Reds Make Good Deal in China," p. 6. Conditions tended to be more difficult in Peking and Nanking than in Shanghai, where the majority of foreign newsmen congregated. In May, 1949 Nanking reporters found that their stories had to be sent to Shanghai by mail or courier for transmission abroad because local telegraph offices would not accept them. Henry R. Lieberman, "China's Reds Scoff at Objective Press," p. 13.

31. 893.83/6-2449, #2470 Cabot, Shanghai, RG 59, NA; "Foreign Papers Have Become Hotbed of Rumors, Readers Should Be Specially Guarded Against Them," *Wen Hui Pao* (connected with the Democratic League), Shanghai, June 21, 1949, Box 4, Gould Papers, Hoover.

32. Gould's controversial story referred to labor troubles at the *Post* as "sud-

den, without warning and in the management's view without provocation." Randall Gould, "If You Fight You May Get Hit," preliminary draft of a report to C. V. Starr, Gould Papers, Box 4, Hoover; Randall Gould to Benjamin Mandel, Research Director, U.S. Senate Committee on the Judiciary, August 23, 1954, Gould Papers, Box 1: Correspondence, Hoover; "Lock-ins, Gould Says, Paved Way for Control of Shanghai by Reds," *Overseas Press Club Bulletin*, January 28, 1950, p. 5, Gould Papers, Box 4, Hoover; Interview with Randall Gould, August 1976.

33. "Reds Censor Press Cables in Shanghai," *Denver Post*, Shanghai AP dispatch, July 17, 1949, p. 16.

34. Fred Hampson, "Shanghai Reds List Censorship Controls," p. 3; Henry R. Lieberman, "Shanghai Censors Foreign Newsmen," p. 39; Interview with Walter Sullivan, *New York Times*, February 2, 1979.

35. Landman and Landman, *Profile*, p. 94; "Chinese Communists and the Foreign Press," *The Economist*, p. 788.

36. *Ibid.*, pp. 788, 790; Interview with Walter Sullivan, February 2, 1979.

37. The reporters involved were Robert P. (Pepper) Martin (*New York Post*, CBS), Amos Landman (NBC, freelance), Julian Schuman (ABC, *Chicago Sun-Times*) and Lynn Chase (freelance, and Landman's wife). They spoke to Gould on June 26, 1949 and were turned down. The left-leaning editor of the *China Weekly Review*, J. B. Powell, made a similar offer on June 29 and was also refused. Gould, "If You Fight,", pp. 39–46. Even before Gould's confrontation with the workers, some correspondents told John M. Cabot that the *Post*'s editorial comments were "unduly hasty and flip." John M. Cabot Diary, June 7, 1949, Washington, D.C.

38. Topping, *Journey*, p. 105.

39. Lieberman, "China's Reds Scoff," p. 13; Barnett, *On the Eve*, p. 355.

40. The Foreign Service Institute stressed the utility of contacts with journalists in the field. Gregory Prince, "The American Foreign Service in China" (Ph.D. diss.), p. 40n35.

41. Few could speak more than a simple conversational Chinese. Re language and other problems: Christopher Rand, "Reporting in the Far East," p. 309. Henry R. Lieberman, among the most respected of the China newsmen, contended that "despite the difficulties of covering China, it is still possible to get a reasonably accurate picture of what is happening." Lieberman, "The Correspondent," p. 72. Lieberman himself spoke conversational Chinese. Interview with Henry R. Lieberman, January 15, 1979.

42. Prince, "American Foreign Service," pp. 76–78. Although more mobility was introduced with the war, foreign service officers still lacked the reporter's freedom to travel. Interview with John Melby, March 26, 1977. The Chinese countryside intimidated many journalists who preferred to remain in relatively comfortable Shanghai. Those who ventured forth included Tillman Durdin and Henry R. Lieberman (*New York Times*), Seymour Topping (AP), A. T. Steele and Christopher Rand (*New York Herald Tribune*), Robert "Pepper" Martin (*U.S. News and World Report*) and Jack Belden (INS). Interview with Dorothy Borg, January 15, 1979; Interview with Henry R. Lieberman, January 15, 1979; Englehardt, "Long Day's Journey," pp. 93–94.

43. John Melby recalled: "When you were talking with a man like Till Durdin of the *New York Times* or Art Steele of the *Herald Tribune*, you knew you were dealing with men who knew China. They probably knew China better than some

of us did." Interview with John Melby, March 26, 1977; Cabot Diary, *passim.* 693.0031/3-1949, #72 Paxton, Tihwa, RG 59, NA, notifies the Department that Paxton has been working in close cooperation with Walter Sullivan of the *New York Times;* 893.00/2-1749, #A-27 Stuart, Nanking, RG 59, NA; Cohen, *Press and Foreign Policy,* p. 144; Interview with Walter Sullivan, February 8, 1979.

44. Although I have not uncovered any evidence of an official intelligence agency connection with the American press in China, journalists have been alleged to have cooperated with the CIA in Japan. CIA sources told Watergate reporter Carl Bernstein in 1977 that "the Company" had worked with several *Newsweek* people. *New York Times* investigations turned up at least four CIA employees at *Newsweek*'s Tokyo bureau during the 1950s. Malcolm Muir, *Newsweek*'s publisher until 1961, admitted that Harry F. Kern, the magazine's foreign affairs editor, met regularly with CIA contacts and Kern himself added "We thought it was admirable at the time." Howard Schonberger, "Of Arms and Men," paper presented at the New England Conference of the Association for Asian Studies, October 21, 1979.

45. Acheson felt that the integrity and intelligence of columnists was unreliable and the experience of most reporters was insufficient to understand international affairs. Nevertheless he asserted that his relations with newsmen— not columnists—were quite good. Moreover, he did conduct private sessions with correspondents not just to explain Department policies but also to hear their views. Princeton Seminar Transcripts, July 2, 1953, p. 10, July 16, 1953, pp. 15–17, July 23, 1953, p. 19, Papers of Dean Acheson, HST.

46. Memorandum Livingston Merchant (FE) to Philip C. Jessup (S/A), July 1950, and Memorandum of Conversation, Livingston Merchant (FE) to Dean Rusk (FE), October 7, 1950, folder: Ranshofer-Ravenholt 1953-48, Box 61, Philip C. Jessup Papers, LC. Butterworth wrote A. T. Steele: "Feel I must let you know how important and significant your post-Peking dispatches have been. Needless say would welcome any personal suggestions or observations you may wish to forward through same channel." #320, May 14, 1944, File 350: Miscellaneous-Political, Hong Kong, RG 84, WNRC.

47. Harrison Forman to Philip C. Jessup, November 30, 1949, Folder: Forman-Fauler 1953–48, Box 56: General Correspondence 1919–59 and Philip C. Jessup to Tillman Durdin, July 11, 1949, Folder: Chronological File, July 1949, Box 48: General Correspondence 1919–58, Jessup Papers, LC. (The subject referred to in the second item cited here may not have been China, but Jessup does thank Durdin for "various suggestions" which have been "enormously helpful.")

48. Joseph Alsop, who was feuding with his one-time friend Dean Acheson, maintained, "In the State Department, Dean has let it be known that he cares more about official discretion, than about informing the public. Hence all men on the working level, who were formerly eager to brief responsible newspapermen about important situations, now fear to talk with any freedom or confidence to the press." Joseph Alsop to Felix Frankfurter, Justice, U.S. Supreme Court, n.d., Folder: January–February 1950, Box 5: General Correspondence, Joseph and Stewart Alsop Papers, LC; Cohen, *The Press and Foreign Policy,* pp. 78–79; William O. Chittick, "The Domestic Information Activities of the Department of State" (Ph.D. diss.), pp. 131–33.

49. 761.93/4-3049 Office Memo Butterworth (FE) to Rusk (G), Webb (U) and Acheson (S), RG 59, NA. Similarly John Davies wrote to Philip Sprouse, George Kennan and Mr. Fisher: "I am much impressed by a point made by A. T. Steel

[*sic*] in his excellent dispatch to the Herald Tribune, published April 25." 893.00/ 4-2649 Memorandum John Davies Jr. (Policy Planning Staff) to Philip Sprouse (CA), George Kennan (Director PPS) and Fisher (FE), RG 59, NA.

50. Cohen, *The Press and Foreign Policy*, p. 141; Richard Aliano, *American Defense Policy from Eisenhower to Kennedy*, p. 148.

51. Bernard C. Cohen, *The Public's Impact on Foreign Policy*, p. 107. The *New York Times, Washington Post, New York Herald Tribune, Wall Street Journal, Christian Science Monitor, Baltimore Sun* and *Washington Evening Star*, because they reached officials on the day of publication and covered foreign affairs in detail, were read for information and analysis. Regional papers including the *St. Louis Post-Dispatch, Louisville Courier-Journal, Milwaukee Journal* and *Minneapolis Tribune* were, in contrast, read primarily for opinion and comment. Cohen, *The Press and Foreign Policy*, pp. 139, 209–10, 221, 233. Some 63% of government information officers, interviewed in a study conducted by Dan D. Nimmo, said they used editorials as sources of public opinion. *Newsgathering in Washington*, p. 187.

52. The "Weekly Summary of Comment on China," which originated with the Office of War Information's wartime service to United States Information Service officers in China, provided domestic and foreign information and policy officers of the State Department with a regular digest of opinion on China in the postwar period. Among the Department personnel who were known to see the summaries were Ambassador-at-Large Philip C. Jessup, Assistant Chief of Chinese Affairs Fulton Freeman, and the Director of the Division of Chinese Affairs, W. Walton Butterworth. It was not clear to Bureau members whether the Secretary or the Undersecretary of State saw their material on a regular basis. Memorandum S. Shepard Jones (PS) to Player (P), December 13, 1949, Folder: China, 1949–52, Box 33, Office of Public Opinion Studies, 1943–65, RG 59, NA; "Opinion Resources of the Public Opinion Studies Staff," Department of State, Bureau of Public Affairs, January 1963, cited by John H. Hedley, "The Truman Administration and the 'Loss' of China" (Ph.D. diss.), pp. 122–24; H. Schuyler Foster to me, February 24, 1979.

53. Quoted in William L. Rivers, *The Opinionmakers*, p. 17. The clipping files in almost any Congressman's papers substantiate this point. For a convincing example see the mammoth scrapbook collection deposited as part of the Patrick McCarran Papers, Holy Names College, Oakland, California.

54. Cohen, *The Press and Foreign Policy*, pp. 215–16. Raymond P. Brandt, chief of the Washington bureau of the *St. Louis Post-Dispatch* from 1934 to 1961, for example, maintained that smart Senators cultivated close relations with Senate reporters. Raymond P. Brandt Oral History Interview, p. 28, September 28, 1970, Oral History Collection, HST.

55. James Reston, *The Artillery of the Press*, p. 63.

56. Aliano, *American Defense Policy*, pp. 148–49. An estimate of the significance which Senators and Representatives accorded news commentators can be made from the volume of their writings inserted into the *Congressional Record*.

57. Harry S Truman, *Memoirs*, 2:176; Herbert L. Williams, "Truman and the Press" (Ph.D. diss.), pp. 246, 347–48, 359–73, 418.

58. Williams, "Truman," pp. 436–37; Truman, *Memoirs*, 2:427.

59. Harry S Truman to Claude Bowers, American Embassy, Santiago, Chile, December 1, 1948, cited by Williams, "Truman," p. 87; Randall L. Murray, "Harry S Truman and Press Opinion, (Ph.D. diss.), pp. 51, 64–65n42. A similar

impression was noted by Arthur Krock in "The President: A New Portrait," p. 48.

60. Truman told Arthur Krock that he enjoyed reading the editorials in the *New York Times, Baltimore Sun, Washington Star,* and the *Washington Post.* Harry S Truman to Arthur Krock, October 10, 1949, cited by Williams, "Truman," p. 419.

61. Truman was known to have read the *Times, Herald Tribune, Star, Sun, St. Louis Post-Dispatch, Kansas City Star,* and the *Chicago Tribune* regularly. The daily clipping digest which had been prepared for Roosevelt was discontinued by Truman in July 1947. There is, however, some evidence in the files of George Elsey, Administrative Assistant to the President, that press opinion summaries prepared by the Bureau of Public Opinion Studies did reach the White House. These summaries also would have been President Truman's prime access to news magazines and radio commentators, for he did not otherwise read or listen to them. Among Truman's friends in the press corps were Joseph Short (*Baltimore Sun*), Eddie Folliard (*Washington Post*), Tony Vaccaro (AP), and Raymond "Pete" Brandt (*St. Louis Post-Dispatch*). Murray, "Truman and Press Opinion," pp. 41–48, 53–66, 235–37, 415; Williams, "Truman," p. 28; Brandt Oral History, p. 16; Jack L. Bell Oral History Interview, January 12, 1971, p. 1, HST; George Elsey Papers, Box 59, Folder: Foreign Affairs—China, HST.

62. Aliano, *American Defense Policy,* pp. 149, 167.

63. Harry S Truman to Burton K. Wheeler, January 7, 1948, cited by Williams, "Truman," p. 63; Merle Miller, *Plain Speaking,* pp. 37–38. Truman, *Memoirs,* 2:176.

64. "Recent Opinion Regarding the Effect of the 'Loss' of China on U.S. Foreign Policy," Special Report on American Opinion, April 22, 1949, and "American Public Discussion and Opinion on U.S. Relations with China and Neighboring Countries," September 26, 1949, and "U.S. Attitudes on Recognition of the Communist Regime in China," Special Report on American Opinion, November 30, 1949, Office of Public Opinion Studies 1943–65, RG 59, NA.

65. Gordon, "The American Press and Recent China Policy," pp. 38–66; "The Secretary of State," *New York Herald Tribune,* January 8, 1947, p. 26.

66. Editorial, *New Orleans Item,* January 3, 1949, and Introduction to Summary, Weekly Summary, December 30, 1948–January 5, 1949; American Opinion Report, December 23, 1948, RG 59, NA.

67. Editorial, Scripps-Howard Newspapers, and Jack Beall, ABC, January 22, 1949, Weekly Summary, January 20–26, 1949.

68. Allen Raymond, dispatch from Nanking, *New York Herald Tribune,* January 23, 1949, Weekly Summary, January 20–26, 1949.

69. "Chiang Kai-shek Returns," editorial, *St. Louis Post-Dispatch,* April 28, 1949, p. 2B. For similar sentiments see "Chiang and Confusion," editorial, *Denver Post,* February 21, 1949, p. 10.

70. Jack Bell, *Miami Herald,* November 28, 1948, Tom Connally Papers, Box 227, folder: S.1063 McCarran, LC.

71. "Bullitt's Amazing Proposals," editorial, *St. Louis Post-Dispatch,* January 8, 1949, p. 9A. The Bureau of Public Opinion Studies noted that Bullitt's idea was received with coolness from radio and press commentators including: *Washington Star* (January 9, 1949), *San Francisco Chronicle* (January 10, 1949), *Chicago News* (January 12, 1949), and *Philadelphia Inquirer* (January 8, 1949). William C.

Bullitt's recommendation came as part of a report he wrote as a consultant to the Congressional Joint Committee on Foreign Economic Cooperation in December 1948. He based his argument on the fact that: "There is not a single Government general who has the military training and technical skill to handle the over-all problems of logistics involved in meeting the attack of a Communist army of more than 2,000,000 men." Report by Consultant William C. Bullitt to the Joint Committee on Foreign Economic Cooperation Concerning China, 80th Cong., 2d sess., December 24, 1948, p. 12, cited by Tsou, *America's Failure*, 2:491.

72. "More Aid to What China?" editorial, *St. Louis Post-Dispatch*, March 12, 1949, p. 4A; "Politicking with China Policy," *ibid.*, April 1, 1949, p. 2C; "The Old Cry," editorial, *Denver Post*, March 19, 1949, p. 10; editorial, *Kansas City Star*, April 27, 1949; editorial, *Des Moines Register*, April 26, 1949; and William Henry Chamberlain in the *Wall Street Journal*, May 4, 1949, Weekly Summary, April 28–May 4, 1949.

73. Elmer Davis, ABC, May 3, 1949, Weekly Summary, April 28–May 4, 1949; Introduction to Weekly Summary, March 10–16, 1949; *Chicago Tribune*, September 19, 1949, Weekly Summary, September 15–21, 1949.

74. Introduction to Weekly Summary, April 14–20, 1949.

75. George Sokolsky, "Conquest by Fear," editorial, *New York Daily Mirror*, April 23, 1949, folder: *New York Daily Mirror*, January 1, 1948–December 31, 1949 editorials, Scrapbooks, George Sokolsky Papers, Butler Library Manuscript Division, Columbia University; editorial, *New York Times*, April 16, 1949, p. 14; see also Weekly Summaries, April 14–20, 1949, and April 28–May 4, 1949.

76. Editorial, *Louisville Courier-Journal*, April 16, 1949, Weekly Summary, April 14–20, 1949.

77. Eric Sevareid, CBS, May 4, 1949, Weekly Summary, May 5–11, 1949, and other continuing opposition to aid proposals: Walter Lippmann and the *Chicago Tribune*, September 19, 1949, and *Milwaukee Journal*, September 16, 1949, Weekly Summary, September 15–21, 1949; "Popular Attitudes Toward U.S. Aid to China," Special Report on American Opinion, June 23, 1949, RG 59, NA.

78. Introduction to Weekly Summary, May 5–11, 1949; Special Report on American Opinion, April 22, 1949, RG 59, NA.

79. Editorial, *Boston Herald*, June 13, 1949; Weekly Summary, June 9–15, 1949 and editorial, *Baltimore Sun*, May 6, 1949, Weekly Summary, May 5–11, 1949.

80. Westmore Wilcox, New York City, to editor, *New York Herald Tribune*, June 14, 1949, refers to column by Stewart Alsop in June 10 edition. Folder: "Matter of Fact Column"—with readers W-Y, 1946–56, Box 23: Special Correspondence, Alsop Papers, LC; column, Stewart Alsop, June 6, 1949, Weekly Summary, June 2–8, 1949.

81. Hallett Abend and Ferdinand Mayer, "Wanted: A New China Policy!" p. 6.

82. Clyde Farnsworth, Scripps-Howard, July 9, 1949, Weekly Summary, July 7–13, 1949, and David Sentner, *Baltimore News-Post*, Weekly Summary, September 8–14, 1949 and Weekly Summaries for 1949, *passim*; 026 China/8-849, Daily Summary of Opinion Developments, no. 1178, August 6–8, 1949, RG 59, NA; 026 China/8-1949, Memorandum for the President, Public and Congressional Reaction to the White Paper on China, RG 59, NA.

83. Daily Summary, no. 1178, August 6–8, 1949, RG 59, NA; 026 China/8-1949 Memo, RG 59, NA.

84. Walter Briggs, *New Republic*, February 21, 1949, Weekly Summary, February 17–23, 1949.

85. Weekly Summary, December 30, 1948–January 5, 1949, January 27–February 2, 1949, and April 21–27, 1949; "Recent Opinion Regarding the Effect of the 'Loss' of China on U.S. Foreign Policy," p. 5. *U.S. News and World Report* has been considered by at least one observer as a magazine "consistent in . . . support of Chiang." Koen, *China Lobby*, p. 50.

86. J. N. Robert, AP, January 5, 1949, Weekly Summary, February 3–9, 1949, and Joseph Phillips, *Newsweek*, May 16, 1949, Weekly Summary, May 12–18, 1949.

87. Edgar Snow and editorial, *Saturday Evening Post*, April 2, 1949, Weekly Summary, March 31–April 6, 1949. Koen also lists the SEP as a pro-Nationalist publication after 1947. *China Lobby*, p. 50.

88. "Mao Again On Record," editorial, *New York Times*, July 2, 1949.

89. "Chiang Steps Down," p. 116.

90. Editorial, *Washington Post*, August 2, 1949, p. 10.

91. Editorial, *Minneapolis Star*, May 31, 1949, Weekly Summary, June 9–15, 1949.

92. Editorial, *New Republic*, December 12, 1949, Weekly Summary, December 8–14, 1949.

93. Special Report on American Opinion, November 30, 1949, RG 59, NA.

94. Special Report on American Opinion, November 30, 1949, RG 59, NA; *New York Times*, November 11, 1949, p. 24.

95. *New York World Telegram* editorials and news coverage on the Ward incident ran in the following issues: November 11, 1949, p. 18; November 12, 1949, p. 14; November 14, 1949, p. 1; November 15, 1949, p. 22; November 16, 1949, p. 1; and November 17, 1949, pp. 1 and 30. The *Washington News*, also a Scripps-Howard paper, proposed a naval blockade of Manchuria and North China, November 12, 1949, Weekly Summary, November 10–16, 1949. The readership of Scripps-Howard publications numbered 2.5 million. The Hearst papers (4.6 million) and the McCormick-Paterson chain (3.5 million) also focused on the Ward case. Thus some 10.6 million readers were potentially exposed to the anti-Chinese Communist, anti-State Department criticism made possible by this incident. Introduction to Weekly Summaries, November 10–16, November 17–23, 1949. There is, of course, debate among analysts on the question of what percentage of newspaper readers actually do read the editorials. A study conducted during the period under consideration here ascertained that more than one third of all male and one quarter of all female readers do, in fact, read the editorials in newspapers. The Continuing Study of Newspaper Reading, no. 138, Study Summary, New York, Advertising Research Foundation, Inc., 1951, which was corroborated in a later study: Chilton R. Bush (comp), *News Research for Better Newspapers*, 5 vols (New York: American Newspaper Publishers Association Foundation, 1966–71), cited by Murray, "Truman and Press Opinion," p. 15.

96. Introduction to Weekly Summary, November 17–23, 1949.

97. Barnett Nover, "Red China Dilemma," editorial, *Denver Post*, June 28, 1949, p. 10; Hedley, "Truman Administration," pp. 156–57; "A Moral Chinese Policy," editorial, *St. Louis Post-Dispatch*, June 27, 1949, p. 2B.

98. Edward R. Murrow, CBS, November 29, 1949, Weekly Summary, November 24–30, 1949.

99. "A New Policy for Asia," editorial, pp. 5–6.

100. "China's Recognition," editorial, p. 483.

101. Column, Walter Lippmann, January 2, 1950, Weekly Summary, December 28–January 4, 1950.

102. Special Report on American Opinion, November 30, 1949, RG 59, NA.

103. Daily Summary of Opinion Developments, no. 1280, January 6, 1950, and no. 1281, January 9, 1950. Elsey Files, HST.

104. "A Summary of Current American Attitudes on U.S. Policy Toward the Far East," Special Report on American Opinion, February 13, 1950, Office of Public Opinion Studies 1943–65, RG 59, NA; Daily Summary of Opinion Developments, no. 1284, January 12, 1950, Truman Papers, George M. Elsey Files, Box 59: Subject File (Foreign Relations, C–M), folder: Foreign Affairs—China, HST.

105. Special Report on American Opinion, February 13, 1950, RG 59, NA.

106. Daily Summary, no. 1281, January 9, 1950, Elsey Files, HST; Ronald Steel, *Walter Lippmann and the American Century*, pp. 466–67.

9. THE PUBLIC, CONGRESS, SCHOLARS

1. American leaders often explained United States policies to unhappy foreign observers by citing the constraints placed on them by American public opinion. According to American diplomatic historian Thomas Paterson "such statements . . . represented a diplomatic device to press foreign officials, rather than a political reality at home." Even special-interest groups did not always influence policymakers successfully. Polish-Americans failed to shape policy toward their homeland because their political influence was splintered, their numbers small, their leaders ineffective and their loyalty to the Democratic Party reasonably reliable. Thomas G. Paterson, "Presidential Foreign Policy, Public Opinion, and Congress," pp. 10–12; Walter LaFeber, "American Policy-Makers, Public Opinion, and the Outbreak of the Cold War," pp. 47–48. Indeed, Professor LaFeber discounts their influence even with Senator Vandenberg, since the Polish-Americans were "rock-ribbed Democrats" whom "Vandenberg had largely ignored . . . in 1940, winning handsomely" nevertheless.

2. Hadley Cantril, the analyst mentioned, worked with the Office of Public Opinion Research at Princeton. Ralph B. Levering, *The Public and American Foreign Policy*, p. 32. A similar assessment has been made by Gabriel Almond, *The American People and Foreign Policy*, pp. 69–71; Paterson, "Presidential Foreign Policy," pp. 5–6; James N. Rosenau, *Public Opinion and Foreign Policy*, p. 35. H. Schuyler Foster, Director of the Public Opinion Studies Staff in the State Department, asserts that according to poll data, little more than half of America's adult population claim a continuing interest in their country's foreign relations. H. Schuyler Foster, "The Role of the Public in U.S. Foreign Relations," p. 825.

3. U.S. Cong., Senate, Committee on Foreign Relations, *Congress, Information and Foreign Affairs* pp. 87–92.

4. Paterson, "Presidential Foreign Policy," p. 17.

5. Bernard C. Cohen, *The Public's Impact on Foreign Policy*, pp. 89–90.

6. American Opinion Report, September 12, 1949, RG 59, NA; John M. Hed-

ley, "The Truman Administration and the 'Loss' of China" (Ph.D. diss.), pp.
165–67. The Office of Public Opinion Studies distributed some 200 of their
monthly opinion reports within the State Department, 200 to other parts of the
Administration and 400 overseas to U.S. Missions. William O. Chittick, "The
Domestic Information Activities of the Department of State" (Ph.D. diss.), p.
208. Brief mention of polls also appeared in the State Department's Weekly
Summary of Comment on China produced by the Office of Public Opinion Studies. See for examples: Weekly Summary, May 26- June 1, 1949, or July 7-13,
1949.

7. National Opinion Research Center survey no. 162, November 1948, Roper
Public Opinion Research Center, University of Connecticut, Storrs, Conn. (hereafter Roper); NORC survey no. 169, September 1949, Roper. Another indicator
of the low interest taken in U.S. China policy can be found in the statistics kept
on mail received at the White House. Mail is considered the poorest index of
public opinion because it is almost always from a negligible percentage of the
adult population and generally written by opponents of an announced policy.
It is significant in this context because compared with letters and telegrams on
various other subjects, the recorded volume of material on China proves pitiful.
Mail on China counted in the White House files for 1948, 1949 and the first half
of 1950 totals 2,681 letters, postcards, and telegrams. The case of Cardinal Min-
dszenty, the Hoover Report on Government Reorganization, and the issue of
sending an American envoy to the Vatican each brought more mail in a single
week than did China in two and one half years. Hedley, "Truman Administration," pp. 124, 168–95.

8. Arthur N. Feraru, "Public Opinion Polls on China," pp. 130–32; Roche,
"Public Opinion," pp. 255–56.

9. "Some Unpublished Gallup Polls on China," Memo H. Schuyler Foster
(FS) to Mr. Fisher (FE), May 2, 1949, Office of Public Opinion Studies, Box 33,
folder: China 1949–1952, RG 59, NA.

10. American Opinion Report, September 12, 1949, RG 59, NA.

11. NORC survey no. 162, November 1948, Roper.

12. American Opinion Report, September 12, 1949, RG 59, NA.

13. American Opinion Report, February 13, 1950, RG 59, NA. The Public
Opinion Studies Staff (POSS) noted: "Discussion of U.S. policy toward the Far
East, highlighted by the heated Congressional and press debate over Formosa,
reached a peak in January which it has not attained in many years . . . [as]
almost every editor, radio commentator and columnist across the country discussed one or another aspect of the situation in Asia. . . . The largest volume
of comment during this time centered on the specific issue of Formosa."

14. "Popular Opinion on U.S. Policy Toward China," Memo Foster (PS) to
Sprouse (CA) and Fisher (FE), July 7, 1949, Office of Public Opinion Studies,
Box 33, folder: China 1949–1952, RG 59, NA; American Opinion Report, No-
vember 30, 1949, RG 59, NA.

15. The totals were as follows: June 1949, 27%; July 1949, 40%; October 1949,
23%; November 1949, 38%; January 1950, 26%; June 1950, 44%. In one of the
two samples in which the group opposed to recognition exceeded 50%—the
January 1950 survey in which the opposition totalled 62%—the question itself
probably had much to do with the high negative response. It did not simply
inquire about reactions to recognition of the CCP, but rather asked about ending
recognition of Chiang Kai-shek and transferring it to the Communists.

16. AIPO #446 T Form, August 1949, Roper; American Opinion Report, September 12, 1949, RG 59, NA.

17. American Opinion Report, September 12, 1949, RG 59, NA; "American Public Discussion and Opinion on U.S. Relations with China and Neighboring Countries," p. 1, September 26, 1949, Office of Public Opinion Studies, Box 33, folder: China 1949–1952, RG 59, NA; Feraru, "Polls on China," pp. 130–32.

18. "Popular Opinion on U.S. Policy Toward China," July 7, 1949, RG 59, NA.

19. American Opinion Report, February 13, 1950, RG 59, NA.

20. LaFeber, "American Policy-Makers," pp. 43–44, 60. This article forcefully argues the point that "By the spring of 1945, President Harry S. Truman and a small number of advisers controlled foreign policy, allowing their final decisions to be determined by neither public opinion nor Congress."

21. Margaret Truman, Harry S. Truman, p. 346. H. Schuyler Foster recalls that "Sometimes [government] commentators reminded [POSS] that American opinion was not an important issue in many foreign policy questions, which turned rather on economic considerations or our relations with other countries in the world—with the American public paying little attention." H. Schuyler Foster to me, February 24, 1979.

22. Robert D. Schulzinger, The Making of the Diplomatic Mind, pp. 134, 153.

23. Princeton Seminars, July 8–9, 1953, Dean Acheson Papers, HST; Cohen, The Public's Impact On Foreign Policy, pp. 58–64. Acheson maintained that a Secretary of State must not be distracted by public opinion from his role as foreign affairs advisor to the Administration. He believed that union, industry, and religious leaders could not develop a Far Eastern policy for the Department but might comment and criticize once an approach had been formulated. They would also be helpful in informing the public of the government's decisions. Oscar W. Perlmutter, "Acheson and American Foreign Policy" (Ph.D. diss.), pp. 80, 149–51; H. Alexander Smith to H. Kenaston Twitchell, July 15, 1949, H. Alexander Smith Papers, Box 98, folder: Correspondence re Far East #1, H. Seeley Mudd Manuscript Library, Princeton University. Acheson reflected some of his exasperation with the State Department's need to deal with the public as early as 1945: "If we have a program for giving out information, we are propagandizing. If we don't give out information promptly and systematically we are cynically denying your right as citizens to know what is going on behind these musty old walls. . . . The Department is damned if it does and it's damned if it doesn't." Dean Acheson, "Government-Citizen Cooperation in the Making of Foreign Policy," p. 894.

24. Margaret Truman, Truman, p. 356.

25. Richard H. Freeland, The Truman Doctrine and the Origins of McCarthyism, pp. 9–11, 89–103, 115–17; Bert Cochran, Harry Truman and the Crisis Presidency, pp. 185–86; Congress, Information and Foreign Affairs, p. 19. To help sell the Truman Doctrine Senator Vandenberg insisted Truman "scare hell" out of the American people. Truman appointed a special cabinet committee under Secretary of the Treasury John Snyder to reach the business community and similarly exaggerate the Soviet threat. Susan M. Hartman, Truman and the 80th Congress, pp. 57–58. Similar activities advanced the Bretton Woods Agreement, see Alfred E. Eckes Jr., A Search for Solvency (Austin: University of Texas Press, 1975).

26. The Gallup Poll: Public Opinion 1935–71, 1(1935–1948): 617, 623, 636–37, 675; LaFeber, "American Policy-Makers," pp. 53–54; Foster, "American Public Opin-

ion," p. 798. The State Department used public opinion polls extensively in planning its information program on the Truman Doctrine, Chittick, "Domestic Information Activities," p. 210.

27. Re Department's failure to prepare the public see Chittick, *ibid.*, p. 96n35, and Kenneth S. Chern, *Dilemma in China*, pp. 212–14. Re willingness of public to follow policy elites Gabriel Almond notes: "The American foreign policy mood is permissive; it will follow the lead of the policy elites if they demonstrate unity and resolution." Almond, *The American People and Foreign Policy*, p. 87.

28. Michael Leigh, *Mobilizing Consent: Public Opinion and American Foreign Policy*, p. 31; Francis H. Russell, "The Function of Public Opinion Analysis in the Formulation of Foreign Policy," pp. 277, 303; MacAlister Brown, "The Demise of State Department Public Opinion Polls," pp. 13–15; H. Schuyler Foster, "American Public Opinion," pp. 796–97. Philip C. Jessup, who served in or in conjunction with the State Department repeatedly after 1924, observed that the Department in the 1940s was particularly anxious to ascertain public opinion. Interview with Philip C. Jessup, September 21, 1977.

29. *United States Relations With China With Special Reference to the Period 1944–1949*, Department of State Publication 3573. The transmittal letter was all that members of the general public read. Additional information on its contents came through media coverage.

30. According to H. Schuyler Foster "most of the time editorial opinion and polls of citizens take the same side of an issue, that is, the majority of editors and majority of citizens share the same attitude (although perhaps in different proportions). But in our experience, when these two indexes of American opinion did point in opposite directions, it was usually the editorial opinion which foretold the eventual action of the government (whether Congress or Executive), rather than the polls reflecting the views of the less-informed man-in-the-street." H. Schuyler Foster to me, February 24, 1979. See ch. 8.

31. Poll results were as follows:

January 1949:47% thought that the United States government should not continue to help Chiang's government; 25% said that the U.S. should continue; 16% had no opinion; 12% hadn't heard of the war ("Some Unpublished Gallup Polls on China," May 2, 1949, RG 59, NA.)

June 1949:48% disapproved of sending military supplies to Chiang' government; 40% approved; 2% had no opinion. The results of this poll may have been influenced by the fact that Chiang's opponents were specified as communists (American Opinion Report, June 28, 1949, RG 59, NA.)

September 1949:45% disapproved of sending aid to China's government in its fight against the communists; 43% approved; 12% had no opinion. When Chiang's government was specified as the recipient the totals shifted to 44% disapproval, 25% approval, and 31% no opinion (American Opinion Report, September 12, 1949, RG 59, NA.)

For *January 1950* results on Formosa see American Opinion Report, February 13, 1950.

32. 893.01/11-2949 James I. Dolliver (R, Ia) to Secretary of State, RG 59, NA; 893.01/11-1649 Representative T. Vincent Quin (R, NY) to Secretary of State, RG 59, NA; Anthony L. Dexter, "What Do Congressmen Hear: The Mail," pp. 16–27; Leila Sussmann, "Mass Political Letter Writing in America," pp. 203–12.

33. Conversation V. K. Wellington Koo, Chinese Ambassador to the United States, with Senator Tom Connally, Chairman Senate Foreign Relations Com-

mittee, February 2, 1949, Box 130: Notes of Conversation 1949, #43, V. K. Wellington Koo Papers, Butler Library Manuscript Division, Columbia University (hereafter Koo Papers); Conversation Koo with Senator Pat McCarran, March 31, 1949, Koo Papers, Box 130, #47; Conversation Koo with Senator William Knowland, August 16, 1949, Koo Papers, Box 130, #67; V. K. Wellington Koo Oral History Collection, I (sec. 2):39, (sec. 3):89–90, (sec 8): 419–20, J (sec 3):191–92, 205, 208–9, 229, East Asian Institute, Columbia University (hereafter Koo Oral History). See also chs 4 and 5.

34. Re Walter Judd's experience see ch 5 on the China Lobby. John Vorys served with Yale-in-China and H. Alexander Smith had a long-term association with the Princeton-Yenching Foundation although his interest remained nominal before 1948. Mike Mansfield served in China with the U.S. Navy, taught Far Eastern history at the University of Montana, and in 1944 went on a fact-finding mission to China for Franklin Roosevelt. Elbert Thomas taught Far Eastern politics at the University of Utah and wrote on the subject as well. Tom Connally visited China in 1935 and during World War II claimed a special interest in Pacific theatre developments. H. Bradford Westerfield, *Foreign Policy and Party Politics*, p. 242; William M. Leary, Jr., "Smith of New Jersey" (Ph.D. diss.), p. 132; Chern, *Dilemma in China*, pp. 31, 57–65; FRUS (1945)7:2–26; Thomas Connally and Alfred Steinberg, *My Name is Tom Connally*, pp. 180, 259.

35. 893.01/4-2649 Office Memo Weigle (FE) to Butterworth and Allison (FE), RG 59, NA; Styles Bridges to Tom Clark, Attorney General of the United States, n.d., Bridges Papers, File 27, folder 30.

36. "Ambassador from Nevada," pp. 23–25; "China and the Silver Bloc," editorial from the *Providence Evening Bulletin* reprinted in the *St. Louis Post-Dispatch*, April 21, 1949, p. 2B; 893.00/4-2649 Office Memo Weigle to Butterworth and Allison (FE), RG 59, NA; Peter Edson, *Washington News*, March 14, 1949, Weekly Summary, March 10–16, 1949; Leary, "Smith of N.J.," p. 137; H. Alexander Smith to Kenaston Twitchell, August 15, 1949, Smith Papers, Box 98, folder: Correspondence re Far East #1; Conversation Koo with Mr. James A. White, Secretary of the Conference of Western Senators, U.S. Senate, Box 166: Personalities, folder: L3 Congress, Koo Papers. McCarran's desire to increase silver production through Chinese demand fitted in nicely with Nationalist wishes. To boost army morale the Chinese government paid its soldiers in silver coins and, therefore, hoped to obtain a silver grant or loan of some seventy million ounces from the United States. Ambassador Koo presented this silver request repeatedly during 1949. Koo Oral History, I (sec 4): 132–35, (sec 6): 263, (sec 8): 422–23. The only point of disagreement between McCarran and the Nationalists was the former's insistence that aid to China be strictly controlled by American administrators. "New Loan Proposal," *North China Daily News*, January 13, 1949, Patrick McCarran Papers, Scrapbook #26, August 4, 1948–January 31, 1949, Holy Names College, Oakland, Ca.

37. Robert A. Taft, among the most powerful men in the 81st Congress, took his stand on China policy largely for political reasons. Taft had never paid much attention to Asian affairs. He adamantly opposed the concept of bipartisanship in foreign policy or in almost anything else. Strong parties, he believed, were the foundation of American politics. Truman's foreign policy as a whole he considered too expensive and too reminiscent of Roosevelt's activism. Even though he believed in a firm anticommunism, Taft generally preferred that the United States abstain from overseas commitments. Re partisanship see James

T. Patterson, *Mr. Republican*, pp. 340, 438–49, 443–46; and John A. Ricks, "'Mr. Integrity' and McCarthyism," (Ph.D. diss.), pp. 56–115. Re isolationism see Joseph Alsop to Paul Bellamy, editor, *Cleveland Plain-Dealer*, January 27, 1950, Joseph and Stewart Alsop Papers, Box 24: Special Correspondence, folder: "Matter of Fact" Col—with publishers—C 1946–56, LC; Henry W. Berger, "A Conservative Critique of Containment: Senator Taft on the Early Cold War Program," in David Horowitz, ed., *Containment and Revolution*, pp. 128, 131; Richard Rovere, "Taft: Is This the Best We've Got?" pp. 294, 298–99; Patterson, *Mr. Republican*, pp. 384, 435–36. Knowland's motives remain obscure but interest in Asian trade may have supplemented his political reasons for becoming involved with the China Lobby and the Japan Lobby. Howard Schonberger, "Of Arms and Men," paper, New England Conference, Association for Asian Studies, October 21, 1979; Schonberger, "The Japan Lobby in American Diplomacy, 1947–52," pp. 327–59.

38. Crisis in Europe, especially the Berlin blockade, also contributed to the low-keyed approach to foreign affairs in the 1948 campaign. Westerfield, *Foreign Policy*, pp. 306–10.

39. Re decision that bipartisanship hurt Republican fortunes: Senator Karl Mundt to Senator Robert Taft, n.d., and "The Report of the Committee on Republican Fundamental Principles of the National Republican Roundup Committee, Chicago, Ill., November 10 and 11, 1949," point 14, Box 868: Legislative Re-Ru, folder: Republican Principles 1950, Taft Papers, LC; Edward A. Harris, "Bipartisan Foreign Policy Buckling at the Joints?" p. 1B; Willard Shelton, "The New Irresponsibles," pp. 313–14; *Congress, Information and Foreign Affairs*, pp. 22–23, 27; *New York Times*, December 26, 1949, pp. 1, 23. The Democrats contributed to a decline in bipartisan feeling after 1948. In the Senate Foreign Relations Committee, for example, they forced through an 8 to 5 division in representation giving the GOP the smallest minority voice legally possible. Leary, "Smith of N.J.," pp. 131–32; Westerfield, *Foreign Policy*, pp. 325–33.

40. Richard Rovere, "The Unassailable Vandenberg," p. 396. James Reston recalled that in 1946 Vandenberg had explained that some areas had to be left out of bipartisan cooperation lest the Republicans having nothing to complain about in the entire area of foreign affairs. James Reston, "Memorandum to General MacArthur," p. 5.

41. Tsou, *America's Failure*, p. 447; Westerfield, *Foreign Policy*, pp. 245–47, 254, 262; Cecil V. Crabb Jr., *Bipartisan Foreign Policy*, p. 102; John R. Skretting, "Republican Attitudes Toward the Administration's China Policy" (Ph.D. diss.), pp. 33–34; James Reston, "Events Spotlight Vandenberg's Dual Role," pp. 51–52; Floyd R. Goodno, "Judd" (Ph.D. diss.), pp. 210–11; Vandenberg, *CR*, 93 (80th Cong., 1st sess., 1947): 3474, 10708. Evidence of Republican concern about China was not entirely lacking. Brief flurries were generated by the Patrick Hurley investigation in 1945 and the "Manchurian Manifesto" of 1946. James A. Fetzer, "Congress and China" (Ph.D. diss.), pp. 55–77.

42. *CR* (May 18, 1949) 95 (pt 4): 6391.

43. The attack on Butterworth was led by Senators Bridges, Knowland, Brewster and Ferguson. Butterworth was passed over fourteen times and finally got confirmation on a highly partisan vote. Westerfield, *Foreign policy*, pp. 347–50; Fetzer, "Congress and China," pp. 191–92; Tsou, *America's Failure*, pp. 499–504; *New York Times*, March 11, 1949, p. 13.

44. The White House did not consult Congressional Republicans before nom-

inating Acheson. They looked upon him as "Truman's creature." Vandenberg, who had enjoyed a close personal relationship with Secretary Marshall, never established personal bonds with Acheson. Opposing his confirmation were Senators Bridges, Jenner, Knowland, Wherry, Langer and Capehart. Virginia Kemp, "Congress and China" (Ph.D. diss.), p. 105. Senator Homer Capehart to Charles Parsons, January 12, 1949, Charles Parsons Papers, Group 387, Series I, Box 20, folder 436, Yale University, Sterling Memorial Library, New Haven, Conn.; Malcolm E. Jewell, *Senatorial Politics and Foreign Policy*, p. 125; Westerfield, *Foreign Policy*, pp. 327–39; Arthur H. Vandenberg Jr., and Joe Alex Morris, eds., *The Private Papers of Senator Vandenberg*, p. 469; David S. McLellan, *Dean Acheson: The State Department Years*, p. 58. Senator Hugh Butler reflected much of this feeling when he said: "I look at the fellow, I watch his smartaleck manner and his British clothes and that New Dealism, everlasting New Dealism, in everything he says and does, and I want to shout, Get Out, Get Out. You stand for everything that has been wrong with the United States for years." Eric F. Goldman, *The Crucial Decade—and After*, p. 125.

45. Robert Griffith, *The Politics of Fear*.

46. Holbert N. Carroll, *The House of Representatives and Foreign Affairs*, pp. 31, 90–93; Westerfield, *Foreign Policy*, pp. 262–63. Vorys reportedly told Vandenberg that the addition of China to the Interim Aid Bill of 1947 by the House Foreign Affairs Committee was necessary to build up its prestige by forcing through a measure against Senate and Administration objections.

47. Ben H. Brown Jr., "Congress and the Department of State," pp. 103–5; Jack K. McFall Oral History Interview, HST; LaFeber, "American Policy-Makers," pp. 60–61; McLellan, *Dean Acheson*, pp. 23, 35; Dean Acheson, "The Parties and Foreign Policy," p. 33; Robert Taft, *A Foreign Policy for Americans*, pp. 21–23. President Truman also believed that Congress should acquiesce in and support foreign policies made by the President. Anthony R. Bullard, "Harry S. Truman and the Separation of Powers in Foreign Affairs" (Ph.D. diss.), pp. 49–50, 283. LaFeber, "American Policy-Makers, pp. 56, 62.

48. 794.00/1-550 Memorandum of Conversation, FRUS (1950)6:258–63; Westerfield, *Foreign Policy*, p. 364. Even Tom Connally and John Kee, chairmen of the Senate Foreign Relations and House Foreign Affairs Committees respectively, did not receive word of the announcement until the day before. Princeton Seminars, July 23, 1953, Dean Acheson Papers, HST.

49. Interview with Everett Case, November 9, 1977; 893.00/8-1749 Memo Howard (H) to Jessup (S/A). RG 59, NA. In the H. Alexander Smith Papers, for instance, there is evidence of repeated efforts made to apprise State Department and other important officials of the Senator's views. After his Autumn 1949 trip to the Far East, for example, he sent his report to Acheson, Kennan, Butterworth, McFall, and the consultant group Jessup, Case and Fosdick. Smith Papers, Box 98, folder: China trip 1949.

50. Eight radio stations used McCarran's fifteen-minute broadcasts. See McCarran Papers, Speeches.

51. William Knowland to Henry E. North, President, San Francisco Chamber of Commerce, CR (October 18, 1949) 95 (pt 2): 14831; James C. Nelson, "The United States Senate and Recognition of Communist China" (Ph.D. diss.), p. 43; Westerfield, *Foreign Policy*, p. 364; "China Policy Critic: Senator William F. Knowland," pp. 33–34.

52. 893.00/4-2849 "Meeting in the President's Office with Senators Wherry

and Bridges on China," RG 59, NA. For a list of Acheson's appearances before Congressional committees concerning China and his private meetings on this same subject with members of Congress see "Dates of Congressional Appearances on China—or other consultations, 1949–1950," Notes For Meetings, Princeton Seminars, Acheson Papers, HST.

53. Off-the-record White House meeting attended by President Truman, Dean Acheson, Senators Vandenberg, Connally, and Barkley, and Representatives Eaton and Bloom. Vandenberg, *Private Papers*, pp. 530–32; Memo National Security Council to Secretary of State, February 7, 1949, PPS Records, Box 13, folder: China 1949, RG 59, NA.

54. Fetzer, "Congress and China," pp. 135–69, 208; Tsou, *America's Failure*, pp. 465–70. Acheson made his promise to Connally in a letter dated July 1, 1949.

55. Re danger of coalition: Kemp, "Congress and China," p. 66; Westerfield, *Foreign Policy*, p. 358; Tsou, *America's Failure*, p. 470. Re economy-mindedness: John Taber was a highly partisan ultraconservative. He considered most foreign aid a waste of American resources and believed the State Department staffed by incompetent appeasers. He had neither interest in nor knowledge of world affairs. Cary Smith Henderson, "Congressman John Taber of Auburn" (Ph.D. diss.), pp. 329–65, 412–23. The proportion of Republicans voting against spending measures grew in the late 1940s. In the 1947–48 Congress 70% of all GOP votes cast on spending amendments favored increases or opposed reductions, but in 1949–50 this percentage fell to 36% and would decline again in the 1951–52 session to 21%. Jewell, *Senatorial Politics*, p. 40. As Senator William Jenner explained, his vote for aid to Greece and Turkey did not signify that "I am committing myself to a future program of depleting our economy on a 'do-good' basis." Jenner to Charles Parsons, April 26, 1947, Parsons Papers, Group 387, Series I, Box 20, folder 472. Re isolationists: Kenneth Wherry approached China policy as did isolationists generally. Wherry used China to strike at Truman's whole foreign policy. He talked blandly of pouring billions into China but, at the same time, voted against all aid to Europe. "The Mess in China," p. 7; Harl Dalstrom, "Kenneth S. Wherry" (Ph.D. diss.), pp. 476–975; Marvin E. Stromer, *The Making of a Political Leader*; Vandenberg, *Private Papers*, p. 466.

56. Senator McCarran headed the Senate Appropriations subcommittee on State Department appropriations. Senator Bridges was the ranking Republican on the Senate Appropriations Committee and chairman of the watchdog committee on foreign aid. His seniority among Republicans in the Senate was second only to that of Arthur Vandenberg. Westerfield, *Foreign Policy*, p. 113; Tsou, *America's Failure*, p. 491.

57. CR (June 27, 1949) 95 (pt 6): 8406-07; Fetzer, "Congress and China," p. 207; Westerfield, *Foreign Policy*, p. 352; Blair Bolles, "Asia Policy and the Election," pp. 221–24.

58. George Fallon (R,Md) to President Truman, November 15, 1949, Truman Papers, Official File 150(1947)-150 Misc (1948), Box 633, folder: 1947–49, HST; Fetzer, "Congress and China," p. 210; Nelson, "U.S. Senate and Recognition," pp. 33–38; CR (October 18, 1949) 95 (pt 2) 14180. Ironically, in May 1949 Senator McCarran had argued in favor of United States recognition of Spain in the following terms: "We do not send ambassadors and ministers to foreign nations for the benefit of those nations, but for the benefit of our own diplomatic position, and for the purpose of securing information for ourselves. . . . If we are going to withdraw our ambassadors from all countries whose forms of govern-

ment we do not completely approve, there will be a great surplus of ex-ambassadors in Washington." Radio Speech, week of May 16, 1949, pp. 11–12, McCarran Papers, Speeches. *CR* (January 5, 1950) 96 (pt 1): 81, January 9, 1950, p. 158, and January 13, 1950, p. 390; Press Release, January 4, 1950, Bridges Papers, File 29, folder: Senator's Statements re China, Korea and Foreign Policy Since August 1949.

59. Westerfield, *Foreign Policy*, p. 361.

60. 893.01/10-2649 Edwin C. Johnson to Secretary of State, RG 59, NA.

61. Chern, *Dilemma in China*, p. 225. Elbert Thomas was a member of the Senate Foreign Relations Committee. Connally opposed hasty recognition but pointed out to opponents of relations with China that the act of recognition did not mean approval of a government but would provide American citizens with protection. Thomas Connally Papers, Box 573: 1949, folder: Speech, November 1949, and Box 569: 1949, folder: Press Conference—December 29, 1949, and Box 570, folder: Press Statement—January 6, 1950, LC.

62. Nelson, "U.S. Senate and Recognition," pp. 38–39; *CR* (January 5, 1950) 96 (pt 1): 87–88.

63. Nelson, "U.S. Senate and Recognition," p. 41; *CR* (January 5, 1950) 96 (pt 1): 93–94. In March 1948 Morse had asked whether China might not be "lost to the same degree under [Nationalist] fascism as it would be lost under communism?" *CR* (March 30, 1948) 94 (pt 3): 3670–71.

64. Westerfield, *Foreign Policy*, p. 361. Vandenberg by this time was too ill to mediate between opposing forces in Congress. Crabb, *Bipartisan Foreign Policy*, p. 122.

65. Re weakness of the China bloc and inability to suggest constructive programs: Bolles, "Asia Policy," pp. 221–24; Fetzer, "Congress and China," p. 227; Goodno, "Judd," p. 227; re Knowland resolution: Tsou, *America's Failure*, p. 501. The depth of China-bloc support from the electorate also came into question. Ambassador-at-Large Jessup questioned Senator Knowland's assertion that Californians strongly opposed recognition, citing his own observations of "a very strong group behind the [pro-recognition Roger] Lapham point of view expressed at the Asilomar Conference of December 1949 and elsewhere. Memo of Conversation Jessup with Knowland, December 20, 1949, John Cabot Papers, folder: China Correspondence, 1948–1949, Manchester, Mass.; Jessup to Butterworth, December 24, 1949, Philip C. Jessup Papers, Box 47, folder: Chronological File, December 1949, Far Eastern trip, LC.

66. McCarthy's influence did not take immediate effect after his Wheeling, West Virginia "debut" on February 9, 1950. At a March 29, 1950 hearing before the Senate Foreign Relations Committee Dean Acheson condemned Chiang Kai-shek's rule on Formosa and asserted "he is not the person who is going to liberate China." The only objection to Acheson's comments came from Senator H. Alexander Smith and all that he said was a mild, "I do not share your conclusions. Now, assuming you can't use him, what are we going to do with Formosa?" This contrasts sharply with the rhetoric after the outbreak of the Korean War. Dean Acheson testimony in Executive Session, March 29, 1950, U.S. Cong., Senate, Committee on Foreign Relations, *Reviews of the World Situation, 1949–1950*, pp. 274–75; Comments by Walter LaFeber, transcript of the Conference on the Causes of the Cold War in Asia and Sino-American Relations, June 9–11, 1978, Mt. Kisco, New York, available at the East Asian Institute, Columbia University.

67. McCarthy had used the communist issue and made charges against John Service before. Richard M. Fried, *Men Against McCarthy*, pp. 42–43. See also Acheson, *Creation*, pp. 363–64; Alan D. Harper, *The Politics of Loyalty*; Earl Latham, *The Communist Controversy in Washington*; Griffith, *Fear*; Koen, *The China Lobby*. Re John Service see E.J. Kahn Jr., *The China Hands*. Other outspoken critics of Truman's misguided actions in China, such as Kenneth Wherry, Senator from Nebraska, displayed a similar ignorance of actual events there. 893.00/4-2849 "Meeting in the President's Office with Senators Wherry and Bridges on China," RG 59, NA; Chern, *Dilemma in China*, p. 94; John Roots to H. Alexander Smith, January 25, 1949, Smith Papers, Box 98, folder: Correspondence re Far East #2.

68. White, *In Search*, p. 50; John M. Lindbeck, *Understanding China*, pp. 30–37. The Far Eastern Association organized in 1941 to publish the *Far Eastern Quarterly* became a membership organization in 1948. In 1956 the FEA changed its name to the Association for Asian Studies.

69. Judith Coburn, "Asian Scholars and Government," pp. 67–68, 73–74; Chittick, "Domestic Information Activities," pp. 56–57.

70. Re Jessup's role in editing the volume see the introduction by Lyman P. Van Slyke to *China White Paper 1949*. Jessup told me that W. Walton Butterworth had done most of the work compiling the volume and that Jessup, was brought in to edit it because of his academic credentials. Interview with Philip C. Jessup, September 21, 1977. Re Peffer consultation see Jessup to Nathaniel Peffer, July 22, 1949, Jessup Papers, Box 48, Chronological File July 1949, General Correspondence 1919–1958. See also Princeton Seminars 1953–1954, July 22–23, 1953, Acheson Papers, HST; Acheson, *Creation*, pp. 302–3.

71. "U.S. Policy Toward China," *Department of State Bulletin* (October 15, 1951) 25:603–7; and Dean Acheson to Everett Case, August 23, 1949, Everett Case Papers in the possession of Mr. Case, Van Hornesville, New York. The original suggestion for the consultant group may have come from Dean Rusk as an alternative to the often-made recommendation that a United States Commission be sent to China. 893.00/4-449 Memorandum Dean Rusk, Assistant Secretary of State, to James E. Webb, RG 59, NA.

72. According to Everett Case the consultants saw all government reports and telegraph traffic germane to the issues they were studying. Interview with Everett Case November 9, 1977. Jessup's letter soliciting memoranda on the China situation, August 18, 1949, Jessup Papers, Subject File, Box 137: Attacks on Jessup, folder: Briefing Book—Sparkman 51, LC.

73. The scholars whose opinions were solicited were: Hugh Borton, Columbia; Claude Buss, Army War College; Isaiah Bowman, Johns Hopkins; Rupert Emerson, Harvard; Charles B. Fahs, Rockefeller Foundation; John Fairbank, Harvard; Carrington Goodrich, Columbia; Kenneth Scott Latourette, Yale; Owen Lattimore, Johns Hopkins; Paul M. A. Linebarger, Columbia; Wallace Moore, Occidental; Cornelius Osgood, Yale; Nathaniel Peffer, Columbia; Roscoe Pound, Harvard; Edwin O. Reischauer, Harvard; David Rowe; Yale; James Shotwell; George Taylor, University of Washington; Amry Vandenbosch, University of Kentucky; Karl A. Wittfogel, Columbia; Mary Wright, Stanford. Jessup received a total of thirty-one replies to his letter. Jessup Papers, Subject File, Box 137, and see also Boxes 47 and 48 for Jessup's acknowledging letters, LC; Raymond Fosdick Papers, Box 9, folder: Papers on China 1949–1950, Princeton.

74. Unsolicited opinions offered by: Kenneth Colegrove, Northwestern; Paul L. Harvey, Mills College; Howard Preston, University of Washington; M. Har-

tley Dodge, Columbia; W. Leon Godshall, Lehigh; Norman Palmer, University of Pennsylvania; and Harold Vinacke, University of Cincinnati. Jessup Papers, Boxes 47, 48 and 61, LC.

75. Both Case and Jessup had been officers of the American Institute of Pacific Relations in the 1930s and early 1940s. Everett Case had visited China in 1931. Interview with Everett Case, September 9, 1977, and Jessup Biographical Note, Jessup Papers, LC; Philip C. Jessup, *The Birth of Nations*, pp. 26–27, 165.

76. The scholars who attended were: Bernard Brodie, Yale; Claude Buss, Army War College; Kenneth Colegrove, Northwestern; Arthur Coons, Occidental; John Fairbank, Harvard; Arthur Holcombe, Harvard; Owen Lattimore, Johns Hopkins; Nathaniel Peffer, Columbia; Harold Quigley, Minnesota University; Edwin O. Reischauer, Harvard; Phillip Talbot, University of Chicago; George Taylor, University of Washington; and Harold Vinacke, University of Cincinnati.

71. Office Memorandum Francis H. Russell (PA) to John Paton Davies and George F. Kennan, October 13, 1949, PPS Records, Box 13: Country and Area Files, folder: China 1949, RG 59, NA.

78. U.S. Department of State, *Round Table*, pp. 101–2 (Colegrove), 151–52 (Lattimore), 170 (Coons), 184–85 (Quigley), 188 (Brodie), 427–28 (Peffer), 428 (Holcombe), 457–58 (Quigley).

79. Columbia University, East Asian Institute luncheon with Owen Lattimore, March 30, 1979.

80. Owen Lattimore, "Our Failure in China," p. 226.

81. The books were: *The United States and China* and *Next Step in Asia*. The periodicals to which he contributed articles included: *Foreign Policy Bulletin, Nation, The Reporter, and Far Eastern Survey*.

82. John K. Fairbank to Philip C. Jessup, October 15, 1951, quotation from *Next Step in Asia*, Jessup Papers, Box 56: Correspondence-alphabetical, folder: Fackenthal-Farrand 1953–1948, LC.

83. John K. Fairbank, *The United States and China*, p. 3, and "What Can U.S. Do If Chiang's Government Falls?" p. 1.

84. Fairbank to Jessup, October 15, 1951, quotation from *The Reporter*, January 3, 1950, Jessup Papers, LC; *America's Town Meeting of the Air*, December 6, 1949, New York City, Styles Bridges Papers, File 81, folder 78: Speech Material China, New England College Library, Henniker, New Hampshire.

85. Charles S. Gardner, President, Far Eastern Association, to the Senate Foreign Relations Committee and the House Foreign Affairs Committee, January 7, 1950, Robert Taft Papers, Box 573: Ch-Ci, folder: China-Formosa, 1950, LC. Professor Biggerstaff noted in a letter to me that in 1949 he favored immediate United States recognition of the People's Republic. He did begin to have some reservations after the seizure of U.S. Consulate property in Peking in January 1950. Knight Biggerstaff, Ithaca, New York, to the author, August 4, 1977. See also Koen, *The China Lobby*, pp. 116–17.

86. Interview with Everett Case November 9, 1977; "Nineteen Statements from Far Eastern Specialists: Summary of Recommendations," September 30, 1949, CA Records, Box 14: 1948–49, folder: United States Policy Toward China and the Far East, RG 59, NA; Roche, "Public Opinion," p. 353.

87. L. Carrington Goodrich, New York to Philip C. Jessup, Washington, September 12, 1949, L. Carrington Goodrich Papers, Catalogued Correspondence Box 1, Butler Library Manuscript Division, Columbia University.

88. 893.01/12-2049 Office Memorandum Foster (PS) to Connors (FE), RG 59, NA.
89. Mary C. Wright, "China Remains Key to U.S. Policy in Asia," pp. 1–2, and Weekly Summary, September 8–14, 1949.
90. Department of State, American Opinion Reports, April 22, 1949, November 30, 1949 and February 13, 1950, Office of Public Opinion Studies 1943–65, Box 33, folder: China 1949–1952, RG 59, NA. The Council on Foreign Relations' survey of 720 leading citizens regarding China found that they favored recognition. Weekly Summary, March 30-April 5, 1950; and Joseph Barber, ed., *American Policy Toward China*.
91. 893.00/2-149 A. Doak Barnett, Peking to Walter S. Rogers, Institute of Current World Affairs, New York, RG 59, NA which circulated through various offices in the Department; Philip C. Jessup to Walter S. Rogers, October 4, 1949, Jessup Papers, Box 48, folder: Chronological File—October 1949, LC; 893.00/6-1950 Jessup to O. Edmund Clubb, RG 59, NA; Dean Rusk, Deputy Undersecretary of State to Jessup, forwarding materials from the New York Study Group on American Far Eastern Policy of the American Institute of Pacific Relations, July 27, 1949, Jessup Papers, Subject File 1924-1959, Box 124, folder: IPR Correspondence, July 1952-1949, LC. The study group—composed of representatives of business, the press, the law, universities, mission groups, and the United Nations—favored the establishment of relations with the Chinese Communists.
92. Robert A. Dahl, *Congress and Foreign Policy*, p. 109; Robert P. Newman, *Recognition of China?* p. 18.

10. THE STATE DEPARTMENT AND THE WHITE HOUSE

1. Goldman, *The Crucial Decade and After*, pp. 91–132. NSC 34/1, approved in January 1949, declared that the United States should regard "efforts with respect to China as of lower priority than efforts in other areas where the benefits to U.S. security are more immediately commensurate with the expenditure of U.S. resources." Cited in Iriye, "Was There a Cold War in Asia?" p. 10; Thomas H. Etzold, "The Far East in American Strategy," pp. 107–8; Dean Acheson testimony in Executive Session, May 1, 1950, U.S. Cong., Senate, Committee on Foreign Relations, *Reviews of the World Situation, 1949–1950*, p. 292.
2. John L. Gaddis, "Harry S. Truman and the Origins of Containment," in Frank J. Merli and Theodore A. Wilson, eds., *Makers of American Diplomacy*, p. 206; Acheson, *Power and Diplomacy* p. 72; McLellan, *Dean Acheson*, p. 115; Smith, *Dean Acheson*, pp. 16, 108–9. General Douglas MacArthur alone among top government and military leaders contended that the Far East was as important a front against communism as Europe. Undersecretary of State Dean Rusk and Ambassador-at-Large Philip C. Jessup viewed events in universalistic terms. Memorandum of Conversation Between General MacArthur and Senator H. Alexander Smith, September 27, 1949, Box 98, folder: Far East Trip, 1949, H. Alexander Smith Papers, Seeley Mudd Library Manuscript Division, Princeton University, Princeton, N.J.; John L. Gaddis, "The Strategic Perspective: the Rise and Fall of the 'Defensive Perimeter' Concept, 1947–1951," in Borg and Heinrichs, eds., *Uncertain Years*, p. 75.

3. Oscar W. Perlmutter, "Acheson and American Foreign Policy," (Ph.D. diss.), p. 71.

4. Norman A. Graebner, "Dean G. Acheson, 1949–1953," in Graebner, ed., *An Uncertain Tradition*, p. 276; Cochran, *Harry Truman and the Crisis Presidency*, pp. 186–250; Truman, *Memoirs*, 2:112, 115, 430.

5.The dearth of information on China in Truman's papers suggests that little consideration of these issues troubled the President. Very important telegrams from China were sent to Clark Clifford for Truman's information. Memo Butterworth to Sprouse and Freeman, November 13, 1948, CA Records, Box 13: 1948, RG 59, NA.

6. Michael Baron, "Notes of Discord: United States Policy Toward China, 1947–48," Certificate Essay, East Asian Institute, Columbia University, 1976.

7. Meeting with the President, October 31, 1949, Records of the Executive Secretariat, 1949–1952, Box 3: Memoranda of Conversations with the President, folder: 1949, RG 59, NA (hereafter Secretariat Records); Memorandum of Conversation, November 14, 1949, and Memorandum for the President, November 17, 1949, CA Records, Box 14: 1948–49, folder: Ward Case, RG, NA; Memo Humelsine to Secretary of State, November 21, 1949 and Memorandum of Conversation, November 21, 1949, Secretariat Records, Box 3, folder: 1949, RG 59, NA.

8. 123 Stuart, #775 Secretary to Stuart, July 1, 1949, and 123 Stuart, Memorandum of a Conversation with the President, July 11, 1949, and 123 Stuart, #852 Secretary to Stuart, July 20, 1949, FRUS (1949)8:769, 780-81, 794. U.S. Cong., Senate, Committee on Foreign Relations, *The United States and Communist China in 1949 and 1950: The Question of Rapprochement and Recognition* pp. 10-11. See also re Nationalist blockade, 393.1115/10-149 Memorandum of Meeting with the President, and Secretariat Records, Box 3, folder: 1949, RG 59, NA; and re possible revision of NSC 41, 693.419/8-2149 Memo Merchant (FE) to Sprouse (CA), RG 59, NA; Memorandum of Conversation with the President, September 16, 1949, Secretariat Records, Box 3, folder: 1949, RG 59, NA. Here again Acheson convinced Truman to let a liberal policy stand. The Administration feared losing support in Congress for the European Recovery Program, Point Four, the Economic Cooperation Administration, Korean aid legislation and United States membership in the International Trade Organization. 893.01/11-749 Memorandum of Conversation, RG 59, NA; Blair Bolles, "Washington Still Undecided on China Policy," p. 1.

9. Quote taken from NSC 7 approved by the President March 30, 1948 and cited by Iriye, "Was There a Cold War in Asia," p. 5. Re Molotov see "Remarks at a Meeting with the American Society of Newspaper Editors," April 17, 1947, *Public Papers of the President, 1947* (Washington, D.C.: Government Printing Office, 1963), pp. 207–10; Truman, *Memoirs*, 1:81-82. Clark Clifford, Truman's primary political adviser, emphasized the Soviet threat in a September 24, 1946 paper entitled "American Relations with the Soviet Union," (actually authored by George Elsey), Iriye, p. 5.

10. According to Philip Jessup, although neither Acheson nor Truman had any interest in East Asia, when China questions arose Acheson influenced Truman, not vice versa. Interview with Philip C. Jessup, September 21, 1977.

11. Gaddis, "Origins of Containment,' pp. 201–2; *The Journals of David Lilienthal*, 2:525; Cabinet Meeting, November 27, 1945, cited by Schaller, *U.S. Crusade* p. 288.

12. 893.00/6-1649 Meeting with the President, RG 59, NA.

13. Maury Maverick to Harry S Truman, November 19, 1949, and Harry S Truman to Maury Maverick, Truman Papers, President's Secretary's Files—Foreign Affairs File (China-1), Box 173, folder: 1949, HST; Harry S Truman to Sam Rayburn, December 17, 1949, Truman Papers, White House Central Files, Confidential Files—State Department Correspondence, Box 37: 1950, folder: 20, HST. Maverick continued to advocate recognition, see Memorandum to Truman, Connally, Kee, Acheson and Rusk, April 5, 1950, Truman Papers, PSF, Subject Files—Foreign Affairs File (China-1), Box 173, folder: 1949, HST.

14. 811.24593/1-549 Memorandum by Director of the Office of Far Eastern Affairs (Butterworth) to Acting Secretary (Webb), FRUS (1949)9:1210.

15. "The President's Special Conference with the Association of Radio News Analysts," October 19, 1949, *Public Papers of the President, 1949* (Washington, D.C.: Government Printing Office, 1964), p. 502. See also 893.01/10-349 Memorandum of Conversation by James E. Webb, RG 59, NA. *Time* magazine (a not unbiased source) contended that according to a "high State Department official" Acheson had "been steadily arguing with Truman to go along on an early recognition of Communist China. Just before Truman left for Key West, Acheson got him to admit the logic of early recognition. Truman said that Acheson made a forceful case. The trouble now isn't with Truman, but in persuading him to override the pressure from congressional and other groups not to recognize." *Time*, October 15, 1951, pp. 22–23.

16. "Conversation with the President," November 17, 1949, Secretariat Records, Box 3, folder: 1949, and copy in PPS Records, Box 13: Country and Area Files, folder: China 1949, RG 59, NA. Also see "Outline of Far Eastern and Asian Policy for Review with the President," November 14, 1949, FRUS (1949)7:1210-14; Interview with Everett Case, November 9, 1977. Professor Case recalls expecting Truman to have a strong anticommunist bias, but found that this was not true.

17. Merle Miller, *Plain Speaking*, pp. 282–83, 289; Lilienthal, *Atomic Energy*, p. 525; Truman *Memoirs*, 2:90; Memorandum of Conversation by Philip Jessup, FRUS (1950)7:180.

18. Memorandum of Conversations with the President, February 4, 1949 and February 7, 1949, Acheson Papers, Box 64: Memoranda of Conversations 1949, folder: January-February 1949, HST; Memoranda for the President by Sidney Souers, Executive Secretary of the National Security Council, February 3, 1949 and February 17, 1949, Truman Papers, PSF-NSC, Box 220: Memoranda for the President, 1948–53, HST.

19. Memoranda of Conversations with the President, June 2, 13, 27, 30, July 11, 14, 1949, Secretariat Records, Box 3, folder: 1949, RG 59, NA. Jessup has asserted that Truman's direct pressure overcame the reluctance of diplomatic personnel in the Department and in the field to see it published. Serious questions were raised as to the propriety of publishing confidential documents and of seemingly pushing the Kuomintang over the brink. Princeton Seminars, July 22-23, 1953, Acheson Papers, HST. The President also pledged Acheson all possible assistance in not letting the military water down the volume. Memorandum of Conversation, July 18, 1949, Secretariat Records, Box 3, folder: 1949, RG 59, NA.

20. Raymond G. O'Connor, "Harry S. Truman: New Dimensions of Power," pp. 40-41. A small amount went for informational activities in China.

308 NOTES FOR PAGES 177–178

21. Maxwell Stewart, "America's China Policy," pp. 174–75; Melby, *The Mandate of Heaven*, p. 273. Re Butterworth see Melby, pp. 169, 229; Interview with Hilda Melby, Butterworth's secretary, July 21, 1977; W. Walton Butterworth Oral History Interview, draft transcript, p. 64, HST. Re Merchant see Recorded Interview by Professor Bianci, June 1967, Livingston Merchant Papers, Princeton. John Cabot, whose prior experience had been in South America and Europe, confided to the American Ambassador in Belgrade that the Shanghai appointment came as quite a shock. He wrote another friend that he didn't want to become "an old China Hand" and hoped his next tour of duty would be in Latin America. John Cabot to William Leonhart, Belgrade, December 9, 1947 and Cabot to Ellis O. Briggs, July 6, 1948, Cabot Papers, folder: China Correspondence 1947–48.

22. Robert P. Browder, *The Origins of Soviet-American Diplomacy, passim*; "Recognition Question," p. 41; 893.01/5-1549, #1025 Stuart, Nanking, FRUS (1949)9:23–24; 893.01/5-1949 Memo Bacon (FE) to Freeman (CA), RG 59, NA. Truman believed Roosevelt was right in giving diplomatic recognition to the USSR in 1933. *Memoirs*, 2:273.

23. 893.00/8-2649, #2155 Kirk, Moscow, FRUS (1949)9:67–68. See also 893.01/10-749, #2538 Kirk, Moscow, FRUS (1949)9:107; 793.02/1-150, #6 Kirk, Moscow, FRUS (1950)6:268n9.

24. 893.01/5-549, #589 Secretary to Stuart, Nanking, FRUS (1949)9:22–23; Meeting of the Executive Secretariat, July 15, 1949, Secretariat Records, Box 1, folder: Minutes, RG 59, NA; *Rapprochement and Recognition*, p. 16. An economic common front proved somewhat easier to impose and sustain. In mid-June 1949 Edwin Martin, Director of the Office of International Trade Policies, traveled to Europe to secure agreement for limits on export of strategic materials to China (e.g., oil, airplane parts). Similar controls already existed on trade with the Soviet Union and Eastern Europe. It should be noted that the primary concern was to prevent transshipment to the USSR, not to deprive China of supplies for normal domestic consumption. Gittings, *The World and China*, pp. 169–70.

25. 893.01/6-149, #111 Foster, Canberra, FRUS (1949)9:32–33; 893.01/6-2849, #1395 Stuart, Nanking, FRUS (1949)9:47; 893.01/10-449, #881 Steere, The Hague, FRUS (1949)9:98–99; 893.01/11-749, #1373 Donovan, New Delhi, FRUS (1949)9:175; 893.01/12-1649 Ernest Bevin, British Foreign Secretary to Acheson, FRUS (1949)9:225. British officials claimed that overwrought feelings in the United States were influencing rational consideration of recognition. Maberly E. Dening, British Assistant Undersecretary of State for Foreign Affairs told a Commonwealth Conference in Singapore that the White Paper provided the best case for recognition. 893.01/12-2849, #422 Langdon, Singapore, FRUS (1949)9:249.

26. Acheson recognized this point, warning that the effort to tie the United States to Chiang Kai-shek would "mobilize the whole of Asia's millions solidly against the United States and destroy the possibility in our time of a friendly power, and friendly peoples, in Asia." Graebner, "Acheson," p. 282. See also CIA 1-50, "Review of the World Situation," January 18, 1950, p. 2, Truman Papers, PSF, Intelligence File, folder: Central Intelligence Reports, HST; 893.01/11-2349, #2652 Cowen, Manila, RG 59, NA; Memoranda of Conversations with Nehru, October 12, 1949 and October 13, 1949, Acheson Papers, Box 64, folder: October-November 1949, HST; James Reston, "Truman Top Aides Divided on What to Do About China," p. 6; 893.01/8-2349, #739 Stanton, Bangkok,

FRUS (1949)9:62–63; 893.01/10-3149, #424 AmEmb Rangoon, RG 59, NA; 893.01/12-2049, #A-505 Day, Rangoon, RG 59, NA; 893.01/5-2049, #2084 Bruce, Paris, RG 59, NA; 893.01/12-2049, #2880 Cowen, Manila, FRUS (1949)9:234.

27. Ambassador Jessup worried that the United States would isolate itself. "Discussion of Far Eastern Affairs in Preparation for Conversations with Mr. Bevin," September 13, 1949, CA Records Box 14, folder: U.S. Policy Toward China and the Far East, RG 59, NA. John Cabot warned as early as May, 1949 that other nations are not "going to wait indefinitely for us to climb on the bandwagon they are already fashioning." 893.00/5-1149 Cabot to Butterworth, RG 59, NA.

28. 894A.20/12-2949, Memorandum of Conversation by the Secretary, FRUS (1949)9:466. See also ch 2.

29. Sulzberger's articles of February 11, 15, 18 and 21, 1949 all were based on briefings by Davies. Cyrus L. Sulzberger, A Long Row of Candles, pp. 384–87; quotes taken from Sulzberger, New York Times, February 18, 1949, p. 8.

30. NSC 41, "U.S. Policy Regarding Trade with China," March 3, 1949, FRUS (1949)9:826–34. Policy reaffirmed on two occasions: Memo Gay (CP) to Davies (S/P), May 11, 1949, CA Records, Box 15, folder: NSC 41, and NSC 41/1, Truman Papers, HST, reprinted in FRUS (1949)9:891–92. See also 893.00/3-2449 Cabot to Butterworth, RG 59, NA, which says that this policy is supported by Consul General Cabot, Counselor of the American Embassy, Nanking, Livingston Merchant, Commercial Attaché Hinke and Consul General McConaughy. Re Sino-Soviet split see ch 2.

31. 611.9331/4-2929, #296 Clark, Canton, FRUS (1949)9:934; 893.00B/6-649, #534 ibid., p. 370 (and even he thought Chou should be encouraged re his démarche); 893.00/7-2749, #829 ibid., pp. 59–61.

32. 893.01/12-2449, #2350 Clubb, Peking, FRUS (1949)9:243; 893.9111RR/10-849, #1710 ibid., p. 112; 893.00B/12-2349, #2341 ibid., 8:644–45; Interview with O. Edmund Clubb, December 21, 1978.

33. John Leighton Stuart, a missionary educator and founder of Yenching University, had spent most of his life in service in China. Almost more Chinese than American in his perspective, he urgently desired a resolution of the civil war which would bring the Chinese peace and stability. Although a long-time friend of Chiang Kai-shek, by 1949 he had come to realize that the Generalissimo was no longer synonymous with the future of his country. Stuart also had established close relations with various members of the CCP during their student days at Yenching. He hoped to use these friendships to keep lines of communication open between the United States and China. Melby, Mandate, pp. 138, 181, 264-65. For examples of Stuart's thought both for and against dealing with the communists in China see: "Notes on a Future American China Policy," July 14, 1949, CA Records, Box 14: 1948–49, folder: U.S. Policy Toward China and the Far East, RG 59, NA and reprinted in FRUS (1949)8:430–35; 893.00/2-549, #44 Stuart, Nanking, ibid., pp. 108–10; 893.01/6-2349, #A-140 Hopper, Hong Kong, RG 59, NA; #2003 Stuart, Nanking cited by Butterworth in a Memo to the Acting Secretary, November 3, 1948, CA Records, Box 13, folder: U.S. Policy Toward China; Stuart, Fifty Years in China, p. 236; V. K. Wellington Koo Oral History Collection, I (sec 8): 442–43; John Leighton Stuart Diary, April 13, 1949, June 3, 1949, November 3, 1949, Washington, D.C.: 893.00/4-1949, #A-84 Stuart, Nanking, RG 59, NA; 711.93/5-349, #921 Stuart, Nanking, FRUS (1949)9:14-15. Contradictions in Stuart's assessments were noted, see #1490 Secretary to

Stuart, October 26, 1948, Clark Clifford Papers, Box 3: China, Coal Case, folder 2: China, HST.

34. Interview with Hilda Melby, secretary to Ambassador J. Leighton Stuart, July 21, 1977; O. Edmund Clubb Oral History Interview, June 26, 1974, p. 81, HST; Interview with O. Edmund Clubb, December 21, 1978; "A New Policy for Asia: An Editorial," p. 5; NSC 41/1, "Report on U.S. Policy Regarding Trade with China," Truman Papers, HST, and FRUS (1949)9:891–92.

35. Butterworth's remarks were made at the October 1949 Round Table Conference. Gittings, *World and China*, p. 177n.

36. These warnings suggested only that Americans lacking compelling reasons to remain consider the advisability of evacuating. The State Department maintained that it did not mean to suggest that key personnel in commerce, industry, religious, or philanthropic enterprises should depart. 811.24593/1-549 Memorandum by the Director of the Office of Far Eastern Affairs (Butterworth) to the Acting Secretary (Lovett), FRUS (1949)9:1212.

37. 893.00/9-1349, #1095 Strong, Canton, RG 59, NA.

38. 393.1115/5-1349, Cabot, Shanghai, FRUS (1949)9:1257; 893.00/12-749 "China," RG 59, NA, and in CA Records, Box 14, folder: Ambassador Jessup's trip; 893.01/12-849 John E. Peurifoy to Helen Gahagan Douglas, RG 59, NA; Acheson to Sidney Souers, Executive Secretary of the NSC, April 4, 1949, Truman Papers, PSF, Box 205: NSC Meetings, no. 35, March 3, 1949, HST; 890.00/11-1749 Memorandum by Charlton Ogburn of the Bureau of Far Eastern Affairs, FRUS (1949)9:161; Memo Jessup (S/A) to Rusk (G), March 23, 1950, Philip C. Jessup Papers, Box 47, folder: Chronological File, March 1950, Report to Board of Directors, United Service to China, Hathaway Watson, Jr., January 25, 1950 to Dean Acheson and Paul V. McNutt, chairman, USC, April 3, 1949, Box 3814, Lot File 53D211, Philip C. Jessup Papers, Department of State, Washington, D.C. (hereafter State). There were still 2,700 Americans in China according to the Secretary of State as of March 1, 1950. *New York Times*, March 2, 1950, p. 20.

39. A Sun Li-jen coup might have materialized had the Korean war not intervened. Interview with Beverly D. Causey, former member of the Reports and Estimates Branch, CIA, June 2, 1978; 893.00/2-2849, #684 Cabot, Shanghai, RG 59 NA; John Cabot Diary, May 3, 1949, Washington, D.C.; Memorandum by W. W. Stuart, undated but apparently early 1950, CA Records, Box 16, folder: Taiwan, RG 59, NA; 893.00/10-1749, #JM88 MacDonald, Taipei, RG 59, NA; 893.24/12-2149, #2332 Clubb, Peking, RG 59, NA; "Change in Political Control of Taiwan," October 13, 1949, Memorandum by Central Intelligence Agency, Washington, D.C.

40. Re Truman's contribution to the growth of public hysteria see Athan G. Theoharis, *The Yalta Myths*, pp. 71-76; Cochran, *Harry Truman*, p. 309. Republican attacks were considered partisan rather than substantive by members of the State Department staff, see Butterworth Oral History, pp. 52–53, 59–61. Indeed many members of the Department looked on Senators and Congressmen with some degree of contempt. Interview with John Melby, March 26, 1977. Acheson, *Creation*, pp. 99–100. George Kennan thought Congress had made flexibility in foreign policy impossible. Stewart Alsop to Marty, April 1, 1950, Joseph and Stewart Alsop Papers, Box 27: Special Correspondence, folder: SEP January-June 1950, LC. Everett Case, China consultant, refused to accompany his old friend H. Alexander Smith on his autumn 1949 Far Eastern trip because he expected

it to be a purely propaganda junket. It was. Interview with Everett Case, November 9, 1977.

41. Gaddis, "Defensive Perimeter," pp. 74–78, 88–89.

42. Harry F. Kern, "Defeat in Asia—The How and Why," p. 43. According to Wellington Koo, Johnson was very friendly with Chiang Kai-shek. Koo Oral History, I (sec 4):194. Secretary of State Acheson, conscious of the pressure Johnson placed on the JCS, suggested at a July 25, 1949 State Department meeting that a paper be redrafted before submission to the NSC in a way which would help channel JCS thinking on the problem. Executive Secretariat Meeting, July 25, 1949, Secretariat Records, Box 1, folder: Minutes, RG 59, NA.

43. JCS 1330/10, "U.S. Military Advisory Group to China," October 22, 1945, FRUS (1945)7:590–98. Objection to large-scale commitment Secretary of State James Byrnes to State–War Coordinating Committee, January 5, 1945, FRUS (1945)10:810–11. Truman favored a smaller group. Truman to the Secretaries of State, War and Navy, February 25, 1946, *White Paper* pp. 339–40.

44. SM-8388, "Study of the Military Aspects of United States Policy Toward China," June 9, 1947, JCS to SWNCC, FRUS (1947)7:838–48; NSC 22, "Possible Courses of Action for the U.S. with Respect to the Critical Situation in China," July 26, 1948, FRUS (1948)8:118–22 and NSC 22/1, August 6, 1948, *ibid.*, pp. 131-35; NSC 37, "The Strategic Importance of Formosa," December 1, 1948, FRUS (1949)9:262.

45. Even before the Soviet bomb the Harmon Report, completed in May 1949, had concluded that the planned atomic air offensive against Russian cities would not prevent loss of Western Europe and parts of the Middle East to the USSR in the event of war. On the other hand, Truman's low defense budget forced the armed services to rely on atomic weaponry and led Secretary Johnson to conceal the Harmon Report from the President. As to the impact of the Russian bomb, no immediate revision of war plans occurred, although several studies were undertaken. Intelligence estimates concluded that, in fact, the United States would not be threatened before 1951 since the Soviets would not have appropriate delivery systems until then. David A. Rosenberg, "American Atomic Strategy and the Hydrogen Bomb Decision," pp. 69–73, 80; Joseph Alsop to William R. Mathews, *Arizona Daily Star*, Tucson, Arizona, July 12, 1950, Alsop Papers, Box 24: Special Correspondence, folder: "Matter of Fact" Column—with Publishers, A 1946–56; Joseph Alsop to Marty," October 16, 1949, Alsop Papers, Box 27; Special Correspondence, folder: SEP June-December 1949, LC.

46. JSC 1769/1, "United States Assistance to Other Countries from the Standpoint of National Security," April 29, 1947, FRUS (1947)1:736–50. In 1948 China dropped to seventeenth place. SANACC 360/11, August 18, 1948, Rusk to Acheson, March 16, 1949, FRUS (1949)1:262.

47. NSC 37/3, "The Strategic Importance of Formosa," February 11, 1949, FRUS (1949)9:285; Memo Johnson to Souers, April 2, 1949, *ibid.*, pp. 307–08; NSC 37/7, "The Position of the United States with Respect to Formosa," August 22, 1949, *ibid.*, p. 377.

48. Memorandum by Marshall S. Carter, February 7, 1949, and Acheson Memo of Conversation with Truman, February 7, 1949, and Memo by Sidney Souers, February 8, 1949, FRUS (1949)9:485–87; Vandenberg, *Private Papers*, pp. 530–31; McLellan, *Dean Acheson*, p. 188n; Acheson, *Creation*, p. 306; Anthony R. Bullard, "Harry S. Truman and the Separation of Powers in Foreign Affairs"

(Ph.D. diss.), p. 173. The State Department was also content to see military aid stop when the funds of Section 404 of the 1948 China Aid Act were fully obligated on April 2, 1949. Memo for Sidney Souers, Executive Secretary of the NSC, April 4, 1949, Truman Papers, PSF, Box 205: NSC Meetings, no. 35, March 3, 1949, HST. Delays in arms shipments continued. 893.24/11-2349 Memo Sprouse to Merchant, RG 59, NA.

49. 893.24/7-2349 Memo Yost to Jessup, RG 59, NA. See also Princeton Seminars, July 22–23, 1959, HST.

50. 893.00/2-1149 Memo on Telephone Conversation by Marshall S. Carter, RG 59, NA and printed in FRUS (1949)8:123; Executive Secretariat Meeting, March 8, 1949, Secretariat Records, Box 1, folder: Minutes, 1949, RG 59, NA.

51. Letter of Transmittal, July 30, 1949, White Paper, pp. iii–xvii.

52. Cohen, "Acheson, His Advisers, and China," in Borg and Heinrichs eds., Uncertain Years, pp. 23–24; Smith, Dean Acheson, pp. 116–17.

53. 894.00/8-449 Memo Department of State to Souers, NSC, FRUS (1949)9:370. This document was circulated as NSC 37/6, "Current Position of the U.S. with Respect to Formosa," August 5, 1949.

54. ORE 76-49, "Survival Potential of Residual Non-Communist Regimes in China," October 19, 1949, Central Intelligence Agency, RG319, WNRC, also excerpts in Department of Defense, United States-Vietnam Relations 1945–1947, VB2: Justification of the War—Internal Commitments, Truman Administration 1945–52, Bk I: 1945–49, p. 245; CIA 1-50, "Review of the World Situation," January 18, 1950, p. 3, Truman Papers, PSF, Intelligence File, folder: Central Intelligence Reports, HST; ORE 7-50, CIA estimate of March 20, 1950, and April 10, 1950, noted in 794A.00/4-1750 Memorandum by Assistant Secretary of State for Far Eastern Affairs to Secretary, FRUS (1950)6:330 (Defense Department dissented from the March appraisal); 893.00/12-749, "China," RG 59, NA and CA Records, Box 14, folder: Ambassador Jessup's Trip, RG 59, NA; 794A.00/5-1750 Strong, Taipei, FRUS (1950)6:340; Circular Airgram, September 23, 1949, 350.2 Taiwan Miscellaneous-Political, Box 912, Consul General Hong Kong, China Post Files, RG 84, WNRC.

55. 794A.00/4-2750, #658 Strong, Taipei, FRUS (1950)6:335–39; 794A.00/5-1750, #759 ibid., p. 340.

56. 894A.20/12-149 Memo by Deputy Assistant Secretary for Far Eastern Affairs Merchant to Assistant Secretary Butterworth, FRUS (1949)9:431–33. For text of the circular telegram: "Policy Information Paper—Formosa," Special Guidance No. 28, December 23, 1949, printed in U.S. Cong., Senate, Committee on Armed Services and Committee on Foreign Relations, Hearings: Military Situation in the Far East, 82d Cong., 1st sess, 1951, pt 3, pp. 1667–69.

57. Dean Acheson testimony in Executive Session, January 13, 1950 and March 29, 1950, U.S. Cong., Senate, Committee on Foreign Relations, Reviews of the World Situation: 1949–1950, pp. 184, 275. Philip Sprouse, Chief of the Office of Chinese Affairs, subsequently asserted that in his meetings with Congress Acheson "was apparently paving the way for eventual serious consideration of recognition" after the CCP had taken Taiwan and the Nationalist Government had ceased to exist. Philip Sprouse to Robert Blum, Committee on Foreign Relations, U.S. Senate, February 8, 1973, Diplomatic History (Spring 1978) 2:215.

58. 793.00/2-1750 Memorandum of Telephone Conversation by Windsor G. Hackler (FE) FRUS (1950)6:313n4; Memorandum, March 3, 1950, CA Records, Box 16, folder: Taiwan, RG 59, NA.

59. *New York Times*, January 3, 1950, p. 1 and January 4, 1950, p. 1; Westerfield, *Foreign Policy*, pp. 362–66; Tsou, *America's Failure* pp. 529–34; Lewis M. Purifoy, *Harry Truman's China Policy*, pp. 141–43; McLellan, *Dean Acheson*, pp. 205–9; 893.00/11-3049 Memorandum of Conversation by McFall, Assistant Secretary for Congressional Relations, FRUS (1949)9:207; Smith, *Dean Acheson* p. 128.

60. NSC 37/9, "Possible United States Military Action Toward Taiwan Not Involving Major Military Forces," December 23, 1949, FRUS (1949)9:460–61; Freda Kirchwey, "China: Blunder Upon Blunder?" p. 2; Harriet D. Schwar, "The Truman Administration and the Problem of Taiwan, 1949–1950," Paper presented at the Third Conference on War and Diplomacy, The Citadel, Charleston, S.C., March 9–10, 1978, pp. 10–12; Gaddis, "Defensive Perimeter," in Borg and Heinrichs, eds., *Uncertain Years*, pp. 82–83. New funds were available under Section 303 of the Mutual Defense Assistance Act of 1949 approved by Congress September 28, 1949. It provided $75 million for use in the general area of China at the President's discretion.

61. Tsou, *America's Failure*, p. 527.

62. Re State Department recommendations for use of the $75 million: 890.20/10-2449 Memo Butterworth to Webb, FRUS (1949)9:570–76. Re State Department rebuttal at NSC meeting: 894A.20/12-2949. Memorandum of Conversation, FRUS (1949)9:463–67. In NSC 37/5, "Supplementary Measures with Respect to Formosa," March 1, 1949, FRUS (1949)9:291–92, it is pointed out that the Department has consistently opposed in the NSC 34 series, NSC 11/12 and NSC 37/1 the establishment of United States military forces on Taiwan as "not only diplomatically disadvantageous" but "a heavy political liability for us." It would not deter communist infiltration and agitation and might well make Taiwan an irredentist issue in China. The President sided with the State Department, see NSC 48/1, "The Position of the United States With Respect to Asia," December 23, 1949, *U.S.-Vietnam Relations*, VB2, BkI, pp. 245–46 which as approved December 30, 1949 became NSC 48/2.

63. Truman was convinced that the CCP could take Taiwan at will. See Memorandum of Conversation with the President, October 31, 1949, Secretariat Records, Box 3, folder: 1949, RG 59, NA.

64. *New York Times*, January 6, 1950, pp. 1, 3.

65. Acheson, "Crisis in Asia," pp. 111–18; Tsou, *America's Failure*, pp. 532–36.

66. U.S. Cong., Senate, Committee on Foreign Relations, *Economic Assistance to China and Korea: 1949–50*, pp. 193–227; Tsou, *America's Failure*, pp. 537–38. This was the first major setback in Congress for the Administration's foreign policy program since the war.

67. Re obstruction of interdepartmental communication see Princeton Seminars, July 22–23, 1953, HST; 893.00/7-2249 Secretary Johnson to Secretary Acheson, RG 59, NA; Livingston Merchant, "Relationship of the Departments of State and Defense in National Security Affairs," December 14, 1962, Merchant Papers, Box 3: Speeches, folder: 1962; Acheson, *Creation*, p. 371; Interview with Philip C. Jessup, September 21, 1977. Re trouble over the White Paper see Memorandum of Conversations, July 21, 1949 and July 25, 1949, Secretariat Records, Box 3, folder: 1949, RG 59, NA; 893.00/7-2149 Johnson to Acheson, RG 59, NA. Against sending the *General Gordon* to Shanghai see 393.1115/8-2749 Johnson to Acheson, RG 59, NA; 393.1115/9-1449 Johnson to Acheson, RG 59, NA. General friction noted by Joseph Alsop in "Real Danger of Acheson, Johnson Row," p.

1B. See also Joseph Alsop to Marty, June 6, 1949, Alsop Papers, Box 26: Special Correspondence, folder: SEP January-May 1949, and Stewart Alsop to Marty, August 5, 1950, Box 27: Special Correspondence, folder: January-June 1950, LC.

68. Omar Bradley, Chairman, JCS, testimony in Executive Session, January 26, 1950, U.S. Cong., Senate, Committee on Foreign Relations, *Reviews of the World Situation: 1949–1950*, pp. 239–45; Gaddis, "Defensive Perimeter," in Borg and Heinrichs, eds., *Uncertain Years*, pp. 77–89; Schwar, "The Truman Administration," pp. 10–12; Memorandum by General MacArthur, June 14, 1950, FRUS (1950)7:161–65; Telegram C56410 from CINCFE for JCS, May 29, 1950, *Declassified Documents Reference System*, R: 52F; 661.93/4-1850 Memo Rusk to Acheson, FRUS (1950)6:333–35. China's weakness meant that it did not pose a military threat to the United States. The JCS concern was to keep Taiwan out of Soviet control. Memo JCS to Secretary of Defense Forrestal, November 24, 1948, FRUS (1949)9:261-62; 894A.00/1-649 Memorandum of Conversation by Counselor of Embasssy in the Philippines, *ibid.*, p. 265. On June 24, 1950 Secretary Johnson, upon returning from a Far Eastern trip with JCS Chairman Omar Bradley, said that they had gotten all the facts regarding the Far Eastern situation from MacArthur and other commanders. *New York Times*, June 25, 1950, p. 18.

69. NSC 37/2, "The Current Position of the United States With Respect to Formosa," February 3, 1949, FRUS (1949)9:281–82; 893.50 Recovery/4-2949 Director of ECA China Program, Harlan Cleveland to Butterworth, *ibid.*, pp. 319–20; 893.50 Recovery/5-449 Merchant, Taipei, *ibid.*, pp. 324–26; 894A.00/5-2449 Memo Merchant to Butterworth, *ibid.*, 337–41.

70. Meetings held October 26 and 27 with Secretary Acheson presiding. 890.00/11-1749 Memorandum by Charlton Ogburn Jr., Bureau of Far Eastern Affairs, FRUS (1949)9:160–61.

71. PPS 53, "United States Policy Toward Formosa and the Pescadores," July 6, 1949, FRUS (1949)9:356–59. On the other hand, John Paton Davies, PPS expert on China, and W. Walton Butterworth warned against sending in American forces lest this action anger the people of Taiwan and give impetus to CCP subversion. Cohen, "Acheson, His Advisers and China," in Borg and Heinrichs, eds., *Uncertain Years*, p. 26.

72. Rusk's proposal: 794A.00/5-3150 Memorandum by Howe, Deputy Special Assistant for Intelligence, to Armstrong, Special Assistant to the Secretary of State for Intelligence and Research, FRUS (1950)6:347–51. Re Rusk's continuing concern with Taiwan, see Executive Secretariat Meetings June 22, 1949 and August 31, 1949, Box 1, folder: Minutes, RG 59, NA. Rusk said he was investigating the possibility of getting retired General Frank Merrill to go to Formosa and talk with Sun Li-jen to work out plans for saving the island. Other Departmental consideration of plans for a United Nations trusteeship included: 501.BB/6-949 Memo Butterworth to Rusk, FRUS (1949)9:346-50 in which Butterworth recommends the "morally unassailable" position of calling for a UN plebiscite on Taiwan; 894A.01/3-2349, #640 Merchant, Nanking, *ibid.*, pp. 302-3; 893.00/11-3049 Memorandum of Conversation by McFall, Assistant Secretary for Congressional Relations, *ibid.*, p. 207 at which Senator H. Alexander Smith conceded such action was probably not practicable; Smith to Omar Bradley, December 6, 1949 and Smith to Herbert W. Wheeler, December 21, 1949, and Smith to Thomas C. Hart, December 23, 1949, and Smith to Acheson, December 27, 1949, Smith Papers, Box 98. Information from U.S. Consul at Taipei Edgar indicated that the "mass of Taiwanese hate KMT, fear Communists and would welcome U.S. mil-

itary occupation." Alternately they looked to an UN trusteeship arrangement. 894A.00/12-2349, #865 Edgar, Taipei, FRUS (1949)9:451–55.

73. 611.00/5-1850 Dulles Memorandum, May 18, 1950, FRUS (1950)1:314–16. Republican senatorial leaders agreed on May 23, 1950 to let Dulles pursue the Taiwan issue with Acheson before they indulged in "fireworks." Gaddis, "Defensive Perimeter," in Borg and Heinrichs, eds., *Uncertain Years*, pp. 86–87. Just as plans for the neutralization of Taiwan required the Korean War to reach fruition, so too did NSC 68, which historians have considered evidence of a developing hard line in the government during the early months of 1950. In fact, this policy reflected the thinking of Paul Nitze and the PPS and a few Defense Department representatives which the President declined to approve in April 1950, see epilogue.

74. *New York Times*, June 25, 1950, p. 18.

75. Acheson, *Creation*, p. 147, 203–10; Notes of Conversations, #48 John Foster Dulles, April 18, 1949 and #54 George C. Marshall, June 6, 1949, Box 130, V. K. Wellington Koo Papers, Butler Library Manuscript Division, Columbia University (hereafter Koo Papers); Koo Oral History, I (sec 2): 47–48 and (sec 4):180, 186–87.

76. 893.00/11-3049 Memorandum of Conversation by McFall, FRUS (1949)9:206–7; Address to the National Press Club by Dean Acheson, January 12, 1950, published as "Crisis in Asia," pp. 115–17. Acheson contended in the December 29, 1949 meeting with the JCS that Formosa's fall would be due less to military assault by the CCP than to internal decay: "With a hostile population, overrun by refugees, a corrupt government, even though K. C. Wu has been brought forward as scenery, it seems likely we will see a continuation of the process which lost the Mainland." 894A.00/12-2949 Memorandum of Conversation by Secretary, FRUS (1949)9:466.

77. Butterworth Oral History, pp. 66–68.

78. Ambassador Stuart pointed out to Huang Hua, Chief of the CCP Office of Alien Affairs in Nanking, that the retention of Western ambassadors in Nanking after the CCP had taken over the city could be considered "as significant" by the Party. 711.93/6-849, #1235 Stuart, Nanking, FRUS (1949)8:752; NSC 34/2, "U.S. Policy Toward China," February 28, 1949, Truman Papers, PSF, HST; Memo Butterworth Through McWilliams to Rusk, March 29, 1949, CA Records, Box 15, folder: NSC 34/2, RG 59, NA.

79. 893.00B/3-1049, #62 Stuart, Nanking, FRUS (1949)8:173–77; 893.00B/4-649, #A-33, Secretary to Stuart, FRUS (1949)9:230–31.

80. Memo for Sidney Souers, NSC, on implementation of NSC 34/2, April 4, 1949, Truman Papers, PSF, Box 205, NSC Meetings, no. 35, March 3, 1949, HST; 890.00/11-1749 Ogburn Memo, FRUS (1949)9:161. See also chapter 7.

81. 123 Clubb, #253 Secretary to Clubb, Peking, FRUS (1950)6:321–22. See also 893.01/10-1949 Memo Jessup to Butterworth, RG 59, NA: 893.01/11-349 Memo Butterworth through Rusk to the Secretary, RG 59, NA. Ambassador-at-Large Jessup, for one, had long been worried about keeping Americans in China because of the possibility of incidents which, with their effect on Congress and public opinion, might result in pressures for action the United States would not otherwise take. 393.1115/7-2849 Jessup to Acheson, RG 59, NA. In fact, the Americans did not finally depart until April, citing CCP delaying tactics. The Chinese denied this, speculating that the United States government might have regretted its decision since "a day will come when it will have to ask our gov-

ernment to permit those who have now been granted permission to leave to return to China and that this will result in a big loss of face." Shih-chieh Chih-shih Ch'u-pan she (comp), *Chung-hua Jen-min Kung-ho Kuo tui-wai kuan-hsi wen-chien chi* [Collected Documents on the Foreign Relations of the People's Republic of China] p. 97, and English translation, "Why Have Large Number of U.S. Official Personnel Not Left China," Hsinhua Daily News Release #279, February 6, 1950, p. 26.

82. Acheson talk with Trygve Lie—January 21, 1950. Lie, *In the Cause of Peace*, p. 255; 026 China/8-2549, #1427 Clubb, Peking, RG 59, NA.

83. 893.01/5-1949 Memo Bacon (FE) to Freeman (CA), RG 59, NA; 893.01/5-1149 Memo Bacon to Butterworth with study "Recent Policy of the U.S. With Respect to Recognition of New Governments or States," RG 59, NA; 893.01/8-249 Memo Bacon to Sprouse (CA), RG 59, NA.

84. Outline of Policy, November 14, 1949, FRUS (1949)7:1213; 893.01/10-1949 Jessup to Butterworth, RG 59, NA; 893.01/12-1049 Jessup to Butterworth, RG 59, NA; Memo Butterworth to Sprouse, December 10, 1949, CA Records, Box 14, RG 59, NA, and on decision against a Jessup visit to Peking, see Philip C. Jessup, *The Birth of Nations*, p. 343; 893.24/11-2349 Memo Fosdick to Sprouse, RG 59, NA; Fosdick to Jessup, August 29, 1949, and October 25, 1949 Raymond Fosdick Papers, Box 9, folder: Papers on China and Southeast Asia, State Department 1949–1950, Princeton; Interview with Philip C. Jessup, September 21, 1977. Ambassador Jessup remarked that although both he and Secretary Acheson agreed on the ultimate necessity of recognition they believed that for the moment it was impossible; Interview with Everett Case, November 9, 1977. According to Professor Case the consultants not only favored recognition but expected it to be extended in the not too distant future—probably during 1950.

85. Allen Griffin to Livingston Merchant, January 18, 1950, January 19, 1950, and January 30, 1950, Allen Griffin Papers, Box 1: Correspondence Series, folder: Merchant, Livingston, 1949–1950, Hoover; Roger Lapham, "The Chinese Situation As I Saw It," speech before the Commonwealth Club of California, September 8, 1949, California Historical Society Archives, San Francisco. Memorandum of Explanation by Roger Lapham, December 28, 1949, John D. Sumner Papers, Box 3: General File folder: Personal files on China—Correspondence 1948–52, HST; Memo Griffin to Jessup, September 19, 1949, Griffin Papers, Box 1, folder: Jessup, Philip C. 1949.

86. Charles Yost, special assistant to Ambassador Jessup in 1949–50, said that the general feeling in the Department was that recognition was practical and would happen. Interview with Charles Yost, December 1, 1977; Charles Yost, *The Insecurity of Nations*, p. 146. Similarly O. Edmund Clubb maintained that most foreign service officers favored recognition. Clubb, remarks, University Seminar on Modern China, November 1978. See 393.1115/4-2749, #1389 Cabot, Shanghai, FRUS (1949)9:1251–52; Cabot Diary, April 27, 1949 and May 2, 1949; 893.00/5-1149 Cabot to Butterworth, RG 59, NA; Cabot to Butterworth, February 17, 1949, and Cabot to Butterworth, December 30, 1948, Cabot Papers, folder: Secret Correspondence, 1947–49; 893.111RR/10-849, # 1710 Clubb, Peking, FRUS (1949)9:112; 893.01/12-2449, #2350 *ibid.*, p. 243; 893.00/9-449, #2000 Jones, Nanking, *ibid.*, p. 71; John Melby, "Idle Reflections on the Question of Recognizing the Chinese Communists," CA Records, Box 16, folder: Recognition 1949, RG 59, NA; Interview with John Melby, March 26, 1977; Speech to the Institute for World Organization, January 12, 1950, Merchant Papers, Box: Speeches, folder:

1950; 893.01/10-1249, #4094 Holmes, London, FRUS (1949)9:124; Memorandum Leonard C. Meeker to Philip C. Jessup, August 22, 1949, Box 1, Lot File 53D211, Jessup Papers, State; 893.01/10-449, #1674 Clubb, Peking, FRUS (1949)9:97–98; "Discussion of Far Eastern Affairs in Preparation for Conversations with Mr. Bevin," September 13, 1949, CA Records, Box 14, folder: U.S. Policy Toward China and the Far East, RG 59, NA; 794A.5/4-2050 Strong to Sprouse, FRUS (1950)6:334n3; 793.00/6-250 Memorandum by Charlton Ogburn, FRUS (1950)6:353.

87. 893.00/8-1749 Memo Sprouse (CA) to Yost (S/A), RG 59, NA; 893.00/8-2449 Memo Sprouse to Jessup, RG 59, NA; 893.00/4-2649 Memo Butterworth to Rusk, RG 59, NA; 893.24/5-1149 Memorandum of Conversation by the Secretary of State, FRUS (1949)8:304. Ambassador Koo found W. Walton Butterworth, Robert Lovett, and other Department personnel hostile to the Nationalist cause. Koo Oral History, H(sec. 1):36 (November 11, 1948), and (sec 4):148–49 (January 13, 1949); I(sec 5):231 (July 8, 1949). Secretary Acheson at a Cabinet meeting remarked that General Chennault's advocacy of aid for the Nationalists proceeded from a misguided loyalty to the reigning families in China by a man who was a better soldier than politician. Cabinet Meeting, May 13, 1949, Truman Papers, Matthew J. Connally Files, Box 1, folder: January 3-December 30, 1949, Set I, HST.

88. Re investigation of financial abuse see Executive Secretariat Meeting, July 5, 1959, Secretariat Records, Box 1, folder: Minutes, RG 59, NA. Re parallel between JCS and KMT proposals see 894A.00/12-2349 Ambassador Koo to Secretary, FRUS (1949)9:457–60; NSC 37/9, "Possible United States Military Action Toward Taiwan Not Involving Major Military Forces," December 23, 1949, ibid., pp. 460–61; 894A.00/12-2849 Memo Butterworth to Secretary, ibid., pp. 461–62. There was also awareness of dishonest practices by military leaders in key areas in China. Merchant Papers, Interview by Professor Bianci.

89. The KMT notable was Hollington Tong, a member of the Central Advisory Committee of the KMT and General Manager of China Broadcasting Corporation. 611.93/5-2550 Memorandum of Conversation, FRUS (1950)6:343–44. Re Dulles' advocacy of aid see New York Times, February 11, 1947, p. 6.

90. This took place on January 17, 1950. Tsou, America's Failure, pp. 532–33, 536–37.

91. The results of the Round Table Conference, Ambassador Jessup's inquiries to thirty Far Eastern specialists and press opinion, were summarized for the Secretary of State in a Memorandum by Gerald Stryker, Office of Chinese Affairs, 893.01/11-249, FRUS (1949)9:155–60. Other informational materials of this sort circulated through the State Department. "A Summary of Current American Attitudes on U.S. Policy Toward the Far East," February 13, 1950, Special Report on American Opinion, Office of Public Opinion Studies 1943–65, Box 33, folder: China 1949–52, RG 59, NA.

92. Cohen, "Acheson, His Advisers and China," in Borg and Heinrichs, ed, Uncertain Years, pp. 50–51.

93. Acheson, Creation, p. 323. Re British view of American attitude: Minister of the British Embassy in Washington, Sir Derick Hoyer Millar, remarked to Allen Griffin that "the British have discarded the mentality of treaty port days with better grace than [the Americans] who never had any treaty ports." Griffin to Merchant, January 30, 1950, Griffin Papers, Box 1, folder: Merchant, Livingston, 1949–50.

94. *New York Times*, September 20, 1949, p. 18. On recognition as a practical matter: PPS 24, "To Establish the Policy of the Department Regarding the Recognition of New Governments," March 15, 1948, and Memo Butterworth to Butler (S/P), March 15, 1948, PPS Records, Box 72: PPS—Working Papers, folder: Recognition 1948–1950, RG 59, NA; Memo on the position the United States should take during the forthcoming discussions with the British with respect to the question of possible recognition of a Chinese Communist regime, CA Records, Box 16, folder: Recognition 1949, and Box 14; 893.00/5-1049, RG 59, NA reaffirms the March 1948 study. Re Acheson's objection to Wilsonianism in foreign affairs, see Norman Graebner, "Dean G. Acheson," p. 269; U.S. Cong., Senate, Committee on Foreign Relations, *Reviews of the World Situation*, pp. 126–27. Not long after Acheson's September speech Winston Churchill told Parliament in strikingly similar terms: "The reason for having diplomatic relations is not to confer a compliment but to secure a convenience." Britain was then less than two months from according the PRC recognition. *House of Commons Debates*, 1949, p. 2226.

95. Position Paper for Bevin Conversations, September 1949, CA Records, Box 16, folder: Recognition 1949, RG 59, NA. See also 893.01/12-849 Memorandum of Conversation by the Secretary, FRUS (1949)9:220; 893.01/12-2049, #1074 Stanton, Bangkok, *ibid.*, p. 231; 893.01/6-749, #1478 Kohler, Moscow, *ibid.*, p. 35.

96. *Rapprochement and Recognition*, pp. 12–13.

97. Text of Dean Acheson's Commonwealth Club of California speech, March 15, 1950, "United States Policy Toward Asia," pp. 56–60; Speech by Loy Henderson, Ambassador to India, *Department of State Bulletin*, April 10, 1950, pp. 565–66. In fact, as early as September 1949 the Office of Chinese Affairs and the Division of Far Eastern Affairs had concluded that the only essential condition for recognition would be definition of the rights of foreign nationals and clarification of the status of foreign-owned property in China. "Recognition of the international obligations of the antecedent government" should be sought "insofar as possible." Position Paper for Bevin Conversations, CA Records, Box 16, folder: Recognition 1949, RG 59, NA. This viewpoint was set forth again in policy reviews before a new set of discussions with the British and the French in November. 893.01/11-549 Memorandum by Troy L. Perkins, CA Records, FRUS (1949)9:168.

98. Re calling the Communist Chinese puppets Raymond Fosdick noted: "According to all reports the Chinese are sensitive on this subject of subserviency to Russia. This is the point at which we should drive—with every resource at our command." 893.00/8-2949, RG 59, NA; John Paton Davies, *Dragon By the Tail*, *passim*. Re Sino-Soviet rift as major focus of policy, see 893.00/12-749 Jessup briefing memo, CA Records, Box 14, folder: Ambassador Jessup's Trip, RG 59, NA; Dean Acheson testimony in Executive Session, March 29, 1950, U.S. Cong., Senate, Committee on Foreign Relations, *Reviews of the World Situation*, pp. 273–74.

99. *Ibid.*, pp. 272, 275.

100. *Ibid.*, p. 273.

EPILOGUE

1. Scholars have proposed a variety of explanations for America's response to the North Korean attack. Ronald Caridi in *The Korean War and American Politics*,

suggests partisan politics as a prime factor. Alexander George and Richard Smoke blame mutual misperceptions of the clash in their study *Deterrence in American Foreign Policy*. Gabriel and Joyce Kolko conceive of the American response in Korea as an effort to defend the international capitalist system, see *The Limits of Power*. To John Spanier, Truman acted to prevent a worldwide upsurge in communist aggression which would upset the international balance of power, see *The Truman-MacArthur Controversy and the Korean War*. For a more detailed discussion of the literature, see Stephen E. Pelz, "America Goes to War, Korea, June 24–30, 1950: The Politics and Process of Decision," working paper for the International Security Studies Program, The Wilson Center, Smithsonian Institution, Washington, D.C. Pelz also offers his own explanation of the Truman Administration's position.

2. 611.00/9-150, #330 Secretary of State to Loy Henderson, New Delhi, Department of State, FRUS (1950)6:479. Fearing Soviet aggression elsewhere in the world while the United States was preoccupied in Korea, Acheson warned, "the Soviets might not intervene themselves in Korea, but might utilize the Chinese communists." Minutes of the 59th meeting of the National Security Council, June 28, 1950, Harry S Truman Papers, President's Secretary's Files, HST. The question of whether the Chinese participated in the planning for the North Korean action remains unanswerable. Moscow clearly took the major part in preparing and directing the offensive. Stalin probably told Mao of his intentions during the treaty negotiations in February but it is also likely that the Chinese did not expect to become directly involved. Whiting, *China Crosses the Yalu*, p. 45.

3. 794A.00/7-2850, #522 Acheson to Douglas, London, FRUS (1950)6:396–97; David S. McLellan and David C. Acheson, eds., *Among Friends: Personal Letters of Dean Acheson*, pp. 100–1.

4. 330/6-2850 Acheson to United Nations Mission, FRUS (1950)7:276; JCS 84681 JCS to MacArthur June 29, 1950, *ibid.*, pp. 240–41; 794A.00/7-2850, #522, FRUS (1950)6:397; 611.94A/8-1450, #144 Rusk to Rankin, *ibid.*, p. 438; 611.00/9-150, #330, *ibid.*, pp. 478–80; Dean Acheson testimony in Executive Session, September 11, 1950, U.S. Cong., Senate, Committee on Foreign Relations, *Reviews of the World Situation, 1949–1950*, p. 354. Historian William Whitney Steuck points out that the U.S. Navy was overcommitted in the western Pacific and could spare little real power to patrol the Straits, making America's pronouncement "largely a bluff." *The Road to Confrontation*, p. 196.

5. Re primary threat Russian control see NSC 37, "The Strategic Importance of Formosa," December 1, 1948, FRUS (1949)9:261–62. Re denying Taiwan to the Russians see Gaddis, "Defensive Perimeter," in Borg and Heinrichs, eds., *Uncertain Years*, p. 81. Preliminary versions of the war plan, subsequently named OFFTACKLE, surfaced in May 1949. OFFTACKLE did not receive formal approval of the Joint Chiefs until December 8, 1949. On January 26, 1950 the JCS determined that it should remain in effect through the middle of 1951.

6. Acheson press conference, January 5, 1950, *Department of State Bulletin*, (January 16, 1950)22:81.

7. Memorandum of Conversation Kennan with MacArthur, March 5 and 21, 1948, appended to PPS 28, "Recommendations with Respect to U.S. Policy Toward Japan," March 25, 1948, FRUS (1948)6:700–1, 709; Gaddis, "Defensive Perimeter," in Borg and Heinrichs, eds., *Uncertain Years*, pp. 61–66; Tsou, *America's Failure* pp. 556–57 Acheson had described the defensive perimeter to the Senate Foreign Relations Committee on January 10, 1950 and Chairman Connally re-

320 NOTES FOR PAGES 197–201

lated the concept to newsmen before the National Press Club appearance. Tsou, pp. 211, 535.

8. *CR*, 81st Cong., 2d sess. (1950)96:644, 649.

9. Four of the five Republicans on the Senate Foreign Relations Committee made statements to the effect that Truman and Acheson had invited the Korean attack. *New York Times*, August 14, 1950, p. 1. The Administration had expected that no more than $10 million of the residual funds for China would actually be spent.

10. Tsou, *America's Failure*, pp. 537–38. Re Taft see *CR* 81st Cong., 2d sess. (1950)96:9319–23. Re Wherry see *New York Times*, August 7, 1950, p. 1, and August 17, 1950, p. 1 (includes quote).

11. The one exception was the American Labor Party representative, Vito Marcantonio (NY). He objected that Truman had usurped Congessional powers and oppressed a national liberation struggle. *New York Times*, June 28, 1950, pp. 1, 5; "Truman's Stand Electrifies Nation," *Newsweek* (July 10, 1950)30:24; "Mr. Truman Would Lose Now," *U.S. News & World Report*, January 12, 1951, p. 23; Larry Elowitz, "Korea and Vietnam: Limited War and the American Political System," (Ph.D. diss.), p. 72; *Gallup Poll: Public Opinion 1935–71*, p. 942.

12. Koen, *China Lobby*, pp. 83–84; Gaddis, "Defensive Perimeter," in Borg and Heinrichs, eds., *Uncertain Years*, p. 90.

13. 795B.5/6-2950 Memo Merchant to Acheson, FRUS (1950)7:239; 795B.5/6-3050 Memorandum of Conversation by Freeman and Aide-Memoire from Chinese Minister Tan Shao-hwa, *ibid.*, pp. 262–63.

14. *New York Times*, August 1, 1950, p. 4, and August 2, 1950, p. 6; Tsou, *America's Failure* pp. 566–67; 795.00/8-150, #180 Secretary to Acting Political Advisor in Japan (Sebald), FRUS (1950)6:405; 794A.00/8-350, #315 Sebald, Tokyo, *ibid.*, p. 415.

15. Cited by Whiting, *China Crosses the Yalu*, p. 89.

16. *Ibid.*, p. 96. For text of the letter see *New York Times*, August 29, 1950, p. 16.

17. Memorandum of Conversation by Philip Jessup, FRUS (1950)7:180.

18. 795.00/8-2550 JCS84737 JCS to MacArthur, FRUS (1950)7:269; 795B.5/6-2950 Secretary of State to Chinese Ambassador Koo, *ibid.*, pp. 276–77; Acheson, *Creation*, pp. 412–13; 795B.5/7-350 Memorandum of Conversation by Rusk, FRUS (1950)7:285. Truman worried at first that Chiang's offer might have to be accepted, since all the other permanent members of the United Nations Security Council were contributing support. Robert H. Ferrell, ed., *Off the Record: The Private Papers of Harry S Truman*, p. 185.

19. 794.00/8-2650 Memorandum by Lucius D. Battle, Special Assistant to Acheson, FRUS (1950)6:453–60; *New York Times*, August 28, 1950, p. 1, and August 29, 1950, pp. 1, 3, 17; Tsou, *America's Failure*, pp. 566–67; McLellan and Acheson, *Among Friends*, pp. 101–2. The CCP did not find Truman's order withdrawing the letter especially reassuring. *Hsin-hua yueh-pao* (November 1950)3:16.

20. 794A.00/9-450, #214 Acheson to Rankin, Taipei, FRUS (1950)6:485; 611.94A/8-1450, #144, *ibid.*, pp. 434–38.

21. Truman, *Memoirs*, 2:339.

22. 794A.00/5-3150 Memorandum by Deputy Special Assistant for Intelligence, Fisher Howe, to the Secretary for Intelligence & Research, W. Park Armstrong, FRUS (1950)6:347–49; 611.94A/5-3050 Extract of Memo by Rusk, *ibid.*, pp. 349–51; Cohen, "Acheson, His Advisors, and China," in Borg and Heinrichs, eds., *Uncertain Years*, pp. 28, 31.

23. 793.00/7-2950 Secretary of Defense to Secretary of State, and reply, FRUS

NOTES FOR PAGES 201–204

(1950)6:401–3; Memo Truman to Secretary of State, July 18, 1950, CA Records, Box 17, folder: U.S. Policy Toward China, RG 59, NA; 611.93/7-2150, #55 Secretary of State to Embassy in China, FRUS (1950)6:385; 795.00/8-850 Extracts of a Memorandum of Conversation, W. Averell Harriman, Special Assistant to the President, with MacArthur, Tokyo, August 6 & 8, 1950, *ibid.* pp. 429–30.

24. "General Policy of the United States Concerning Formosa," July 27, 1950, FRUS (1950)6:392–94; NSC 37/10 "Immediate United States Courses of Action With Respect to Formosa," August 3, 1950, *ibid.*, pp. 413–14. This was a reversal for the JCS. As late as May and June of 1950, they had reaffirmed their opposition to an American defense of Taiwan. Pelz, "America Goes to War," p. 38.

25. 794A.5/8-2550 Truman to Acheson, FRUS (1950)6:414*n*4. Truman told Acheson that he had allocated to the Defense Department $14,344,500 from Mutual Defense Assistance funds, section 2(a) of P.L.627 approved July 31, 1950 to carry out section 303(a) of the 1949 Mutual Defense Assistance Act. The aid to the Nationalists was meant to be for defensive, not aggressive, buildup. 611.00/9-150, #330, FRUS (1950)6:480.

26. Warner R. Schilling, et al., *Strategy, Politics, and Defense Budgets*, p. 147.

27. Robert Jervis, "The Impact of the Korean War on the Cold War," p. 568; "Domestic Impact of Budget Ceilings for the Fiscal Year 1951," Memorandum by Edwin G. Nourse to NSC, September 30, 1949, FRUS (1949)1:394–96. Nourse's comments pertained to NSC 52/2: Government Programs in National Security and International Affairs for the Fiscal Year 1951 which recommended raising the overall budget ceiling as much as $2 billion.

28. Just before the war the House raised it to $13.8 billion. The Senate had not yet acted on June 25, 1950. Schilling, et al., *Strategy, Politics*, pp. 332–33.

29. *Ibid.*, pp. 292, 306, 309–13.

30. S/S NSC Files: Lot 63D351: NSC 68 Series, FRUS (1950)1:234–35; Pelz, "America Goes to War," pp. 33, 60n66. Truman, Pelz argues, was worried about falling tax receipts and the national debt ceiling, particularly with an election only months away.

31. Jervis, "Impact of the Korean War," pp. 563–92.

32. Memorandum Livingston Merchant to Dean Rusk, Checklist on China and Formosa, June 29, 1950, Box 17 folder: U.S. Policy Toward China, CA Records, RG 59, NA; 795.00/7-450 Memorandum of Conversation by Merchant, FRUS (1950)7:298–99; and see FRUS (1950)6:619–90.

33. *Report of the 37th National Foreign Trade Convention, New York, October 30, 31 & November 1, 1950*, pp. 207–11: Tozer, "Last Bridge to China," pp. 64-78; James H. Dolsen, "Big Steel Firm Urges Recognition of China," p. 4.

34. *New York Times*, December 10, 1950, p. 34.

35. Letter to the editor, *New York Times*, August 28, 1950, p. 16.

36. Michael P. Rogin, *The Intellectuals and McCarthy*, p. 243; Acheson, *Creation*, pp. 364–66, 370; Adam Ulam, *The Rivals*, p. 173. According to Eben Ayers, assistant press secretary, Truman had been optimistic about discrediting McCarthy in April but by early June he had lost faith in the efficacy of the Tydings investigation. Pelz, "America Goes to War," pp. 18–19.

37. *New York Times*, June 29, 1950, p. 13; 795.00/6-2950 and 501/6-3050 Secretary of State to All Diplomatic Missions and Certain Consular Offices, FRUS (1950)7:231–32, 255–57.

38. Steuck, *Road to Confrontation, passim*; 795.00/6-2650, #773 Chapin, Netherlands, FRUS (1950)7:186.

39. Acheson, *Creation*, pp. 416–20; 795.00/7-750 Bevin to Acheson, FRUS

(1950)7:329–30; 795.00/7-1050, #132 Acheson to Bevin, *ibid.*, pp. 347–51; 330/7-1350 Memo by McGhee, Assistant Secretary for Near Eastern, South Asian and African Affairs, *ibid.*, pp. 372–73; 795.00/8-1150 Memorandum of Conversation by James N. Hyde, U.S. Mission to the UN, *ibid.*, pp. 555–56.

40. *New York Times*, August 12, 1950, p. 3, and August 18, 1950, p. 10; 330/6-2850, #955 Henderson, New Dehli, FRUS (1950)7:218; 795.00/7-1150, #241 and 795.00/7-1450, #291 Douglas, London, *ibid.*, pp. 361, 381–82.

41. 661.00/8-1550 Minutes of Meeting by Representatives of France, the United Kingdom and the United States, August 4, 1950, FRUS (1950)6:421.

42. Direct U.S. war procurements totaled $145 million in the second half of 1950, $592 million in 1951, $824 million in 1952, and $806 million in 1953. Jon Halliday, *A Political History of Japanese Capitalism*, pp. 196–97, 384n185.

43. 795.00/6-2750, #I.E. No. 7, Intelligence Estimate Prepared by Estimates Group, Office of Intelligence & Research, State Department, FRUS (1950)7:151–52. For Japanese reaction to the war as reported by American and British observers, see: 83816 (FJ 10111/46) #599 Gascoigne, Tokyo, July 8, 1950 and (FJ 10111/48) #214 Gascoigne, Tokyo, July 11, 1950, British Foreign Office Records, Public Records Office, Kew, Surrey, Great Britain.

44. On March 29, 1949, the *New York Times* estimated that there were 35 Catholic missionaries of all nationalities in Communist Chinese prisons. No similar estimate of Protestant missionaries is available, but in view of the greater hostility of the CCP toward the Catholic Church, the number of Protestants incarcerated was probably smaller. In 1953 eight of the ten American Protestant missionaries still in China were in prison. Richard C. Bush Jr., *Religion in Communist China*, p. 48; *New York Times*, March 29, 1949, p. 9. As recently as July 1970 a Catholic prisoner, Bishop James E. Walsh, was released after signing a confession that said he had been a spy "in the legal sense of your laws." *New York Times*, July 11, 1970, p. 1, and July 16, 1970, p. 4.

45. As of December 1949 nearly 2,000 Protestant missionaries from the United States, Canada, and Great Britain still resided in China. Also present were 192 Maryknoll missionaries and a smaller number of American Catholics from such other orders as the Dominicans, Jesuits, and Vicentians. "Report on Protestant Missions," *Monthly Report*, December 31, 1949, p. 24; Statement of Reverend Coleman to me, November 20, 1974.

46. Bush, *Religion*, p. 77.

47. Whiting, *China Crosses the Yalu*, pp. 62–64; *People's China* (July 16, 1950) 2:4.

48. Tsou, *America's Failure*, pp. 561–62; *Hsin-hua yueh-pao* (July 1950) 2:525; Whiting, *China Crosses the Yalu*, pp. 64–65.

49. Whiting, *China Crosses the Yalu*, passim.

50. Truman Special Message to Congress, July 19, 1950, and Radio and Television Report to the American People on the Situation in Korea, September 1, 1950, in *Public Papers of the Presidents of the United States: Harry S Truman, 1950* (Washington, D.C.: Government Printing Office, 1965), pp. 527, 613; 611.00/9-150, #330 Secretary of State to Embassy in India, FRUS (1950)6:479–80; Dean Rusk, "Fundamentals of Far Eastern Policy," *Department of State Bulletin*, (September 18, 1950) 23:465–68. Acheson and other American leaders genuinely seemed to believe that China should be reassured by their statements, see Spanier, *Truman-MacArthur Controversy*, p. 97.

Bibliography

MANUSCRIPT COLLECTIONS

Acheson, Dean Papers. Harry S Truman Library. Independence, Mo.

Alsop, Joseph and Stewart Papers. Library of Congress. Washington, D.C.

American Institute of Pacific Relations. China Reading Room Files. Lehman Library, Columbia University. New York, N.Y.

Ballantine, Joseph W. Papers. Hoover Institution on War, Revolution and Peace. Stanford, Ca.

Bridges, Styles Papers. New England College. Henniker, N.H.

Cabot, John M. Papers. In possession of Cabot Family, Manchester, Ma.

Case, Everett N. Papers. In possession of Everett N. Case, Van Hornsville, N.Y.

Chennault, Claire L. Papers. Library of Congress. Washington, D.C.

Clayton, William L. Papers. Harry S Truman Library. Independence, Mo.

Clifford, Clark M. Papers. Harry S Truman Library. Independence, Mo.

Connally, Thomas Papers. Library of Congress. Washington, D.C.

Connelly, Matthew J. Files. Harry S Truman Library. Independence, Mo.

Council on Foreign Relations Archives. New York, N.Y.

Cross, Rowland M. Papers. Hoover Institution on War, Revolution and Peace. Stanford, Ca.

Dennison, Robert L. Papers. Harry S Truman Library. Independence, Mo.

Dollar, Robert Papers. Bancroft Library. University of California. Berkeley, Ca.

Elsey, George M. Papers. Harry S Truman Library. Independence, Mo.

Far East-America Council of Commerce and Industry Files. New York, N.Y.

Feis, Herbert Papers. Library of Congress. Washington, D.C.

Foreign Missions Conference of North America Files. Far Eastern Joint Office, China Program. Interchurch Center. New York, N.Y.

Fosdick, Raymond Papers. Seeley Mudd Manuscript Library. Princeton University. Princeton, N.J.

Goodrich, L. Carrington Papers. Butler Library Manuscript Division. Columbia University. New York, N.Y.

Gould, Randall Papers. Hoover Institution on War, Revolution and Peace. Stanford, Ca.

Greater San Francisco Chamber of Commerce Collection. California Historical Society Archives. San Francisco, Ca.

Griffin, R. Allen Papers. Hoover Institution on War, Revolution and Peace. Stanford, Ca.

Hornbeck, Stanley K. Papers. Hoover Institution on War, Revolution and Peace. Stanford, Ca.

IT&T Corporation Archives. New York, N.Y.

Jessup, Philip C. Papers. Library of Congress. Washington, D.C.

Johnson, William R. Papers. Yale Divinity School Library. New Haven, Conn.

Koo, V. K. Wellington Papers. Butler Library Manuscript Division. Columbia University. New York, N.Y.

Lapham, Roger D. Papers. Hoover Institution on War, Revolution and Peace. Stanford, Ca.

Latourette, Kenneth Scott Papers. Yale Divinity School Library. New Haven, Conn.

McCarran, Patrick Papers. Holy Names College. Oakland, Ca.

MacMurray, John V. Papers. Seeley Mudd Manuscript Library. Princeton University, Princeton, N.J.

Merchant, Livingston Papers. Seeley Mudd Manuscript Library. Princeton University, Princeton, N.J.

Mobil Oil Corporation Library. New York, N.Y.

National Council of the Churches of Christ in the U.S.A. Papers. Division of Overseas Ministries. China Program Files. Interchurch Center. New York, N.Y.

National Foreign Trade Council Files. New York, N.Y.

Parsons, Charles Papers. Sterling Memorial Library. Yale University. New Haven, Conn.

Scott, Roderick Papers. Hoover Institution on War, Revolution and Peace. Stanford, Ca.

Shanghai Power Company Files. Boise Cascade Company. Boise, Id.

Smith Family Papers. Yale Divinity School Library. New Haven, Conn.

Smith, H. Alexander Papers. Seeley Mudd Manuscript Library. Princeton University. Princeton, N.J.

Sokolsky, George E. Papers. Butler Library Manuscript Division. Columbia University. New York, N.Y.
Snyder, John W. Papers. Harry S Truman Library. Independence, Mo.
Sumner, John D. Papers. Harry S Truman Library. Independence, Mo.
Taft, Robert A. Papers. Library of Congress. Washington, D.C.
Truman, Harry S Papers. Harry S Truman Library. Independence, Mo.
United Presbyterian Church in the United States of America Central Files. Interchurch Center. New York, N.Y.
Wilbur, Ray Lyman Papers. Hoover Institution on War, Revolution and Peace. Stanford, Ca.
Willauer, Whiting Papers. Seeley Mudd Manuscript Library. Princeton University. Princeton, N.J.
Young Men's Christian Association Archives. National Headquarters. New York, N.Y.

PUBLIC RECORDS

Unpublished Documents

Agency for International Development. Record Group 286. General Archives Division. Washington National Records Center. Suitland, Md.
Army Intelligence Document Files. Record Group 319. General Archives Division. Washington National Records Center. Suitland, Md.
Assistant Secretary and Undersecretary of State Office Records. Lot Files. National Archives Building. Washington, D.C.
Assistant Secretary of State for Economic Affairs, 1944-1950, Office Files. Harry S Truman Library. Independence, Mo.
British Foreign Office Records. Public Records Office. Kew, Richmond, Surrey, England.
China Post Files. Record Group 84. General Archives Division. Washington National Records Center. Suitland, Md.
Chinese Affairs Office Records. National Archives Building. Washington D.C.
Commerce Department Records. Record Groups 40 and 151. National Archives Building. Washington, D.C.
Executive Secretariat Records, 1949-1952. Lot Files. National Archives Building. Washington, D.C.
Foreign Claims Settlement Commission Files. Washington, D.C.
    CN-0353 Norwood Francis Allman and Mary Louise Allman
    CN-0340 American Express International Banking Corporation
    CN-0492 Ault & Wiborg (Far East) Ltd.

CN-0278   Bank of America National Trust and Savings Association
CN-0249   Caltex (Asia) Ltd.
CN-0362   Anna Chan Chennault
CN-0288   Esso Standard Eastern, Inc.
CN-0440   First National City Bank
CN-0292   General Electric Company
PL87-846 General Electric Company, War Claim
CN-0067   Henningsen Produce Co.
CN-0285   International Telephone & Telegraph
CN-0072   Metro-Goldwyn Mayer, Inc.
CN-0380   Michaelian & Kohlberg, Inc.
CN-0463   Reliance Motors
CN-0088   Robert Dollar Co.
CN-0280   Shanghai Power Co.
CN-0416   Shanghai Wharf and Warehouse Co.
CN-0323   Triangle Trading Co.
CN-0357   Universal Leaf Tobacco Co.
CN-0439   Warner Brothers (FE) Inc.
CN-0291   Western District Power Co.

Philip C. Jessup Papers. Lot File 53D211. Department of State. Washington, D.C.

Policy Planning Staff Records, 1947-1953. National Archives Building. Washington, D.C.

Special Reports on American Opinion. Office of Public Opinion Studies, 1943-1965. National Archives Building. Washington, D.C.

State Department Records. Decimal File. General Record of the Department of State. Record Group 59. National Archives Building. Washington, D.C.

Weekly Summary of Comment on China. Office of Public Opinion Studies, 1943-1965. National Archives Building. Washington, D.C.

White House Central Files. Harry S Truman Library. Independence, Mo.

White House Official Reporter Records. Harry S Truman Library. Independence, Mo.

Published Documents

Great Britain. Parliament. *Parliamentary Debates* (House of Commons).
    vol 450, May 1948.
    vol 459, December 1948.
    vol 469, November 1949.
    vol 475, May 1950.

U.S. Commission on Foreign Economic Policy. *Report to the President and the Congress, 1954* (The Randall Report). Washington, D.C.: Government Printing Office, 1954.

U.S. Commission on Foreign Economic Policy. *Staff Papers*. Washington, D.C.: Government Printing Office, 1954.

U.S. Congress. House. Committee on Foreign Affairs. Hearings Before the Subcommittee on the Far East and the Pacific. *Claims of Nationals of the United States Against the Chinese Communist Regime*. 89th Cong., 2d sess., 1966.

U.S. Congress. House. Committee on Foreign Affairs. *Hearings on Emergency Foreign Aid*. 80th Cong., 1st sess., 1947.

U.S. Congress. House. Committee on Foreign Affairs. *Hearings: Military Assistance Act of 1949*. 81st sess., July-August 1949.

U.S. Congress. House. Committee on Foreign Affairs. *Hearings: United States Foreign Policy for a Post-war Recovery Program*. 80th Cong., 2d sess., 1948.

U.S. Congress. Joint Committee on the Economic Cooperation Administration. *Report Concerning China* by William C. Bullitt. 80th Cong., 2d sess., December 1948.

U.S. Congress. Senate. Committee on Appropriations. *Hearings: Third Supplemental Appropriations Bill for 1948*. 80th Cong., 1st sess., 1947.

U.S. Congress. Senate. Committee on Foreign Relations. *Congress, Information and Foreign Affairs*. Washington, D.C.: Government Printing Office, 1978.

U.S. Congress. Senate. Committee on Foreign Relations. *Economic Assistance to China and Korea: 1949-50*. Washington, D.C.: Government Printing Office, 1974.

U.S. Congress. Senate. Committee on Foreign Relations. *Executive Sessions*. 81st Cong., 1st and 2d sess., 1949-1950 (Historical Series). Washington, D.C.: Government Printing Office, 1976.

U.S. Congress. Senate. Committee on Foreign Relations. *Reviews of the World Situation: 1949-1950*. Hearings in Executive Session. 81st Cong., 1st and 2d sess., (Historical Series). Washington, D.C.: Government Printing Office, 1974.

U.S. Congress. Senate. Committee on Foreign Relations. *The United States and Communist China in 1949 and 1950: The Question of Rapprochement and Recognition*. Washington, D.C.: Government Printing Office, 1973.

U.S. Congress. Senate. Subcommittee of the Committee on Foreign Relations. *Hearings on the Nomination of Philip C. Jessup to be United States Representative to the Sixth General Assembly of the United Nations*. 82d Cong., 1st sess., 1951.

U.S. Congress. Senate. Committees on Foreign Relations and Armed Services. *Hearings: Military Situation in the Far East:* 82nd Cong., lst sess., 1951.

U.S. Congress. Senate. Committee on the Judiciary. *Hearings on the Institute of Pacific Relations.* 82nd Cong., 1st and 2d sess., 1951-52.

U.S. Department of Commerce. Bureau of the Census. *Historical Statistics.* 1960.

U.S. Department of Commerce. Office of Business Economics. *Census of American Direct Investments in Foreign Countries.* Washington, D.C.: Government Printing Office, 1951.

U.S. Department of Commerce. Office of International Trade. *World Trade Developments in 1948 in Selected Countries.* Washington, D.C.: Government Printing Office, 1949.

U.S. Department of Commerce. Office of International Trade. International Economic Analysis Division. *Foreign Trade of the U.S., 1936-49.* Washington, D.C.: Government Printing Office, 1951.

U.S. Department of Defense. *United States-Vietnam Relations, 1945-47.* Washington, D.C.: Government Printing Office, 1971.

U.S. Department of State. *A Decade of Foreign Policy, 1941-1949.* Washington, D.C.: Government Printing Office, 1950.

U.S. Department of State. *Foreign Relations of the United States.*
   1944, vol 6: *The Far East: China.* Washington, D.C.: Government Printing Office, 1967.
   1945, vol 7: *The Far East: China.* 1969.
   1946, vol 9: *The Far East: China.* 1972.
   1946, vol 10: *The Far East: China.* 1972
   1947, vol 1: *General; The United Nations.* 1973.
   1947, vol 6: *The Far East.* 1972.
   1947, vol 7: *The Far East: China.* 1972.
   1948, vol 6: *The Far East & Australia.* 1974.
   1948, vol 7: *The Far East: China.* 1973.
   1948, vol 8: *The Far East: China.* 1973.
   1949, vol l: *National Security Affairs, Foreign Economic Policy.* 1976.
   1949, vol 7: *The Far East & Australia.* 1976.
   1949, vol 8: *The Far East: China.* 1978.
   1949, vol 9: *The Far East: China.* 1975.
   1950, vol 1: *National Security Affairs, Foreign Economic Policy.* 1977.
   1950, vol 6: *East Asia and the Pacific.* 1976.
   1950, vol 7: *Korea.* 1976.

U.S. Department of State. *Transcript of the Round Table Discussion on American Policy Toward China,* October 6, 7, and 8, 1949. Washington,

D.C.: Government Printing Office, 1949, and also appears as appendix to IPR Hearings.

U.S. Department of the Treasury. Office of the Secretary. *Census of American Owned Assets in Foreign Countries.* Washington, D.C.: Government Printing Office, 1947.

INTELLIGENCE REPORTS

R&A 119. "Chinese Politico-Military Factions," n.d. Office of Strategic Services/State Department Research & Intelligence Reports. Reel I, Pt III: China & India. University Publications of America, Inc. Washington, D.C.

R&A 108. "Stabilization and Silver in American Aid to China," December 31, 1941. OSS/State Department Reports. Reel I, Pt III.

R&A 951. "China's Destiny by Chiang Kai-shek, a Political Bible for the New China," July 15, 1943. OSS/State Department Reports. Reel I, Pt III.

R&A 1753 "Kwangsi-Kwangtung Leaders," February 26, 1944. OSS/State Department Reports. Reel II, Pt III.

R&A 2228. "The Present Stability of the Chinese Government," June 10, 1944. OSS/State Department Reports. Reel II, Pt III.

R&A 2336S. "Scope and Operation of Censorship in China," January 19, 1945. OSS/State Department Reports. Reel II, Pt III.

R&A 3211 "Yen Hsi-shan's Political Position in North China," July 16, 1945. OSS/State Department Reports. Reel II, Pt III.

OIR 4217. "Estimate of the Petroleum Situation in China," May 7, 1947. OSS/State Department Reports. Reel IV, Pt III.

OIR 4378. "The April 1947 Reorganization of the Chinese Government," May 26, 1947. OSS/State Department Reports. Reel IV, Pt III.

OIR 4256. "Biographies of Leading Members of Minority Political Groups in China," August 29, 1947. OSS/State Department Reports. Reel IV, Pt III.

OIR 4657. "Religious Intolerance in Communist China," April 9, 1948. OSS/State Department Reports. Reel IV, Pt III.

OIR 4608. "Popular Reactions to Chinese Communist Rule," April 15, 1948. OSS/State Department Reports. Reel IV, Pt III.

OIR 4729. "Biographic Data on Members of the Politburo and the Central Executive Committee of the Chinese Communist Party," August 20, 1948. OSS/State Department Reports. Reel IV, Pt III.

OIR 4835. (PV). "Economic Developments in China, 1948," December 14, 1948. OSS/State Department Reports. Reel IV, Pt III.

OIR 4862 (PV). "U.S. Involvement with the Nationalist Government of China," January 10, 1949. OSS/State Department Reports. Reel IV, Pt III.

OIR 4848. "Chinese Communist Commercial Policy," January 17, 1949. OSS/State Department Reports. Reel IV, Pt III.

OIR 4867. "The Effect of a Communist-Dominated China on Other Areas of the Far East," January 24, 1949. OSS/State Department Reports. Reel IV, Pt III.

OIR 4910 (PV). "New Light on Chinese Communism from a Disillusioned Party Member, " March 22, 1949. OSS/State Department Reports. Reel IV, Pt III.

ORE 29-49. "Prospects for Soviet Control of a Communist China," April 15, 1949. Central Intelligence Agency. Intelligence Document Files. Record Group 319. General Archives Division. Washington National Records Center. Suitland, Md.

ORE 45-49. "Probable Developments in China," June 16, 1949. CIA. ID Files. RG 319. WNRC.

OIR 5009 (PV). "Considerations Relevant to the Formulation of Conditions for U.S. Recognition of a Communist Government of China," July 1949. OSS/State Department Reports. Reel IV, Pt III.

OIR 5017 (PV). "Prospects for Renewed Peace Negotiations Between the Chinese Communists and the Kwangsi Clique," July 25, 1949. OSS/State Department Reports. Reel IV, Pt III.

OIR 5011 (PV). "Problems of Domestic and Foreign Policy Confronting the Chinese Communists," July 28, 1949. Office of Intelligence Research, General Records of the Department of State, Record Group 59. National Archives Building. Washington, D.C.

CIA 8-49. "Review of the World Situation," August 17, 1949. Central Intelligence Agency. Harry S Truman Papers. President's Secretary's Files. Harry S Truman Library. Independence, Mo.

OIR 5050 (PV). "Prospects for Cooperation Between Chiang Kai-shek and Other Non-Communist Leaders in China," September 19, 1949, OSS/State Department Reports. Reel IV Pt III.

OIR 5037. "Nature and Extent of Governmental Authority in China as of August 30, 1949," September 21, 1949. OSS/State Department Reports. Reel IV, Pt III.

ORE 78-49. "Factors Affecting the Status of Hong Kong (to September 1950)," October 4, 1949. CIA. ID Files. RG 319. WNRC.

ORE 76-49. "Survival Potential of Residual Non-Communist Regimes in China," October 19, 1949. CIA. ID Files. RG 319. WNRC.

OIR 5077. "Initial Chinese Communist Reaction to the U.S. White Paper on China," November 3, 1949. OSS/State Department Reports. Reel IV, Pt III.

OIR 5111. "Current British Policy Toward Communist China," November 15, 1949. OSS/State Department Reports. Reel IV, Pt III.

CIA 12-49. "Reviews of the World Situation," December 21, 1949. CIA. Truman Papers. Harry S Truman Library. Independence, Mo.

OIR 5101. "The Status of Mao Tse-tung as Theoretician and Leader," December 22, 1949. OSS/State Department Reports. Reel IV, Pt III.

CIA 1-50. "Review of the World Situation As It Relates to the Security of the United States," January 18, 1950. CIA. Truman Papers. Harry S Truman Library. Independence, Mo.

UNPUBLISHED PAPERS

Anderson, Irvine H. "Petroleum As A Strategic Commodity in American-East Asian Relations." Paper prepared for the Conference on American-East Asian Economic Relations. Mt. Kisco, N.Y. June 25–27, 1976.

"Caltex in China." Provided to the author by J. M. Voss, Chairman of the Board, Caltex Petroleum Corporation. November 29, 1976.

Chen Chu-yuan. "U.S. Petroleum Trade with China, 1876–1949." Paper prepared for the Conference on American-East Asian Economic Relations. Mt. Kisco, N.Y. June 25–27, 1976.

Cohen, Warren I. "Dean Rusk." Paper presented at the Conference of the Organization of American Historians, April 1978. New York, N.Y.

Hoyt, Frederick B. "Protection Implies Intervention: The State Department Versus the American Catholic Mission at Kanchow, Kiangsi, 1921–34." Paper presented at the Midwest China Seminar. Washington University. St. Louis, Mo. March 9, 1974.

Pelz, Stephen E. "America Goes to War, Korea, June 24–30, 1950: The Politics and Process of Decision." Working paper no. 10. International Security Studies Program. The Wilson Center. Smithsonian. Washington, D.C.

Schaller, Michael. "A Road Not Taken: The United States and the Chinese Communists, 1943–1945." Paper presented at the Conference of the American Historical Association, December 1976. Washington, D.C.

Schonberger, Howard. "Of Arms and Men: Harry F. Kern and the Corruption of Postwar Japan." Paper presented at the New England Conference of the Association for Asian Studies. October 21, 1979.

Schran, Peter. "The Significance of Commercial Relations Between the United States and China, ca. 1850–1931." Paper presented to the Conference on American-East Asian Economic Relations. Mt. Kisco, N.Y. June 25–27, 1976.

Schwar, Harriet D. "The Truman Administration and the Problem of Taiwan, 1949–1950." Paper prepared for the Third Conference on War and Diplomacy, The Citadel, Charleston, S.C. March 9–10, 1978.

Shaw Yu-ming. "Rev. John Leighton Stuart: A Missionary Politician in China, 1937–1941." Paper presented to the annual Conference of the American Society of Church History. December 28, 1976.

Stein, Guenther. "American Business with East Asia." Paper for the Tenth Conference of the Institute of Pacific Relations. Stratford-upon-Avon, England. September 1947.

Strong, Robbins. "The Stronghold." Foochow, China. January 1, 1949.

"Trade Relations, China, 1913–1949." Provided to the author by J. W. Kinnear, Caltex Petroleum Corporation. December 6, 1976.

Yoshitsu, Michael. "Tokyo Tilts Toward Peking: 1951–1952."

DISSERTATIONS AND THESES

Adler, Leslie K. "The Red Image: American Attitudes Toward Communism in the Cold War Era." Ph.D. dissertation, University of California, Berkeley, 1970.

Babcock, Fenton. "Issues of China Policy Before Congress, September 1945 to September 1949." Ph.D. dissertation, Yale University, 1956.

Barnett, Irving "UNRRA in China: A Case Study in Financial Assistance for Economic Development." Ph.D. dissertation, Columbia University, 1956.

Baron, Michael. "Notes of Discord: United States Policy Toward China, 1947–1948." Certificate Essay, East Asian Institute, Columbia University 1976.

Bibber, Joyce K. "The Chinese Communists As Viewed by the American Periodical Press, 1920–1937." Ph.D. dissertation, Stanford University, 1969.

Bullard, Anthony R. "Harry S Truman and the Separation of Powers in Foreign Affairs." Ph.D. dissertation, Columbia University, 1972.

Carpenter, Thomas E. "The IPR and American Foreign Policy." Ph.D. dissertation, Fletcher School, 1968.

Chan, Marjorie M. "A Survey of the American Automobile Market in China." M.A. thesis, Columbia University, 1948.

Chang Tsung-che. "American Investments and Industrial Development in Postwar China." M.A. thesis, Columbia University, 1948.

Chen Chin-yuen. "American Economic Policy Toward Communist China, 1950–1970." Ph.D. dissertation, Columbia University, 1972.

Cheng Peter Ping-chi. "A Study of John Foster Dulles' Diplomatic Strategy in the Far East." Ph.D. dissertation, Southern Illinois University, 1964.

Chittick, William O. "The Domestic Information Activities of the Department of State." Ph.D. dissertation, Johns Hopkins University, 1964.

Chrone, Ruth B. "An Inquiry Into a Possible Relationship Between Propaganda and the Fall of Shanghai." Ph.D. dissertation, New York University, 1960.

Dalstrom, Harl A. "Kenneth S. Wherry." Ph.D. dissertation, University of Nebraska, 1965.

Dinegar, Caroline A. "Some Aspects of the Use of the Recognition of New Governments as an Instrument of U.S. Foreign Policy, 1900–1960." Ph.D. dissertation, Columbia University, 1963.

Dodge, Dorothy R. "Recognition of the P.R.C.: Legal and Political Aspects." Ph.D. dissertation, University of Minnesota, 1955.

Eismann, Bernard N. "The Emergence of 'Two Chinas' in American Foreign Policy, 1950–59." M.A. thesis, Columbia University, 1959.

Ellison, Duane C. "The United States and China 1913–1921: A Study of the Strategy and Tactics of the Open Door Policy." Ph.D. dissertation, George Washington University, 1974.

Elowitz, Larry. "Korea and Vietnam: Limited War and the American Political System." Ph.D. dissertation, University of Florida, 1972.

Fetzer, James. "Congress and China, 1941–1950." Ph.D. dissertation, Michigan State University, 1969.

Goldstein, Steven M. "Chinese Communist Perspectives in International Affairs." Ph.D. dissertation, Columbia University, 1972.

Goodno, Floyd R. "Walter H. Judd: Spokesman for China in the United States House of Representatives." Ph.D. dissertation, Oklahoma State University, 1970.

Gordon, Morton. "The American Press and Recent China Policy, 1941–1949." M.A. thesis, University of Chicago, 1950.

Greenwalt, Bruce S. "Missionary Intelligence from China: American Protestant Reports 1930–1950." Ph.D. dissertation, Chapel Hill, 1974.

Hamilton, William C. "The Development of Foreign Policy Attitudes in Certain American Pressure Groups." Ph.D. dissertation, Yale University, 1955.

Hedley, John H. "The Truman Administration and the 'Loss' of China: A Study of Public Attitudes and the President's Policies from the Marshall Mission to the Attack on Korea." Ph.D. dissertation, University of Missouri, 1964.

Henderson, Cary Smith. "Congressman Taber of Auburn: Politics and Federal Appropriations, 1923–62." Ph.D. dissertation, Duke University, 1964.

Jonas, Gilbert. "American Aid to China as Part of a Policy, 1945–49." Certificate Essay, East Asian Institute, Columbia University, 1953.

Kemp, Virginia M. "Congress and China, 1945–1959." Ph.D. dissertation, University of Pittsburgh, 1966.

Kennedy, Thomas L. "The Treatment of Americans in Red China Prior to the Korean War." M.A. thesis, Georgetown University, 1961.

King, James T., Jr. "United States Policy of Recognition of the Communist Government of China." M.A. thesis, Georgetown University, 1961.

Kliesch, Ralph E. "History and Operations of the McGraw-Hill World New Service." Ph.D. dissertation, University of Minnesota, 1968.

Lacy, Creighton. "Protestant Missions in Communist China." Ph.D. dissertation, Yale University, 1953.

Leary, William M. Jr. "Smith of New Jersey: A Biography of H. Alexander Smith United States Senator from New Jersey, 1944–1959." Ph.D. dissertation, Princeton University, 1966.

Long, F. M. S. Brother Ronald B. "The Role of American Diplomats in the Fall of China, 1941–1949." Ph.D. dissertation, St. John's University, 1961.

Martin Ben L. "Interpretations of U.S. Policy Toward the Chinese Communists, 1944–1968: Survey and Analysis." Ph.D. dissertation, Fletcher School, 1968.

Murray, Randall L. "Harry S Truman and Press Opinion, 1945–1953." Ph.D. dissertation, University of Minnesota, 1973.

Nelson, James C. "The U.S. Senate and Recognition of Communist China." M.A. thesis, University of Chicago, 1954.

Perlmutter, Oscar W. "Acheson and American Foreign Policy: A Case Study in the Conduct of Foreign Affairs in a Mass Democracy," Ph.D. dissertation, University of Chicago, 1959.

Prince, Gregory. "The American Foreign Service in China, 1935–1941: A Case Study of Americans Observing China." Ph.D. dissertation, Yale University, 1973.

Pritchard, Ross. "Will Clayton: Industrial Statesman." Ph.D. dissertation, Fletcher School, 1956.

Ricks, John A. " 'Mr. Integrity' and McCarthyism: Senator Robert A. Taft and Senator Joseph R. McCarthy." Ph.D. dissertation, Chapel Hill, 1974.

Roche, George C. "Public Opinion and the China Policy of the United States, 1941–1951." Ph.D. dissertation, University of Colorado, 1965.

Rozanski, Mordechai. "The Role of American Journalists in Chinese-American Relations, 1900–1925." Ph.D. dissertation, University of Pennsylvania, 1974.

Siegler, Sylvia H. "American Views of the Chinese Communists, 1945–1947." M.A. thesis, Claremont Graduate School.

Skretting, John R. "Republican Attitudes Toward the Administration's China Policy, 1945–1949." Ph.D. dissertation, University of Iowa, 1952.

Smith, Cordell A. "The Marshall Mission: Its Impact Upon American Foreign Policy Toward China, 1945–1949." Ph.D. dissertation, Oklahoma University, 1963.

Stopsky, Fred C. "An Analysis of the Conflict Within the United States Federal Government in the Period 1949–1956 Concerning U.S. Policy Toward China." Ph.D. dissertation, New York University, 1969.

Thomas, Samuel B. "The Doctrine and Strategy of the CCP; Domestic Aspects 1945–1956." Ph.D. dissertation, Columbia University, 1964.

Tidd, J. Thomas. "The Formulation of U.S. Policy Toward China 1945–1950." M.A. thesis, University of Denver, 1950.

Wang Cheng. "The Kuomintang: A Sociological Study of Demoralization." Ph.D. dissertation, Stanford University, 1953.

Weiss, Lawrence. "Storm Around the Cradle: The Korean War and the Early Years of the People's Republic of China, 1949–1953." Ph.D. dissertation, Columbia, 1981.

Whitehead, Raymond L. "Christian Response to People's China: Documentation of a Moral Failure." Th.D. thesis, Union Theological Seminary, 1969.

Williams, Frederick B. "The Origins of Sino-American Conflict, 1949–1952." Ph.D. dissertation, University of Illinois, 1967.

Williams, Herbert L. "Truman and the Press (April 12, 1945–January 20, 1953)." Ph.D. dissertation, University of Missouri, 1954.

Yoshitsu, Michael. "Peace and Security for Japan." Ph.D. dissertation, Columbia University, 1979.

Yu, Frederick T. C. "The Treatment of China in Four Chicago Daily Newspapers, July 1 through December 31, 1949." Ph.D. dissertation, University of Iowa, 1951.

INTERVIEWS

Bates, M. Searle, New York, winter 1972.
Cabot, John M., Washington, D.C., November 29, 1977.
Case, Everett N., New York, November 9, 1977.
Causey, Beverly D. Jr., Geneva, N.Y., June 2, 1978.
Clubb, O. Edmund, New York, December 21, 1978.
Coleman, Reverend, telephone interview, November 20, 1974.
Fugh, Philip, Washington, D.C., February 21, 1977 and July 21, 1977.
Gould, Randall, Mill Valley, Ca., August 1976.
Hopkins, Peter, New York, July 11, 1977.
Hosokawa, Bill, Denver, Co., July 12, 1976.
Hoyt, Palmer, telephone interview, Denver, Co., July 15, 1976.
Jessup, Philip C., New York, September 21, 1977.
Lieberman, Henry R., New York, January 15, 1979.
Loh, P.Y. Pichon, New Jersey, April 17, 1978.
Melby, Hilda, Washington, D.C., July 21, 1977.
Melby, John F., New York, March 26, 1977.
Rosen, Arthur, New York, February 4, 1976.
Smith, Wilfred J., Washington, D.C., November 1977.
Sullivan, Walter, New York, February 8, 1979.
Wedemeyer, Albert C., Maryland, November 30, 1977.
Yost, Charles W., Washington, D.C., December 1, 1977.

ORAL HISTORIES

Acheson, Dean. Butler Library Manuscript Division. Columbia University New York.
Alsop, Stewart. John Foster Dulles Oral History Project. Seeley Mudd Manuscript Library. Princeton University.
Ballantine, Joseph. Butler Library Manuscript Division. Columbia University.
Barnett, Robert W. Harry S Truman Library. Independence, Mo.
Bell, Jack L. Harry S Truman Library. Independence, Mo.
Benton, William. Butler Library Manuscript Division. Columbia University.
Brandt, Raymond P. Harry S Truman Library. Independence, Mo.
Brown, Winthrop G. Harry S Truman Library. Independence, Mo.
Butterworth, W. Walton, Draft Interview. Harry S Truman Library. Independence, Mo.
Butterworth, W. Walton. John Foster Dulles Oral History Project. Seeley Mudd Manuscript Library. Princeton University.

Ch'en Kuang-fu (K. P. Ch'en). Chinese Oral History Project. Butler Library Manuscript Division. Columbia University.

Childs, Marquis. Butler Library Manuscript Division. Columbia University.

China Missionary Oral History Project. Claremont Colleges. Pomona, Ca.

Clubb, O. Edmund. Harry S Truman Library. Independence, Mo.

Daniel, Jonathan. Harry S Truman Library. Independence, Mo.

Dennison, Robert L. Harry S Truman Library. Independence, Mo.

Drummond, Roscoe. John Foster Dulles Oral History Project. Seeley Mudd Manuscript Library. Princeton University.

Folliard, Edward T. Harry S Truman Library. Independence, Mo.

Fox, Joseph A. Harry S Truman Library. Independence, Mo.

Greene, Charles J. Harry S Truman Library. Independence, Mo.

Ho Lien. Chinese Oral History Project. Butler Library Manuscript Division. Columbia University.

Judd, Walter H. Eisenhower Administration Project. Butler Library Manuscript Division. Columbia University.

Judd, Walter H. Harry S Truman Library. Independence, Mo.

Kent, Carleton. Harry S Truman Library. Independence, Mo.

Koo, V. K. Wellington. East Asian Institute. Columbia University.

Krock, Arthur. Butler Library Manuscript Division. Columbia University.

Li Tsung-jen. Chinese Oral History Project. Butler Library Manuscript Division. Columbia University.

Locke, Edwin A. Harry S Truman Library. Independence, Mo.

Lowry, W. McNeil. Harry S Truman Library. Independence, Mo.

McFall, Jack K. Harry S Truman Library. Independence, Mo.

Merchant, Livingston. Eisenhower Administration Project. Butler Library Manuscript Division. Columbia University.

Merchant, Livingston. John Foster Dulles Oral History Project. Seeley Mudd Manuscript Library. Princeton University.

Murphy, Charles S. Harry S Truman Library. Independence, Mo.

Princeton Seminars, 1953–1954. Dean Acheson Papers. Harry S Truman Library. Independence, Mo.

Riggs, Robert L. Harry S Truman Library. Independence, Mo.

Ringwalt, Arthur R. Harry S Truman Library. Independence, Mo.

Robertson, Walter S. Eisenhower Administration Project. Butler Library Manuscript Division. Columbia University.

Salant, Walter S. Harry S Truman Library. Independence, Mo.

Smith, H. Alexander. Butler Library Manuscript Division. Columbia University.

Sokolsky, George E. Butler Library Manuscript Division. Columbia University.
Spingarn, Stephen J. Harry S Truman Library. Independence, Mo.
Strout, Richard L. Harry S Truman Library. Independence, Mo.
Swope, Gerard. Butler Library Manuscript Division. Columbia University.
Trohan, Walter. Harry S Truman Library. Independence, Mo.
Tsiang Ting-fu. Chinese Oral History Project. Butler Library Manuscript Division. Columbia University.
Tso Shun-sheng. Chinese Oral History Project. Butler Library Manuscript Division. Columbia University.
Weigle, Richard D. Harry S Truman Library. Independence, Mo.
Wu Kuo-cheng (K. C. Wu). Chinese Oral History Project. Butler Library Manuscript Division. Columbia University.
Young, Arthur N. Harry S Truman Library. Independence, Mo.

ANNUAL REPORTS AND YEARBOOKS

Abbott Laboratories. *Annual Reports 1948–1950*. Scudder Collection, Business School Library. Columbia University.
American and Foreign Power Company, Inc. *Annual Reports 1948–1950*. Scudder Collection, Business School Library. Columbia University.
American Board of Commissioners for Foreign Missions. *Annual Reports 1948–1951. Yearbooks 1949–1951*. Missionary Research Library. Union Theological Seminary, New York.
Associated Press. *Annual Volumes 1949–1950*. Journalism Library. Columbia University.
Bank of America. *Annual Reports 1949–1950*. Scudder Collection, Business School Library. Columbia University.
British-American Tobacco Company. *Reports of the Directors 1948–1951*. Scudder Collection, Business School Library. Columbia University.
Chase National Bank of the City of New York. *Annual Reports 1948–1950*. Scudder Collection, Business School Library. Columbia University.
China Council of the Presbyterian Church in the United States of America. *35th Annual Meeting*. Hong Kong, 1949. Interchurch Center. New York.
China Yearbook. Taipei: China Publishing Co., 1940–43, 1950.
Editor and Publisher Yearbook, 1948 and 1951. Journalism Library. Columbia University.
Evangelical United Brethren Church. Executive Committee. *Mission Yearbook: Reports and Journals of the Annual Meeting of the Board of Missions*. Dayton, Ohio, 1948–1950. Interchurch Center. New York.

Foreign Missions Conference of North America. *Report of the 55th Annual Meeting* of the Conference of Foreign Mission Boards in Canada and in the United States. Buck Hill Farms, Pa. January 4–7, 1949. Interchurch Center. New York.

General Electric. *Annual Reports 1948–1950.* Scudder Collection, Business School Library. Columbia University.

Interchemical Corporation. *Annual Reports 1940–1942, 1945–1950.* Inmont Corporation Library. Clifton, N.J.

International Standard Electric Corporation. *Annual Reports 1948–1950.* IT&T Corporation Files. New York.

IT&T Corporation. *Annual Reports 1948–1950.* IT&T Corporation Files. New York.

Ketcham, George F. ed. *Yearbook of American Churches, 1949.* Lebanon, Pa.

Lutheran Global Missions. *Annual Reports 1947–1951.* Missionary Research Library. Union Theological Seminary. New York.

Methodist Church. Division of Foreign Missions. Executive Secretary. *Report.* Cincinnati. 1948–1949. Interchurch Center. New York.

National Foreign Trade Council. *Report of the 34th National Foreign Trade Convention.* St. Louis. October 20–22, 1947. New York: NFTC, 1948.

National Foreign Trade Council. *Report of the 36th National Foreign Trade Convention.* New York. October 31, November 1 and 2, 1949. New York: NFTC, 1950.

National Foreign Trade Council. *Report of the 37th National Foreign Trade Convention.* New York. October 30, 31, and November 1, 1950. New York: NFTC, 1951.

North American Council of the College of Chinese Studies. *Report of a Meeting.* New York, April 19, 1950.

Northwest Airlines, Inc. *Annual Report to the Shareholders 1948–1950.* Scudder Collection, Business School Library. Columbia University.

Pan American World Airways. *Wings Over the World Annual Reports 1948–1950.* Scudder Collection, Business School Library. Columbia University.

Presbyterian Church in the United States of America. *Minutes of the General Assembly.* Cincinnati, 1950–1951. Interchurch Center. New York, NY.

Standard Oil of California. *Annual Reports 1948–1950.* Scudder Collection, Business School Library. Columbia University.

Standard Oil Company (New Jersey). *Annual Reports 1948, 1950.* Scudder Collection, Business School Library. Columbia University.

Universal Leaf Tobacco Co., Inc. *Annual Statements 1947–1950.* Scudder Collection, Business School Library. Columbia University.

Women's Division of Christian Service of the Board of Missions and Church Extension of the Methodist Church. Cincinnati. *Annual Reports 1948–1950*. Interchurch Center. New York, NY.

MISCELLANEOUS

Cabot, John M. Diary. In possession of Cabot Family, Washington, D.C.

Forrestal, James V. Diaries. Seeley Mudd Manuscript Library. Princeton University.

Stuart, John Leighton Diary. Washington, D.C.

Ahlers, John, La Jolla, Ca. to this author, January 28, 1977.

Biggerstaff, Knight, Ithaca, N.Y., to this author, August 4, 1977.

Clubb, O. Edmund, New York, to Robert Blum, Committee on Foreign Relations, U.S. Senate, February 25, 1973.

Foster, H. Schuyler, Washington, D.C. to this author, February 24, 1979.

Sprouse, Philip, Orinda, Ca., to Robert Blum, Committee on Foreign Relations, U.S. Senate, February 8, 1973, *Diplomatic History* (Spring 1978) 2:214–17.

Roper Public Opinion Research Center. Public Opinion Poll Data. University of Connecticut. Storrs, Connecticut.

Gerli, Paolino. Comments at East Asian Institute Research Luncheon, May 31, 1977, Columbia University.

Lattimore, Own. Comments at East Asian Institute Research Luncheon, March 30, 1979, Columbia University.

Luce, Clare Boothe. "The Mystery of American Policy in China." Address at the testimonial dinner honoring the Most Reverend Paul Yu-pin, Archbishop of Nanking, June 14, 1949, New York.

Mansfield, Michael J. "The Chinese Policy of the United States." 1947 speech transcript sent to the author by Senator Mansfield.

United States. Declassified Documents Reference System.

United States. Joint Publications Research Service.

PERIODICALS AND NEWSPAPERS

America: A Catholic Review of the Week, January 1948–December 1949.

Business Week, January 1949–May 1950.

China Bulletin of the Foreign Missions Conference of North America. Far Eastern Joint Office. January 1947–December 1950.

China Digest 1948–1950.

China News Letter. Shanghai. Lutheran World Federation. December 1947–June 1950.

Chinese Press Review. U.S. Consulate General, Shanghai. March–September 1949, no. 860–982.
  U.S. Consulate General, Hong Kong. 1948–1949.
  U.S. Embassy, Nanking. January–August 1948, no. 602–753.
Chinese Press Survey. Millard Publishing Co., Shanghai. January 1949–June 1950.
Christian Herald, January 1949–June 1950.
Christian Science Monitor, 1948.
Congressional Record, 1947–1950, 1952, selectively.
Current History, 1949.
Denver Post, January 1949–June 1950.
Department of State Bulletin, 1949–1950.
Far Eastern Survey, 1949–1952.
Far Eastern Quarterly, November 1949–August 1950.
Foreign Broadcast Information Service, January 1948–June 1950.
Foreign Commerce Weekly, October 1948–June 1950.
Foreign Policy Bulletin, October 1948–October 1950.
Harvard Business Review, selectively.
Jen-min jih-pao, January 1949–June 1950, selectively.
Missionary Herald: At Home and Abroad, January 1948–November 1949.
Monthly Report: A Monthly Newsletter. Millard Publishing Co., Shanghai. 1949–1950.
Nation, January 1949–June 1950.
New York Times, 1948–1950.
New China News Agency *Daily Bulletin,* 1950.
New China News Agency *Daily New Release,* 1949–1950.
New China News Agency *Weekly Bulletin,* 1949.
Quarterly Notes: Being the Bulletin of the International Missionary Council, January 1948–January 1950.
St. Louis Post-Dispatch, January 1949–June 1950.
Time, 1949–1951.

ARTICLES

"A New Policy for Asia." *New Republic* (September 26, 1949) 121:5–7.
Abend, Hallett and Ferdinand L. Mayer. "Wanted: A New China Policy." *Current History* (July 1949) 17:1–6.
Acheson, Dean. "American Policy Toward China." *Department of State Bulletin,* (June 18, 1951) 24:963–74.
―――― "Attacks on United States Shipping by the Chinese." *Department of State Bulletin* (December 12, 1949) 21:908.

—— "Crisis in Asia—An Examination of United States Policy." *Department of State Bulletin* (January 23, 1950) 22:111–18. Also appears as "Relations of the Peoples of the United States and the Peoples of Asia." *Vital Speeches of the Day* (February 1950) 16:238–44.

—— "Further Details on Closure of U.S. Missions in China." *Department of State Bulletin*, (March 20, 1950) 22:462.

—— "Government-Citizen Cooperation in the Making of Foreign Policy." *Department of State Bulletin* (December 2, 1945) 13:893–94.

—— "Parties and Foreign Policy." *Harper's* (November 1955) 211:29–34.

—— "Problems in American Foreign Policy." *Department of State Bulletin*, (October 31, 1949) 21:668–69.

—— "U.S. Good Neighbor to Asia." *U.S. News & World Report* (January 20, 1950) 28:21–22.

—— "United States Policy Toward Asia." Text of address, March 15, 1950. *U.S. News & World Report* (March 24, 1950) 28:56–60, and reprinted in *Department of State Bulletin*, (March 27, 1950) 22:467–72.

—— "U.S. Protests to CCP in Smith-Bender Case," *Department of State Bulletin* (December 12, 1949) 21:908.

—— "What a Secretary of State Really Does." *Harper's* (December 1954) vol. 209.

Adler, Kenneth P. and Davis Bobrow. "Interest and Influence in Foreign Affairs." *Public Opinion Quarterly* (Spring 1956) 20:89–101.

Allen, Robert S. "U.S. Oil Firms Shipping to Reds in China." *St. Louis Post-Dispatch*, November 8, 1949, p. 1B.

—— "U.S. Recognition of China Wins Backing." *St. Louis Post-Dispatch*, October 18, 1949, p. 1B.

—— "White Paper on China to Aim at New Yorker." *St. Louis Post-Dispatch*, July 6, 1949, p. 1B.

Alsop, Joseph. "Real Danger of Acheson, Johnson Row." *St. Louis Post-Dispatch*, August 9, 1949, p. 1B.

—— "U.S. Now Ready to Draw a Line to Halt Soviet Expansion in Asia." *St. Louis Post-Dispatch*, May 24, 1949, p. 1B.

—— "Why We Lost China," *Saturday Evening Post* (January 7, 1950) 222:16–17; and (January 21, 1950):30.

—— and Alsop, Stewart. "Truman Faces Great Ruins of Victory." *Denver Post*, March 21, 1949, p. 10.

Alsop, Stewart. "British Mobilization in Hong Kong Warning to Reds They Will Fight." *St. Louis Post-Dispatch*, May 18, 1949, p. 1c.

—— "Death of a City." *Denver Post*, May 15, 1949, p. 2c.

—— "Hope Out of China." *New York Herald Tribune*, June 8, 1949.

———— "Shanghai a Frightened City, Observer Finds." *St. Louis Post-Dispatch*, May 13, 1949, p. 1c.

———— "Still Some Chance." *Denver Post*, June 8, 1949, p. 10.

———— "We Are Losing Asia Fast." *Saturday Evening Post* (March 11, 1950) 222:29.

———— "West in Position to Dictate Trade Terms to Chinese Reds, Promote Nation's Independence of Kremlin." *St. Louis Post-Dispatch*, June 10, 1949, p. 1c.

"Ambassador from Nevada." *Reporter*, September 13, 1949, pp. 23–25.

"America's New Policy on Red China, May Day Parade." *Newsweek*, (May 9, 1949) 33:19.

"American Espionage Ring in Manchuria." *China Digest* (December 14, 1949) 7:9.

"American Spy Ring in Mukden." *China Digest* (June 28, 1949) 6:17–18.

"An Old China Hand." *New Republic* (May 2, 1949) 120:8.

Ascoli, Max. "Starting the Job." *Reporter* (April 15, 1952) 6:2.

"Asia Plan: Forget Formosa, Beef Up South." *Business Week*, January 14, 1950, pp. 101–2.

Baldwin, Hanson. "U.S. Groping in China." *New York Times*, September 18, 1949, p. 7.

"Banking Rules for Communist China." *Far Eastern Survey* (June 1, 1949) 18:123.

Barnett, A. Doak. "Chinese Reds Winning Support of People Near Peiping by Policy of Treading Softly, Visit Reveals." *St. Louis Post-Dispatch*, January 2, 1949, p. 3D.

———— "Report on Red China: Communist Long-Range Policies Intensify Economic Crisis, Many Face Starvation Before Year End." *St. Louis Post-Dispatch*, September 6, 1949, pp. 1B, 10B.

———— "Report on Red China: New Rulers Trying to Orient Nation to Pro-Russian Position, Propaganda Brands U.S. as Enemy." *St. Louis Post-Dispatch*, September 8, 1949, pp. 1B, 7B.

———— "Report on Red China: One of Greatest Sales Campaigns in History as Communists Attempt to Sell Party Line to the Chinese." *St. Louis Post-Dispatch*, September 9, 1949, p. 1D.

Bates, M. Searle. "The Protestant Enterprise in China, 1937–1949." In Wilbur C. Harr, ed. *Frontiers of the Christian World Mission Since 1938*. New York: Harper, 1962.

Bayar, Charles H. "The Blocked Chinese Assets: Present Status and Future Disposition." *Virginia Journal of International Law* (Summer 1975) 15:959–1008. Abbreviated version: "China's Frozen Assets in the U.S." *U.S. China Business Review* (September–October 1975) 2:31–44.

Beech, Keyes. "M'Arthur Aides Favor Trade With Red China." *St. Louis Post-Dispatch*, September 1, 1949, p. 1B.

Benson, Lee, "An Approach to the Scientific Study of Past Public Opinion." *Public Opinion Quarterly* (Winter 1967–68) 31:522–67.

Biggerstaff, Knight. "The Nanking Press: April–September 1949." *Far Eastern Survey* (March 8, 1950) 19:50–54.

Blaisdell, Donald C. "Pressure Groups, Foreign Policies, and International Politics." *Annals of the American Academy of Political and Social Science* (September 1958) 319:150–57.

Blum, Robert M. "The Peiping Cable: A Drama of 1949." *New York Times Magazine*, August 13, 1978, pp. 8–10, 53–58.

Bodde, Derk. "China Under Red Rule." Letter to the editor, *New York Times*, May 27, 1950, p. 16.

——— "Deadline Here for U.S. Decision on China." *Foreign Policy Bulletin* (January 6, 1950) 29:1–2.

——— "Notes on Cultural Activities in Peiping; News of the Profession." *Far Eastern Quarterly* (February 1950) 9:195–98.

——— "Report on Communist China." *Far Eastern Survey* (November 16, 1949) 18:265–69.

Bolles, Blair. "Asia Policy and the Election." *Far Eastern Survey* (December 6, 1950) 19:221–24.

——— "Problem of China." *Foreign Policy Bulletin* (November 5, 1948) 28:1.

——— "Washington Still Undecided on China Policy." *Foreign Policy Bulletin* (December 2, 1949) 29:1–2.

Bonilla, Frank. "When Is Petition 'Pressure'?" *Public Opinion Quarterly* (Spring 1956) 20:39–48.

Borg, Dorothy. "America Loses Chinese Good Will." *Far Eastern Survey* (February 23, 1949) 18:37–45.

——— "Economic Cooperation Administration and U.S. Policy in China." *Far Eastern Survey* (August 24, 1949) 18:197–99.

——— "The China Market." *Far Eastern Survey* (July 2, 1947) 16:150–53.

Borton, Hugh. "The Allied Occupation of Japan, 1945–47." In F. C. Jones, Hugh Borton, and B. R. Pearn. *The Far East 1942–1946*. London: Oxford University Press, 1955, pp. 307–428.

Braisted, William R. "The United States and the American China Development Company." *Far Eastern Quarterly* (February 1952) 11:147–66.

Briggs, Herbert W. "American Consular Rights in Communist China." *American Journal of International Law* (1950) 44:243–50.

"The Brothers Alsop." *Newsweek*, March 13, 1950, p. 55.

Brown, Ben H. Jr. "Congress and the Department of State," *Annals of* the *American Academy of Political and Social Science* (September 1953) 289:100–7.

Brown, MacAlister. "The Demise of State Department Public Opinion Polls: A Study in Legislative Oversight." *Midwest Journal of Political Science* (February 1961) 5:1–17.

Brown, Philip M. "The Legal Effects of Recognition." *American Journal of International Law* (1950) 44:617–40.

Buck, Pearl. "A Warning About China." *Life*, May 10, 1943, pp 53–56.

Buhite, Russell D. "'Major Interests': American Policy Toward China, Taiwan, and Korea, 1945–1950." *Pacific Historical Review* (August 1978) 47:425–51.

Bullitt, William C. "A Report to the American People on China." *Life* (October 13, 1947) 23:35–37, 139–51.

Burdette, Franklin L. "The Influence of Noncongressional Pressures on Foreign Policy." *Annals of the American Academy of Political and Social Science* (September 1953) 289:92–95.

Bush, Richard. "Succession in the Kuomintang, 1925–1937." *Contemporary China* (November 1976) 1:31–34.

"Businessmen in China." *Economist* (December 31, 1949) 157:1459.

Butterfield, Fox. "A Missionary View of the Chinese Communists (1936–39)." *Papers on China*. Cambridge: Harvard University Press, 1961.

Cabot, John M. "American Answer to Chinese Communist Propaganda." *Department of State Bulletin* (February 13, 1949) 20:179–83.

——— "American Community Activities Continue in Shanghai." *Department of State Bulletin* (June 12, 1949) 20:765.

"Canadians, Americans Confer on Far East." *Far Eastern Survey* (February 8, 1950) 19:28–30.

Cantile, K. "RR Construction in China and its Effect on Recent History." *Eastern World* (May 1950) 4:35–37 and (June 1950) 4:37–40.

Cartwright, Frank T. "Protestant Missions in Communist China." *Far Eastern Survey* (December 28, 1949) 18:301–5.

Celler, Emmanuel. "Pressure Groups in Congress." *Annals of the American Academy of Political and Social Science* (September 1958) 319:1–9.

Chamberlain, William Henry. "A Lost Battle." *Wall Street Journal*, December 13, 1949, p. 8.

——— "Oriental Retribution." *Wall Street Journal*, November 1, 1949, p. 6.

Chao, Yi-ya. "Kuo-chi chu-i hsüeh-hsi t'i-kan" [Study Principles of Internationalism], *Hsüeh-hsi* (December 1949) 1:7–9.

Chen I. "T. V. Soong's New Mission," *Newsweek* (Shanghai), May 19, 1949.

Chennault, Claire L. "Eleventh Hour in China." *America* (December 3, 1949) vol. 82.

"Chiang Steps Down." Editorial, *Nation*, (January 29, 1949) 168:115–16.

"Chiang's Fall Within a Year." *China Digest* (November 30, 1948) 5:5.

Childs, Marquis. "Chinese in U.S. Politics." *Washington Post*, April 15, 1952, p. 10.

——— "Chinese Puzzle." *Denver Post*, March 30, 1949, p. 2c.

——— "Mr. Truman Does His Best for the U.S." *Denver Post*, March 16, 1949, p. 10.

"China and the Silver Bloc." Editorial, *Providence Evening Bulletin* reprinted in the *St. Louis Post-Dispatch*, April 21, 1949, p. 2B.

"China and U.S. Far East Policy, 1945–67." *Congressional Quarterly*. Washington, D.C.: Government Printing Office, 1967.

"China and U.S. Foreign Policy." *Congressional Quarterly*. Washington, D.C.: Government Printing Office, 1973.

"China, Asia and the U.S." *New Republic* (July 18, 1949) 121:5.

"China: Economic Conditions, Situation in Recent Months." *Foreign Commerce Weekly* (Department of Commerce publication) (June 27, 1949) 35:18–20; (October 10, 1949) 37:15–17; (December 5, 1949) 37:18–20.

"China: Economic Conditions: Striking Developments in January and February." *Foreign Commerce Weekly* (April 18, 1949) 35:20–22.

"The China Lobby: A Case Study." *Congressional Quarterly Special Supplement*, (June 29, 1951) vol. 9. Reprinted in *Congressional Record*, 82nd Cong., 2nd sess. 98:6795–6804.

"China-Policy Critic: Senator William F. Knowland." *U.S. News & World Report* (January 13, 1950) 28:33–34.

"China: Tariff and Trade Controls: New Chinese Communist Tariff Policy Announced." *Foreign Commerce Weekly* (April 3, 1950) 39:19.

"China: Tariff and Trade Controls. Regulations for Promotion of East China Export Trade Announced by Communist Government." *Foreign Commerce Weekly* (August 8, 1949) 36:11.

"China Tightens Trade Controls." *Journal of Commerce*, December 12, 1950.

"China Under the Communists." *Economist* (June 25, 1949) 156:1189–90.

"China White Paper: A Tale of American Failure." *Newsweek* (August 15, 1949) 34:38.

"China Without Chiang." *Economist* (January 29, 1949) 156:180–81.

"China's Recognition." *Nation* (November 19, 1949) 169:483.

"Chinese Communists and the Foreign Press." *Economist* (October 8, 1949) 157:788, 790.

"Chinese Communists Regulate Foreign Trade." *Far Eastern Survey* (April 20, 1949) 18:92.

"Chinese Export-Import Rules Cabled Here From Shanghai." *Journal of Commerce*, June 22, 1949.

"Chinese Paper Urges British Ships Go T'sin." *North China Daily News*, January 25, 1949, p. 2.

"Chinese Puzzle." *Wall Street Journal*, October 4, 1949, p. 6.

Chiu Hungdah. "Suspension and Termination of Treaties in Communist China's Theory and Practice." *Osteuropa-Recht*, September 1969, pp. 169–90.

"Christians Under the Chinese Communist State." *The Church* (Hong Kong), June 1949.

Chu Keh-tai. "After Nanking, What About Kwangtung?" *Sinwen Tienti* (Shanghai), April 28, 1949.

Cleveland, Harlan. "Economic Aid to China." *Far Eastern Survey*, January 12, 1949, pp. 2–6.

Clubb, O. Edmund. "Chinese Communist Strategy in Foreign Relations." *Annals of the American Academy of Political and Social Science* (September 1951) 277:156–66.

—— "Formosa and the Offshore Islands in American Policy 1950–1955." *Political Science Quarterly* (December 1959) 74:517–31.

—— "'Titoism' and the Chinese Communist Regime: An American View." *The World Today* (December 1952) 8:521–31.

Coburn, Judith. "Asian Scholars and Government: The Chrysanthemum on the Sword." In Edward Friedman and Mark Selden, eds. *America's Asia*, New York: Vintage, 1971, pp. 67–107.

Cohen, Jerome A. "Chinese Law and Sino-American Trade." In Alexander Eckstein, ed. *China Trade Prospects and U.S. Policy*, New York: Praeger, 1971.

Cohen, Warren I. "The Study of Sino-American Relations: Where Are We Now and Where Must We Go From Here." In Milton O. Gustafson, ed. *Conference on the National Archives and Foreign Relations Research.* Papers and proceedings, Athens: Ohio University Press, 1975.

"Communism's March Through China." *Business Week*, November 20, 1948, pp. 125–29.

Costello, William. "Could Japan Go Communist?" *Nation*, May 14, 1949, pp. 554–56.

Coxe, Spencer. "Quakers and Communists in China," *Far Eastern Survey* (June 29, 1949) 18:152–55.

Crane, Burton. "Chiang Gave Fund to Formosa Regime." *New York Times*, February 2, 1950, p. 5.

Dalleck, Robert. "The Truman Era." In Ernest R. May and James C. Thomson Jr., eds. *American-East Asian Relations.* Cambridge: Harvard University Press, 1972, pp. 356–76.

Daniels, William H. "The People's Republic and the Church." *The Messenger*, October 24, 1950, p. 16.

Davis, Elmer. "The Crusade Against Acheson." *Harper's* (March 1951) 202:23–29.

Dernberger, Robert F. "The Role of the Foreigner in China's Economic Development, 1840–1949." In Dwight Perkins, ed. *China's Modern Economy in Historical Perspective*. Stanford: Stanford University Press, 1975, pp. 19–47.

"Development in the Pacific Pact Plan." *Shih Shih Hsin Pao*, May 18, 1949.

Dexter, Lewis A. "What Do Congressmen Hear: The Mail." *Public Opinion Quarterly* (Spring 1956) 20:16–27.

"Diplomacy and Friendship." *People's China* (January 16, 1950) 1:3.

"Dollar in Red China." *Newsweek* (June 13, 1949) 33:64–67.

Dolsen, James H. "Big Steel Firm Urges Recognition of China." *Daily Worker*, February 16, 1951, p. 4.

Dower, John W. "Occupied Japan and the American Lake, 1945–50." In Edward Friedman and Mark Selden, eds. *America's Asia*. New York: Vintage, 1971, pp. 186–206.

Dugan, George. "Reds in China Seen Accepting Church." *New York Times*, December 7, 1949, p. 19.

Durdin, Tillman. "China's Reds Face Internal Disputes." *New York Times*, September 17, 1949, p. 5.

—— "China Reds Warn Against Brutality." *New York Times*, April 26, 1949, p. 12.

—— "Nationalist Funds Dwindle in China." *New York Times*, September 26, 1949, p. 12.

—— "New Plan Offered on China ECA Fund." *New York Times*, September 14, 1949, p. 16.

—— "Radical Wing Held on Top in China." *New York Times*, September 18, 1949, p. 26.

Eckel, George. "Talk With Soviet Urged by Stassen." *New York Times*, February 19, 1950, p. 24.

Edwards, Willard. "'China Lobby' Aided Truman, Sen. Cain Says." *Washington Times Herald*, June 10, 1952.

"11th Hour in China," *Economist* (April 23, 1949) 156:731–32.

Eliot, George Fielding. "How Reds Can Be Kept Out of Southern China." *St. Louis Post-Dispatch*, May 10, 1949, p. 1B.

Engelhardt, Tom. "Long Day's Journey: American Observers in China, 1948–1950." In Bruce Douglass and Ross Terrill, eds. *China and Ourselves*. Boston: Beacon Press, 1969–70, pp. 90–121.

Etzold, Thomas H. "The Far East in American Strategy." In Etzold, ed.

Aspects of Sino-American Relations Since 1784. New York: New Viewpoints, 1978, pp. 102–26.

"Facts About Ward Case." *China Digest* (December 14, 1949) 7:6–8.

"Facts That Dim Forecast of Big Trade with China." *U.S. News & World Report* (June 18, 1948) 24:17.

Fairbank, John K. "America and the Chinese Revolution." *New Republic,* (August 22, 1949) 211–13.

────── "Pinpricks or Policy?" *Nation* (May 20, 1950) 170:488–89.

────── "Toward a Dynamic Far Eastern Policy." *Far Eastern Survey* (September 7, 1949) 18:209–12.

────── "Toward a New China Policy." *Nation* (January 1, 1949) 168:5–8.

────── "U.S. Reviews China Policy in Light of White Paper." *Foreign Policy Bulletin* (August 12, 1949) 28:1–2.

────── "What Can U.S. Do if Chiang's Government Falls?" *Foreign Policy Bulletin* (November 19, 1948) 28:1–2.

Fairbank, Wilma. "The College of Chinese Studies, Peiping, China; News of the Profession." *Far Eastern Quarterly* (November 1949) 9:78–79.

────── "U.S. Government Offices in Washington Which Use Far Eastern Specialists; News of the Profession." *Far Eastern Quarterly* (February 1950) 9:192–95.

Faulkner, James M. "Foreign Insurance in China." *Far Eastern Survey* (September 3, 1947) 16:188–89.

Federal Council of the Churches of Christ in America, Executive Committee. "The Churches and American Policy in the Far East." *Far Eastern Survey* (December 28, 1949) 17:305–6.

Fenton, John H. "Asia Aid Program Urged by Stassen." *New York Times,* April 2, 1949, p. 1.

Feraru, Arthur. "Public Opinion Polls on China." *Far Eastern Survey* (July 12, 1950) 19:130–32.

Fetzer, James A. "The Case of John Paton Davies, Jr." *Foreign Service Journal* (November 1977) 54:15–22, 31–32.

Fischer, John. "Mr. Truman's Politburo." *Harper's* (June 1951) 102:29–36.

Fleeson, Doris. "China Issue Faces Congress," *Denver Post,* January 9, 1950, p. 10.

────── "Lucas-Wherry Clash in Senate Result of Break in Majority." *St. Louis Post-Dispatch,* April 6, 1949, p. 1B.

────── "Wherry Enjoys Current Job as Chieftain." *Denver Post,* April 4, 1949, p. 10.

Fletcher, Henry P. "China and Bipartisanism." *Human Events* (December 14, 1949) 6:1–2.

"Foreign Papers Have Become Hotbed of Rumors, Readers Should be Specifically Guarded Against Them." *Wen Hui Pao*, June 21, 1949.

"The Foreign Service and the Correspondents." *American Foreign Service Journal* (August 1948) 25:7–9, 33.

Foster, H. Schuyler. "American Public Opinion and U.S. Foreign Policy." *Department of State Bulletin* (November 30, 1959) 41:796–803.

———— "The Role of the Public in U.S. Foreign Relations." *Department of State Bulletin* (November 28, 1960) 43:823–31.

Fox, Howard. "Oil Resources in the Far East." *Eastern World* (October 1949) 111:32–34.

Freeman, Howard E. and Morris Showel. "Differential Political Influence of Voluntary Associations," *Public Opinion Quarterly* (Winter 1951–52) 15:703–14.

"Freeze-out of Exporters in China: Discrimination Against Westerners and Growth of Government Monopolies." *World Report*, September 9, 1947, pp. 24–25.

Friendly, Alfred. "Man Behind the Man Who Is Accusing Lattimore." *Washington Post*, April 23, 1950, sec. II, pp. 1,3.

"From Stilwell to Marshall." *Amerasia* (December 1945) 9:311–27.

Fromm, Joseph. "Shanghai Communists Put Girl Entertainers to Sewing Uniforms, And Anybody Caught Playing Mah Jong Has to Sweep the Streets." *U.S. News & World Report* (February 10, 1950) 28:28.

Frondorf, Robert U. "Ault & Wiborg (Far East)." *Interchemical Review* (Summer 1948) 7:52–59. In-house publication, Inmont Corporation Library, Clifton, N.J.

"The Future of British Business in China." *Economist* (September 24, 1949) 157:676.

Gaddis, John L. "Was the Truman Doctrine a Real Turning Point?" *Foreign Affairs* (January 1974) 52:386–402.

———— "Containment: A Reassessment." *Foreign Affairs* (July 1977) 55:873–87.

Gibson, Tony. "Life in the Communist Hinterland." *Eastern World* (December 1949) 3:4–5.

Gittings, John. "New Light On Mao." *China Quarterly* (December 1974) 60:750–66.

Gordon, Walter. "New Chinese Wall: American Businessmen Returning to China." *Collier's* (October 11, 1947) 120:49–54.

Gordon, William E. "Economic Growth and Foreign Trade of Asia." In Robert J. Barr, ed. *American Trade With Asia and the Far East*. Milwaukee: Marquette University Press, 1959, pp. 247–89.

Gould, Randall. "China Outlook: A Business View." *Far Eastern Survey* (April 20, 1949) 18:90–92.

———— "Reds Harass U.S. Bank." *Denver Post*, October 29, 1950, pp. 1,3.

———— "Shanghai During the Takeover, 1949." *Annals of the American Academy of Political and Social Science* (September 1951) 277:182–92.

Graebner, Norman A. "Changing Perceptions of China Since Midcentury." In John Chay, ed. *The Problems and Prospects of American-East Asian Relations*. Boulder, Co.: Westview Press, 1977, pp. 51–73.

Green, O. M. "Shanghai Faces Ruin." *Eastern World* (May 1950) 4:16–17.

Gwertzman, Bernard. "The Hostage Crisis—Three Decades Ago." *New York Times Magazine*, May 4, 1980, pp. 41–44, 101–6.

Hamburger, Philip. "Profile: Mr. Secretary." *New Yorker* (November 12 and 19, 1949) 25:39–53, and 40–60.

Hamilton, William C. "Some Problems of Decision-making in Foreign Affairs." *Department of State Bulletin* (September 9, 1957) 37:432–36.

Hampson, Fred. "China Reds Gag Reporters." *Denver Post*, February 27, 1949, p. 1.

———— "Reds Make Good Deal in China." *Denver Post*, June 8, 1949, p. 6.

———— "Shanghai Communists Ask Ouster of Foreign 'Vermin.'" *Denver Post*, July 21, 1949, p. 4.

———— "Shanghai Hoping Reds Hurry Up As Nationalists Start 'Looting.'" *Denver Post*, May 20, 1949, p. 5.

———— "Shanghai Reds List Censorship Controls." *Denver Post*, July 16, 1949, p. 3.

Harris, Don R. "Re-thinking Our China Policy." *Survey*, August 1949.

Harris, Edward A. "Aid-China 'Angel' A Donor to Bridges' Campaign Fund." *St. Louis Post-Dispatch*, September 21, 1949, pp. 1,6.

———— "Bipartisan Foreign Policy Buckling At the Joints?" *St. Louis Post-Dispatch*, August 21, 1949, p. 1B.

———— "Men Behind McCarthy," *New Republic* (April 24, 1950) 122:10–11.

Hauser, E. O. "China Needs a Friendly Nudge." *Saturday Evening Post*, August 26, 1944, pp. 28–29.

Hightower, John M. "Acheson to Discuss New U.S. Policy in Far East With Bevin This Week." *St. Louis Post-Dispatch*, September 12, 1949, p. 1B.

———— "Solid Front on China U.S. Goal." *Denver Post*, May 25, 1949, p. 6.

———— "U.S. Britain Likely to Link Policies on China and the Far East." *St. Louis Post-Dispatch*, August 11, 1949, p. 1B.

Ho Ping. "What Is the Kwangsi Clique Planning to Do?" *Hai Chao*, February 11, 1949.

Hobbs, Malcolm. "Chiang's Washington Front," *Nation* (December 24, 1949) 169:619–20.

Hornbeck, Stanley. "Recognition of Governments." *America Society of International Law Proceedings* (1950) 44:181–92.

Horoth, V. L. "The Economic and Political Significance of the Chinese Communist Victories." *Magazine of Wall Street* (September 24, 1949) 84: 631–33.

——— "Our Dilemma: What China Policy Now?" *Magazine of Wall Street* (December 18, 1948) 83:279–81, 304–5.

Horton, Philip. "The China Lobby—Part II." *Reporter* (April 26, 1952) 6:5–22.

"Hostages in Shanghai." *Newsweek* (March 27, 1950) 35:39.

Hoyt, Frederick B. "The Summer of '30: American Policy and Chinese Communism." *Pacific Historical Review* (May 1977) 46:229–49.

Hsiao Min. "An Inventory of T. V. Soong's Estate." *China Daily Tribune* (Shanghai), May 16, 1949.

Hsu We-yu. "Signal for the Collapse of the CC Financial Group." *Niu Shih* (Shanghai), February 11, 1949.

Hu Nung-chih. "Will Kan Chieh-hou Become Foreign Minister?" *Shih Shih Hsin Pao* (Shanghai), May 15, 1949.

Huang Pin. "Faction Strife in the Kuomintang." *New Hope Weekly* (Shanghai), March 21, 1949.

Ickes, Harold. "Acheson vs. Acheson." *New Republic* (February 13, 1950) 122:23.

——— "Keeping Out of Formosa." *New Republic* (January 30, 1950) 122:19.

——— "Truman's Formosa Policy." *New Republic* (January 23, 1950) 122:17.

"The Ideal Papers." *Newsweek*, May 19, 1952.

"Insiders Get Rich on China Aid." *U.S. News & World Report*, August 26, 1949, pp. 15–17.

"I.T. & T. Properties in Orient Returned in Operating Condition." *International Review of the International Telephone & Telegraph Corporation* (October 1945) 1:26–27.

Iriye, Akira. "Was There A Cold War In Asia?" In John Chay, ed. *The Problems and Prospects of American-East Asian Relations*. Boulder, Co: Westview Press, 1978, pp. 3–24.

"Is New China Anti-Foreign?" *China Digest* (July 27, 1949) 6:11.

Isbrandtsen. "China Trade." *Journal of Commerce*, September 21, 1949.

Israel, Jerry. "'Mao's Mr. America': Edgar Snow's Images of China." *Pacific Historical Review* (February 1978) 47:107–22.

Jao Shu-shih. "How New China Fights US-KMT Blockade." *China Digest* (August 24, 1949) 6:14–15.

Jen Pi-shih. "Kung-shang-yeh cheng-ts'e." *Chung-kuo jen-min chieh-fang-chün ju-ch'eng cheng-ts'e* ["Industrial and Commercial Policy." Chinese People's Liberation Army Policy for Entering the Cities] n.p.: New China Bookstore, 1949.

Jervis, Robert. "The Impact of the Korean War on the Cold War." *Journal of Conflict Resolution* (December 1980) 24:563–92.

Johnson, Gerald W. "Great Newspapers, If Any." *Harper's*, June 1948, pp. 542–46.

Johnson, William R. "The United States Sells China Down the Amur." *China Monthly* (December 1947) vol. 8.

Kahn, E. J. Jr. "Foresight, Nightmare, and Hindsight: Profile of John Service." *New Yorker*, April 8, 1973, pp. 43–95.

Kaim, J. R. "Trade Prospects in China." *Far Eastern Survey* (June 1, 1949) 18:121–24.

Kalischer, Peter. "U.S. Fleet Sails From Whangpoo." *Denver Post*, May 19, 1949, p. 5.

Kennan, George F. "The International Situation." *Department of State Bulletin* (September 15, 1949) 21:323–24.

Kern, Harry F. "Defeat in Asia—The How and Why." *Newsweek* (April 24, 1950) 35:36–38.

Keswick, John. "Review of the Situation in China: Report by the Chairman of British Chamber of Commerce in Shanghai." *Far Eastern Economic Review* (May 12, 1948) 4:454–58.

Kirchwey, Freda. "Appeasement's Tragedy." *Nation*, April 8, 1950, pp. 312–13.

——— "China: Blunder Upon Blunder?" *Nation* (January 7, 1950) 170:1–2.

Knowles, Clayton. "U.S. Has Large Stake in Trade With China." *New York Times*, December 4, 1949, p. 6E.

K'o Pai-nien. "Hsin-min chu-yi ti wai-chiao cheng-ts'e" [The Foreign Policy of New Democracy] *Hsüeh-hsi* (October 15, 1949) 1:13–15.

——— "Su-lien tsai shih-yüeh ko-ming hou ch'u-ch'i tsen-yang yü ti-kuo chu-i tso tou-cheng" [How the Soviet Union Struggled With Imperialism in the Initial Period After the October Revolution] *Hsüeh-hsi* (November 1949) 1:12–14.

Kohlberg, Alfred. "Stupidity and/or Treason." *China Monthly* (June 1948) 9:151.

"Kohlberg's Klan." Editorial, *Washington Post*, April 13, 1950, p. 12.

Krock, Arthur. "The President: A New Portrait." *New York Times Magazine*, April 7, 1949, p. 48.

Ku Jen. "The Influence of American Aid and the Pacific Pact on the Peace Talks." *Ho Ping Jih Pao* (Shanghai), April 13, 1949.

Kung Sun-wang. "Peace Talks in China Before the World's Gathering Storm." *Sinwen Tienti* (Shanghai), April 21, 1949.

Kuo Mo-jo. "Closer Ties Between China and the USSR." *China Digest* (August 24, 1949) 6:6, 23.

—— "'Pai-wan-hsiung-shih kuo ta-chiang' tu Mao chu-hsi hsin fa-piao-te shih-tz'u" ["An Army of One Million Crosses the Great River" upon reading one of the newly published poems of Chairman Mao] *Hung-ch'i* (1964) 1.

LaFeber, Walter. "American Policy-Makers, Public Opinion, and the Outbreak of the Cold War, 1945-1950." In Yōnosuke Nagai and Akira Iriye, eds. *The Origins of the Cold War in Asia.* New York: Columbia University Press, 1977, pp. 43-65.

Landman, Amos. "Behavior of Reds Wins Shanghai's Confidence." *Denver Post*, May 26, 1949, p. 4.

—— "Red Army Rule Changes Life in Shanghai." *Denver Post*, July 10, 1949, pp. 1c, 3c.

Landman, Amos and Lynn Chase. "Left and Right in China Bitter About America." *Denver Post*, May 29, 1949, pp. 1c, 3c.

—— "Shanghai—Communist Prize in Asia." *Denver Post*, April 17, 1949, p. 1c

Lasky, Victor. "Rally Warns U.S. to Bar Recognition of Red China." *New York World Telegram*, November 29, 1949.

Lattimore, Owen, "Our Failure in China: White Paper on China." *Nation* (September 3, 1949) 169:223-26.

Lawrence, David. "Recognition." *U.S. News & World Report* (January 27, 1950) 28:27.

Lee, Rensselaer W. "General Aspects of Chinese Communist Religious Policy With Soviet Comparisons." *China Quarterly* (July/September 1964) 19:161-73.

Lees, Lorraine M. "The American Decision To Assist Tito, 1948-1949." *Diplomatic History* (Fall 1978) 2:407-22.

Levine, Steven I. "A New Look at American Mediation in the Chinese Civil War: The Marshall Mission and Manchuria." *Diplomatic History* (Fall 1979) 3:349-75.

—— "If My Grandmother Had Wheels She'd Be A Trolley, or Reflections On the 'Lost Chance in China.'" *Contemporary China* (December 1976) 1:31-32.

Li Li-san. "Policy Toward Private Capital." *China Digest* (May 31, 1949) 6:9.

Lieberman, Henry R. "British, Americans Differ in Shanghai." *New York Times*, August 12, 1949, p. 3.

———— "China's Reds Scoff At Objective Press." *New York Times*, June 1, 1949, p. 13.

———— "Chinese Assembly Postpones Ballot." *New York Times*, April 26, 1948, p. 12.

———— "Chinese Chamber Backs Li, Snubs Sun." *New York Times*, March 5, 1949, p. 6.

———— "Chinese Refugees Mass in Formosa." *New York Times*, February 15, 1949, p. 1.

———— "Communists Confronted With Great Tasks in China." *New York Times*, January 16, 1949, p. 5.

———— "Correspondent Versus the News in China." *New York Times Magazine*, December 15, 1948, pp. 11, 62–72.

———— "Li Acts to Speed China's Peace Talks." *New York Times*, February 5, 1949, p. 5.

———— "Population Shift in Shanghai Urged." *New York Times*, July 16, 1949, p. 6.

———— "Russia Offers Only Modest Aid to China's Economy." *Foreign Policy Bulletin* (March 3, 1950) 29:2–3.

———— "700 Told to Quit China's Assembly." *New York Times*, March 28, 1948, p. 23.

———— "Shanghai Censors Foreign Newsmen." *New York Times*, July 17, 1949, p. 39.

Lieberthal, Kenneth. "Mao Versus Liu? Policy Towards Industry and Commerce, 1946–1949." *China Quarterly*, July/September 1971, pp. 496–519.

Lin Piao. "Chung-kuo jen-min ke-ming chan-cheng-te sheng-li shih Mao Tse-tung ssu-hsiang-te sheng-li" [The Victory of the Chinese People's Revolutionary War Is the Victory of the Thought of Mao Tse-tung] *Jen-min jih-pao*, September 30, 1960.

Lindley, Ernest K. "Bipartisan China Policy." *Newsweek* (August 15, 1949) 34:20.

———— "General Marshall's Responsibility." *Newsweek* (May 1, 1950) 35:25.

Linebarger, Paul M. A. "The Failure of Secret Diplomacy in China." *Far Eastern Survey* (September 7, 1949) 18:212–14.

———— "Outside Pressures on China, 1945–50." *Annals of the American Academy of Political and Social Science* (September 1951) 277:177–81.

Lippmann, Walter. "The White Paper: Mr. Acheson's Conclusion." *New York Herald Tribune*, September 6, 1949, p. 19.

Liu Shih-chih. "Press Censorship in Shanghai." *Sinwen Tienti* (Shanghai), May 10, 1949.

"Liu Shao-ch'i's May Day Address." *Hsin Hua Yüeh Pao* (May 1, 1950) 2:5–10.

"Living With the Chinese Communists." *New Republic* (December 12, 1949) 121:5–7.

Lu Ying-hua. "The Delicate Relations Among Li Tsung-jen, Sun Fo, and Chang Chih-chung." *Niu Shih* (Shanghai), February 11, 1949.

Lyon, Jean. "When the Communists Entered Peking." *Harper's* (February 1950) 200:78–86.

"MacKay Asks U.S. to Recognize Chinese Regime." *Religious News Service*, January 5, 1950, p. 1.

McKee, Frederick. "Our Stand on China." Letter to the editor, *New York Times*, May 1, 1949, p. 8E.

"Make a Class Analysis of Factionalism." *Peking Review* (May 10, 1968) vol. 11.

Mark, Eduard M. "The Question of Containment." *Foreign Affairs* (January 1978) 56:430–41.

——— "What Kind of Containment?" In Thomas G. Patterson, ed. *Containment and the Cold War*. Reading, Mass.: Addison-Wesley, 1973, pp. 96–109.

Martin, Robert P. "China's Chiang Has Some Aces In His Sleeve." *Denver Post*, February 20, 1949, pp. 1c, 3c.

Masland, John W. "Commercial Influence Upon American Far Eastern Policy, 1937–1941." *Pacific Historical Review* (1942) 2:281–99.

——— "Missionary Influence on United States Policy." *Pacific Historical Review* (September 1941) 10:279–96.

May, Ernest R. "An American Tradition in Foreign Policy: The Role of Public Opinion." In William H. Nelson, ed. *Theory and Practice in American Politics*. Chicago: University of Chicago Press, 1964, pp. 101–22.

Melby, John F. "The Origins of the Cold War in China." *Pacific Affairs* (Spring 1968) 41:19–33.

Meng, C. Y. W. "What A Chinese Thinks of Aid to China." *China Weekly Review*, March 19, 1949.

"Mess in China: White Paper." *New Republic* (August 5, 1949) 121:7.

Messer, Robert L. "Paths Not Taken: The United States Department of State and Alternatives to Containment, 1945–1946." *Diplomatic History* (Fall 1977) 1:297–319.

Milks, Harold E. "Close Links With Moscow Seen in Moves of Chinese Communists." *Denver Post*, April 27, 1949, p. 4.

Miller, Warren E. and Donald E. Stokes. "Constituency Influence in Congress." *American Political Science Review* (March 1963) 57:45–56.

Moore, John Bassett. "Fifty Years of International Law." *Harvard Law Review* (January 1937) 50:395–448.

Moosa, Spencer. "Chinese Reds Resisting Lure of Easy Wealth." *St. Louis Post-Dispatch*, June 15, 1949, p. 1c.

Morley, Felix. "China and the Election: Recognition of the Reds Would Threaten More Than Security." *Barron's* (October 3, 1950) 30:3.

"Morse Seeks 'Lie' Probe of Chiang Envoys." *Washington Post*, June 10, 1952, p. 3.

Morse, Wayne. "China Lobby." *Washington Post*, August 1952.

Mortenson, Ralph. "China Bible House Still Going Strong." *China News Letter*, July–August 1950, pp. 3–4.

"Mr. Acheson vs. Mr. Acheson." *Barron's* (September 25, 1950) 30:5.

Nathan, Andrew J. "Imperialism's Effects on China." *Bulletin of Concerned Asian Scholars*, December 1972, pp. 3–8.

Neumann, William L. "Determinism, Destiny, and Myth in the American Image of China." In George L. Anderson, ed. *Issues and Conflicts: Studies in 20th Century American Diplomacy*. Lawrence: University of Kansas Press, 1959.

—— "How to Merchandise Foreign Policy." *American Perspective* (September 1949) 3:183–93.

"NCNA Analytical Refutation of American White Paper." *China Digest* (September 7, 1949) 6:10–18.

NCNA editorial. "Good-Bye, Leighton Stuart!" *China Digest* (September 7, 1949) 6:3–5.

NCNA editorial. "Washington's Reluctant Confession." *China Digest* (August 24, 1949) 6:3.

"No Smoke-Screen Round Taiwan." *People's China* (January 16, 1950) 1:4.

"NWA Plans to Continue in China." *North China Daily News*, February 15, 1949, p. 2.

Nover, Barnett. "Far East Plan Drags." *Denver Post*, January 4, 1950, p. 14.

—— "Red China Dilemma." *Denver Post*, June 28, 1949, p. 10.

O'Connor, Raymond G. "Harry S Truman: New Dimensions of Power." In Edgar E. Robinson, ed. *Powers of the President in Foreign Affairs*. San Francisco: Lederer, Street & Zeus, 1966, pp. 17–76.

Okabe Tatsumi. "The Cold War and China." In Yōnosuke Nagai and Akira Iriye, eds. *The Origins of the Cold War in Asia*. New York: Columbia University Press, 1977, pp. 224–51.

Olsen, Arthur S. "Visiting Team in Peking." *China News Letter*, May–June 1950, p. 3.

"On the Question of Stalin—Comment on the Open Letter of the Central Committee of the CPSU." *Peking Review* (September 20, 1963) 6:8–15.

"Overseas Employees Are Leaving China." *Stanvac Meridian* (September 1949) 1:4.

Pakenham, C. "Calendar of Chaos." *Newsweek* (March 14, 1949) 33:34ff.

——— "Doing Business With Reds." *Newsweek* (April 25, 1949) 33:38.

——— "Night Over Shanghai," *Newsweek* (January 17, 1949) 33:34–35.

Paine, Robert Treat. "Stop the Bombing." *New Republic* (May 29, 1950) 122:4.

Palmer, Norman D. "Hazards Seen in U.S. Relations With Communist China." *Foreign Policy Bulletin* (October 21, 1949) 29:1–2.

Paterson, Thomas G. "If Europe, Why Not China? The Containment Doctrine, 1947–49." *Prologue* (Spring 1981) 13:19–38.

——— "Presidential Foreign Policy, Public Opinion, and Congress: The Truman Years." *Diplomatic History* (Winter 1979) 3:1–18.

Pearson, Drew. "Cables Show Chiang's War Effort." *Washington Post*, June 4, 1952, p. 37B.

——— "Chinese Communists May Take Nationalists Into Their Cabinet." *Denver Post*, June 3, 1949, p. 11.

——— "Senator Bridges Challenges Vandenberg." *Denver Post*, April 27, 1949, p. 11.

——— "State Department Hushed Up Chinese-Soviet Bargaining." *Denver Post*, June 21, 1949, p. 11.

——— "State Department Suddenly Tones Down Criticism of Chiang." *Denver Post*, July 14, 1949, p. 15.

——— "Truman's Political Strength." *Denver Post*, March 19, 1949, p. 10.

Peffer, Nathaniel. "China Crisis Is a Crisis for U.S." *New York Times Magazine*, November 14, 1948, pp. 12–13.

Peurifoy, John E. "The Department of State: A Reflection of U.S. Leadership." *Department of State Bulletin* (October 31, 1949) 21:671–74.

Philips, Cabell. "Is There a China Lobby? Inquiry Raises Question." *New York Times*, April 30, 1950, p. 7D.

Phillips, Joseph B. "Chinese Communists Sugarcoat a Pill." *Newsweek* (August 15, 1949) 34:39.

"Pootung Terminal Damage Protested by State Department." *Stanvac Meridian* (March 1950) 1:1.

Powell J. B. "Missouri Authors and Journalists in the Orient." *Missouri Historical Review* (October 1946) 41:45–55.

Prickett, James R. "Some Aspects of the Communist Controversy in the CIO." *Science and Society* (Summer/Fall 1969) 33:299–321.

"Problem for Chinese Communists: Cotton-Textile Industry." *Business Week*, May 21, 1949, pp. 128–30.

"Proletarian Internationalism is the Banner of the Workers of All Countries." excerpts from the *Kommunist*, May 1964, in *China Quarterly* (July/September 1964) 19:191.

"Prospects in China." *Economist* (September 3, 1949) 157:512–13.

Rand, Christopher. "Reporting in the Far East." In Louis M. Lyons, ed. *Reporting the News*. Cambridge: Harvard University Press, 1965, pp. 303–12.

Rankin, Mary Backus. "The Ku-t'ien Incident (1895): Christians Versus the T'sai-hui." *Papers on China*. Cambridge: Harvard University Press, 1961.

Ravenholt, Albert. "Communists Can Seize Shanghai But May Delay Until They Decide How to Cope With Its Problems." *St. Louis Post-Dispatch*, April 28, 1949, p. 1B.

—— "Formosa Looms as Trouble Spot; Rightwing Chinese Hope America Will Protect It Against Communists." *St. Louis Post-Dispatch*, April 7, 1949, p. 1B.

—— "Hong Kong Is Revising Its Hope of Business Deals With Red China." *St. Louis Post-Dispatch*, May 9, 1949, p. 1B.

—— "Reds Ignoring Nationalist Troops to Take Intact Economic Prizes Such as Plants, Railways in China." *St. Louis Post-Dispatch*, May 24, 1949, p. 1B.

Reardon-Anderson, James. "The Case For the 'Lost Chance in China.'" *Contemporary China* (December 1976) 1:33–34.

"Recognition Question." *Newsweek* (October 17, 1949) 34:40–41.

"Recognizing Mao's China." *Economist* (November 19, 1949) 157:1117–18.

"The Record," *Time*, October 15, 1951, p. 23.

Reischauer, Edwin O. "U.S. Must Define Long-term Objectives in Asia." *Foreign Policy Bulletin* (September 30, 1949) 28:3–4.

Reston, James. "Events Spotlight Vandenberg's Dual Role." *New York Times Magazine*, March 28, 1948, pp. 10, 49–52.

—— "Memorandum to General MacArthur." *New York Times Magazine*, April 22, 1951, pp. 5, 61, 63.

—— "Truman Top Aides Divided On What to Do About China." *New York Times*, December 30, 1949, p. 6.

"Retiring Gov't Troops Seize Foreign Property for Billets." *North China Daily News*, January 18, 1949, p. 1.

"Return to Peking." *Economist* (October 22, 1949) 157:903–4.

"Review of the Present Economic Condition of China." *Far Eastern Economic Review* (May 26, 1948) 4:505–7.

Riggs, Fred W. "U.S. Weighs Alternatives in China's Debacle." *Foreign Policy Bulletin* (December 24, 1948) 28:1–2.

Robertson, Walter S. "An Untold Chapter in the Loss of China." *U.S. News & World Report,* January 1, 1954, pp. 31–33.

Rosenberg, David A. "American Atomic Strategy and the Hydrogen Bomb Decision." *Journal of American History* (June 1979) 66:62–87.

———— "The U.S. Navy and the Problem of Oil in a Future War: The Outline of a Strategic Dilemma, 1945–1950." *National War College Review,* Summer, 1976.

Rosinger, Lawrence K. "Nanking Weakened As Urban Morale Declines." *Foreign Policy Bulletin* (October 22, 1948) 28:3–4.

———— "Victories Bring Chines Communists New Problems" *Foreign Policy Bulletin* (May 13, 1949) 28:1–2.

Ross, Nancy L. "Disputed China Claims Involve Bonds Plot." *Washington Post,* June 1, 1977, p. 1E.

Roth, Andrew. "Chiang Under Fire." *Nation* (January 8, 1949) 168:35–36.

———— "China and the 'Foreign Devils.'" *Nation* (March 12, 1949) 168:295–97.

———— "China: the Communists' Plan." *Nation* (February 5, 1949) 168:156–58.

———— "The Chinese Revolution." *Nation* (April 30, 1949) 168:500–2.

———— "The Fall of Peiping." *Nation* (January 29, 1949) 168:125.

———— "Hong Kong: Prosperous But Worried." *Nation* (July 30, 1949) 169:107–9.

———— "How the Communists Rule." *Nation* (November 19, 1949) 169:488–91.

———— "Manchurian Mystery." *Nation* (July 9, 1949) 169:35–36.

———— "Peiping's New Look." *Nation* (March 5, 1949) 168:274–75.

———— "Shanghai Awaits the Communists." *Nation* (January 15, 1949) 168:70–72.

Rovere, Richard. "'Taft' Is This the Best We've Got?" *Harper's* (April 1948) 196:289–99.

———— "The Unassailable Vandenberg." *Harper's* (May 1948) 196:394–403.

Rowe, David N. "American Policy Toward China." *Annals of the American Academy of Political and Social Science* (January 1948) 255:136–45.

———— "Where Can We Stand In Asia?" *Virginia Quarterly Review* (Autumn 1949) 25:526–43.

Russell, Francis H. "The Function of Public Opinion Analysis in the Formulation of Foreign Policy." *Department of State Bulletin* (March 6, 1949) 20:275–77, 303.

Salisbury, Laurence E. "Support of the Status Quo." *Far Eastern Survey* (October 24, 1945) 14:297–99.

Schonberger, Howard. "American Labor's Cold War in Occupied Japan." *Diplomatic History* (Summer 1979) 3:249–72.

—— "The Japan Lobby in American Diplomacy, 1947–52." *Pacific Historical Review* (August 1977) 46:327–59.

Schuman, Julian. "Reds Have Been Slow to Change Communist China's Administration." *Denver Post*, March 6, 1949, p. 1C.

—— "Shanghai Business Asks Quick Peace with Reds." *Denver Post*, March 13, 1949, pp. 1C, 3C.

—— "South China Awaits Commies." *Denver Post*, May 8, 1949, p. 1C.

"Scripps-Howard Papers On Business with Reds." *North China Daily News*, January 25, 1949, p. 2.

Shelton, Willard. "The New Irresponsibles." *Nation*, April 8, 1950, pp. 313–14.

Shui Chieh-tan. "A Study of the Sino-Soviet Local Commercial Pact." *Ta Kung Pao*, February 5, 1949.

"Sino-Japan Trade to Continue." *North China Daily News*, January 8, 1949, p. 6.

Smith, Gaddis. Review of *Dean Acheson* by David S. McLellan. *New York Times Book Review*, September 12, 1976, p. 7.

Snow, Edgar. "China's Fighting Generalissimo." *Foreign Affairs* (July 1938) 16:612–25.

—— "In China the People Decided." *New Republic* (November 7, 1949) 121:18–19.

—— Obituaries: *New York Times*. February 16, 1972. *Nation* (February 28, 1972) 214:261.

—— "Recognition of the PRC." *Annals of the American Academy of Political and Social Science* (July 1959) 324:75–85.

—— "What We Could Do About Asia." *Nation* (January 28, 1950) 170:75–79.

—— "Weak China's Strong Man." *Current History* (January 1934) 39:402–8.

—— "Will China Become a Russian Satellite?" *Saturday Evening Post* (April 9, 1949) 221:30–31.

Sokolsky, George E. "Chiang Speaks His Mind." *New York Daily Mirror*, July 11, 1949.

—— "Conquest By Fear." *New York Daily Mirror*, April 23, 1949.

"Soviet Plans Further Aggression From Its China Base." *Labor's Monthly Survey* (April–May 1950) 2:5.

"S.S. Fillmore Arrives From Taku Bar." *North China Daily News*, February 25, 1949, p. 1.

"Stanvac Follows U.S. Government Policy." *Stanvac Meridian* (July 1950) 1:1.

Steiner, H. Arthur. "Chinese Communist Urban Policy." *American Political Science Review* (March 1950) 44:47–48.

Stevens, Harley. "Business and Politics in China." *Far Eastern Survey* (September 25, 1946) 15:295–98.

Stewart, Maxwell. "America's China Policy." *Nation* (February 12, 1949) 168:174–75.

Stokes, Richard L. "Under Secretary of State James E. Webb in Charge of Reorganization." *St. Louis Post-Dispatch*, March 27, 1949, p. 1B.

Stone, I. F. "Chungking and Washington." *Nation*, April 5, 1941, pp. 400–1.

"Stop Reds in China Now, Bullitt Urges." *Houston Chronicle*, April 27, 1949.

"The Story of the China Electric Company," *International Review of the International Telephone & Telegraph Corporation* (February 1946) 2:14–20.

Sullivan, Mark. "China's Plight and U.S. Guilt." *Manchester Morning Union*, April 9, 1949.

Sullivan, Walter. "Americans Fear Losses in China." *New York Times*, January 4, 1949, p. 72.

—— "Chiang Aides Seen in New Manuever." *New York Times*, February 11, 1949, p. 8.

—— "Chinese Reds Urge U.S. Firms to Stay." *New York Times*, December 28, 1948, pp. 1, 12.

—— "News That Comes From Inside China." *New York Times*, June 25, 1950, p. 5D.

—— "Shanghai Freezes All Bank Accounts." *New York Times*, June 1, 1949, p. 12.

—— "Soviet Bank Seeks to End in Shanghai." *New York Times*, June 9, 1950, p. 13.

Sulzberger, C. L. "Soviet Held Wary of Mao Bid in South." *New York Times*, February 18, 1949, p. 8.

—— "U.S. Appears to Expect a Nationalist Red China." *New York Times*, February 15, 1949, p. 12.

—— "U.S. China Policy Is Held One Of 'Watchful Waiting.'" *New York Times*, February 11, 1949, p. 8.

—— "'Wait-and-See' China Policy Is Defended in Washington." *New York Times*, February 21, 1949.

"Summary of Discussions Regarding Private Schools." *Ta Kung Pao*, June 11, 1949.

Sussmann, Leila. "Mass Political Letter Writing in America." *Public Opinion Quarterly* (Summer 1959) 22:203–12.

Taylor, George E. "An Effective Approach in Asia." *Virginia Quarterly Review* (Winter 1950) 26:28–43.

Terrill, Ross. "John Carter Vincent and the American 'Loss' of China." In Bruce Douglass and Ross Terrill, eds. *China and Ourselves*. Boston: Beacon Press, 1969–70, pp. 122–54.

Ti Ch'ao-pai. "The Meaning and Method of Sino-Soviet Economic Cooperation." *Jen-min jih-pao*, April 21, 1950.

Timperely, J. J. "Makers of Public Opinion About the Far East." *Pacific Affairs* (June 1936) 9:223–25.

"To Recognize or Not." *Wall Street Journal*, December 1, 1949, p. 8.

Topping, Seymour. "American Businessmen in China Expressing Desire to Trade With Communists." Associated Press Dispatch, December 8, 1949.

Tozer, Warren W. "Last Bridge to China: The Shanghai Power Company, the Truman Administration and the Chinese Communists." *Diplomatic History* (Winter 1977) 1:64–78.

"Trade With Communist China." *Economist* (November 19, 1949) 157:1138.

Truman, Harry S. "Public Opinion and American Foreign Policy." *Department of State Bulletin* (August 1, 1949) 21:145–47.

"2,500 U.S. Businessmen Sticking It Out in Shanghai." *North China Daily News*, January 3, 1949, p. 3.

"25,000 Chiang Press Agent Seeks More Cash For China." *Baltimore Sun*, September 19, 1949.

"Twilight in Shanghai." *Newsweek* (May 15, 1950) 35:42.

"Underdeveloped Inland China: Heavy Taxation." *North China Daily News*, January 21, 1949, p. 7.

"Unlimited Commercial Potential of Far East." *North China Daily News*, January 4, 1949, p. 1.

"U.S. and Red China." *Nation* (July 30, 1949) 169:100.

"U.S. Imperialists Never Learn." *People's China* (February 1, 1950) 1:3.

"U.S. Protests to Chinese Communists in Smith-Bender Case." *Department of State Bulletin* (December 12, 1949) 21:908.

"U.S. Trade Opportunities in China." *Commercial and Financial Chronicle* (April 18, 1946) 163:2083.

Van Alstyne, Richard W. "The White Paper and China." *Current History* (October 1949) 17:193–201.

Warner, Geoffrey. "America, Russia, China and the Origins of the Cold War, 1945–1950." In Joseph M. Siracusa and Glen St. John Barclay, eds. *The Impact of the Cold War: Reconsiderations*. Port Washington, NY: Kennikat Press, 1977, pp. 144–62.

364 BIBLIOGRAPHY

Watt, D. C. "Britain and the Cold War in the Far East, 1945–58." In Yōnosuke Nagai and Akira Iriye, eds. *The Origins of the Cold War in Asia.* New York: Columbia University Press, 1977, pp. 89–122.

Weiner, Walter H. "Local Branch of Bank of America Opens." *North China Daily News,* January 29, 1949, p. 9.

Weintal, E. "Recognition Build-Up." *Newsweek* (October 31, 1949) 34:30.

"Wen-t'i chieh-ta," [Questions and answers] *Hsüeh-hsi* (May 1, 1950) vol. 2.

Wertenbaker, Charles. "The China Lobby." *Reporter* (April 15, 1952) 6:4–24.

Whelan, Joseph G. "The United States and Diplomatic Recognition: The Contrasting Cases of Russia and Communist China." *China Quarterly* (January–March 1961) 5:62–89.

"Where U.S. Had Foreign Investments, 1945–1948." *Business Week,* February 25, 1950, pp. 129–30.

Wiley, Alexander. "The Committee on Foreign Relations." *Annals of the American Academy of Political and Social Science* (September 1953) 289:58–65.

Woodhouse, Charles E. and David S. McLellan. "American Business Leaders and Foreign Policy: A Study in Perspectives." *American Journal of Economics and Sociology* (July 1966) 25:267–80.

Wright, Mary C. "China Remains Key to U.S. Policy in Asia." *Foreign Policy Bulletin* (September 9, 1949) 28:1–2. Reprinted as "What Shall We Do About China?" *St. Louis Post-Dispatch,* September 29, 1949, p. 2B.

Wu, Donald. "United States and Red China: Reply." *Nation* (August 20, 1949) 169:191.

Yen Sun. "The Kwangsi Clique On The Brink of a Precipice." *Far Eastern Bulletin,* April 9, 1949.

Zagoria, Donald S. "Choices in the Postwar World: Containment and China." In Charles Gati, ed. *Caging the Bear: Containment and the Cold War.* New York: Bobbs-Merrill, 1974, pp. 109–27.

—— "Mao's Role in the Sino-Soviet Conflict." *Pacific Affairs* (Summer 1974) 47:141–46.

BOOKS

Abell, Tyler, ed. *Drew Pearson Diaries, 1949–50.* New York: Holt, Rinehart & Winston, 1974.

Acheson, Dean. *A Citizen Looks At Congress.* New York: Harper, 1957.

—— *Power and Diplomacy.* Cambridge: Harvard University Press, 1958.

—————— *Present at the Creation*. New York: W. W. Norton, 1969.

Advertising Research Foundation, Inc. *The Continuing Study of Newspaper Reading*, no. 138. Study Summary, New York, 1951.

Aitken, Thomas. *A Foreign Policy For American Business*. New York: Harper, 1962.

Aliano, Richard A. *American Defense Policy From Eisenhower to Kennedy*. Athens: Ohio University Press, 1975.

Allen, George C. and Audrey G. Donnithorne. *Western Enterprise in Far Eastern Economic Development: China and Japan*. New York: Macmillan, 1954.

Allison, Graham. *Essence of Decision*. Boston: Little Brown, 1971.

Almond, Gabriel A. *The American People and Foreign Policy*. New York: Praeger, 1960.

Ambrose, Stephen. *Rise to Globalism*. New York: Penguin, 1976.

America and American Firms in China. Shanghai: Shanghai Evening Post & Mercury, 1946.

Anderson, Irvine H. Jr. *The Standard-Vacuum Oil Company and United States East Asian Policy, 1933–1941*. Princeton: Princeton University Press, 1975.

Angel, Juvenal L. *Looking For Employment in Foreign Countries*. New York: World Trade Academy Press, 1954.

Auerbach, Jerold S., ed. *American Labor: The Twentieth Century*. New York: Bobbs-Merrill, 1969.

Bachrack, Stanley D. *The Committee of One Million: "China Lobby" Politics, 1953–1971*. New York: Columbia University Press, 1976.

Ball, George W., ed. *Global Companies: The Political Economy of World Business*. Englewood Cliffs, N.J.: Prentice-Hall, 1975.

Barber, Joseph, ed. *American Policy Toward China: A Report on the Views Of Leading Citizens in Twenty-Three Cities*. New York: Council on Foreign Relations, 1950.

Barnett, A. Doak. *China on the Eve of Communist Takeover*. New York: Praeger, 1963.

Barr, Robert J., ed. *Conference on American Trade with Asia and the Far East*. Milwaukee: Marquette University, 1959.

Barrett, David. *Dixie Mission*. Berkeley: University of California Press, 1970.

Bates, M. Searle, ed. *China in Change*. New York: Friendship Press, 1969.

Bauer, Raymond A., Ithiel de Sola Pool, and Lewis A. Dexter. *American Business and Public Policy*. New York: Atherton Press, 1963.

Baum, Willa K. *Oral History for the Local Historical Society*. Nashville, Tenn.: American Association for State and Local History, 1977.

Beardsley, Frank G. *A History of American Revivals*. New York: American Tract Society, 1904.

Belden, Jack. *China Shakes the World*. New York: Monthly Review Press, 1949.

Bell, Coral. *Negotiating From Strength*. New York: Alfred A. Knopf, 1963.

Bianco, Lucien. *Origins of the Chinese Revolution, 1915–1949*. Stanford: Stanford University Press, 1967.

Billington, Ray A. *The Protestant Crusade, 1800–1860*. New York: Rinehart, 1938.

Bingle, E. J., and Kenneth G. Grubb. *World Christian Handbook, 1952*. London, 1952.

Blough, Roy. *International Business*. New York: McGraw-Hill, 1966.

Boardman, Robert. *Britain and the People's Republic of China 1949–74*. New York: Macmillan, 1976.

Bohlen, Charles E. *Witness to History, 1929–69*. New York: Norton, 1973.

Boorman, Howard L. and Richard C. Howard, eds. *Biographical Dictionary of Republican China*. New York: Columbia University Press, 1968.

Borg, Dorothy. *American Policy and the Chinese Revolution, 1925–28*. 2d ed. New York: Octagon, 1968.

———— *The United States and the Far Eastern Crisis of 1933–38*. Cambridge: Harvard University Press, 1964.

———— and Waldo Heinrichs, eds. *Uncertain Years: Chinese-American Relations 1947–50*. New York: Columbia University Press, 1980.

Borisov, C. B. and B. T. Koloskov. *Soviet-Chinese Relations, 1945–1970*. Bloomington: Indiana University Press, 1975.

Borton, Hugh. *Japan's Modern Century*. New York: Ronald Press, 1970.

Boyle, Samuel E., ed. *The Church in Red China "Leans to One Side": A Documented Study of the Influence of Communism on the Protestant Churches in China*. Hong Kong, 1950.

Brandt, Conrad. *Stalin's Failure in China*. New York: W. W. Norton, 1958.

Browder, Robert P. *The Origins of Soviet-American Diplomacy*. Princeton: Princeton University Press, 1953.

Brugger, William. *Democracy and Organization in the Chinese Industrial Enterprise (1948–1953)*. New York: Cambridge University Press, 1976.

Bundy, McGeorge. *The Pattern of Responsibility*. Boston: Houghton Mifflin, 1952.

Burns, Richard D. and Edward M. Bennett, eds. *Diplomats in Crisis: United States-Chinese-Japanese Relations, 1919–1941*. Santa Barbara, Ca.: ABC-Clio, 1974.

Bush, Chilton R., comp. *News Research for Better Newspapers*. New York: American Newspaper Publishers Association Foundation, 1966–71.

Bush, Richard C. Jr. *Religion in Communist China.* New York: Abingdon Press, 1970.

Caridi, Ronald. *The Korean War and American Politics: The Republican Party As a Case Study.* Philadelphia: University of Pennsylvania Press, 1968.

Carroll, Holbert. *The House of Representatives and Foreign Affairs.* Pittsburgh: University of Pittsburgh Press, 1958.

Carter, Paul A. *The Decline and Revival of the Social Gospel.* Ithaca, N.Y.: Cornell University Press, 1954.

Caute, David. *The Great Fear.* New York: Simon & Schuster, 1978.

Chang Chia-sen (Carsun Chang). *The Third Force in China.* New York: Bookman Associates, 1952.

Chay, John, ed. *The Problems and Prospects of American-East Asian Relations.* Boulder, Co.: Westview Press, 1977.

Chen Ch'en. *Chung-kuo chin-tai kung-ye shih tsu-liao* [Historical Data on China's Modern Industry], Peking, 1958.

Cheng Yu-kwei. *Foreign Trade and Industrial Development of China.* Washington, D.C.: University Press, 1956.

Chennault, Claire L. *Way of a Fighter.* New York: G. Putnam's Sons, 1949.

Chern, Kenneth S. *Dilemma in China.* Hamden, Conn.: Archon Books, 1980.

Chiang Kai-shek. *China's Destiny.* New York: Roy Publishers, 1947. (Original publication, 1943.)

Chieh-fang-hou Shanghai Kung-yün tsu-liao [Materials on the Shanghai Workers Movement After Liberation]. Shanghai: Ying-tung ch'u-pan she, 1950.

Ch'ien Tuan-sheng. *The Government and Politics of China.* Cambridge: Harvard University Press, 1950.

China Handbook, 1950. New York: Rockport Press, 1950.

Chinese Communist Party. *Biographies of Kuomintang Leaders.* Mimeographed by Committee on International and Regional Studies, Harvard University, February 1948.

Chow Ching-wen. *10 Years of Storm.* New York: Holt, Rinehart, 1960.

Churchill, Winston S. *The Second World War.* Vol. 4. *The Hinge of Fate.* Boston: Houghton Mifflin, 1950. Vol. 5 *Triumph and Tragedy*, 1953.

Clayton, James L., ed. *The Economic Impact of the Cold War.* New York: Harcourt, Brace & World, 1970.

Clubb, O. Edmund. *The Witness and I.* New York: Columbia University Press, 1974.

Coblentz, Edmund D., ed. *William Randolph Hearst: A Portrait in His Own Words.* New York: Simon & Schuster, 1952.

Cochran, Bert. *Harry Truman and the Crisis Presidency*. New York: Funk & Wagnalls, 1973.

―――― *Labor and Communism*. Princeton: Princeton University Press, 1977.

Cohen, Benjamin J., ed. *American Foreign Economic Policy*. New York: Harper & Row, 1968.

Cohen, Bernard C. *The Influence of Non-Governmental Groups on Foreign Policy-Making*. Princeton: Princeton University Press, 1959.

―――― *The Press and Foreign Policy*. Princeton: Princeton University Press, 1963.

―――― *The Public's Impact on Foreign Policy*. Boston: Little Brown, 1973.

Cohen, Warren I. *America's Response to China*. New York: John Wiley, 1971.

―――― *The Chinese Connection*. New York: Columbia University Press, 1978.

―――― *Dean Rusk*. Totowa, N.J.: Cooper Square, 1980.

Cole, Charles C. Jr. *The Social Ideas of the Northern Evangelists, 1826–1860*. New York: Octagon, 1966.

Common Program and Other Documents of the First Plenary Session of the Chinese People's Consultative Conference. Peking, 1950.

Conference of Scholars on the Administration of Occupied Areas, 1943–1955. April 10–11, 1970, Harry S Truman Library, Independence, Mo.

Connally, Thomas and Alfred Steinberg. *My Name Is Tom Connally*. New York: Thomas Y. Crowell, 1954.

Cooke, Alistair. *A Generation on Trial*. New York: Alfred A. Knopf, 1952.

Cornelius Vander Starr, 1892–1968. New York: C. V. Starr & Co., 1970.

Crabb, Cecil V. *Bipartisan Foreign Policy: Myth or Reality?* White Plains, N.Y.: Row, Peterson, 1957.

Crozier, Brian. *The Man Who Lost China: The First Full Biography of Chiang Kai-shek*. New York: Charles Scribner's Sons, 1976.

Curti, Merle. *Ameican Philanthropy Abroad*. New Brunswick, N.J.: Rutgers University Press, 1963.

Dahl, Robert A. *Congress and Foreign Policy*. New York: Harcourt, Brace, 1950.

Daniels, Jonathan. *The Man of Independence*. New York: J. B. Lippincott, 1950.

Davies, John Paton, Jr. *Dragon By the Tail*. New York: W. W. Norton, 1972.

―――― *Foreign and Other Affairs*. New York: W. W. Norton, 1964.

Davis, Forrest and Robert A. Hunter. *The Red China Lobby*. New York: Fleet Publishing, 1963.

Dedijer, Vladimir. *Tito Speaks*. London: Weidenfeld & Nicholson, 1953.

Dietrich, Ethel B. *Far Eastern Trade of the United States.* New York: Institute of Pacific Relations, 1940.

Directory of the China-America Council of Commerce and Industry: A Guide to Nearly 400 American Companies Interested in Developing Trade Between China and the USA. New York: China-America Council of Commerce and Industry, 1946.

Directory of the Far East-America Council of Commerce and Industry. New York, 1948.

Directory of the Protestant Christian Movement in China. New York: National Christian Council, 1950.

Directory of Selected American Companies with Foreign Operations (Preliminary), NYS School of Industrial and Labor Relations, Cornell University, 1953.

Divine, Robert A. *Foreign Policy and U.S. Presidential Elections.* New York: New Viewpoints, 1974.

Djilas, Milovan. *Conversations with Stalin.* New York: Harcourt, Brace & World, 1963.

Donovan, John F. *The Pagoda and the Cross.* New York: Scribner, 1967.

Donovan, Robert J. *Conflict and Crisis: The Presidency of Harry S Truman 1945–1948.* New York: W. W. Norton, 1977.

Dulles, Foster Rhea. *American Policy Toward Communist China, 1949–69.* New York: Thomas Y. Crowell, 1972.

Dunn, Robert W. *American Foreign Investments.* New York: Viking, 1926.

Eastman, Lloyd E. *The Abortive Revolution—China Under Nationalist Rule 1927–37.* Cambridge: Harvard University Press, 1972.

Eckstein, Alexander, ed. *China Trade Prospects and United States Policy.* New York: Praeger, 1971.

Engler, Robert. *The Politics of Oil: A Study of Private Power and Democratic Institutions.* New York: Macmillan, 1961.

Esherick, Joseph W., ed. *Lost Chance in China: The World War II Dispatches of John S. Service.* New York: Random House, 1974.

Etzold, Thomas H. and John L. Gaddis, eds. *Containment: Documents on American Policy and Strategy, 1945–1950.* New York: Columbia University Press, 1978.

Exporter's Encyclopedia. New York: Thomas Ashwell, 1945–1948.

Fairbank, John K. *Missionary Enterprise in China and America.* Cambridge: Harvard University Press, 1974.

———— *Next Step in Asia.* Cambridge: Harvard University Press, 1949.

———— *The United States and China.* New York: Viking, 1958.

Fairbank, John K., Edwin O. Reischauer, and Albert Craig. *East Asia: The Modern Transformation.* Cambridge: Harvard University Press, 1955.

Fairbank, Wilma. *America's Cultural Experiment in China, 1942–49*. Washington, D.C.: Government Printing Office, 1976.

Farrell, Tom, ed. *The Working Press of the Nation*. New York: Farrell Publishing, 1947.

Feis, Herbert. *The China Tangle*. Princeton: Princeton University Press, 1953.

———— *Contest Over Japan*. New York: W. W. Norton, 1967.

———— *Churchill-Roosevelt-Stalin: The War They Waged and the Peace They Sought*. Princeton: Princeton University Press, 1957.

Ferguson, Mary E. *China Medical Board and Peking Union Medical College: A Chronicle of Fruitful Collaboration, 1914–1951*. New York: Medical Board of New York, 1970.

Ferrell, Robert H., ed. *Off the Record: The Private Papers of Harry S Truman*. New York: Harper & Row, 1980.

Filene, Peter G. *Americans and the Soviet Experiment, 1917–1933*, Cambridge: Harvard University Press, 1967.

Fishel, Wesley, R. *The End of Extraterritoriality in China*. Berkeley: University of California Press, 1952.

Fitch, Geraldine. *China Lob-Lolly*. New York: Devin Adair, n.d.

Flash, Edward S. Jr. *Economic Advice and Presidential Leadership: The Council of Economic Advisers*. New York: Columbia University Press, 1965.

Forman, Harrison. *Report From Red China*. New York: Henry Holt, 1945.

Freeland, Richard H. *The Truman Doctrine and the Origins of McCarthyism*. New York: Alfred A. Knopf, 1972.

Fried, Richard M. *Men Against McCarthy*. New York: Columbia University Press, 1976.

Gaddis, John L. *The United States and the Origins of the Cold War, 1941–1947*. New York: Columbia University Press, 1972.

Gallup Poll: Public Opinion 1935–71. 2 vols, New York: Random House, 1972.

Gardner, Lloyd C. *Architects of Illusion: Men and Ideas in American Foreign Policy 1941–1949*. Chicago: Quadrangle Books, 1970.

George, Alexander and Richard Smoke. *Deterrence in American Foreign Policy*. New York: Columbia University Press, 1974.

Gillin, Donald. *Warlord: Yen Hsi-shan in Shansi Province, 1911–1949*. Princeton: Princeton University Press, 1967.

Gittings, John. *The World and China, 1922–1972*. New York: Harper & Row, 1974.

Goldman, Eric F. *The Crucial Decade and After*. New York: Vintage, 1960.

Gould, Randall. *China in the Sun*. New York: Doubleday, 1946.

Graebner, Norman A., ed. *An Uncertain Tradition: American Secretaries of State in the Twentieth Century*. New York: McGraw-Hill, 1961.

Grassmuck, George. *Sectional Biases in Congress on Foreign Policy*. Baltimore: Johns Hopkins Press, 1951.

Greene, Felix. *A Curtain of Ignorance*. Garden City, N.Y.: Doubleday, 1964.

Greene, Robert W. *Calvary in China*. Garden City, N.Y.: Doubleday, 1964.

Griffith, Robert. *The Politics of Fear*. Lexington: University of Kentucky Press, 1970.

Griggs, Thurston. *Americans in China: Some Chinese Views*. Washington, D.C.: Foundation for Foreign Affairs, 1948.

Griswold, A. Whitney. *The Far Eastern Policy of the United States*. New Haven, Conn.: Yale University Press, 1966.

Hahn, Emily. *The Soong Sisters*, Garden City, N.Y.: Garden City Publishing Co., 1941.

Halliday, Jon. *A Political History of Japanese Capitalism*. New York: Pantheon, 1975.

Hamby, Alonzo L. *Beyond the New Deal: Harry S. Truman and American Liberalism*. New York: Columbia University Press, 1973.

Han Ssu. *K'an! Cheng-hsüeh hsi* [Look! The Political Study Clique]. Hong Kong: Hua-nan ch'u-pan she, 1947.

Harper, Alan D. *The Politics of Loyalty*. Westport, Conn.: Greenwood Press, 1969.

Harrison, James P. *The Long March to Power*. New York: Praeger, 1972.

Hart, Hornell. *McCarthy Versus the State Department*. Durham, N.C.: Duke University Press, 1952.

Hartman, Susan M. *Truman and the 80th Congress*. Columbia: University of Missouri Press, 1971.

Hazelton, Anne, ed. *The Story of the Year 1949: God of the Valleys, China Inland Mission*. Philadelphia, 1950.

Hero, Alfred O. Jr. *American Religious Groups View Foreign Affairs*. Durham, N.C.: Duke University Press, 1973.

Hohenberg, John. *Between Two Worlds: Policy, Press, and Public Opinion in Asian-American Relations*. New York: Praeger, 1966.

———— *Foreign Correspondence: The Great Reporters and Their Times*. New York: Columbia University Press, 1964.

Hoopes, Townsend. *The Devil and John Foster Dulles*. Boston: Little, Brown, 1973.

Horowitz, David, ed. *Containment and Revolution*. Boston: Beacon Press, 1967.

———— *Corporations and the Cold War*. New York: Monthly Review Press, 1969.

Hosokawa, Bill. *Thunder in the Rockies: The Incredible Denver Post.* New York: William Morrow, 1976.

Hou Chi-ming. *Foreign Investment and Economic Development in China, 1840–1937.* Cambridge: Harvard University Press, 1965.

Hsu, Immanuel C. Y. *The Rise of Modern China,* New York: Oxford University Press, 1970.

Hsu Kai-yu. *China's Gray Eminence.* Garden City, N.Y.: Doubleday, 1969.

Hsüeh Chün-tu, ed. *The Chinese Communist Movement, 1921–49: An Annotated Bibliography of Selected Works in the Chinese Collection of the Hoover Institution.* 2 vols. Stanford: Stanford University Press, 1960.

Hua-shang Pao, ed. *Chieh-fang ch'ü mao-i hsü-chih* [Trade Information From the Liberated Areas]. Hong Kong: Hua-shang pao, 1949.

Huai Hsiang (pseud). *Lun Li Tsung-jen yü Chung-Mei fan-tung p'ai* [A Discussion of Li Tsung-jen and the Sino-American Reactionary Clique], Hong Kong, 1948.

Hudson, Winthrop S. *Religion in America.* New York: Scribner, 1965.

Hunt, Michael. *Frontier Defense and the Open Door.* New Haven, Conn.: Yale University Press, 1973.

Hyde, Charles C. *International Law Chiefly as Interpreted and Applied by the United States.* Boston: Little, Brown, 1947.

The Important Documents of the First Plenary Session of the Chinese Political Consultative Conference. Peking: Foreign Language Press, 1949.

Iriye, Akira. *Across the Pacific.* New York: Harcourt, Brace & World, 1967.
———— *The Cold War in Asia.* Englewood Cliffs, N.J.: Prentice-Hall, 1974.

Isaacs, Harold. *Images of Asia.* New York: Capricorn Books, 1962.
———— *The Tragedy of the Chinese Revolution.* New York: Atheneum, 1966.

Jacobs, Paul. *Old Before Its Time: Collective Bargaining at 28.* Santa Barbara, Ca.: Center for the Study of Democratic Institutions, 1963.

Jain, J. P. *China in World Politics.* New Delhi: Radiant Press, 1976.

Jessup, Philip C. *The Birth of Nations.* New York: Columbia University Press, 1974.

Jewell, Malcolm E. *Senatorial Politics and Foreign Policy.* Lexington: University of Kentucky Press, 1962.

Johnson, Arthur M. *Winthrop W. Aldrich.* Boston: Harvard University Press, 1968.

Johnson, Chalmers. *Peasant Nationalism and Communist Power.* Stanford: Stanford University Press, 1962.

Johnson, William R. *China, Key to the Orient—and to Asia.* Polo, II., 1950.

Jones, Francis P., ed. *Documents of the Three Self Movement.* New York, 1963.

Kahn, E. J. Jr. *The Big Drink: The Story of Coca-Cola.* New York: Random House, 1960.

——— *The China Hands: America's Foreign Service Officers and What Befell Them*. New York: Viking, 1972.

Katkoff, V. *Soviet Economy 1940–1965*. Baltimore: Dangary, 1961.

Kawai Kazuo. *Japan's American Interlude*. Chicago: University of Chicago Press, 1960.

Keeley, Joseph C. *The China Lobby Man: The Story of Alfred Kohlberg*. New Rochelle, N.Y.: Arlington House, 1969.

Kennan, George F. *Memoirs, 1925–1950*. Boston: Little Brown, 1967.

Kirkendall, Richard S., ed. *The Truman Period as Research Field*. Columbia: University of Missouri Press, 1967.

Klein, Donald W., and Anne B. Clark. *Biographic Dictionary of Chinese Communism, 1921–1965*. Cambridge: Harvard University Press, 1971.

Kluckhorn, Frank L. *The Drew Pearson Story*. Chicago: Chas. Hallberg, 1967.

Koen, Ross. *The China Lobby in American Politics*. New York: Harper & Row, 1974.

Kolko, Gabriel. *The Politics of War*. New York: Harper & Row, 1972.

Kolko, Gabriel and Joyce Kolko. *The Limits of Power*. New York: Random House, 1968.

Kuan-yu ch'eng-shih cheng-ts'e te chi-ko wen-hsien [Some Documents on City Policy]. N.p.: Hua pei hsin hua shu-t'ien, 1949.

Kubek, Anthony. *How the Far East Was Lost*. Chicago: Henry Regnery, 1963.

Kung-fei ti yi-ge wu-nien chi-hua chih yen-chiu [Study of the First Five Year Plan of the Communist Bandits]. Taipei, 1959.

LaFeber, Walter. *America, Russia, and the Cold War 1945–1975*. New York: John Wiley, 1976.

Landman, Lynn and Amos. *Profile of Red China*. New York: Simon & Schuster, 1951.

Larson, Henrietta M., Evelyn H. Knowlton, and Charles S. Popple. *History of the Standard Oil Company*. Vol 3: *New Horizons 1927–1950*. New York: Harper, 1971.

Lary, Diana. *Region and Nation*. New York: Cambridge University Press, 1974.

Latham, Earl. *The Communist Controversy in Washington*. Cambridge: Harvard University Press, 1966.

———*The Meaning of McCarthyism*. Boston: D.C. Heath, 1965.

Latourette, Kenneth Scott. *Christianity in a Revolutionary Age*. Vol 5: *The Twentieth Century Outside Europe*. New York: Macmillan, 1962.

Lattimore, Owen, *Ordeal By Slander*, Boston: Little, Brown, 1950.

Leary, William M. Jr. *The Dragon's Wings: The China National Aviation*

Corporation and the Development of Commercial Aviation in China. Athens: University of Georgia Press, 1976.

Lee, R. Alton. *Truman and Taft-Hartley*. Lexington: University of Kentucky Press, 1966.

Leigh, Michael. *Mobilizing Consent: Public Opinion and American Foreign Policy, 1937–1947*. Westport, Conn.: Greenwood Press, 1976.

Leuchtenburg, William E. *A Troubled Feast: American Society Since 1945*. Boston: Little Brown, 1973.

—— *Franklin Delano Roosevelt and the New Deal*, New York: Harper & Row, 1963.

Levering, Ralph B. *American Opinion and the Russian Alliance, 1939–1945*. Chapel Hill: University of North Carolina Press, 1976.

—— *The Public and American Foreign Policy, 1918–78*. New York: William Morrow, 1978.

Liang Sheng-chün. *Chiang-Li tou-cheng nei-mu* [The Inside Story of the Struggle Between Chiang and Li], Hong Kong: Union Asia Press, 1954.

Lie, Trygve. *In the Cause of Peace*. New York: Macmillan, 1954.

Lilienthal, David. *The Journals of David E. Lilienthal*. Vol 2: *The Atomic Energy Years, 1945–1950*. New York: Harper & Row, 1964.

Lindbeck, John M. H. *Understanding China*. New York: Praeger, 1971.

Linebarger, Paul M. A. *The China of Chiang Kai-shek*. Boston: World Peace Foundation, 1941.

Link, Arthur S. *Woodrow Wilson and the Progressive Era, 1910–1917*. New York: Harper & Row, 1954.

Liu Kwang-ching. *Americans and Chinese*. Cambridge: Harvard University Press, 1963.

Liu Kwang-ching, ed. *American Missionaries in China*. Cambridge: Harvard University Press, 1966.

Liu Shao-ch'i. *Collected Works, 1945–1957*. 3 vols. Hong Kong: Union Research Institute, 1969.

—— *Lun Kuo-chi chu-i yü min-tsu chu-i* [On Internationalism and Nationalism]. Hong Kong: Hsin min chu-i ch'u-pan she, 1949.

Liu Shao-ch'i, et al. *Hsin min-chu chu-i ch'eng-shih cheng-ts'e* [The New Democratic City Policy. Hong Kong: Hsin min chu-i ch'u-pan she, 1949.

Loh, P. Y. Pichon. *The Early Chiang Kai-shek*. New York: Columbia University Press, 1971.

Loh, Robert. *Businessmen in China*. Hong Kong: Viewpoints, 1960.

—— *Escape From Red China*. New York: Coward-McCann, 1962.

Loth, D. G. *Swope of General Electric*. New York: Simon & Schuster, 1958.

Luard, Evan. *Britain and China*. London: Chatto & Windus, 1962.

Lundberg, Ferdinand. *Imperial Hearst*. New York: Equinox Cooperative Press, 1936.

Lutz, Jessie. *China and the Christian Colleges, 1850–1950*. Ithaca, N.Y.: Cornell University Press, 1971.

Lutz, Jessie, ed. *Christian Missions in China: Evangelists of What?* Boston: D.C. Heath, 1965.

McCammon, Dorothy S. *We Tried to Stay*. Scottsdale, Pa.: Herald Press, 1953.

MacInnis, Donald. *American Response to the Chinese Revolution: 1970*, New York: China Program Report, 1970.

McLellan, David S. *Dean Acheson: The State Department Years*. New York: Dodd, Mead, 1976.

McLellan, David S. and David C. Acheson, eds. *Among Friends: Personal Letters of Dean Acheson*. New York: Dodd, Mead, 1980.

Magdoff, Harry. *The Age of Imperialism: The Economics of United States Foreign Policy*. New York: Monthly Review Press, 1969.

Mao Tse-tung. *Mu-ch'ien Hsing-shih ho Wo-men-ti Jen-wu* [The Present Situation and Our Tasks]. N.p.: Chieh-fang she, 1949.

———— *Selected Works*. 5 vols, Peking: Foreign Language Press, 1967–77.

Martinson, Harold H. *Red Dragon Over China*. Minneapolis: University of Minnesota Press, 1956.

Marty, Martin E. et al., eds. *The Religious Press in America*. New York: Holt, Rinehart & Winston, 1963.

Mary Victoria, Sister. *Nun in Red China*. New York: McGraw-Hill, 1953.

Maryknoll Mission Letters. New York, 1923 and 1927.

May, Ernest R. *"Lessons" of the Past*. New York: Oxford University Press, 1973.

———— *The Truman Administration and China, 1945–1949*. New York: J. B. Lippincott, 1975.

Mazuzan, George T. *Warren R. Austin at the United Nations, 1946–1953*. Kent, Ohio: Kent State University Press, 1977.

Melby, John F. *The Mandate of Heaven: Record of a Civil War 1945–1949*. Toronto: University of Toronto Press, 1968.

Merli, Frank J. and Theodore A. Wilson, eds. *Makers of American Diplomacy*. New York: Scribner, 1974.

Miller, Merle. *Plain Speaking: An Oral History of Harry S. Truman*. New York: G. P. Putnam's Sons, 1973.

Millis, Walter E., ed. *The Forrestal Diaries*. New York: Viking, 1951.

Moore, John Bassett. *A Digest of International Law*. Washington, D.C.: Government Printing Office, 1906.

Murphey, Rhoads. *Shanghai: Key to Modern China*. Cambridge: Harvard University Press, 1953.

Nathan, Andrew J. *Peking Politics, 1918–1923*. Berkeley: University of California Press, 1976.

New China News Agency. *The Truman Doctrine in China*. Peking, 1949.

New York Times Biographical Edition. Vol 4. New York: Times Publishing Company, 1973.

Newman, Robert P. *Recognition of Communist China?* New York: Macmillan, 1961.

Nimmo, Dan D. *Newsgathering in Washington*. Englewood Cliffs, N.J.: Prentice-Hall, 1964.

North, Robert C. *Kuomintang and Chinese Communist Elites*. Stanford: Stanford University Press, 1952.

Oppenheim, L. F. L. *International Law*. Vol 1. New York: Longmans Green, 1920.

Oss, John. *Mission Advance in China*. Nashville, Tenn.: Southern Publishing Assoc., 1949.

Paddock, Paul. *China Diary: Crisis Diplomacy in Dairen*. Ames: Iowa State University Press, 1977.

Passin, Herbert. *The Legacy of the Occupation—Japan*. New York: East Asian Institute Occasional Paper, 1968.

Paterson, Thomas G., ed. *The Cold War Critics*. Chicago: Quadrangle Books, 1971.

Patterson, James T. *Mr. Republican: A Biography of Robert A. Taft*. Boston, Houghton Mifflin, 1972.

Payne, Robert. *Chiang Kai-shek*. New York: Weybright & Talley, 1969.

Peffer, Nathaniel. *The Far East*. Ann Arbor: University of Michigan Press, 1958.

Pepper, Suzanne. *Civil War in China*. Berkeley: University of California Press, 1978.

Perkins, Dexter. *The Diplomacy of a New Age: Major Issues in U.S. Foreign Policy Since 1945*. Bloomington: University of Indiana Press, 1967.

Perkins, Sara. *Red China Prisoner*. Westwood, N.J.: Revell, 1963.

Phillips, Cabell. *The Truman Presidency*. New York: Macmillan, 1966.

Pollard, James E. *The Presidents and the Press*. Washington, D.C.: Public Affairs Press, 1964.

Porter, Brian E. *Britain and the Rise of Communist China*. New York: Oxford University Press, 1967.

Public Papers of the President: Harry S. Truman. 8 vols. Washington, D.C.: Government Printing Office, 1961–66.

Purifoy, Lewis M. *Harry Truman's China Policy: McCarthyism and the Diplomacy of Hysteria, 1947–51*. New York: New Viewpoints, 1976.

Rankin, Karl L. *China Assignment*. Seattle: University of Washington Press, 1964.

Ravenholt, Albert. *Christianity and the Chinese Communists*. New York, 1963.

Reardon-Anderson, James. *Yenan and the Great Powers*. New York: Columbia University Press, 1980.

Remer, Carl F. *Foreign Investments in China*. New York: Macmillan, 1933.

Reston, James. *The Artillery of the Press: Its Influence on American Foreign Policy*. New York: Harper & Row, 1966.

Reynolds, Hubert and Harriet. *What Christian Approach to the Chinese?* Indianapolis, Ind., n.d.

Rivers, William L. *The Opinionmakers*. Boston: Beacon Press, 1965.

Robinson, Edgar E. *Powers of the President in Foreign Affairs, 1945–65*. San Francisco: Commonwealth Club of California, 1966.

Rogin, Michael P. *The Intellectuals and McCarthy*. Cambridge: MIT Press, 1967.

Rosenau, James N. *Public Opinion and Foreign Policy*. New York: Random House, 1961.

Rosenau, James N., ed. *Domestic Sources of Foreign Policy*. New York: Free Press, 1967.

Rosinger, Lawrence K. *China's Wartime Politics, 1937–1944*. Princeton: Princeton University Press, 1944.

Rovere, Richard H. *Senator Joe McCarthy*. New York: Meridian, 1966.

Schaller, Michael. *The United States and China in the Twentieth Century*. New York: Oxford University Press, 1979.

——— *The U.S. Crusade in China, 1938–1945*. New York: Columbia University Press, 1979.

Schilling, Warner R., Paul Y. Hammond, and Glen H. Snyder. *Strategy, Politics, and Defense Budgets*. New York: Columbia University Press, 1962.

Schram, Stuart. *Mao Tse-tung*. Baltimore: Penguin, 1970.

——— *The Political Thought of Mao Tse-tung*. New York: Praeger, 1970.

Schram, Stuart, ed. *Chairman Mao Talks to the People*. New York: Pantheon, 1974.

Schulzinger, Robert D. *The Making of the Diplomatic Mind*. Middletown, Conn.: Wesleyan University Press, 1975.

Schurmann, Franz. *Logic of World Power*. New York: Pantheon, 1974.

Schwartz, Harry. *Russia's Soviet Economy*. Englewood Cliffs, N.J.: Prentice-Hall, 1954.

Scovel, Myra. *The Chinese Ginger Jars*. New York: Harper, 1962.

Service, John. *The Amerasia Papers*. Berkeley: University of California Press, 1971.

Shaw, Henry I. *The United States Marines in North China, 1945–1949*. Washington, D.C.: Government Printing Office, 1962.

Sherwin, Martin J. *A World Destroyed*. New York: Alfred A. Knopf, 1975.

Shewmaker, Kenneth E. *American and Chinese Communists, 1927–1945: A Persuading Encounter*. Ithaca, N.Y.: Cornell University Press, 1971.

Shih-chieh Chih-shih Ch'u-pan she (comp). *Chung Hua Jen-min Kung-ho Kuo tui-wai kuan-hsi wen-chien chi* [Collected Documents on the Foreign Relations of the People's Republic of China], 1. 1949–1950. Peking: Shih-chieh Chih-shih, 1957.

Simpson, Smith. *Anatomy of the State Department*. Boston: Houghton Mifflin, 1967.

Smedley, Agnes. *Battle Hymn of China*. New York: Alfred A. Knopf, 1943.

Smith, Arthur R. *The Tiger in the Senate: The Biography of Wayne Morse*. Garden City, N.Y.: Doubleday, 1962.

Smith, Gaddis. *Dean Acheson*. New York: Cooper Square, 1972.

Smith, Timothy L. *Revivalism and Social Reform in Mid-Nineteenth-Century America*. New York: Abingdon Press, 1957.

Snow, Edgar. *Red Star Over China*. New York: Grove Press, 1978.

Solomon, Richard H. *Mao's Revolution and the Chinese Political Culture*. Berkeley: University of California Press, 1971.

Spanier, John. *The Truman-MacArthur Controversy and the Korean War*. Cambridge: Harvard University Press, 1959.

Spencer, Cornelia. *Chiang Kai-shek: Generalissimo of Nationalist China*. New York: John Day, 1968.

Stebbins, Richard P. *The United States in World Affairs, 1949–53*. New York: Council on Foreign Relations, 1950–54.

Steel, Ronald. *Walter Lippmann and the American Century*. Boston: Little Brown, 1980.

Steele, A. T. *The American People and China*. New York: McGraw-Hill, 1966.

Steiger, George N. *China and the Occident*. New Haven: Conn.: Yale University Press, 1927.

Stein, Guenther. *The Challenge of Red China*. New York: McGraw-Hill, 1945.

Steinberg, Alfred. *The Man from Missouri*. New York: G.P. Putnam's Sons, 1962.

——— *Sam Rayburn*. New York: Hawthorne Books, 1975.

Stoessinger, John G. *Nations in Darkness: China, Russia and America*. New York: Random House, 1971.

Strang, Lord. *Home and Abroad*. London: Andre Deutsch, 1956.

Stromer, Marvin E. *The Making of a Political Leader: Kenneth S. Wherry and the United States Senate*. Lincoln: University of Nebraska Press, 1969.

Stuart, John Leighton. *Fifty Years in China*. New York: Random House, 1954.

Stueck, William Whitney Jr. *The Road to Confrontation: American Policy Toward China and Korea, 1947–1950.* Chapel Hill: University of North Carolina Press, 1981.

Sulzberger, C. L. *A Long Row of Candles.* New York: Macmillan, 1969.

Sutter, Robert G. *China-Watch.* Baltimore: Johns Hopkins University Press, 1978.

Swanberg, W. A. *Luce.* New York: Scribner, 1972.

Swenson, Victor E. *Parents of Many.* Rock Island, Ill., 1959.

Taft, Philip. *The A. F. of L. From the Death of Gompers to the Merger.* New York: Harper, 1959.

———— *Defending Freedom: American Labor and Foreign Affairs.* Los Angeles: Nash Publishing, 1973.

Taft, Robert A. *A Foreign Policy for Americans.* Garden City, N.J.: Doubleday, 1951.

Talbot, Strobe, trans. *Khrushchev Remembers.* Boston: Little, Brown, 1970.

———— *Khrushchev Remembers: The Last Testament.* Boston: Little, Brown, 1974.

Tan, Chester. *The Boxer Catastrophe.* New York: W. W. Norton, 1967.

Tang Tsou. *America's Failure in China, 1941–1950.* Chicago: University of Chicago Press, 1963.

Tanzer, Michael. *The Political Economy of International Oil and the Underdeveloped Countries.* Boston: Beacon Press, 1969.

Tebbel, John. *The Life and Good Times of William Randolph Hearst.* New York: Paperback Library, 1952.

Tennien, Mark. *No Secret Is Safe.* New York: Farrar, Straus & Young, 1952.

Theoharis, Athan. *Seeds of Repression: Harry S Truman and the Origins of McCarthyism.* Chicago: Quadrangle Books, 1971.

———— *The Yalta Myths.* Columbia: University of Missouri Press, 1970.

Thomson, James C. Jr. *While China Faced West: American Reformers in Nationalist China, 1928–1937.* Cambridge: Harvard University Press, 1969.

Thorne, Christopher. *Allies of a Kind.* New York: Oxford University Press, 1978.

Tien Hung-mao. *Government and Politics in Kuomintang China, 1927–1937.* Stanford: Stanford University Press, 1972.

Topping, Seymour. *Journey Between Two Chinas.* New York: Harper & Row, 1972.

Truman, Harry S *Memoirs.* Vol I: *Year of Decision,* Garden City, N.Y.: Doubleday, 1955, Vol 2: *Years of Trial and Hope,* 1956.

Truman, Margaret. *Harry S Truman.* New York: William Morrow, 1973.

Tuchman, Barbara. *Notes From China.* New York: Collier Books, 1972.

—— *Stilwell and the American Experience in China.* New York: Macmillan, 1971.

Tung Shih-chin. *Kung-ch'ü hui-i hsü-p'ien* [Reminiscences of Communist Rule], Kowloon: Tzu-yu, 1952.

Tung, William M. *The Political Institutions of Modern China.* The Hague: Martinus Nijhoff, 1968.

—— *Revolutionary China.* New York: St. Martin's Press, 1973.

—— *V. K. Wellington Koo and China's Wartime Diplomacy.* New York: St. John's University Press, 1977.

Ulam, Adam. *The Rivals.* New York: Penguin, 1971.

United Nations. *Economic Survey of Asia and the Far East.* New York: United Nations, 1949.

United States Marine Corps. *The United States Marines in North China, 1945–1949.* Marine Corps Historical Reference Series Number 23, Washington, D.C., 1962.

Utley, Freda. *Last Chance in China.* Indianapolis, Ind.: Bobbs-Merrill, 1947.

Vandenberg, A. H. Jr. and Joe A. Morris, eds. *The Private Papers of Senator Vandenberg.* Boston: Houghton-Mifflin, 1952.

Van Slyke, Lyman P. *The China White Paper, August 1949.* 2 vols, Stanford: Stanford University Press, 1967.

—— *Enemies and Friends: The United Front in Chinese Communist History.* Stanford: Stanford University Press, 1967.

Varg, Paul. *Missionaries, Chinese and Diplomats.* Princeton: Princeton University Press, 1958.

Walton, Robert J. *Henry Wallace, Harry Truman and the Cold War.* New York: Viking, 1976.

Wedemeyer, Albert C. *Wedemeyer Reports!* New York: Devin Adair, 1958.

Wehrle, Edmund S. *Britain, China and the Antimissionary Riots, 1891–1900.* Minneapolis: University of Minnesota Press, 1966.

Weinstein, Allen. *Perjury.* New York: Alfred A. Knopf, 1978.

Westerfield, H. Bradford. *Foreign Policy and Party Politics.* New Haven: Yale University Press, 1955.

White, Theodore. *In Search of History.* New York: Harper & Row, 1978.

—— *Making of the President, 1960.* New York: Atheneum, 1961.

White, Theodore and Annalee Jacoby. *Thunder Out of China.* New York: William Sloane Associates, 1946.

Whiting, Allen S. *China Crosses the Yalu.* Stanford: Stanford University Press, 1960.

Wilkins, Mira. *The Maturing of Multinational Enterprise: American Business Abroad From 1914–1970.* Cambridge: Harvard University Press, 1974.

Wilkins, Mira and Frank E. Hill. *American Business Abroad: Ford on Six Continents*. Detroit: Wayne State University Press, 1964.

Wilson, Joan Hoff. *American Business and Foreign Policy, 1920–1933*. Lexington: University of Kentucky Press, 1971.

Wittenbach, H. A. *Christianity and Communism in China*. London, 1949.

Wu Chao-kwang. *The International Aspect of the Missionary Movement in China*. Baltimore: Johns Hopkins University Press, 1930.

Yin Shih (pseud). *Li-Chiang Kuan-hsi yü Chung-kuo* [The Li-Chiang Relationship and China]. Hong Kong: Freedom Press, 1954.

Yost, Charles. *The Age of Triumph and Frustration*. New York: R. Speller, 1964.

———— *The Conduct and Misconduct of Foreign Affairs*. New York: Random House, 1972.

———— *The Insecurity of Nations*. New York: Praeger, 1968.

Index

ABC (American Broadcasting Company), 84, 146–48, 171
Abend, Hallett, 135, 148
Abortive Revolution, The (Eastman), 64
Academic community, 92–93, 156, 168–72, 190, 257*n*60, 303*n*73, 304*n*76
Acheson, Dean, 1–7, 9, 11, 13–18, 43, 100, 173–75, 181, 183–94; Asia, 308*n*26; British policy in China, 2, 24, 191; Chennault, Claire, 317*n*87; Chiang Kai-shek, 302*n*66, 308*n*26; China Lobby, 95–96, 98; Chinese Titoism, 16–17, 32; Congress, 4, 14, 154–55, 164–67, 185, 299*n*44, 302*n*66; disengagement from Nationalist China, 181, 187, 190–91, 193, 197; Europe, focus on, 2, 11, 17–19, 174, 306*n*10; journalists and the media, 142–43, 147–48, 150, 289*nn*45,48; Korean War, 195–200, 202, 204–5, 319*n*2; Kuomintang, opinion of, 187–88; Marshall, George C., relations with, 9, 187–88; missionaries, 5; Nationalist Chinese air raids, 185; Pacific defense union, 73; priorities of foreign policy, 11, 14; public opinion, 3–4, 154, 159, 161, 191, 296*n*23; recognition issue, 38–39, 150, 183, 188–94, 307*n*15, 312*n*57, 316*n*84; scholars, 169; Soviet-Chinese alliance, 28, 32, 212*n*32; Taiwan, 55–58, 152, 185, 192–93, 315*n*76; Ward Incident, 14–16
ACPA, *see* American China Policy Association
AFL, *see* American Federation of Labor
Alien Affairs Office, Chinese Communist, 47, 50, 57
Allied Syndicates, Inc., 97, 260*n*87

Alsop, Joseph, 98, 252*n*7, 289*n*48
Alsop, Stewart, 98, 148, 250*n*81, 252*n*7
America, 88, 255*n*41
American Association of Shanghai, 121, 274*n*35
American Bureau for Medical Aid to China, 85
American Chambers of Commerce, in China, 115, 120–21, 123, 125, 283*n*80
American China Policy Association (ACPA), 76, 85, 88, 93–94, 126, 254*n*35
American Express Company, 127, 277*n*48
American Federation of Labor (AFL), 87, 249*n*77, 254*nn*31, 32, 33
American Historical Association, 171
American Legion, 15, 92
American Legion Magazine, 92
American President Lines, 86, 118, 120, 286*n*6, 270*n*17
American Technical and Military Advisory Group, 91
American Volunteer Group (Flying Tigers), 96
America's Town Meeting of the Air, 91, 129, 170
Amethyst Incident, 218*n*30
Anaconda Copper dealership, 116
Anderson, Meyer & Co., 118, 121, 123, 268*n*6, 275*nn*37,42, 283*n*78
Anticommunism, *see* Communism, American fear of, and obsession with
AP, *see* Associated Press
Ascoli, Max, 80
Asia, Western nations' status in, 20
Associated Press (AP), 31, 139–43, 149
Atlantic Charter, 20
Atlanta Constitution, 152

Quirino, Elpidio, 66, 73

Rand, Christopher, 288*n*42
Rankin, Karl, 200
Ravenholt, Al, 143
Raymond, Allen, 146
Red Star Over China (Snow), 137, 285*n*8
Religion, in China, 102–3; *see also*
    Missionaries
Religious bodies: China Lobby, 87–88, 95;
    see also Missionaries
Reporter magazine, 80
"Report to the American People on
    China, A" (Bullitt), 84
Republican party, 2–3, 12–13, 59, 163,
    181–85, 189, 193, 197–98, 299*n*4,
    301*nn*55, 56, 315*n*73, 320*n*9
Republic Steel Corporation, 127
Reston, James, 144
Reuters, 143
Reynolds, William, 86
Reynolds Metals Company, 86, 253*n*28
Rhee, Syngman, 73
Ringwalt, Arthur, 217*n*27
Roberts, J. N., 149
Roderick, John, 139
Roman Catholicism, 102, 104–6, 110–11,
    267*n*58; assets, 102, 262*n*7; China
    Lobby, 87–88, 95; Chinese Communist
    hostility, 262*n*8; recognition, 264*n*34;
    treatment by Chinese Communists,
    104–5; view of Chinese Communism,
    106
Roosevelt, Franklin D., 7–8, 12;
    anticolonial views, 20; China policy, 21–
    22, 33, 216*n*14, 298*n*34; Chinese attitude
    toward, 44–45; Kohlberg, Alfred, 86;
    recognition of USSR, 177, 254*n*31; self-
    determination, 20
Roschin, N. V., 61
Rowe, David Nelson, 92, 257*n*60, 303*n*73
Rusk, Dean, 72, 143, 187, 189, 199–200,
    305*n*2, 314*n*72
Rutherford, H. R., 91

St. Louis Post-Dispatch, 146–47, 171,
    290*n*51, 291*n*61
San Francisco Chamber of Commerce,
    128, 165, 259*n*70, 284*n*81
San Francisco Chronicle, 128, 152, 291*n*71

Saturday Evening Post, 98, 137, 149
SCAP, *see* Supreme Commander of the
    Allied Powers in the Pacific
Schelke, C. V., 121
Scholars, American, 6, 92–93, 156, 168–
    72, 190
Schwellenbach, Lewis B., 89
Scripps-Howard newspapers, 82, 84–85,
    94, 146, 148, 150–51, 153, 293*n*95
Sebald, William J., 37
Self-determination, principle of, 20
Senate, U.S., *see* Congress, U.S.
Senate Committee on Interstate and
    Foreign Commerce, 130
Senate Foreign Relations Committee, 89,
    165–67, 171, 185, 193, 204, 302*n*66,
    320*n*9
Sentner, David, 98, 148
Service, John, 44–45, 167, 231*n*18, 251*n*3,
    303*n*67
Sevareid, Eric, 147
Seventh Fleet, U.S., 58, 91, 195–96, 199–
    200, 319*n*4
Shanghai air raids, 74–75, 122, 185
Shanghai Evening Post & Mercury, 51, 117,
    123, 140–41, 275*n*39
Shanghai Power Company, 71, 115, 120–
    21, 125, 128, 203, 248*n*69, 268*n*6, 269*n*7,
    276*n*46, 278*nn*52,53, 283*n*76, 286*n*16,
    287*n*32, 288*n*37; *see also* Hopkins, Peter
Shansi Military Clique, 68
Shantelco (Shanghai Telephone), 115, 120,
    268*n*6, 274*n*33, 276*n*46
Sherman, Forrest P., 91
Shih Shih Hsin Pao, 69
Shun Pao, 240*n*9
Singapore Conference, 25
Sinkiang, 29, 42
Sino-American relations, *see* China-
    American relations
Sino-American Treaty for the
    Relinquishment of Extraterritorial Rights
    in China (1943), 49
Sino-Japanese War, 28–29, 241*n*13
Sino-Soviet Friendship Treaty (1945), 16,
    28, 71; (1950), 19, 31–32, 42, 54–55, 195,
    237*n*59
Sino-Soviet relations, *see* China-Soviet
    relations
Smith, H. Alexander, 76, 94–96, 98, 143,

Contemporary American History Series
WILLIAM E. LEUCHTENBURG, GENERAL EDITOR

Lawrence S. Wittner, *Rebels against War: The American Peace Movement,
1941–1960,* 1969.

Davis R. B. Ross, *Preparing for Ulysses: Politics and Veterans during World
War II,* 1969.

John Lewis Gaddis, *The United States and the Origins of the Cold War,
1941–1947,* 1972.

George C. Herring, Jr., *Aid to Russia, 1941–1946: Strategy, Diplomacy,
the Origins of the Cold War,* 1973.

Alonzo L. Hamby, *Beyond the New Deal: Harry S. Truman and American
Liberalism,* 1973.

Richard M. Fried, *Men against McCarthy,* 1976.

Steven F. Lawson, *Black Ballots: Voting Rights in the South, 1944–1969,*
1976.

Carl M. Brauer, *John F. Kennedy and the Second Reconstruction,* 1977.

Maeva Marcus, *Truman and the Steel Seizure Case: The Limits of Presidential
Power,* 1977.

Morton Sosna, *In Search of the Silent South: Southern Liberals and the Race
Issue,* 1977.

Robert M. Collins, *The Business Response to Keynes, 1929–1964,* 1981.

Robert M. Hathaway, *Ambiguous Partnership: Britain and America,
1944–1947,* 1981.

Leonard Dinnerstein, *America and the Survivors of the Holocaust,* 1982.

Lawrence S. Wittner, *American Intervention in Greece, 1943–1949,* 1982.

Nancy Bernkopf Tucker, *Patterns in the Dust: Chinese-American Relations
and the Recognition Controversy, 1949–1950,* 1983.